T0211673

Lecture Notes in Computer Science 12763

More information about this subseries at http://www.springer.com/series/7409

Masaaki Kurosu (Ed.)

Human-Computer Interaction

Interaction Techniques and Novel Applications

Thematic Area, HCI 2021
Held as Part of the 23rd HCI International Conference, HCII 2021
Virtual Event, July 24–29, 2021
Proceedings, Part II

Springer

Editor
Masaaki Kurosu
The Open University of Japan
Chiba, Japan

ISSN 0302-9743 ISSN 1611-3349 (electronic)
Lecture Notes in Computer Science
ISBN 978-3-030-78464-5 ISBN 978-3-030-78465-2 (eBook)
https://doi.org/10.1007/978-3-030-78465-2

LNCS Sublibrary: SL3 – Information Systems and Applications, incl. Internet/Web, and HCI

This Springer imprint is published by the registered company Springer Nature Switzerland AG
The registered company address is: Gewerbestrasse 11, 6330 Cham, Switzerland

Foreword

Human-Computer Interaction (HCI) is acquiring an ever-increasing scientific and industrial importance, and having more impact on people's everyday life, as an ever-growing number of human activities are progressively moving from the physical to the digital world. This process, which has been ongoing for some time now, has been dramatically accelerated by the COVID-19 pandemic. The HCI International (HCII) conference series, held yearly, aims to respond to the compelling need to advance the exchange of knowledge and research and development efforts on the human aspects of design and use of computing systems.

The 23rd International Conference on Human-Computer Interaction, HCI International 2021 (HCII 2021), was planned to be held at the Washington Hilton Hotel, Washington DC, USA, during July 24–29, 2021. Due to the COVID-19 pandemic and with everyone's health and safety in mind, HCII 2021 was organized and run as a virtual conference. It incorporated the 21 thematic areas and affiliated conferences listed on the following page.

A total of 5222 individuals from academia, research institutes, industry, and governmental agencies from 81 countries submitted contributions, and 1276 papers and 241 posters were included in the proceedings to appear just before the start of the conference. The contributions thoroughly cover the entire field of HCI, addressing major advances in knowledge and effective use of computers in a variety of application areas. These papers provide academics, researchers, engineers, scientists, practitioners, and students with state-of-the-art information on the most recent advances in HCI. The volumes constituting the set of proceedings to appear before the start of the conference are listed in the following pages.

The HCI International (HCII) conference also offers the option of 'Late Breaking Work' which applies both for papers and posters, and the corresponding volume(s) of the proceedings will appear after the conference. Full papers will be included in the 'HCII 2021 - Late Breaking Papers' volumes of the proceedings to be published in the Springer LNCS series, while 'Poster Extended Abstracts' will be included as short research papers in the 'HCII 2021 - Late Breaking Posters' volumes to be published in the Springer CCIS series.

The present volume contains papers submitted and presented in the context of the Human-Computer Interaction (HCI 2021) thematic area of HCII 2021. I would like to thank the Chair, Masaaki Kurosu, for his invaluable contribution to its organization and the preparation of the proceedings, as well as the members of the Program Board for their contributions and support. This year, the HCI thematic area has focused on topics related to theoretical and methodological approaches to HCI, UX evaluation methods and techniques, emotional and persuasive design, psychological and cognitive aspects of interaction, novel interaction techniques, human-robot interaction, UX and technology acceptance studies, and digital wellbeing, as well as the impact of the COVID-19 pandemic and social distancing on interaction, communication, and work.

I would also like to thank the Program Board Chairs and the members of the Program Boards of all thematic areas and affiliated conferences for their contribution towards the highest scientific quality and overall success of the HCI International 2021 conference.

This conference would not have been possible without the continuous and unwavering support and advice of Gavriel Salvendy, founder, General Chair Emeritus, and Scientific Advisor. For his outstanding efforts, I would like to express my appreciation to Abbas Moallem, Communications Chair and Editor of HCI International News.

July 2021   Constantine Stephanidis

HCI International 2021 Thematic Areas
and Affiliated Conferences

Thematic Areas

- HCI: Human-Computer Interaction
- HIMI: Human Interface and the Management of Information

Affiliated Conferences

- EPCE: 18th International Conference on Engineering Psychology and Cognitive Ergonomics
- UAHCI: 15th International Conference on Universal Access in Human-Computer Interaction
- VAMR: 13th International Conference on Virtual, Augmented and Mixed Reality
- CCD: 13th International Conference on Cross-Cultural Design
- SCSM: 13th International Conference on Social Computing and Social Media
- AC: 15th International Conference on Augmented Cognition
- DHM: 12th International Conference on Digital Human Modeling and Applications in Health, Safety, Ergonomics and Risk Management
- DUXU: 10th International Conference on Design, User Experience, and Usability
- DAPI: 9th International Conference on Distributed, Ambient and Pervasive Interactions
- HCIBGO: 8th International Conference on HCI in Business, Government and Organizations
- LCT: 8th International Conference on Learning and Collaboration Technologies
- ITAP: 7th International Conference on Human Aspects of IT for the Aged Population
- HCI-CPT: 3rd International Conference on HCI for Cybersecurity, Privacy and Trust
- HCI-Games: 3rd International Conference on HCI in Games
- MobiTAS: 3rd International Conference on HCI in Mobility, Transport and Automotive Systems
- AIS: 3rd International Conference on Adaptive Instructional Systems
- C&C: 9th International Conference on Culture and Computing
- MOBILE: 2nd International Conference on Design, Operation and Evaluation of Mobile Communications
- AI-HCI: 2nd International Conference on Artificial Intelligence in HCI

List of Conference Proceedings Volumes Appearing Before the Conference

1. LNCS 12762, Human-Computer Interaction: Theory, Methods and Tools (Part I), edited by Masaaki Kurosu
2. LNCS 12763, Human-Computer Interaction: Interaction Techniques and Novel Applications (Part II), edited by Masaaki Kurosu
3. LNCS 12764, Human-Computer Interaction: Design and User Experience Case Studies (Part III), edited by Masaaki Kurosu
4. LNCS 12765, Human Interface and the Management of Information: Information Presentation and Visualization (Part I), edited by Sakae Yamamoto and Hirohiko Mori
5. LNCS 12766, Human Interface and the Management of Information: Information-rich and Intelligent Environments (Part II), edited by Sakae Yamamoto and Hirohiko Mori
6. LNAI 12767, Engineering Psychology and Cognitive Ergonomics, edited by Don Harris and Wen-Chin Li
7. LNCS 12768, Universal Access in Human-Computer Interaction: Design Methods and User Experience (Part I), edited by Margherita Antona and Constantine Stephanidis
8. LNCS 12769, Universal Access in Human-Computer Interaction: Access to Media, Learning and Assistive Environments (Part II), edited by Margherita Antona and Constantine Stephanidis
9. LNCS 12770, Virtual, Augmented and Mixed Reality, edited by Jessie Y. C. Chen and Gino Fragomeni
10. LNCS 12771, Cross-Cultural Design: Experience and Product Design Across Cultures (Part I), edited by P. L. Patrick Rau
11. LNCS 12772, Cross-Cultural Design: Applications in Arts, Learning, Well-being, and Social Development (Part II), edited by P. L. Patrick Rau
12. LNCS 12773, Cross-Cultural Design: Applications in Cultural Heritage, Tourism, Autonomous Vehicles, and Intelligent Agents (Part III), edited by P. L. Patrick Rau
13. LNCS 12774, Social Computing and Social Media: Experience Design and Social Network Analysis (Part I), edited by Gabriele Meiselwitz
14. LNCS 12775, Social Computing and Social Media: Applications in Marketing, Learning, and Health (Part II), edited by Gabriele Meiselwitz
15. LNAI 12776, Augmented Cognition, edited by Dylan D. Schmorrow and Cali M. Fidopiastis
16. LNCS 12777, Digital Human Modeling and Applications in Health, Safety, Ergonomics and Risk Management: Human Body, Motion and Behavior (Part I), edited by Vincent G. Duffy
17. LNCS 12778, Digital Human Modeling and Applications in Health, Safety, Ergonomics and Risk Management: AI, Product and Service (Part II), edited by Vincent G. Duffy

38. CCIS 1420, HCI International 2021 Posters - Part II, edited by Constantine Stephanidis, Margherita Antona, and Stavroula Ntoa
39. CCIS 1421, HCI International 2021 Posters - Part III, edited by Constantine Stephanidis, Margherita Antona, and Stavroula Ntoa

http://2021.hci.international/proceedings

Human-Computer Interaction Thematic Area (HCI 2021)

Program Board Chair: **Masaaki Kurosu,** *The Open University of Japan, Japan*

- Salah Ahmed, Norway
- Valdecir Becker, Brazil
- Nimish Biloria, Australia
- Maurizio Caon, Switzerland
- Zhigang Chen, China

- Yu-Hsiu Hung, Taiwan
- Yi Ji, China
- Alexandros Liapis, Greece
- Hiroshi Noborio, Japan
- Vinícius Segura, Brazil

The full list with the Program Board Chairs and the members of the Program Boards of all thematic areas and affiliated conferences is available online at:

http://www.hci.international/board-members-2021.php

HCI International 2022

The 24th International Conference on Human-Computer Interaction, HCI International 2022, will be held jointly with the affiliated conferences at the Gothia Towers Hotel and Swedish Exhibition & Congress Centre, Gothenburg, Sweden, June 26 – July 1, 2022. It will cover a broad spectrum of themes related to Human-Computer Interaction, including theoretical issues, methods, tools, processes, and case studies in HCI design, as well as novel interaction techniques, interfaces, and applications. The proceedings will be published by Springer. More information will be available on the conference website: http://2022.hci.international/:

General Chair
Prof. Constantine Stephanidis
University of Crete and ICS-FORTH
Heraklion, Crete, Greece
Email: general_chair@hcii2022.org

http://2022.hci.international/

Contents – Part II

Human-Robot Interaction

Digital Wellbeing

HCI in Surgery

Novel Interaction Techniques

Performance Evaluation and Efficiency of Laser Holographic Peripherals

Alexander Fedor, Mulualem Hailom, Talha Hassan, Vu Ngoc Phuong Dinh, Vuong Nguyen, and Tauheed Khan Mohd(✉)

Augustana College, Rock Island, IL 61201, USA
{alexanderfedor18,mulualemhailom17,talhahassan18,
vungocphuongdinh17,vuongnguyen18,tauheedkhanmohd}@augustana.edu

Abstract. The introduction of virtual and voice recognition technologies have been at the forefront of HCI development in the last decade. The tech world has embraced the user experience when it comes to design and innovation. The way we communicate with computers has evolved over the years, things are moving from the more manual way of passing information to the computer into a more virtual style. Keyboards and mouses have been the two most important tools for doing this job, and innovation has transitioned them from the standard setups into virtual and holographic setups that take up minimal space. They are a part of green computing which promotes recycling and less plastic and electronic wastes. This paper would explore the evolution of the keyboard and explain how the new technology works. The paper would analyze both the hardware and the software to observe the design and the inner workings of two selected virtual devices: A virtual keyboard and ODin holographic mouse. There are several approaches used to process the information such as 3D optical ranging, the paper would include details about the mechanism behind it. An important concern is whether these virtual machines are accurate enough when it comes to performance and durability as compared to the standard styles. This paper would discuss the experiment performed to determine the user experience and accuracy based on monitored tasks that were repeated on the standard version as well. Deep Learning, Recurrent neural networks, in particular, is another important feature of this paper with their ability to improve the devices.

Keywords: Virtual · Keyboard · Mouse · Laser · Image processing · Webcam · Deep learning

1 Introduction

HCI has expanded vastly by incorporating multiple disciplines, such as computer science, cognitive science, Artificial Intelligence, Machine Learning and human-factors engineering. HCI is seen as having great potential in revolutionizing the experience between a user and a computer. Computer devices are becoming increasingly linked with our everyday life; we interact with computers through different means such as audio, vision, motion, voice, etc. However, the most popular form of interaction between people

© Springer Nature Switzerland AG 2021
M. Kurosu (Ed.): HCII 2021, LNCS 12763, pp. 3–16, 2021.
https://doi.org/10.1007/978-3-030-78465-2_1

and computers is through the QWERTY keyboard [27]. QWERTY keyboard can vary from mechanical keyboard to touch keyboard on the mobile phone or the holographic keyboard. Similarly, a computer mouse, whether it is a mechanical, optical, or holographic mouse, is another important device in the communication between people and computers. A computer mouse can vary from mechanical, optical mouse to holographic mouse [24]. The innovative progress of our methods of communication with a computer is at the front line of our development of HCI and deep learning.

As technology becomes more widespread, the adaptation of more user-friendly interfaces and portable lifestyles is being preferred. Keyboards and mouses are expected to replace their physical builds with virtual ones. The virtual keyboard is designed to be smaller and thus more convenient to carry around. With different technical methods such as laser and webcam processing, the base would project a full-size QWERTY keyboard on a flat surface. Despite the smaller size, it carries the same functionality as the standard keyboard.

A virtual keyboard is a great tool for using mobile phones or any portable devices; the keyboards on these devices are relatively small for many people, such as people with larger fingers, making it difficult to tap into the correct key [19]. The virtual keyboard is also helpful for people with technological syndromes such as Carpal Tunnel Syndrome, Mouse Shoulder, or Cervical Syndrome [23]. Using a hand at a poor angle or putting intense and long-time pressure on the shoulders results in these syndromes [22]. People with these syndromes would have a hard time using a physical keyboard or mouse; continuing to use these devices can also aggravate their condition. With a virtual keyboard or mouse, the wrist is at a much more comfortable and natural angle; this would help reduce stress on those areas.

Another reason for the appearance of virtual computer keyboard and mouse is green computing. Green computing focuses on reducing the wastes related to computer products [14]. The standard keyboard and mouse may contain toxic components, which are difficult to dispose of or recycle correctly. Using a virtual keyboard and mouse instead would reduce plastic waste. This would help minimize the adverse effect on human and environmental health [13].

This article would explore the development of the keyboard from a type-writer to a virtual keyboard. It gives insights into the different techniques used by scientists in building virtual keyboards and the holographic mouse. This article specifically focuses on AGS Laser Projection Bluetooth Virtual Keyboard, with English QWERTY layout. The laser projection keyboard easily pairs with iPhone, Ipad, Smartphone, laptop, or tablet via Bluetooth. The article also provides a study into some common keyboard types and the different kinds of virtual keyboards and mouses available in the market. The article also focuses on ODiN - Virtual Laser Holographic Mouse - World's First Projection Trackpad. It is lightweight, compact, and could easily be connected with any computer device via Bluetooth. This mouse turns any flat surface into a trackpad and provides multipoint controls that support a range of gestures. Through various experimental tests, the article compares the accuracy of the virtual keyboards with the standard keyboard. By evaluating the results, the article provides predictive analysis on the future of virtual keyboards and mouses.

2 Related Work

2.1 The Development of Keyboard

The approach taken to enter and edit text has evolved over the years. The modern-day standard keyboard could be seen as inherited from the typewriter. The most popular layout has been the QWERTY keyboard layout, designed by Sholes and his partner James Densmore in 1878. This model is globally recognized and its popularity could be credited to its efficiency and familiarity. The earlier models were dependent on the teletype machines or keypunches. The problem with them was that having myriad mechanical steps to transmit data between the keyboard and computer, delayed the time taken to visualize text. To resolve that issue, VDT technology, and electric keyboards were introduced. The keys could now send electronic impulses directly to the computer and save time. It has been over a century since the QWERTY keyboard has been designed. QWERTY has been monopolizing the market with its unique style that does not leave room for other layouts. Despite these concerns, the QWERTY layout was recognized as the standard keyboard design when it comes to communicating with keyboard [12]. In modern technology, user experience is expected to impose minimal cognitive load on the user. An average user has already become accustomed to the QWERTY layout and a new layout can not attract users on a massive scale [26].

The QWERTY keyboard layouts are usually used with soft keyboards. Other types include the FITALY, Cuban, and OPTI soft keyboards. Through the last decade, voice recognition technologies have greatly advanced and have been integrated into the text entry system but it would be fair to say that voice recognition has not replaced soft keyboards. The current voice recognition systems are usually far from perfect, and the probability that a spoken word would be misrecognized is increased as the vocabulary supporting it increases [17].

As technology has progressed, developers have tried to introduce smaller portable keyboards. However, the major issue has been that with decreased size user finds it hard to press the key of interest. One type of the commonly used keyboard is the mechanical keyboard comprising mechanical keys activated by physically depressing them with a finger. In comparison to the standard style typewriters, each key is closer to the other keys increasing the chance of pressing an unintended key. Efforts to make portable keyboards, that could be folded into multiple sub-sections, have been made. Despite the convertible property, these keyboards remain relatively thick after folding and are not convenient for people to carry in a bag. Such models do not have support for folding junctions, allowing the keyboard to get loose and elevate unevenly. It is also noted that notation marks on the keyboard tend to wear off [7].

A virtual touch-sensitive display screen can be considered another type of keyboard. Touch screens are widely used for communicating with computers. Most people rely on the touch screen when using tablets as compared to attaching a keyboard. An interesting feature offered by touch-screen keyboard is detection of multiple touches occurring at about the same time and tracking their respective locations [11]. This has been one of the big reasons for the success of touch screen smartphones.

There are two common types of keyboards found on the market today: mechanical and virtual keyboards. While both keyboards allow the person to add text inputs to the computer system, they use different techniques to work.

2.2 Mechanical Keyboard Types

Mechanical keyboards are widely available in the market and used throughout the globe. The keyboard is designed with the standard QWERTY layout; in some cases, additional keys are built-in above the numeral keys. These extra keys are added to have an adjustable function in which each button would run different commands. Usually, these extra keys control volume, screen brightness, and have a shortcut button to turn off the computer [9].

Mechanical keyboards are pressure sensitive. This means the signals to create text input are made through pressure on the keys. This process pressure interaction. Each pressure interaction generates signals from the circuits under the keys. Signals from tweaking a key refer to a specific text character [3].

Despite being popular among users, the mechanical keyboard has its drawbacks. The downsides include the lack of portability, noise issues that originate while tweaking the key, easily damaged or loose keys, keystroke logging, hardware requirement, and language barrier [15].

2.3 Introduction of Virtual Keyboard

While mechanical keyboard work mostly the same, Virtual keyboards can be divided into three groups: Vision-based, wearable, and others.

Vision-Based Virtual Keyboard. A vision-based virtual keyboard is a keyboard that can receive and transmit a signal when a key, identified by a camera, is activated by the user. An example of this type of keyboard is the holographic keyboard. This keyboard creates a projection of a keyboard layout, usually on a flat surface, the projected keys are light-sensitive. The keyboard registers a detection, a "pressed key" when there is an alteration in the flow of ambient light between the flat surface and the camera. This paper also focuses on this type of keyboard and the pros and cons are going to be discussed deeply in other lower sections of this paper [8, 21].

Wearable Virtual Keyboards. Another type of virtual keyboard is a wearable virtual keyboard that uses Io T motion-recognition rings and a paper keyboard. This type of keyboard uses two to four motion-recognition rings per hand and a paper keyboard template. The main features for the keystrokes to be recognized are attitude angle and acceleration of fingers while typing. This keyboard has high accuracy, low-cost, and is customized to the person [27]. However, there are a few disadvantages: The keyboard is hard to share with a partner because it requires wearing the rings on fingers. It also requires different sizes of rings because different people have different sizes of fingers. Designing size adjustable rings would make this a better product and a more popular keyboard.

Other Virtual Keyboard. Another way to impute letters and words into the computer system is touch typing smart screens. This process is different enough from the mechanical keyboards and other virtual keyboards to be its category. While typing on the smartphone or tablet, the input can be by pressure interaction or by sensing a particular point at which a figure tip would touch the screen display [16].

2.4   How Virtual Keyboard and Mouse Function

For developing the virtual experience of keyboard and mouse, typically a webcam was proposed as the device to simulate the action. Two different webcams are used; one is for noticing when the user hits the key on the keyboard (event detection) and the other is to locate the position where the user hits (location detection). With this technique, two webcams are used to optimize the process [10].

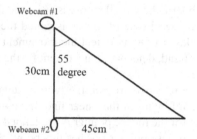

Fig. 1. Webcam virtual keyboard layout

As you can see from Fig. 1, two webcams are placed at 90° to each other. The borderline is used to check the user's finger, the borderline triggers when the user crosses the line. The second webcam (event detection) is placed at the lowest position to increase the accuracy of finding which finger crossed the borderline. The first webcam needs to set up at a higher position than the second one since it has to get the x and y-coordinates (location detection) to identify the key pressed.

However, the webcam is not the only tool to locate the key. Another device used for the same purpose is called CMOS wireless camera and it has three parts. The first part is the sensor with an Infrared bandpass filter and it limits the camera sensing capacity to only Infrared light. It is used as it is the least interfering light in any environment. The second part of the design is the keyboard projector. As the name suggests, this part projects a fixed designed keyboard by showing a visible laser beam passing through a biconcave lens and a holographic keyboard layout plate. The third part is the Infrared laser diode. It generates a layer of linear Infrared light which is parallel to the surface where the keyboard is projected. The height between the projector and camera should be 3 cm [18].

The Fig. 2 is the model of the Laser Projection Keyboard kit, which is another type of Laser Projection Keyboard kit, it has three main parts: an infrared light camera, a keyboard pattern projector, and a linear laser. The model locates the tip of the finger that touches the keyboard by detecting the light plane created by the linear laser. The infrared light camera captures the images of the finger that the user press on the keyboard and sends these images to the signal processing software which transforms them into the right key on the virtual keyboard [21].

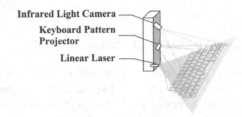

Fig. 2. The Laser projection keyboard kit design [21]

Besides the virtual keyboard, the virtual mouse is also used for inputting information to the computer. One widely used type of mouse is called the optical mouse, it relies on the Light Emitting Diodes (LEDs) to detect the movement on the flat surface. The virtual mouse, on the other hand, detects the movement by the hand gesture of the user [24].

For the cursor of mouse to move around, the two rectangular boxes, as shown in Fig. 3, are used to find the midpoint in the linear line that connects those boxes. This midpoint acts as the tracker for the mouse pointer A predefined point is set and activates the mouse cursor when the mouse pointer reaches this point. When the user intends to make a click, the two boxes corner closer, as shown in the 4, to create a bounding box. The system performs a left-click when the bounding box becomes 20% of its initial size. If the user holds onto the same position for 5 s, the mouse identifies it as a double click. For a right-click, simply one finger is enough, the webcam detects one fingertip color cap and a right button click is performed. The scrolling system works by using three fingers with the color cap. For the scroll up function, three fingers need to be moving up simultaneously and down for the scroll-down function [20] (Fig. 4).

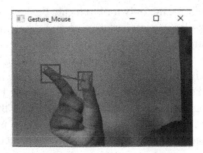

Fig. 3. Mouse movement (open gesture)

Fig. 4. Left click (close gesture)

2.5   How Virtual Keyboard and Mouse Process the Information

The captured image is expected to be a mirror image of the original image. The image frames that are developed from the camera consists of infrared images as the camera lens is integrated with an infrared bandpass filter. The region where the intended key has been touched contains a lot of noise and a very high frequency.

In a projection keyboard, the following steps work coherently to project and take input from a keyboard.

- A filter is used to remove white noise.
- Threshold frequency is used to identify the region touching the surface. Once the input has been identified, a series of steps happen to process the information [18].
- In the image capture module connection between the image sequence buffer and the Web Camera is established [25].
- Images of touching movements are captured and stored in a buffer.
- The buffer acts as a queue and images are popped from it.
- The next step is the character identification module. The image selected from the queue now goes through several image processing techniques to extract relevant information from it.
- The whole keyboard is analyzed to identify specific key locations and finally the letter/object associated with the designated key is generated.
- Edges of the keyboard are detected using the image. The height and width are noted and compared with the height and width of the key touched on the projection.
- The next step is positioning mapping intending to transform the position detected into a keyboard input.
- The minimum difference of displacement between stored and identified coordinates is found, and a tree structure is used for comparison [18].
- The position could be seen in terms of x and y coordinates. The x and y values are compared to the values already stored with each key and the virtual key code established is used to generate the letter.
- The character identification module sends the virtual key code to the server.
- The signal is forwarded to the keyboard device driver which further sends the signal to the appropriate window where it is finally displayed (Fig. 5).

Laser Projection Display

Interactive LED Lighting

Infrared Sensor for
Motion Detection

90 Degree Infrared
Beam

Fig. 5. ODiN labelled diagram

The idea of operation behind the holographic mouse is that it would capture the image of the projected screen, store it, and then accurately detect the laser pointer and identify its corresponding position on the projected screen and move the mouse cursor accordingly on the displayed screen. The following steps take place after the webcam capture the input given to the holographic mouse.

- The captured image has noises that would adversely affect the accuracy of the program. Filters are applied to take care of the unwanted noise. Gaussian filter, a common filter that has the property of no overshoot to a step function input and the ability to minimize the rise and fall time, could be applied. To achieve this Gaussian Blur function is used [24].
- The image is then passed to the image processing module. The standard image-processing techniques are applied, an image is observed as two dimensional signal and standard signal processing techniques are applied to it.
- From here, the image is passed to the laser detecting module.
- The module looks for the laser dot on the image (if there is any) and returns the position of the laser pointer on the image.
- The algorithm for the detection works with the assumption that the brightest point is the one referring to the point the user wants to be processed and displayed.
- Similar to the virtual keyboard, the holographic mouse carefully takes notes on the detected position.
- The x and y coordinates are noted and compared with the threshold values to accurately predict the right spot.

3   Experimental Setup

The experiment performed for testing the accuracy of keyboards and mouse have two different parts. Part one tests the performance and accuracy of 3 different keyboards and mouses by statistically comparing them with each other. The experiment would determine if a virtual keyboard and mouse could function as well as the physical ones. Since the technology varies between these products so our hypothesis is that their performance would vary as well.

For comparing the keyboards, the experiment used a mechanical key-cap keyboard, a membrane key-cap keyboard, and a holographic keyboard. For the mouses, a normal computer mouse, a laptop touchpad, and a holographic mouse were used.

The standard mouse uses Lighting Emitting Diodes (LEDs) technology to determine the movement of the mouse on the flat surface [24]. The laptop touchpad uses a cursor sensor to detect the finger movement [4]. The mechanical key-cap keyboard is used by determining the pressure put on the springs under each switch while the membrane key-cap keyboard is used by determining the pressure put on the rubber membrane under the whole keyboard. The holographic keyboard and mouse both use an infrared laser to project a normal keyboard or mouse on the flat surface; then they would use a webcam to detect the finger movement for each key (Figs. 6 and 7).

Fig. 6. Holographic Mouse (left) and Keyboard (right) used in experiment

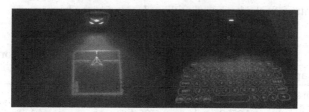

Fig. 7. Holographic Keyboard and Mouse used in experiment with no light

Two different websites were used for testing the performance and accuracy of the keyboard and mouse. For keeping the consistency and correctness one person ran the experiment on both websites and all the selected devices. If the experiment was performed by different people, it would have generated systematic errors because each person would have different skills and timing in using keyboard and mouse so the result is expected to be varied.

The website 10fastfingers.com [2] is used to test for the keyboard's performance. On this website, users have to type many sentences or a sequence of words in a given amount of time; if there is a wrong letter in a word, it would be counted as a wrong word. From that, the website calculates the keystroke, accuracy, and the number of correct and wrong words.

Another website mouseaccuracy.com [1] tests for mouse accuracy. This website renders click points with different sizes and locations; the point would change to a new location after a small amount of time so users would need certain and fast mouse movement to click the point correctly and on time. Then, the website calculates the click accuracy, target efficiency, and the number of clicks and targets performed.

For part two, after analyzing different virtual and physical keyboards, the experiment would try to find possible improvements in the virtual keyboard and the holographic mouse. For conducting this experiment, virtual devices from different brands may be used and more data points may be calculated. This part would use the spellchecker program, which is used to correct the wrong spelling word into a correct word. The experiment would aim at improving the performance of the virtual devices through deep learning techniques.

4   Experimental Result

4.1   Keyboard Experiment Results

The Fig. 8 and 9 contains the results of comparing the three keyboards 10 times on 10fast fingers.com [2]. The average words per minute (WPM) for the mechanical and Membrane keyboard were very similar and much higher than that of the holographic keyboard. The holographic keyboard also was noticeably less accurate than the other two keyboards, with about 20% less accuracy comparatively. While conducting the experiment it was observed that when attempting to press one key, the keyboard would often read the input as a different key, slowing down progress as the error then needed to be corrected. The holographic keyboard also lacked a physical sensation, it was very difficult for the user to find their position on the keyboard without looking at the keys.

	Average WPM	Keystrokes Correct	Keystrokes Incorrect
Holographic	16	79.9	16.3
Membrane	106.8	533.6	9.9
Mechanical	107.3	535.4	11.3

Fig. 8.   Keyboard results part 1

	Correct Words	Wrong Words	Accuracy
Holographic	15.3	3	75%
Membrane	102.1	1.9	95.7%
Mechanical	101.4	2	95.3%

Fig. 9.   Keyboard results part 2

4.2 Mouse Experiment Results

For the mouse, the experiment was conducted on mouseaccuracy.com [1], the Fig. 10 and 11 contain the averages of the results for the three mouses. Targets appeared on the screen at a rate of 1.8 per second for 90 s which the user than needed to click on. The normal computer mouse performed the best, far ahead of both the holographic mouse and the laptop touchpad. While the holographic mouse did not hit as many targets due to the longer time needed to lift your hand from the table and then tap compared to the pressing of a button on the other devices, its accuracy was similar to the other mouses. The less complex nature of a mouse easily lent itself to allowing this device to still retain a good modicum of the accuracy and performance of physical hardware. The holographic mouse also did feel more comfortable to use, as after performing the 10 tests one after another it did not put as much of a strain on the user's arm due to the more natural position.

	Targets Hit	Targets Missed	Efficiency
Holographic	59	102	36.4%
Laptop Touchpad	108	53	67%
Computer Mouse	147	14	81%

Fig. 10. Mouse results part 1

	Clicks Hit	Clicks Missed	Clicks Per Second	Accuracy
Holographic	59	7	0.73	88.2%
Laptop Touchpad	108	14	1.36	89%
Computer Mouse	147	23	1.91	86.5%

Fig. 11. Mouse results part 2

4.3 Possible Improvements in Hardware

– The Webcam should have a stronger lens to obtain a better image quality for the image processing.
– The webcam should have the infrared filter installed in it.
– The device may have a button to control the intensity of the projection so the user can choose how bright the keyboard appears based on preference and surrounding light.
– An option could be provided to alter the projection distance so the projection appears where the user wants it to.
– Projection keyboard size control could be given. Availability of different sizes of keyboards can allow the user to choose the keyboard he wants to use based on the work he is doing. A user may not want a separate numeric keypad on the right side.
– A user may choose from a few languages and layouts he wants to be projected.
– Additional Cameras may be installed in the device to help with key recognition and timing.

4.4 Possible Improvements Through AutoCorrect and RNN-LM

As described, the holographic keyboard leaves a lot of room for improvement compared to other physical devices. A possible improvement that we looked into was the use of an auto-correct program in order to correct any errors that could occur through the use of the holographic keyboard.

The python package fsondej, imported by importing speller from autocorrect library, could be used for improvement. The experiment could not incorporate this package as the two aforementioned sites were not compatible with it. The auto-complete function could also be used to improve the functionality of the device. A user may find it beneficial to have the inputted word be completed before all the alphabets are typed. For example, "keyb" could be recognized as "keyboard" and a suggestion can pop out on the screen. Similarly, alternate words can be presented, for example, if the user types "fore", words such as "forecast", "foremost", "forensic" etc. could be predicted by the keyboard.

There are some cases that the same letters appear many times or too many wrong letters in a word, the auto-correct program would be unable to catch that error. The holographic keyboard was inaccurate to the point that such mistakes were common even with the careful use of the device. However, there is another way that this autocorrect program could be improved to help with the device. The recurrent neural networks (RNNs) are highly effective models of natural language [6]. It looks at the relationship between the words and makes predictions. RNN uses parameter sharing to train data. It provides flexibility and has the potential to incorporate different kinds of information such as temporal order [5]. In the case of processing writing patterns, they can come handy as RNN would provide accurate and chronologically sound recommendations. Through the use of a Recurrent Neural Network based Language Model (RNN-LM), the computer would be able to use a mass of information on spelling and common errors to help check for errors. It can also analyze the word while the users are writing and suggest the closest and correct word; this way would avoid further errors. This still does not solve the hardware issues because the auto-correct is just a tool to improve the processed key input. However, this is a possible improvement for the input of text from the keyboard.

5   Conclusion

The virtual form of communicating with the computer is growing to be a crucial part of HCI. Features such as portability and eco-friendliness make the product better. Research shows that, unlike the standard keyboards and mouse, virtual ones are safer when it comes to technological syndromes resulted from wrong postures when using computers. Despite the positives, we have to consider the results from the experiments that were conducted to test the accuracy of two selected virtual devices. As explained in the experimental result section, the products performed fairly poorly in comparison to the non-virtual models when it comes to the accuracy of detecting the keys and the time it takes to process them. This suggests that there is still a lot of improvement needed before these products replace the standard non-virtual style products. More work needs to be done for improving the identification of the intended user key and neglecting the finger shadow as the input.

Suggestions have been made for improvement through deep learning, particularly Recurrent Neural Networks RNN and Convolutional Neural Networks CNN, which would allow for better results. CNN would allow us to better identify the details and relationship of each element on the image. From this, it is expected to detect and analyze the finger shadow so that when image processing is used, there is no confusion between finger movement and finger shadow. RNN, on the other hand, would help with the auto-correct and spelling of the inputted text.

The big tech companies, such as Apple, Asus, Lenovo, Huawei, hp, Logitech, etc. need to take interest in re-designing these virtual products to make them more user-friendly, attractive, and cheaper for the masses. This would allow the virtual keyboard and mouse to progress and possibly replace the standard keyboard and mouse someday.

References

1. Mouse accuracy. https://mouseaccuracy.com/. Accessed 20 Jan 2021
2. Test amp; improve your typing speed with our free typing games. https://10fastfingers.com/. Accessed 20 Jan 2021
3. Bocirnea, R.C.: Pressure-sensitive keyboard and associated method of operation, February 26 2013. uS Patent 8,384,566
4. Conte, C., et al.: Kinematic and electromyographic differences between mouse and touchpad use on laptop computers. Int. J. Ind. Ergon. **44**(3), 413–420 (2014)
5. Donkers, T., Loepp, B., Ziegler, J.: Sequential user-based recurrent neural network recommendations. In: Proceedings of the Eleventh ACM Conference on Recommender Systems, pp. 152–160 (2017)
6. Dyer, C., Kuncoro, A., Ballesteros, M., Smith, N.A.: Recurrent neural network grammars. arXiv preprint arXiv:1602.07776 (2016)
7. Fang, J.: Membrane keyboard, July 1 2003. uS Patent 6,585,435
8. Feldman, S.: Holographic keyboard, June 13 2002. uS Patent App. 09/734,874
9. Fullerton, R.L.: Handheld computer keyboard system, August 22 2000. uS Patent 6,108,200
10. Hernanto, S., Suwardi, I.S.: Webcam virtual keyboard. In: Proceedings of the 2011 International Conference on Electrical Engineering and Informatics, pp. 1–5. IEEE (2011)
11. Hotelling, S.P., Zhong, J.Z.: Touch-sensitive display, December 18 2008. uS Patent App. 11/818,498
12. Keislar, D.: History and principles of microtonal keyboards. Comput. Music J. **11**(1), 18–28 (1987)
13. Kiddee, P., Naidu, R., Wong, M.H.: Electronic waste management approaches: an overview. Waste Manage. **33**(5), 1237–1250 (2013)
14. Kumar, P.M.: Method, metrics and motivation for a greener approach to comput- ing, creating virtual monitor, keyboard and mouse environments (vmkm)
15. Noyes, J.: The qwerty keyboard: a review. Int. J. Man-Mach. Stud. **18**(3), 265–281 (1983)
16. Paasovaara, S.: Method, apparatus and computer program product for providing a word input mechanism, June 17 2014. uS Patent 8,756,527
17. Porter, E.W.: Voice recognition system, May 9 1989. uS Patent 4,829,576
18. Roy, S., Singh, A.K., Mittal, A., Thakral, K.: Virtual wireless keyboard system with co-ordinate mapping. Int. J. Adv. Eng. Technol. **7**(3), 1003 (2014)
19. Shah, S., Patel, D., Patel, J., Patel, R.: A survey of virtual keyboard with its senses. Int. J. Recent Trends Eng. Res. **3**, 184–190 (2017)

20. Shibly, K.H., Dey, S.K., Islam, M.A., Showrav, S.I.: Design and development of hand gesture based virtual mouse. In: 2019 1st International Conference on Advances in Science, Engineering and Robotics Technology (ICASERT), pp. 1–5. IEEE (2019)
21. Team, R.: Laser projection keyboard kit calibration and usage manual. http://image.dfrobot.com/image/data/KIT0030/V2/LaserProjectionKeyboardKitv2−calibrationanduse.pdf
22. Thomsen, J.F., Gerr, F., Atroshi, I.: Carpal tunnel syndrome and the use of computer mouse and keyboard: a systematic review. BMC Musculoskelet. Disord. 9(1), 1–9 (2008)
23. Tiric-Campara, M., et al.: Occupational overuse syndrome (technological diseases): carpal tunnel syndrome, a mouse shoulder, cervical pain syndrome. Acta Inform. Med. 22(5), 333 (2014)
24. Wan, C.S.: Virtual mouse. Ph.D. thesis, UTAR (2016)
25. Wijewantha, N.S., Amarasekara, C.: VISTAKEY: a keyboard without a keyboard–a type of virtual keyboard. Final year project thesis. Informatics Institute of Technology, Wellawatta, Sri Lanka (2004)
26. Zhai, S., Kristensson, P.O.: The word-gesture keyboard: reimagining keyboard interaction. Commun. ACM 55(9), 91–101 (2012)
27. Zhao, Y., Lian, C., Zhang, X., Sha, X., Shi, G., Li, W.J.: Wireless IoT motion-recognition rings and a paper keyboard. IEEE Access 7, 44514–44524 (2019). https://doi.org/10.1109/ACCESS.2019.2908835

Using Real-Pen Specific Features of Active Stylus to Cope with Input Latency

Roman Kushnirenko(iD), Svitlana Alkhimova(iD), Dmytro Sydorenko(iD),
and Igor Tolmachov$^{(\boxtimes)}$ (iD)

Samsung R&D Institute Ukraine (SRK), Kyiv, Ukraine
{r.kushnirenk,s.alkhimova,dm.sidorenko,i.tolmachev}@samsung.com

Abstract. Despite the growing quality of touch screen mobile devices, most of them still suffer from input latency. This paper presents a new way to cope with this problem for users who use an active stylus to perform pointing tasks. It is based on the usage of real-pen specific features of an active stylus that can be obtained without any additional wearables. To assess latency compensation that uses orientation, tilt, and pressure values, two studies are conducted. The first study shows that using these features decreases prediction error by 2.5%, improves the distribution of deviation angle from the target direction, and has a good ability to reduce lateness and wrong orientation side-effect metrics by 9.4% and 3.3%, respectively. The second study reveals that users perceive fewer visual side-effects with latency compensation using real-pen specific features of the active stylus. The obtained results prove the effectiveness of utilizing orientation, tilt, and pressure to cope with the latency compensation problem.

Keywords: Touch screen · Touch input · Latency · Prediction · Neural network

1 Introduction

Most modern devices use touch screens as the main way to receive input from users. These screens are designed to work with fingers and are very comfortable for basic device control. However, in the case of writing or drawing, finger input can cause quite an unusual experience. It could feel like putting a finger into ink and trying to write or draw with it. To make this input more comfortable, people use a stylus that works just like a real pen. The latter makes styli very popular among creators and artists because this allows the transferring of human common writing and drawing behaviors, which is not possible with finger input [1]. The simplicity and speed of handwriting over typing result in active usage of a pen and paper for making notes during work meetings and casual tasks that was shown by the survey conducted by NeoLAB Convergence Inc., a manufacturer of smartpens [2]. Therefore, input behavior similar to real-pen one is preferable, and this provides good reasoning for the manufacturers to produce devices with pen-based input.

The stylus popularity increases alongside with rising popularity of so-called phablets (class of mobile devices combining or straddling the size format of smartphones and

© Springer Nature Switzerland AG 2021
M. Kurosu (Ed.): HCII 2021, LNCS 12763, pp. 17–31, 2021.
https://doi.org/10.1007/978-3-030-78465-2_2

tablets) and other devices with extended screen size. There are some classic stylus-equipped product lines like the Samsung Galaxy Note and LG Stylus series that are relevant nowadays and completely new devices like the Motorola Moto G Stylus, launched this year. All these devices have a stylus stored inside the case, making it handy for daily tasks and minimizing the risk of its loss. Also, a lot of modern tablets, like Apple iPad, Microsoft Surface, and Samsung Galaxy Tab, are sold with or can be additionally equipped with a stylus.

Even though the usage of a stylus can be embarrassing in some scenarios, this fact cannot outshine the advantages of stylus input. In particular, a stylus brings the following advantages:

- Stylus nib does not cover a point of contact, whereas fingertip does
- Stylus allows for more precise input due to the smaller contact area
- Stylus, if it is active, can produce real-pen specific features such as tilt, orientation, pressure to enhance stroke rendering process and make it more realistic

On the one hand, these benefits bring more comfortable input. Still, on the other hand, stylus usage on latency-prone systems causes user performance to suffer due to more noticeable latency [1]. Depending on its amount and variation over time, latency can degrade the action-perception loop and make the whole system feel less responsive and interactive [3–5].

The factors mentioned above form a strong motivation for struggling with latency to make stylus input more natural. Therefore, the object of our study is the effectiveness of latency compensation, while usage of real-pen specific features provided by an active stylus is considered as a novel way for more accurate prediction results.

2   Background and Related Work

2.1   Nature of Touch Screen Input Latency

Since handwriting and drawing input speed can be very high in real life, the technology behind the touch screen interaction should have an extremely high response rate to be able to reproduce the stroke shapes from what we input without latency [1].

Latency on touch screen mobile devices is caused by different hardware and software factors. Usually, it has three main sources [6]: 1) sensors that capture touch events (i.e., input hardware component), 2) software components that process touch events and generate output to be displayed, and 3) a screen itself (i.e., visualization hardware component). Decrease of system latency on touch screen mobile devices requires addressing latency issues in all three of these components and is thus a significant challenge.

Hardware latency is caused by the low responsiveness of input and visualization components. Software latency has a much more complex nature. To begin with, any mobile operating system (OS) takes a particular sequence of steps to show user input on a screen. The most popular modern mobile OSs do these steps in the same way for all kinds of interactions [7, 8]. Any user input goes through an event manager, an application, and a buffer manager until shown on a screen. Since OS has to provide all applications with a consistent frame rate and absence of frame drops or tearing effect, it controls all these steps except the application one.

Nowadays, hardware capabilities of typical touch screen mobile devices are mainly locked in at 60 Hz of screen refresh rate. It means that the event-polling loop generally has a delay of ~16.6 ms to synchronize with screen updates. At the same time, triple-buffer rendering is widely used to get frame rate stabilization (smoothness) with no tearing effect. This technique allows the program to have two buffers (backbuffers) to be filled with data while the third one (screenbuffer) is being placed on the screen. As a result, the swap chain with three buffers can be a software source of three-frame duration input latency (i.e., 50 ms with a screen update rate of 60 Hz). However, when the system is loaded, latency can be more durable, but three frames duration is a minimum amount to be decreased on such devices.

Equipping devices with more responsive components can reduce hardware latency. Such improvements will decrease latency within the fixed range, which highly depends on the quality of sensors embedded in the screen. At the same time, it mainly leads to higher power consumption and a high cost of touch screen technology.

Software-based approaches to cope with latency are divided into latency reduction and latency compensation. Both of them offer a possibility to achieve even better results with no cost of hardware complexity. Latency reduction approaches imply system-level solutions to optimize intervals or delays between requesting of touch screen state, synchronizing sensor driver events, and screen refreshing. However, latency reduction implementations influence the whole system and can produce side effects, such as jittering or tearing in certain cases. Latency compensation approaches assume prediction of the future touch position, based on the sequence of the previous input events. Latency compensation approaches are more flexible and can be applied to a specific application or service without influence on the whole system.

Given all the above, it can be summarized that latency is an important problem to solve as it degrades user performance. Existing approaches to cope with latency have their advantages and disadvantages. Hardware-based latency reduction improves user performance, but there will always be sources of software latency due to heavy application side computations, complex high-end graphics, or network delays. At the same time, the influence on the whole system somewhat weakens the interest in software-based latency reduction. Therefore, it is reasonable to improve existing software-based latency compensation approaches or create new ones that help to solve this problem completely or at least to decrease latency to levels perceived by users as low.

2.2 Focus of Input Latency Studies

The research into the effects of latency is typically focused on 1) the perception of delay, 2) impacts on the outcome of an activity, and 3) changes in user behavior. Such studies have been explored widely.

According to Miller [9], the response time of the system on any user interaction should be within 100 ms; otherwise, the system would be perceived as slow. However, recent studies show that even the difference, as small as a few milliseconds, is noticeable when utilizing touch screen devices. Jonathan Deber et al. [5] reported that detectable thresholds in the case of dragging (11 ms) are lower than for tapping direct input (69 ms).

Albert Ng et al. [1] found that, while users performed dragging and scribbling tasks with a stylus, they can perceive very low levels of latency (i.e., ~1 ms for dragging and ~7 ms for scribbling). Michelle K. Annett et al. [4] reported that latency perception for inking tasks is worse (~50 ms) than perception for non-inking ones when a stylus is being used. At the same time, hiding the input instrument from users' eyes and showing only output on a separate display, makes latency perception even weaker (up to 97 ms) on inking scenarios.

2.3 Latency Compensation Approaches

Related studies that are listed below proposed different approaches aimed at latency compensation.

Cattan et al. [10, 11] used a simple linear prediction model to compensate device latency on simple object dragging tasks. They found out that on the system with a lag of 25 ms, latency's negative effects could be decreased with linear extrapolation. However, on the system with a lag above 42 ms, their approach is not precise enough to increase performance. Nancel et al. [12, 13] compared more complicated prediction models, like Taylor series, curve fitting, and some heuristic approach, based on pointer speed and acceleration. Their general finding was that the upper mentioned methods bring side effects, which disturb users even more than perceiving latency. As a result, they proposed a predictor that behaves according to the current pointer velocity to eliminate the most probable side effects for every velocity range. Even though their predictor showed better results than compared approaches, its efficiency was not tested in the perspective of stylus usage. It was not compared to neural network approaches due to a lack of accessible calibration procedures.

Alternatively to mathematical methods, mentioned above, Henze et al. [14, 15] used neural networks to predict the finger's future position based on the latest trajectory of a finger. Received results showed that the usage of neural networks for latency compensation is more precise than simple extrapolations, but they had limited success. Their research on different machine learning prediction algorithms resulted in PredicTouch (a hybrid software-hardware approach), which increased the prediction performance by considering data from a wrist-worn inertial measurement unit [16]. In contrast to the results mentioned above, the current research is aimed at latency compensation improvement that can be achieved not by improving the neural network architecture and not by utilizing additional data from wearables, but by using available information obtained from an active stylus.

3 Orientation, Tilt, Pressure for Latency Compensation

Until now, all neural network models, designed to cope with latency compensation problem, used only three parameters to predict future position [14, 15]. These parameters are x/y coordinates and timestamps of previous touch events. We propose to use such real-pen specific features of the active stylus as orientation, tilt, and pressure to compensate input latency with an approach based on neural networks.

3.1 Real-Pen Specific Features of Active Stylus

The orientation value indicates the direction of the stylus tilt in relation to the vertical axis of the screen. Orientation values are defined as directional inputs over 360° around a reference point. As stylus orientation varies continuously during the input, it can be actively used for prediction enhancement in all input scenarios. Of course, orientation values depend on user handedness, but all the cases can be easily generalized because of hand anatomy and the relativeness of the input system.

Tilt refers to the angle of the stylus during the input process, and it is tightly related to its work-plane orientation. This angle can vary from the value when the stylus is held perpendicular to the touch screen surface to value when it lies flat on the surface. We supposed that utilizing tilt can help to predict the future position of stylus nib on latency-prone systems. If the tilt of the stylus for some trajectory has a pattern, this pattern can be used to form further changes in the trajectory.

Pressure value indicates the force applied to the surface by the stylus nib. Input pressure values can continuously change within a different range that depends on device calibration and varies from one touch screen device to another. Leaving aside the influence of user mental state on input pressure, we hypothesized that the strategy of controlling stylus pressure stays the same while the user performs input of a particular stroke pattern, e.g., a specific letter shape or sketch graphics.

3.2 Dataset and Preprocessing

To collect strokes with logged information about orientation, tilt, and pressure values, we developed an Android application that instructed participants on how to perform different input scenarios and provided the possibility to record all touch events data.

The dataset was collected from 40 participants (30 male, 10 female), 23–51 years old (avg. 32.8), 7 left-handed. All of the participants owned a touch screen mobile device and used touch input at least one hour per day. Participants were not compensated.

In total, the collected data contains 20.8 million touch events from 264.3 thousand strokes of writing and drawing inputs with an active stylus on Galaxy Note 9 devices (US and EU market models).

All collected data were preprocessed in the way described below.

Initially, we filtered out consecutive touch events that had no changes in x/y coordinates since they were produced when stylus remained motionless. Touch events obtained not with a stylus (caused by some random screen touches, canvas scrolling, or even palm resting on the touch screen) were also skipped. It should be mentioned that to avoid stroke breaking, we did not filter touch events, which happened to be outside the input area.

After the filtering, we calculated differences between x/y and timestamp values obtained from each pair of neighboring touch events. The same procedure was performed with values of orientation, tilt, and pressure.

We also converted x/y differences to millimeters to avoid dependency on screen resolution.

All differences were normalized to 0–1 range to enable better convergence of the neural network solution.

3.3 Implementation Details

To verify the fact that the usage of real-pen specific features of the active stylus improves latency compensation, we implemented GRU-CNN neural network
architecture according to [17] using Tensorflow 2.0 library.

To derive a set of samples for neural network models training, we applied a sliding-
window technique on touch events. Each sample was in the form of two vectors.

An input vector contained information on 19 consecutive differences (this value was
determined with a grid search). While the first dimensionality of the input vector was
equal to 19, the second one was 3 for latency compensation using only trajectory and 6
for latency compensation using real-pen specific features of the active stylus. As a result,
we had 19×3 and 19×6 input vectors.

An output vector represented a spatial shift (x/y coordinates) from the last touch
event in the input vector to the future position of a stylus nib within the canvas area. As
a result, we had 1×2 output vectors.

To demonstrate the impact of real-pen specific features of active stylus on prediction
accuracy, we conducted two studies: quantitative and qualitative.

In both studies, we used two models with the same GRU-CNN architecture. The only
difference was data given to them: the first model was trained with using all real-pen
specific features of the active stylus, whereas the second one was trained without it. Both
models were aimed to cope with three-frame duration input latency on devices with a
screen update rate of 60 Hz (i.e., 50 ms). As was mentioned above, it is a minimal amount
to be compensated for applications that use the swap chain with three buffers (according
to the triple-buffer rendering technique). The models training was done similar to the
procedure in [17].

All data and results are obtained with applications developed for Android OS due
to its open-source availability and popularity on the mobile device market. Despite that,
many of the concepts could probably be useful on other platforms where active stylus
interactions are supported.

4 Study 1: Latency Compensation Accuracy

This study is aimed at latency compensation assessment with quantitative metrics. In
addition to the common metric used to evaluate the accuracy of prediction (prediction
error) and custom one (distribution of deviation angle), we calculated metrics that allow
quantification of visual side-effects perceived by users.

4.1 Apparatus

We developed an Android application that provides an opportunity for the user to perform input tasks under different scenarios (Fig. 1). The application instructs participants
on how to input in different scenarios and provides a mechanism to log touch event
information given by active stylus; thus, we can collect appropriate data.

We used Galaxy Note 9 devices for both US (Qualcomm Snapdragon 845, 4 ×
2.8 GHz & 4 × 1.7 GHz cores, Adreno 630) and EU (Exynos 9810, 4 × 2.7 GHz & 4 ×
1.8 GHz cores, Mali-G72 MP18) markets. All devices have a screen refresh rate equal
to 60 Hz and an input sampling rate equal to 360 Hz.

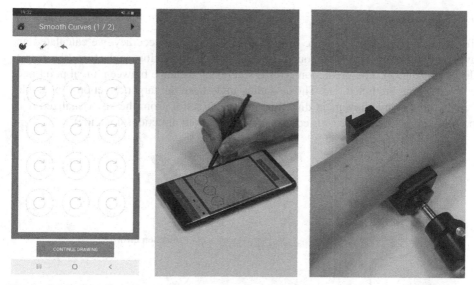

Fig. 1. Study 1 outline. Screenshot of the user interface for the representative task (left); a participant inputs in the proposed scenario (middle); cuff for forearm immobilization (right).

4.2 Participants

We involved 9 participants (5 male, 4 female), 23–35 years old (avg. 28.1), 1 left-handed. All of the participants owned a touch screen mobile device, and all of them used touch input at least one hour per day. Participants were not compensated.

4.3 Task and Procedure

Participants gave a consent form and were briefed on the tasks they should perform. These tasks include replicating closed circular curves (below referred to as *smooth curves*), 15°, 35°, 55°, 75° angles (*acute angles*), 105°, 125°, 145°, 165° angles (*obtuse angles*), drawing a simple sketch (*usual drawing*) and writing a text with Latin characters (*usual writing*).

In *smooth curves*, *acute angles*, and *obtuse angles* tasks, participants inputted data in two ways according to [18]. One way implied only finger movements, whereas the other way also allowed wrist movements. While performing these tasks, participants were asked to replicate each shape in the direction depicted by an arrow.

In *usual drawing* task, participants were asked to input an arbitrary sketch. In *usual writing* task, participants inputted any text they wanted. Each participant spent on average 1 min (SD 0.3) performing *usual drawing* task and on average 0.5 min (SD 0.1) performing *usual writing* task.

Participants sat in a comfortable position and inputted at their usual speed; similar to [18] their forearms were immobilized with a cuff to avoid accidental movements.

4.4 Measurements

To assess how real-pen specific features affect prediction accuracy, we calculated an average prediction error and found a distribution of deviation angle from the target direction (Fig. 2). The prediction error is Euclidean distance between a real point and corresponding predicted one. The deviation angle from the target direction is an angle between the stylus movement direction and the direction from the last visualized real point to the predicted one (it is equal to zero when both directions coincide).

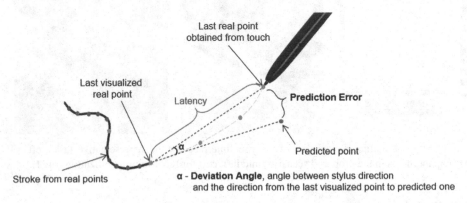

Fig. 2. Schematic presentation of the evaluation method.

We also calculated a set of metrics introduced by Nancel et al. [12]. This set of metrics was shown to be able to estimate the perceptual probability of the seven most common visual side-effects perceived by users in cases of input with latency compensation. We used the code provided[1] by Nancel et al. to calculate lateness, over-anticipation, wrong orientation, jitter, and jumps metrics. We did not report the spring effect metric since obtained values were equal to 0 for this metric in all cases. A higher score for each calculated metric corresponds to a higher chance that users notice corresponding visual side-effect. Thus, a better prediction approach should provide lower scores.

4.5 Results and Discussion

Metrics were calculated using 450 thousand touch events that were produced from 1080 strokes collected in *smooth curves*, *acute angles*, and *obtuse angles* tasks and 736 strokes collected in *usual writing* and *usual drawing* tasks. Data collected from *usual drawing* and *usual writing* tasks were preprocessed by excluding the 5% shortest and 5% longest strokes in duration (similar to the procedure in [12]).

Results of prediction error comparison (Table 1) indicated that utilizing real-pen specific features of active stylus affected prediction more positively in cases of *usual writing* and *usual drawing* tasks.

Two reasons can explain it. First, the input in *smooth curves*, *acute angles*, and *obtuse angles* tasks had some synthetic nature caused by certain precision requirement. Second,

---

[1] http://mjolnir.lille.inria.fr/turbotouch/predictionmetrics/.

Table 1. Prediction error comparison; data presented are absolute values, mm (improvement compare to utilizing only X/Y coordinates, %).

Features	Smooth curves	Acute angles	Obtuse angles	Usual drawing	Usual writing
X/Y	0.3336	0.2833	0.2912	0.1450	0.4223
Orientation	0.3318(+0.54)	0.2829(+0.14)	0.2910(+0.07)	0.1436(+0.97)	0.4199(+0.57)
Tilt	0.3319(+0.51)	0.2839(−0.21)	0.2919(−0.24)	0.1433(+1.17)	0.4217(+0.14)
Pressure	0.3283(+1.59)	0.2802(+1.09)	0.2858(+1.85)	0.1414(+2.48)	0.4206(+0.40)

data collecting with only finger movements was inconvenient for most participants, and it led to input trajectory subject to frequent errors. The last one also can explain that tilt had insignificant positive or even negative impact in mentioned tasks.

Despite the slight improvements with prediction error, results on all collected data showed that deviation angle became less scattered (Fig. 3).

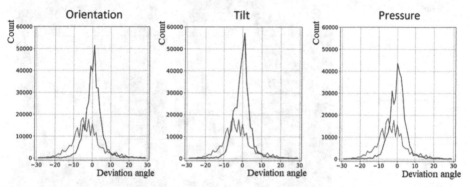

Fig. 3. Deviation angle from the target direction obtained in case of utilizing only X/Y coordinates (red) and in case of additional utilizing one of the real-pen specific features (blue). (Color figure online)

Analysis of variance (ANOVA) was conducted to compare the effect of considering real-pen specific features of active stylus on prediction error. It revealed a significant main effect of orientation ($F_{1, 16} = 451.48$, $p = 3.75 \cdot 10^{-13}$, $\eta^2 = 0.94$), tilt ($F_{1, 16} = 60.67$, $p = 7.83 \cdot 10^{-7}$, $\eta^2 = 0.62$) and pressure ($F_{1, 16} = 6535.85$, $p = 2.49 \cdot 10^{-22}$, $\eta^2 = 0.99$) usage.

As lateness, over-anticipation, wrong orientation, jitter, and jumps metrics are used to assess the perception of visual side-effects, these metrics were calculated on data obtained in cases of usual input (*usual writing* and *usual writing* tasks). Pairwise comparison showed that compensation utilizing both trajectory and all real-pen specific features of the active stylus has a good ability to reduce lateness and wrong orientation cases; it also positively affects jitter and jumps. Lateness was reduced from 1.09 to 0.99, wrong orientation from 7.61 to 7.37, jitter from 1.48 to 1.46, jumps from 1.21 to 1.19. At the same time, over anticipation showed a higher score: 2.58 vs. 2.60. It can be explained by the fact that lateness and over-anticipation have contrary nature so that effective lateness treatment can cause degradation in over-anticipation.

5 Study 2: Users' Perception of Latency

This study is aimed at questionnaire data obtaining since latency compensation assessment is not only determined by good quantitative results. The primary reason for conducting the survey was to determine if users could notice prediction improvement caused by considering real-pen specific features of the active stylus.

5.1 Apparatus

We developed an Android application to conduct a survey and to get feedback on how real-pen specific features of active stylus affect latency compensation (Fig. 4).

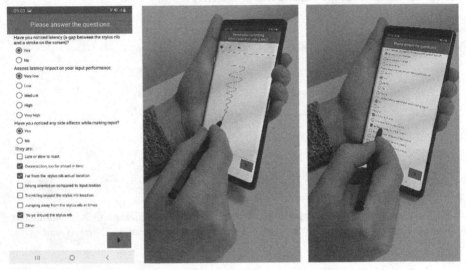

Fig. 4. Study 2 outline. Screenshot of survey user interface (left); a participant performs input to assess latency (middle) and takes a survey (right).

We used the same Galaxy Note 9 devices as in Study 1.

Rendering of our application was done using the swap chain with three buffers (according to the triple-buffer rendering technique). To get evidence that this causes input latency with at least three-frame duration (50 ms in our case), we determined an average latency using the method of Ng et al. [6]. We used Galaxy Note 9 stock camera application to record 960 fps video at 1280×720. To obtain movements across the screen at a rate as constant as possible, we changed the originally proposed scenario with finger to scenario with stylus mounted on the computer numerical control machine (Fig. 5). We determined an average input latency of 58.1 ms (SD 2.3) in the case with no latency compensation.

Fig. 5. Inputting with stylus mounted on the computer numerical control machine.

In our application, we rotated the screen vertically and set the resolution to 2220 × 1080 pixels; the actual size was 145 × 70 mm, with 0.065 mm/pixel resolution.

The application rendering mechanism replaced each predicted point with the corresponding real one once the latter was being processed by the OS (at least after 50 ms in our case). This behavior represents the objective of latency compensation to make visual feedback more responsive, not to corrupt the shape of inputted stroke.

5.2 Participants

We involved 23 participants (18 male, 5 female), 26–50 years old (avg. 32.1), 2 left-handed. Similar to Study 1, all of the participants owned at least one touch screen mobile device and actively used it according to their work needs. All of this study participants reported that they used touch input at least three hours per day. Participants were not compensated.

5.3 Task and Procedure

After having explained the goals of the study to participants, we received their consent forms. To be able to describe their experience, participants were provided with basic latency-terminology.

We presented participants with an application that allows them to perform such pointing tasks as writing or drawing, and assess latency during the input process (Fig. 4). The task given to participants was to input arbitrary text or sketch. We did not limit time for them to perform the task.

The participants were given two consecutive trials that differed on whether input latency was compensated or not. Since we studied two approaches to compensate latency, during each trial the application could be executed in one of three modes: 1) with compensation utilizing only previous trajectory (below referred to as *simple latency compensation*), 2) with compensation utilizing trajectory and real-pen specific features (*advanced latency compensation*), and 3) without latency compensation (*without latency compensation*). Only two trials, instead of three, guaranteed that the answers were not affected with the knowledge of the modes chosen by the randomizer. Moreover, a three-mode comparison would be less exact comparing to a two-mode.

The three modes mentioned above gave nine different two-mode combinations. Combinations with the same modes were taken into consideration to ensure that participants perceive them as equal. However, these combinations should be relatively rare and were drawn with a 10% probability (i.e., with a 3.33% probability per each of three combinations). The remaining six combinations with distinct modes were drawn with a 90% probability (with a 15% probability per each combination).

After having spent some time inputting in each mode, the participants were asked to assess latency impact (if any) on their input performance with *very low*, *low*, *medium*, *high*, and *very high* values.

We were also interested if the participants have noticed some side effects during the input process. To be able to classify participants' answers, we provided all participants with the list of side-effects described by Nancel et al. [12]: lateness, over-anticipate, wrong distance, wrong orientation, jitter, jumps, and spring effect. To make the process of side-effects description easier, we presented participants with descriptions of each side-effect that were adapted to pointing input with the active stylus as follows:

- Lateness as "late, or slow to react" case
- Over-anticipate as "overreaction, too far ahead in time" case
- Wrong distance as "far from the stylus nib actual location" case
- Wrong orientation as "not going in the same direction compared to input motion" case
- Jitter as "trembling around the stylus nib location" case
- Jumps as "jumping away from the stylus nib at times" case
- Spring effect as "yo-yo around the stylus nib" case

If the participants noticed any side-effect, we asked them to estimate its disturbance between 1 (not disturbing at all) and 5 (unacceptable) according to [12].

5.4 Results and Discussion

In the current study, we got 16 cases of input with *simple latency compensation*, 15 cases of input with *advanced latency compensation*, and 15 cases of input *without latency compensation*.

The whole group of participants noticed the changes in latency according to the scenario proposed to them during two consecutive input trials. First, this result indicates that even lower input latency than reported in [4] can be noticed while performing such pointing tasks as writing or drawing. Additionally, this provides an outline of the key drawback in human-computer interaction caused by the triple-buffer rendering technique. The utilization of this technique as a common rendering approach inevitably leads to noticing input latency on devices with a 60 Hz screen update rate.

It has been pointed out, that in cases of input *without latency compensation* 33.3% of participants assessed latency impact as *very low*, 20% as *low*, 33.3% as *medium*, 13.3% as *high*, and 0% as *very high*.

Although participants noticed similar visual side-effects in both cases of input with latency compensation, the *advanced latency compensation* case showed a lower amount of side-effect occurrences. Table 2 provides occurrence and aggregated disturbance rankings of side-effects where applicable.

Table 2. Side-effects reported by participants; data presented are occurrence, %, and aggregated disturbance ranking between 1 (not disturbing at all) and 5 (unacceptable), median (mode).

Side-effect	Simple compensation		Advanced compensation	
	Occurrence	Disturbance	Occurrence	Disturbance
Lateness	3	2 (2)	1	1 (1)
Over-anticipate	3	2 (2)	0	–
Wrong distance	1	2 (2)	1	3 (3)
Wrong orientation	5	3 (4)	1	3 (3)
Jitter	3	1 (1)	2	1 (1)
Jumps	2	3 (3)	1	3 (3)
Spring effect	1	2 (2)	0	–

It should be mentioned that in the case of *advanced latency compensation* disturbance of such side-effects as wrong distance and wrong orientation was noticed by the same participant. The scenario proposed to this participant was input *without latency compensation* in the first trial and input with *advanced latency compensation* in the second one. Visual side-effects noticed in the second trial could not be identified by the participant among the mentioned visual side-effects.

Although each participant noticed the changes in input latency, not all of them noticed visual side-effects resulting from latency compensation approaches.

Having analyzed the answers of the participants, we found out that input speed affected the number of side-effects noticed by participants. The observations revealed that participants who inputted more slowly observed fewer side-effects than participants who inputted faster.

6   Conclusion and Future Work

Our contribution is in the considering of real-pen specific features as a new way to cope with input latency more effectively.

Comparing to the latency compensation involving only trajectory, additional usage of real-pen specific features of active stylus allowed us to reduce prediction error by 2.5% and significantly improve the distribution of deviation angle from the target direction. At the same time, values of metrics for quantifying visual side-effects were decreased by 9.4% for lateness, 3.3% for wrong orientation, 1.4% for jitter, and 1.3% for jumps. It should be mentioned that these results were achieved with no additional data from wearables but with data solely obtained from the active stylus, which was an input tool.

Obtained results demonstrated that quantitative metrics values, as well as user satisfaction, were improved in case of compensation utilizing real-pen specific features of the active stylus. However, latency compensation accuracy, or more precisely, prediction accuracy is not still perfect. Therefore, new experiments can be performed to make input prediction more robust. Moreover, new approaches to process and display prediction data can be considered. For example, the idea to combine prediction results for a period of one, two, and three frames duration merits careful consideration. Such an approach might prove useful for more natural stroke construction.

References

1. Ng, A., et al.: In the blink of an eye: investigating latency perception during stylus interaction. In: Proceedings of the SIGCHI Conference on Human Factors in Computing Systems, pp. 1103–1112. ACM, New York (2014). https://doi.org/10.1145/2556288.2557037
2. New Survey Shows Professionals Prefer Pen and Paper Note Taking for Increased Productivity and Retention. Press release (2015). https://www.neolab.net/en/news/press-releases/new-survey-shows-professionals-prefer-pen-and-paper-note-taking-for-increased-productivity-and-retention. Accessed 21 Jan 2021
3. Jota, R., Ng, A., Dietz, P., Wigdor, D.: How fast is fast enough?: a study of the effects of latency in direct-touch pointing tasks. In: Proceedings of the SIGCHI Conference on Human Factors in Computing Systems, pp. 2291–2300. ACM, New York (2013). https://doi.org/10.1145/2470654.2481317
4. Annett, M., et al.: How low should we go?: under-standing the perception of latency while inking. In: Proceedings of Graphics Interface 2014, pp. 167–174. Canadian Information Processing Society, Toronto (2014)
5. Deber, J., Jota, R., Forlines, C., Wigdor, D.: How much faster is fast enough?: user perception of latency & latency improvements in direct and indirect touch. In: Proceedings of the 33rd Annual ACM Conference on Human Factors in Computing Systems, pp. 1827–1836. ACM, New York (2015). https://doi.org/10.1145/2702123.2702300
6. Ng, A., et al.: Designing for low-latency direct-touch input. In: Proceedings of the 25th Annual ACM Symposium on User Interface Software and Technology, pp. 453–464. ACM, New York (2012). https://doi.org/10.1145/2380116.2380174
7. Yun, M.H., He, S., Zhong, L.: POLYPATH: supporting multiple tradeoffs for interaction latency. arXiv preprint arXiv:1608.05654v1 (2016)
8. Yun, M.H., He, S., Zhong, L.: POLYPATH: reducing latency by eliminating synchrony. In: Proceedings of the 26th International Conference on World Wide Web, pp. 331–340. International World Wide Web Conferences Steering Committee, Republic and Canton of Geneva (2017). https://doi.org/10.1145/3038912.3052557
9. Miller, R.B.: Response time in man-computer conversational transactions. In: Proceedings of the December 9-11, 1968, Fall Joint Computer Conference, Part I, pp. 267–277. ACM, New York (1968). https://doi.org/10.1145/1476589.1476628
10. Cattan, E., Rochet-Capellan, A., Perrier, P., Bérard, F.: Reducing latency with a continuous prediction: effects on users' performance in direct-touch target acquisitions. In: Proceedings of the 2015 International Conference on Interactive Tabletops & Surfaces, pp. 205–214. ACM, New York (2015). https://doi.org/10.1145/2817721.2817736
11. Cattan, E., Rochet-Capellan, A., Bérard, F.: A predictive approach for an end-to-end touch-latency measurement. In: Proceedings of the 2015 International Conference on Interactive Tabletops & Surfaces, pp. 215–2018. ACM, New York (2015). https://doi.org/10.1145/2817721.2817747

12. Nancel, M., et al.: Next-point prediction metrics for perceived spatial errors. In: Proceedings of the 29th Annual Symposium on User Interface Software and Technology, pp. 271–285. ACM, New York (2016). https://doi.org/10.1145/2984511.2984590

13. Nancel, M., et al.: Next-point prediction for direct touch using finite-time derivative estimation. In: Proceedings of the 31st Annual ACM Symposium on User Interface Software and Technology (UIST '18), pp. 793–807. ACM, New York (2018). https://doi.org/10.1145/324 2587.3242646

14. Henze, N., Funk, M., Shirazi, A.S.: Software-reduced touchscreen latency. In: Proceedings of the 18th International Conference on Human-Computer Interaction with Mobile Devices and Services, pp. 434–441. ACM, New York (2016). https://doi.org/10.1145/2935334.2935381

15. Henze, N., Mayer, S., Le, H.V., Schwind, V.: Improving software-reduced touchscreen latency. In: Proceedings of the 19th International Conference on Human-Computer Interaction with Mobile Devices and Services, pp. 1–8. ACM, New York (2017). Article no. 107. https://doi. org/10.1145/3098279.3122150

16. Le, H.V., Schwind, V., Göttlich, P., Henze, N.: PredicTouch: a system to reduce touchscreen latency using neural networks and inertial measurement units. In: Proceedings of the 2017 ACM International Conference on Interactive Surfaces and Spaces, pp. 230–39. ACM, New York (2017). https://doi.org/10.1145/3132272.3134138

17. Kushnirenko, R., Alkhimova, S., Sydorenko, D., Tolmachov, I.: Active stylus input latency compensation on touch screen mobile devices. In: Stephanidis, C., Antona, M. (eds.) HCII 2020. CCIS, vol. 1224, pp. 245–253. Springer, Cham (2020). https://doi.org/10.1007/978-3-030-50726-8_32

18. Schomake, L.R.B., Réjcan, P.: The relation between pen force and pen-point kinematics in handwriting. Biol. Cybern. 63(4), 277–289 (1990). https://doi.org/10.1007/BF00203451

Comparing Eye Tracking and Head Tracking During a Visual Attention Task in Immersive Virtual Reality

Jose Llanes-Jurado$^{(\boxtimes)}$, Javier Marín-Morales, Masoud Moghaddasi, Jaikishan Khatri, Jaime Guixeres, and Mariano Alcañiz

Instituto de Investigación e Innovación en Bioingeniería (i3B),
Universitat Politècnica de València, 46022 Valencia, Spain
jllajur@i3b.upv.es

Abstract. The use of eye tracking (ET) and head tracking (HT) in head-mounted displays allows for the study of a subject's attention in virtual reality environments, expanding the possibility to develop experiments in areas such as health or consumer behavior research. ET is a more precise technique than HT, but many commercial devices do not include ET systems. One way to study visual attention is to segment the space in areas of interest (AoI). However, the ET and HT responses could be similar depending on the size of the studied area in the virtual environment. Therefore, understanding the differences between ET and HT based on AoI size is critical in order to enable the use of HT to assess human attention. The purpose of this study was to perform a comparison between ET and HT technologies through the study of multiple sets of AoI in an immersive virtual environment. To do that, statistical techniques were developed with the objective of measuring the differences between the two technologies. This study found that with HT, an accuracy of 75.37% was obtained when the horizontal and vertical angular size of the AoIs was 25°. Moreover, the results suggest that horizontal movements of the head are much more similar to eye movements than vertical movements. Finally, this work presents a guide for future researchers to measure the precision of HT against ET, considering the dimensions of the AoI defined in a virtual scenario.

Keywords: Head-mounted display · Eye-tracking · Head-tracking · Virtual-reality · Area of interest

1 Introduction

Virtual Reality (VR) is a powerful tool in many research fields, including consumer behavior, psychological assessment, education, and health care, as it reproduces or creates different realistic situations under controlled laboratory conditions. This technology can design virtual environments that evoke cognitive processes and emotions similar to real environments [1]. Naturally, it also allows free-navigation emulating real-world movement. Recently, head-mounted displays (HMDs) have been achieving a high level

© Springer Nature Switzerland AG 2021
M. Kurosu (Ed.): HCII 2021, LNCS 12763, pp. 32–43, 2021.
https://doi.org/10.1007/978-3-030-78465-2_3

of immersion and fidelity. HMDs enable the most realistic experience during the performance of the experiment in the virtual environment, as they isolate the subject in the environment. VR can also be combined with many different technologies, such as eye tracking (ET) or head tracking (HT). These technologies are not only used to measure certain features of the subject's performance in the virtual environment, some studies have also implemented them to assess reactive scenarios from the user's measurement feedback. Renaud et al. [2] developed an environment using ET features that was able to change when the subjects indicated visual avoidance, in order to prevent a decrease in therapy effectiveness. The use of these technologies not only allows for the study of subject behavior but can also improve the interaction of a subject with the virtual environment.

The use of ET or HT in HMDs improves the assessment of a subject's attention and inspection [3]. Both technologies have many applications in the study of human interaction in such fields as therapy [4] and consumer behavior research. Indeed, this type of technology is often preferred in clinical research over others due to its ease of use and the information that it provides [5]. For example, ET is usually used to detect autism in children. The work of Bekele et al. [6] used a VR environment in which the eye gazes of children with autism were tracked to study variations between different groups of children. Other research has used ET for academic purposes, including the work of Deans et al. [7] that studied attention deficit hyperactivity disorder (ADHD) through subjects' reading or visual inspection training in VR [8]. On the other hand, HT has been used for the study of driver attention recognition [9]. Another study used this technology to control a power wheelchair. There have also been studies that use both technologies. Zito et al. [10] studied HT and ET to assess the behavior of young and old people in street-crossing scenarios in VR.

Even though both technologies measure visual attention and can be used simultaneously, HT is a simpler technology that does not require integration of eye tracker systems in the HMD. HT technology is included in the HMD and does not require special equipment [11]. On the other hand, ET requires tracker system integration, which not many commercial HMDs have. This increases the cost of ET. However, ET is much more precise than HT. ET obtains eye gaze points from corneal reflections and pupil movements. In the case of HT, the computation of the head gaze comes from the interpolation of the position of the head and its direction. It offers less precision than ET in gaze measurement. Indeed, HT does not require previous calibration to be used. Despite the difference between ET and HT being commonly known, the quantification of these differences in VR is still an open issue. Some studies have compared ET and HT technologies. For example, Pfeil et al. [12] compared HT and ET in two groups of people, one group performing a task in VR and the other group in physical reality (PR). The conclusion was that people in VR perform more movements than people in PR, indicating a possible difference in the formation of a subject's natural responses. Qian et al. [13] also performed a comparison study between HT and ET, in which the subjects wore HMDs displaying a desktop screen. The subjects used gaze to select certain spheres of different sizes in the environment. Surprisingly, the results showed that HT achieved the best performance. Indeed, the authors highlighted correct calibration of the ET as a limitation in the study, as two subjects were excluded due to calibration problems. However, to the best of our knowledge, there are no studies that explore the accuracy and similarity between ET and HT sensors in an immersive virtual environment. The measurement of accuracy for sensor type could guide future research by providing a quantifiable method for choosing ET or HT sensors depending on the precision needed in each application. It could also increase the interaction level of the subject in the VR displayed.

This study aimed to measure under which conditions the measurement of ET and HT were similar. We proposed different types of analysis to evaluate the similitude between ET and HT technologies. The main objective of this work was to measure the threshold size of an area of interest (AoI) that achieved a high accuracy for both technologies. To do that, a range of different angular sizes for horizontal and vertical sides of the AoI was set. Similarities between the gaze trajectories of ET and HT were also compared in a virtual environment. A final set of recommendations were identified from the results of this work.

2 Materials and Methods

2.1 Participants

A group of 57 subjects (27 females and 30 males) with corrected-to-normal vision, participate in this study. The mean age of the participants was 25.36 (SD = 4.97). The inclusion criteria were as follows: Spanish nationality, age between 18 and 36 years, and no previous VR experience. All experimental protocols and methods were performed in accordance with the regulations and guidelines of the local ethics committee of the Polytechnic University of Valencia.

2.2 Virtual Environment and Data Collection

The virtual environment was displayed using an HMD with the ET- and HT-integrated HTC Vive Pro Eye system (see Fig. 1). This display offers a field of view of $110°$. The scene has a maximum refresh rate of 90 Hz with a total resolution of 2880×1600. The ET data were obtained from the Unity VR using the ET software development kit (SRanipal). It has a maximum frequency of 120 Hz and an accuracy of $0.5°-1.1°$. The computer used was an Intel Core i7-770 CPU 3.60 GHz with an NVIDIA GeForce GTX 1070. To perform the study, an immersive 3D scenario using the Unity 3D platform was developed. This featured a room modeled by an occlusive Cube Map, which was a Unity object that captured and ensured that all the possible ET and HT rays impacted against an element in the virtual scenario.

The virtual room included two equal-dimension panels. Each panel displayed a matrix of 4×4 numbers. Every square was identified by a number sequence from 1 to 16 in the first panel, and 17 to 32 in the second. Each square included a background color to ensure contrast between the cells and focus the subject's attention (see Fig. 2). The initial location of the viewer was above a marked orange point in the scene, in front of the first panel. The location of this orange point was established to provide frontal and diagonal gazes in each subject. The first panel, from the subject's point of view, had an angular horizontal position that started at $-14.93°$ and went to $14.93°$, whereas the

Fig. 1. Subject using the experimental setup, an HTC Vive Pro Eye developed for the study.

Fig. 2. Virtual scenario from subject perspective.

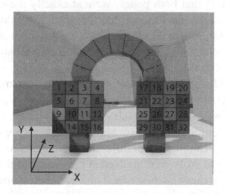

Fig. 3. Frontal view of the virtual environment indicating the axis orientation inside it.

second panel went from 25.02° to 45.00°. This ensured that the subject's head moved in multiple directions during the experiment.

A predetermined and identical sequence for all subjects was designed and followed to facilitate attention directed in different locations within the scenario. The subjects were instructed to look at the illuminated squares during the task. The sequence was created randomly according to the following criteria:

- The sequence had to begin in the first panel.
- The four diagonals and the center of the central panel had to be explored.
- The subject had to look at the nearest and furthest point of the second panel.
- Certain squares had to be illuminated alternating between the two panels.

The result was the following sequence: 1, 16, 4, 13, 6, 11, 7, 10, 17, 32, 22, 10, 20, 5, and 30. The subjects were asked to freely explore the environment for 5 s to adapt to it. After that, the subjects were instructed to look at each square when it was illuminated, which remained brightened for 3 s. Every illuminated square was defined as an AoI. The total time of the task was less than 60 s.

The raw ET and HT data included the 3D position of the impact of the gaze ray in the environment's system of coordinates, which are fix coordinates. x-axis indicated horizontal position, y-axis indicated vertical position, and z-axis indicated the depth of the gaze position in the environment. This was the data used for statistical analysis. The virtual environment also provided a file that recorded the specific illumination time of a square (for example, square 1; time 5 s–8 s). This file was used to synchronize the gaze data with the illuminated sequence protocol for each AoI. Only ET and HT gaze data that was between the illuminated and shutdown times for each AoI was taken into account.

2.3 Comparison Between Head-Tracking and Eye-Tracking

The first analysis performed was to measure the similitude between ET and HT through the trajectory of both in the x-, y-, and z-axes. However, the z-axis was removed from the analysis due to the fact that both panels were at exactly the same distance, in this component, from the subject. This meant that the depth component depended on the display of the virtual environment and did not provide any relevant information. Next, the two trajectories were compared by use of regression and statistical metrics including root mean square error (RMSE), mean absolute error (MAE), and cross-correlation. Moreover, in order to evaluate if both curves were statistically similar or not, a one-way analysis of variance (ANOVA) test was performed for the average position per second for both technologies. A p-value higher than 0.05 was used to determine if the distributions are not statistically different. In either case, both distributions are statistically different.

The accuracy of both technologies for different-sized rectangular AoIs was also evaluated. These variably sized AoIs were located at the center of the illuminated squares of the environment. For a range of horizontal and vertical angular sizes, the software identified if eye and head gazes were located in the defined AoIs. This was studied for every subject according to the sequence of illumination of each AoI. In other words, eye and head gaze were only compared for each AoI when it was illuminated. The horizontal and vertical angular ranges began at $0°$ and terminated at $100°$ each $5°$. However, the frequency record of both technologies was different, making analysis difficult as it would require analyzing each subject individually. To avoid this inconvenience, each eye and head gaze position was averaged every 0.1 s from the beginning of each AoI's illumination. These mean positions were included in analysis if they occurred during the same AoI illumination. Accuracy metric was chosen to measure the agreement between eye and head gaze. Comparison of the obtained accuracy for horizontal and vertical rectangular AoIs was also performed. Finally, the results obtained for squared AoIs were shown.

3 Results

First of all, the eye and head gaze trajectories in the x-, y-, and z-axis were compared. This comparison is shown in three plots: Fig. 4, which refers to the x-axis, and Fig. 5, which refers to the y-axis. Figure 4 shows a high correlation between the head and eye gazes in the x-component at a descriptive level, despite the AoIs being in different panels. The y-component illustrated in Fig. 5 shows less similarity than the x-component, although a higher similarity for downward movements than for upward ones is evident. Figure 5 shows a good correlation between head and eye gazes until the end of the sequence in the first panel. After that, the movement between panels desynchronizes both trajectories. Indeed, after this point, the HT is never fixed again with respect to the subject in the virtual environment.

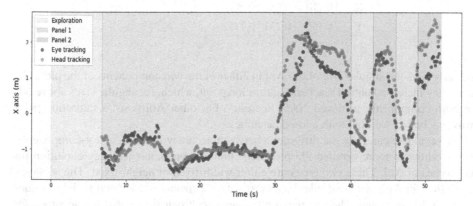

Fig. 4. Graphical representation of the x-axis trajectory during the experimentation of eye (blue) and head (orange) gazes. This plot also illustrates the mean time it took for subjects to look at the different panels (pink for first panel and purple for second panel). The initial exploratory phase of the experiment is also included (grey). (Color figure online)

The statistical comparison between the ET and HT trajectories of the three axes is shown in Table 1. As can be seen, RMSE, MAE, and cross-correlation metrics showed higher similarity for x- than for y- and z-components. The p-value was not statistically significant (p-value > .05) for the x-component whereas for the y-component a p-value less than .001 was found indicating a statistical difference between ET and HT.

The evolution of ET and HT accuracy with regard to the different horizontal and vertical angular sizes is shown in Fig. 6. This plot shows how the accuracy increased

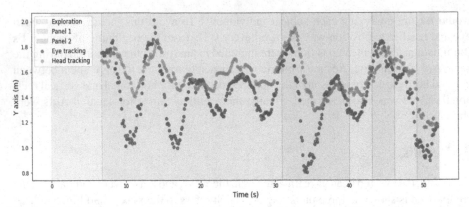

Fig. 5. Graphical representation of the y-axis trajectory during the experimentation of eye (blue) and head (orange) gazes. (Color figure online)

Table 1. Regression and statistical metrics of the comparison between eye and head gazes. The p-value column indicates the statistical significance according with the following: * p-value $< .05$, ** p-value $< .01$ and *** p-value $< .001$.

Axis	RMSE	MAE	Cross. Correlation	p-value
X	0.110	0.083	0.951	–
Y	0.156	0.121	0.717	***

linearly with the angular size of the AoI in either of the two components of the plot. The accuracy increased until it reached a saturation point, which, for angular sizes above 60° in both components, achieved 100% accuracy. For other AoI sizes, a saturation point was reached as well but with a lower accuracy.

To evaluate carefully the difference between accuracy in the x- and y-components, Fig. 7 shows a more detailed 2D plot. This plot compares the accuracy evolution for two types of AoI. These two types are either width-fixed or height-fixed. The accuracy evolution for AoIs with one side fixed (vertical or horizontal) in 10° and with both sides fixed in 20° is shown. The comparison between each pair shows that the accuracy for vertical AoIs was higher than the accuracy for horizontal AoIs. The saturation point achieved by vertical and horizontal AoIs was also significant. For example, in the case of an AoI whose horizontal size measured 10°, an accuracy was achieved that saturated at 39.53%, whereas the vertical accuracy saturated at 47.50%. In the case of AoI's with a maximum size of 20°, this difference went from 72.83% accuracy for horizontal and 77.67% accuracy for vertical. Figure 7 also illustrates the accuracy evolution for squared AoIs. The results indicate that for squared AoIs with an angular size of 20°, the obtained accuracy was 60.74% between HT and ET. The accuracy of squared AoIs was lower than for rectangular AoIs for small angular amplitudes. However, a saturation point of 100% accuracy was achieved for an angular size of 80°.

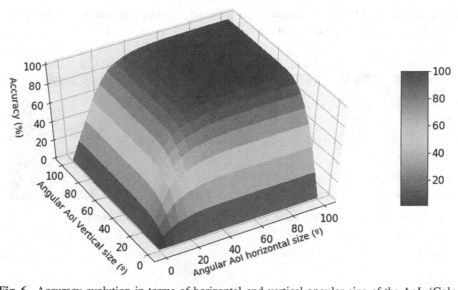

Fig. 6. Accuracy evolution in terms of horizontal and vertical angular size of the AoI. (Color figure online)

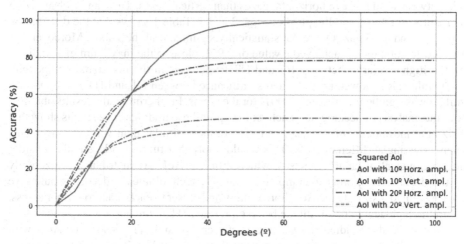

Fig. 7. Accuracy evolution for different AoIs sizes. The x-axis indicates the angular size of the AoI in degrees. The y-axis indicates the percentage of accuracy between ET and HT for a particular AoI size. The orange and pink lines indicate a variable-sized AoI with a fixed height of 10° and 20°, respectively. The red and purple lines indicate a variable-sized AoI with a fixed width of 10° and 20°, respectively. The blue line shows the accuracy evolution for a squared AoI of equal width and height. (Color figure online)

Figure 8 reports the obtained accuracy value for different angular sizes up to a squared AoI size of 50°. The reported accuracy values show that AoIs with a higher vertical angular amplitude achieved a higher accuracy than those with a higher horizontal angular amplitude. As the plot shows, the accuracy saturated at different values (not always 100%) as the angular amplitude increased.

	Vert. size 5°	Vert. size 10°	Vert. size 15°	Vert. size 20°	Vert. size 25°	Vert. size 30°	Vert. size 35°	Vert. size 40°	Vert. size 45°	Vert. size 50°
Horz. size 5°	7.53%	13.98%	18.02%	20.00%	21.98%	22.93%	23.36%	23.62%	23.78%	23.83%
Horz. size 10°	12.46%	24.46%	33.54%	38.47%	42.25%	44.30%	45.54%	46.37%	46.83%	47.07%
Horz. size 15°	16.25%	32.28%	45.15%	52.66%	57.98%	61.13%	62.91%	64.28%	65.28%	65.82%
Horz. size 20°	17.78%	35.48%	50.59%	60.74%	67.86%	71.95%	74.30%	75.95%	77.08%	77.67%
Horz. size 25°	18.85%	37.83%	54.49%	66.84%	75.37%	80.07%	82.77%	84.88%	86.38%	87.27%
Horz. size 30°	19.47%	38.99%	56.64%	70.37%	80.39%	85.42%	88.73%	90.87%	92.46%	93.39%
Horz. size 35°	19.63%	39.47%	57.76%	72.07%	82.70%	88.14%	91.71%	93.96%	95.58%	96.54%
Horz. size 40°	19.67%	39.52%	58.05%	72.54%	83.24%	88.99%	92.66%	95.01%	96.67%	97.65%
Horz. size 45°	19.67%	39.53%	58.24%	72.82%	83.63%	89.40%	93.08%	95.43%	97.09%	98.12%
Horz. size 50°	19.67%	39.53%	58.25%	72.83%	83.64%	89.41%	93.08%	95.44%	97.09%	98.13%

Fig. 8. Accuracy value, in percentage, for different AoIs sizes.

4 Discussion

From the obtained results two conclusions can be made. First, there was a higher similitude between head and eye horizontal gazes than vertical gazes. This can be observed in the results of Table 1 and the plots of Figs. 3 and 4. Table 1 shows that the distribution of the eye and head gazes were not statistically significant in the x-axis. Moreover, the cross-correlation metric achieved a value of 0.951, close to the maximum of 1, indicating the high similarity between ET and HT trajectories in the horizontal component. The p-value also showed no statistical significance between ET and HT for the x-axis, while it was significant (p-value $< .001$) for the y-axis. Furthermore, the results obtained from the analysis of accuracy for each AoI support these findings. The results show that horizontal movements of the head and eye are more similar than vertical movements when assessing at different AoIs. This would imply that future works should consider the development of environments in which different AoIs are distributed horizontally around the subject in order to compare ET and HT technologies. Indeed, it would give more insight to distribute the AoIs horizontally and closer to each other to further assess, due to the high degree of similitude between ET and HT in the horizontal plane.

This work also studied the accuracy between ET and HT sensors for AoIs with different angular sizes. As can be seen from the results of Fig. 7, these values saturate at a certain accuracy value, independent of the magnitude of the AoI sides. The size of the AoI only determined when the accuracy would saturate, with a sooner saturation for small AoIs compared to larger AoIs. Figures 6 and 7 suggest that AoIs with one side fixed at 10° or less, will not obtain accuracies above 25% for head and eye gazes. This shows that very large horizontal or vertical AoIs do not guarantee to achieve a high similitude between ET and HT. On the other hand, Figs. 6 and 7 also show an interesting result. As the amplitude of the AoI increased, the accuracy was a slightly higher for horizontal AoIs than vertical ones. However, after both accuracy evolution curves cross, the vertical AoI overtakes the horizontal one in accuracy. For example, Fig. 6 shows the evolution of the AoI fixed at 20° in the horizontal and the vertical sides (purple and pink lines, respectively). Before the curves cross, the horizontal AoI has a slightly higher accuracy than the vertical one. The curves cross when both AoIs are equal because both are squared AoIs. After this point, the vertical one achieves a higher accuracy. Indeed, the saturation point of both curves is different, with the horizontal AoI saturating sooner. These results suggest that future research should consider better vertical AoIs than horizontal ones, with large AoI angular sizes such as 15° and 25° or above. These AoIs also guarantee an accuracy range between 45% and 60% for both technologies. For smaller AoIs, the use of horizontal or vertical AoI would be inconsequential, though the horizontal ones are slightly more accurate. However, an AoI below 15° would show a low accuracy for ET and HT (less than 45%). Finally, AoIs with larger sizes, greater than 25° or 30°, would achieve high accuracies above 80% for both technologies. For these types of AoIs, ET and HT technologies could achieve almost an equal performance in the virtual environment.

There are some limitations to this work. For example, the experimental methodology consists of a guided task, in which it is indicated where the subject had to look each time. Thus, it would be interesting to compare non-guided experiments to the achieved results. Random AoI sequences for each subject could also be tested, as well as different virtual scenarios. This would avoid some possible bias in the design of the sequence and scenario of this experimentation. For example, the distribution of both panels horizontally, in the present environment, could bias the results of the x-component. Future studies could be designed with panels in different dimensions. All in all, more research is needed in order to further and validate the results found in this work.

The results of this study suggest a set of indications that could help future research to perform improved AoI studies using ET and HT. These indications include the consideration of AoI with an angular size between 20° and 25° that would achieve an accuracy between 60% and 80%, and the development of AoI with a larger size in the vertical component rather than in the horizontal one. The results show that the use of HT could be comparable to ET under certain conditions. For objects with a square size of 25°, both technologies could be compared and achieve similar results, with an accuracy of 75.37%. The obtained results could be used for glasses that do not have ET integration but can measure HT. With the use of HT, for objects above an angular size of 15°, assessment of visual attention is similar to ET, with a high degree of precision. The obtained results can be also used for non-virtual reality environments such as images or videos in 360°. The distribution of the virtual environment is similar to the distribution found in a 360° image. This is due to the fact that the subject stays at a fixed point in the scenario. Consequently, the present results could be used for 360° images in different contexts such as visual inspection training, tourism, or marketing. These types of contexts often use 360° images and videos. These results could help in the design of future scenarios in these areas. For example, the findings of this work suggest the ability to design scenarios with a horizontal distribution of the objects rather than vertical. Indeed, these contexts use AoIs with angular sizes that could be easily higher than 20° or 25° in the environment. For this reason, the use of ET and HT could be, under these circumstances, indistinguishable.

5 Conclusions

In conclusion, the present study has shown a set of similarities between the use of ET and HT. This work suggests new thresholds for AoI size in a virtual environment in order to compare the performance of both technologies. An accuracy above 75% is obtained for AoIs with a size greater than 25°. Moreover, this study has shown that horizontal trajectories are much more similar between ET and HT than vertical ones. The findings of this work could suggest and improve the design of future virtual reality experiments. Moreover, these results could also be extrapolated to semi-immersive scenarios such as 360° images and videos or cave automatic virtual environment.

Acknowledgment. This work was supported by the European Commission (Project RHUMBO H2020-MSCA-ITN-2018-813234), by the Generalitat Valenciana funded project "Rebrand," grant number PROMETEU/2019/105, and by the European Regional Development Fund program of the Valencian Community 2014–2020 project "Interfaces de realidad mixta aplicada a salud y toma de decisiones," grant number IDIFEDER/2018/029.

References

1. Riva, G., et al.: Affective interactions using virtual reality: the link between presence and emotions. Cyberpsychol. Behav. Impact Internet Multimedia Virtual Real. Behav. Soc. **10**, 45–56 (2007)
2. Renaud, P., Joyal, C., Stoleru, S., Goyette, M., Weiskopf, N., Birbaumer, N.: Real-time functional magnetic imaging-braincomputer interface and virtual reality. Promis. Tools Treat. Pedophilia. Prog. Brain Res. **192**(2), 63–72 (2011)
3. Henderson, J., Hollingworth, A.: High-level scene perception. Annu. Rev. Psychol. **50**, 243–271 (1999)
4. Lutz, O., et al.: Application of head-mounted devices with eye-tracking in virtual reality therapy. Curr. Dir. Biomed. Eng. **3**(1), 53–56 (2017)
5. Al-Rahayfeh, A., Faezipour, M.: Eye tracking and head movement detection: a state-of-art survey. IEEE J. Transl. Eng. Health Med. **1**, 2100212 (2013)
6. Bekele, E., Zheng, Z., Swanson, A., Crittendon, J., Warren, Z., Sarkar, N.: Understanding how adolescents with autism respond to facial expressions in virtual reality environments. IEEE Trans. Vis. Comput. Graph. **19**(4), 711–720 (2013)
7. Deans, P., O'Laughlin, L., Brubaker, B., Gay, N., Krug, D.: Use of eye movement tracking in the differential diagnosis of attention deficit hyperactivity disorder (ADHD) and reading disability. Psychology **1**, 238–246 (2010)
8. Duchowski, A.T., Medlin, E., Gramopadhye, A., Melloy, B., Nair, S. Binocular eye tracking in VR for visual inspection training. In: Proceedings of the ACM Symposium on Virtual Reality Software and Technology, pp. 1–8. Association for Computing Machinery, New York (2001)
9. Ahlstrom, C., Victor, T., Wege, C., Steinmetz, E.: Processing of eye/head-tracking data in large-scale naturalistic driving data sets. IEEE Trans. Intell. Transp. Syst. **13**(2), 553–564 (2012)
10. Zito, G.A., Cazzoli, D., Scheffler, L.: Street crossing behavior in younger and older pedestrians: an eye- and head-tracking study. BMC Geriatr. **15**, 176 (2015)
11. Zapała, D., Balaj, B.: Eye tracking and head tracking – the two approaches in assistive technologies (2012)

12. Pfeil, K., Taranta, E.M., Kulshreshth, A., Wisniewski, P., LaViola, J.J.: A comparison of eye-head coordination between virtual and physical realities. In: Proceedings of the 15th ACM Symposium on Applied Perception, no. 18, pp. 1–7. Association for Computing Machinery, New York (2018)
13. Qian, Y.Y., Teather, R.: The eyes don't have it: an empirical comparison of head-based and eye-based selection in virtual reality. In: Proceedings of the 5th Symposium on Spatial User Interaction, pp. 91–98. Association for Computing Machinery, New York (2017)

Investigation of Motion Video Enhancement for Image-Based Avatars on Small Displays

Tsubasa Miyauchi$^{(\boxtimes)}$, Wataru Ganaha, Masashi Nishiyama⑩, and Yoshio Iwai⑩

Graduate School of Engineering, Tottori University, 101 Minami 4-chome, Koyama-cho, Tottori 680-8550, Japan
{nishiyama,iwai}@tottori-u.ac.jp

Abstract. We investigate a method for enhancing the motion video sequences of an image-based avatar so that the body motion can be perceived as natural on a small display. If some avatar motions are too small, then the users cannot perceive those motions when the avatar is viewed on a small display. In particular, the motion of an upright posture that the avatar uses when waiting to start interacting with the user is very small. In this paper, we enhance the motion of the upright posture so that the user naturally perceives the movement of the avatar as human-like, even on a small display. To do this, we use an existing method for phase-based video motion processing. This method allows us to control the amount of avatar movement using a pre-defined enhancement parameter. The results of our subjective assessment show that the users sometimes perceived the avatar's motion as natural on a small display when the body sway motions of the avatar were appropriately enhanced to the extent that no significant noise was included.

Keywords: Avatar · Body sway · Motion video enhancement

1 Introduction

Interactive systems that use human-like avatars are an active topic in human-agent interaction research and have many potential applications, such as conversational avatars in a museum [1], avatars who talk about the past [2], and speechinteractive guidance avatars [3]. These avatars can utilize the large displays that we often see in many places (e.g., in stations, shopping plazas, office entrances, and airports), and they can automatically communicate with users without the constraints of time and place (e.g., at an automatic information desk late at night). In particular, we focus on navigation systems that synthesize human-like realistic avatars by exploiting an image-based technique [2,4] in which video sequences interact with users. To develop such navigation systems, it is important to provide a navigation guide that is intuitive for users, such

© Springer Nature Switzerland AG 2021
M. Kurosu (Ed.): HCII 2021, LNCS 12763, pp. 44–55, 2021.
https://doi.org/10.1007/978-3-030-78465-2_4

Fig. 1. Overview of our navigation system using image-based avatars on large and small displays.

as people who are not familiar with complex technology, to use. In this paper, we focus on the use of image-based techniques to generate realistic human-like avatars that can interact with users naturally.

Figure 1 shows an overview of our navigation system using image-based avatars. We use such an avatar on a large display as digital signage. A user stands in front of an avatar on this display and talks to it to receive directions. In our system, an avatar interacts with a user using human-like behavior. Here, we consider a situation in which it will be difficult for the user to remember these directions (e.g., a path to the destination is very complex). To help the user in this situation, our system then guides the user on his/her mobile device, such as a smartphone, after the user has finished talking with an avatar on a large display. Existing research [5] shows that an avatar that points at a map significantly increases the likeability of the system. Therefore, our system displays an avatar and a map on the user's mobile device. The avatar on the small display continues to guide the user until the destination is reached to prevent the user becoming lost en route.

We consider how to generate an intuitive video sequence of an image-based avatar, which is an important element in a navigation system. We divide the video generation into generation for large displays and generation for small displays. Because a life-sized avatar can be displayed on a large display, we can easily reproduce the movement of a real person in the avatar. In contrast, when displaying an avatar on a mobile device, the avatar motions become too small because the screen size of the mobile device is much smaller. As a result, the user cannot naturally perceive the avatar's motions. So that the avatar motions can be perceived by the user, we need to adaptively control the amplitude of the avatar's movement. Here, we consider a situation in which an avatar with an upright posture waits to start interacting with the user before providing directions. The avatar may appear to be completely stationary, that is, moving little or not at all, on a small display. In this situation, a user incorrectly feels that the avatar system is broken and interaction cannot begin. Therefore, we need to design a video generation method for displaying an avatar with a natural-looking upright posture on a mobile device.

When we observe the motions of standing people with an upright posture, their bodies constantly swing around a certain position. In these motions, people are subconsciously swinging their bodies to avoid overloading some muscles. A method for reproducing body sway motions in an image-based avatar has previously been proposed [6]. It generates continuous and natural body sway from a short video sequence of an avatar with an upright posture. However, the existing method was designed for an image-based avatar on a large display. If we use the existing method on a small display, a user may perceive the avatar motions as very small and unnatural. We therefore need to enhance avatar motions with an upright posture on a small display so that a user feels that the motions are more natural.

In this paper, we investigate the intuitive video generation of image-based avatars with an upright posture on a small display. Specifically, we employ an existing method for phase-based video motion processing and evaluate an enhancement parameter used in the method. To do this, we test the following hypothesis.

Hypothesis: Users perceive the motion of an image-based avatar as more natural if it is enhanced using an enhancement parameter of phase-based video motion processing that is appropriate for a small display.

2   Importance of an Upright Posture for Avatars

Existing research [6,7] has found that, to synthesize realistic avatars for interactive systems, the states of the avatar must be considered. Two states of the avatar are important for the avatars of interactive systems. The first is the action state, in which the avatar speaks with a user, and the second is the wait state, in which the avatar maintains a standing pose. In particular, the wait state has an important role in the interaction between avatars and users because the avatars do not continuously communicate with the users. In contrast, the wait state is needed to handle periods before and after interaction. For example, if the wait state is not adequately applied in the avatars, the users cannot judge whether to begin communication with the avatars or not.

The wait state of the avatars enhances the nonverbal communication between users and avatars, as illustrated in Fig. 2. To achieve this, we synthesize human-like micro movements. Consider a standing pose in the wait state; we often see

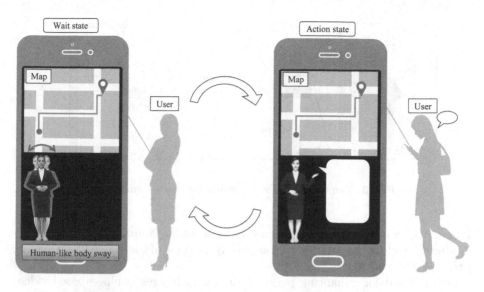

Fig. 2. We consider the body sway of an image-based avatar in the wait state to enhance the nonverbal communication between it and a user in an interactive system.

standing receptionists at airports, hotels, and information offices. When people maintain a standing pose, they continuously move their body slightly around its center line. As described in [8], people unconsciously spread the burden of standing across their muscles by making micro movements to avoid overloading one set of muscles. This physiological phenomenon is called body sway.

We consider reproducing body sway in an image-based avatar. Body sway is a very small movement. When the image-based avatar is displayed on a large display, the user can visually recognize the movement of the body sway, so we can reproduce the body sway motions of an actual human in the image-based avatar. When displaying the image-based avatar on a small display, the user cannot visually perceive the body sway motions of an actual human. Then, the user misunderstands that the image-based avatar is stopping and the navigation system is out of order. We therefore need to enhance body sway motions of the image-based avatar on a small display so that a user feels that the motions are more natural.

3   Method for Enhancing Body Sway Motions

Here, we explain the method of enhancing body sway motions in an image-based avatar. In the most basic approach to this method, a data set is created by taking images of an image-based avatar standing upright with a large body sway motions. However, this method would need to use different data sets depending on whether a large or small display is used, and a large amount of data sets would need to be prepared. In addition, body sway is performed unconsciously

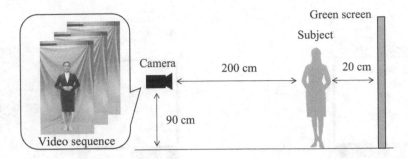

Fig. 3. Camera setup for acquiring the avatar images.

by humans, so it is difficult to consciously increase the amplitude of body sway motions. Therefore, we enhance the body sway motions of the image-based avatar in the images instead.

One method for enhancing periodic motion in images is phase-based video motion processing [9]. In this paper, we use this method to enhance body sway motions. One study [10] found that the frequencies of most body sway movements range from 0 to 1.5 Hz. Here, we measure the actual body sway motions of an image-based avatar in the images, and the frequencies of the body sway are investigated. Figure 3 shows the setup for obtaining the image-based avatar images. The person region of the image-based avatar is extracted from the image-based avatar images using background subtraction. The body sway motions are measured by comparing the person regions in the images on the time axis. Specifically, we measure the difference between the person region of the image at the reference time and the person region at the comparison time. Figure 4 (a) shows the result for head motions in the image (one man and one woman). The vertical axis of the graph represents the difference in the person regions of the reference and comparison images. Figure 4 (b) shows the results for body sway frequency obtained using the fast Fourier transform (FFT) of the difference results. We confirmed that the frequencies of body sway movements range from 0 to 1.5 Hz from the results for both the male and female avatars. Similar results were obtained for parts other than the head. Therefore, phase-based video motion processing enhances frequencies in the range of 0 to 1.5 Hz. We control the amplitude of motion enhancement using parameter alpha, where a larger value of alpha generates larger motions.

4   Subjective Assessment

4.1   Conditions of the Subjective Assessment

We conducted a subjective assessment in which we displayed image-based avatars with enhanced motions. We set the frequencies to range from 0 to 1.5 Hz, which represents most body sway movements, as described in previous section. We used both male and female image-based avatars in the subjective assessment.

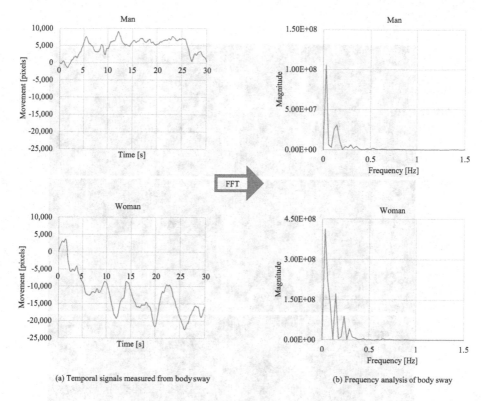

(a) Temporal signals measured from body sway   (b) Frequency analysis of body sway

Fig. 4. Measured results of body sway and the FFT results of body sway.

Figures 5 and 6 show the video sequences of the male and female image-based avatars, respectively. The length of each video was 20 s. We compared the following experimental conditions:

M1: No motion enhancement.
M2: Enhancement using an alpha of 0 to generate a few motions.
M3: Enhancement using an alpha of 1 to generate weak motions.
M4: Enhancement using an alpha of 2 to generate relatively large motions.
M5: Enhancement using an alpha of 3 to generate very large motions.

We used the paired-comparisons method. Twenty-two participants (17 males and five females, with a mean age of 22.2 years) evaluated five avatars (M1, M2, M3, M4, and M5) presented on displays. The avatars were adjusted to the following sizes:

Time

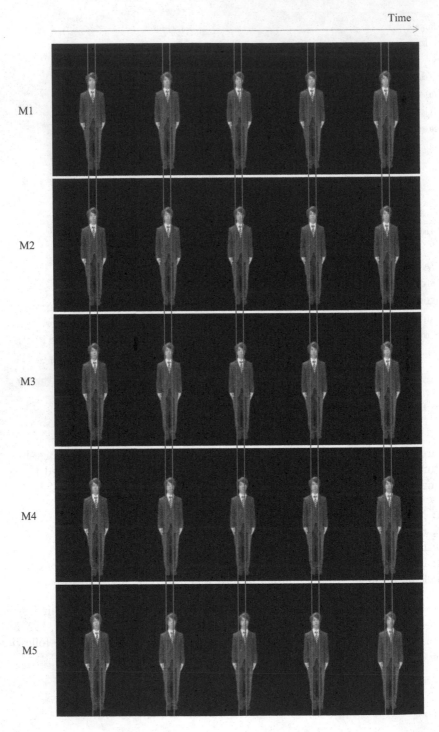

M1

M2

M3

M4

M5

Fig. 5. Examples of video sequences of the male avatar used in our subjective assessment.

Time

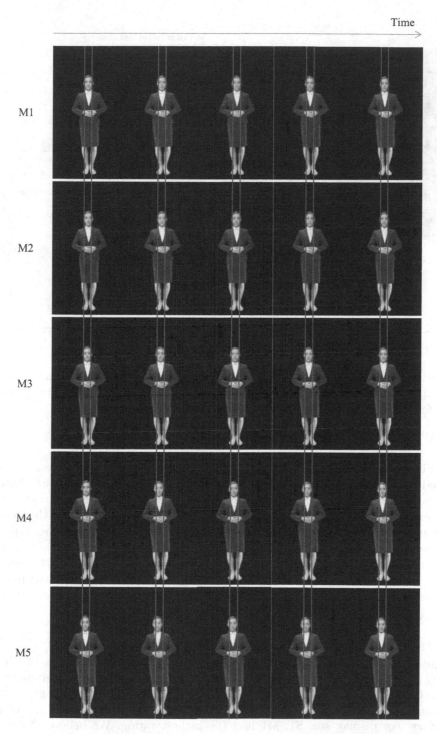

M1

M2

M3

M4

M5

Fig. 6. Examples of video sequences of the female avatar used in our subjective assessment.

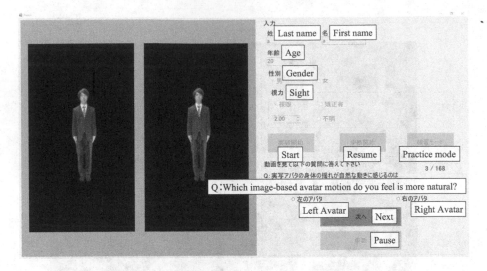

Fig. 7. Questionnaire used in our subjective assessment.

S1: 71.8 mm in height
S2: 44.2 mm in height

That is, S1 was half as large as a 4-in. display, and S2 was half as large as a
6.5-in. display. We displayed pairs of avatars and asked the subjects to answer
the following question:

Q: Which image-based avatar motion do you feel is more natural?

Figure 7 shows the question form. The participants evaluated the two image-
based avatars displayed on the left side of the question form. Figure 8 shows
the setup for each participant in our subjective assessment. The participants
sat in a chair and used the question form displayed on the PC on the desk.
The participant's eyes were 115 cm from the ground and 61 cm from the display
on average. The average angle of the display was 119°. The participants were
presented with randomly generated pairs of five avatars ($_5C_2 = 10$) of two sizes
and two types of avatar (male and female), 40 times in total. The participants
then selected the video sequence in the pair that he or she felt was more natural.

4.2   Result of Subjective Assessment

Figure 9 shows the result of the subjective assessment of the five types of body
sway motion enhancement. The graphs express one axis of subjective evaluation
from the number of votes obtained. A higher subjective score indicates agreement
among the subjects, and vice versa. First, we focus on the results of the male
avatars. For display size S1, M1 had the highest rating. We believe that the
participants felt that the body sway motions of the avatar were sufficient without

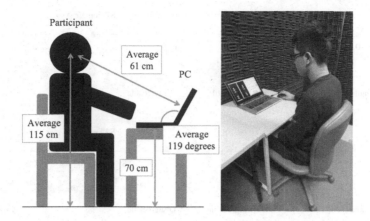

Fig. 8. Experimental setting for our subjective assessment.

motion enhancement. In contrast, for S2, M3 and M4 had a higher rating than M1. We believe that the participants felt that the motion enhancement was agreeable when the display size was smaller. The avatar with very large motion enhancement, M5, was unnatural because of continuous motions, so it received a low rating. M2 also received a low rating because it was too small.

Next, we focus on the results of the female avatars. For display size S1, M1 had the highest rating. Again, we believe that the participants felt that the body sway motions of the avatar were sufficient without motion enhancement. For display size S2, the ratings of M2, M3, and M4 were close to the rating of M1, but M1 had the highest rating. We believe that this result was caused by the shortcomings of the phase-based video motion processing. When enhancing motions, phase-based video motion processing introduces noise into the movie, and it can generate a large amount of noise depending on the movie. Figure 10 shows the noise of the female image-based avatar. When we enhanced motions of the female image-based avatar, high levels of noise were generated in the videos for M3, M4 and M5. Therefore, M3, M4, and M5 had ratings lower than that of M1. M2 received a low rating because the avatar's motion was too small.

In the results of the male avatar, M3 and M4 had a higher rating than M1 for S1. In the results of the female avatar, the ratings of M3 and M4 were closer to that of M1 in S2 than in S1. If we could enhance the body sway motion of the image-based avatar without adding noise, the participants might perceive the avatar motion as natural. In conclusion, the participants may have perceived the avatar motion as natural when it was enhanced with the appropriate value of alpha.

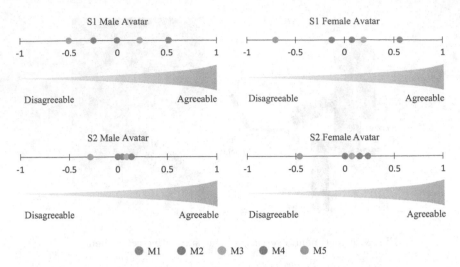

Fig. 9. Results of the subjective assessment. We used the paired comparisons method.

Fig. 10. Noise introduced when generating video sequences of the female avatar used in our subjective assessment.

5   Conclusion

We enhanced the motions of an avatar with an upright posture on a small display so that a user feels that the motions are more natural. We used phase-based video motion processing to enhance the body sway motions. In a subjective experiment, the participants perceived the avatar motion as natural on a small display when we enhanced body sway motion of the image-based avatar and there were low levels of noise. In contrast, the participants did not perceive the avatar motion as natural when high levels existed in the video.

As part of our future work, we plan to develop a method for enhancing the body sway motion of image-based avatars that does not introduce noise.

References

1. Robinson, S., Traum, D., Ittycheriah, I., Henderer, J.: What would you ask a conversational agent? Observations of human-agent dialogues in a museum setting. In: 6th International Conference on Language Resources and Evaluation (LREC), pp. 28–30 (2008)
2. Artstein, R., et al.: Time-offset interaction with a holocaust survivor. In: 19th International Conference on Intelligent User Interfaces (IUI), pp. 163–168 (2014)
3. Lee, A., Oura, K., Tokuda, K.: MMDAgent–a fully open-source toolkit for voice interaction systems. In: IEEE International Conference on Acoustics, Speech, and Signal Processing (ICASSP), pp. 8382–8385 (2013)
4. Jones, A., et al.: An automultiscopic projector array for interactive digital humans. In: ACM SIGGRAPH Emerging Technologies, p. 6:1 (2015)
5. Inoue, M., Shiraiwa, A., Yoshimura, H., Nishiyama, M., Iwai, Y.: Evaluating effects of hand pointing by an image-based avatar of a navigation system. In: 20th International Conference on Human-Computer Interaction (HCII), Part II, pp. 370–380 (2018)
6. Nishiyama, M., Miyauchi, T., Yoshimura, H., Iwai, Y.: Synthesizing realistic image-based avatars by body sway analysis. In: 4th International Conference on Human-Agent Interaction (HAI), pp. 155–162 (2016)
7. Miyauchi, T., Ono, A., Yoshimura, H., Nishiyama, M., Iwai, Y.: Embedding the awareness state and response state in an image-based avatar to start natural user interaction. IEICE Trans. Inf. Syst. **E100-D**, 3045–3049 (2017)
8. Mark, L.S., Warm, J.S., Huston, R.L.: Ergonomics and Human Factors: Recent Research. Springer, New York (1987). https://doi.org/10.1007/978-1-4612-4756-2
9. Wadhwa, N., Rubinstein, M., Durand, F., Freeman, W.: Phase-based video motion processing. ACM Trans. Graph. **32** (2013)
10. Kim, J., Eom, G., Kim, C., Kim, D., Lee, J., Park, B., Hong, J.: Sex differences in the postural sway characteristics of young and elderly subjects during quiet natural standing. J. Geriatr. Gerontol. Int. **10**, 192–198 (2010)

Sound Symbolic Words as a Game Controller

Yuji Nozaki⊙, Shu Watanabe, and Maki Sakamoto(⊠)⊙

Department of Informatics, University of Electro-Communications, 1-5-1 Chofugaoka, Chofu, Tokyo 182-8585, Japan
Maki.sakamoto@uec.ac.jp

Abstract. We developed a game system driven by sound symbolic words that given by a user. While most of other voice-interactive games released in the past focused on making a communication between a player and in-game characters by understanding the meaning of speech, our game system interprets sounds of voice into operable commands. The player's character can move around in a 2D side-scrolling platform game runs on Unity, and its action is controlled by the degree of dynamically and elasticity expressed in the sound symbolic words given by the user. We conducted experiments on 18 subjects to evaluate the difference in user experience between the operation with a conventional game controller and proposed method. As the result of an analysis on questionnaires, it was found that proposed method can provide new experiences to users and can make the game more enjoyable though the difficulty of the game increases by the unfamiliar controlling method.

Keywords: Sound symbolism · Sound symbolic word · Voice interaction

1 Introduction

Voice-controlled gaming has a long history. However, voice interaction remains an understudied modality. Despite a huge number of titles released in gaming industry for the last several decades, there exists few numbers of games that featured voice control, even though most of modern gaming console are technologically capable of handling speech recognition. In general, most of the voice interaction games focused on understanding the orders of the player by analyzing the meaning of words with a speech recognition. Unlike that, we focused on "sounds" of words that the player provides. In other words, instead of replacing existing control schemes, we designed our game to bring new modality by a voice interaction.

Sound symbolism, synesthetic associations between sounds and person's sensory experiences has been demonstrated in a variety of languages [1–3]. The *takete–maluma* effect [4] and the *bouba/kiki* effect [5], are the ones of the most well-known studies in this field. SSWs (Sound symbolic words) can differentiate individual's perceptual experience with a finer resolution than can be achieved with adjectives. Regarding Japanese language, it has been reported that there are about 300 SSWs related to the sense of touch [6]. This number is about twice the number of adjectives in Japanese language. Our objective is to introduce SSWs for a gaming control and to analyze what kind of new modality they can bring to a game.

© Springer Nature Switzerland AG 2021
M. Kurosu (Ed.): HCII 2021, LNCS 12763, pp. 56–64, 2021.
https://doi.org/10.1007/978-3-030-78465-2_5

2 Method

2.1 Game Design

Intuitive movements can be expressed by SSW. To utilize this excellent characteristic for movement instructions, we developed a 2D side-scrolling platform game which is well known by Super Mario Bros series released by Nintendo.

The player operates a red player character and traverses the stage until reaching the goal or touching a treasure chest at the right end of the stage. Figure 1 shows the stage map that used in the experiment.

The stage has several obstacles such as steps, platforms, and pits. Figure 2 shows a typical screen with objects and indicators. Steps and platforms can be jumped on. And falling into a pit results in returning player character to the point in front of the pit. Thus, to reach the goal, the player is required to control the character to jump over these obstacles. Also, there are several coins in the stage. Playing time and the number of coins collected are used to evaluate user experience.

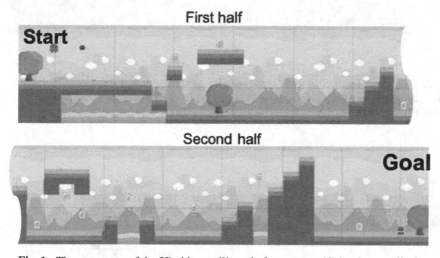

Fig. 1. The stage map of the 2D side-scrolling platform game. (Color figure online)

2.2 Game System

Figure 3 shows the overview of our gaming system used in experiments. As shown in the figure, our system consists of 4 components: dictation software, SSW analyzer, command generator, and game engine. All the software programs are installed in a desktop personal computer. The desktop computer also employs necessary human computer interfaces for game play, such as a microphone, a mouse, and a keyboard. Figure 4 shows the experimental scene of this study. A voice input from a user is converted into text base data by the dictation software, and then analyzed by the SSW analyzer, which we previously developed, to extract "Dynamicity" and "Resiliency" from the input SSW. The command generator decides a type of action, it's direction, and the degree of the action based on the dynamicity and the resiliency of SSW and give the information to the game engine as the command input.

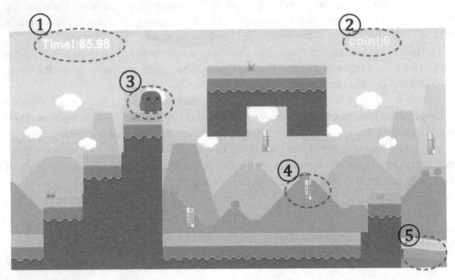

Fig. 2. Examples of indicators and objects. (1) Time from game start, (2) The number of coins collected by a player, (3) Player character, (4) Coin. A player character can get a coin by touching, (5) Pit. Falling into a pit results in returning a player to the point in front of the pit.

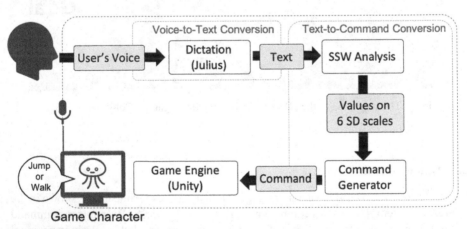

Fig. 3. The Overview of the gaming system. A voice of a user will convert into text data by the dictation software (Julius), and then converted into command to control the in-game character.

In the experiment, Julius [7] is used for the dictation software. To improve the precision of dictation for SSW, we customized its original dictionally. Specifically, we

Fig. 4. An experimental scene.

eliminated several of Japanese words which causes wrong conversion for frequently used SSWs. Since platform games requires a real-time response to the player, the latency of voice input is significantly important for user's experience. As original parameters of Julius are optimized for ordinally daily Japanese conversations, we have heuristically tuned parameters of Julius so that it can efficiently recognize very short sentence such as SSW. Table 1 shows the list of configured parameters and their values that used at our gaming system. As our measurement, the latency to the completion of voice input to its reflection in the character's operation was measured to be approximately 0.16 s.

For the SSW analyzer, we used a mathematical model we previously developed [8, 9]. The model converts a SSW into numerical values on sensory scales, such obtained with the Semantic Differential (SD) method [10]. The SD method is one of the most used methods for estimating the fine quality of sensory aspects from objects. Specifically, our model is a multiple regression model that decomposes given SSW into phonemes and calculates the score for each sensory scale on each phoneme considering the order and structure [11]. The model was made by analyzing correspondences between phonemes and morphologies of SSWs and the score of SD method obtained in sensory tests (For the details of our regression model, please refer [9]). The model can calculate more than forty sensory scales on a scale of −1 to 1. Among these scales, two scales which are considered especially related to movement were used (see Table 2).

Table 1. Parameters and values for dictation software

Option	Description	Value
Headmargin msec	Margin time from the beginning of audio recording. Audio that inputted between this margin will be discarded	300
Tailmargin msec	Margin time from the ending of audio recording. Audio that inputted between this margin will be discarded	100
Rejectshort msec	Threshold time for rejection. Audio input that is shorter than this value will be discarded	100
Overflow pop time	Threshold for the number of expansion hypotheses to be judged as solution search termination	10

Table 2. List of scales

Polar adjectives
Static – Dynamic
Elastic – Nonelastic

The command generator takes two numerical values as an input and converts into a command to give a game engine. A value of "Static-Dynamic" contained in SSW corresponds to "walk right" command, and its value is used to calculate the length of walk. In the same manner, "Elastic -Nonelastic" corresponds to "jump" command and its value is tied to height of jump. Taking an SSW "*dada-dada*" for example, it's value om "Static - Dynamic" is calculated to be 0.45 by our model. This means that the given SSW include much amount of dynamicity, thus make a player character walk long distance. As another example, an SSW "pyon", which the value of "Elastic - Nonelastic" is calculated to be −0.3, results in jumping of middle height. In this way, it is possible to operate the character by freely inputting the SSW without depending on the Bag-of- words-based method nor the wizard of Oz method [12]. A 2D side-scrolling platform game developed on Unity [13] takes commands and gives the game character movements.

3 Experiment

3.1 Experiment Design

To evaluate a user experience of the game, we conducted an experiment on 20 participants. 20 healthy participants (18 males, 2 females) between the ages of 18 to 24 were participated in this study. All participants were a student in The University of Electro-Communication and were recruited as a paid study participant. Most of participants are familiar with video games, and none of them had ever experienced a video game.

All players were provided the same instructions at the experiment, that is, (1) the objective of the game is to obtain a treasure crate, or to reach the right end of the stage,

(2) a player is required to achieve the objective as quickly as possible while collecting coins as many as possible, (3) a player is required to play the game with two different type of game control method, one is with voice-control, and the other is with ordinally game controller with a directional pads and multiple buttons. Then, the participants are given instructions of the game operation.

The total time played, and the number of coins collected are used as performance indicator in the later analysis. To evaluate subjective satisfaction survey, we use a questionnaire with 5 questions which shown in Table 3. All participants answered the questions on two conditions, with and without voice-control enabled. The questionnaire is given in Japanese language in the original experiment. To qualify the effect of voice-interaction, the participants also played the same game with a gamepad as a control. Subjects are divided into two groups and played games with and without voice control in different orders.

Table 3. Questions for subjective satisfaction survey

	Questions	Answers
Q1	Comfortableness and easiness of operation	1 (bad) 7 (good)
Q2	Difficulty of the game	1 (easy) 7 (difficult)
Q3	Degree of entertaining of the game	1 (boring) 7 (fun)
Q4	Novelty of the game	1 (ordinary) 7 (novel)
Q5	Do you want to play the game once again?	Yes/No

4 Result and Discussion

4.1 Result

We compared the in-game indicators for two types of control mode, that is, controlling by voice input and the controlling by a game controller. Table 4 shows the mean and the standard deviation calculated on all subjects. As shown in the table, while the average play time increases about 3.86 times when a user plays the game with voice control, the rate of coin acquisition remains the same (Welch's t test, $p > 0.38$).

Table 4. Comparison of in-game indicators for the two controlling methods

Control mode	Time to game clear [second]	Coin acquisition [%]
Game controller	20.0 ± 1.2	76.7 ± 5.3
Voice control	77.3 ± 9.1	70.6 ± 4.1
p value (t test)	4.38×10^{-7}	0.38

Figure 5 shows a box plots of participants' answer for the questionnaire. As shown in the figure, statically significant differences were observed in all questions (Welch's t test, $p < .05$). This means that playing with an ordinally game controller makes the difficulty of game easier, but on the other hand, playing with voice is more interesting and novel, and there is a tendency to want to play again.

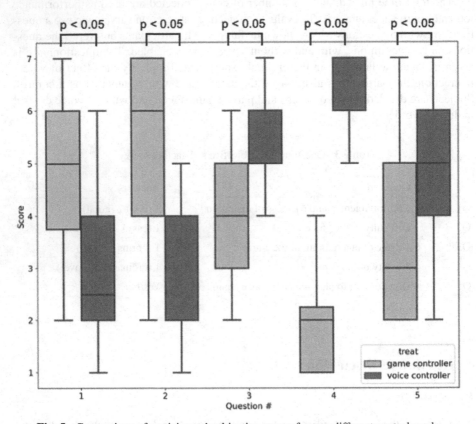

Fig. 5. Comparison of participants' subjective scores for two different control mode.

4.2 Discussion

In this section we consider the result of the experiments. First, we consider the average play time to finish the game. There are several possible causes for increasing in play time of the game by the participants. One is that when speech recognition by SSW is enabled, there is a latency of 0.16 s to convert a voice input into a command for the game engine. Since it takes about 30 operations to clear the game, it consumes about 4.8 s assuming the case of all voice inputs are properly recognized. Furthermore, the time required for the utterance itself also requires more time than the key input that made by the controller. The time required to complete one SSW is about 0.8 s longer than that of the key input, so typically another 24 s (0.8 s × 30 times) shall be added to play time. The success rate of SSW recognition by the dictation software was about 60% throughout the experiment. Taking this number into consideration, the estimated shortest time to clear the game by voice control is calculated to be 48 s longer than the case of operation by a game controller, which is roughly in agreement with this result. It can be easily imagined that such latency, slow input of voice, and recognition rate adversely affect the player's game experience.

There is no statistically significant difference between the two operation methods in the average rate of in-game coin acquisition which is one of the key indices for knowing whether the user has performed the desired operation. This suggests that the concept of this research, SSWs can be used as the controller of a real time game, has experimentally been realized.

As the results of a questionnaire of the user's gaming experience, the scores for two types of control method were significantly different for all five questions. Regarding the first two questions, the operability and the difficulty level of the game, there were remarkable differences between the case of using a general game controller and the case of using the control by voice input. The difference in operability is relatively smaller than that in difficulty, which is consistent with the result that coins were obtained with almost the same rate. In the next three questions about the degree of fun and novelty of the game, the score was significantly higher when using voice input.

In summary, our proposed gaming system works correctly as we intended. And the result of experiment showed that proposed method provides the newness to user's game experiences and makes the game more enjoyable though the difficulty of the game increases by the unfamiliar controlling method that takes any kind of voice (SSWs) from a user.

Acknowledgement. This work was supported by a Grant-in-Aid for Scientific Research on Innovative Areas "Shitsukan" (Nos. 23135510 and 25135713) from MEXT Japan and JSPS KAKENHI Grant Number 15H05922 (Grant-in-Aid for Scientific Research on Innovative Areas "Innovative SHITSUKSAN Science and Technology") from MEXT, Japan.

References

1. Jespersen, O.: Symbolic value of the vowel I. Verlag nicht ermittelbar (1921)
2. Sapir, E.: A study in phonetic symbolism. J. Exp. Psychol. **12**(3), 225–239 (1929). https://doi.org/10.1037/h0070931
3. Wertheimer, M.: The relation between the sound of a word and its meaning. Am. J. Psychol. **71**(2), 412–415 (1958). https://doi.org/10.2307/1420089
4. Köhler, W.: Gestalt Psychology. H. Liveright, New York (1929)
5. Ramachandran, V.S., Hubbard, E.M.: Synaesthesia–a window into perception, thought and language. J. Conscious. Stud. **8**(12), 3–34 (2001)
6. Sakamoto, M., Watanabe, J.: Effectiveness of onomatopoeia representing quality of tactile texture: a comparative study with adjectives. Papers from the National Conference of the Japanese Cognitive Linguistics Association, pp. 473–485 (2013)
7. Julius: https://julius.osdn.jp/index.php?q=dictation-kit.html. Accessed 19 Dec 2020
8. Sakamoto, M., Watanabe, J.: Visualizing individual perceptual differences using intuitive word-based input. Front. Psychol. **10** (2019). https://doi.org/10.3389/fpsyg.2019.01108

9. Sakamoto, M.: System to quantify the impression of sounds expressed by onomatopoeias. Acoust. Sci. Technol. **41**(1), 229–232 (2020). https://doi.org/10.1250/ast.41.229
10. Osgood, C.E., Suci, G.J., Tannenbaum, P.H.: The Measurement of Meaning. University of Illinois Press, Champaign (1957)
11. Hamano, S.: The Sound-Symbolic System of Japanese. The Center for the Study of Language and Information Publications, Stanford, California, Tokyo (1998)
12. Moore, R., Morris, A.: Experiences collecting genuine spoken enquiries using WOZ techniques. In: Proceedings of the Workshop on Speech and Natural Language, USA, February 1992, pp. 61–63 (1992). https://doi.org/10.3115/1075527.1075540
13. Unity Technologies: Unity real-time development platform|3D, 2D VR & AR Engine. https://unity.com/. Accessed 19 Dec 2020

Towards Improved Vibro-Tactile P300 BCIs

Rupert Ortner[1]([✉]), Josep Dinarès-Ferran[1], Danut-Constantin Irimia[2],
and Christoph Guger[3,4]

[1] g.tec Medical Engineering Spain, Carrer del Plom 5, 08038 Barcelona, Spain
ortner@gtec.at
[2] Gheorge Asachi Technical University of Iaşi, Iaşi, Romania
[3] g.tec Medical Engineering GmbH, Sierningstraße 14, 4521 Schiedlberg, Austria
[4] Guger Technologies OG, Herbersteinstraße 60, 8020 Graz, Austria

Abstract. The vibro-tactile P300 based Brain-Computer Interface is an interesting tool for severe impaired patients which cannot communicate using the
muscular and visual vias. In this study we presented an improved tactile BCI for
binary communication that reduces the wrong answers by adding a threshold to
the decision value to achieve a valid answer, otherwise, the BCI gives an indecisive
answer to the question. The threshold is calculated using a statistical test on the
EEG, data recorded during the question to the patient. In total 7 tactile stimulators
were placed on different parts of the subject's body. We tried the new BCI with
4 healthy subjects and using the statistical test they were able to get no wrong
answers after 10 questions asked to each participant. The spelling accuracy and
information transfer rate with and without statistical test are presented as well as
examples of event related potentials.

Keywords: DOC · P300 speller · BCI

1 Introduction

Brain-Computer Interfaces are devices which allow a person to control in some way a
computer or a device connected to that computer. By definition there is no means of
movement or other muscular activity necessary for that control [1]. Comparing such an
interface to classic human-computer interfaces, like a computer mouse, keyboard, touchscreen or voice control, it is pretty clear that the BCI provides an inferior information
transfer rate (ITR) and control accuracy. Bearing that in mind, but adding the fact that no
motor control is necessary it seems clear that today's most BCI applications are thought
for patients whose motor abilities are affected in one way or another. One of the first
BCIs for communication was created by Niels Birbaumer and colleagues in 1999 [2].
They used slow cortical potentials (SCPs) for two patients suffering amyotrophic lateral
sclerosis (ALS). To measure SCPs one needs only one EEG electrode, the drawback is
that the voluntary control of those shifts in cortical potentials are very time consuming
to be learned. In the publication of Birbaumer et al. two patients received more than
300 training sessions before they started free spelling, where one training day consisted
of 6–12 sessions. For that reason, other control strategies were used in the following

© Springer Nature Switzerland AG 2021
M. Kurosu (Ed.): HCII 2021, LNCS 12763, pp. 65–74, 2021.
https://doi.org/10.1007/978-3-030-78465-2_6

years for BCI communication, most time based on event related potentials (ERP). These are electrical potentials, generated by the brain, that are related to specific internal or external events (e.g., stimuli, responses, decisions) [3]. Such events can be auditory-, tactile-, visual-, olfactory stimuli and even heat or pain. One can provide stimuli in a fast repetitive way with distinct frequencies or patterns and look for those patterns in the EEG. Such approaches are called SSVEP (see [1]), or code based visual evoked potentials (c-VEP, [4]). For SSVEPs Guger et al. demonstrated that 53 subjects reached a grand average accuracy of 95.5% after only a few minutes of training [5]. Volosyak et al. calculated a mean information transfer rate (ITR) of 40.23 bit/min and an accuracy of 97.83% with their c-VEP speller [6].

Another approach to utilize the ERP is done with P300 paradigms. There, the BCI is detecting a part of the ERP, the so called P300, which appears only after the user is focusing on a certain target stimulus. Hence, the trick is to present a series of distinguishable stimuli while the user waits for his pre-selected target stimulus to appear. As soon as this happens, the P300 will be generated, which can be detected and as a result the system knows which one was the target stimulus the user just chose. It is important to mention that one needs also nontarget stimuli, sometimes also called distractor stimuli for this approach to work. For a visual based P300 BCI one can use a big number of different characters, for example all the keys of computer keyboard and still gain high classification accuracy. For example Guger et al. found a mean accuracy of 91% with a 36 character speller and 81 participants [7].

BCIs using visual stimuli require the user to be able watching a computer screen or an array of LEDs and to shift his or her gaze from one point to another. Heavily impaired people may not be able to control a BCI in such a way. For those persons one could use other kinds of stimuli, for example auditory or tactile.

With a tactile P300 BCI, Eidel and Kübler recently reached 95% accuracy and 9.5 bits/min ITR after 5 sessions of training on 16 healthy participants [8]. In their first session they reached an ITR of 3.1 bits/minute and 65% accuracy. These results emphasize the influence of training even on P300 based BCIs. The same publication of Eidel and Kübler also presents an overview of recent tactile P300 publications with ITRs ranging mostly between 0.5 and 8 bits/minute and one publication showing an ITR of 20.73 bits/minute [9]. Auditory P300 provide a similar range of ITRs and accuracy, for example Halder et al. reached 2.46 bits/minute and accuracies of 78.6% [10]. It seems clear that the tactile and auditory paradigms cannot reach the same ITR as visual P300 BCI, because one cannot use as many classes as with a visual spelling matrix.

In 2014 we presented a tactile P300 BCI, using either two or three vibrotactile stimulators, placed on the users' body [11]. With the spelling paradigms, 6 locked-in patients reached an average accuracy of 55.3%. Possible results with the speller were YES, NO or an indecisive result in case the distractor stimuli received the highest classification result. For that work, we identified several problems that could have had negative influence on the performance. Firstly, we wanted to provide the user the possibility of an indecisive answer which is neither YES or NO. Such results would not only show if the user may not want to answer YES or NO, but it could also indicate that the user is currently just not attending the task. To implement this indecisive answer, we allowed the distractors to be classified as well. The distractor stimuli were provided with higher probability than the two YES or NO stimuli, therefore the chance level of correctly choosing an answer was only 12.5%, which puts the reached 55.3% accuracy in a better light. But still, such an accuracy level must be considered questionable to be useful for a real communication task with patients. The second identified problem was that the distractor stimuli were provided all by the same vibrotactile stimulator. This could result in participants just ignoring the distractors, or rather not recognizing them in the sequence of stimuli, which could lead to a lower P300 amplitude after target stimuli.

For the current publication, we therefore thought on how to enhance the paradigm. We changed the classification in a sense that a distractor could not be longer a valid classification result. But, for still allowing patients to provide indecisive answers, we further introduced a statistical test, hence only a YES or NO answer, reaching a statistical threshold is considered a valid answer. Furthermore, we increased the number of vibrotactile stimulators from 3 to 7, distributed over the whole participant's body. The new paradigm was tested on 4 healthy participants. The accuracy as well as the ITR was calculated twice: with and without the statistical test. Examples of ERP plots are shown to demonstrate that subjects were able to generate distinct ERP patterns for each class (YES and NO), which can be detected by a classification algorithm.

2 Methods

2.1 Subjects

Four persons (all male, age 31.5 ± 6.5 years, see also Table 1) participated to the study. All participants signed an informed consent, the study was conducted in accordance with the guidelines of the Declaration of Helsinki and approved by the responsible ethics committee (Ethikkommission des Landes Oberösterreich).

2.2 Materials and Methods

The BCI was implemented using a computer running a Simulink model in g.HIsys (g.tec medical engineering, Austria). A biomedical amplifier (g.USBamp, g.tec medical engineering, Austria) was connected to the computer in order to acquire EEG data from the subject. The EEG cap used by the subject had 16 active electrodes. Figure 1A shows the positions according to the extended international 10/20 system. Red positions show the active electrodes, the yellow electrode marks the position of the ground, the reference electrode was placed to the right earlobe (blue) of the subject.

Seven vibro-tactile stimulator units (g.VIBROstim, g.tec medical engineering, Austria) were placed on different parts of the subject's body, see Fig. 1B. The grey positions mark the places for the distractor stimulations: one on each ankle and shoulder, and another one near the navel. The green spot in the same figure marks the tactor positions that was used to provide the answer YES (users' left hand). The red spot marks the position to provide the answer NO (right hand).

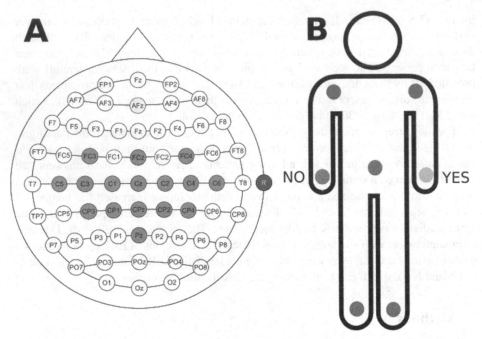

Fig. 1. A: Positions of the acquired EEG. Red spots are active electrodes, blue is the reference and yellow shows the position of the ground. B: Positions of the vibro-tactile stimulators. The green and red dots mark the two possible target positions and the grey dots the distractor positions. (Color figure online)

2.3 Stimulation Sequence

The sequence of stimuli for generating the ERPs was a sequence of vibrations of the vibro-tactile stimulators, doing so in a pseudorandomized order. Before the start of each session, it was explained that the participant should focus on the sequence of stimuli. If one wanted to express the answer YES, one should count each stimulus that was felt on the left hand. For selecting the answer NO, one was supposed to count the stimuli that were felt on the right hand. The counting of target stimuli helped the participants to remain focused on the task and created the P300 components that were used for classification.

One vibration stimulus with any stimulator lasted 100 ms, the inter-stimulus interval was 75 ms. For a precise recording of the timing, the stimulation device sent in parallel a trigger impulse to the digital input of the amplifier each time it switched on a stimulator.

One question was composed of 25 cycles, and each cycle had 8 trials. One trial represents a single stimulus of one of the vibro-tactile stimulators. In every cycle there was at least one trial belonging to one of the seven stimulators, and only one belonging to each of the left and right stimulators.

2.4 One Session

Each participant did one training run, followed by 10 online communication runs. The training run was a sequence of 6 questions where the participant shall select 3 time the answer YES and 3 times NO. In each communication run, the participant was asked one questions with known answer, for example "Do you currently live in Vienna".

The training run lasted 5 min, including short pauses between the questions. One run (question) of the online communication test lasted 37 s.

2.5 Feature Expression and Classification

EEG data were acquired with a sample rate of 256 Hz. Applied filters were a highpass with cutoff frequency at 0.5 Hz, a lowpass at 30 Hz and additionally a notch filter at 50 Hz to suppress power line interference.

After that, the data was triggered into single trials. One trial contained 100 ms before the stimulus onset and 600 ms after that. The segment before each stimulus was used for an individual baseline correction of each trial and channel, by subtracting the mean value of that baseline from the whole trial data.

Consecutively, data got down-sampled by factor 24, using a lowpass filter before to not violate the Nyquist criterium. With the remaining samples, we generated the feature space (6 samples per channel). Classification was done using the time-variant linear discriminant analysis according to Grünwald et al. [12]. This method uses a time-variant feature space, accounting different phases of the ERP. Since 25 trials of each target were used for classification, the single LDA distances got summed up to generate one final decision of each character.

2.6 Indecisive Answers

To decide if an answer was indecisive, a threshold was calculated. If the LDA was below the threshold, the answer was considered indecisive. For that, a gaussian distribution of LDA distances was created by splitting up the test-data and using a bootstrapping approach. Having the gaussian distribution of LDA distances one can decide if the LDA distance calculated with the whole set of test data is withing the percentile 45 and 55, then the answer is indecisive, otherwise not.

2.7 ERP Plots

For the ERP plots the single trials, as described above, got averaged after baseline correction. The plot show target trials in blue and distractor trials in red-dashed line. Additionally, Mann-Whitney significance tests has been done to indicate areas with significant difference between the lines. Those areas are marked in green in the ERP plots.

2.8 ITR

To calculate the ITR, one needs to calculate the average transferred information per answer and the time needed to select one answer. The transferred information depends on the number of correctly provided answers, in worst case, if this is only about 50% then the answer is not better than random, hence no information would be transferred. The number of bits (B) is calculated with the following formula:

$$B = \log_2 N + P \log_2 P + (1 - P)\log_2 \frac{1 - P}{N - 1}$$

Where N is the number of possible answers, and P the reached accuracy. Since the subject were always asked to either answer yes or no, N was set to 2. The accuracy P was calculated for each participant with the number of correct answered questions divided by the number of asked questions. Having calculated B, one can calculate the ITR with:

$$ITR = B/T_{average}$$

$T_{average}$ is the average time needed to provide one answer which is either yes or no. Hence, that value was constant when only binary classification is allowed (37 s). If indecisive classification is allowed too, the average time is calculated with:

$$T_{average} = \frac{asked\ questions}{yes\ and\ no\ answered\ questions} 37\ s$$

3 Results

Table 1. Results of the four subjects calculated two times with the same data. Left: accuracy and ITR if no indecisive answers were allowed, Right: indecisive answers were allowed.

ID	Age (y)	No indecisive answers		Indecisive answers	
		Acc. (%)	ITR (B/min)	Acc. (%)	ITR (B/min)
S1	40	100	1.6	100	1.5
S2	33	90	1.4	100	1.5
S3	26	100	1.6	100	1.5
S4	27	90	1.4	100	1.3
MEAN	31.5	95	1.5	100	1.4
STD	6.5	5.8	0.1	0	0.1

Table 1 shows the four subjects with their age, accuracy in percent and ITR in bits/minute. The accuracy and ITR was calculated two times on the same data. The first time (left part of the table) each question resulted in an answer YES or NO, so the test for indecisive answers was not applied. In the second case (right part of the table) that test was applied and answers got classified indecisive if they did not reach the threshold. S2 and S3 could increase their accuracy from 90% to 100% because their one wrong answer was classified indecisive in the second case.

Indecisive answers are not considered wrong for the accuracy calculation. The change of wrong answers to indecisive answers is further visualized in Fig. 2. The bars marked with A show the results without indecisive answers. Bars marked with B show the results with calculation of possible indecisive answers. The number of correct answers is indicated with green color, the number of wrong answers is indicated with red color and the indecisive answers are plotted in grey color. The ITR of both calculations can be seen in Table 1.

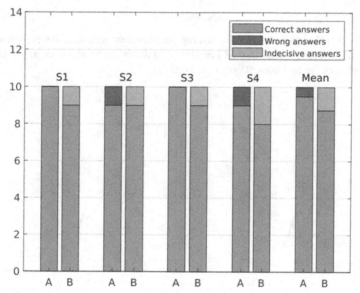

Fig. 2. Number of correctly provided answers of the four participants. The two last columns show the mean values of all subjects. Bars marked with A: no indecisive answers allowed, B indecisive answers allowed. (Color figure online)

Figures 3 and 4 show the ERP plots of participant S3 on position Cz. To generate the plots EEG data of the training run was used, where each participant shall focus for three questions on the left hand stimuli and for three questions on the right hand stimuli. In Fig. 3 one sees the averaged trials of left hand stimuli (blue line) and the averaged distractor data from the same two questions (red dashed line). These stimuli were used to provide the answer yes. The green marked areas show the significant differences between the two lines. The vertical dashed line at 0 s shows the onset time of the stimuli. There is a big positive peak at 100 ms and a broad positive peak around 300 ms after the stimulus onset. Figure 4 shows the other two questions. The shape of averaged target trials is quite different to the ones in Fig. 3.

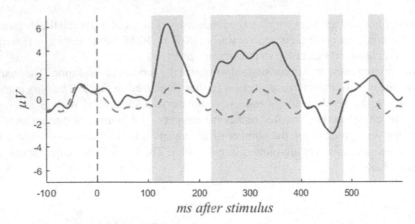

Fig. 3. ERP of S3 at location Cz. Blue line: averaged trials when target stimuli were delivered with the tactor on the left hand. Red - dashed line: averaged distractor trials. Green areas: significant differences between the two lines. (Color figure online)

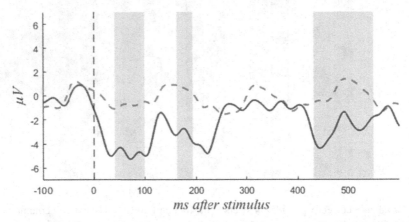

Fig. 4. ERP of S3 at location Cz. Blue line: averaged trials when target stimuli were delivered with the tactor on the right hand. Red, dashed line: averaged distractor trials. Green areas: significant differences between the two lines. (Color figure online)

4 Discussion

With this publication, we would like to demonstrate two things: First, the classification accuracy of our new paradigm and secondly the influence of a new approach that shall only present an answer if the results have a strong enough tendency towards one result or the other, and otherwise mark the result as indecisive. In future, the BCI shall be used by heavily impaired patients, who cannot use visual P300 speller or other means of communication. Therefore, we rather focus on the spelling accuracy than speed, which seems more important in our point of view for these applications. Also, the indecisive answers are thought to be useful for users who may not be able to indicate to the outer world if they currently do not want to use the tool at all, or just don't want to say yes or no to a specific question.

The accuracy could be increased from 95% to 100% with the statistical test for indecisive answers, but the ITR decreased from 1.5 to 1.4 bits/minute. This is consistent with our defined goals, to have the best possible accuracy, even if the speed suffers. In a real scenario an indecisive answer could mean that one has to ask the same question again to wait if a significant classification result could be reached.

The ITR of 1.4 bits/minute is worse compared to most of other studies as presented in Eidel and Kübler [8]: between 0.5 and 20.73 bits/minute. But those results were often achieved after several sessions of training and none reached the 100% accuracy our approach showed.

Maybe the biggest caveat for our study is that the future target user group, people with impairments have not been covered by the participants of this study. But we wanted to first validate if the system works at all, and shows a good performance, before going to patients. It is clear though that the achieved results of ITR and accuracy will not be perfectly transferable to patients.

The example plot of ERP in Fig. 3 shows a late P100 and a broad P300 peak for target stimuli. This broad peak goes in accordance to our previous work where the same tactile stimulators were used for generating ERP, see for example [13]. The ERP in Fig. 4 are of the same subject, but with the target stimuli presented on the right hand instead of the left hand. The ERP looks quite unusual, especially for a healthy control. We chose these plots on purpose because they demonstrate something worth discussing. For reaching a good spelling accuracy one does not need to generate textbook like ERPs, or at least not for both classes. If the subject's ERPs for right hand target stimulation would be the same as for distractor stimulation, while the ERPs for left hand stimulation are as shown in Fig. 3, the classifier would be still perfectly able to distinguish the two classes. We did not test if users can, on purpose, elicit an indecisive answer by trying to ignore the stimulation sequence. We could speculate that such a user as S3 could have troubles in doing so. Something that could be investigated deeper in future studies.

Our next step is to validate the approach on a bigger number of healthy users, and eventually adapt it, based on the lessons learned with that data. After that having done successful, we would like to recruit patients for tests.

Acknowledgements. This work was supported by funds of the European Union under the MSCA-IF-EF-SE grant DOC-Stim (No. 839234) and by a grant of the Romanian Ministry of Education and Research, CNCS - UEFISCDI, project number PN-III-P1-1.1-TE-2019-1753, within PNCDI III.

References

1. Wolpaw, J.R., Birbaumer, N., McFarland, D.J., et al.: Brain–computer interfaces for communication and control. Clin. Neurophysiol. **113**, 767–791 (2002). https://doi.org/10.1016/S1388-2457(02)00057-3
2. Birbaumer, N., Ghanayim, N., Hinterberger, T., et al.: A spelling device for the paralysed. Nature **398**, 297–298 (1999)

3. Luck, S.J: An Introduction to the Event-Related Potential Technique. MIT Press, Cambridge (2014)
4. Bin, G., Gao, X., Wang, Y., et al.: VEP-based brain-computer interfaces: time, frequency, and code modulations [Research Frontier. IEEE Comput. Intell. Mag. **4**, 22–26 (2009). https://doi.org/10.1109/MCI.2009.934562
5. Guger, C., Allison, B.Z., Großwindhager, B., et al.: How many people could use an SSVEP BCI? Front. Neurosci. **6** (2012). https://doi.org/10.3389/fnins.2012.00169
6. Volosyak, I., Rezeika, A., Benda, M., et al.: Towards solving of the Illiteracy phenomenon for VEP-based brain-computer interfaces. Biomed. Phys. Eng. Express **6**, 035034 (2020). https://doi.org/10.1088/2057-1976/ab87e6
7. Guger, C., Daban, S., Sellers, E., et al.: How many people are able to control a P300-based brain–computer interface (BCI)? Neurosci. Lett. **462**, 94–98 (2009). https://doi.org/10.1016/j.neulet.2009.06.045
8. Eidel, M., Kübler, A.: Wheelchair control in a virtual environment by healthy participants using a P300-BCI based on tactile stimulation: training effects and usability. Front. Hum. Neurosci. **14** (2020). https://doi.org/10.3389/fnhum.2020.00265
9. Herweg, A., Gutzeit, J., Kleih, S., Kübler, A.: Wheelchair control by elderly participants in a virtual environment with a brain-computer interface (BCI) and tactile stimulation. Biol. Psychol. **121**, 117–124 (2016)
10. Halder, S., Rea, M., Andreoni, R., et al.: An auditory oddball brain–computer interface for binary choices. Clin. Neurophysiol. **121**, 516–523 (2010). https://doi.org/10.1016/j.clinph.2009.11.087
11. Lugo, Z.R., Rodriguez, J., Lechner, A., et al.: A vibrotactile p300-based brain–computer interface for consciousness detection and communication. Clin. EEG Neurosci. **45**, 14–21 (2014)
12. Gruenwald, J., Znobishchev, A., Kapeller, C., et al.: Time-variant linear discriminant analysis improves hand gesture and finger movement decoding for invasive brain-computer interfaces. Front. Neurosci. **13**, 901 (2019). https://doi.org/10.3389/fnins.2019.00901
13. Ortner, R., Spataro, R., Scharinger, J., et al.: Vibro-tactile evoked potentials for BCI communication of people with disorders of consciousness and locked-in syndrome. In: Proceedings of the Graz Brain-Computer Interface Conference 2017 (2017)

Talking Through the Eyes: User Experience Design for Eye Gaze Redirection in Live Video Conferencing

Wooyeong Park[1]($\boxtimes$), Jeongyun Heo[1]($\boxtimes$), and Jiyoon Lee[2]($\boxtimes$)

[1] Kookmin University Jeongneung-ro, Seongbuk-gu, Seoul, Republic of Korea
yuniheo@kookmin.ac.kr
[2] Monash University, 900 Dandenong Rd, Caulfield East, VIC 3145, Australia
jiyoon.lee@monash.edu

Abstract. In the post-corona era, more institutions are using videoconferencing (VC). However, when we talked in VC, we found that people could not easily concentrate on the conversation. This is a problem with computer architecture. Because the web camera records a person looking at a computer monitor, it appears as if people are staring at other places and having a conversation. This was a problem caused by overlooking eye contact, a non-verbal element of face-to-face conversation. To solve this problem, many studies focused on technology in literature. However, this study presented ER guidelines in terms of user experience: the function of selecting the direction of the face, the function of selecting a 3D avatar face divided into four stages through morphing, and a guideline on the function of intentionally staring at the camera using the teleprompter function.

Keywords: Eye-gaze based interaction · UX (user experience) · Video conferencing

1 Introduction

People who are unfamiliar with untact (un + contact) in the post-corona era are also adjusting to the untact era. The environment in workplaces and schools has changed rapidly due to social distancing. Owing to the coronavirus pandemic, the common method of face-to-face communication has been actively replaced with videoconferencing (VC). Classes, meetings, and telecommuting were carried out using VC without having sufficient time to make systematic preparations for it. As found in this study, the differences between the VC environment and face-to-face communication are considerable. In general, we talk with our eyes facing each other's when we have a conversation [1]. Eye contact is a very important factor to increase the concentration within a conversation [1]. Eye contact enriches communication and makes it more efficient. It plays an important role in improving reliability and business transactions [2]. Eye contact creates social cues between people and increases participation rate. It also helps indicate the focus and context of the conversation [3]. However, due to the location of the cameras, we found

© Springer Nature Switzerland AG 2021
M. Kurosu (Ed.): HCII 2021, LNCS 12763, pp. 75–88, 2021.
https://doi.org/10.1007/978-3-030-78465-2_7

the phenomenon of disagreement in the VC environment [4]. The absence of eye contact makes for an awkward and unnatural situation for communication [5].

Most group VC systems do not accurately communicate the eye's gaze [6] during a conversation in a VC environment. Therefore, many studies have developed eye redirection (ER) technologies to solve the eye contact issue in the VC environment. The existing ER guidelines were largely divided into hardware and software. In the case of hardware, ER was performed by matching the lens of a camera to the user's eye movements using a semi-transparent screen [7].

In case of software, users were photographed through a camera and ER was performed using machine learning [8]. Focusing on user experience, a study attempted to imitate the non-verbal element of eye contact in videoconferencing [9]. This study recognized that users of the ER guidelines in the VC environment are not awkward in communication and that it is a natural situation based on the need to be provided from the perspective of user experience to use the ER guideline. As such, existing researchers have been studying ER function to solve ER in a systemic aspect.

Unlike existing literature that divides ER functions into hardware and software, this study proposes elements necessary for ER functions in terms of user experience rather than technology. Therefore, this study conducted interviews and surveys to approach ER from the perspective of user research.

First, we conducted a literature survey in Sect. 2 and found that there is lack of research on ER guidelines centered on user research. In Sect. 3, information on the necessity of eye contact in a VC environment, eye contact method of VC users, and preference of the user's face angle photographed by the camera were identified for graduate students with VC experience.

In Sects. 4 and 5, the survey was conducted based on the Pain Point for VC found in the first in-depth interview. Through the questionnaire, we obtained insights into the elements required for the ER guidelines from a user experience perspective. In Sect. 6, based on the insights obtained through the questionnaire, the following were presented: (1) 3D morphing avatar selection, (2) face angle selection, and (3) new ER guidelines with teleprompter function.

2   Related Work

2.1   No Eye Contact in VC

When we converse in VC, we talk while looking at the screen, which is different from the usual eye contact. In case of VC, the webcam or laptop's built-in camera is located at the top or bottom of the monitor. Unlike general eye contact and conversation, the integrated camera of a laptop or a webcam is located at the top and bottom of the monitor. Therefore, it is difficult to have a face-to-face conversation, and the camera location disrupts smooth communication between speakers [4, 10]. In particularly, the conditions for eye gaze are not met due to the location of the integrated camera or webcam installed in the computer (See Figs. 1, 2). Previous studies mainly used hardware and software to solve the e-contact problem in VC.

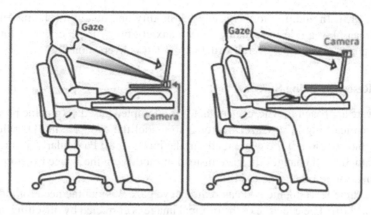

Fig. 1. Eye gaze does not match with the location of the integrated camera [4, 10].

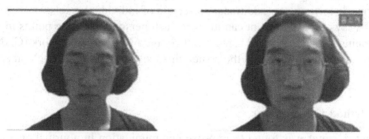

Fig. 2. Example of down gazing (The left picture). Example of looking directly at the camera to engage with the viewer (The right picture).

2.2   ER Function Using Hardware

First, the ER function for eye contact in VC was approached with a stereo matching [7, 11], a kinect camera [12], and a hardware method using a half-slivered mirror. Vertegaal et al., used a half-slivered mirror to reduce or eliminate angular deviation. The camera was placed in the optical path of the display to achieve eye gaze [6]. And Chen made that a VC screen was placed under the webcamera positioned on top of the monitor. When staring at the other person in the VC, the gaze does not go down because the VC screen is located at the top of the monitor [13]. That is, because the VC screen is located close to the camera, it is possible to induce to gaze at the front.

Yang, et al., found it difficult to solve the eye contact problem with a single camera [14]. They photographed two angles of the subject using stereo cameras, one at the top and another at the bottom of a computer. They also synthesized a stereo technique combined with a personalized face model and graphics hardware to make a virtual video that makes eye contact. The generated image was synthesized using a view morphing technique.

Teleprompters are generally used in professional environments such as news and broadcasting. The teleprompter is a device that matches the position of the prompter and the position of the camera to make it look as if the speaker is looking continuously at the camera [15]. In addition to increasing the fluidity and quality of the presentation, prompters can play a role in reducing speech anxiety by easing the fear of forgetting important points or even the overall structure of their conversation [16].

2.3   ER Research Using Software

As a software approach for ER, eye contact was attempted based on graphic processing such as deep learning [17]. GazeDirector is to model the eye gaze in 3D, rather than predicting the position of the eye directly in the image [18]. Particularly, it transforms the eyes into 3D and changes the gaze instead of modifying the image by morphing or compositing it with other images [18].

The machine learning method can redirect eye gaze without the need for individual training data [16]. The eye gaze of the original image is corrected by offsetting the other eye image to the original image [19]. DeepWarp is also a method of correcting the gaze through image learning based on machine learning [20]. DeepWarp is a deep architecture that performs distortion after additional correction of individual pixels.

NVIDIA says face alignment can identify each person's key face points in a video call and reanimate the user's face using a Generative Adversarial Network (GAN). You can also rotate your faces to align them such that they appear to face each other during a call [21].

2.4   ER Method Using Avatar

A user-created avatar was found to improve communication in a virtual environment. [22] Garau et al. designed eye contact in the form of image 3D using avatars during a conversation [23]. The results of revealed that the eye gaze was similar to the modified avatar's dialogue participation and face-to-face dialogue. In their study, avatar VC showed non-verbal feedback on the participants' faces, although the avatar used only one non-verbal action, gaze. This suggests that avatars make a significant contribution to a positive perception of communication without detailed facial expressions.

Dialogue using avatars showed high communication and cooperation in education. Using VC, a high level of communication can be achieved through dialogue between avatars [24]. It is also reported that communication via avatars is well transferred to anthropomorphic avatars and the reliability and attractiveness are as high as ordinary conversations [25]. However, not all avatars have a positive effect on communication. There are complex interactions in the appearance and behavior of avatars [26]. User responses to high-quality avatars are positively affected, but more abstract avatars are negatively affected [26].

The method of dividing the image step by step by morphing the actual and avatar faces helps determine the morphing image stage that people perceive closer to their own face. As a study on the negative effects of abstract avatars, Gonzalez-Franco et al., animated real faces and 3D avatars in 8 steps using the morphing technique [27]. From Step 1 to 8, an experiment was conducted to stop at the stage where the experimenter was perceived as himself/herself by showing the image sequence morphing in 3D on the real face. The results of their study revealed that the avatars' self-awareness was maximized when using facial animation.

2.5 Summary

Much research has been conducted on eye gaze redirection using 3D and communication research using 3D avatars. However, research on user guidelines for the VC ER function is insufficient. From the user experience perspective, our ER guidelines were based on existing literature and content from in-depth interviews and surveys. Furthermore, it differs from previous studies in that it approaches the ER guidelines from the user perspective or experience.

3 Methods

See (Fig. 3).

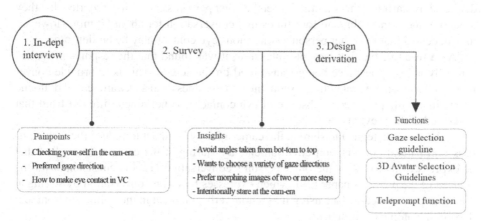

Fig. 3. Structure of the methods

3.1 User Research Design

The previous study was conducted on the technical aspects of the ER function. In other words, extant research on ER function in terms of user experience was insufficient. Therefore, the main purpose of the user-experience-oriented research is to improve the convenience of the ER function presented from the user's viewpoint. The study investigated eye contact for a one-to-one VC situation. A questionnaire was created based on the Pain Points for VC found in the in-depth interview. A survey was conducted to determine whether the user is most comfortable with the angle of gaze, insights on camera shooting, and intentional eye contact.

3.2 Interview with VC Users

The first interview was conducted with five people who had experience using VC. The subjects were five students from Kookmin University's graduate school master's program who took Zoom classes from March to December 2020. The subjects were two males and three females in their 20 s.

In the conversation with all five people, the most important factor was eye contact. In case of VC, it can be seen that the conversation was more awkward and unnatural than face-to-face conversation because eye contact was not properly formed. In a question about the change in the shape of the face according to the camera installation angle, an interviewee reported as follows. "I am worried about my own appearance on the screen through the camera. There were times when I missed the conversation. I could see that I was constantly checking myself through the screen."

In particular, an interviewer who had experience using an integrated camera installed in a laptop computer reported, "I hate the appearance of myself as the chin is emphasized from the bottom up. So, the interviewee replied "Move the camera to the desired angle" to solve the angle problem. As another payoff point, the interviewee replied that he was deliberately staring at the camera to meet the other person's eyes. They reported that they looked at the camera three to four times in a conversation for about 20 min. However, they accepted that the other person's continuous eye contact may be burdensome.

As a result of the first in-depth interview, it was found that the respondent looked carefully at his appearance being transmitted on the screen. This is to provide convenience by using a 3D avatar. In addition, the unnaturalness and awkwardness of dialogue according to the presence or absence of eye contact was not much different from that described in the previous study [9].

In VC, people tended to stare at the camera for eye contact to reduce the awkwardness and natural conversation environment. By staring at the camera, he replied that he expressed his focus on the other person's conversation. This is consistent with the content of the previous paper [28], which expresses focus on conversation by staring at the other person face-to-face using it as a non-verbal element in the online environment despite the online environment.

4   Survey

A questionnaire was written based on the content of the in-depth interview. Survey subjects are those who have had online meetings or video calls in the last month. A one-on-one conversation situation was assigned and investigated. A total of 50 participants were surveyed, with 31 subjects in their 20s, 18 in their 30s and 1 in their 40s.

The questionnaire questions could be classified into three major categories: the degree of awkwardness of the self-image taken by the camera, the camera face angle desired by the user, and the experience of staring at the camera for intentional eye contact.

4.1   The Degree to Which You Care About Yourself Photographed on the Camera

First, the degree of awkwardness of the self-photography on the camera was investigated on the Likert 7-point scale. Using real faces and morphed 3D avatars to replace their own appearance, participants' preferred image levels were investigated.

First, "Luvatar" application of NSI (HOLDINGS LIMITED) was used to provide guidelines for face angles such as front and side. Luvatar can take a picture of the user's face and turn it in an avatar [29].

Next, a four-step image was designed using the morphing technique. This method extracts feature points from each image and synthesizes the face image through the average vector of the parts recognized as faces in the two images [30].

The extracted image of the front face of the 3D avatar, created through the Luvatar application, was morphed using the smartphone application Face Morph (envy soft). The front photo of the real face was designated as step 1, and the 3D avatar extracted from Luvatar was set to step 4. Morphing settings were 0%, 25%, 75%, and 100%. A 4-step image guideline was provided by morphing the 3D avatar image from 0% without morphing to 25% to 75% and 100% of the front face of the 3D avatar, created through the Luvatar application, was morphed using the smartphone application Face Morph (Fig. 4).

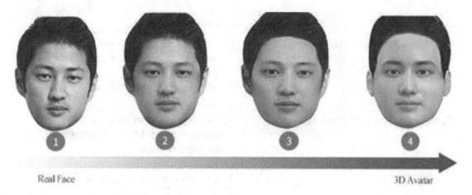

Real Face   3D Avatar

Fig. 4. Four steps for morphing 3D avatar image.

4.2 Camera Face Angle Desired by the User

The level of awkwardness of the user due to the unwanted angle of the face was measured on the Likert 7-point scale. Next, the participants' preferences were investigated using the photo below to find out which face angle the participant thought was the most comfortable (See Fig. 5). The face angle of the avatar was adjusted directly from the Luvatar application to determine the front, left, right, right. A total of 9 face angles were made: upward, left upward, right downward, and left downward.

4.3 Camera Gaze Experience for Intentional Eye Contact

Finally, the importance of eye contact was investigated. In addition, we analyzed whether there was any experience of intentionally staring at the camera to make eye contact with the other party in VC (Table 1).

Fig. 5. Select guideline of facial angles

Table 1. Survey questionnaire

Classification	Questionnaire
– The degree to which you care about yourself being photographed on the camera	1. Check the experience that was uncomfortable with the appearance on the screen 2. Step 4 morphing preference for avatar image
– Camera face angle desired by the user	1. The degree of awkwardness of your appearance on the monitor depending on the camera angle 2. Each person's preferred face angle 3. The most avoided face angle
– Camera gaze experience for intentional eye contact	1. The importance of eye contact with the other party in face-to-face conversation 2. Whether you have intentionally stared at the camera to meet the other person's gaze

5   Result

5.1   Degree of Awkwardness About the Self-shot on the Camera

All the survey participants confirmed their concern about the appearance on the screen. As a result of checking through the Likert 7-point scale, it was found that 39 out of 50 participants cared about their own image captured by the camera. This was the same as the content in which the participant was concerned about his image taken on the camera in the pre-interview.

In the 3D morphing step 4 image category, they prefer a 3D image that suits their tastes rather than a single morphing image with 26% of the image in the first step, 34% of the image in the second step, 22% of the image in the third step, and 18% in the fourth step.

In addition, it was found through a survey that they prefer to display avatars and their morphed images (74%) into the VC environment rather than actual images (26%). In other words, it was judged that the participant preferred the image of the second stage or higher.

In addition, during video calls or online meetings with the other party, among the images of the other party, the images considered to be the most convenient for conversation were images of level 2 or higher (72%).

These survey results support the findings of Gonzalez-Franco, et al. [27]. In the morphing image that changes from a real face to an avatar, participants recognized the avatar resembling themselves the most when the morphing was applied was ~30%. Based on the aforementioned study [27] and these s0urvey results, the 2 steps avatar was the one where people recognized themselves best.

5.2 Face Angle Preference

Of the participants, 76% answered that they felt that their appearance was awkward depending on the camera angle. Participants showed that they did not like all compositions 1, 2, and 3 (See Fig. 5), in which the camera was tangled from the bottom to the top. Those excluding angles 1, 2, 3, and angles 4, 5, 6, 7, 8, 9 were selected (See Fig. 5).

The face angle that the participants most preferred was the front (58%). The angle of the other person's gaze, which the interviewee thinks is the most comfortable, also appeared in the front (76%). This is similar to the way participants gaze at the other person in real life by choosing the front view and this finding was consistent with previous studies.

5.3 Experience of Intentional Camera Gaze

62% of the survey participants had experience of intentionally staring at the camera to make eye contact with the other party during an online meeting or video call. It was judged that this was for people to take advantage of the non-verbal element of eye contact in the VC environment [8].

6 User Experience-Oriented ER Guideline Proposal

Based on the interview contents and questionnaire, the Eye-contact ER guideline for the one-on-one conversation situation in the VC environment was proposed. The guidelines are expressed in Figs. 6, 7, and 8.

6.1 3D Source for 3D Face Angle

As shown in Fig. 6, six face angle guidelines were provided by adjusting the front, right, left, and 45-degree angles in the avatar made using Luvatar. Based on the results of the survey, it was determined that the angle photographed from the bottom to the top was not desired, and a guideline was proposed to suggest the remaining angles excluding angles 1, 2, and 3 (See Fig. 7). We intend to provide a guideline interaction that the user can use to select from the face angle presented through the 3D face angle selection function.

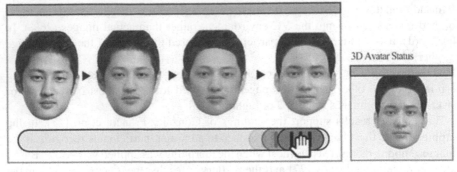

Fig. 6. Guidelines for choosing a 3D face.

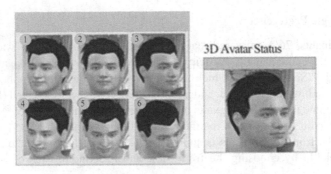

Fig. 7. Guidelines for choosing a face angle.

Fig. 8. Place the red dot close to the camera to guide your gaze to the camera. (Color figure online)

6.2   3D Face Selection with Morphing Image Step 4

Users can create highly realistic avatars in VR environments using user face avatars [27]. Therefore, by dividing into 3D avatars in 4 stages, the user can select a morphed face without Uncanny Valley Presented. By providing the user with a four-step 3D face, the most natural face and face angle that the user thinks is directly selected so that VC can use his or her appearance without difficulty.

6.3 Teleprompter

Third, by utilizing the teleprompter function, we intend to provide a guideline for the user's natural eye contact in a meeting or class environment. In addition, through the first interview, it was confirmed that continuous eye contact during offline meetings or classes can create an uncomfortable situation.

When presenting in an online environment, a point that the presenter can recognize in the middle of the speech was placed near the camera, giving the effect of looking at the camera during speech to look into the audience's eyes. In addition, the prompter function is not continuously activated, but dots appear at intervals so that the presenter consciously looks into the eyes of the listener in the middle. Through this, we tried to increase the concentration on the conversation.

7 Conclusion and Future Studies

This study attempted to increase the convenience of using ER through ER guidelines in a one-on-one VC conversation from the perspective of user experience. In particular, functional studies on ER have been actively conducted through prior studies. However, as a result of interviews and surveys, 3D Avatar selection guidelines, face angle selection guidelines, and teleprompter functions were needed from the viewpoint of user experience.

First, from the user's point of view on the ER function, we studied what information to give to the user through the guideline. As a result of the survey, they preferred to take a face-to-face gaze, but there were other participants who chose a different direction of gaze. This does not want only the focus of the eyes to be corrected, and it is necessary to improve the user experience by providing a choice for the direction of the gaze.

When the second user uses a 3D avatar face, it is necessary that the Uncanny Valley effect is not generated for his/her avatar by giving the avatar face option. As a result of the survey, it was confirmed that among the morphed avatars, preferred morphing avatars were different for each participant. Similar to the guideline for selecting the direction of gaze, the user showed that there is a need for the degree to which he or she has become avatar.

The teleprompter, which is mainly used for the third presentation or speech, was used as a material for ER guidelines in a general VC environment. This provided convenience to induce users who purposefully stare at the camera in VC to gaze at the camera when a red dot appears without being aware of the camera.

Finally, through the results of this study, it is expected that better VC communication will be achieved if the user does not simply edit the focus of the eyes, but it provides an experience that the user can select himself from the perspective of the user. In addition, it is expected that a more comfortable VC environment will be established by utilizing the improved eye contact guidelines to increase the concentration of real-time online video lectures and online meetings through the VC guidelines.

As a future study, the three guidelines proposed in this study will be verified through further empirical experiments. In addition, although this study focused on the character's preference level and preference for the gaze method compared to the live-action method centered on the face, the following study intends to identify additional elements including gestures that can expand the experience of empathy in VC. In other words, in addition to eye contact, which is a non-verbal element, we plan to study gestures that are used in actual conversation as a method that can be used to better impart one's own communication in VC. This research result is expected to be utilized in the future system development for VC.

Acknowledgments. This research was partially supported by SK Telecom.

References

1. McCarthy, A., Lee, K.: Children's knowledge of deceptive gaze cues and its relation to their actual lying behavior. J. Exp. Child Psychol. **103**(2), 117–134 (2009). https://doi.org/10.1016/j.jecp.2008.06.005
2. Bohannon, L.S., Herbert, A.M., Pelz, J.B., Rantanen, E.M.: Eye contact and video-mediated communication: a review. Displays **34**(2), 177–185 (2013). https://doi.org/10.1016/j.displa.2012.10.009
3. Jones, A., et al.: Achieving eye contact in a one-to-many 3D video teleconferencing system. ACM Trans. Graph. **28**(3), 1–8 (2009). https://dl.acm.org/doi/abs/10.1145/1531326.1531370
4. Ebara, Y., Kukimoto, N., Koyamada, K.: Evaluation experiment on eye-to-eye contact in remote communication with tiled displays environments. In: 22nd International Conference on Advanced Information Networking and Applications - Workshops (Aina worshops 2008), pp. 1017–1022. Gino-wan, Japan (2008). https://doi.org/10.1109/WAINA.2008.157
5. Kuster, C., Popa, T., Bazin, J.C., Gotsman, C., Gross, M.: Gaze correction for home video conferencing. ACM Trans. Graph. **31**(6), 1–6 (2012). https://doi.org/10.1145/2366145.2366193
6. Vertegaal, R., Weevers, I., Sohn, C., Cheung, C.: GAZE-2: conveying eye contact in group video conferencing using eye-controlled camera direction. In: Proceedings of the SIGCHI Conference on Human Factors in Computing Systems, pp. 521–528. Association for Computing Machinery, New York, NY, USA (2003). https://doi.org/10.1145/642611.642702
7. Criminisi, A., Shotton, J., Blake, A., Torr, P.H.: Gaze manipulation for one-to-one teleconferencing. In: Proceedings Ninth IEEE International Conference on Computer Vision, vol. 1, pp. 191–198. IEEE, Nice, France (2003). https://doi.org/10.1109/ICCV.2003.1238340
8. Baron-Cohen, S., Wheelwright, S., Jolliffe, T.: Is there a "Language of the Eyes?" evidence from normal adults, and adults with autism or asperger syndrome. Vis. Cogn. **4**(3), 311–331 (1997). https://doi.org/10.1080/713756761
9. Grayson, D.M., Monk, A.F.: Are you looking at me? Eye contact and desktop video conferencing. ACM Trans. Comput.-Hum. Interact. **10**, 221–243 (2003). https://doi.org/10.1145/937549.937552
10. Liu, X., Cheung, G., Zhai, D., Zhao, D.: Sparsity-based joint gaze correction and face beautification for conferencing video. In: 2015 Visual Communications and Image Processing (VCIP), pp. 1–4 (2015). https://doi.org/10.1109/VCIP.2015.7457830
11. Ho, Y., Jang, W.: Eye contact technique using depth image based rendering for immersive videoconferencing. In: 2014 International Conference on Information and Communication Technology Convergence (ICTC), Busan, Korea (South), 2014, pp. 982–983 (2014). https://doi.org/10.1109/ICTC.2014.6983350

12. Giger, D., Bazin, J., Kuster, C., Popa, T., Gross, M.: Gaze correction with a single webcam. In: 2014 IEEE International Conference on Multimedia and Expo (ICME), pp. 1–6 (2014). https://doi.org/10.1109/ICME.2014.6890306
13. Leveraging the asymmetric sensitivity of eye contact for videoconference. In: Proceedings of the SIGCHI Conference on Human Factors in Computing Systems, Inneapolis, Minnesota, USA (2002). https://dl.acm.org/doi/abs/10.1145/503376.503386?casa_token=2YovNqnOT bYAAAAA:YehVv9litc1PwArEXxJ1y4dTManjJf8vEaDR4KRVfbaWN7lx-QJKkvvOya 9ToiTbc8FOs7ZxG-DkaEg. Accessed 26 Feb 2021
14. Ruigang, Y., Zhengyou, Z.: Eye gaze correction with stereovision for video-teleconferencing. IEEE Trans. Pattern Anal. Mach. Intell. **26**, 956–960 (2004). https://doi.org/10.1109/TPAMI. 2004.27
15. Parsons, M.M.: PowerPoint as visual communication pedagogy: relative differences in eye tracking and aesthetic pleasure (2020). https://ttu-ir.tdl.org/handle/2346/85826
16. Asadi, R., Trinh, H., Fell, H.J., Bickmore, T.W.: IntelliPrompter: speech-based dynamic note display interface for oral presentations. In: Proceedings of the 19th ACM International Conference on Multimodal Interaction, pp. 172–180. ACM, Glasgow, UK (2017). https://doi.org/ 10.1145/3136755.d3136818
17. Kononenko, D., Ganin, Y., Sungatullina, D., Lempitsky, V.: Photorealistic monocular gaze redirection using machine learning. IEEE Trans. Pattern Anal. Mach. Intell. **40**, 2696–2710 (2018). https://doi.org/10.1109/TPAMI.2017.2737423
18. Wood, E., Baltrušaitis, T., Morency, L.-P., Robinson, P., Bulling, A.: GazeDirector: fully articulated eye gaze redirection in video. Comput. Graph. Forum **37**, 217–225 (2018). https:// doi.org/10.1111/cgf.13355
19. Massé, B.: Gaze direction in the context of social human-robot interaction (2018). https://tel. archives-ouvertes.fr/tel-01936821
20. Ganin, Y., Kononenko, D., Sungatullina, D., Lempitsky, V.: DeepWarp: photorealistic image resynthesis for gaze manipulation. In: Leibe, B., Matas, J., Sebe, N., Welling, M. (eds.) ECCV 2016. LNCS, vol. 9906, pp. 311–326. Springer, Cham (2016). https://doi.org/10.1007/978-3-319-46475-6_20
21. Maxine Hompage. https://developer.nvidia.com/maxine. Accessed 2 Nov 2020
22. Dodds, T.J., Mohler, B.J., Bülthoff, H.H.: Talk to the virtual hands: self-animated avatars improve communication in head-mounted display virtual environments. PLoS ONE **6**, (2011). https://doi.org/10.1371/journal.pone.0025759
23. Garau, M., Slater, M., Bee, S., Sasse, M.A.: The impact of eye gaze on communication using humanoid avatars. In: Proceedings of the SIGCHI Conference on Human Factors in Computing Systems, pp. 309–316. Association for Computing Machinery, New York, NY, USA (2001). https://doi.org/10.1145/365024.365121
24. Salmon, G., Nie, M., Edirisingha, P.: Developing a five-stage model of learning in second life. Educ. Res. **52**(2), 169–182 (2010). https://doi.org/10.1080/00131881.2010.482744
25. Kang, S.H., Watt, J.H.: The impact of avatar realism and anonymity on effective communication via mobile devices. Comput. Hum. Behav. **29**, 1169–1181 (2013). https://doi.org/10. 1016/j.chb.2012.10.010
26. Bente, G., Rüggenberg, S., Krämer, N.C., Eschenburg, F.: Avatar-mediated networking: increasing social presence and interpersonal trust in net-based collaborations. Hum. Commun. Res. **34**(2), 287–318 (2008). https://doi.org/10.1111/j.1468-2958.2008.00322.x
27. Gonzalez-Franco, M., Steed, A., Hoogendyk, S., Ofek, E.: Using facial animation to increase the enfacement illusion and avatar self-identification. IEEE Trans. Vis. Comput. Graph. **26**(5), 2023–2029 (2020). https://doi.org/10.1109/TVCG.2020.2973075
28. Greiner, B., Caravella, M., Roth, A.E.: Is avatar-to-avatar communication as effective as face-to-face communication? An ultimatum game experiment in first and second life. J. Econ. Behav. Organ. **108**, 374–382 (2014). https://doi.org/10.1016/j.jebo.2014.01.011

29. Luvatar Homepage. https://www.luvatar.com/. Accessed 2 Nov 2020
30. Areeyapinan, J., Kanongchaiyos, P.: Face morphing using critical point filters. In: 2012 Ninth International Conference on Computer Science and Software Engineering (JCSSE), pp. 283–288, Bangkok, Thailand (2012). https://doi.org/10.1109/JCSSE.2012.6261966

Evaluating the Accuracy and User Experience of a Gesture-Based Infrared Remote Control in Smart Homes

Heinrich Ruser[1]([✉]) [iD], Susan Vorwerg[2], Cornelia Eicher[2], Felix Pfeifer[3], Felix Piela[3], André Kaltenbach[4], and Lars Mechold[4]

[1] Institute for Applied Physics and Measurement Technology, Universität der Bundeswehr München, 85577 Neubiberg, Germany
heinrich.ruser@unibw.de
[2] Geriatrics Research Group, Charité – Universitätsmedizin Berlin, 13347 Berlin, Germany
[3] August & Piela Konstruktiv GbR, 10829 Berlin, Germany
[4] Laser Components GmbH, 82140 Olching, Germany

Abstract. To enhance user experience while satisfying basic expectations and needs is the most important goal in the design of assistive technical devices. As a contribution, the user experience with the *SmartPointer*, a novel hand-held gesture-based remote control for everyday use in the living environment, is being explored in comprehensive user tests. The concept and design of the *SmartPointer* exploits the user's familiarity with TV remotes, flashlights or laser pointers. The buttonless device emits both an infrared (IR) and a visible (VIS) laser beam and is designed to be universally and consistently used for a large variety of devices and appliances in private homes out of arm's reach. In the paper, the results of three user studies regarding recognition rates and usability issues are summarized. Study One was a mixed-method study in the pre-implementation stage with 20 older adults, gathering the expectations towards a gesture-based remote control and exploring simple, quasi-intuitive controlling gestures. In Study Two, the acceptance and usability of a prototype of the SmartPointer remote control was verified and compared with a group of 29 users from the target group, exploring 8 most frequently used gestures from Study One. In Study Three, comprehensive gesture-recognition tests with an updated version of the remote were carried out with a group of 11 younger adults in various light conditions, postures and distances to the operated device. All three studies confirm the feasibility of the underlying principle, the usability and satisfaction among the participants and the robustness of the technical solution along with a high success rate of the recognition algorithm.

Keywords: Gesture control · User experience · Smart home · Ageing–in–place · Design-for-all

1 Introduction

Ageing-in-place is a valuable concept supporting the desire of older adults to stay and live in their home as long as possible. Ageing-in-place, however, requires for the older

© Springer Nature Switzerland AG 2021
M. Kurosu (Ed.): HCII 2021, LNCS 12763, pp. 89–108, 2021.
https://doi.org/10.1007/978-3-030-78465-2_8

person to be still able to perform various basic daily activities in the familiar domestic environment independently and safely. Seemingly simple activities like switching on a light, raising a blind or opening a window behind a sofa can get increasingly difficult, with these devices uncomfortable to reach and strenuous to handle, especially when the user is plagued by different physical constraints or mobility impairments.

In recent years, many technical solutions have been made available and affordable, which intend to greatly simplify the operation of household appliances. Many household appliances are made operable from a distance, whether using a device-specific remote control or, for example, via a smartphone app. In a 'connected home' or 'smart home' environment, a central control panel with a touchscreen – wall-mounted or on a smart-phone or mobile tablet – serves to overlook and operate all the devices and appliances. Regarding the status quo, all of these options – a number of special purpose remotes, smartphone apps or a central touchscreen panel – are often not the best solution from the user's perspective:

- To handle a number of different device-specific remote controls can be very annoying, with the particularly one often not at the right place. Small buttons can be hard to find and press.
- Central control panels to operate interconnected household devices are (apart from not being widespread in use) often not at hand and too complex when just a simple action like switching on the light is desired.
- To operate a home device with a smartphone (or tablet) app generally requires switch-ing on the hand-held device, selecting the right app and directing oneself through a number of menus and forms. This process often seems disproportionate to the simple task at hand. (An unconventional solution is proposed in [34].) And, as our studies ver-ified once again, the use of smartphone or tablets is not prevalent among older adults. For many elderly, modern smartphones are generally perceived as being cumbersome, costly, bulky and heavy-weight. They require care – above all frequent recharging – and are not very robust; the fear of elderly users of dropping and damaging them further reduces their use.
- As experience shows, to select and press the right 'analog' button at a remote or 'digital' buttons on a touchscreen can be physically or cognitively unpleasant or strenuous and sometimes almost impossible, not only for older adults but also when in a hurry, with dry, wet, cold or trembling hands, without glasses, in a dark room etc.

The seemingly obvious alternative to button-related devices would be to use one of the commercially successful voice control interfaces. However, in many situations these solutions fail the usability test, starting from the requirement of an existing and stable internet connection over stressful performance drops due to disturbances from ambient noise or unclear pronunciation (frequently found among elderly people) or the hesitation to speak to a technical device altogether, up to, last but not least, concerns related to privacy issues. As our usability studies with different groups of older adults showed (see Sect. 5), if given a choice, elderly people like to rely on other modalities than voice to feel comfortable and safe in their homes.

As a consequence, a universal, very easy-to-use remote control consistently opera-ble for a large variety of technical devices in homes under various circumstances and in different mood would be most desirable. Cost-effective and small-sized and hence ubiquitously available, it would not only empower mobility-constrained persons but would be enjoyable also for all other user groups. To approach this goal, a gesture-based, buttonless, hand-held infrared remote control we call *SmartPointer* is being designed and tested [1–4].

The basic concept of the system is shown in Fig. 1. The hand-held device ('*Smart-Pointer*') emits an invisible infrared laser dot pattern. The operation principle of the gestural remote control is based on detecting the motion of that pattern (i.e. the hand motion) in two dimensions at a small receiver close to or in every device to be operated. After the hand's trajectory is recognized in the receiver box as one of the specified gestures, it will be translated into the appropriate device-specific command and transferred to the device to be remotely controlled (lights, blinds, TV set, radio, telephone etc., but also 'non-classical' applications e.g. in the bathroom).

The device in various distances from an arm length up to about 8 m is selected and switched on/off by simply pointing at it (or broadly in its direction) with the *SmartPointer*. Subsequently, the essential functions of the selected device can be remotely operated by hand or arm motions using only a small number of simple, quasi-intuitive mid-air gestures. A brief presentation of the basic hardware components of the system along with important design parameters and signal-processing issues will be given in Sect. 3.

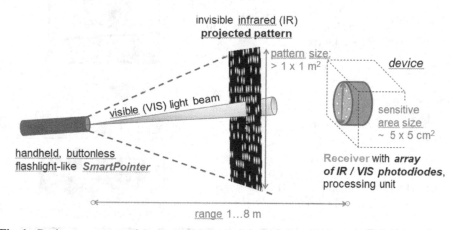

Fig. 1. Basic components of the *SmartPointer* gesture-based remote control: 1) buttonless hand-held device ('SmartPointer') projecting a large invisible randomly dotted pattern and a smaller visible laser light spot and 2) Receiver in or near the device to be remotely operated (comprising an array of photodiodes and the processing unit).

In the paper, the stepped efforts to evaluate and improve the user experiences with the novel interaction device are consistently summarized. Based on the results of two previous user studies regarding many different usability aspects – Study One, first presented in detail in [2], and Study Two, based on it and presented in [3] and [4] – a new comprehensive Study Three was recently conducted. Many interesting results of the latter study will be presented and discussed in detail here for the first time.

Study One was a mixed-method study in the pre-implementation stage, gathering the expectations from 20 older adults towards the gesture-based remote control and exploring simple, quasi-intuitive controlling gestures. In *Study Two*, the acceptance and usability of a first built-up SmartPointer remote control was verified and compared with a group of 29 users from the target group, using 8 of the most frequently suggested gestures from Study One to operate 4 typical home appliances: (1) switch a light on/off, (2) raise/lower window blind, (3) increase/decrease the temperature of a heating device and (4) open/close a door, see Table 2. In the new *Study Three*, comprehensive gesture-recognition tests of 6 of these gestures were carried out with a group of 11 younger adults under varies influencing factors, hereby characterizing the robustness of the gesture recognition algorithm. In Table 1, the three studies are briefly summarized.

Table 1. Overview over user studies conducted in the Usability Lab of the Geriatrics Research Group at Charité – Universitätsmedizin Berlin.

User Study	Participants	No. of gestures	No. of classes (referents)	Situations during the experiments
Study One [2]	20 (10f/10m) 74.7 ± 4.9 yrs	417 + 330	~30	
Study Two [3,4]	29 (15f/14m) 74.9 ± 4.7 yrs	642	8	
Study Three	11 (8f/3m) 33.5 ± 7.0 yrs	1,870	6	

The remaining part of the text is organized as follows: In Sect. 2, related work regarding usability issues, gesture-elicitation studies and commercial solutions for gestural interaction with smart home devices is reviewed and summarized. In Sect. 3, an overview over the hardware and software concept of the new *SmartPointer* system is given. In Sect. 4, the experimental design of three of our user studies, their objectives and goals are briefly introduced. In Sect. 5, important results of these studies regarding usability, accuracy and user experience are presented. The text concludes with a discussion and an outlook to next steps.

2   Related Work

2.1   Gestures for Entertainment and Work

Gestures give the promise of natural interaction with technical devices by exploiting ubiquity, human experience and imagination. Free-hand 'mid-air' gestures drawn in the air with one or two arms or the fingers of one or two hands were found well-suited for various application scenarios such as gaming and entertainment, mobile computing, or interacting with large displays (see e.g. [5–8] and the references within).

Indeed, it looks as if gestures have permeated into many facets of modern life, from smartphones, smart watches, up to game controllers and various emerging AR/VR applications. Several devices supporting gestural interaction have been successfully commercialized, like Microsoft's game controller Kinect® relying on an optical 3D viewing solution developed by PrimeSense, Nintendo's Wiimote® or the DepthSensor® from SoftKinetic. Amazing solutions like LeapMotion®, GestureTek®, eyeSight® or Point-Grab® - all based on powerful image processing - have come up, utilizing a laptop or smartphone camera but no other hardware. Although many of these camera-based approaches are increasingly optimized and made suitable for low-resource, low-energy embedded systems (e.g. [9, 10]), posture, occlusions or fast changing ambient light conditions can still be very challenging and the detection range is usually smaller than an arm's range. The primary goal of these solutions is to replace keypads or keyboards and enable quick formalized data entry.

Many other principles and modalities to track gestures have been proposed and commercialized, like data gloves based on accelerometers, camera installations detecting optical markers at finger rings or bracelets, electromagnetic 'myo' wristbands measuring the arm muscles tensions to sense gestures, as well as sophisticated approaches of large range/low-resolution ultrasound or high-resolution/low range radar waves [11].

2.2   Gestures in the Home Environment

As gesture-based technologies have shown to be useful and practical in many different applications, gestural interfaces have been proposed and commercialized also for home entertainment devices, foremost for the TV set as still one of the most commonly used technical devices in homes. A number of gesture elicitation studies for TV control tasks have been published over the years (e.g. [12–14]), promising a whole new user experience.

Studies of installations and assistive techniques designed for gesture control of a larger number of varies devices and appliances in private homes are surprisingly rare. Three recent, large surveys [15–17] exploring 47, 216 and 250 mid-air gesture elicitations studies (= studies to define consistent vocabularies), resp., found merely a handful of projects addressing gestural interfaces for a larger set of home devices (e.g. [18–20]). Although many empirical findings in all of these studies indicate a great benefit from gestural interaction in private homes, application prospects are still scarce.

One of the reasons might be that most approaches rely on capturing and recognizing free-hand gestures with 2D or 3D cameras, thus inheriting all the problems and limitations for image processing under challenging conditions, like low visibility, fast changing ambient light, fast moving targets of varying size and velocity in varying distances, occlusions etc. Recognizing free-hand gestures under these natural circumstances can be very complex [5, 6], severely affecting the recognition rate and hence the perceived usability. (The concerns of privacy issues linked to the extensive use of cameras will be discussed later in Sect. 5, evaluating our user studies.)

The more severe aspect when thinking of gesture-based control of various devices is how to design gestures appropriate to the task at hand. Researchers continue to investigate how to maximize gesture utility as well as how to best recognize gesture patterns (e.g. [21–25]). A vocabulary of appropriate free-hand gestures have to be agreed on and be easily remembered by all potential users. In [12], a set of 19 "referents" (according to the accepted terminology proposed in [22]) have been defined from extensive user tests. [26] found a basic vocabulary of 21 freehand gestures that would be needed to operate common TV functions.

Moreover, touchless interfaces are governed by constraints, which can be opaque to users. Unlike traditional inputs via buttons or clicks, gestures provide users with a large degree of flexibility in how to perform them. The review of 216 different gesture elicitation studies [16] involving almost 5,000 participants revealed that out of a total of 150,000 gestures, only approx. 10,000 gestures could be agreed on by almost all participants. Such flexible input still has to be successfully mapped onto a limited set of gesture classes.

3   Hardware Concept and Realization

The novel gesture-based universal remote control (cf. Fig. 1) consists of (1) the haptically shaped handheld, buttonless, battery-powered *SmartPointer* (Fig. 2 left) which emits a) a visible light spot to point in the direction of a particular device and select it and b) an invisible, spatially structured IR light pattern to operate the device; (2) a receiver box (Fig. 2 right) in or near the device which detects the trajectory of motion of the projected pattern (and hence the user's hand) and converts the identified gesture into device-specific commands.

The user holds the *SmartPointer* like a small flashlight or laser pointer and performs in-air gestures by moving that arm or forehand. Moving the invisible IR light pattern across the light entrance window of the small receiver box changes the light intensities at its photodiodes in a specific way, from which the pattern's trajectory and hence the gesture is reconstructed and – by assigning it to one of the predefined gesture classes – recognized [1].

Noticeable properties of the developed *SmartPointer* system - punctuating its practical use - are the small sizes of both the hand-held device and the receiver unit, the wide projection angle and high operating range up to 10 m also in bright sunlight or intense artificial light – all at fairly low laser light intensities such as to fulfill the safety regulations (laser class 1) with a large margin. The buttonless device emits invisible "structured" infrared light with a pseudo-random spatial pattern projected by a diffractive optical element (DOE) which is a low-cost commercial component widely used for a large variety of holography and spatial vision applications [27].

The *SmartPointer* needs to be active only when it is in the user's hand. For this purpose, a simple acceleration sensor is included in the handheld device which awakes

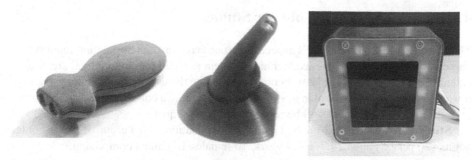

Fig. 2. (Left) Two version of the handheld, buttonless, battery-powered *SmartPointer*, based on user-centered design: a slim 'cross' (left) and a bulbous 'pipe' (right), with charging cradle. (Right) Receiver box with the array of IR sensitive photodiodes behind the optical filter (black square) to block ambient light, and a ring of in green and red LED for visual feedback. (Color figure online)

it from sleep-mode, ensuring to keep the power consumption of the battery-powered device low.

We developed a fast algorithm for high performance of gesture recognition (i.e. low classification errors) independently of the user even for large inter- and intra-personal variabilities of the gesture almost in real-time, using a sliding-window technique and a simplified pattern-matching algorithm. Based on extensive simulations and typical gestures obtained from initial user tests, fundamental design parameters for a highly satisfactory performance have been optimized [28]. From the sampled electrical signals of all photodiodes, the intended gesture have to be found automatically discarding the delivery and final movements of the user's hand motion (since no 'opt-in' and 'opt-out' gestures will be used), see Fig. 3.

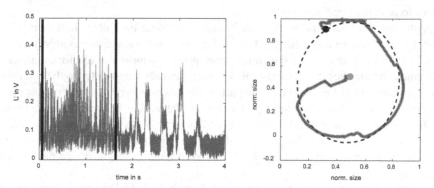

Fig. 3. Exemplary electrical signal of one of the photodiodes within a time frame of 4 seconds (left) and reconstructed motion trajectory (right) calculated from the signals of all photodiodes within the (adaptive) time frame marked by vertical black lines [28].

4   Experimental Design of User Studies

The consequences of how a user's expectations and needs are met by the functionality and perceived usability of a designed technical system in a certain environment are widely called user experience (UX) [29]. In order to evaluate the users' needs and expectations towards gesture-based control in the home environment, we conducted several extensive user studies. Three of them will be reported on in the sequel.

Study One was a mixed-method qualitative evaluation with a group of healthy older adults (20 persons aged 74.7 ± 4.9 years, 10 females/10 males) comprising.

1. detailed interviews about expectations, needs and wishes with regard to a gesture-based remote control to be used in their homes with pleasure; the results of the expressed views were subsequently translated into technical requirements for the system to be developed,
2. practical user tests with a common laser pointer (a substitute resembling the device to be developed from the user's perspective), enabling video recording of a) the visible light spot on a screen while executing gestures with the laser pointer towards the screen (for later reconstruction of the trajectory) and (b) observations of the hand and arm posture during execution of gestures,
3. evaluation of user experiences gained from this new approach to control home appliances, assessments of its usability and how it meets the expectations.

The participants were first asked to describe what technical devices in the household they use (and how often) and to articulate practicability issues when handling these devices. Next, the participants were asked to list devices in their homes and basic functions they would like to be controllable by gestures from a distance. Consequently, an image of the 'tech affinity level' arose, but also of 'non-classical' applications of gesture control to be considered, see Table 2.

In the practical part, the participants were asked to sit on a chair in a distance of about 2 m opposite to a screen (1.20 m $\times$ 1.50 m), take a standard laser pointer and 'draw' gestures onto that screen they found appropriate and most intuitive for a number of commands given to them by the assistant. These commands were related to the control of the basic functions of those devices the participants mentioned in the first part as being important to them. Both, the point projections of the visible laser spot on the screen and the according arm or hand movements of the participants were video-recorded. In post-processing the videos, the position of the light spot was calculated with subpixel precision based on a simple threshold operation to identify bright pixels on the dark blackboard.

Afterwards, the opposite exercise was conducted: We asked the participants to tick from a predefined gesture catalog that particular gesture they found most appropriate to remotely operate each of the devices and functions via mid-air gestures.

In total, 417 gestures were drawn by the 20 participants and subsequently 330 gestures were chosen by them from the gesture catalog [2].

Straight motion gestures such as horizontal (right/left) or vertical (up/down) lines and circular movements (clockwise/counterclockwise) were by far the most frequently used

Table 2. Devices in private homes and their functions remotely controllable by gestures which were most frequently proposed by the 20 participants of Study One (adopted from [2]).

Device(s)	Functions	Suggested forearm gestures
TV	on/off; louder/lower; channel forward/back channel selection	Point at it, small circle; left-right; digit
Music system/radio	on/off; volume up/down; song forward/back function selection	Point at it, small circle; left-right; digit
Telephone	make/end call; volume up/down	Point at it; digit
Heating	on/off; warmer/colder	Left-right; circle
Lights	on/off; brighter/darker	Point at it; "tick" sign; up/down; circle
Blinds	up/down	Up/down
Door	open/close; unlock/lock	Left/right; circle; "tick" sign

uni-stroke gestures. From the gesture catalog, horizontal, vertical and circled gestures were also predominantly (>70%) chosen as the most favorable.

The subsequent survey focused on the expectations towards the hand-held device to be developed, regarding size, haptics, design, material or the way how to recharge the battery powered device. Based on those findings (see Sect. 5), two differently shaped hand-held devices were designed and built, see Fig. 2.

Study Two was based on the findings of Study one and focused on a series of user tests with a built-up prototype of the *SmartPointer* system and a group of 29 healthy older adults aged 66...85 years (74.9 ± 4.7, 15 females/14 males). A small number of participants in Study Two had already taken part in Study One.

To test their cognitive abilities, all participants performed the Mini-Mental State Examination (MMSE) [30] with 30 items, indicating cognitive impairments if the MMSE index is lower than 25. No cognitive anomalies were detected (MMSE: 29.2 ± 0.9). To determine with high validity whether a person had a noticeable tremor, the force of the dominant hand was measured using a hand dynamometer. The coordinative or fine-motor abilities of the dominant hand were examined conducting a Grooved Pegboard Test.

For the experiments, four typical scenarios regarding remote control of household appliances were chosen: (1) To switch the light on or off, (2) to lower or raise the blind, (3) to increase/decrease the temperature of a heating device, and (4) to open or close a door. To support the imagination of the users and to test the interaction and feedback, four small demonstrator devices (light, blind, heater, door) were built and put in front of the users [3]. For each application a specific pair of simple straightforward symmetric motion gestures was assigned, see Table 3.

At the beginning of a test series, each test person chose one of two hand-held devices they preferred and sat on a chair in a distance of about 3 m from the demonstrator devices. Next, the test person was briefly introduced in the procedure of the measurements and the approximate size of the imaginary 'sensitive' area behind the devices to be operated. The test person learned that since the overall size of the projected pattern is large (min.

Table 3. Gesture lexicon used in Study Two with a group of 29 older adults and associated functions (adopted from [3]).

Gesture (referent)			Associated with	
No.	Action	Trajectory	Device	Function
1	Point at it	—	Lamp	Switch on
2	Point at it	—		Switch off
3	Move hand or arm straight bottom-up	Line bottom-up	Blind	Lift/open
4	Move hand or arm straight top-down	Line top-down		Lower/close
5	Move hand or arm straight left-to-right	Line left-to-right	Door	Open
6	Move hand or arm straight right-to-left	Line right-to-left		Close
7	Turn/rotate hand or arm to the right	Circle or ellipse clockwise	Heater	Warmer
8	Turn/rotate hand or arm to the left	Circle or ellipse counterclockwise		Colder

1.5 m × 1.5 m in the working distance of approx. 3 m to the receiver), parts of the pattern will cover the receiver while carrying out a gesture describing "a trajectory in the air" by arm or hand motion even when not targeted directly. Next, the person was told that she/he had time to perform the gesture of up to 6 s after the starting signal.

Then each time the assistant announces the task to perform an appropriate dynamic gesture to initiate an action of a specific device. While a test person was carrying out the gesture, the electrical signals from of all photodiodes of the receiver unit were synchronously recorded. Each person repeated a specific gesture to be used to control a specific application for light, blind, heating, and doors (Wizard-of-Oz experiment) up to three times with one of two differently shaped remote controls chosen be the test person to be used. Overall, 642 gestures from 29 participants were recorded and analyzed. Participants made an average of 2.70 gestures per gesture class (referent).

Study Three comprised extensive tests with a group of 11 younger adults (aged 25...46 years (33.5 ± 7.0 years), 8 females/3 males) with an improved version of the *SmartPointer* device. The tests were conducted on two consecutive days in one large hall-sized room (approx. 12 m × 6 m × 3.50 m) with unobstructed view towards the receiver. The small receiver box (8 cm × 8 cm) was placed on a table close to the center of one of the shorter sides of the room. The participants were positioned facing the receiver in 5 different distances to it (2 m, 3 m, 4 m, 6 m, 8 m), in two postures (sitting on a chair and standing) and two different ambient light conditions (without and with artificial ambient light). In all tests, the hand-held SmartPointer device was of bulbous shape ('pipe').

The tests were conducted in time slots of roughly one hour for every test person. Starting the session, a brief introduction was given to the test person, particularly about the rough size of the imaginary 'sensitive area' around the receiver box into which the gestures have to be 'drawn' and the time window during which the signals would be recorded. For each series of gestures, the test person was assigned to a fixed position in a predefined distance to the receiver and a certain posture. Then the test person was asked to execute the specific gesture corresponding to a short spoken command ('stroke left-to-right', 'stroke top-down', 'circle clockwise' etc.) given by the computer.

After the voice command was given, the participants had time for 3 s to execute the gesture. (It turned out that most of the participants performed a large part of the gestures much faster.) Immediately after finishing the recording, the trajectory was reconstructed and the gesture automatically recognized as to belong to one of the 6 predefined classes (or otherwise marked as 'unclassified'). The decision whether the executed gesture was correctly recognized or not was given to the test person without noticeable delay (less than 1 s for a decision) via an audio sequence from the computer. After that, the next gesture was announced to be executed by the test person etc.

The commands for the gestures to be executed were given (a) in regular order, (b) in randomized order and number, to put slightly more (time) pressure on the participants and keep them focused. In about 30 min, 170 gestures were recorded from each test person, in total 1,870 gestures. Participants made an average of 28.0 gestures per gesture class (referent).

5 Results of User Tests

5.1 User Experience

User experience is highly dependent on the overall user's familiarity with a range of technical devices and procedures as well as expectations resulting from it. In our interviews we gathered expectations expressed by two groups of older adults (16 and 29 persons) regarding a) the kinds and functions of devices in their home environment they would like to be controllable by gesture, b) a list of gestures they would find appropriate (because these gestures would be easy to execute and easy to remember) and c) practical concerns regarding feedback and safety issues. A multitude of expectations and desires towards gesture-based remote controls could be identified and taken into account during the development of the *SmartPointer* system. The most interesting findings are summarized below.

Household Devices to be Remotely Controlled. Among the mentioned household devices desired for simple mid-air gesture control were (in this order) TV sets, lights, hi-fi systems/radios and doors plus a number of 'non-classical' (with respect to gestural interaction) devices, e.g. in the bathroom. Functionalities imagined by the interviewees included switching the TV/radio on and off, adjusting its volume, switching between TV and radio channels and directly choosing the favorite channel (e.g. be "drawing" a digit in the air), dimming the lights and opening/closing and locking/unlocking doors. Additional functions were imagined for temperature settings at heating devices, the position of window blinds, digits to make telephones calls or functions to browse through TV media libraries and internet boxes [3].

Free-Hand Gestures or Hand-Held Device? Fundamentally, we wanted to learn from the participants how they would imagine the use of gestures to control different technical devices in their homes. Given the alternatives a) to flexibly use their plain hand (or both hands) but be observed by a camera at all times (or rather a set of cameras; for simplicity, appropriate camera-friendly postures, distances or lighting etc. are omitted here) or b) to perform gestures on behalf of a hand-held device (with no need for any camera), the vast majority of participants rejected the idea of free-hands gestural interaction and preferred a gesture interaction with a hand-held device. In the first place this originated in the understandable reluctance or outright rejection to be observed and tracked by cameras, but – interestingly - also because of subliminally feeling overwhelmed by the vast flexibility of dynamic free-hand gestures, fearing to forget how to perform a specific gesture correctly or to comply with the necessary conditions for a camera-based recognition (regarding posture, distance, occlusions, light etc.).

The preferred choice of a hand-held device to 'point' in the direction of the device to be controlled and then 'draw' gestures with it is also most understandable out of common practice to use remote controls for TV and other entertainment devices or to use laser pointers for presentations. As numerous studies showed and common sense indicates, users will not be interested in an assistive device they have to learn a lot of how to use it, unless there is a clear and obvious increase in efficiency.

Gesture Vocabulary. Having made the point that a hand-held device would be used for remotely controlling different devices in the home, it meant that gestures would be basically confined to forearm motions of the dominant hand. The next question evaluated was about the catalog of preferred gestures to be performed with such a hand-held remote.

In Study One, based on the gestures drawn by the participants with the laser pointer during the task-based investigation and their ticks in the proposed gesture catalog, the popularity of certain dynamic gestures was determined. It turned out that the most frequently used gestures were horizontal and vertical lines, arc and circular movements and pointing gestures (to target a chosen device). Symmetrical gestures such as horizontal left-to-right and right-to-left movements, vertical top-down or bottom–up movements and clockwise or counter-clockwise circular movements were by far the most frequently proposed by the interviewed participants and chosen from the gesture catalog as most favorable.

In general, it was observed that most gestures were borrowed from well-known familiar patterns and that there were clear tendencies towards the use of certain 'pantomimic' gestures. For example, the participants predominantly chose vertical top-down and bottom-up movements to lower or raise the blind or to increase or decrease the intensity of the ceiling light. We also observed that most participants repeatedly chose the same gestures for the same function, regardless of the type of device to be remotely controlled. That was also the case when the gestures of different participants were compared: For a specific task like increasing or decreasing the volume of a TV set or radio or dimming the light, many test persons chose the same dynamic gestures. This is not surprising and consistent with other studies, but nevertheless an important outcome of the study indicating that there might be a large consensus from experience about what motion gestures to choose in order to initiate several fundamental actions.

A great concern of many participants was to forget the specific commands. This would not mean to lose power to control the devices (since traditional touch switches would not be removed) but, as a consequence, we agreed – at least in this initial state, without much training – that the gesture vocabulary should be as short and quasi-intuitive as possible. From the gestures proposed and ticked by the participants, 6 basic gestures were chosen for the test on the *SmartPointer* system in this early stage of involvement. This is in perfect agreement with the often claimed number of 7 ± 2 objects an average human can hold in short-term memory (Miller's law). The 6 gestures are 'left-to-right' (LR), 'right-to-left' (RL), 'bottom-up' (UP), 'top-down' (DN), 'circle clockwise' (CR) and 'circle counter-clockwise' (CL).

Performing a Gesture. As the interviews had revealed, the vast majority of the participants was not familiar with any gesture-based device or game console. All test persons, however, did immediately understand how to 'draw' a stroke or circle 'in the air' with the flashlight-like *SmartPointer*. In the case of 'straight line' gestures ('top-down' or 'left-to-right') most test persons tended to perform the gestures fast, requiring only little physical effort and minimal time. Most linear gestures lasted less than 2 s. Circular forms (arcs, circles, ellipses) were drawn more cautiously taking more time to perform them (in general more than 3 s). Although we observed the tendency that younger test persons performed many gestures faster than older test persons, especially regarding swiping or linear gestures that was not the rule. Many older persons often performed swiping gesture quite hastily.

Pointing at a Device. An interesting question arose around the agreement on how to choose a device to be controlled and how to switch it on (i.e. how to awake it from stand-by mode). To indicate a selection, most people would immediately point at something remotely in a distance. In full agreement with this intuitive finding, the majority of the test persons pointed in a certain direction to select an imaginary device and moved the laser pointer vertically or drew a small circle to switch it on or off. We suggested that both actions (selecting a device and switching it on/off) could be easily combined by just pointing at it for a longer while (1...2 s) since it was already agreed on that every device would have its own receiver.

Feedback. All participants desired to get a feedback from the system indicating that a certain device was selected and that the gesture was recognized and its meaning transmitted to the chosen device. According to the majority of the participants, a visual feedback or a combination of visual and audible feedback would be preferable.

With the aim to meet two goals, 1) the expectation to use a quick, simple and intuitive gesture to select a device and switch it on or off with 2) the understandable desire for some kind of feedback (although for an experienced user and a reliable recognition it would not be needed) the following solution was proposed and successfully tested by the participants in Study Two: A visual light beam would be included in the *SmartPointer* and be detected by photodiodes in the receiver box to a) visually indicate the direction the hand-held devices points to, b) to select a device when pointed at it for a longer while and c) to switch it on or off (depending on the current state) when selected. This light spot should be clearly visible on different surfaces and it size should be larger than that of a laser pointer spot such that the precision required for targeting the receiver at the selected device is greatly reduced compared to using a laser pointer.

Design of the Hand-Held Device. Since the preferred gesture-based remote control is said to be used similarly to a laser pointer, questions towards the functionality and design of such a hand-held device arose: The process of designing the hand-held device followed the guidelines of participatory design with potential users.

In the interviews we asked about their preferences regarding parameters influencing the haptic like size, shape, weight and surface material. We learned that the size of the *SmartPointer* should be smaller than that of common TV remotes, that the shape should be slim but not too slim, so that it cannot slip out of the hand easily, that the device should be lightweight but not too light (supposedly for the same reason) and that it should have a pleasant touch with a surface easy to clean but not slippery. Most importantly, the remote control should come without any button, so it could be comfortably usable also in a hurry, in a dark room, with trembling hands etc. As a result, a lightweight (~70 g), small-sized (~10 cm), buttonless haptic interface was designed and built in two shapes: a slim 'cross' and a bulbous 'pipe'. (Weight and size of both are about half of that of conventional remotes.). To switch it on, it just has to be taken into the hand: an acceleration sensor included in the handheld device awakes it from sleep-mode. The battery-powered device should be easily rechargeable. Charging cradles prepared for wireless inductive charging were designed for both shapes.

It is interesting to note that when choosing a specifically shaped hand-held device (slim 'cross' and a bulbous 'pipe'), clear preferences could be observed among the 29 participants of Study Two. In a free choice with no other differences between the two *SmartPointers*, after some initial trials female participants predominantly (10 of 15) chose the slim 'cross', whereas male participants had no preference: 7 of 14 chose the bulbous 'pipe'. The choice was also age-related: 12 of 14 persons under 75 years chose the 'cross' for the tests, 10 of 15 persons 75 years and older the 'pipe' (the number of females and males being nearly equal in both age groups).

Satisfaction. The subjective satisfaction, commonly equaled with the perceived usability, is often assessed based on a System Usability Survey (SUS), a questionnaire comprising 10 items, each with five response options on a Likert scale ranging from "strongly disagree" to "strongly agree" [31]. Lower scores indicate lower perceived usability. The *Smartpointer*'s usability was assessed by all 29 participants in Study Two. Based on the SUS scale, more than 75% of the participants rated the usability as 'good' or 'very good', the remaining as 'OK'. A second measure influencing the satisfaction is related to the perceived workload required to solve a task or initiate an action. The workload rating the task complexity and ease of task control can be assessed on behalf of the Task Load Index (NASA-TLX), a questionnaire with subscales evaluating the mental, physical and temporal demands, the perceptual strain and related situational stress, distraction or frustration on a 0-to-100 scale (low-to-high workload). The 29 participants of Study

Two rated the overall workload to use the *SmartPointer* as 'pretty low' (TLX mean value of 17.5, in the lower 20%).

5.2 Accuracy

The accuracy of the gesture recognition is given for both experimental studies, Study Two and Study Three. All participants in both studies repeated each of the 6 gestures 'left-to-right' (LR), 'right-to-left' (RL), 'bottom-up' (UP), 'top-down' (DN), 'circle clockwise' (CR) and 'circle counter-clockwise' (CL) several times (up to 3 time in Study Two, up to 30 times in Study Three). The performance of the multi-class classification problem is characterized by the average recognition rate (true positive rate TPR, referred to as "sensitivity") as the number of correctly recognized gestures to all performed gestures. A recognition is correct, when the predicted gesture (class) corresponds to the expected (known) gesture ('true class') and incorrect otherwise. If a gesture is not contributed to any class it is assigned to the class 'unclassified' (UN).

In Fig. 4, the recognition results of Study Three from different situations (postures and distances of the participants to the receiver) are listed. The results reveal that performing gestures from close distance (2 m) in sitting position was most error-prone. A histogram of the durations of all 1,853 recorded gestures of Study Three (17 of the 1,870 gestures were performed outside the recording time) shows that the majority of gestures was performed in less than 2 s.

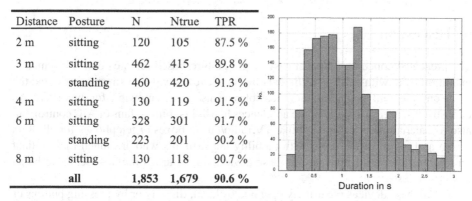

Distance	Posture	N	Ntrue	TPR
2 m	sitting	120	105	87.5 %
3 m	sitting	462	415	89.8 %
	standing	460	420	91.3 %
4 m	sitting	130	119	91.5 %
6 m	sitting	328	301	91.7 %
	standing	223	201	90.2 %
8 m	sitting	130	118	90.7 %
	all	**1,853**	**1,679**	**90.6 %**

Fig. 4. (Left) Recognition results of Study Three for different postures and distances of the participants to the receiver (N: number of gestures for that condition; Ntrue: number of correctly recognized gestures; TPR: true positive rate). (Right) Histogram of the durations of all 1,853 gestures of Study Three. The large bar on the right edge indicates that many gestures were truncated after the recording time of 3 s (mostly circular motions).

In Fig. 5, the detailed recognition results are given, as achieved by the current template-based algorithm for the 6 gesture classes from a) 508 gestures performed by 29 older adults in Study Two (in total 642 gestures were recorded, the remaining being pointing gestures) and b) 1,853 gestures performed by 11 younger adults in Study Three.

The average recognition rates for both age groups were similar: almost 89% for all gestures performed by the group of older adults and almost 91% for all gestures performed by the group of younger adults. The recognition rates per participant rated from 73% up to 99%.

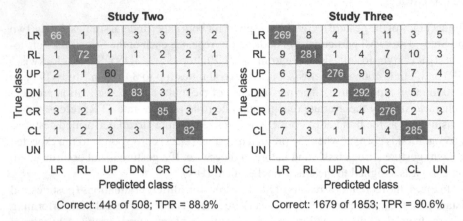

Study Two

True class	LR	RL	UP	DN	CR	CL	UN
LR	66	1	1	3	3	3	2
RL	1	72	1	1	2	2	1
UP	2	1	60		1	1	1
DN	1	1	2	83	3	1	
CR	3	2	1		85	3	2
CL	1	2	3	3	1	82	
UN							

Predicted class

Correct: 448 of 508; TPR = 88.9%

Study Three

True class	LR	RL	UP	DN	CR	CL	UN
LR	269	8	4	1	11	3	5
RL	9	281	1	4	7	10	3
UP	6	5	276	9	9	7	4
DN	2	7	2	292	3	5	7
CR	6	3	7	4	276	2	3
CL	7	3	1	1	4	285	1
UN							

Predicted class

Correct: 1679 of 1853; TPR = 90.6%

Fig. 5. Overall recognition results for 6 gesture classes from (left) 508 gestures performed by 29 older adults in Study Two and (right) 1,853 gestures performed by 11 younger adults in Study Three. (UN: unclassified gesture; TPR: true positive rate).

6 Discussion

The presented concept of a novel easy-to-use gesture-based remote control is aimed at making the life with existing technical objects of everyday use in smart homes (and the home environment in general) more feasible and also more enjoyable for their users. An unobstructed access to basic home appliances like lights, blinds, fans or A/C control, but also to entertainment equipment like TV/radio/music boxes or telephones for all users – also and foremost for those with mobility impairments who are much more reliant on remotes to control for many of these devices out of arm's range –, seems to be an obvious necessity.

All of these devices are usually operated by hand, directly or by pressing buttons or touching displays; up to now, few of them are operable by a comfortable tool always in reach. One fundamental option promising a novel, rich experience would be for users to use their hands, gesticulating without touch in direction of chosen devices comfortably from the actual position.

Hand gesture vocabularies for various framed HCI applications often result from an ad-hoc choice made by the designers to trigger certain pre-assigned actions (like e.g. clapping one's hands to turn on the computer). Their primary goal is to replace keypads, keyboards or touchscreen to enable quick formalized data entry without touch. The vocabularies are often designed for their ease of implementation to facilitate distinctive recognition and segmentation. However, these gestures have to be trained and their association be well remembered by potential users, which undermines the purpose of using hand gestures as a way to facilitate intuitive and natural interaction [32].

What makes touchless gestures natural and intuitive? In a conversation with another person, human beings besides language habitually and unconsciously use 'pantomimic' gestures with their hands in order to communicate a 'transitive' action to that person (instructing an immediate action to be undertaken, like "Put that there!"). These 'pantomimic' gestures are frequently used by all of us because they are easily and naturally performed, and they are perceived as predictable (i.e. similar in various situations) and transparent (clear and understandable). Predictability, transparency and naturalness are also the key guiding principles for effective HCI systems [21].

The *SmartPointer* approach is based on such natural dynamic 'pantomimic' gestures. It borrows from the observation of how people would communicate with other people to 'show' them via a simple sign language what action they should be undertaken. It makes use of a small set of typical simple but required hand or arm motions to manipulate physical objects via direct contact.

In equipping the user with a familiar assistive tool to operate something from a (variable) distance – resembling a well-accustomed alas buttonless TV remote, a laser pointer or a conductor's baton – it leads her/him to simplify and formalize the remote interaction with a specific device and helps making that interaction predictable, transparent and natural. "Gestures triggering manipulation of objects are often dynamic iconic representations of the motion required for the manipulation, rather than static iconic hand poses." [33].

As a consequence, evaluating the user studies we were not surprised to see most of the volunteering participants frequently showing very instinctive gestures for imaginary remote operation of several everyday household devices like e.g. selecting the window blind by pointing at it and then making the blind to go down by drawing a line top-down or making the blind to go up by drawing a line bottom-up.

We therefore believe that simple 'pantomimic' dynamic gestures performed with a familiar handheld device, based on the intuitive experience and interpreted by all users in the same way (basal gestures without dependence on age, constitution, gender or cultural context) greatly enhance both the applicability and the user experience. The elaboration of (quasi-) intuitive gestures is important because they shall allow to use the novel remote control without prior explicit learning of rules and procedures. This makes the proposed *SmartPointer* approach very different from previously known solutions.

7   Conclusion and Next Steps

In this paper, the results from three practical studies with in total over 50 participants (predominantly older adults, but also younger adults) evaluating the *SmartPointer*, a novel hand-held optical gestural remote control, was presented and discussed in terms of accuracy of gesture recognition and overall user experience and usability. The lightweight, buttonless *SmartPointer*, used similar to a familiar flashlight or laser pointer, is designed to be a general-purpose, user-friendly alternative to existing touch, voice or camera-based smart home interfaces which are sometimes perceived as awkward. A universal remote control usable for many different devices shall substantially simplify the independent life specifically for older adults and persons with mobility impairments and improve their well-being every day.

The design and results of three recent user studies to evaluate the user experience, robustness and accuracy of the proposed solution were presented. The results of all three studies confirm the feasibility and applicability of the proposed quasi-intuitive user interface to perform and recognize hand gestures to remote operate home appliances, its usability and satisfaction among the participants and the robustness of the technical solution along with a high success rate of the recognition algorithm, widely unaffected by the speed of gesture execution, varying distances to the device to be remotely controlled or the ambient light conditions.

For the time being, based on extensive mixed-methods studies aimed to evaluate the status quo and the expectation and needs of potential users with respect to remote controls, 6 uni-stroke gestures and 2 pointing gestures were examined in laboratory set-ups with 40 volunteers and a total number of more than 2,500 gestures. The gestures were executed from distances of up to 8 m form the devices to be controlled using one of two differently shaped hand-held devices, complying a user-centered design.

In one of our next development steps, this 'lexicon' for 2D (or essentially 3D) gestures will be enlarged. 'Referents' of fundamental and quasi-intuitive gestures could include, for example, also chopping gestures or multi-stroke gestures (e.g. digits), to operate more devices with more functions. Note that not only 'binary' settings (on/off, open/close etc.) but also continuous, 'intermediate' settings are addressed: An indicator of how much to change a regulator value could be the length of the gesture.

We envisage that the proposed *SmartPointer* approach could be adapted to other contexts of mid-air interactions with multiple devices, beyond the smart home or nursery home, like for example larger-range gestural interactions in workshops or factory halls, technology-enhanced public spaces, etc. with the aim to improve its usability, intuitiveness and experience. User case studies in real-world scenarios will further validate the methodology and its performance and determine the achieved improvements in user experiences.

Acknowledgments. This work was supported by the German Federal Ministry of Education and Research (BMBF) in the SME-Innovative Human-Technology Interaction Program.

References

1. Ruser, H., Kaltenbach, A., Mechold, L.: SmartPointer: buttonless remote control based on structured light and intuitive gestures. In: Proceedings of 6th int Workshop on Sensor-Based Activity Recognition and Interaction (iWOAR). Association for Computing Machinery, New York (2019)
2. Vorwerg, S., et al.: Requirements for gesture-controlled remote operation to facilitate human-technology interaction in the living environment of elderly people. In: Zhou, J., Salvendy, G. (eds.) HCII 2019. LNCS, vol. 11592, pp. 551–569. Springer, Cham (2019). https://doi.org/10.1007/978-3-030-22012-9_39

3. Ruser, H., Vorwerg, S., Eicher, C.: Making the home accessible - experiments with an infrared handheld gesture-based remote control. In: Stephanidis, C., Antona, M. (eds.) HCII 2020. CCIS, vol. 1226, pp. 89–97. Springer, Cham (2020). https://doi.org/10.1007/978-3-030-50732-9_13

4. Vorwerg, S., Eicher, C., Ruser, H., Piela, F., Obée, F., Mechold, L.: Vergleichsstudie zur Akzeptanz und Usability eines gestengesteuerten Smart Home Systems mit Personen im späten Erwachsenenalter (Comparative study on acceptance and usability of a gesture-controlled smart home system with persons in late adulthood); In: AAL-Kongress 2020, as part of 54th Annual Conference of the German Society for Biomedical Engineering (BMT), Leipzig, Germany (2020)

5. Rui, L., Zhenyu, L., Jianrong, T.: A survey on 3D hand pose estimation: cameras, methods, and datasets. Pattern Recogn. **93**, 251–272 (2019)

6. Vuletic, T., Duy, A., Hay, L., Mcteague, C., Campbell, G., Grealy, M.: Systematic literature review of hand gestures used in human computer interaction interfaces. Int. J. Hum.-Comput. Stud. **129**, 74–94 (2019)

7. Koutsabasis, P., Vogiatzidakis, P.: Empirical research in mid-air interaction: a systematic review. Int. J. Hum. Comput. Interact. **35**(18), 1747–1768 (2019)

8. Oudah, M., Al-Naji, A., Chahl, J.: Hand gesture recognition based on computer vision: a review of techniques. J. Imaging **6**(73) (2020)

9. Krupka, E., Karmon, K., Bloom, N.: Toward realistic hands gesture interface: keeping it simple for developers and machines. In: Proceedings of CHI 2017, Denver, USA (2017)

10. Vatavu, R.-D., Anthony, L., Wobbrock, J.O.: $Q: a super-quick, articulation-invariant stroke-gesture recognizer for low-resource devices. In: MobileHCI 2018, pp. 231–239, Barcelona, Spain (2018)

11. Rise, K., Alsos, O.: The potential of gesture-based interaction. In: Kurosu, M. (ed.) HCII 2020. LNCS, vol. 12182, pp. 125–136. Springer, Cham (2020). https://doi.org/10.1007/978-3-030-49062-1_8

12. Dong, H., Danesh, A., Figueroa, N., El. Saddek, A.: An elicitation study on gesture references and memorability toward a practical hand-gesture vocabulary for smart televisions. IEEE Access **3**, 543–555 (2015)

13. Carvalho, D., Silva, T., Abreu, J.: Interaction models for iTV services for elderly people. In: Abásolo, M.J., Silva, T., González, N.D. (eds.) jAUTI 2018. CCIS, vol. 1004, pp. 89–98. Springer, Cham (2019). https://doi.org/10.1007/978-3-030-23862-9_7

14. Wu, H., Yang, L., Fu, S., Zhang, X.: Beyond remote control: exploring natural gesture inputs for smart TV systems. J. Ambient Intell. Smart Environ. **11**(4), 335–354 (2019)

15. Vogiatzidakis, P., Koutsabasis, P.: Frame-based elicitation of mid-air gestures for a smart home device ecosystem. Informatics **6**(23), MDPI (2019)

16. Villarreal-Narvaez, S., Vanderdonckt, J., Vatavu, R.-D., Wobbrock, J.O.: Systematic review of gesture elicitation studies: what can we learn from 216 studies? In: ACM Designing Interactive Systems Conference (DIS 2020), Eindhoven, Netherlands, pp. 855–872 (2020)

17. Vatavu, R.-D., Vanderdonckt, J.: What gestures do users with visual impairments prefer to interact with smart devices? In: ACM Designing Interactive Systems Conference (DIS 2020), Eindhoven, Netherlands, pp. 85–90 (2020)

18. Kühnel, C., Westermann, T., Hemmert, F., Kratz, S., Müller, A., Möller, S.: I'm home: defining and evaluating a gesture set for smart-home control. Int. J. Hum.-Comput. Stud. **69**, 693–704 (2011)

19. Choi, E., Kwon, S., Lee, D., et al.: Towards successful user interaction with systems: focusing on user-derived gestures for smart home systems. Appl. Ergon. **45**(4), 1196–1207 (2014)

20. Hoffmann, F., Tyroller, M., Wende, F., Henze, N.: User-defined interaction for smart homes: voice, touch, or mid-air gestures? In: Proceedings of 18th International Conference on Mobile and Ubiquitous Multimedia (MUM 2019), Pisa, Italy (2019)

21. Nielsen, M., Störring, M., Moeslund, T.B., Granum, E.: A procedure for developing intuitive and ergonomic gesture interfaces for HCI. In: Camurri, A., Volpe, G. (eds.) GW 2003. LNCS (LNAI), vol. 2915, pp. 409–420. Springer, Heidelberg (2004). https://doi.org/10.1007/978-3-540-24598-8_38

22. Wobbrock, J.O., Morris, M.R., Wilson, A.D.: User-defined gestures for surface computing. In: 27th Conference on Human Factors in Computing Systems (CHI 2009). ACM Press, New York (2009)

23. Stern, H., Wachs, J., Edan, Y.: A method for selection of optimal hand gesture vocabularies. In: Sales Dias, M., Gibet, S., Wanderley, M.M., Bastos, R. (eds.) GW 2007. LNCS (LNAI), vol. 5085, pp. 57–68. Springer, Heidelberg (2009). https://doi.org/10.1007/978-3-540-928 65-2_6

24. Pereira, A., Wachs, J., Park, K., Rempel, D.: A user-developed 3-D hand gesture set for human-computer interaction. Hum. Fact. **57**(4), 607–621 (2015)

25. Honig, Sh., Oron-Gilad, T.: Comparing laboratory user studies and video-enhanced web surveys for eliciting user gestures in human-robot interactions. In: 2020 ACM/IEEE International Conference on Human-Robot Interaction (HRI 2020). ACM (2020)

26. Zaiti, I., Pentiuc, S., Vatavu, R.-D.: On free-hand TV control: experimental results on user-elicited gestures with leap motion. Pers. Ubiquitous Comput. **19**, 821–838 (2015)

27. Katz, S., Kaplan, N., Grossinger, I.: Using diffractive optical elements - DOEs for beam shaping – fundamentals and applications. Optik&Photonik **4**, 83–86 (2018)

28. Ruser, H., Kaltenbach, A., Mechold, L., Obée, F., Piela, F.: Low-cost gestural interaction based on motion estimation of a projected dot pattern. In: Proceedings of IEEE Sensors Conference, Rotterdam, Netherlands (2020)

29. Hassenzahl, M., Tractinsky, N.: User experience – a research agenda. Behav. Inf. Technol. **25**(2), 91–97 (2006)

30. McDowell, I.: Measuring Health - A Guide to Rating Scales and Questionnaires. Oxford University Press, Oxford (2006)

31. Bangor, A., Kortum, P., Miller, J., An empirical evaluation of the system usability scale. Int. J. Hum.-Comput. Interact. **24**(6), 574–594 (2008)

32. Ferron, M., Mana, N., Mich, O.: Designing mid-air gesture interaction with mobile devices for older adults. In: Sayago, S. (ed.) Perspectives on Human-Computer Interaction Research with Older People. HIS, pp. 81–100. Springer, Cham (2019). https://doi.org/10.1007/978-3-030-06076-3_6

33. Grandhi, S.A., Joue, G., Mittelberg, I.: Understanding naturalness and intuitiveness in gesture production: insights for touchless gestural interfaces. In: 29th Conference on Human Factors in Computing Systems (CHI 2011), pp. 821–824. ACM (2011)

34. Kirsh, I., Ruser, H.: Phone-pointing remote app: Using smartphones as pointers in gesture-based IoT remote controls. In: Proceedings of 23rd HCI International Conference (HCII'21), CCIS 1420, Springer (2021). https://doi.org/10.1007/978-3-030-78642-7_3

Detection of Finger Contact with Skin Based on Shadows and Texture Around Fingertips

Yuto Sekiya$^{(\boxtimes)}$, Takeshi Umezawa, and Noritaka Osawa

Chiba University, Chiba, Japan
ut_sekiya@chiba-u.jp

Abstract. This paper proposes a method to detect contact between fingers and skin based on shadows and texture around fingertips. An RGB camera installed on a head-mounted display can use the proposed method to detect finger contact with the body. The processing pipeline of the method consists of extraction of fingertip image, image enhancement, and contact detection using machine learning. A fingertip image is extracted from a hand image to limit image features to those around fingertips. Image enhancement reduces the influence of different lighting environments. A contact detection utilizes deep learning models to achieve high accuracy. Datasets of fingertip images are built from videos recording where a user touches and releases the forearm with his/her fingers. An experiment is conducted to evaluate the proposed method in terms of image enhancement methods and data augmentation methods. Results of the experiment show that the proposed method has a maximum accuracy of 97.6% in cross-validation. The results also show that the proposed method is more robust to different users than different lighting environments.

Keywords: Touch detection · Flexible surface · Single RGB camera

1 Introduction

Virtual reality (VR) systems for consumers have become widespread, and content using VR technology has been actively developed in recent years. However, it is difficult to use existing devices and input methods such as a mouse and keyboard in VR environments because a user who wears a closed (non-transparent) head-mounted display (HMD) cannot see the mouse and keyboard. Therefore, devices and input methods suitable for VR environments are required.

This paper focuses on the input method of touching the skin with a finger because finger touch does not require any input devices on the hand, and users can naturally obtain haptic feedback. The method captures an image of fingers and skin of a hand or arm using a camera installed on an HMD, recognizes contact between the finger and the skin, and estimates a point of the contact. Previous studies used depth cameras to detect contact based on depth information, but the detection accuracy was insufficient.

We propose a contact detection method based on images from an RGB camera and Convolutional Neural Network (CNN). The method detects contact by analyzing

© Springer Nature Switzerland AG 2021
M. Kurosu (Ed.): HCII 2021, LNCS 12763, pp. 109–122, 2021.
https://doi.org/10.1007/978-3-030-78465-2_9

the shadows and texture around fingers in an RGB image, which change as the finger touches the skin.

We conducted an experiment to evaluate the proposed method with combinations of image conversions and data augmentation. We also analyze the effects of image enhancement methods and data augmentation by comparing the results of combinations.

2 Related Work

2.1 Operations and Inputs in Virtual Reality Environments

Controller-based input methods are widely used in consumer VR systems, and ray casting [1] is the most common interaction method with controllers. In the method, a virtual ray emitted from a controller is used to select a region, such as a key on a virtual keyboard. Drum-like input interfaces have also been developed [2]. The virtual sticks extending from the controllers are used to tap virtual buttons like drums.

Hand-gesture-based input methods [3] do not require users to hold specific devices and, therefore, can take advantage of free hand movement. AirTarget [4] is a system that detects the fingertips with a camera installed on an HMD and allows a user to specify virtual or real objects. There is also research on typing by directly touching the virtual keyboard interface in the air with fingers [5].

Glove-based input methods [6, 7] recognize pinch gestures with a glove-type device worn on the hands. The methods also have the advantage of sensing the touch position and pressure.

Input methods using physical keyboards enable a user to use the same typing ability as in real environments [8]. Projection of the real keyboard and hands into an HMD is being investigated to reduce typing errors [9]. Bridge [10] tracks the keyboard position, captures the hands with cameras mounted on an HMD, and displays the keyboard and hands in VR environments.

2.2 Input Methods Using Finger Contact with Body

We focus on methods to use contact between a finger and the skin because they can provide high input performance in allowing free movement in a VR environment. A user does not need to wear or hold a specific device, and thus the user's position and posture are not restricted. The methods allow the user to use other input methods such as gestures. Moreover, haptic feedback by touch is expected to improve an input speed and reduce an input error rate.

Kawaguchi et al. [11] proposed a method that recognizes the hand and fingers' position using a depth camera (LeapMotion) attached to an HMD. The method enables a user to manipulate a virtual flick-keyboard interface projected on the palm with his/her fingers. The method needs a finger to be lifted 15 mm from the keyboard for accurate contact detection. That is a limitation and causes a high input error rate (Corrected Error Rate: 37%). The error is attributed to the misrecognition of the handshape by LeapMotion.

Harrison et al. [12] proposed OmniTouch, a shoulder-worn system that combines a depth sensor and a projection device. The system projects an interaction interface onto a hand, arm, wall, or table and detects when a finger touches it. The study employed a depth-map fill algorithm to recognize contact, but the recognition fails where the distance between the finger and the control surface was between 1 and 2 cm.

When a finger touches the skin, it depresses the flexible surface, casts a shadow around the finger, and changes the fine texture of the skin. Therefore, we use the RGB color information instead of the depth information. We process and analyze an RGB image with CNN machine learning to detect the finger contact. We think that our method can accurately detect the moment of contact since a unique shadow of contact appears only when the finger touches the skin.

3 Proposed Method

Our proposed method detects contact between a finger and skin based on an RGB image in which fingers of a hand stay above or on a forearm. The method does not require any specific device on the hand or the forearm. Our method expects an RGB camera installed at the front side of an HMD, which captures images of the user's fingers and forearm. We use a CNN machine learning model to detect contact based on the shadows and colors around a fingertip captured in an RGB camera image.

Figure 1 shows the processing pipeline of the proposed method. The pipeline consists of three processing phases: fingertip extraction, image enhancement, and contact detection. In the fingertip extraction phase, the hand image is cropped, and the images only around the fingertip are extracted. The extracted images will be referred to as fingertip images. In the image enhancement phase, statistical image enhancement methods are applied to fingertip images to correct their contrast and color. In the contact detection phase, a CNN machine learning model detects finger contacts from the enhanced images.

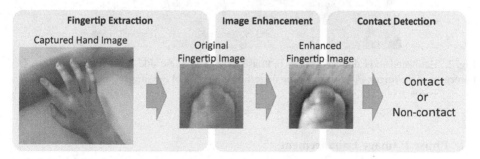

Fig. 1. The processing pipeline

4 Prototype Implementation

This section describes a prototype implementation of the proposed method for the experiments.

4.1 Phase 1: Fingertip Extraction

Fingertip images are extracted from the input motion videos.

A fingertip image is an $S \times S$ pixels square image whose upward direction is adjusted to the finger's direction D, and its center is the fingertip position P (Fig. 2). We set S, the size of one side of the fingertip image, to be twice the finger's width.

S, D, and P are calculated based on the skeletal information estimated from the hand image. Our implementation used MediaPipe Hands [13], a hand position estimation and tracking model provided by Google, to estimate the hand's skeletal information. MediaPipe Hands can estimate the XYZ coordinates of the wrist, 5 fingertips, and 15 finger joints for each hand image. A fingertip position estimated by MediaPipe is used as P. D is a direction to the fingertip from the first joint. We set $S = L \times 0.355$ based on statistical data of Japanese hand and finger size by the National Institute of Advanced Industrial Science and Technology [14]. L is the finger's length calculated by adding the lengths from the fingertip to the third joint.

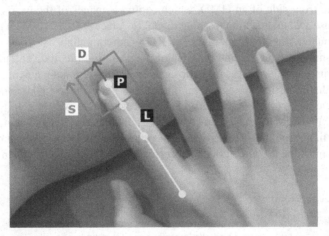

Fig. 2. Estimated and calculated values in Phase 1 (S: Size of one side of the fingertip image, D: Direction of the finger, P: Position of the fingertip, L: Length of the finger)

4.2 Phase 2: Image Enhancement

A statistical image enhancement method is applied to fingertip images to improve the accuracy of contact detection. The following 6 conversion methods (no enhancement and 5 enhancement methods) are tested for improvement in detection accuracy. A pixel can be represented by (r, g, b). r, g, and b are component values of RGB color channels, respectively. Each component in a pixel has an 8-bit value. c represents one of the component values. r^*, g^*, b^*, and c^* are the pixel component values during conversion, and r', g', b', and c' are the pixel component values from 0 to 1 after the final conversion. Normalization is also applied to color channels so that the component values of color channels fall within a range of 0 to 1. min_C, max_C, $\overline{C}$, and s_C respectively represent the minimum value, the maximum value, an average, and a standard deviation of the color channel C. In addition, we define the following function as normalization.

$$norm(v, \textit{offset}, \textit{deviation}) = \frac{v - \textit{offset}}{\textit{deviation}}$$

The following describes six conversion methods.

I.   Baseline without enhancement
     No enhancement is applied to the image.
     $c' = norm(c, 0, 255)$

II. Min-max normalization
     Each color channel is normalized so that the maximum component value is 1 and the minimum component value is 0.
     $c' = norm(c, min_C, max_C - min_C s)$

III. Standardization (z-score normalization)
     Each color channel is standardized. We set the mean to 0.5 and the standard deviation to 0.166 so that the range between $\overline{C} - 3s_C$ and $\overline{C} + 3s_C$ is included in 0 to 1. The component values are clipped from 0 to 1.
     $c^* = norm(c, \overline{C}, s_C) \times 0.166 + 0.5$
     $c' = \max(\min(c^*, 1), 0)$

IV. Standardization and Min-max normalization
     Each color channel is standardized as in method *III* and then normalized as in method *II*. min_{C^*} and max_{C^*} respectively represent the minimum value, maximum value of the color channel C during conversion.
     $c^* = norm(c, \overline{C}, s_C) \times 0.166 + 0.5$
     $c' = norm(c^*, min_{C^*}, max_{C^*} - min_{C^*})$

V.   Grayscale conversion
     Every pixel is converted to grayscale by calculating the luminance using the formula in ITU-R Rec BT.601.
     $c' = 0.299 \times \frac{r}{255} + 0.587 \times \frac{g}{255} + 0.114 \times \frac{b}{255}$

VI. Min-max normalization and Grayscale conversion
     Each color channel is normalized as in method *II* and then converted to grayscale.
     $c^* = norm(c, min_C, max_C - min_C)$
     $c' = 0.299 \times r^* + 0.587 \times g^* + 0.114 \times b^*$

4.3 Phase 3: Contact Detection

The CNN model structure for contact detection is shown in Table 1. This model takes a converted fingertip image resized to 50×50 pixels as input and performs binary classification between contact and non-contact.

We used Adamax as an optimizer and binary cross-entropy as a loss function.

Table 1. Structure of CNN model for finger contact detection

Layer	Size	Output shape	Activation	
Input	-	(50, 50, 3)	-	
Convolution 2D	(3, 3)	(50, 50, 32)	Relu	
Convolution 2D	(3, 3)	(48, 48, 32)	Relu	
MaxPooling 2D	(2, 2)	(24, 24, 32)	-	Dropout = 0.25
Convolution 2D	(3, 3)	(24, 24, 64)	Relu	
Convolution 2D	(3, 3)	(22, 22, 64)	Relu	
MaxPooling 2D	(2, 2)	(11, 11, 64)	-	Dropout = 0.25
Flatten	-	(7744)	-	
Full connected	-	(512)	Relu	Dropout = 0.5
Full connected	-	(1)	Sigmoid	

5   Dataset

This section describes datasets for experiments.

5.1   Recoding Input Motion Videos

We recorded the input motion of touching the forearm with the fingers. An RGB camera placed at about 20 cm above the desk captures a hand on the arm placed on the desktop (Fig. 3). The recorded video format is 24-bit RGB, 1080×1920 pixels, and 30 fps. Touching and releasing the fingers were repeated at intervals of about 1 s, and a video of about 30 s was recorded. We collect a video $V_{n,e}$ from subject n in lighting environment e. In this experiment, the number of subjects N is 3, the number of environments E is 5, and the total number of videos V is $N \times E = 15$.

5.2   Data Augmentation and Datasets

This section summarizes the data used in the experiment.

Fingertip images were manually labeled with binary values of contact (T) or non-contact (H). The number of labels B is 2.

$D_{n,e,a}$ is a dataset extracted from Video $V_{n,e}$ where n, e, and a respectively represent a subject, an environment, and a data augmentation method. A subject id n is 1 to N, An

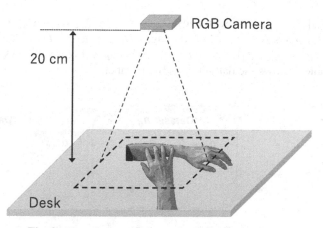

Fig. 3. Recoding environment for input motion videos

environment id e is 1 to E, and A data augmentation method id a is one of no augmentation (O), position-shifting (P), or color-shifting (C). $I_{n,e,f,b}$ is a set of 49 original fingertip images of finger type f and contact label b. The number of finger type F is 4, excluding a thumb since a thumb is not used for input operation in our method. $D_{n,e,O}$ contains $|I_{n,e,f,b}| \times F \times B = 392$ images. $D_{n,e,P}$ and $D_{n,e,C}$ are datasets, which are the same size as $D_{n,e,O}$, created by position-shifting and color-shifting augmentation.

- Position-shifting
  Position-shifting is performed by adding a displacement to the fingertip position when extracting in the fingertip extraction phase. A displacement for each axis is a uniform random number in the range of -S/4 to S/4, where S is the size of one side of a square fingertip image. The center position for extraction (x', y') is represented by

$$(x', y') = \left(x + u\left(-\frac{S}{4}, \frac{S}{4}\right), y + u\left(-\frac{S}{4}, \frac{S}{4}\right)\right),$$

  where (x, y) is the estimated fingertip position. $u(lower, upper)$ is a uniform random number in the range between *lower* and *upper*. This data augmentation is expected to improve robustness to errors in fingertip position estimation.
- Color-shifting
  Color-shifting is performed by randomly shifting each RGB color channel of a fingertip image. The amount of the shift is a uniform random number in the range of -16 to 16 for each color channel and independent for each channel and each image. The pixel value, after color-shifting, (r', g', b') is represented by

$$(r', g', b') = (r + u(-16, 16), g + u(-16, 16), b + u(-16, 16)).$$

Then, a value range of a pixel component is limited between 0 to 255. This data augmentation is expected to improve robustness to different lighting environments.

To verify effectiveness of data augmentation, we built three datasets: Original Dataset (D_O), Position-shift Dataset (D_P), Color-shift Dataset (D_C). D_O consists of $D_{n,e,O}$ and contains $|D_{n,e,O}| \times N \times E = 5880$ images. D_P consists of $D_{n,e,O}$ and $D_{n,e,P}$ and contains $(|D_{n,e,O}| + |D_{n,e,P}|) \times N \times E = 11760$ images. D_C consists of $D_{n,e,O}$ and $D_{n,e,C}$ and contains $(|D_{n,e,O}| + |D_{n,e,C}|) \times N \times E = 11760$ images. Figure 4 shows an overview of datasets. Table 2 shows the dataset sizes by the label.

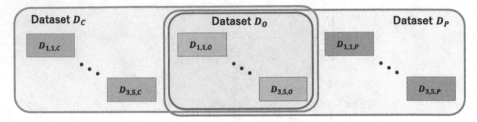

Fig. 4. Overview of datasets

Table 2. The number of fingertip images contained in datasets

Dataset	Contact (T)	Non-contact (H)
Original (D_O)	2940	2940
Position-shift (D_P)	5880	5880
Color-shift (D_C)	5880	5880

6   Experiments

This section describes experiments to evaluate the performance of our proposed method.

6.1   Experiment 1: Performance Evaluation of Contact Detection Model

Condition. We performed V-fold cross-validation to evaluate the performance of our contact detection model. We always used an original dataset $D_{n,e,O}$ as test data. The training datasets are a subset $\cup_{(n',e') \neq (n,e)} D_{n',e',O}$ of D_O, a subset $\cup_{(n',e') \neq (n,e)} (D_{n',e',O} \cup D_{n',e',P})$ of D_P, and a subset $\cup_{(n',e') \neq (n,e)} (D_{n',e',O} \cup D_{n',e',C})$ of D_C. The training period was 50 epochs. Figure 5 shows an overview of data where the test data is $D_{1,1,O}$.

Results. Figure 6 shows test accuracies of combinations of conversion method and dataset. The highest accuracy in Experiment 1 is $R_{1,VI,P} = 97.6\%$, where $R_{x,m,a}$ is an accuracy with using conversion method m and data augmentation method a in experiment x.

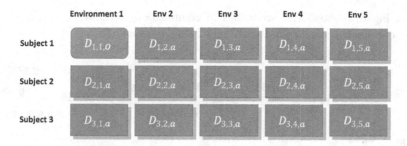

Fig. 5. Overview of training and test data when $D_{1,1,O}$ in orange is used for testing. The datasets in blue are the training data.

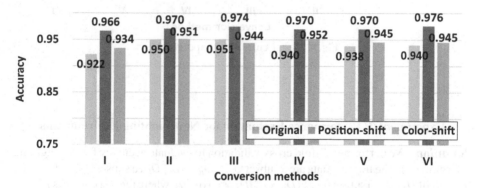

Fig. 6. Test accuracies in Experiment 1

6.2 Experiment 2: Performance Evaluation for New Users

Condition. We performed N-fold cross-validation to evaluate accuracy for new users. The training data are a subset $\cup_{n' \neq n} D_{n',e,O}$ of D_O, a subset $\cup_{n' \neq n}(D_{n',e,O} \cup D_{n',e,P})$ of D_P, and a subset $\cup_{n' \neq n}(D_{n',e,O} \cup D_{n',e,C})$ of D_C, where the test data was $D_{n,e,O}$. The training period was 50 epochs. Figure 7 shows an overview of data where the test data is $D_{1,*,O}$.

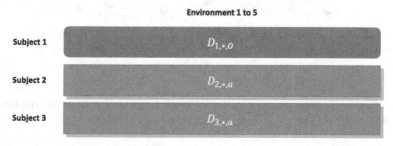

Fig. 7. Overview of training and test data where $D_{1,*,O}$ in orange is used for testing. $D_{2,*,a}$ and $D_{3,*,a}$ in blue are the training data.

Results. Figure 8 shows test accuracies of combinations of conversion method and dataset. The highest accuracy in Experiment 2 is $R_{2,VI,P} = 96.9\%$.

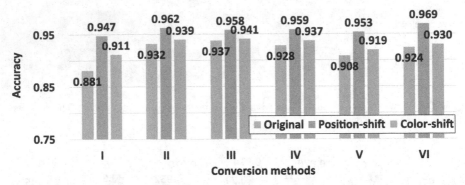

Fig. 8. Test accuracies in Experiment 2

6.3 Experiment 3: Performance Evaluation for New Lighting Environments

Condition. We performed E-fold cross-validation to evaluate accuracy for new lighting environments. The training data are a subset $\cup_{e' \neq e} D_{n,e',O}$ of D_O, a subset $\cup_{e' \neq e}(D_{n,e',O} \cup D_{n,e',P})$ of D_P, and a subset $\cup_{e' \neq e}(D_{n,e',O} \cup D_{n,e',C})$ of D_C, where the test data was $D_{n,e,O}$. The training period was 50 epochs. Figure 9 shows an overview of data where the test data is $D_{*,1,O}$.

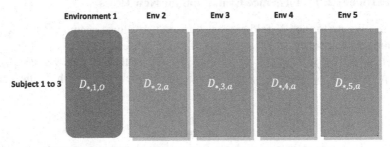

Fig. 9. Overview of training and test data where $D_{*,1,O}$ in orange is used for testing. The datasets in blue are the training data.

Results. Figure 10 shows test accuracies of combinations of conversion method and dataset. The highest accuracy in Experiment 3 is $R_{3,III,P} = 95.5\%$.

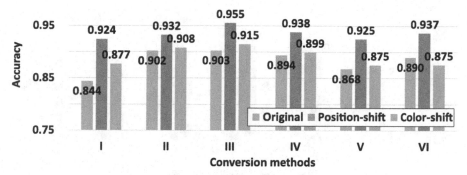

Fig. 10. Test accuracies in Experiment 3

6.4 Experiment 4: Performance Evaluation for New Users and Lighting Environments

Condition. We performed V-fold cross-validation to evaluate accuracy for new users in new lighting environments. The training data are a subset $\cup_{\substack{n' \neq n \\ e' \neq e}} D_{n',e',O}$ of D_O, a

subset $\cup_{\substack{n' \neq n \\ e' \neq e}} (D_{n',e',O} \cup D_{n',e',P})$ of D_P, and a subset $\cup_{\substack{n' \neq n \\ e' \neq e}} (D_{n',e',O} \cup D_{n',e',C})$ of

D_C, where the test data was $D_{n,e,O}$. The training period was 50 epochs. Figure 11 shows an overview of data where the test data is $D_{1,1,O}$.

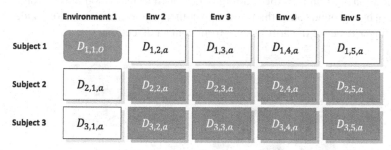

Fig. 11. Overview of training and test data where $D_{1,1,O}$ in orange is used for testing. The datasets in blue are the training data. The datasets in white are not used.

Results. Figure 12 shows test accuracies of combinations of conversion method and dataset. The highest accuracy in Experiment 4 is $R_{4,III,P} = 93.0\%$.

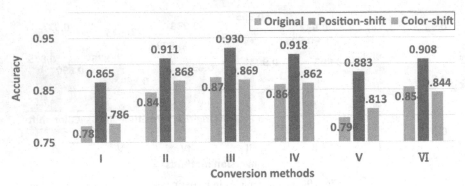

Fig. 12. Test accuracies in Experiment 4

6.5 Discussion

The accuracy of a model based on D_P is the highest in all models based on combinations of datasets and conversion methods. Figure 13(a) shows an example of fingertip images that were correctly detected only in a model based on D_P, regardless of the conversion method. The finger's position tends to be out of alignment with the center of the image in some images. The model built with D_P is robust against finger misalignment, and position-shifting effectively improves an accuracy.

Figure 13(b) shows an example image with a background other than an arm. Such images tended to be falsely detected in methods *I*, *II*, and *III*, which include Min-max normalization. One countermeasure against this false detection is to add fingertip images with various backgrounds to the training data, which trains a model to be robust to the presence of backgrounds other than an arm. Another countermeasure is to exclude images where a finger is out of the arm's range from contact detection.

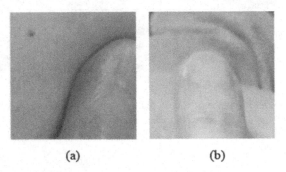

(a)   (b)

Fig. 13. Examples of fingertip images

For all combinations of conversion methods and data augmentations, the accuracies in Experiment 2 are lower than those in Experiment 1. However, the difference between $R_{1,VI,P}$ and $R_{2,VI,P}$, which are the best accuracies in Experiment 1 and 2, is 0.7% points (pp), indicating that our method has the same accuracy level even for new users who are not in the training data.

The difference between accuracies of models based on D_C and those based on D_O is the largest, where conversion method I is used in both Experiment 2 and 3. The difference between $R_{2,I,O}$ and $R_{2,I,C}$ is 3.0pp, and that between $R_{3,I,O}$ and $R_{3,I,C}$ is 3.3pp, and they are small. We expected that color-shifting improves accuracy when detecting data in new lighting environments, but the result is different from the expectation. $R_{2,I,C}$ and $R_{3,I,C}$ suggest that color-shifting is effective only when conversion method I is used. The results suggest that the effectiveness of color-shifting is reduced by the enhancement methods.

The accuracies for all combinations of conversion and data augmentation methods in Experiment 3 is lower than that in Experiment 2, even though the size of training data used in Experiment 3 was larger than that used in Experiment 2. These suggest that the image features focused on in this study, such as shadows and textures around fingertips, are more diverse in environments than in users. The result suggests that training data with different lighting environments will more effectively contribute to accuracy improvement.

The maximum accuracy in Experiment 4 is $R_{4,III,P} = 93.0\%$, which is 4.6pp lower than $R_{1,VI,P} = 97.6\%$, the maximum accuracy in Experiment 1. Since the input motion videos are 30 fps, an accuracy of 93.0% means that 2.1 frames per second on average are misclassified, which is not sufficiently accurate as an input method. We will build a larger training dataset, especially data in a new lighting environment, to improve classification accuracy in the future. Our current method detects contact in each frame and does not utilize multiple frames in the sequence. We will utilize time-series data to train a machine learning model. We think that utilization of features in multiple frames will enhance the proposed method.

7   Conclusion

This study investigates the detection of touching the skin with a finger as an input method in a virtual reality environment. To solve the problem in contact detection based on depth information in previous work, we proposed a method to detect contact from RGB images based on shadows and textures using a CNN model.

We conducted experiments to evaluate combinations of image conversion and data augmentation methods and obtained a maximum accuracy of 97.6% in 15-fold cross-validation.

The results suggest that the processing pipeline in our method is robust to different users. On the other hand, the results show that the image features used in the contact detection of our method are highly dependent on the lighting environments.

We have a plan to incorporate multiple frames in time sequence into the estimation model to enhance the proposed method.

References

1. Lee, Y., Kim, G.J.: Vitty: virtual touch typing interface with added finger buttons. In: Lackey, S., Chen, J. (eds.) VAMR 2017. LNCS, vol. 10280, pp. 111–119. Springer, Cham (2017). https://doi.org/10.1007/978-3-319-57987-0_9

2. Ravasz, J.: Keyboard input for virtual reality. https://uxdesign.cc/keyboard-input-for-virtual-reality-d551a29c53e9 (2017)
3. Microsoft HoloLens. https://docs.microsoft.com/en-gb/hololens/hololens2-basic-usage (2019)
4. Irie, H., et al.: AirTarget: a highly-portable markerless user interface using optical see-through HMD. IPSJ Journal **55**(4), 1415–1427 (2014)
5. Komiya, K., Nakajima, T.: A Japanese input method using leap motion in virtual reality. In: 2017 Tenth International Conference on Mobile Computing and Ubiquitous Network (2017)
6. Bowman, D.A., Rhoton, C.J., Pinho, M.S.: Text input techniques for immersive virtual environments: an empirical comparison. In: Human Factors and Ergonomics Society Annual Meeting Proceedings, vol. 46, no. 26, pp. 2154–2158 (2002)
7. Whitmire, E., et al.: DigiTouch: reconfigurable thumb-to-finger input and text entry on head-mounted displays. In: Proceedings of the ACM on Interactive, Mobile, Wearable and Ubiquitous Technologies, vol. 1, no. 3, Article no. 113 (2017)
8. Grubert, J., Witzani, L., Ofek, E., Pahud, M., Kranz, M., Kristensson, P.O.: Text entry in immersive head-mounted display-based virtual reality using standard keyboards. In: 2018 IEEE Conference on Virtual Reality and 3D User Interfaces (2018)
9. Walker, J., Li, B., Vertanen, K., Kuhl, S.: Efficient typing on a visually occluded physical keyboard. In: Proceedings of the ACM Conference on Human Factors in Computing Systems, pp. 5457–5461 (2017)
10. Bovet, S., et al.: Using traditional keyboards in VR: SteamVR developer kit and pilot game user study. In: 2018 IEEE Games, Entertainment, Media Conference, pp. 132–135 (2018)
11. Kawaguchi, K., Isomoto, T., Shizuki, B., Takahashi, S.: Flick-based Japanese text entry method on palm for virtual reality. In: Proceedings of the Human Interface Symposium (2019)
12. Harrison, C., Benko, H., Wilson, A.D.: OmniTouch: wearable multitouch interaction everywhere. In: Proceedings of the 24th Annual ACM Symposium on User Interface Software and Technology, pp. 441–450 (2011)
13. Zhang, F., et al.: MediaPipe hands: on-device real-time hand tracking. arXiv:2006.10214 (2020)
14. Kouchi, M.: 2012 AIST Japanese hand dimensions data (2012). https://www.airc.aist.go.jp/dhrt/hand/index.html. (in Japanese)

Character Input Method Working on 1-in. Round Screen for Tiny Smartwatches

Ojiro Suzuki[✉], Toshimitsu Tanaka, and Yuji Sagawa

Meijo University, Shiogama, 1-501, Tenpaku, Nagoya, Japan
`203426010@ccmailg.meijo-u.ac.jp`

Abstract. We have developed a method for entering Japanese hiragana characters using a 1-in. circular screen. The circumference of the smartwatch screen is divided every 90°. Hiragana is divided into 10 groups of 5 characters each, so the first half of the group is assigned to the left segment and the second half is assigned to the upper segment.

First, select a segment in the slide-in, which is the operation that first touch a finger to the outside of the screen then move it inside the screen as it is. The slide-in crosses the edge of the screen, so it can be detected in contour areas that are only 2 mm wide. As your fingertips pass through the segments, the screen is divided into five areas, each displaying one of the five group names assigned to the passed segment. The group displayed in the central area is selected when you release your finger in that area. The surrounding group is selected by slide-out in that direction. The slide-out is the operation that sliding outward beyond the screen edge while touching the screen. Then, the five hiragana characters that are members of the selected group are displayed. The letter in the center is entered by tapping, and other letters are entered by flicking to each direction.

The input speed for beginners was 23.1 CPM after using for about 14 min. The speed exceeded 30 CPM after 1 h of use. The error rate was about 3%.

Keywords: Character input · Smartwatch · Slide-in · Slide-out · User interface

1 Introduction

Since a smartwatch is paired to a smartphone, it is easy to send text to the smartwatch from the smartphone. However, it is troublesome to take the smartphone out of your pocket or bag every time you enter text, so if the text is short, I want to enter it directly.

Speech recognition is one choice. But it is inability to use it in environments where silence is required, such as museums and theaters. Its recognition rate is down in noisy places like crowded places or trains. In addition, privacy is not kept secret. Because what people say is heard by the people around them.

It is possible to use a flick keyboard on a smartwatch. But each key becomes too small because the flick keyboard needs the keys in four rows by five columns. As the result mistyping increases. In addition, most of the screen is occupied by the keyboard. For example, the Google flick keyboard [5] displayed on a smartwatch occupies 90% of the screen.

© Springer Nature Switzerland AG 2021
M. Kurosu (Ed.): HCII 2021, LNCS 12763, pp. 123–134, 2021.
https://doi.org/10.1007/978-3-030-78465-2_10

FlickKey Mini keyboard [6] and Flit keyboard [13] have reduced keys by using 8-way flicks to assign 9 characters to a single key. However, the Flit keyboard still uses 62% of the screen and the FlickKey Mini keyboard uses 50%. To reduce screen occupancy, keyboards that place keys around the screen (TouchOne keyboard [7], HARI keyboard [8], Black Phone Flick [9], etc.) have been developed. However, but all of them require more than 10 keys. According to the report of Akita et al. [1], these keyboards use almost half of the screen. ZoomBoard [11] scales the keyboard in stages before selecting characters, so the key size is large enough. However, half of the screen is required to display the minimized QWERTY keyboard. The 5-TILES keyboard [10] arranges 5 keys on a horizontal row. This keyboard has a high occupancy on a circular screen. This is because the keys in a row must be closer to the center to display the keys in a touchable width.

The SliT method developed by Akita et al. [1] can narrow the width of the keys, so it occupies about 25% of the screen, which is lower than other methods. However, the length of the keys becomes insufficient when the screen size is small. Because the method divides the circumference of the smartwatch screen into eight equal parts and it assigns keys to each.

The typical screen size of smartwatches on the market today is about 1.5 in. The case size will exceed 40 mm if the screen is circular. Many users want a smaller smartwatch because this size is comparable to the larger size of a regular men's wristwatch. The case size of women's wristwatches ranges from 26 to 35 mm [12], so small smartwatches with a screen size of less than 1 in. (25.4 mm) are expected to be sold in the future. When the screen size is reduced to 2/3, the key size of the current smartwatch character input method is smaller than the fingertip size. As a result, the number of incorrect inputs increases and the input speed slows down. To solve this problem, we have developed a character input method with a small number of keys that can be used stably even on a 1-in. round screen.

2 Previous Research

Figure 1 shows the screen layout of SliT [1] developed by Akita et al. Figure 1(a) is the screen in the standby state before starting character input. 2 mm from the edge of the screen is divided into 45° sections, each of which is a key. The key width can be narrowed because the key is selected by slide-in. Slide-in is an action in which a finger that touches the outside of the screen slides directly onto the screen, and since the fingertip crosses the key without fail, passage can be detected even with a narrow width. To reduce the number of keys, to each of keys, two groups of hiragana (two rows of the syllabary table of the fifty sounds of the Japanese language) are assigned, from the lower left section in a clockwise direction. The lower right key is used to switch between symbol mode and alphanumeric mode. The lower area is divided into three sections of 30°, and from left to right, Backspace (BS), Space (SP), and Enter (ENT) are assigned.

First, select one group of hiragana that is a row in the Japanese syllabary table. In Fig. 1(a), you make slide-in from the key where the row name of the character you want to input is written. As your finger crosses the screen edge, the screen splits into two, and the row names assigned to the key are displayed one by one. If you move your finger to the side you want to select while touching the screen, the area will turn green as shown in Fig. 1(b). If you release your finger, the row written in the area will be selected.

(a) The standby screen of   (b) The screen when making   (c) The screen for selecting
        SliT.   slide-in and selecting the "   characters on the "た" row.
                                              た" row.

Fig. 1. These are screens of SliT. (a) is the standby screen before starting to input text. Two groups of hiragana are assigned to each key, clockwise from the lower left segment. Here the group is one row of the syllabary table of the fifty sounds of the Japanese language. (b) is the screen when sliding in from the key at the upper of the left side. The screen is split and the group names assigned to the keys are displayed for each. The area will turn green by moving your finger into it. Release your finger from the screen to select the group. (c) shows the screen after the "た" group is selected. 5 characters belong the group is displayed. Tap a character to select it. (Color figure online)

Then select one character which is a member of the selected row. When a row is selected, the screen is divided into eight directions as shown in Fig. 1(c). Characters belonging to the selected row are displayed one in each area. Tap on any of these to enter that character. In this way, character input consists of two steps, group selection and character selection, in order to reduce the number of keys displayed on the screen at the same time.

In SliT, both steps split the screen into 45° to form the keys. For a 1.5-in. diameter screen, the key length is about 15 mm at the edge of the screen. It is longer than the width of the fingertip, which is about 10 mm. However, if you reduce the screen diameter to 1 in., the key length will be less than 10 mm, so the finger will hide the key during selecting it. As a result, you are more likely to have fat finger problems, such as accidentally tapping a surrounding key.

3 Proposed Method

In this study, we refined the key layout and character selection gestures of Akita's SliT, and develop a character input method named SlioF (Slide in to out, then Flick) that can be used on a 1-in. diameter screen. This method also reduces the number of keys displayed on the screen by selecting one character in the two steps like SliT.

3.1 Key Layout at Standby Status

The standby screen of SlioF is shown in Fig. 2(a). In order to make the keys longer than the width of the fingertip, the angle per key was changed to 90° (that is twice as large as that of SliT). As the result, the length of the key is 17 mm, even if the diameter of the screen is 1 in. It is larger than the fingertip, so selecting it is easy.

The key layout of SliT, which assigns the area with fixed width of the screen edge to keys, is better to reduce the screen occupancy. However, round areas are not convenient for displaying text. So, a square inscribed in a circular screen, that is the largest square area, is used as the text display area. And the rest is used as a keyboard. The screen occupancy of this key layout is 36%, which is lower than most smartwatch keyboards. This ratio is higher than SliT, but under the condition of displaying text in a square area on a 1-in. screen, it can display 41% more characters than SliT.

The reduction in the number of keys is compensated for by assigning five rows of hiragana to each key. The left section is used for "あ" to "な" rows, and the upper section for "は" to "わ" rows. The right key is used to switch to alphanumeric mode. The lower key is used to enter the Backspace (BS), Space (SP), and Enter (ENT) keys.

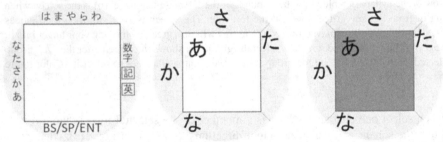

(a) The standby screen of (b) The screen after sliding (c) The screen when a finger
      SlioF.   in from the left key.   moves into the center area.

Fig. 2. These are screens of SlioF. (a) is the standby screen before starting to input character. Each five rows of hiragana are assigned to the left key and the top key. (b) is the screen when you make slide-in from the left key. The screen is divided to 5 areas and row names written in the left key of (a) are displayed in each area. (c) Background color of the area turns green when the fingertip moves into the area. The center area is selected by releasing the finger from the screen in the area. The others are selected by sliding out toward that direction. (Color figure online)

3.2 Selection of a Row of Hiragana

In the screen of the standby state, you make slide-in your finger across the key written with the row name (name of a hiragana group) in which the letter you want to enter is a member. When the finger crosses the key, the screen changes to display five rows assigned to the key. Figure 2(b) shows the screen when sliding in from the left side. The row name "あ" is displayed in the center. The row names "か", "さ", "た", and "な" are shown on the left, upper, right, and lower, respectively. Figure 2(b) is for right-handed users. The row names are offset to the upper left so they will not be hidden by the users' fingertips touching from the lower right.

If the fingertip is within the square area in the center, the background changes to green (Fig. 2(c)). If you release your finger in this state, you can select the "あ" row. The other rows are selected by making slide-out beyond the section where each name is written. The slide-out is the motion of your finger outwards across the edge of the screen while still touching the screen. The slide-out ensures that fingertips pass through the edge of the screen, so the passage can be detected with a narrow key. If the screen is 1 in. in diameter, the thickest part of the surrounding area is 5 mm, so you can select the area without fail by the slide-in. Also, the size of the central square is 15 mm × 15 mm in this case, so it's easy to stop your fingertip in it.

3.3 Selection of a Character

When a row is select, the screen for selecting one character from the members of the selected row is displayed. Figure 3(a) shows the screen when the "た" row is selected.

A cross key is placed in the center of the screen, and each cell displays one hiragana character contained in the "た" row. Tap the character in the center to select it. Other characters are selected by flicking in each direction.

Four button painted blue are placed in the four corners. Tap the button at the bottom right to change the displayed characters to voiced or lowercase, if existing. Tap the button in the upper right to display the lowercase characters of "や" row following the character in the "い" column of the selected row are displayed. For example, when tap the upper right button after selecting the "た" row, "ち ゃ", "ち ゅ", and "ち ょ" are displayed. These buttons can be used in combination. The displayed characters can be selected in the same way as normal characters. The buttons also are used to back to the normal characters.

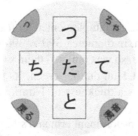
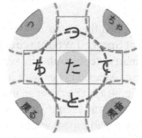

(a) The member selection belonging the "た" row

(b) Finger detection areas for near the center and buttons in the four corners

Fig. 3. (a) is the screen after selecting a row. You can select one character by tapping to the center or flicking from the center to one of four directions. Tap the buttons in the four corners are used to change display. The dotted circle in (b) shows the fingertip detection area of them. The diameter of the circle is 12 mm (when the screen diameter is 1 in.), so even if the fingertips are slightly misaligned, touches on them can be detected. (Color figure online)

The upper left button is assigned the function to directly enter "っ" (lowercase of "つ") when the "た" row is selected. According to "Hatena Diary Kana Frequency Data for 4.52 Million Characters [2]", the frequency of appearance of "っ" in Japanese texts is 1.66%. The rate is relatively high. However, in order to enter "っ" with SliT, it was necessary to add one tap to the normal character input procedure. So, I installed this function. The lower left button is used to cancel the character input and return to the standby screen.

The green circle in the center (the target you touch when selecting a character) and the surrounding buttons are small. However, the actual touch detection area is larger than the displayed area because it is inside the red or blue dotted lines in Fig. 3(b). The reason for making the size smaller is to encourage the user to touch it accurately. The diameter of the detection area is 12 mm (for a screen diameter of 1 in.), so touches can be detected even if the fingertip is out of position a little.

Once the touch in the center area is detected, the buttons in the four corners are no longer needed, so their detection areas are disabled. Therefore, even if a finger enters the area of a button during a flick motion, the button will not be accidentally selected. Also, no matter where you touch inside the red dotted circle, there is space to move your finger up, down, left and right, so flicking in all four directions will be possible.

4   Input Speed and Error Rate of Beginners

4.1   Experimental Condition

Since character input on a smartwatch is likely to be used for entering short sentences, the usage time will be short. For this reason, we thought it was important for the user to be able to input characters easily from the beginning of use. Therefore, we investigated the changes in input speed and input error rate among five university students (four males and one female, aged 20–22) who were not familiar with the proposed method. All of these students were familiar with the use of smart phones, but had no experience using smartwatches.

We developed the proposed system in Android Wear and implemented it on a smartwatch, Fossil Sport FTW6024 (circular screen, 1.22 in. in diameter, 390 × 390 pixels). Since the smartwatches with 1 in. screen are not for sale, so we emulated them by attaching a thin ring-shaped cover with an inner diameter of 1 in. on the screen. Its photo is shown in Fig. 4(a). The cover is made of resin and has a thickness of 1 mm, so touch input does not occur even if you touch the cover.

Experiment participant wear this device on their non-dominant arm and sit in a chair in a natural position. Then place their arm on the desk and operate with their dominant hand. Which finger to use is chosen by each participant.

4.2   Experimental Procedure

The procedure of this experiment is shown below.

1. Listen an explanation of how to operate the system in about 5 min.

(a) Photo of the smartwatch.   (b) Screen shot of the task.

Fig. 4. Smartwatch used in the experiment. (a) is the photo. Small-screen smartwatches are not for sale, so we emulated them by attaching a thin ring-shaped cover with an inner diameter of 1 in. on the screen. (b) is the screenshot of the task performed in the experiment. The task word is displayed at the top of the text area. The entered characters appear below the word.

2. Perform the task of entering 5 hiragana words.
3. Take a break for 3 min.
4. Repeat steps 2 and 3 above 10 times.

First, explain to participants how to operate the system and the procedure of this experiment, with PowerPoint and videos. At this time, we ordered them to input the characters as correct as possible. After that, they wear the smartwatch on their non-dominant arm and perform the task. There is no practice in advance.

The experiment is started by tapping the center of the screen (the area where the text is displayed). At the top of the text area, one word for the task appears in hiragana, as shown in Fig. 4(b). Participants type the letters of the word and then input Enter to complete this word. Following, the next word is appeared. When five words have been entered, this task ends. 10 tasks were performed with a 3-min break, and the input speed and error rate were measured for each task.

The words used in the task were selected from the frequency list of the Balanced Corpus of Contemporary Written Japanese (BCCWJ) of the National Institute for Japanese Language and Linguistics [3]. First, we extracted 100 nouns (excluding numerals and particles) with 4, 5, or 6 characters in hiragana, in descending order of frequency. Next, words with the same hiragana notation (words with the same reading, such as "九州" and "吸収") are combined into a single word. The frequency of words after merging is the sum of the frequencies of words before merging.

The most frequent 50 words are selected from each list of 4, 5, and 6 characters. In this way, a total of 150 words are selected for the experiment. The words that have been presented are recorded in the list. At the beginning of each task, this list is referred to and the used words are removed from the candidate words. After that, the program shuffles the candidate words randomly and present to participants. Therefore, the experiment will not present the same word to one participant twice.

The experimental system is equipped with a log function that records the time when the screen is tapped and the characters entered. From this log, we determine for each word the time when the task was displayed and the time when Enter was input. The time difference between these two times is defined as the input time for one word, and the total input time for each word is defined as the input time for the task. The total input time for each word is the input time for the task. The input time includes the time for correction (erasing with Backspace and redoing the input). The number of characters per minute (CPM) is calculated by dividing the number of characters entered in the task by the input time of the task (in seconds) and multiplying by 60. The rate of incorrect input is also evaluated in the same way. The total error rate [4] is calculated by dividing the total number of incorrectly entered characters, including the characters corrected in the task, by the number of characters in the task.

4.3 Experimental Result

Figure 5 shows the average input speed and the average error rate for the five participants for each task. The average input speed increased from 12.5 CPM in the first trial, to 23.1 CPM in the 10th trial. The speed slowed down on the fifth trial, but then increased monotonically. The average error rate on the first trial was 9.2%. It was constantly reduced until the fourth trial, and the error rate reached the minimum of 1.7%. However, in the fifth trial, the error rate increased significantly. This is because the two participants made many mistakes at the same time. As the result, the input speed has decreased. After that, the rate declined monotonically and eventually fell below 2%.

The average total number of characters for the 10 tasks was about 245, and the average input time was about 844 s. The input speed at this point is about 1.8 times faster than the first time the participants touched the system, and the error rate has decreased to 1.6%. These results suggest that the input method of the proposed method is easy to understand.

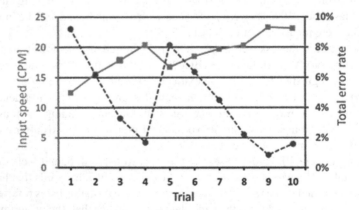

Fig. 5. Average input speed and error rate of beginners. In the first trial, the average input speed was 12.5 CPM (Characters Per Minute). In the final trial, the speed reached to 23.3 CPM. The total error rate was 1.6% at the final trial.

There are two possible reasons for the increased input speed. One is to remember the key layout. This reduces the time it takes to find the key and allows the key selection stroke to begin earlier. The other is to speed up the movement of your fingertips. This is achieved by repeat actions for selecting characters. In the case that participants preferentially learn the key layout, more accurate key selection is expected. As a result, input errors are reduced and input speed is improved. In the case that the movement speed of the fingertip increases before layout learning, it is expected that the input speed will temporarily decrease due to an increase in incorrect input such as touching the wrong position. In this experiment, the ratio of the latter participants was high, so it is probable that the input speed temporarily decreased.

Figure 7 show the error rate for each participant. The error rate for the fifth trial of participant A is 18.2%, and that of participant C is 18.5%. These rates are very high. However, the remaining three participants, B, D, and E, have an error rate of 0.0%, 4.0%, and 0.0%, respectively. It can be said that the reason why the average error rate is high in the 5th to 7th trials is that participants A and C made many incorrect inputs. As shown in Fig. 6, which plots the input speed of each participant, the input speed of participants A and C decreased in the fifth trial. It caused the down of the average input speed down shown in Fig. 5.

The error rate of participant C decreased steadily after the sixth trial and became zero after the eighth trial. This suggests that in the process of getting used to the system, his finger movements became rough and error input increased. Therefore, it is considered a temporary phenomenon. Figure 6 shows that the input speed of participant C is always faster than other participants. Therefore, participant C is considered to have increased the speed of fingertip movement before learning the key layout. Participant A has the same tendency.

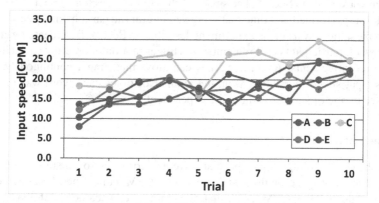

Fig. 6. The input speed for each participant. The speed generally increased in proportion to the number of trials. However, the speed of participants A and C temporarily slowed in the fifth attempt due to increased misoperation.

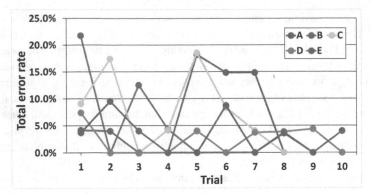

Fig. 7. The total error rate for each participant. Values vary widely from participant to participant. The error rates for participants A and C increased once during this experiment, while that for other participants generally decreased with the number of trials.

5   A 30-Day Experiment

5.1   Experimental Condition

In the beginner's experiment in Sect. 4, the input speed tended to increase even in the final trial. Therefore, the change in input speed was measured over a long period of time. In this experiment, 10 words entered once a day for 30 days. This setting expects the user to enter short text daily, such as a reply to an email.

Participants in the experiment are three male university students aged 21 to 22 who used the system for the first time in this experiment. They did not participate in the experiments described in Sect. 4. The smartwatch is the same as that in Sect. 4. The word input task was performed at a time that is convenient for the participants. The words are chosen in the same way as in the experiment described in Sect. 4. By repeatedly entering the same word, participants will remember the finger motion of entering each character as a series of movements. As a result, they can move their finger continuously, which improves input speed. For this reason, the number of times each word was presented was limited to one or less throughout the experiment.

5.2   Experimental Result

Figure 8 shows the average input speed and average error rate for the three participants each day. The input speed on the first day was 12.5 CPM, but on the 21st day it reached the highest value of 34.9 CPM. After that, the input speed became about 30 CPM. The dotted line in this figure is a logarithmic approximation of the input speed. The formula is $y = 5.99 \times \ln x + 11.67$. According to the approximation curve the speed reaches the upper limit of about 35 CPM. Since the average input time for 30 days is 62 min and 11 s, it can be said that the time required to master this system is short.

The error rate was 10% or more on the first day, but it is about 3% after the 20th day. The error rate rose to 7.6% on the 24th day, due to two participants happening to make a mistake. According to the input log, one participant made several mistakes in

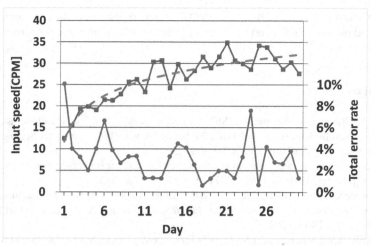

Fig. 8. Average input speed and error rate for the 30-day experiment. The red line shows the average input speed. The dotted line is the logarithmic approximation curve. The formula is *Inputspeed* $= 5.99 \times \ln(Days) + 11.67$. The blue line is the average error rate. (Color figure online)

selecting characters without noticing the mistake in row selection. Another participant misread some words (for example, "にゅうようじ" was mistaken for "にゅうじょう"), so many characters were wrong. These errors are not due to a flaw in the input method because the participant did not understand how to use the input method or the task word was confused.

6 Conclusion

In this research, we developed a character input method that can be applied to a smart-watch with a screen diameter of 1 in. The number of keys on the standby screen has been reduced to four in order to reduce the screen occupancy of the keyboard and perform touch operation with a fingertip with a width of about 10 mm.

First five rows of the Japanese syllabary table (rows "あ", "か", "さ", "た", and "な") are assigned to the left key. And the second half (rows "は", "ま", "や", "ら", and "わ") is assigned to the top key. Slide-in from one of the keys to select a row group. Then release the finger in the center of the screen or slide out to one of the four directions to select one row. After that, five hiragana characters belong the row will be displayed on the screen, so tap or flick to select one. Voiced, semi-voiced, or lowercase letters can be entered with a single tap of a button in the four corners before selecting a character. This system is designed to allow the user to enter hiragana with a small number of operations.

Experiments for beginners have shown that the input speed after use for about 14 min averages 23.1 CPM. The final error rate is about 3%. Therefore, it can be said that the system is easy to use even for beginners. In the 30-day experiment, the total usage time was only about 1 h, but on the last day all of three participants achieved an input speed of about 30 CPM and an input error rate of about 3%. This keyboard occupies only 36%

of the 1-in. circular screen, so it has a lower rate than competitors' methods. In this way, the proposed method allows you to enter characters on the 1-in. screen of smartwatches at a practical speed.

References

1. Akita, K., Tanaka, T., Sagawa, Y.: SliT: character input system using slide-in and tap for smartwatches. In: Kurosu, M. (ed.) HCI 2018. LNCS, vol. 10903, pp. 3–16. Springer, Cham (2018). https://doi.org/10.1007/978-3-319-91250-9_1
2. Kana-connection frequency data in Hatena Diary for 4.52 million characters. https://ena.hat enablog.jp/entry/20101011/1286787571. Accessed 22 Jan 2020
3. The Balanced Corpus of Contemporary Written Japanese (BCCWJ) of the National Institute for Japanese Language and Linguistics. http://pj.ninjal.ac.jp/corpus_center/bccwj/freq-list. html. Accessed 18 Dec 2020
4. Soukoreff, R.W., MacKenzie, I.S.: Metrics for text entry research: an evaluation of MSD and KSPC, and a new unied error metric. In: Proceedings of ACM CHI 2003, pp. 113–120 (2003)
5. Google Japanese Input. https://play.google.com/store/apps/details?id=com.google.android. inputmethod.japanese&hl=ja&gl=US. Accessed 16 Dec 2020
6. FlickKey Mini Keyboard. http://www.flickkey.com/. Accessed 18 Dec 2020
7. TouchOne Keyboard. https://www.kickstarter.com/projects/790443497/touchone-keyboard-the-first-dedicated-smartwatch-k?lang=ja. Accessed 18 Dec 2020
8. Saito, K., Oku, H.: HARI Keyboard: A Japanese Input Keyboard for Ultra-small Touch Panel Terminals. Information Processing Society of Japan, Interaction 2016, pp. 701–703 (2016)
9. Nishida, K., Kato, T., Yamamoto, S.: A Prototype of Japanese Kana Input Interface for Smartwatches. Information Processing Society of Japan, Interaction 2017, pp. 897–902 (2017)
10. 5-TILES. https://ja-jp.facebook.com/fivetiles. Accessed 18 Dec 2020
11. Oney, S., Harrison, C., Ogan, A., Wiese, J.: A diminutive QWERTY soft keyboard using iterative zooming for ultra-small devices. In: Proceedings of ACM CHI 2013, pp. 2799–2802 (2013)
12. BLAND WATCH MANIAX. https://watchmania.jp/casesize/. Accessed 18 Dec 2020
13. Flit Keyboard. https://sites.google.com/site/flitkeyboard/home. Accessed 11 Jan 2021

One Stroke Alphanumeric Input Method by Sliding-in and Sliding-out on the Smartwatch Screen

Toshimitsu Tanaka$^{(\boxtimes)}$, Hideaki Shimazu, and Yuji Sagawa

Department of Information Engineering, Faculty of Science and Technology, Meijo University, Nagoya, Japan
toshitnk@meijo-u.ac.jp

Abstract. We have developed a character input method for smartwatches with circular screen, that allows you to enter one alphanumeric character with a single stroke. With this method, characters are selected by the combination of the start and end positions of the stroke.

On the standby screen, a square inscribed inside the circular display is assigned to the text area. The left, top, and right of the remaining area is split in two, with each segment used as a key. As a result, the key length is longer than the fingertip size of 10 mm. The screen occupancy of the keyboard is 36%.

Each key is selected by slide-in, which is the operation of moving the fingertip that touches the outside of the screen inward. The slide-in ensures that it crosses the edge of the screen, so that passing of the fingertip can be detect with very thin keys. As the fingertip passes the edge of the screen, the screen is separated to 12 areas. Each area is assigned one alphanumeric character or symbol. By moving the fingertip to one area then releasing from the screen, the character assigned to that position is entered.

The key assignment is based on the telephone keyboard. The two keys on the telephone keyboard are combined into one key in our method. As the slide-in passes through a key, the two numbers assigned to the key and the 6 or 7 alphabets associated with those numbers are displayed in each split area.

Keywords: Smartwatch · Software keyboard · Character input · 1-stroke gesture · Alphanumeric

1 Introduction

On the smartwatch screen, text data such as schedules and e-mails can be displayed. These texts are usually entered from the smartphone to which the smartwatch is connected. However, it is a hassle to remove your smartphone from your pocket or bag every time typing a short sentence, so a way to type text directly into the smartwatch is required.

The software keyboard is the most common way to enter characters to a touch device. However, the flick keyboard, which is popular on smartphones, occupies almost the entire screen of a smartwatch because it requires 20 or more keys. Speech recognition is also

© Springer Nature Switzerland AG 2021
M. Kurosu (Ed.): HCII 2021, LNCS 12763, pp. 135–146, 2021.
https://doi.org/10.1007/978-3-030-78465-2_11

available on many devices, but it doesn't protect your privacy because your input is heard by people nearby.

Methods have been developed to draw and enter characters in the air using a glove-type device [1] or a ring-type device [2, 3]. These methods are intuitive to used but the input speed will be slower because the arm needs to be moved a lot.

There are methods of using the user's hands as a virtual keyboard. One such method, SkinTrack [4], detects the position of a finger by touching the bare skin with a finger wearied with a ring-shaped transmitter. The FingersT9 [5] and DigiTouch [6] use fingers as a keyboard by adhered a touch sensor to each node of fingers. Finger tactile [7] projects the virtual keyboard from the device attached to the user's wrist onto the hand. Haier's Asu Smartwatch [8] also projects a virtual keyboard onto the back of the hand. With the plate-shaped device TAP [9], a letter is selected by tapping with a combination of five fingers. These methods require to always wear a dedicated device. Also, some methods require to learn the gestures assigned to letters.

Software keyboards are better because they don't require extra devices and are easy to use. The disadvantage of software keyboards is their high screen occupancy. Therefore, we are developing a software keyboard with a low screen occupancy.

2 Related Researches

Keys smaller than the fingertips cause the fat finger problems [10]. Therefore, to run on the small screen of a smartwatch, it is needed to reduce number of keys. The FlickKey Mini keyboard [11] and Flit keyboard [12] have reduced keys by using 8-way flicks to assign 9 characters to a single key. However, the Flit keyboard still uses 62% of the screen and the FlickKey Mini keyboard uses 50%.

Table 1. Screen occupancy of software keyboard for smartwatch. "Square" and "Circle" in the table mean the shape of the screen. A blank cell means that the keyboard does not support that screen shape.

Screen shape	Square	Circle
Google flick	90%	
Flit keyboard	62%	
TouchOne	61%	56%
FlickKey Mini, Zoom Board, Zshift	50%	
HARI		48%
5-TILES	30%	41%
SliT	26%	22%

Zoom Board [13] uses the QWERTY key layout. However, since it is a method of enlarging the area around the touch position of the first tap and selecting one character with the second tap, the key is large enough to be selected with a fingertip. The ZShift keyboard [14] uses the QWERTY reduced keyboard as it is, but the user can enter characters by moving his/her fingertip while looking at the pop-up window that displays the key being touched. These methods require half the screen as shown in Table 1, to display the QWERTY keyboard.

The TouchOne keyboard [15] places eight keys around the screen, assigning three or four letters to each key. This method works on both square and circular screens. The user selects one character with the touched key and the direction of movement of the fingertip. Since this method allocate mode selection buttons on screen in additional, the screen occupancy is high.

The HARI keyboard [16] is another method that places keys on the edges of the round screen. Tap any of the 10 keys and perform a stroke gesture from there to select a single character. This method does not require any other keys, so it occupies less screen than the TouchOne keyboard. However, the ratio is 46%, which is almost half of the screen.

The 5-TILES keyboard [17] arranges 5 keys horizontally and assigns 5 to 6 alphabets to one key. The user touches one of the keys, moves his/her fingertip to another key as needed, and then leaves it off the screen. A combination of the two keys selects one character. This keyboard works on both square and circular screens. However, circular screens have a higher screen occupancy. This is because the keyboard needs to be closer to the center to display the keys in a touchable width.

The SliT [18] we developed has the advantage of low screen occupancy. This method assigns 2 mm wide keys around the screen, shown in Fig. 1(a). A key is selected by slide-in, which is the operation of first touching the outside of the screen with the fingertip and then moving to the inside of the screen. It ensures that the fingertip passes the edge of the screen so the crossing can be detected with a width of only 2 mm.

1st step: Slide-in then select a group.   2nd step: select a letter.

Fig. 1. SliT screen display when entering alphabets. (a) In the standby state, the keys are allocated at the border of the screen. First, the selects one key by slide-in. (b) When the fingertip passes a key of the screen, two character-groups bound to the key are displayed. Move the fingertip off the screen in either area. (c) The screen is divided into eight areas, and the alphabet of the selected group is displayed in each area. Tap one to enter.

The SliT is designed for entering Japanese character. There are 46 basic characters in Japanese hiragana, so there are too many to select in one stroke. Therefore, one character is selected in the two steps. To make the input procedure the same, the alphabet is also input in two steps, shown in Fig. 1. In the first step, select a group of letters by combining the keys selected in the slide-in with the position releasing the fingertip from the screen. In the next step, select one letter in the group by a tap.

3 Proposed Method

We have developed a one-stroke alphanumeric input method that uses slide-in and slide-out. SliT requires two steps to select one of the 46 hiragana characters. On the other hand, since the alphabet has only 26 characters, one can be selected with one stroke if the input characters are limited to the alphabet. However, the key layout must be changed.

This method displays the text in a square inscribed in the circular display, as shown in Fig. 2 (a). The SliT keyboard shown in Fig. 1 (a) is suitable for reducing screen occupancy. However, text is usually displayed in a rectangular area, so a round area is awkward and difficult to read. Therefore, it makes sense to first allocate the largest square area for the text display. Keys are assigned around the text area. Even with this layout, the keyboard screen occupancy is 36%. This rate is higher than the SliT rate, but lower than the other methods. On the other hand, if the smartwatch screen has a diameter of 1.4 inches, the area of the largest rectangle that can display text is increased by 27% compared to SliT.

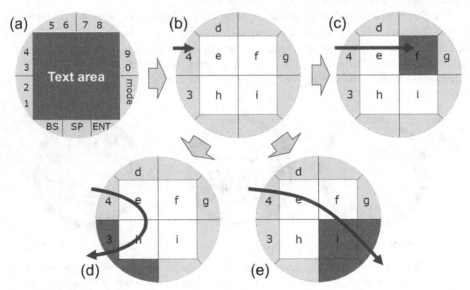

Fig. 2. The key layout of the proposed method and strokes for selecting characters. (a) In standby mode, keys are assigned to the four areas around the text area. (b) When the slide-in intersects the key, the screen is divided into 12 areas and the characters assigned to the key are displayed. (c) Release the fingertip in the square area and enter the character written in that area. (d) and (e) Slide the finger beyond the screen edge to enter the surrounding characters.

The 26 alphabets and some symbols are divided into 10 groups. Each group is linked to a different single-digit number. This assignment is based on the telephone keyboard.

The telephone keypad has been attached to push-button phones since the 1960s. As shown in Fig. 3, each key from "2" to "9" is assigned three or four alphabets. This alphabet assignment is also widely used in software keyboards for smartphones. Therefore, our method follows this assignment.

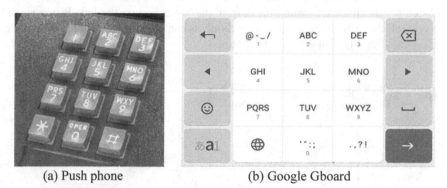

(a) Push phone   (b) Google Gboard

Fig. 3. Character arrangement on the telephone keyboard. It has been used for a long time in push phones. It is also common on smartphone software keyboards.

On a keyboard that is displayed in standby mode, the left edge, top edge, and right edge are each divided into two segments and used as keys. As shown in Fig. 2(a), a pair of numbers is written in each of the keys. To them alphabetic characters are linked, just like the telephone keyboard. For example, D, E, F, G, H, and I are linked to the upper key on the left edge where 3 and 4 are written. However, these alphabetic characters are not written because the segment is small.

Select any key in the slide-in. As the fingertip moves inward beyond the edge of the screen, the screen is divided into 12 areas as shown in Fig. 2 (b). This figure shows the character assignment as the fingertip crosses the upper key of the left side. The numbers (3 and 4) written on the key where the finger passes and the characters (d, e, f, g, h, and i) linked to the numbers are written in each area.

The character written inside each of the white squares is selected by moving the fingertip into the area and then away from the screen. As shown in Fig. 2 (c), the area turns green while the fingertip is within the area. By checking this color change and then releasing the finger, the error in character selections can be reduced.

Select the surrounding characters by the slide-out. The slide-out is an operation that moves the fingertip outward beyond the edge of the screen while maintaining contact with the screen.

Select the surrounding characters by the slide-out. The slide-out is an operation that moves the fingertips outward beyond the edges of the screen while maintaining contact with the screen. Like slide-in, slide-out can be detected with the narrow area. Therefore, the square areas were enlarged by thinning the surrounding areas.

To the blank areas where no character is written, the nearby character is assigned. This is the reason that multiple areas are green in Figs. 2 (d) and (e). The number 3 is assigned to the two green areas of Fig. 2 (d) and the letter i is assigned three green areas of (e). This multiple assignment is to reduce the failure that no character is selected.

The placement of characters after the slide-in depends on the key of the initial screen selected by slide-in. Some examples are shown in Fig. 4. Figure 4 (a) shows the placement when sliding from the right key on the top border. Each character is assigned to an area near the key or an area that can be reached by a smooth travel path. (b) shows the placement when sliding from the upper key on the right side. Caps Lock and Shift are placed in this character group. (c) is from the lower key on the left. It is assigned some symbols that often appear in the text. Symbols can be entered in the symbol mode, including the symbols contained in this figure.

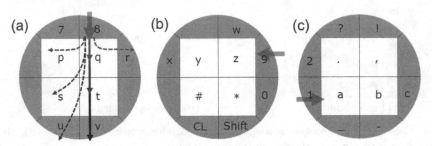

Fig. 4. Examples of character placement. (a) shows the characters when sliding from the right key on the upper border of Fig. 1 (a). Characters are assigned to areas near the starting position and areas reachable by a smooth travel path. (b) shows when sliding from the upper key on the right side. Caps Lock and Shift are placed in this character group. (c) is from the lower key on the left side. It is assigned some symbols that often appear in the text.

Slide in from the lower right key labeled "mode" in Fig. 2 (a) to shift to symbol mode. Here, the screen is divided into 8 sectors at 45-degree intervals. Symbols are displayed in 5 sectors. Other sectors are assigned Forward, Back, and Cancel. The symbol is replaced by tapping the Forward/Back. When the symbol wanted to enter is displayed, tap it.

4 Experiment

4.1 Experiment Preparation

This experiment uses the FOSSIL Q MARSHAL FTW2106 smartwatch with a 1.4 in. diameter, 320 × 290 pixel circular screen. Wear this smartwatch on the subject's non-dominant arm, sit in a chair and lift the arm horizontally. Each experimental subject selects a finger to use to enter characters. The thumb or index finger is usually used.

One task word appears at the top of the text area, as shown in Fig. 5. The letters entered appear just below the word. The subjects of experiments are Japanese. English is not their native language. So, it is necessary to use well-known words for experiments. Therefore, we chose 400 test words from the approximately 1200 words used in Japanese junior high school English textbooks posted on this site [19]. These words are 3–9 letters, with an average of 5.3 letters.

If all the alphanumeric characters are written to the keys on the standby screen, the font size will be too small to read. For this reason, the alphabet is not written. Therefore,

Fig. 5. Smartwatch for experiments (left) and screenshot of word entry task (right).

it is necessary to know the assignment of characters to numbers defined by the telephone keyboard. However, this assignment is not well known to Japanese. So, prior to the experiment, each subject used Google Gboard to enter 70 test words daily for four days and learned the correspondence between numbers and the alphabet on the tele-phone keyboard.

4.2 Input Speed and Error Rate of Beginners

Each smartwatch is typically used by connecting it to a smartphone. In this case, the smartwatch is not used to enter long sentences. The usage time is also shortened. Therefore, we thought that the input speed of beginners is important.

The subjects are five university students who have never used the character input system running on a smartwatch. In the experiment, subjects first watch a 10-min. video to understand how to use our character input system. Then they perform the task of entering the 5 words displayed on the smartwatch screen 5 times with a 3-min. break. This experiment uses 123 words which are 3 to 5 letters. They were selected from the 400 test words. The words are randomly sorted before the experiment for each subject, and then presented in order from the beginning. Therefore, no subject will enter the same word twice during this experiment.

Figure 6 shows the average input speed and error rate of the five subjects. The average input speed for the first task was 18.4 [CPM (characters/minute)]. By the third task the speed had increased to 26 [CPM] and remained the same for the rest of the tasks. The reason for the constant speed after the third task is expected to be an increase in input errors. The input speed did not increase, because the movement control was not accurate although the movement speed of the finger increased. The average total usage time for the five tasks was 320 [seconds].

Input error is evaluated with a Total Error Rate (TER) [20]. TER is calculated by dividing the sum of the number of wrong characters and the number of corrected characters by the total number of the characters in the task words. The wrong characters are characters eventually entered incorrectly. The corrected characters are characters which were entered in mistake but deleted by the backspace.

If the subjects notice that they have selected the wrong key in the slide-in, they must enter any character, then delete it, and enter the correct character. As a result, if subjects don't remember the character assignments of the telephone keyboard, they often choose

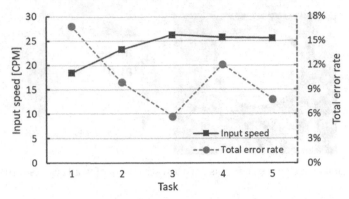

Fig. 6. Average input speed and average error rate for five beginners. Each subject entered 5 words in one task. The total usage time of the five tasks averaged 320 s.

the wrong key, resulting in a high error rate. In post-experimental interviews, some subjects reported that they were sometimes confused when choosing a key.

4.3 Long-Term Experiment

From the experimental result of beginners, it seems that five tasks are not enough to learn the assignment of alphabets to numbers. Therefore, I conducted an experiment to input many words. The subject of this experiment is one student who had never used a smartwatch before. He is not the subject of the beginner experiment.

The equipment and conditions are the same as for the beginner experiment. However, all 400 test words are used. The words are randomly reordered before starting this experiment, and then presented in order from the beginning. In this experiment, 25 words are entered in one task. Every day, this task is repeated 3 times with 3-min. break. The term of this experiment is 14 day. Therefore, a total of 1050 words will be entered. When the list of test words becomes empty, the 400 words are randomly reordered to create a new word list. As a result, every word appears 2 or 3 times in 14 days.

Figure 7 shows the input speed and error rate. The values in the graph are the average of the day, that is, the average of the 75 words entered in one day. The speed on the first day is about the same as the fifth task of the beginner experiment. The speed increased almost continuously and reached to 60 [CPM] at the last day. The total operation times was 122 min. and the number of characters was 5518. The approximate curve, the red dotted line in Fig. 7, tends to speed up even on the last day. The error rate varies widely from day to day. On the 9th day, it exceeded 6%. But for the final four days, it was almost 2–4%.

4.4 Input Speed and Error Rate of the Expert

To find the top speed, we conducted a long-term experiment described in the previous section with one of the developers of this system. The results are shown in Fig. 8. The expert is familiar with this system, so the input speed is 56 [CPM] from day one. The

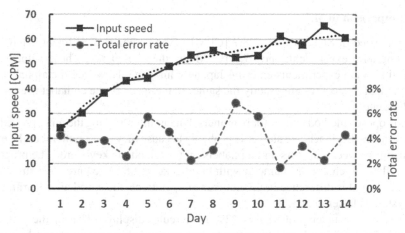

Fig. 7. Input speed and error rate for the long-term experiment with one beginner. He entered 75 words daily for 14 days. The total usage time was 122 min.

speed increased day by day, but slowly. The final day reached 87 [CPM]. The approximate curve on the last day is almost flat. Therefore, a stable top speed is expected to be 80 [CPM]. The error rate after the 5th day was almost less than 2%.

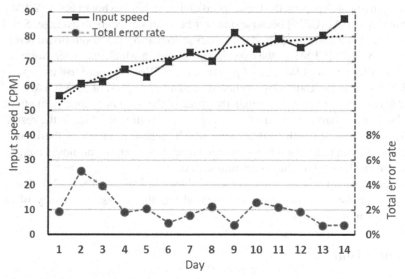

Fig. 8. Input speed and error rate of the expert. This is the result of a long-term experiment conducted with an expert of our system as subjects.

4.5 Comparison to SliT

The input speed of SliT [18] was 28.7 [CPM] in the beginner experiment, 51 [CPM] in the long-term experiment, and 67.7 [CPM] by the SliT expert. These values were measured in some experiments entering Japanese hiragana. However, the alphabet and hiragana input procedures are exactly the same, so the speed of the alphabet is expected to be the same.

The proposed method is slow for beginners, but fast after training the input procedure. The reason why beginners are slower is probably because they don't remember the exact relationship between numbers and alphabets on the telephone keyboard. The proposed method allows to enter one character with one stroke, but SliT requires one stroke and one tap. Due to this difference in the number of operations, the speed after learning the input system is faster than SliT.

The screen occupancy of SliT is 22% for circular displays. That of the proposed method is 36%. SliT is lower than the proposed method when compared by screen occupancy. However, when displaying text in a rectangular area, the area of the proposed method is 1.27 times the area of SliT. This is because the proposed method assigns the square inscribed to the circular display, that is the largest square area, is assigned to displaying text.

4.6 Comparison to the Other Related Method

According to research papers, the input speed of the Flickey keyboard is 9.4 [WPM]. The value translates to 47 [CPM] because one word contains 5 letters in average. Similarly, the input speed of ZShift is reported to be 50.5 or 36 [CPM] and Zoom Board is reported to be 38, 43.5, or 39 [CPM]. In the experiment we did, in which characters were entered one by one after a total of 90 min. of practice, the 5-Tilse keyboard had an input speed of 43.3 [CPM] and the TouchOne keyboard had an input speed of 55.3 [CPM].

The above input speed is faster than the speed of the beginner experiment after using 5 min, but slower than the speed of the long-term experiment which is the result after using 122 min. It is difficult to determine which method is faster, as the input speed usually increases in proportion to the practice time. However, the proposed method is at least not much slower than the competing method.

The screen occupancy for each method is shown in Table 1 in Sect. 2. In the screen occupancy comparisons, the proposed method has the lowest occupancy of all the methods shown in this section.

5 Comparison

We have developed a one-stroke alphanumeric input method for smartwatches with a circular display. This method assigns a square inscribed in the circular display to the text area and then sets a key around the square. Therefore, the screen occupancy of our method is 36%. The left, top, and right areas are divided into two keys. Although these keys are very narrow, they can be selected definitely by sliding-in.

Each key is assigned two numbers and several alphabets. Grouping numbers and alphabets is the same as for telephone keyboards. As the slide-in crosses the key, the screen is divided into 12 areas, each displaying the number and alphabet assigned to the key. Characters written in any of the four inner areas are selected by moving the fingertip into that area and then away from the screen. Characters written in the surrounding area are selected by sliding-out.

The input speed of the developed method was 26 [CPM] after using it in 5.3 min., 60 [CPM] after using it in 122 min, and 80 [CPM] after sufficient practice. The current specifications do not allow users to cancel the slide-in. So even if they notice that the wrong key is selected in the slide-in, they still must enter one character and delete it. This slows down the input speed for beginners who don't remember the key bindings on the telephone keyboard correctly. Therefore, we plan to assign the escape function to one of the 12 areas. The users can cancel the slide-in by moving their fingertip off the screen in the escape area. This change reduces the time it takes to remove the wrong character with the backspace key.

References

1. Fujitsu develops glove-style wearable device. http://www.fujitsu.com/global/about/resources/news/press-releases/2014/0218-01.html. Accessed 11 Jan 2021
2. Ring-type wearable device enables users to write in the air with finger. https://journal.jp.fujitsu.com/en/2015/02/10/01/. Accessed 11 Jan 2021
3. Ring zero. https://logbar.jp/en/index.html. Accessed 11 Jan 2021
4. Zhang, Y., Zhou, J., Laput, G., Harrison, C.: SkinTrack: using the body as an electrical waveguide for continuous finger tracking on the skin. http://www.gierad.com/assets/skintrack/skintrack.pdf. Accessed 11 Jan 2021
5. Wong, P., Zhu, K., Fu, H.: FingerT9: leveraging thumb-to-finger interaction for same-side-hand text entry on smartwatches. In: Proceedings of CHI 2018, Paper No. 178 (2017)
6. Whitmier, E., et. al.: DigiTouch: reconfigurable thumb-to-finger input and text entry on head-mounted displays. In: Proceedings of ACM IMWUT 2017, Vol. 1, No. 3, Article 133 (2017)
7. Finger touching. http://www.yankodesign.com/2007/10/02/wearable-mobile-device-for-enhanced-chatting/. Accessed 11 Jan 2021
8. Haier Asu Smartwatch. https://www.digitaltrends.com/smartwatch-reviews/haier-asu-review/. Accessed 11 Jan 2021
9. Tap. http://www.tapwithus.com. Accessed 11 Jan 2021
10. Siek, K., Rogers, Y., Connelly, K.: Fat finger worries: how older and younger users physically interact with PDAs. In: IFIP Conference on Human-Computer Interaction, pp. 267–280 (2005)
11. Akita, K., Tanaka, T., Sagawa, Y.: SLiT: character input system using slide-in and tap FlickKey mini. http://www.flickkey.com/FlickKey_Mini.html. Accessed 11 Jan 2021
12. Flit keyboard. https://sites.google.com/site/flitkeyboard/home. Accessed 11 Jan 2021
13. Oney, S., Harrison, C., Ogan, A., Wiese, J.: ZoomBoard: a diminutive QWERTY soft keyboard using iterative zooming for ultra-small devices. In: ACM CHI 2013, pp. 2799–2802 (2013)
14. Leiva, L., Sahami, A., Catala, A., Henza, N., Schmodt, A.: Text entry on tiny QWERTY soft keyboards. In: Proceedings of CHI 2015, pp. 669–678 (2015)
15. TouchOne keyboard. https://twitter.com/touchonekey. Accessed 11 Jan 2021
16. Saito, K., Oku, H.: HARI keyboard: ultra-small touch panel devices for Japanese input keyboard. Proc. IPSJ Interact. **2016**, 701–703 (2016). (in Japanese)
17. 5-tiles keyboard targets wearables to hunt the post-qwerty holy grail. https://techcrunch.com/2014/05/24/5-tiles-keyboard/. Accessed 11 Jan 2021

18. Akita, K., Tanaka, T., Sagawa, Y.: SliT: character input system using slide-in and tap for smartwatches. In: HCI 2018: Human-Computer Interaction. Interaction Technologies, pp. 3–16 (2018)
19. eigo-duke.com List of English words. http://www.eigo-duke.com/tango/tangoindex.html. Accessed 7 Jan 2021
20. Soukoreff, W., MacKenzie, I.: Metrics for text entry research: an evaluation of MSD and KSPC, and a new unified error metric. In: Proceedings of ACM CHI 2003, pp. 113–120 (2003)

Research on Hand Detection in Complex Scenes Based on RGB-D Sensor

Jin Wang[✉], Zhen Wang, Shan Fu, and Dan Huang

School of Aeronautics and Astronautics, Shanghai Jiao Tong University, Shanghai,
People's Republic of China
b2wz@sjtu.edu.cn

Abstract. Human gesture has the characteristics of intuitive, natural and informative, and is one of the most commonly used interaction methods. However, in most gesture interaction researches, the hand to be detected is facing detection camera, and experiment environment is ideal. There is no guarantee that these methods can achieve perfect detection results in practical applications. Therefore, gesture interaction in complex environments has high research and application value. This paper discusses hand segmentation and gesture contour extraction methods in complex environments and specific applications: First, according to the characteristics of depth map, an adaptive weighted median filtering method is selected to process depth data; then use depth information to construct background model which can reduce interference of noise and light changes, and combine RGB information and depth threshold segmentation to complete hand segmentation; finally, region grow method is used to extract precise gesture contour. This paper verifies the proposed method by using vehicle environment material, and obtains satisfactory segmentation and contour extraction results.

Keywords: Gesture based interaction · Depth data · Hand segmentation · Contour extraction · Real sense

1 Introduction

1.1 Research Background

Human-Computer Interaction (HCI) has become an important part of daily life, and been the basis for touch screens, smart homes, and virtual reality technologies [22]. Compared with other interactive methods, gesture interaction method is more efficient and convenient. In addition to specific operations that have been widely used, such as sliding and touching, hands can easily perform a variety of actions with rich connotations, such as fingers expressing numbers, thumbs expressing praise, waving hands expressing negation, and more complicated sign language and army codes, and so on. These dynamic gestures are more intuitive than touching and sliding, and are very close to human instinctive interaction methods: using body language to enhance the content to be expressed.

© Springer Nature Switzerland AG 2021
M. Kurosu (Ed.): HCII 2021, LNCS 12763, pp. 147–158, 2021.
https://doi.org/10.1007/978-3-030-78465-2_12

The application fields of gesture recognition are very extensive, including almost all aspects of human life. For example, in smart home life, gesture recognition can help user complete smart home functions such as control, selection and determination, switching, and rotation. Another example, in car driving, assisted driving system based on gestures and voice can help driver operate other devices without contact while keeping his eyes on the road, avoid distraction and reduce traffic accidents. In driverless technology, gesture recognition can help driving system recognize gestures given by driver or traffic police. In addition, sign language recognition systems can help deaf-mute people communicate more smoothly with the outside world; hand behavior analysis, such as pilot hand operation analysis, can improve interaction quality between pilots and cockpit; in public places such as supermarkets, hospitals and banks, gesture recognition applications can also be mounted on service-oriented devices or robots.

In a hand detection system, hand segmentation and contour extraction technology greatly affects accuracy of gesture classification. This paper discusses hand detection in practical applications, implements a hand segmentation and contour extraction module that is robust to various complex environments, and verifies effectiveness of the proposed method through experiments in vehicle driving environment.

1.2 Related Research Statuses

To achieve accurate gesture recognition, hand segmentation and gesture contour extraction are very important. In current research on hand segmentation, there are mainly technical solutions such as skin color threshold segmentation, pixel clustering, foreground and background segmentation, and region growth, but each has different problems including calculation speed, scene adaptability and segmentation accuracy.

Skin color threshold segmentation has strong robustness to scale, rotation, deformation, and shooting direction, but it is susceptible to interference from actual environment (light, occlusion, skin color differences of different races and skin-like areas, etc.). Clustering segmentation method divides image into regions according to certain rules, judges regions to which the pixels belong, and marks and divides them. Commonly used clustering methods include: K-means algorithm [9], FCM algorithm and SLIC clustering [10]. Region grow [21] continuously aggregates pixels or sub-regions into larger regions to form regional blocks and then achieve segmentation, according to the growth rules (growth neighborhood and judgment threshold). But growth needs a lot of time and computational cost, which is not suitable for real-time segmentation, but can be used to extract contours in small regions.

Foreground and background segmentation methods mainly include inter-frame difference method, optical flow method and background difference method. Frame difference method [11, 12] extracts moving objects by subtracting adjacent frames, which greatly depends on frame interval. Optical flow method [14] uses optical flow characteristics of moving target with time to extract the moving target, but has complex calculation process. Background difference method needs to first model background image, and then make difference between real-time image and the background model to extract moving foreground. Literature [13] uses three-frame difference method to combine background subtraction to track multiple moving targets. Literature [15] proposed a traffic video background modeling method based on inter-frame differences and statistical histograms, and obtained background images that match the real background in urban road traffic scenes.

Vision-based methods mentioned above use RGB information for hand segmentation and gesture extraction, which were susceptible to interference from factors such as illumination and occlusion, and could not be extended to daily life. Compared with color information, depth information is more suitable for hand detection in complex scenes, depth data get better detection results in dim and light changing environments. With the advent of depth cameras, research on visual segmentation began to develop rapidly. Literature [4] uses Kalman filter to achieve real-time 3D gesture tracking method based on depth information. Literature [5] uses Kinect's depth image for hand tracking. Literature [6] uses Kinect sensor to collect depth images and color images, and then uses skin color model to perform secondary segmentation to obtain quite accurate hand segmentation. Literature [7, 8] adds a limitation of the number of pixels to the hand area segmented by depth threshold, and reduce the noise effect of depth image. And, RGB-D gesture recognition methods that combine color and depth information have emerged one after another, such as [1], but in these studies, the hand to be detected is facing the camera and within a suitable distance range. The effect in actual application is not good. Or extract hand model from depth information separately, and then use a classifier to classify gestures, such as [2]; or convert depth image to a three-dimensional point cloud space, and use neural networks for gesture estimation, such as [3], but data processing and extraction process of these methods are relatively complicated. For hand segmentation in complex environments, only a few researchers do some research on specific application scenarios. Zhao [23] uses depth camera for hand click experiment to locate palm center. Konda [16] applied gesture recognition to outdoor robots and analyzed the influence of scene lighting conditions. Fujimura [17] studied hand segmentation algorithms at different distances and different directions.

In commercial applications, there are also gesture human-computer interaction products based on depth information. Leap Motion sensor can instantly track user's finger within a specific positioning distance, and is often used for sign language recognition. Kinect2.0, a somatosensory sensor from Microsoft, can identify human skeleton nodes. There are also technology companies such as Google and Sony that have released exclusive 3D vision sensors and supporting gesture recognition software.

1.3 Research Content

Research on gesture recognition technology in complex scenarios is helpful to improve robustness of applications based on hand, as well as usability, practicability. Hand segmentation and contour extraction play an important role in the gesture recognition system, and have a great impact on the accuracy of gesture classification results. However, existing related research methods cannot solve the interference problem of light changes. And, skin color detection cannot extract accurate gesture contours. In response to these problems, this paper uses depth map background difference method to reduce the interference of light on detection processing. Then, on the basis of skin color detection, the extracted gesture contour is optimized through region grow of a small area on depth map.

Therefore, this paper takes hand segmentation as research object, and designs an algorithm module for hand segmentation and gesture contour extraction with high efficiency, scene adaptability and high accuracy. At the same time, the effectiveness of algorithm is verified through the on-board scene.

2   Method of Hand Segmentation and Contour Extraction

This paper implements hand segmentation and gesture contour extraction based on depth and color information. The focus of the proposed method is:

1. Use depth information to enhance the adaptability and accuracy of hand segmentation in different scenes;
2. On the basis of determining region of interest (ROI) where the hand is located, use skin color segmentation and region grow to extract accurate gesture contour.

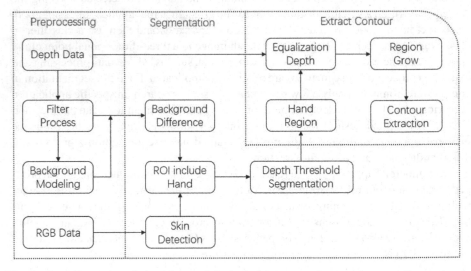

Fig. 1. Specific process of algorithm module, includes reprocessing part, segmentation part and contour extraction part.

In preprocessing stage, use an adaptive median filter to remove noise and smooth the image.

In hand segmentation stage, this paper adopts the method which is mainly based on background modeling and difference, supplemented by skin color detection method. The combined method can ensure accuracy and computational efficiency of segmentation algorithm and obtain a sufficiently small ROI including hands. In background modeling method, inter-frame difference method is first used to find background area, and multi-frame average is used to establish background from the image with holes removed. Then, using background difference to obtain region of interest (ROI) of motion foreground.

After that, use skin color detection and morphological processing to eliminate non-skin color interference. Finally, the ROI of hands is determined by adaptive depth threshold segmentation.

In contour extraction stage, histogram equalization is performed on depth image first. And then perform region growth in depth image. Finally, extract precise gesture contour and gesture center point.

The specific process of algorithm module is shown in Fig. 1.

2.1 Data Acquisition Equipment

Now, depth cameras on the market can collect depth images and color images as auxiliary data. There are three types of depth cameras commonly used for gesture analysis: Kinect, Leap Motion, and Real Sense. Choose Real Sense camera as the depth camera for method design and experiment.

Real Sense is relatively suitable for the indoor depth and some outdoor depth. The camera this research using is Intel RealSense Depth Camera D435. The maximum distance captured by lens can reach 10 m, and the effect is good in outdoor sunlight. And it supports the output of 1280×720 resolution depth images.

2.2 Preprocessing

The noise level of depth image is relatively high. Source of noise mainly includes phase drop at sudden change of depth, light intensity saturation, infrared light refraction and so on. Therefore, the quality of depth image needs to be improved, by removing noise and smoothing image through filters.

Standard median filter cannot do a good balance between suppressing image noise and protecting image details. According to the characteristics of Real Sense depth images, this paper adopts adaptive [18] weighted median filter algorithm for depth map preprocessing.

The adaptive weighted median filter is specifically divided into three steps.

Count the Number of Noise Points. Noise detection: Use a 3×3 filter window to slide on the depth map to be processed, when depth values of center point is the maximum or minimum value among points in the window, and difference between center depth and average depth of the window is greater than pre-set detection threshold, the window center point is considered as a noise point.

The detection threshold adopts the noise sensitivity coefficient d_{ij}, related to human eye characteristics [19]. And calculation method is:

$$d_{ij} = \frac{1}{3} \sqrt{\sum_{k=-1}^{1} \sum_{r=-1}^{1} [f(i+k, j+r) - Aver_{ij}]^2} \tag{1}$$

Where, $f(i, j)$ represents depth value at point (i, j), and $Aver_{ij}$ represents depth average in the window.

Adaptive Filter Kernel. After noise detection, retain original depth value for all non-noise points, and then the size of filter kernel corresponding to each noise point is determined according to the number of noise points in each small area.

The adaptive of size of filter kernel can ensure that filter function can smooth image and remove noise while retaining edge details and image gradient in the area with few noise points. In a 3 × 3 area with a noise point as center, if the number of noise points is less than 4 among all the points except center point, then the window size of weighted median filter is 3. If the number of noise points is less than 7, window size is set to be 5. If the number of noise points is greater than 7, and 7 is set to window size.

Weighting. Calculate the similarity between each point in filter window and center point (noise point to be updated). And calculation method is:

$$S(i+k,j+r) = \frac{1}{1 + (f(i+k,j+r) - f(i,j))^2} \tag{2}$$

Where, $f(i+k,j+r)$ and $f(i,j)$ are depth values of the corresponding points $(i+k,j+r)$ and (i,j) respectively.

Then, these points are sorted according to its similarity, and the point most similar to center point is given largest weight.

Weighted Median Filtering. Finally, perform weighted median filtering [20].

2.3 Background Modeling

This paper uses depth images to model a depth background image, which has a good effect on eliminating interference from light changes and glare at night. At the same time, in order to make hand segmentation algorithm applicable to multiple scenarios, the background modeling process needs to be completed automatically. Therefore, the method of background modeling includes frame difference and multi-frame average. Modeling process has two steps.

Extract the Pending Background Area. Assuming that the number of video frames used to construct background image is n, divide these n frames into n-1 groups: (1, 2), (2, 3), (3, 4), (4, 5) … (n − 1, n). In each group, a foreground part is obtained by inter-frame difference, and then the foreground part is subtracted from the previous frame to obtain pending background area corresponding to the group. The background image is updated every time a new pending background area appears, and finally a complete background image can be obtained after n-1 pending background areas are calculated.

Calculate the Background Image. Remove the point with a depth value of 0 in pending background area obtained by difference. Then calculate non-zero average value of each pixel point as depth value of corresponding point in background image, until all points in the background image are determined.

2.4 Hand Segmentation Method

Step1: Extract ROI from background difference. Within the set height and width range, calculate absolute value of the difference between depth values of each pixel in current frame and background image.

Step2: Morphological processing. After background difference, obtained ROI area is basically the foreground part of movement, including hand that needs to be segmented, other subtle motion contours into camera lens, shooting noise, light change noise, and so on. Through continuous opening and closing operations in morphological processing, small noise areas are eliminated and holes are filled in preparation for subsequent detection.

Step3: Skin detection. To remove non-skin color areas, adapt a method which uses the H component in HSV color space and the CrCb component in YCrCb color space. Before skin color detection, align depth frame and color frame.

Step4: Adaptive threshold segmentation. The skin and skin-like parts are further extracted by threshold segmentation method, but general threshold segmentation cannot guarantee adaptability. In this paper, depth threshold interval is selected adaptively by constructing depth histogram in ROI area. And in the current ROI area, the number of pixels included in hand to be detected should be the largest, so the midpoint of threshold segmentation interval can be adaptively selected through histogram peak.

First draw depth histogram of the current ROI area and eliminate the burrs by filtering; then find the two largest extreme points in histogram as the midpoint of threshold interval; finally, select suitable threshold range based on empirical data, and update segmented area as new ROI area.

The physical thickness of a human hand is about 2–3 cm. Considering that palm plane is not always perpendicular to the optical axis of depth camera, so the algorithm in this paper takes hand depth interval to be 7 cm.

2.5 Contour Extraction Method

Through above process, the region of operator's hands can been obtained. However, gesture region at this time is obtained by skin color detection, and there may be some holes or depressions caused by strong light. Therefore, region grow on depth map is used to fill and optimize gesture contour, and then use canny contour extraction operator to draw gesture contour.

Region grow [21] is an image segmentation method which has been widely used, and is able to obtain connected regions with same characteristics and provide good boundary information. The region grow algorithm in this paper includes three steps:

1. Select each center point of ROI area extracted above as a seed point for grow.
2. Perform 8 neighborhood expansion at each seed point. If any neighboring pixel meet grow conditions, this neighboring point is included in hand area and become a new seed point for next grow.
3. Until there is no seed point in seeds set.

The grow threshold is selected as 15 mm, which corresponds to the depth image after filtering and histogram equalization, the pixel threshold is 3.

3 Experimental Verification and Result Analysis

To evaluate the proposed method, completed hand segmentation and contour extraction algorithm is applied to actual driving scenario. And some complex scenes such as illumination transformation were investigated. In experiment, driver will complete a driving operation in a changing light environment, including turning, clicking, operating throttle lever, and putting on a seat belt.

3.1 Results in Complex Scenario

The hand segmentation and contour extraction under normal driving conditions are shown in Fig. 2. When the driver performs quick operations, hands can still be completely extracted and the outline of gesture can be drawn. In figures (c)–(d), the light is constantly changing. It can be seen that the proposed method in this paper can resist the interference of light to a certain extent.

3.2 Evaluation Parameters

Consider the following two evaluation parameters:

1. The proportion of correct segmentation in the output result;
2. The proportion of the complete contour in all the frames which obtain correctly segmented result;

Consider: the frame with correct hand center point is considered as a correct segmentation result, and hand segmentation of the remaining frames fails; the frame with complete hand contour is considered as a correct contour extraction result, and contour extraction of the remaining frames fails.

Count detection result of a video of a driver's turning operation. The duration is 30 s and the total number of frames is 900. The statistical results are shown in Table 1. Because driver's left hand is at the edge of the image, only part of it appears in the depth camera in most frames. The edge part is close to car window and is directly irradiated by sunlight. The detection result of left hand obtained is not ideal. Therefore, the results in Table 1 are only detection result of driver's right hand.

In hand segmentation results, correct segmentation results were obtained in 80.4% of the video frames. This is a satisfactory detection result in an environment where strong light changes, fast movement, and the camera shakes due to bumps. By comparing detection result and the input video, it is found that there are three main reasons for segmentation failure: the right hand is not completely captured by the camera; most region of hand is illuminated by strong light; there will be 1–2 frames of target loss between correct segmentation sequences. Among them, the third type of detection failure

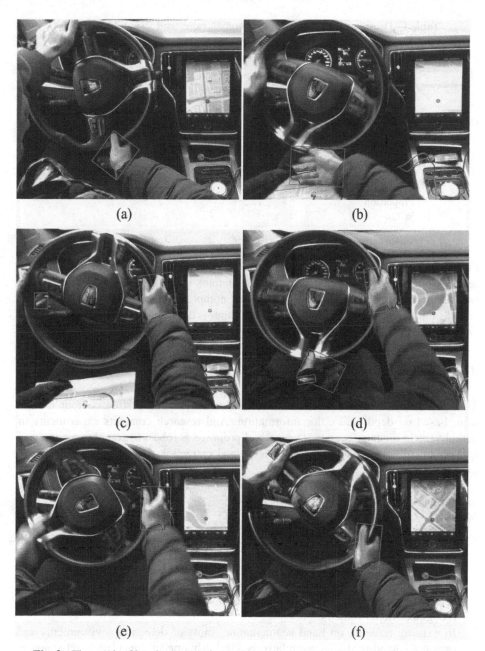

(a)   (b)

(c)   (d)

(e)   (f)

Fig. 2. The result of hand segmentation and contour extraction in actual vehicle scene.

accounts for one-third of the number of failures, and target loss can be handled by target tracking algorithms.

In the frames where right hand is correctly segmented, that is, the correct center point of right hand is obtained, a complete contour can be extracted in 72.5% of the frames.

Table 1. Detection result of a turning operation video with 30 s and 900 frames

	Fail detection	Correct detection	
Number of frames	176	724	
Proportion in 900	19.6%	80.4%	
		Effective contour	Invalid contour
Number of frames		613	111
Proportion in 724		72.5%	27.5%

For correctly segmented video frames, the contour extraction method can get satisfying result. Comparing with input video, invalid contours include: the hand is divided into two parts, resulting in discontinuous contours; complete contour includes interference such as the steering wheel; only part of the contour is drawn, such as the thumb contour and the index finger contour.

4 Conclusion

This paper implements a method of hand segmentation and gesture contour extraction, based on depth and color information. And research conducts experiments in actual vehicle-mounted scenes. The method proposed is robust to complex scenes, and can obtain sufficient accurate segmentation and extraction results in the verification experiment.

The proposed method in this paper differs from other hand segmentation and contour extraction methods as follows:

1. Use depth maps for background modeling. Compared with color images, depth images can provide additional longitudinal distance information and increase the dimension of gesture features in recognition process. Depth data also reduces the complexity of segmentation process. Compared with other similar products, the selected RealSense depth camera is more suitable for most life scenes in terms of recognized depth value range.
2. In existing research on hand segmentation, most of detection environments and operator's hand positions are relatively ideal. This paper considers hand status in actual application scenarios and designs algorithms for complex scenes, which has certain practical application value.

But the current algorithm module still has some shortcomings:

The calculation speed is not fast enough to output the detection results in real time with the video input. To optimize this problem, algorithm needs to be further optimized;

In a very severe change in strong light or in a dim environment, detection results cannot achieve expected results. It is necessary to do some color equalization processing on the color image, or select the appropriate color space component threshold for skin color detection according to actual ROI area, which can improve detection effect in strong light or dim environment.

References

1. Yao, Z., Pan, Z., Xu, S.: Wrist recognition and the center of the palm estimation based on depth camera. In: International Conference on Virtual Reality and Visualization, pp. 100–105. IEEE (2013)
2. Smedt, Q.D., Wannous, H., Vandeborre, J.P.: Skeleton-based dynamic hand gesture recognition. In: IEEE Conference on Computer Vision and Pattern Recognition Workshops (CVPRW) (2016)
3. Ge, L., Liang, H., Yuan, J., et al.: Robust 3D hand pose estimation in single depth images: from single-view CNN to multi-view CNNs, pp. 3593–3601 (2016)
4. Park, S., Yu, S., Kim, J.: 3D hand tracking using Kalman filter in depth space. EURASIP J. Adv. Signal Process. **2012**(1), 1–18 (2012)
5. Hong yong T, Youling, Y.: Finger tracking and gesture recognition with Kinect. In: IEEE, International Conference on Computer and Information Technology, pp. 214–218 (2012)
6. Gang, N.: Research on human hand gesture detection and recognition method. Nanjing University of Posts and Telecommunications (2019)
7. Klompmaker, F., Nebe, K., et al.: d Sensing NI: a framework for advanced tangible interaction using a depth camera. In: International Conference on Tangible, pp. 217–224. ACM (2012)
8. Li, Z., Jarvis, R.: Real time hand gesture recognition using a range camera (2009)
9. Celebi, M.E., Kingravi, H.A., Vela, P.A.: A comparative study of efficient initialization methods for the k-means clustering algorithm. Expert Syst. Appl. (2013)
10. Achanta, R., Shaji, A., Smith, K., et al.: SLIC super pixels compared to state-of-the-art super pixel methods. IEEE Trans. Pattern Anal. Mach. Intell. **34**(11), 2274–2282 (2012)
11. Lipton, A.J., Fujiyoshi, H., Patil, R.S.: Moving target classification and tracking from real-time video. In: IEEE Workshop on Applications of Computer Vision. IEEE Computer Society (1998)
12. Zhang, J., Cao, J., Mao, B.: Moving object detection based on non-parametric methods and frame difference for traceability video analysis. In: Procedia Computer Science (2016)
13. Silpaja Chandrasekar, K., Geetha, P.: Multiple objects tracking by a highly decisive three-frame differencing-combined-background subtraction method with GMPFM-GMPHD filters and VGG16-LSTM classifier. J. Vis. Commun. Image Represent. (2020)
14. Zhang, Y., Zheng, J., Zhang, C., Li, B.: An effective motion object detection method using optical flow estimation under a moving camera. J. Vis. Commun. Image Represent. (2018)
15. Qia, W., Qi, Y.: Traffic video background modeling method based on frame difference and statistical histogram. Comput. Sci. **47**(10), 174–179 (2020)
16. Konda, K.R., Königs, A., Schulz, H., et al.: Real time interaction with mobile robots using hand gestures. In: ACM/IEEE International Conference on Human-Robot Interaction, pp. 177–178. IEEE (2012)
17. Fujimura, K., Liu, X.: Sign recognition using depth image streams. In: International Conference on Automatic Face and Gesture Recognition, pp. 381–386. IEEE (2006)
18. Zhang, X.: Adaptive median filtering for image processing. J. Comput. Aid. Des. Comput. Graph. (2005)

19. Piva, A., Barni, M., Bartolini, F., et al.: DCT-based watermark recovering without resorting to the uncorrupted original image. In: International Conference on Image Processing (1997)
20. Qi, Z., Li, X., Jia, J.: 100+ times faster weighted median filter (2014)
21. Songhua, W.: Research on image region growing segmentation algorithm. Science and Technology Innovation Guide (2015)
22. Wei, C., Wang, Z., Fu, S., et al.: Usability evaluation of car cockpit based on multiple objective measures. In: Engineering Psychology and Cognitive Ergonomics. Cognition and Design, Held as Part of the 22nd HCI International Conference, HCII 2020 (2020)
23. Zhao, Y., Wang, Z., Lu, Y., et al.: A visual-based approach for manual operation evaluation. engineering psychology and cognitive ergonomics. In: Mental Workload, Human Physiology, and Human Energy, Held as Part of the 22nd HCI International Conference, HCII 2020 (2020)

It's a Joint Effort: Understanding Speech and Gesture in Collaborative Tasks

Isaac Wang[1]([⊠]), Pradyumna Narayana[2], Dhruva Patil[2], Rahul Bangar[2], Bruce Draper[2], Ross Beveridge[2], and Jaime Ruiz[1]

[1] Department of CISE, University of Florida, Gainesville, FL 32611, USA
wangi@ufl.edu
[2] Department of Computer Science, Colorado State University, Fort Collins, CO 80523, USA

Abstract. Computers are evolving from computational tools to collaborative agents through the emergence of natural, speech-driven interfaces. However, relying on speech alone is a limitation; gesture and other non-verbal aspects of communication also play a vital role in natural human discourse. To understand the use of gesture in human communication, we conducted a study to explore how people use gesture and speech to communicate when solving collaborative tasks. We asked 30 pairs of people to build structures out of blocks, limiting their communication to either *Gesture Only*, *Speech Only*, or *Gesture and Speech*. We found differences in how gesture and speech were used to communicate across the three conditions and found that pairs in the *Gesture and Speech* condition completed tasks faster than those in *Speech Only*. From our results, we draw conclusions about how our work impacts the design of collaborative systems and virtual agents that support gesture.

Keywords: Gesture · Speech · Multimodal · Communication · Collaboration

1 Introduction

Interaction with computers has become increasingly natural through the emergence and near-ubiquity of speech-driven interfaces, such as Apple's Siri [1] and Amazon's Alexa [2]. These dialogue-based systems have enabled computers to become more like collaborative agents rather than computational tools. Any user can now talk and interact with these systems much as they would with another human, making interactions more natural.

However, these interfaces lack the richness and multimodality of human-to-human communication. Our everyday discourse encompasses much more than just speech; throughout the course of a conversation, we may use gesture, expression, body language, and/or context to communicate our feelings, thoughts, and actions [3–7]. Thus, the use of speech as the sole medium of communication with speech-driven interfaces is a limitation. Computers must utilize nonverbal channels of communication if they are to function effectively as collaborative partners by emulating human interactions.

Thus, we need to identify and model how gestures and speech are used in human-to-human communication. Prior work has studied gesture interaction quite extensively

© Springer Nature Switzerland AG 2021
M. Kurosu (Ed.): HCII 2021, LNCS 12763, pp. 159–178, 2021.
https://doi.org/10.1007/978-3-030-78465-2_13

Fig. 1. Example showing two people collaborating to build a structure. The Signaler (left) is gesturing to the Actor (right).

(e.g., [8–11]), and has also investigated the use of multimodal interaction (e.g., [12–15]). Other studies have focused on understanding how to support remote collaboration between people by supporting the coordination of mutual knowledge through common ground [16–19]. These studies have mainly concentrated on the usefulness of shared visual information [18, 20, 21] and nonverbal information other than gesture, such as gaze [22–24]. Our goal, however, is to motivate and inform the development of multimodal interfaces and collaborative agents that incorporate the use of gesture. We work toward this goal by studying the natural interaction between two people working to solve a collaborative task (Fig. 1).

In this paper, we present an exploratory study observing the natural dyadic communication between two people collaborating to build structures out of blocks. We limit the communication allowed across three conditions: *Gesture Only*, *Speech Only*, and *Gesture and Speech*. Our work provides the following main contributions:

1. We describe *differences in the usage of speech and gesture* when the two are used together, or when one is present and the other is not.
2. We show how *communication was predominantly multimodal* when people were given the option to use both gesture and speech.
3. We present data showing a *quantifiable performance benefit from the inclusion of gesture with speech*.
4. From our findings, we derive *insights and design implications* into how the inclusion of gesture can benefit collaboration and the design of collaborative virtual agents.

These contributions highlight the importance of integrating the use of speech and gesture when designing collaborative technology and collaborative virtual agents.

2 Related Work

There has been an ongoing effort in HCI on integrating both speech and gesture in multimodal computer interaction since the introduction of the point-and-manipulate "Put-that-there" system by Bolt [25]. In this section, we focus on prior gesture research that motivates our work. This includes research on gesture in the domains of psychology and HCI as well as research on multimodal communication and collaboration.

2.1 Gesture in Psychology

Research in multimodal gesture and speech interaction began with psychological and cognitive studies (e.g., [3, 7, 26, 27]). For instance, Kendon's gesture classification scheme [7, 27] describes five categories of gestures that range from gesticulation, which appears in the presence of speech, to sign languages, which appear in the complete absence of speech. Additionally, McNeill [7] emphasized that gesture and speech are closely intertwined and both are critical to organization and generation of thought. Other work by Kendon details how gesture is used in everyday conversation to refer to objects and to add expressiveness to language by demonstrating events or actions [6]. These gestures co-occur with speech and may contain redundant or complementary information. Both Kendon and McNeill emphasize that gesture contains information. Therefore, it is likely that understanding both speech and gesture can help a system better interpret what a person is trying to convey.

Kendon and McNeill focused on the descriptive use of gesture in the context of narration and conversation. Gestures also play a more functional role in communication, such as conveying spatial information [6, 28, 29]. Gestures and other nonverbal cues arc also valuable in conversational grounding, i.e. the process of establishing a mutual understanding in communication [4, 5, 30]. The use of gesture also helps manage the flow of a conversation by functioning as a signal for turn-taking and providing a "back-channel" for communicating attention and turn-taking [26, 31]. Additionally, Argyle [3] noted how gestures have social functions, such as their use in simple greetings or their conveyance of emotional state.

The concepts and theories derived from these studies help motivate our work in designing systems that incorporate the use of gesture. These studies illustrate how gesture is an important and natural part of human communication, both in interacting with other humans and in helping to organize and express thoughts. Therefore, designing systems that recognize and understand gesture is vital if we wish to create collaborative technology and virtual agents that are more natural and versatile.

2.2 Gesture in HCI

In HCI, there has been a large effort in creating systems focused on gesture interaction. There is a large body of prior work on designing and developing gesture input techniques and recognition, ranging from mobile devices [8, 10, 32, 33] to large-screen displays [11, 34, 35], as well as research on multimodal interaction [12–15, 36, 37]. This body of work focuses on using gesture as an alternative means of providing input commands to a system.

In contrast, other work focuses on the use of gesture and other nonverbal expressions in a more communicative manner, emphasizing how gesture can also be used to convey information. For instance, Grandhi et al. [38] saw how people used pantomime to directly paint images of objects and actions (i.e., holding imaginary objects and pretending to perform a task) rather than attempt to use abstract gestures to describe the task or object.

Holz and Wilson [9] showed that pantomimes can describe the specific spatial features of 3D objects. Likewise, Sowa and Wachsmuth [39] detailed a method to allow users to select objects using gestures by inferring this spatial information from their hands.

Gesture can also convey information alongside speech. Epps et al. [40] conducted a study on multimodal expressions for photo manipulation tasks, and found that gestures provided complementary information (e.g., pointing to an object and giving a verbal command) and redundant information (e.g., a rotational gesture along with speech describing the rotation). Furthermore, other studies [41–43] also noted and explored the varying co-expressiveness and redundancy of gesture and speech. Our work extends these studies by similarly looking at how speech and gesture are used together to communicate and convey information, but also compares how using gesture and speech separately differs from a multimodal usage.

2.3 Multimodal Communication and Collaboration

As our work focuses on the use of speech and gesture in the context of collaboration, we not only draw from prior work on gesture and multimodal interaction but also work on collaboration and computer-mediated communication. For instance, Bekker et al. [44] conducted an analysis of gestures in a face-to-face design session and found that gestures are naturally used to describe actions, depict spatial relations, and refer to specific items. They also found that gestures help manage the flow of conversations, similar to Duncan and Niederehe's [26] results that showed how people use gestures to signal when they want to speak. Similarly, in observing interactions between people across video, Isaacs and Tang [45] pointed out that video helps express and enhance understanding through the conveyance of nonverbal information, such as facial expression and occasionally gesture. Others have looked at shared gaze information to help resolve references when collaborating [22–24].

Several studies also emphasize the value of providing shared visual information (such as a shared workspace) when supporting virtual collaboration between people [18, 20, 21, 46]. These studies hold that allowing people to share a view of task objects and actions performed on those objects helps with grounding and is thus critical to collaboration. Building off of these studies, Fussell et al. [16] explored ways of using "embodiments of gesture," or the use of alternatives such as pointers or pen drawings in place of natural gestures through body motions. Similarly, Kirk et al. [17] showed how allowing people to gesture at objects by projecting their hands onto the workspace can also help facilitate grounding.

We seek to extend these studies by understanding how the modalities of speech and gesture are used in face-to-face interactions. We recognize the benefit of a shared workspace, and therefore include a shared view in all conditions. Our goal is then to understand and show the added benefit of gesture *in addition to* the shared workspace. To our knowledge, no prior work has investigated how gesture and speech are used separately and together when supporting a natural face-to-face interaction in the context of a shared visual workspace.

3   Method

We conducted an exploratory study asking pairs of adults to collaboratively build different pre-determined structures using wooden blocks.

3.1   Participants

We recruited 60 participants (10 pairs per condition) from computer science classes at a local university and through word-of-mouth recruiting. Participants were between the ages of 19 and 64 (mean = 24.2, SD = 7.7), and 17 participants were female. Out of the 60 participants, six were left-handed, and one person was ambidextrous. Half of all participants had prior experience with motion gesture systems such as the Microsoft Kinect. Out of the 30 pairs of participants, 16 pairs were previously acquainted with each other. All participants received a $10 Amazon gift card as compensation. Our study was approved by our Institutional Review Board.

3.2   Procedure

Each pair of participants was randomly assigned to one of the experimental conditions at the start of the study. They were then split up into the separate rooms, each with a computer and a display that allowed them to communicate. One participant was assigned the role of *Actor*, and the other, the role of *Signaler*. For each trial, the Signaler was given a picture of a *block layout*, depicting an arrangement of blocks that represented the end goal. The Actor was provided a set of blocks. The task was for the Signaler to direct the Actor to arrange the blocks to match the goal layout.

The pair was asked to complete two sessions. For each session, they were asked to complete up to 10 tasks within 30 min. We ended the session if time expired. After the first session, the participants switched roles and attempted another session for a total of up to 20 tasks. The tasks used for each pair were randomly selected without replacement from a corpus of 80 unique layouts.

Since we wanted to observe natural communication in action, participants were not allowed to talk or strategize beforehand and were given no instruction on how to speak or gesture. A trial began when the experimenter presented a new block layout to the Signaler and ended when the Actor replicated the block layout. The time taken to complete each task was measured, and video of both the Actor and Signaler was recorded for later analysis.

3.3   Apparatus

The Signaler and Actor both interacted with similar systems during the study. Each participant stood in front of a table facing a TV screen on the opposite end of the table (Fig. 2). A Microsoft Kinect v2 sensor [47] was also set up on the opposite end, facing the participant. These were connected to a computer that drove the display and collected data from the Kinect. We developed software to stream live video (and audio) from the Kinect sensors between the two setups. High-quality video (1080p) was streamed at

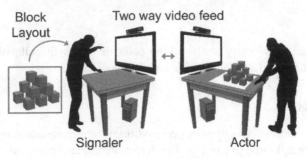

Fig. 2. The experiment setup. The participant on the left (Signaler) was asked to direct the other participant (Actor) to construct a block layout.

30 FPS with no noticeable latency. Because the Kinect sensors capture a mirror image (horizontally reflected; left appears as right, and vice versa), we corrected the image when streaming between the two setups. The Kinect sensors were also used to record RGB video, depth data, and motion capture skeletons.

This full-duplex video link allowed the Signaler and Actor to communicate with each other as if they were facing each other at opposite ends of the same table. The table acted as a shared workspace, as blocks placed on the table could be seen by both participants (from opposite perspectives).

The blocks used in the study were wood cubes with 4-in. sides (10.6 cm). The Actor was provided with 12 blocks total; however, not all 12 blocks were used in every layout. These blocks were kept off the table and placed on the Actor's right-hand side. Blocks were removed from the table and reset between trials. Participants stood approximately 5 feet (1.5 m) away from the screen, allowing for a visible workspace of around 5 × 2.5 feet (1.5 × 0.76 m) on the table.

3.4 Block Layouts

We used a set of 80 different block layouts for the study. Crowdsourcing was used to quickly collect a large variety of layouts that would also afford different intents. For instance, an arrangement of blocks with multiple layers may involve gestures or speech to stack blocks on top of each other, and an arrangement with rotated blocks would involve gestures or speech specifically to rotate blocks. Thus, using a crowdsourced collection of layouts in our study allowed us to capture gestures and utterances for a wide range of possible intents.

To collect layouts, we developed and deployed a web-based game in which submitted layouts were scored based on how closely the position and rotation of blocks matched those in previously submitted layouts. The game simulated the arrangement of blocks in a virtual 3D environment (Fig. 3a). Block physics were also simulated, allowing blocks to support each other and lean against each other in different orientations, further opening possibilities for creative arrangements. We distributed the game to local computer science classes, asking students to submit their own layouts and compete for the high score. We collected a corpus of over 200 layouts in three weeks. Out of these, we first excluded layouts that were unstable (or fell over) or were not unique, and then randomly selected

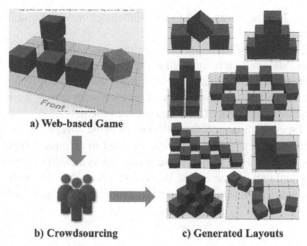

Fig. 3. We (a) deployed a web-based blocks game to quickly (b) crowdsource a diverse corpus of (c) block layouts.

a set of 80 distinct layouts for this experiment. The layouts used varied in their difficulty and complexity (Fig. 3c).

3.5 Conditions

We restricted the participants' communication modalities based on the following conditions:

- *Gesture Only:* Participants could only see each other using the video presented on the TVs; the audio was muted, restricting participants to using only non-verbal communication to accomplish tasks.
- *Speech Only:* Participants were not able to see each other and could only rely on speech to communicate; the video feed was restricted so that both participants could only see the blocks on the table. This was done to remove the ability to communicate through gestures while still retaining a shared workspace.
- *Gesture and Speech:* Both audio and video were enabled, allowing participants to use any natural combination of speech and gesture they wished.

3.6 Data Analysis

To compare gesture use between the *Gesture Only* and *Gesture and Speech* conditions, we annotated the video recordings to label the occurrences of different gestures. Our focus was on how required actions and specific features of the layout were communicated. Therefore, we focused on the gestures made by the Signaler. We followed the gesture analysis procedure detailed by Wang et al. [48]. Using the video annotation tool described in their paper, we marked the start and end of each observed gesture and assigned it a label that described the physical motion of body parts that were involved in making the gesture.

A specific labeling language was used to keep labeling consistent and descriptive. See [48] for further details.

Additionally, the implied intent of each gesture was annotated, e.g., a gesture was given the intent of "slide left" if it signified that the current block(s) needed to be moved left. Intents included labels for sliding/moving blocks, stacking, signifying "OK," "stop," etc. Labels used for gesture and intent were kept consistent across the two conditions, to facilitate comparing instances of gestures between them.

We generated speech transcripts from the videos in the *Speech Only* and *Gesture and Speech* conditions in order to analyze speech. We used an automatic speech recognition (ASR) service by IBM Watson [49] to retrieve transcripts as well as timing information for the beginning and end of utterances. We also ran the videos through Google Cloud Speech [50] to compare ASR accuracies and found the accuracies to be similar to Watson.

4 Results

Using both our labeled gesture data and generated transcripts, we analyzed how speech and gesture were used in the different conditions, and whether the modality used in each condition influenced task performance.

4.1 Differences in Gesture Use

We labeled 24,503 gesture instances across all trials. Additionally, we note that there were 15,222 (62.1%) gestures in the *Gesture Only* condition and only 9,281 (37.9%) in the *Gesture and Speech* condition. Our dataset had 5,060 unique gesture labels and 187 unique intent labels. However, due to the nature of our gesture labels as compound physical descriptions, many of these only occurred once in the entire set. Only 1,427 gestures occurred two or more times, and only 110 gestures occurred at least twenty times and were used by more than one participant.

Due to the large number of unique gestures and intents (caused by the level of detail in our labels), we preprocessed the data by filtering, grouping, and categorizing gestures to decrease the number of items to a manageable set. This was done to extract themes to compare gesture use between the *Gesture Only* and *Gesture and Speech* conditions.

We first filtered the list of unique gestures and intents to include only those that were performed by at least four people and were observed to have occurred in at least 20 instances across the entire set. This allowed us to take a high-level look at the gestures and intents that were commonly used. Similar gestures and intents were grouped into 25 discrete actions and organized into four types: Numeric (counting gestures), Command (translate, rotate, etc.), Reference (this block, there, here, etc.), and Social Cues (start, done, OK, no, stop, etc.). It is important to note that we also included the absence of action ("wait" and "think") under Social Cues, to also look at potential differences in how the Signaler paused to think or waited for the Actor to complete an action. For each action, we compared the number of times the action occurred in the *Gesture Only* condition against the number of times it occurred in the *Gesture and Speech* condition. These frequencies are presented in Table 1.

Table 1. Comparison of action frequencies between the *Gesture Only* and *Gesture and Speech* conditions. Shaded actions occur at least four times more in *Gesture Only*

	Action	Gesture Only	Gesture & Speech
Numeric	one	85	18
	two	64	9
	three	26	4
	four	21	5
	five	29	8
Command	separate	126	125
	translate	234	73
	continual translate	206	44
	translate towards	35	20
	together	83	38
	rotate	225	67
Reference	that / there	150	106
	here / this	111	42
	this group	86	28
	this block	240	94
	these blocks	24	20
	this stack	38	16
	this column	52	13
Social Cues	start	100	51
	ok	693	225
	wait	1582	1555
	think	400	246
	done	81	47
	no	109	11
	emphasis	17	27

We discovered that seven actions were used at least four times more often in the *Gesture Only* condition than in *Gesture and Speech* (highlighted in Table 1). Four of them were the numeric gestures one through four, so these were grouped together, giving us four distinct groups:

- Numeric gestures ("one" through "four"): referring to a quantity by holding up the number of fingers.
- "Continual translate": the act of continually translating an object in a direction until feedback (as in a stop or OK sign) is given.
- "This column": referring to a series of blocks arranged outwardly, as opposed to vertically or horizontally.
- "No": a Social Cue used to give negative feedback.

4.2   Differences in Speech Use

We analyzed speech use between the *Speech Only* and *Gesture and Speech* conditions with the goal of identifying high-level themes by looking for patterns in common phrases people used. Due to the nature of speech, many words or phrases only appeared once or twice, impeding direct comparison between the two conditions. Thus, we looked at the most common bigrams and trigrams retrieved from the transcripts and compared their frequencies. Results from this analysis showed that the most common bigrams described spatial relations through prepositional phrases such as "in the" or "on top." We also looked for items that appeared at least four times more often in either condition, similar to our analysis of gestures. Given these criteria, we did not find any major differences in speech use between the two conditions. There may be additional information gained from looking at the speech acts used or how turn-taking was accomplished, but any deeper linguistic analysis is beyond the scope of this paper.

When comparing the occurrences of trigrams, we gain more insight into how speech was used. We saw the use of prepositional phrases to describe where to place blocks in relation to one another. This paints a clear picture of their use, with phrases such as "in the middle" and "on top of." We also see a large use of the phrases "a little bit" and "little bit more," used to describe small movements or continuations of movements such as *"now go forward a little bit"* (P15) and *"little bit more up and then pushed in a little bit"* (P29).

When examining the top 20 trigrams, we find only a few that appeared much more often in the *Speech Only* condition than *Gesture and Speech*. The trigram "there you go" appears 7.5 times more often in *Speech Only*; however, upon further analysis, this was due to a participant (P57) inflating the occurrence count by repeatedly using the phrase in a trial. The trigrams "going to be" and "little bit more" were used five times and four times more often, respectively. The larger occurrence of "going to be" (e.g., *"it's going to be on your left side"* – P27) is not particularly meaningful, and may just be a nuance of speech (this was not caused by an inflated count, unlike "there you go"). For "little bit more," we note that it is related to "a little bit," so possibly there were more cases where the Signaler needed to make finer adjustments to achieve the goal. We also note the larger occurrence of "I want you" and "want you to" in the *Gesture and Speech* condition. This was also due to a participant (P41) constantly repeating the phrase and inflating the count.

4.3   Co-expression of Speech and Gesture

We took a closer look at the *Gesture and Speech* condition, to identify how the two modalities were used together. Using both our labeled gesture data and transcribed utterance timings, we conducted an analysis following the methodology used by Oviatt and colleagues [15, 36, 40], correlating instances of gesture with specific utterances. This was accomplished by comparing the instances in which gestures occurred with the times where utterances occurred and counting the instances where they overlapped.

We observed a total of 8,473 multimodal and unimodal constructions. Of these, 66.5% (5,638 constructions) were multimodal and 33.5% (2,835) were unimodal. Of the unimodal constructions, 43.2% (1,226) used speech alone and 56.8% (1,609) used gesture alone (Fig. 4). These results mirror those detailed by Epps et al. [40], with the exception that we saw a larger number of gesture only constructions than speech only constructions.

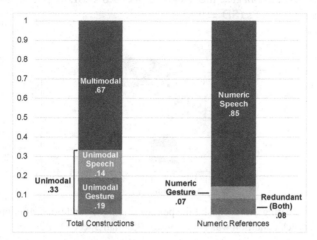

Fig. 4. Proportion of total multimodal/unimodal constructions (left) and numeric references (right) in the *Gesture and Speech* condition.

Our results on gesture use showed that the participants in the *Gesture and Speech* condition used fewer numeric gestures. To determine if speech was being used instead of gestures to refer to numbers, we took a closer look to see if one modality was used more than the other for expressing numbers. The right-most barchart in Fig. 4 depicts the proportions of numeric references using speech, gesture, or both. First, we saw that there was a total of 946 different times where the Signaler referred to a number (849 multimodal constructions, 97 unimodal), either for specifying the number of blocks to add or referring to a group of blocks already on the table. Out of these, an overwhelming majority (807, 85.3%) relied on speech alone to refer to numbers (no numeric gestures were observed concurrently), as opposed to 61 (6.4%) instances that relied on gesture alone to specify a number. There were also a few instances where gesture and speech were used redundantly, representing 78 (8.3%) of the constructions. These instances represented cases where participants verbally stated a number while also holding up the corresponding number of fingers. However, the majority of constructions relied on speech rather than gesture.

4.4 Task Performance

We compared task completion times to determine whether modality had an impact on task performance. As the number of trials differed between participants, task performance was evaluated by taking the average trial/task completion time for each session, resulting in two average times per pair (one for each Signaler/Actor assignment). We found one outlier (greater than three standard deviations away from the mean) in the *Gesture Only* condition. This was due to one pair (P39 & P40) having extreme difficulty with the task, resulting in an average task completion time that was eight standard deviations above the mean (299.1 s). Completion times for this pair were removed from further analysis. For the *Gesture Only* condition, the average trial time for a participant was 89.1 s (SD = 26.7), for *Gesture and Speech*, the average was 69.6 s (SD = 33.5), and for *Speech Only*, the average was 97.4 s (SD = 39.5).

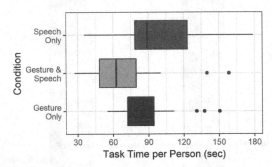

Fig. 5. Boxplots comparing average task time per person across conditions, after outlier removal. The Gesture and Speech condition was faster (*p* < 0.05) than Speech Only.

Analysis of variance (ANOVA) revealed a significant effect of condition on trial/task completion time ($F_{2,55} = 3.531, p < 0.05$). Post-hoc analysis using Bonferroni correction revealed that the *Gesture and Speech* condition was significantly faster than *Speech Only* (*p* < 0.05). However, we found no significant difference for completion time between *Gesture Only* and the two other conditions (*p* > 0.25 in both cases). Figure 5 shows the task completion times per person across conditions.

5   Discussion

We saw that participants predominantly communicated using both modalities simultaneously if given the option, as opposed to using either speech or gesture alone. Our results also suggest that speech use was the same in both speech conditions. Thus, we attribute the inclusion of gesture to the faster completion times found in the *Gesture and Speech* condition. We first discuss the differences in gesture and speech use and then focus on the ways that gesture improved communication between pairs.

5.1   Different Strategies for Different Modalities

From prior work [7, 51], we would expect that gesture use changes accordingly with the presence and absence of speech. This is in alignment with our results, which suggest that the use of gesture changes in the presence of speech. We interpret these findings as different communication strategies for different modalities. For instance, our results showed that numeric gestures were used less often in the *Gesture and Speech* condition. When communicating multimodally, speech was the dominant channel for communicating numbers. If numeric gestures were used, they were often redundant, with participants still using speech to specify numbers. It was likely easier to verbally state the number of blocks than perform a numeric gesture. Speech is also more powerful in this case because the Signaler could easily speak any number from one to twelve, but gesturing via finger counting has a limit of ten. This is supported by our data, which shows that every number from one to twelve was spoken at least once.

Similarly, it would likewise be easier or more understandable for the Signaler to say "no" or verbally correct the Actor than to shake their head or rapidly shake their hands back and forth to quickly stop or undo the current action (which is a drastic action in the videos, much like engaging the emergency brakes when the Actor performs an incorrect move). Furthermore, representing "this column" and "continual translate" through gestures may not be necessary because there are better words to describe the actions of specifying a column or continually translating an object. It is possible that gestures for "continual translate" were supplanted with phrases such as "a little" or "little bit more," avoiding the use of a continual movement in favor of fine-grained incremental movements.

When given the ability to use both speech and gesture, people used multimodal expressions two times more frequently than unimodal expressions. We observed that, when gesture was used with speech, it was often used to convey supplementary information as opposed to redundant information. We saw that gestures were used in the *Gesture and Speech* condition almost as often as in the *Gesture Only* condition. Signalers used these referential gestures (here, there, etc.) to depict or point to objects, along with speech to describe how to manipulate those objects. This is illustrated in Fig. 6, where the Signaler is pointing to a group of three blocks while saying, "Put *that* on the other side." In this case, gesture is used to resolve the verbal reference "that."

These results demonstrate how a multimodal system would need to adapt to support interaction in environments where one modality becomes unavailable. For example, if a user of a multimodal system is likely to encounter environments where speech becomes impractical (e.g., noisy environments), then the system must be prepared to recognize additional gestures that would not appear when speech is present.

5.2 Speech and Gesture for Resolving Orientation

We also saw how speech was used in conjunction with gesture to resolve orientation between pairs. When analyzing the videos, we noticed that people used several different reference frames and perspectives when communicating. For example, sometimes when the Signaler referred to "left" in either gesture or speech, they meant their own left. Other times, "left" referred to the Actor's left. Likewise, there was confusion regarding the "front" and "back" orientations, which could also refer to either the Signaler's perspective or the Actor's perspective. This was further compounded when front and back used a different perspective than left and right. For instance, front and back could refer to the Signaler's perspective while at the same time left and right would refer to the Actor's perspective.

Due to the different perspectives used, participants needed to first achieve common ground with respect to orientation. While we found that both gesture and speech could be ambiguous when conveying direction and orientation, possessives could be used in

Fig. 6. In this example, the Signaler clarified orientation by saying "your right" while also pointing in the correct direction.

speech (e.g., "your" or "my") to quickly specify the perspective of the direction (e.g., "your left" or "my left"). In contrast, gesture lacks this precision and required pairs to resolve perspective and orientation first, which could be difficult to communicate with gesture alone. Ideally, speech can be used to augment gesture to clarify a precise orientation, helping the pair communicate quickly. Figure 6 illustrates an example where the Signaler used both speech and gesture to clarify an ambiguous direction.

Our work emphasizes that people use speech to resolve issues revolving around the use of different perspectives when giving directions, similar to observations by Schober [52]. While our work shows that resolving perspectives continues to be a challenge, it also demonstrates that the problem is more difficult than previously stated because users will assume different perspectives for different directions and orientations, requiring the use of speech and gesture to negotiate perspective. Only after resolving perspective could a person use the full spatial capabilities of gesture in conjunction with the precise nature of speech.

5.3   Improved Performance with Gesture

Our results showed that task completion time in the *Gesture and Speech* condition was significantly faster than *Speech Only*. People were naturally utilizing both speech and gesture to their advantage, when given the ability to use both channels of communication. This is evident by the fact that we saw that people used multimodal expressions more frequently than unimodal expressions, using gesture and speech together to resolve references and disambiguate orientation. Our results also suggest that there is information encoded in gesture and other nonverbal communication, which aligns with prior work [19, 41, 42].

Additionally, information can be conveyed through iconic gestures to visually show how to manipulate a block (such as translating or rotating) or through gestural social cues. These social cues included explicit cues such as "no" (e.g., shaking the head from side to side) and "ok" (a nod or thumbs up gesture), but also included subtler actions such as moving closer to the table/other person to signify "start" or moving away from the table to signify "done." The lack of motion or gesture can also convey information, as we saw the Signaler stop moving when thinking or waiting for the Actor to complete an action (the lack of motion likely indicated to the Actor that they "had the floor" and could perform an action or communicate back to the Signaler). Regardless of the exact information conveyed, we saw that including video of both people helped pairs complete tasks faster.

Our finding that pairs in the *Gesture and Speech* condition had faster task completion times than those in the *Speech Only* condition contradicts prior work. Although prior work [18, 20, 21, 53] states that gestures can be used efficiently to refer to task objects, they did not find any improved task performance. We attribute the observed benefit to two characteristics of our study:

1. Our study used a single video to view the shared workspace and the collaborator. Prior studies [20, 46, 54] required users to split their attention between a video of the shared workspace and a video of the collaborator.
2. Our study enabled participants to see each other in the context of the shared workspace. This mimicked a face-to-face interaction between people. This is in contrast with work by Fussell et al. [20, 46], which used video to mimic a side-by-side collaboration setup. In their setup, the camera and display placements did not mimic what each person would naturally see if they were situated in context.

Together, these characteristics allowed participants to identify their spatial relation to the blocks and the other participant, supporting the use of referential gestures to efficiently refer to objects on the table.

6 Implications for Design

Based on our results and discussion, we summarize the following recommendations for designing systems that support gesture interaction, multimodal communication, and virtual collaboration.

Design Virtual Agents to Utilize Human Gesture: Virtual agents should be designed to perceive and understand users' gestures. By taking advantage of the information encoded in a person's gestures, an agent can better understand human intent and function as a more effective communicator and collaborator. This may also include understanding social cues (e.g., subtle cues such as walking up to the table to begin interaction, or responding to acknowledgements such as ok/no). Such social cues are critical in communicating feedback before, during, and after a task. Although not as prominent as other gestures (such as deictic pointing), they are still useful and communicative.

Design Around Ambiguous Orientation: People may assume different perspectives when referring to objects, causing ambiguity when using speech or gesture to describe orientation. Systems that recognize either modality should be designed in a way to determine the user's intended frame of reference (through mechanisms such as looking for positive or negative feedback, or explicitly grounding by asking if this was the intended direction). Resolving orientation should be flexible and adapt to the user's mental model, whether references are from their perspective or another perspective. If the agent has a visual embodiment, the agent should be designed to use gesture in conjunction with speech to refer to objects in the task, providing additional information for humans to leverage.

Include Views of People, Situated in Context: When designing systems that support collaboration, ensure that all parties can fully see each other. Likewise, when designing a virtual agent to collaborate with humans, designers should situate the agent to mimic where a real person would stand or sit. This allows for the full multimodal use of gesture and other nonverbal communication, which can give people multiple ways for referring to and describing objects, helping them more effectively collaborate on tasks. It is also important to maintain a shared visual workspace for tasks, and, if possible, use views that enable people to see each other in the context of the workspace, mimicking how they would be able to see each other in real life.

Design for Different Modalities: Systems that use multimodal gesture and speech interaction should adapt to work even when limited to one modality by understanding that the use of gesture will change in the absence of speech, and thus the system will need to adapt to different communication strategies. This will ensure that an interaction system or virtual agent can help accomplish tasks even in suboptimal modalities and enable natural user interaction in diverse scenarios. For example, people are not always able to speak and/or gesture, such as when the hands/arms are occupied or when situated in a quiet/noisy environment where speech is not an option. Although we presented differences in gesturing strategies for a physical collaborative task, further work is necessary to understand the communication differences for all tasks and scenarios.

7   Conclusion

In this paper, we described the results of a study exploring how pairs of people use gesture and speech to communicate in collaborative physical tasks. We highlighted differences in gesturing strategies when used in the absence or presence of speech and looked at how gesture and speech were used multimodally. We showed that supporting the use of both gesture and speech by including views of both people resulted in faster task completion times. Additionally, we described how gesture and speech were used together to resolve ambiguity in expressing direction and orientation. From these results, we presented design implications for systems and virtual agents that support gestures, communication, and collaboration.

Acknowledgements. This work was partially funded by the U.S. Defense Advanced Research Projects Agency and the U.S. Army Research Office under contract #W911NF-15-1-0459.

References

1. iOS - Siri – Apple. http://www.apple.com/ios/siri/. Accessed 11 Jan 2017
2. Amazon Alexa. http://alexa.amazon.com/spa/index.html. Accessed 11 Jan 2017
3. Argyle, M.: Bodily Communication. Methuen, London; New York (1988)
4. Clark, H.H., Brennan, S.E.: Grounding in communication. In: Resnick, L.B., Levine, J.M., Teasley, S.D. (eds.) Perspectives on Socially Shared Cognition, pp. 13–1991. American Psychological Association, Washington, DC, US (1991)

5. Clark, H.H., Wilkes-Gibbs, D.: Referring as a collaborative process. Cognition **22**, 1–39 (1986). https://doi.org/10.1016/0010-0277(86)90010-7
6. Kendon, A.: Gesture: Visible Action as Utterance. Cambridge University Press, Cambridge, New York (2004)
7. McNeill, D.: Hand and Mind : What Gestures Reveal About Thought. University of Chicago Press, Chicago (1992)
8. Harrison, C., Hudson, S.E.: Abracadabra: wireless, high-precision, and unpowered finger input for very small mobile devices. In: Proceedings of the 22nd Annual ACM Symposium on User Interface Software and Technology, pp. 121–124. ACM, New York, NY, USA (2009). https://doi.org/10.1145/1622176.1622199
9. Holz, C., Wilson, A.: Data miming: inferring spatial object descriptions from human gesture. In: Proceedings of the SIGCHI Conference on Human Factors in Computing Systems, pp. 811–820. ACM, New York, NY, USA (2011). https://doi.org/10.1145/1978942.1979060
10. Ruiz, J., Li, Y., Lank, E.: User-defined motion gestures for mobile interaction. In: Proceedings of the SIGCHI Conference on Human Factors in Computing Systems, pp. 197–206. ACM, New York, NY, USA (2011). https://doi.org/10.1145/1978942.1978971
11. Walter, R., Bailly, G., Valkanova, N., Müller, J.: Cuenesics: using mid-air gestures to select items on interactive public displays. In: Proceedings of the 16th International Conference on Human-computer Interaction with Mobile Devices & Services, pp. 299–308. ACM, New York, NY, USA (2014). https://doi.org/10.1145/2628363.2628368
12. Brewster, S., Lumsden, J., Bell, M., Hall, M., Tasker, S.: Multimodal "Eyes-free" interaction techniques for wearable devices. In: Proceedings of the SIGCHI Conference on Human Factors in Computing Systems, pp. 473–480. ACM, New York, NY, USA (2003). https://doi.org/10.1145/642611.642694
13. Keates, S., Robinson, P.: The use of gestures in multimodal input. In: Proceedings of the Third International ACM Conference on Assistive Technologies, pp. 35–42. ACM, New York, NY, USA (1998). https://doi.org/10.1145/274497.274505
14. Madhvanath, S., Vennelakanti, R., Subramanian, A., Shekhawat, A., Dey, P., Rajan, A.: Designing multiuser multimodal gestural interactions for the living room. In: Proceedings of the 14th ACM International Conference on Multimodal Interaction, pp. 61–62. ACM, New York, NY, USA (2012). https://doi.org/10.1145/2388676.2388693.
15. Oviatt, S., DeAngeli, A., Kuhn, K.: Integration and synchronization of input modes during multimodal human-computer interaction. In: Proceedings of the ACM SIGCHI Conference on Human Factors in Computing Systems, pp. 415–422. ACM, New York, NY, USA (1997). https://doi.org/10.1145/258549.258821
16. Fussell, S.R., Setlock, L.D., Yang, J., Ou, J., Mauer, E., Kramer, A.D.I.: Gestures over video streams to support remote collaboration on physical tasks. Hum. Comput. Interact. **19**, 273–309 (2004). https://doi.org/10.1207/s15327051hci1903_3
17. Kirk, D., Rodden, T., Fraser, D.S.: Turn it this way: grounding collaborative action with remote gestures. In: Proceedings of the SIGCHI Conference on Human Factors in Computing Systems, pp. 1039–1048. ACM, New York, NY, USA (2007). https://doi.org/10.1145/1240624.1240782
18. Kraut, R.E., Gergle, D., Fussell, S.R.: The use of visual information in shared visual spaces: informing the development of virtual co-presence. In: Proceedings of the 2002 ACM Conference on Computer Supported Cooperative Work, pp. 31–40. ACM, New York, NY, USA (2002). https://doi.org/10.1145/587078.587084
19. Veinott, E.S., Olson, J., Olson, G.M., Fu, X.: Video helps remote work: speakers who need to negotiate common ground benefit from seeing each other. In: Proceedings of the SIGCHI Conference on Human Factors in Computing Systems, pp. 302–309. ACM, New York, NY, USA (1999). https://doi.org/10.1145/302979.303067

20. Fussell, S.R., Kraut, R.E., Siegel, J.: Coordination of communication: effects of shared visual context on collaborative work. In: Proceedings of the 2000 ACM Conference on Computer Supported Cooperative Work, pp. 21–30. ACM, New York, NY, USA (2000). https://doi.org/10.1145/358916.358947

21. Gergle, D., Kraut, R.E., Fussell, S.R.: Action as language in a shared visual space. In: Proceedings of the 2004 ACM Conference on Computer Supported Cooperative Work, pp. 487–496. ACM, New York, NY, USA (2004). https://doi.org/10.1145/1031607.1031687

22. Brennan, S.E., Chen, X., Dickinson, C.A., Neider, M.B., Zelinsky, G.J.: Coordinating cognition: the costs and benefits of shared gaze during collaborative search. Cognition 106, 1465–1477 (2008). https://doi.org/10.1016/j.cognition.2007.05.012

23. D'Angelo, S., Gergle, D.: Gazed and confused: understanding and designing shared gaze for remote collaboration. In: Proceedings of the 2016 CHI Conference on Human Factors in Computing Systems, pp. 2492–2496. ACM, New York, NY, USA (2016). https://doi.org/10.1145/2858036.2858499

24. Gergle, D., Clark, A.T.: See what I'M saying?: Using dyadic mobile eye tracking to study collaborative reference. In: Proceedings of the ACM 2011 Conference on Computer Supported Cooperative Work, pp. 435–444. ACM, New York, NY, USA (2011). https://doi.org/10.1145/1958824.1958892

25. Bolt, R.A.: "Put-that-there": Voice and gesture at the graphics interface. In: Proceedings of the 7th Annual Conference on Computer Graphics and Interactive Techniques, pp. 262–270. ACM, New York, NY, USA (1980). https://doi.org/10.1145/800250.807503

26. Duncan, S., Niederehe, G.: On signalling that it's your turn to speak. J. Exp. Soc. Psychol. 10, 234–247 (1974). https://doi.org/10.1016/0022-1031(74)90070-5

27. Kendon, A.: How gestures can become like words. In: Cross-Cultural Perspectives in Nonverbal Communication, pp. 131–141. Hogrefe, Toronto; Lewiston, NY (1988)

28. Alibali, M.W.: Gesture in spatial cognition: expressing, communicating, and thinking about spatial information. Spat. Cogn. Comput. 5, 307–331 (2005). https://doi.org/10.1207/s15427633scc0504_2

29. Bergmann, K.: Verbal or visual? How information is distributed across speech and gesture in spatial dialog. In: Proceedings of Brandial 2006, the 10th Workshop on the Semantics and Pragmatics of Dialogue, pp. 90–97 (2006)

30. Dillenbourg, P., Traum, D.: Sharing solutions: persistence and grounding in multimodal collaborative problem solving. J. Learn. Sci. 15, 121–151 (2006). https://doi.org/10.1207/s15327809jls1501_9

31. Young, R.F., Lee, J.: Identifying units in interaction: reactive tokens in Korean and English conversations. J. Socioling. 8, 380–407 (2004). https://doi.org/10.1111/j.1467-9841.2004.00266.x

32. Butler, A., Izadi, S., Hodges, S.: SideSight: Multi-"Touch" interaction around small devices. In: Proceedings of the 21st Annual ACM Symposium on User Interface Software and Technology, pp. 201–204. ACM, New York, NY, USA (2008). https://doi.org/10.1145/1449715.1449746

33. Kratz, S., Rohs, M.: Hoverflow: Exploring around-device interaction with ir distance sensors. In: Proceedings of the 11th International Conference on Human-Computer Interaction with Mobile Devices and Services, pp. 42:1–42:4. ACM, New York, NY, USA (2009). https://doi.org/10.1145/1613858.1613912

34. Müller, J., Bailly, G., Bossuyt, T., Hillgren, N.: MirrorTouch: combining touch and mid-air gestures for public displays. In: Proceedings of the 16th International Conference on Human-Computer Interaction with Mobile Devices & Services, pp. 319–328. ACM, New York, NY, USA (2014). https://doi.org/10.1145/2628363.2628379

35. Walter, R., Bailly, G., Müller, J.: StrikeAPose: revealing mid-air gestures on public displays. In: Proceedings of the SIGCHI Conference on Human Factors in Computing Systems, pp. 841–850. ACM, New York, NY, USA (2013). https://doi.org/10.1145/2470654.2470774

36. Oviatt, S., Coulston, R., Lunsford, R.: When do we interact multimodally?: Cognitive load and multimodal communication patterns. In: Proceedings of the 6th International Conference on Multimodal Interfaces, pp. 129–136. ACM, New York, NY, USA (2004). https://doi.org/10.1145/1027933.1027957

37. Voida, S., Podlaseck, M., Kjeldsen, R., Pinhanez, C.: A study on the manipulation of 2D objects in a projector/camera-based augmented reality environment. In: Proceedings of the SIGCHI Conference on Human Factors in Computing Systems, pp. 611–620. ACM, New York, NY, USA (2005). https://doi.org/10.1145/1054972.1055056

38. Grandhi, S.A., Joue, G., Mittelberg, I.: Understanding naturalness and intuitiveness in gesture production: insights for touchless gestural interfaces. In: Proceedings of the SIGCHI Conference on Human Factors in Computing Systems, pp. 821–824. ACM, New York, NY, USA (2011). https://doi.org/10.1145/1978942.1979061

39. Sowa, T., Wachsmuth, I.: Interpretation of Shape-related Iconic Gestures in Virtual Environments. In: Wachsmuth, I., Sowa, T. (eds.) GW 2001. LNCS (LNAI), vol. 2298, pp. 21–33. Springer, Heidelberg (2002). https://doi.org/10.1007/3-540-47873-6_3

40. Epps, J., Oviatt, S., Chen, F.: Integration of speech and gesture inputs during multimodal interaction. In: Proceedings of the Australian Conference on Human-Computer Interaction (2004)

41. Pfeiffer, T.: Interaction between Speech and Gesture: Strategies for Pointing to Distant Objects. In: Efthimiou, E., Kouroupetroglou, G., Fotinea, S.-E. (eds.) GW 2011. LNCS (LNAI), vol. 7206, pp. 238–249. Springer, Heidelberg (2012). https://doi.org/10.1007/978-3-642-34182-3_22

42. Quek, F., et al.: Multimodal human discourse: gesture and speech. ACM Trans. Comput-Hum Interact 9(3), 171–193 (2002). https://doi.org/10.1145/568513.568514

43. Ruiz, N., Taib, R., Chen, F.: Examining the redundancy of multimodal input. In: Proceedings of the 18th Australia Conference on Computer-Human Interaction: Design: Activities, Artefacts and Environments, pp. 389–392. ACM, New York, NY, USA (2006). https://doi.org/10.1145/1228175.1228254

44. Bekker, M.M., Olson, J.S., Olson, G.M.: Analysis of gestures in face-to-face design teams provides guidance for how to use groupware in design. In: Proceedings of the 1st Conference on Designing Interactive Systems: Processes, Practices, Methods, & Techniques, pp. 157–166. ACM, New York, NY, USA (1995). https://doi.org/10.1145/225434.225452

45. Isaacs, E.A., Tang, J.C.: What video can and can't do for collaboration: a case study. In: Proceedings of the First ACM International Conference on Multimedia, pp. 199–206. ACM, New York, NY, USA (1993). https://doi.org/10.1145/166266.166289

46. Fussell, S.R., Setlock, L.D., Kraut, R.E.: Effects of head-mounted and scene-oriented video systems on remote collaboration on physical tasks. In: Proceedings of the SIGCHI Conference on Human Factors in Computing Systems, pp. 513–520. ACM, New York, NY, USA (2003). https://doi.org/10.1145/642611.642701

47. Kinect for Xbox One|Xbox, https://www.xbox.com/en-US/accessories/kinect. Accessed 19 Sep 2017

48. Wang, I., et al.: EGGNOG: a continuous, multi-modal data set of naturally occurring gestures with ground truth labels. In: 2017 12th IEEE International Conference on Automatic Face Gesture Recognition (FG 2017), pp. 414–421 (2017). https://doi.org/10.1109/FG.2017.145

49. Watson Speech to Text, https://www.ibm.com/watson/services/speech-to-text/. Accessed 16 Sep 2017

50. Speech API – Speech Recognition, https://cloud.google.com/speech/. Accessed 18 Sep 2017

51. Goldin-Meadow, S.: The two faces of gesture: language and thought. Gesture **5**, 241–257 (2005). https://doi.org/10.1075/gest.5.1.16gol
52. Schober, M.F.: Spatial perspective-taking in conversation. Cognition **47**, 1–24 (1993). https://doi.org/10.1016/0010-0277(93)90060-9
53. Whittaker, S.: Things to talk about when talking about things. Hum. Comput. Interact. **18**, 149–170 (2003). https://doi.org/10.1207/S15327051HCI1812_6
54. Kraut, R.E., Fussell, S.R., Siegel, J.: Visual information as a conversational resource in collaborative physical tasks. Hum. Comput. Interact. **18**, 13–49 (2003). https://doi.org/10.1207/S15327051HCI1812_2

Human-Robot Interaction

Analysing Action and Intention Recognition in Human-Robot Interaction with ANEMONE

Beatrice Alenljung(✉) ⓘ and Jessica Lindblom ⓘ

University of Skövde, Skövde, Sweden
`beatrice.alenljung@his.se`

Abstract. The ANEMONE is a methodological approach for user experience (UX) evaluation of action and intention recognition in human-robot interaction that has activity theory as its theoretical lens in combination with the seven stages of action model and UX evaluation methodology. ANEMONE has been applied in a case where a prototype has been evaluated. The prototype was a workstation in assembly in manufacturing consisting of a collaborative robot, a pallet, a tablet, and a workbench, where one operator is working in the same physical space as one robot. The purpose of this paper is to provide guidance on how to use ANEMONE, with a particular focus on the data analysis part, through describing a real example together with lessons learned and recommendations.

Keywords: Human-Robot Interaction · Human-Robot Collaboration · User-centered · Evaluation · Action Recognition · Intention Recognition · Activity Theory · Seven Stages of Action Model · User Experience (UX)

1 Introduction

The user experience (UX) evaluation framework denoted ANEMONE provides a methodological approach for action and intention recognition in human-robot interaction (HRI) that guides how to measure, assess, and evaluate this issue in several ways [1]. In this paper, we present how the planning and analysis phases can be carried out in more details, which are exemplified from a case in a larger research project on human-robot collaboration in industry.

Robots have been part of our world for decades but mostly placed in specialised safety zones in automated industrial settings. Now they are entering all kinds of areas with a variety of purposes [2], for example, rescuing robots in emergency areas [3], robots as actors in theatre [4], assisting robots in retail [5], and robots used in therapy for children in the autism spectrum [6]. When robots become part of the human world the need for smooth and pleasant human-robot interaction increases [7–9].

An important aspect to enable interaction and coexistence of humans and robots that are situated in the same physical and social context to be positively experienced by humans is the possibility for them to mutually recognise the actions and intentions of each other [1, 10, 11]. From a human perspective it is important to perceive that the

© Springer Nature Switzerland AG 2021
M. Kurosu (Ed.): HCII 2021, LNCS 12763, pp. 181–200, 2021.
https://doi.org/10.1007/978-3-030-78465-2_14

robot is about to do something, correctly interpret it and understand how to act upon its actions, which facilitates the human to experience predictability and comfort [1].

Designing for high-quality action and intention recognition in HRI is not an easy endeavour. Like UX design in general an iterative process is needed where systematic UX evaluations are conducted. The focal point of ANEMONE is on how to distinguish the likelihood for humans to perceive, understand, and predict the intentions and actions of a robot, as well as assist in understanding why something works or not in the interaction between human and robot [1].

Although ANEMONE provides guidance on how to carry out a UX evaluation from planning to organisation of identified problems more details are needed to support an inexperienced evaluator, not least regarding how to apply the theoretical lenses of activity theory and seven stages of action model when analysing the collected data. More concrete recommendations are needed to increase the usefulness of ANEMONE [1]. Furthermore, ANEMONE has not yet been systematically tested in practice [1]. The aim of this paper is to contribute to the testing of ANEMONE in practice and the development of clear-cut guidance. More specifically, the purpose is to assist evaluators in how to use ANEMONE, with a focus on the data analysis stage, by demonstrating an application of ANEMONE in a real case and identify challenges and how to deal with them.

The paper is organised as follows. An introduction of ANEMONE and its theoretical foundations is presented in Sect. 2. Thereafter, in Sect. 3, the practical application of ANEMONE is described phase by phase. Section 4 consists of lessons learned and recommendations. The paper ends with some concluding remarks in Sect. 5.

2   ANEMONE

The theoretical and methodological foundations of ANEMONE are activity theory [12–15] the seven stages of action model [16, 17], and UX evaluation methodology [18–22]. Activity theory is here used as a lens, similar to a pair of dark glasses that when you put them on tint the world in a way that brings some objects into sharper contrast, while it makes others fade away [23]. We here briefly present some core aspects of activity theory that are applied in this paper, without providing the bigger picture.

It is acknowledged that activity theory has since the mid-1990s been widely and successfully applied in human-technology interaction, and it is stressed in ANEMONE that activity theory is a promising theoretical foundation also for HRI research. Activity theory enables the framing of HRI within a meaningful context, providing opportunities to better grasp the mutual ways robots affect – and are affected by – individuals and groups, as well as elucidating the underlying meaning of robot usage [1, 24]. Law and Sun [25] view activity theory as specifically promising to shed light onto the understanding of UX by considering the users' motives and needs that are in turn shaped by the socio-cultural context in which the users are situated within.

A central principle in activity theory is the hierarchical structure of activity that organises an activity into three levels: activity, action, and operation, which are related to motive, goal, and condition [24]. The top-level is the activity itself that is carried out to fulfil a motive. The middle level action is described as conscious processes subordinated to the activity. Actions correspond to what must be done and are directed at specific goals, which could be decomposed into sub-goals, sub-sub-goals etc., meaning that multiple actions and operations may be nested to fulfil the activity. The bottom level refers to operations and these function as lower-level units of actions. As such, they do not have their own goals but are rather a result of prior actions that have been transformed into automated operation [24]. While actions are about what must be done, operations concern how it can be done and are usually routine parts of an action and one that has been trained to such a level that it no longer requires the subject's attention. Operations are oriented toward the conditions under which the user is trying to reach a certain goal, and are commonly subconscious to the user.

Another principle is tool mediation, which is the core of Russian cultural-historical psychology, having roots in Vygotsky's [15] seminal work. The tool concept is broadly applied, and it embraces both material, physical tools (e.g., hammer, computer, phone, screws, ruler, tablet, screwdriver) and psychological tools (e.g., signs, symbols, language), shaping the ways users interact with the world. Putting tool mediation in the broader social context implies that mediation enables various forms of acting in the world. It should be stressed that a robot is typically not an object of activity but rather the main mediating artefact/tool. Instead, the object of activity is the actual setting and meaningful context in which the robot is used, e.g., manufacturing site. This means that humans per se are not interacting with robots, but interact with the world through them.

Internalisation-externalisation is also a central principle in activity theory that stresses that human activity has a double nature, because every activity has both an external and internal side. Hence, the internalisation-externalisation principle is characterised by the ongoing shifting back and forth between what happens internally "in the head" and what happens practically and externally "in the open" in human activity. It should be acknowledged that internal and external sides of activity are being gradually more intertwined in human work and life from a developmental perspective.

The foundation of activity theory has been elaborated to the activity system model [12], which encompasses that the interactions between subject (user), object (context), and community (society level) are mediated by specific kinds of mediating artefact and tools/instruments for the subject-object interaction (e.g., robots, instructions, tools, and other digital artefacts,), rules (e.g., norms, safety regulations, and legislation) for the subject-community interaction, and division of labour for the community-object interaction. Furthermore, the model includes the outcome of the activity system as a whole, namely, the transformation of the object that is generated by the activity in question into a suggested outcome. This way of visualising highlights the continuous process of transformation and development over a time horizon (see Fig. 1).

To summarise, viewing human activity as a three-layer systems offers the possibility of doing a combined analysis of motivational, goal-directed, and operational aspects of human activity in the socio-cultural and material world, by interrelating the issues of "why", "what", and "how" within a coherent framework that could include the broader activity system model perspective. One of the main challenges in applying activity theory is to identify the proper level of activity. A tentative way forward to overcome this challenge is addressed in ANEMONE, where it is suggested to focus on the action level where Norman's [16, 17] seven stages of action model provides support. As pointed out in ANEMONE, Norman's seven stages of action model is aligned with an activity theory

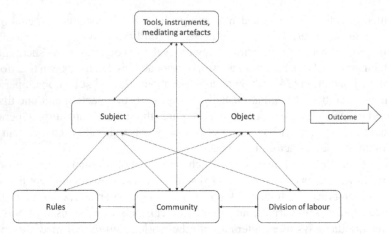

Fig. 1. The activity system model (modified from [12, p. 63]).

approach, and the arguments for our activity theory inspired view of Norman's model is the focus of actions, being aligned to the basic principles of hierarchical structuring of activity, tool mediation, and externalisation/internalisation.

ANEMONE comprises a phase-by-phase procedure, where generic UX evaluation methodology constitutes the base. Together, activity theory and the seven stages of action model provides the added focus on action and intention, where their theoretical lenses give guidance both in planning and analysis phases [1].

3   Practical Application of ANEMONE

The structure of this section follows the phases of ANEMONE in order to illustrate how it can be applied. The phases are 1) preparation, 2) selection of evaluation type, 3) plan and conduct the UX evaluation, 4) analysis of collected data and identifying UX problems, and 5) organising the identified UX problems in scope and severity.

3.1   Phase 1: Preparation

Identification of Case: Identifying the Area of Interest and Defining the Context.
The long-term purpose of the project was to introduce workstations in assembly in manufacturing where a collaborative robot and an operator are working in the same physical space as one robot. The goal of the project was to develop a demonstrator with the purpose of functioning as a test bed for these kinds of industrial workstations. The robot delivers components to the operator in the correct order and the human does the assembly according to instructions available on a closely placed tablet (see Fig. 2). There are several safety regulations that regulate the work and the workspace.

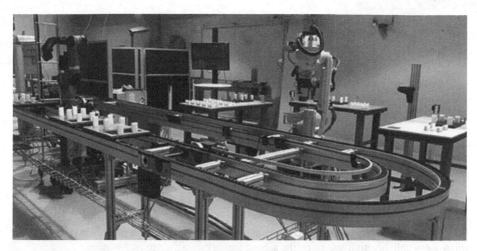

Fig. 2. The workstation prototype for human-robot collaboration (photos by the second author).

The prototype that was used in the presented study was an earlier version of the final demonstrator, which to a large extent are the same but where some improvements were made based on the results of the evaluation. Only a subset of the complete evaluation is described, since the focus in this paper is on illustrating application of ANEMONE not presenting the obtained results. A video of the demonstrator is available: http://www.symbio-tic.eu/index.php?option=com_k2&view=item&id=734:symbio-tic-final-video&Itemid=33.

Specify UX and Evaluation Goals. The long-term purpose of the collaborative robot in manufacturing assembly is to make the assembly more efficient and reduce the need for the human operator to do frequent lifting of heavy components. The end-user group are novice and experienced operators that have no previous practice of working with collaborative robots. With help of instructions on a closely based tablet the operator assembles the components the robot delivers one at a time. On the tablet, the operator marks when a step is finished and that he/she is ready for the next. The work station will be one of many on a shop floor. The shop floor environment will be noisy, and people and trucks will move around in the area. The operators will rotate among the work stations. The context of the evaluation is different from the real. The workstation prototype is located in an area dedicated for testing and is not in an actual shop floor (see Fig. 3). The evaluation context is to a large extent without surrounding disturbances.

With the long-term purpose in mind, three overall UX goals were specified:

- The interaction with the robot should be experienced by the operator as smooth in terms of effectiveness, efficiency, and flow.
- The interaction with the robot should be perceived by the operator as predictable, trustworthy, controllable and safe.
- The robot should be experienced by the operator as providing future prospects.

Fig. 3. One of the participants situated in front of the workbench at the workstation prototype for human-robot collaboration (photo by the second author).

In addition, based on the seven stages of action model the AIRatt evaluation questions was formulated as follows:

- Is it possible for the operator to **perceive the intention** of the robot to perform an action, i.e., perceive the robot's status in its context?
- Is it possible for the operator to **predict** what **sequence of actions** that will take place, i.e., interpret the robot's status in its context?
- Is it possible for the operator to **assess the robot's actions in relation to their goal**, i.e., evaluate the interpretation in relation to the goals?
- Is it possible for the operator to **determine** if any **measures** need to be taken in relation to the robot in order to reach the goal, i.e., forming an intention to act?
- Is it possible for the operator to **specify** a proper **sequence of actions** in relation to the robot, i.e., understand and determine what it is possible to do in order to reach the goal?
- Is it possible for the operator to **perform** the chosen **sequence of actions** in relation to the robot, i.e., execute the sequence of actions?

3.2   Phase 2: Selection of UX Evaluation Type

Evaluation Scope. There are three interrelated layers of user needs involved in UX evaluation: the ecological layer, the interaction layer, and the emotional layer. This evaluation covers two of them: the interaction and the emotional layers.

Characterisation of Analytical and Empirical UX Evaluation. The robot arm that is used in the evaluation is commercially available, but the current setting is a functioning prototype of a work station located in a test area. Thus, it was possible to carry out an empirical evaluation following a UX testing approach.

3.3 Plan and Conduct the UX Evaluation

Analytical UX Evaluation of Action and Intention Recognition. In this evaluation an analytical UX evaluation was not performed.

Empirical UX Evaluation of Action and Intention Recognition. The data gathering techniques used were observation documented with video recording, interview, and questionnaire according to the evaluation matrix (see Table 1) to collect quantitative and qualitative data as well as objective and subjective data.

The complete evaluation consisted of 27 participants, but only five of them are included in the analysis presented in this paper. The selection of participants were Master students and PhD students in engineering and informatics at the University of Skövde who were recruited via email by a colleague at the School of Engineering. All participants signed a consent form before the sessions started.

Before the scenario was initialised, the participants were informed about the safety issues for the prototype. All had to wear safety wests. During the interactions with the prototype, one person from the research team was allocated only to consider safety issues and could halt the robot arm by pressing a stop button.

The evaluation task was to collaboratively assemble the components of a mass balancing system (MBS), which is a component that later on is assembled on a car engine with the robot at the assembly station. The participants were given a short oral description of the task, i.e., assembling the MBS together with the robot, but no details were revealed. The idea was that the scenario, i.e., the collaboration with the robot and the instructions on the tablet, should provide enough support to complete the task. The scenario included 15 steps (see Table 2). The same task was carried out twice by each participant to reduce first-encounter effects. There were no formal training sessions.

The procedure for each session went as follows. First, the participant received only a short description of the overall aim with the evaluation as well as information about safety issues. Then the first round started in which the participant carried out the task in the scenario. After completing it, the participant filled in a modified SUS questionnaire that consisted of predefined statements. Thereafter, the second round started, in which the same task in the same scenario was performed. After completing the task, the participant filled in the same questionnaire once more, only focusing on the last session when completing the questionnaire. Next, a semi-structured post-test interview was carried out. The interview consisted of open questions regarding both rounds and focused on the participants' subjective experiences of interacting with the collaborative robot at the workstation. The interview was audio-recorded and later transcribed. In total, each session took approximately 45 min to complete for the participants. A pilot test was conducted on a colleague, in which the scenario was carried out once.

3.4 Phase 4: Analysis of Collected Data and Identifying UX Problems

Strategies for Analysis of the Collected Data and Identifying Problems. The basis for the analysis are video recordings of how the participants and the robot collaboratively carried out the tasks in the two rounds of the scenario, two sets of post session

Table 1. Evaluation matrix.

UX focal points	UX metrics	Data gathering techniques
Effectiveness	Task accomplishment	Observation
	Claims of being supported to complete the task	Interview
	Subjective rating of level of support of achievement of task	Questionnaire
Efficiency	Time to conduct task and number of errors	Observation
	Claims of perceived efficiency	Interview
	Subjective rating of complexity of robot, easy to use and cumbersome to use	Questionnaire
Flow	Number of hesitations	Observation
	Claims of flow	Interview
	Subjective rating of smoothness of collaboration	Questionnaire
Predictability	Number of activity in advance/in line with/reactive	Observation
	Claims of predictability	Interview
	Subjective rating of easy to learn for others, possibility to understand the robot's intentions, and predictability of the robot's actions	Questionnaire
Trustworthiness	Claims of trustworthiness	Interview
Perceived safety	Claims of perceived safety	Interview
	Subjective rating of danger to collaborate with the robot and risk for collision with robot	Questionnaire
Perceived control	Claims of perceived control	Interview
	Subjective rating of confidence in using the robot	Questionnaire
Providing future prospects	Claims of positive attitude	Interview
	Subjective rating of believe to like to use the robot frequently	Questionnaire

subjective ratings of UX- as well as action and intention-specific aspects and post-test interview transcripts regarding their experience of interacting with the robot and carrying out the tasks and their views on perceiving the robots actions and intentions.

Table 2. The steps carried out in the scenario.

Step	Who	Content
1	Robot	The robot picks up the MBS bottom from the pallet and puts it down on the workbench
2	Robot	After putting it down, the robot withdraws and stands still for a short while
3	Human	The human examines the surface of MBS bottom
4	Robot	The robot moves towards the pallet and picks up the MBS top
5	Robot	The robot moves toward the workbench, then stops and holds the MBS top in front of the human
6	Human	The human examines the surface of the MBS top
7	Robot	The robot puts the MBS top on the workbench
8	Robot	Then the robot moves and picks up the first rod at the workbench
9	Robot	The robot puts the first rod in the MBS bottom and then withdraws to a still position
10	Human	The human takes the second rod from the workbench and puts it into the MBS bottom
11	Human	The human checks that the rods are aligned
12	Human	The human takes the MBS top from the workbench and puts it on the MBS bottom
13	Human	The human identifies and puts screws into 6 of 12 holes in the MBS top
14	Human	The human tightens the 6 screws with the screwdriver and then commands the robot to pick up the MBS via the tablet
15	Robot	The robot grasps the assembled MBS, and then puts it back on the pallet

The analysis of the UX part was carried out as follows. The video-recordings were watched several times to state if the task was completed or not, time how long the human was in an active state, count errors, identify occurrences of hesitations, and to count the number of times the participants acted in advance, in line with or acted reactively. The mean values of the participants' ratings of statements were calculated and assessed as either positive or negative in relation to the UX focal points. The interview transcripts were coded with UX focal points, i.e., the quotes with relevant content were marked as belonging to one or more UX focal points. All quotes for a UX focal point were then grouped for deepened analysis in which the claims for each participant were assessed as positive, negative or unclear. An interpretation of the meaning of the claims was also made. After that the results for each UX focal point were triangulated in order to state their conditions. Below, the triangulated results for each UX focal point is described and the results are compared to the specified overall UX goals.

Effectiveness. All participants were able to complete the scenarios in both rounds. The mean value of the rating five-graded Likert scale 1 strongly disagree – 5 strongly agree (which was the same for all questionnaire statements) of the statement *"I felt that the robot provided a good level of support to me to enable a successful achievement of the collaborative tasks"* were 4.2 after the first round and 4.4 after the second round. Thus, both the observational and questionnaire data strongly support a claim of high effectiveness of the prototype. However, the interview data paints another picture. Three of the participants said that they did not find the robot supportive, mainly because the process was sequential and that the robot was working separate from them. One experienced the robot to be supportive and one found it difficult to answer if the robot was supportive or not. It is therefore not possible to make a strong claim regarding the effectiveness. There seems to be good potential of achieving high effectiveness, but more work on the prototype is needed.

Efficiency. The time it took to conduct the scenarios differed between the first and the second round. The mean time of the human part of the first scenario was 02:42 min and the second was 01:43. Thus, the mean improvement time was 00:59 min. The robot part had a constant time of 03:14 min. Two participants made one error each in the first round and no errors were made in the second round. The mean values of the rating of the efficiency-related statements are as follows: *"I found the robot unnecessarily complex."* were 2.2 after the first round and 2.4 after the second round, *"I thought the robot was easy to use."* were 4.4 after the first round and 5 after the second, and *"I found the robot very cumbersome to use."* were 2 after the first and 1.2 after the second round. Taken together this claims that the prototype is sufficiently efficient. However, the interviews show something else. Four participants had a negative experience finding the robot very slow and the work situation therefore got boring. However, they said that the low speed was understandable from a safety and test perspective, but not long-term viable. One participant had a positive experience saying it was very smooth and time efficient. In sum, the current efficiency from a UX perspective is questionable, although there are indications of possibility to improve in terms of the human being able to conduct the task more swiftly and correctly since reduced time spent and errors made when being more experienced. Nonetheless, the robot speed is a problem from a UX efficiency point of view.

Flow. There were hesitations observed among three participants in the first round, where one hesitated five times and two participants hesitated one time each. No hesitations were observed in the second round. Those who did not hesitate showed some surprise when the robot did not start directly in the last step. The mean value of the ratings of the statement *"I felt that the collaboration with the robot unfolded smoothly."* were 3.8 after the first round and 3.6 after the second. Three participants thought it was too much waiting for the robot to do its part. There were also some delays on the robot's side when the participants interacted with it, which negatively impacted the flow. The movements of the robot were sometimes jerky. One participant emphasised that the interaction on the whole was very smooth, although sometimes a bit slow. One participant was uncertain. This person found the flow to be good, but at the same time mentioned it to be too slow and too much waiting. Taken together, it can be interpreted that the flow is weak and needs to be improved.

Predictability. The activities of four participants were observed to constantly be in line with the scenario in both rounds. The activities of one participant were reactive in the whole first round. In the second round, the activities of one participant were in advance of scenario at one occasion and in line with in the rest. The mean value of the ratings of the predictability-related UX statements are: *"I would imagine that most people would learn to use this robot very quickly."* were 4.8 after the first round and 5.0 after the second one, *"I felt that I could understand the robot's intentions."* were 4.0 after the first and 4.6 after the second round, and *"I felt that the robot's actions were predictable."* were 3.2 after the first round and 4 after the second one. According to the observations and the subjective ratings the predictability can be considered high. However, the interview claims were reversed. There were three participants that talked about predictability and they experienced that it was difficult to understand what the robot was going to do next or if it had finished its operations. The lack of predictability had a negative impact on trust and perceived safety. Furthermore, the participants sometimes found it unclear if they had finished their own actions. Thus, there is room for improvement with respect to predictability.

Trustworthiness. Four participants perceived that the robot was fairly trustworthy, since it was slow and that the movements were relatively controlled and predictable. According to the participants, the trust would have been larger if the robot had been more predictable. One participant perceived a low level of trust because of the unpredictability of the robot's next steps. The available data says that the robot is trustworthy. However, there is no observational and questionnaire data regarding this UX focal point and, hence, triangulation is not possible. This claim is therefore weak and needs to be studied more.

Perceived Safety. The mean value of the ratings of the statements related to perceived safety are as follows: *"I felt it was dangerous to collaborate with the robot."* were 2 after the first round and 1.4 after the second, and *"I felt that the risk for collision with the robot was minimal."* were 3.6 after the first round and 4.2 after the second. Three participants perceived that they were safe, since they were standing at a distance from the robot and not in its working area and that the robot moved slowly. Although, stating perceived safety some participants admitted that some insecurity was lurking. One participant reported feeling unsafe, although not exposed to danger. This person said it was because of not knowing where to be positioned in relation to the robot so that it would not come too close. One participant spoke in an ambiguous way of perceived safety. The person said that he/she adjusted his/her behaviour but did not feel to be in danger. This implies that the participants perceive to be safe but that the feeling is not strong and risk to change into perceived unsafety. Since this perceived safety is vital, not least in an industrial setting, this has to be improved.

Perceived Control. The mean value of the ratings of the statement *"I felt very confident using the robot."* were 3.8 after the first round and 4.8 after the second. In the interviews two participants said that they perceived to be in control, since they had the tablet to direct and sign the robot. Three participants perceived to be a "passenger" and the robot to be the "driver", and, thus, did not feel to be in control. The data points in different directions, some participants perceived to be in control and others not. Thus, perceived control is not sufficient, although not critical.

Providing Future Prospects. The mean value of the statement *"I think that I would like to use this robot frequently."* were 4.4 after the first round and 4.8 after the second. All participants were positive to this kind of robot and workstation, believing that it provides future prospects from an ergonomic and productive perspective. Thus, there are strong claims that the prototype provides future prospects.

UX Goals. For all but one UX focal point it is apparent that the quantitative data from observations and the questionnaires are more positive, in terms of successfully addressing the UX focal points, compared to the qualitative data from the interviews that are more negative. Thus, the first two specified UX goals are not to a satisfying extent reached, i.e., *"The interaction with the robot should be experienced by the operator as smooth in terms of effectiveness, efficiency, and flow."* and *"The interaction with the robot should be perceived by the operator as predictable, trustworthy, controllable and safe."* The third goal is achieved, i.e., *"The robot should be experienced by the operator as providing future prospects."*

Analysis and Problem Identification of Action and Intention Recognition.
The first part of the evaluation revealed that there are, from a UX-centred perspective, issues in the HRI that need to be improved before this kind of workstation can be successfully implemented in an industrial production line. The next step was to identify the critical occasions and do an in-depth analysis of them.

The first-hand observations as well as the video recordings of the ten sessions revealed that there are two critical occasions that have a negative impact on the action and intention recognition between the human and the robot. These occasions happened mostly in the transition between steps 9–10 as well as between steps 14–15 primarily during the first encounter (see Table 2). A micro-analysis was made of these two critical occasions. Below, first an example of micro-analysis is presented, second a description of the first critical occasion is provided, and third the second critical occasion is depicted.

Example of Micro-Analysis. There is not enough space in the paper to fully describe the micro-level analysis of the two occasions. Instead, a segment of the analysis of one of the occasions for one of the participants is chosen as an illustration.

The overall goal in the scenario is to complete the joint assembly task and the sub goal of the segment is to assemble rod two on the MBS bottom. The action to take place in order to complete the segment sub goal is the turn-taking when the operator is to switch from non-active to active, thus, taking over from the robot. The segment unfolds during about five seconds and is analysed with help of the AIRatt evaluation questions (see Table 3).

To illustrate the micro-analysis, a frame-by-frame visualisation is depicted in Fig. 4. The visualisation reveals that the participant is struggling to perceive the robot's intention and predict the sequence of actions in order to assess the robot's action (standing still) in relation to the goal, by reading the frames from the upper left to the bottom right. As it becomes apparent in the last two frames in the bottom row, he finally grasps that it is his turn to continue the assembly of the MBS, when taking a step forward, guided by the instructions on the tablet, and then grasping the second rod.

Table 3. Analysis of segment in critical occasion with AIRatt evaluation questions.

AIRatt evaluation questions	Analysis	Problem spot
Perceive the intention	The robot is empty and is moving away from the operator after leaving rod one on the MBS bottom. The gaze of the operator is focused on the robot and he perceives what is happening	No
Predict sequence of actions	The gaze of the operator begins to flatten between the robot, the belt, the screen and the workbench. He does not seem to be able to interpret what the robot's sequence of actions means and what comes next	Yes
Assess the robot's actions in relation to their goal	The operator can state from the situation as a whole that the goal has not been reached, but cannot assess what the next step is	Yes
Determine measures	At first, the operator cannot decide what is expected of either himself or the robot, which is evident from both the fact that the gaze flutters and that the bodily movement pattern when the torso rocks. Then this is changed by clues in the context, which is evident from the operator taking a step towards the workbench	Yes
Specify proper sequence of actions	Yes, it is possible through instructions from the screen	No
Perform sequence of actions	The operator performs the next step	No

Although this sequence depicted above only lasted about five seconds, it was apparent that the task-switching between the robot and the human was not that intuitive or fluent. I should be acknowledged that the above findings are from the first round. In the second round, the participant effortlessly could perceive when it was his turn to continue the assembly by putting the second rod into the MSB bottom. Hence, the robot's action is then predictable.

First Occasion. The first occasion (steps 9–10) is when the task-allocation should shift from the robot to the human regarding the placing of the rods in the MBS bottom. The robot places the first rod in the MBS bottom and then the human is supposed to take the second rod and place it correctly aligned with the first rod in the MBS bottom. It was revealed that this change in task-allocation is not that obvious for the humans to grasp, especially not when the robot has conducted several steps by itself for a rather long period of time and then stands still in front of them. The participants seemed puzzled

Fig. 4. The frame-by-frame analysis that illustrates how the participant struggles to perceive the robot's intention before he realises that it is his turn to continue the assembly of the MBS (the frames should be read from top left to right, middle left to right, and bottom left to right).

that the robot continued to stand still, and some of them looked hesitant about what should happen next or what were expected from them. Several of them were patient for a short period of time, but when the robot did not start to move, they begun to look around for some contextual cues, looking back and forth between the robot, the workstation, the pallet, and the tablet. Some of them rather soon understood that the tablet provided some instructions that informed them that it was their turn to put the second rod in the MBS bottom. During the second round less hesitations occurred, although the participants did not know in beforehand that they should perform the same scenario twice, i.e., they could not expect that the robot should behave exactly the same during the second round. The participants almost immediately looked at the tablet, and did not show any problems to grasp that it was their turn and what to do.

Second Occasion. The second occasion is at the end of the scenario (steps 14–15). The human has performed several steps of manual assembly of placing and tightening screws to connect the MBS top and bottom. When this task is finished the human commands the robot via the tablet to pick up the assembled MBS to put it on the pallet. It was revealed that the human did not have any problems grasping that they should use the tablet to make the command. The between the human and the robot occurred when the robot continued to be standing still, although the command was correctly given. The participants seemed puzzled and looked back and forth between the robot and the tablet, trying to figure out why the robot did not start to move. The robot was delayed by four seconds before making a pushing sound and then started to move. In this particular situation four seconds are experienced as a rather long delay, and resulted in an "interruption" of the interaction flow. To conclude, these two identified turn-takings happened in both situations when there was a major shift in task-allocation between human and robot.

3.5   Phase 5: Organising the Identified UX Problems in Scope and Severity

The analysis with the help of the AIRatt evaluation questions shows that in spite of the robot's actions being clearly perceivable they are not obvious to read in a way that makes them predictable and assessable. This also makes it more difficult for the operator to determine what measures that need to be taken. The reasons behind these problems are the robot's somewhat jerky movements and movement delays. The scope of problems are global in the sense that if these aspects of the robot's movements are not resolved there is a risk that it will be implemented in other similar workstations. The severity of the problem is low both since the operator fairly quickly gets a grip of the situation and can successfully complete the task and since this is mostly a first-time encounter issue that will shortly disappear.

A problem that is global and of high severity is the robot's slow motions. This causes long non-active periods for the operator that in the long-term risk to be a working environment problem. Having operators standing passively beside a robot and just waiting for it to finish its parts run the risk of being an unsustainable working condition.

Putting on the activity theory lens, there are several aspects that can be highlighted. As pointed out by Halverson [23], the concepts used in activity theory provide a structure for guiding the analysis as well as describing and explaining the identified problems. First, the tool mediating principle pays attention to the robot as the *main mediating artefact*, although the tablet serves as another central *mediating tool*. It appears that the relationship between these tool mediating artefacts is not totally obvious for the participants, i.e., in what order to use them to grasp that it is his/her turn to act.

Closely related to the tool mediation principle is the *externalisation-internalisation principle*, which here is manifested in the ongoing internal interpretation of the external cues provided from the robot's actions and the instructions presented on the tablet. When the experienced gap between the external and internal sides becomes more aligned, he/she understands what to do. This principle highlights the possibility to go beyond the 'bounds of the brain' to explain the overall activity, making it a bit easier to study what happens on a fly 'here and now' instead of only trying to mind-read what the participant might be perceiving. This broadened unit of analysis could then be mapped into an activity system model, in which the theoretical concepts are applied to the actual case (see Fig. 5), including the participant (subject), the object (accomplishment of the action in the workstation), tools (the robot and the tablet), community (the team members), rules (norms, safety regulations, and work practices), division of labour (task-allocation and turn-taking), and outcome (e.g., positive and/or negative UX).

The activity system model could then be used to highlight where the minor interaction 'breakdown' occurred, visualised with a red cross in the figure, that the cause for the critical occasion was a contradiction about the division of labour between the human and the robot that affects other parts in the model via its interconnected relations. The minor breakdown could also be further analysed via the hierarchical structure of activity where several of the now present actions will be transformed to operations through prolonged

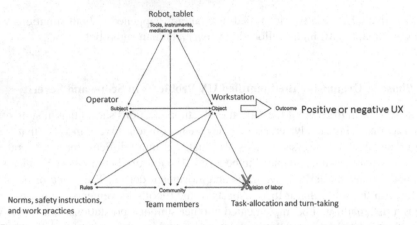

Fig. 5. The above activity system model is a visualisation of the minor breakdown for the task-allocation that affects other parts of the activity system.

assembly practice. Some initial signs of this transformation was identified between the first and second rounds of the assembly scenario when the fluency of interaction was improved, implying that less conscious effort was needed to engage in the particular actions when becoming more used to them.

4   Lessons Learned and Recommendations

There are a number of lessons learned and recommendations regarding data analysis in an ANEMONE-driven evaluation. However, first we want to emphasise the importance of **collecting different kinds of data** and **use multiple data collections techniques**. This means that both subjective and objective data as well as quantitative and qualitative data are necessary, which should be collected with observations, interviews, and questionnaires. The significance of this was apparent in the analysis of UX focal points since the different data sets pointed in separate directions. If only one source had been used, then the results would have been askew. Related to data collection we also want to stress that the **observations need to be recorded**. It is very hard to do a run-time analysis and take notes that are detailed enough.

It is beneficial to **begin by analysing the UX focal point data**, before doing the action and intention recognition analysis. The UX focal point analysis provides an overall understanding from the user's perspective, which guides what needs to be focused on in the next analysis. The AIR analysis is partly conducted on a micro level, and it is most likely not necessary to do a second-by-second analysis on all recorded material.

To use the seven stages of action for analysis may beforehand seem to be straightforward since it is described in an uncomplicated manner. However, to become skilled in doing analysis with **seven stages of action requires practice**. A challenge is to identify the meaningful sequences of actions and define the proper level of analysis. A sign that the significant sequence and suitable level have not been found is when a problem does not reveal itself and cannot be understood. Then you can **change the level of granularity** or **expand the sequence**.

In the seven stages of action, the goal is important since both the user's execution and evaluation of action is put in relation to it. Defining the goal, though, is not always obvious because there are most often multiple goals at work simultaneously, such as in terms of perspective, time frame, and abstraction level. It can be constructive to **think in terms of headline goal and sub goals** to be able to state a goal that is relevant and functioning for the sequences that are to be analysed.

Furthermore, there can be a risk that a "turn" in the seven stages of action is mistaken to be a sequence of actions. **To analyse a sequence of actions several turns is needed**, as a turn is an action (although its granularity can differ). A number of turns forms together a sequence of actions.

Activity theory provides a vocabulary that makes it possible to map the data to central concepts and principles. These principles provide more theoretical explanations for the underlying behavioural patterns of the analysed data. Although the central concepts at a first glance seems rather trivial, there are some risks of confusion between some of the central concepts, such as 'object' and 'mediating artefact'. **The robot should not be denoted as the object, given that the robot is the main mediating artefact.** The concept 'object' denotes the meaningful context in which the activity occurs.

Moreover, the activity theory concept 'outcome' depends on the perspective taken, but in the ANEMONE context, **the outcome is the resulting positive or negative UX when accomplishing the activity** (being based on the hierarchical structure of activity). Once this initial step is done, these central concepts form a unit of analysis, in which the relations between these central concepts are organised. Activity theory thus makes it possible to focus on the relations between the central concepts.

The activity system model makes the relations between the central concepts even more salient through its visualisation. It should be mentioned that **the activity as such is not denoted in the activity system model visualisation, so it could easily be neglected**. UX problems often occur when these relations are not well-aligned, e.g., there can be a workaround or a breakdown between two or more concepts in the activity system model. The severity and scope of these workarounds or breakdowns has an impact on the UX. Hence, activity theory can function as a diagnostic tool to identify alterations in UX that have roots in 'breakdowns' in the action and intention recognition. Breakdowns can also be identified in the seven stage of action model, but activity theory sheds light over why they occur from a more systematic and broader perspective. In other words, **activity theory, and particularly the activity system model, can be applied to clarify the root causes** and not only the symptoms of the experienced unpredictability of action and intention recognition while interacting with the robot.

Moreover, activity theory can also support the categorisation of the severity of UX problems from minor ('confused but can continue the task rather smoothly') and moderate ('there are occasional stops in the assembly with longer delays but the task is completed'), to severe ('the interaction breaks down and the assembly is not completed'). UX problems are often complex and can be nested, and the **hierarchical structure of activity enables a closer and more detailed analysis to unwind nested action and intention recognition-based UX problems** in HRI.

UX is complex in its nature, whether or not it is UX per se that is studied, all so called smooth or fluent robot usage has an implicit and associated UX. This implies that it is hard and even **inappropriate to study the UX of action and intention recognition in HRI without taking the usage context into account**. Hence, activity theory provides a meaningful context for studying UX in HRI within an activity. Finally, the UX is dynamic and unfolds over a time horizon where negotiations between the human and the robot are taking place, in which the **breakdowns could be viewed as contradictions that function as the driving force for development and learning**.

5   Concluding Remarks

In this paper, we illustrate how the methodological approach ANEMONE [1] can be applied, where a particular attention is paid to the data analysis part. The purpose of ANEMONE is to guide UX evaluation of action and intention recognition in HRI. Its foundations are activity theory [12–15] as its theoretical lens, seven stages of action [16, 17] and UX evaluation methodology [18–22]. Guidance of how to use the methodology is provided by presenting a real example how ANEMONE can be used together with lessons learned and recommendations.

So far, we, as the creators of ANEMONE, have only used it ourselves in order to get first-hand experience and an understanding of the difficulties of using the methodology. There is future work to be done to further assist evaluators to effectively and efficiently utilise ANEMONE, such as providing more concrete empirical examples, develop elaborate guidelines, and empirically validate the methodology with evaluators. Nonetheless, the application in a real case that is described in this paper has strengthened our confidence of the relevance and usefulness of ANEMONE.

Acknowledgements. We wish to thank the participants that have contributed to our UX evaluation. We also want to thank our colleagues Wei Wang, Magnus Holm, Richard Sennington, and Bernard Schmidt who have provided assistance during data collection and configured the robot platform used in the present study. We also thank Christine Lindblom for designing Fig. 4. This work was financially supported by the Knowledge Foundation, Stockholm, under SIDUS grant agreement no. 20140220 (AIR, action and intention recognition in human interaction with autonomous systems) as well as the European Commission under the Horizon 2020 Programme under grant agreement no. 637107 (SYMBIO-TIC).

References

1. Lindblom, J., Alenljung, B.: The ANEMONE: theoretical foundations for UX evaluation of action and intention recognition in human-robot interaction. Sensors **20**, 4284 (2020). https://doi.org/10.3390/s20154284
2. Nouwen, R., van Rooij, R., Sauerland, U., Schmitz, H.-C.: Introduction. In: Nouwen, R., van Rooij, R., Sauerland, U., Schmitz, H.-C. (eds.) VIC 2009. LNCS, vol. 6517, pp. 1–12. Springer, Heidelberg (2011). https://doi.org/10.1007/978-3-642-18446-8_1
3. Kulichenko, A.D., Polovko, S.A., Yu Smirnova, E., Shubin, P.K., Ulanov, V.N.: Ontology for group of rescuing robots. In: IOP Conference Series: Earth and Environmental Science 539, 012121 (2020). https://doi.org/10.1088/1755-1315/539/1/012121

4. Lytridis C., et al.: Social robots as cyber-physical actors in entertainment and education. In: International Conference on Software, Telecommunications and Computer Networks (Soft-COM), Split, Croatia, pp. 1–6. IEEE (2019). https://doi.org/10.23919/SOFTCOM.2019.890 3630
5. Mankodiya, K., Gandhi, R., Narasimhan, P.: Challenges and Opportunities for Embedded Computing in Retail Environments. In: Martins, F., Lopes, L., Paulino, H. (eds.) S-CUBE 2012. LNICSSITE, vol. 102, pp. 121–136. Springer, Heidelberg (2012). https://doi.org/10.1007/978-3-642-32778-0_10
6. Esteban, P.G., et al.: How to build a supervised autonomous system for robot-enhanced therapy for children with autism spectrum disorder. Paladyn J. Behav. Robot. **8**, 18–38 (2017). https://doi.org/10.1515/pjbr-2017-0002
7. Boden, M., et al.: Principles of robotics: regulating robots in the real world. Connect. Sci. **29**, 124–129 (2017). https://doi.org/10.1080/09540091.2016.1271400
8. Chen, M., Nikolaidis, S., Soh, H., Hsu, D., Srinivasa, S.: Trust-aware decision making for human-robot collaboration: model learning and planning. ACM Trans. Hum.-Robot Interact. **9**, 9 (2020). https://doi.org/10.1145/3359616
9. Kahn, P.H., Jr., et al.: What is a human? Toward psychological benchmarks in the field of human–robot interaction. Interact. Stud. **8**, 363–390 (2007). https://doi.org/10.1075/is.8.3.04kah
10. Stephanidis, C., et al.: Seven HCI grand challenges. Int. J. Hum.-Computer Interact. **35**, 1229–1269 (2019). https://doi.org/10.1080/10447318.2019.1619259
11. Vernon, D., Thill, S., Ziemke, T.: The Role of Intention in Cognitive Robotics. In: Esposito, A., Jain, L.C. (eds.) Toward Robotic Socially Believable Behaving Systems - Volume I. ISRL, vol. 105, pp. 15–27. Springer, Cham (2016). https://doi.org/10.1007/978-3-319-31056-5_3
12. Engeström, Y.: Learning by Expanding: An Activity-Theoretical Approach to Developmental Research, 2nd edn. Cambridge University Press, New York, NY, USA (2015)
13. Leontiev, A.N.: Activity, Consciousness, and Personality. Prentice-Hall, Englewood Cliffs, NJ, USA (1978)
14. Leontiev, A.N.: The problem of activity in psychology. In: Wertsch, J.V. (ed.) The Concept of Activity in Soviet Psychology, pp. 37–71. M.E. Sharpe, Armonk, NY, USA (1972/1981)
15. Vygotsky, L.S.: Mind in Society: The Development of Higher Psychological Processes. Harvard University Press, Cambridge, MA, USA (1978)
16. Norman, D.: Cognitive engineering. In: Norman, D.A., Draper, S.W. (eds.) User Centred System Design, pp. 31–61. Lawrence Erlbaum, Hillsdale, NJ, USA (1986)
17. Norman, D.: The Design of Everyday Things. Basic Books, New York, NY, USA (2013)
18. Dumas, J.S., Redish, J.: A Practical Guide to Usability Testing. Ablex Publishing, Norwood, NJ, USA (1999)
19. Hartson, R., Pyla, P.: The UX Book: Agile UX Design for Quality User Experience. Morgan Kaufmann, Amsterdam, The Netherlands (2018)
20. Hassenzahl, M.: User experience and experience design. In: Soegaard, M., Dam, R.F., (eds.) The Encyclopedia of Human-Computer Interaction, 2nd edn. The Interaction Design Foundation, Aarhus, Denmark (2013). https://www.interaction-design.org/literature/book/the-encyclopedia-of-human-computerinteraction-2nd-ed/user-experience-and-experience-design
21. Lindblom, J., Alenljung, B., Billing, E.: Evaluating the User Experience of Human–Robot Interaction. In: Jost, C., et al. (eds.) Human-Robot Interaction. SSBN, vol. 12, pp. 231–256. Springer, Cham (2020). https://doi.org/10.1007/978-3-030-42307-0_9
22. Wallström, J., Lindblom, J.: Design and Development of the USUS Goals Evaluation Framework. In: Jost, C., et al. (eds.) Human-Robot Interaction. SSBN, vol. 12, pp. 177–201. Springer, Cham (2020). https://doi.org/10.1007/978-3-030-42307-0_7

23. Halverson, C.A.: Activity theory and distributed cognition: or what does CSCW need to do with theories? Comput. Support. Coop. Work **11**, 243–267 (2002). https://doi.org/10.1023/A:1015298005381

24. Kaptelinin, V.: Activity theory. In: Soegaard, M., Dam, R.F., (eds.) The Encyclopedia of Human-Computer Interaction, 2nd edn. The Interaction Design Foundation, Aarhus, Denmark (2013). https://www.interaction-design.org/literature/book/the-encyclopedia-of-human-computer-interaction-2nd-ed/user-experience-and-experience-design

25. Law, E.L.C., Sun, X.: Evaluating user experience of adaptive digital educational games with activity theory. Int. J. Hum Comput Stud. **70**, 478–497 (2012). https://doi.org/10.1016/j.ijhcs.2012.01.007

A Robot that Tells You It is Watching You with Its Eyes

Saizo Aoyagi[1,2(✉)], Yoshihiro Sejima[3], and Michiya Yamamoto[1]

[1] Faculty of Information Networking for Innovation and Design, Toyo University, Tokyo, Japan
aoyagi@kwansei.ac.jp
[2] School of Science and Technology, Kwansei Gakuin University, Nishinomiya, Japan
[3] Faculty of Informatics, Kansai University, Suita, Japan

Abstract. The eyes play important roles in human communication. In this study, a robot tells a user it is watching her/him in a shopping scenario . First, we conducted experiments to determine the parameters of the eyes on the screen of the robot . Next, we conducted a scenario experiment, assuming a shopping scene, to demonstrate the effectiveness of the eye-based interaction compared to common push-type interaction. The results showed that the robot achieved modest and casual interaction in a shopping scene.

Keywords: Eyes · Gaze · Tablet-based robot · Human-robot interaction · Social robot

1 Introduction

Today, a typical role of social robots that of is sales staff in public spaces. Researchers have focused on robots as sales staff (e.g. [1, 2]). Also, commercial robots function as sales staff in Japan. For example, a lot of Pepper of SoftBank [3] is trying to attract people to shops. A common strategy of robots is a push-type interaction. The robots actively start talking to people before people can approach them, and keep talking noisily.

Nevertheless, the push-type interaction is not always appropriate. An interaction strategy should be selected depending on the context in which a robot and a user are embedded. In Japan, *Omotenashi* is a key concept of service. It resembles hospitality, a Western concept of service. Nevertheless, *Omotenashi* places greater emphasis on modesty, casualness, and distance from customers [4]. The push-type interaction is the opposite of *Omotenashi*. More modest and casual interaction strategies of social robots can be useful in Japan.

In this study, the authors focused on the role of eyes in interactions between a user and a robot in a shopping context. It has been stated that the eye is the window of the soul; eyes play important roles in human communication. Also, some studies have reported the effectiveness of eyes as tools in robot interaction strategies. Kuratomi et al. showed that a twinkle in the eyes makes a robot attractive and affords a good impression [5]. Kawamoto et al. reported that an eye-formed robot could create novel communication [6]. In addition to, eye-based interaction is silent and easily ignored. It can be a modest

© Springer Nature Switzerland AG 2021
M. Kurosu (Ed.): HCII 2021, LNCS 12763, pp. 201–215, 2021.
https://doi.org/10.1007/978-3-030-78465-2_15

and casual interaction strategy for robots as sales staff, relative to the noisy push-type interaction.

The purpose of this study is to develop and evaluate robot that tells a user it is watching her/him with eyes in a shopping scenario. First, a concept of the eye-based interaction of social robots was proposed. Next, a method of user position estimation was developed for implementation of the eye-based interaction. Then, the eye-based interaction was completed through a parameter evaluation experiment (Experiment 1). Sizes, movements, and user's position expressions using eyes were determined through Experiment 1. Finally, the eye-based interaction was evaluated, ralative to common push-type interaction in a shopping scenario experiment (Experiment 2).

2 Related Studies

2.1 Effects of Eyes on Communication

Eyes play important roles in human communication. According to Mehrabian, visual information is responsible for about half of all human communication [7]. Abe et al. [8] showed that humans tend to pay attention to objects that look like eyes, so an illustration of eyes on a poster can reduce the number of illegally parked bicycles. Bateson et al. showed that customers paid more when there is an image of eyes at a coffee shop, compared to that there is an image of plants [9]. As the above examples show, a human generally pays attention to eyes because eyes have social meanings. In particular, Japanese people can easily read emotions from human eyes [10, 11].

2.2 Eyes of Social Robots

A social robot can have one of three typical types of eyes. The first type is physical eyes. Kismet [12] is a typical example. The second type are camera eyes or screen eyes in a physical face. Papero of NEC [13] and Pepper of Softbank [3] are examples. The third type is eyes on a screen, which includes Tapia of mji [14], unibot [15], and jibo [16]. The authors have developed KiroPi v2 through past studies [17, 18] and it has eyes of the third type. In this study, we use KiroPi v2 in the experiment, because it is easier to control the expression of the eyes on the screen.

2.3 Eyes and Human-Robot Interaction

Some studies investigated human-robot interaction with eyes. Takahashi et al. showed that eye contact between a robot and a human can be established [19]. Yonezawa et al. supported joint attention between a plush robot and a user [20]. Kojima et al. developed Keepon, wich is capable of paying joint attention to objects with babies and children [21]. These studies have focused on joint attention or eye contact with robots. This study, on the other hand, focused on the robot's role of declaring that it is watching a user.

2.4 Social Robots in Public Spaces

The uses of robots as sales staff have been investigated. Shi et al. revealed the effectiveness of robotic sales staff in comparison to humans [22]. Okada et al. developed a robot guide base on how humans guide and introduced it to a real museum [23]. Murakami et al. evaluated the effectiveness of robot gestures in a shopping center and showed that gestures could attract people [24]. Few studies have focused on eyes, and on the use of robots as sales staff.

3 Proposal of an Eye-Based Interaction

3.1 KiroPi V2

The authors have investigated embodied interaction with social robots and have developed a table-based robot KiroPi v2 [5]. A KiroPi v2 was used as a testbed for the eye-based interaction proposed in this study.

An outline and overview of KiroPi v2 are shown in Fig. 1. The hardware of KiroPi v2 is a landscape orientation tablet (iPad Air 2 of Apple) and two robotic arms with tree servo motors (HS-5034HD of Hitec) connected to it. Also, there is a front camera near the right arm that enables KiroPi v2 to capture users. Screen drawing is controlled by iOS SDK, and the servo motors are controlled by Raspberry Pi 3 Model B and Windows IoT SDK.

Size	245 x 255 x 100 mm
Weight	1592 g
Servo	HS-5045HHD x 6
Arms	SONY, KOOV x6
CPU board	Raspberry Pi 3 Model B
Screen	Apple iPad Air 2

Fig. 1. Outline of KiroPi v2

3.2 Concept

In this study, an eye-based robot's interaction strategy, telling a user it is watching her/him with eyes, was proposed. In the context of thestrategy, the robot's eyes represent users' position, including distance and angle. A traditional push-type robot actively starts talking to people and keeps talking noisily. In contrast, a robot using the proposed strategy talks relatively little and simply looks at a user to tell convey recognition of that user.

To implement this natural interaction, a KiroPi v2 was employed as a testbed; it uses a camera to capture users and show eyes at positions on a screen corresponding to users' distance and angle.

4 Development

4.1 User Position Estimation

This section describes how a KiroPi v2 determines the distance and angle of users. First, a face recognizer of iOS SDK (CIDetector) extracts the position (f_x and f_y) and the size (f_x) of a face from a camera image, as shown in Fig 2.

Fig. 2. A camera image with a face.

The distance X (cm) and the angle R (deg) are given as Eqs. 1 and 2, where t is a conversion factor from pt to cm (0.0192). The distance was calculated from the results of preliminary measurements of the face size at distances of 1 m and 2 m assuming the average face size is 16 cm. The angle was calculated from the center position of the face on the screen, which was normalized by the screen width, and the angle of view of the camera.

$$X = 978 * t * \left(\frac{16}{(f_s * t)} \right) \tag{1}$$

$$R = 55 * \left(\frac{f_x + f_s/2}{1024} \right) - 35 \tag{2}$$

This estimation method was evaluated through an experiment. We asked ten experimental participants to stand at specific points, and then we calculated distances and angles. Evaluated points were a combination of three distances (1 m, 1.5 m, and 2 m from the robot) and five angles (-20, -10, 0, $+10$, and $+20°$ from the front of the robot). The left side of the robot was plus. Figure 3 shows the results. Positions and angles varied little, estimations were thought to have sufficient accuracy.

4.2 Sizes and Positions of Eyes

Another experiment was conducted to determine the expression of the eyes. The experimental software of KiroPi v2 has four slide bars as shown in Fig. 4. A user can change sizes and horizontal positions of scleras (white parts of the eyes) and irises (black parts of the eyes) using the four slide bars.

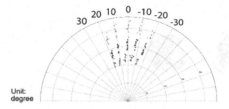

Fig. 3. Calculated user's positions.

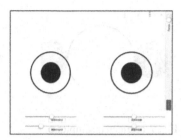

Fig. 4. Sliders to change eyes' sizes and positions.

The experiment was conducted as a public demonstration for four days starting on September 19th, 2019 at GRAND FRONT OSAKA, a building near the Osaka station. Ninety-nine people (57 males and 42 females) participated in the experiment. Each participant sat in front of a desk with a KiroPi v2 and operated the slide bars to determine appropriate sizes and positions of the eyes as shown in Fig. 5. The distance from a participant to the robot was about 30 cm.

Fig. 5. An experimental scene in GRAND FRONT OSAKA.

Participants' determinations of positions and size of eyes varied as shown in Fig. 6. Some samples of eyes were rejected because they were unrecognizable as eyes, such as irises beging outside of scleras as shown in Fig. 7. Finally, valid samples from 76 participants (44 males, and 32 females) were used. Figure 8 shows the medians of the valid samples of the parameters, and Fig. 9 shows a face using the medians of the parameters.

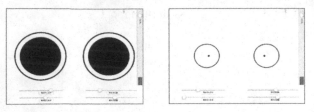

Fig. 6. Samples of eyes created by participants.

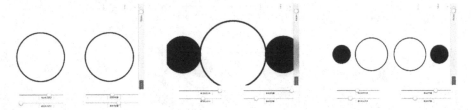

Fig. 7. Rejected samples of eyes.

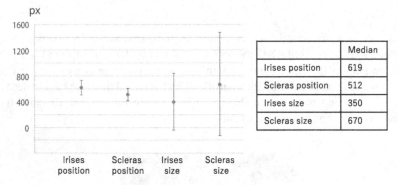

	Median
Irises position	619
Scleras position	512
Irises size	350
Scleras size	670

Fig. 8. Sample medians of the parameters.

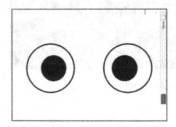

Fig. 9. A face using the medians of the parameters

4.3 Telling Distance

The parameters established by the experimental participants in 0 were detemined when the distance between a KiroPi v2 and the participants was 30 cm. Figure 9 shows a convergence angle (called positions of iris in 0) was large. In terms of human visual characteristics, the effect of the convergence angle shrinks when the distance exceeds 1 m [25–27].

Therefore, we determined that the robot represents their distance from a user using the convergence angle of eyes. The greater the distance, the smaller the convergence angle. We adopted a model in which the distance and the convergence angle are inversely proportional. The convergence angle is 619 px when the distance is 30 cm and is 0 px when the distance is 2 m. Figure 10 shows the model.

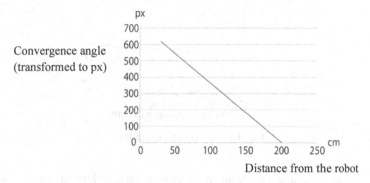

Fig. 10. Inversely proportional model of convergence angle with distance

4.4 Telling Angle

We conducted another experiment to find angles at which users feel their eyes meet those of a robot. An experimental system that enables a user to move the horizontal position of the irises of a KiroPi v2's eyes using a remote controller was developed. Figure 11 shows an overview of the system. Next, 10 participants (6 males and 6 females) were asked to stand at 10° and 20° from the front of the robot. The distance from the robot was always 2 m. Then, the participants were asked to move the irises of the robot using the remote controller until their eyes met those of the robot. The degree of movements of both eyes was the same.

Figure 12 shows the results of iris movements. When they stood at 10°, the median of movements was 6 px, which is corresponded to 2°. When they stood at 20°, the median of movements was 12 px, which is corresponded to 4°. The angle at which participants felt their eyes met is more inward than than the angle in reality. This may be because the eye movements appear more pronounced than they are in reality. This may be because the eye movements appear more pronounced than they are.

5 Experiment 1: Eyes Expression Evaluation

5.1 Convergence Angle and User's Shadow

When a person looks at another person one person's irises reflect the other person's shadows. These shadows operate as the robot's expressions of "watching you" as shown

Fig. 11. Eye movement using a remote controller

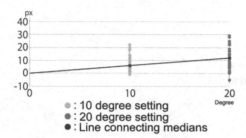

● : 10 degree setting
● : 20 degree setting
● : Line connecting medians

Fig. 12. Eye contact positions

in Fig. 13. So, an experiment to evaluate the effectiveness of human shadows was conducted. In this experiment, the effect of convergence angles was evaluated at the same time.

Experimental conditions are a combination of with/without convergence angles and with/without human shadows; A: without convergences angle and human shadows, B: without convergences angle and with human shadows, C: with convergences angle and without human shadows, D: with convergences angle and human shadows. In each condition, the robot repretents angles of a participant using movements of irises.

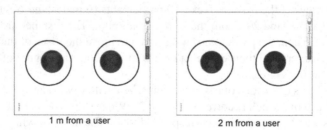

Fig. 13. Representing distances from a user using superimposing human shadows in eyes

A KiroPi v2 was set on a desk, and experimental participants were able to move in a fan-shaped gray area in Fig. 14. The distance from the robot is between 1 m and 2 m, and the angle from the front of the robot is 20° to each side.

Twenty-four experimental participants (12 males and 12 females) were asked to move freely inside the fan-shaped area, look at the screen of the robot, and evaluate it. Then the robot randomly showed two conditions four conditions and paired comparisons

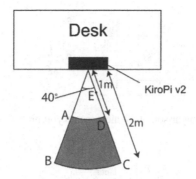

Fig. 14. The layout of Experiment 1.

of "which responds to your movement," "which one do you prefer," and "which is more natural" were conducted. Figure 15 shows a scene of the experiment.

Fig. 15. A scene of Experiment 1.

Figure 16, Fig. 17, and Fig. 18 show the results of "Which corresponds to your movement.", "Which one do you prefer.", and "Which is more natural." respectively. A values in tables refers selected numbers in the paired comparisons. Charts show π ("strength") of each condition calculated using the Bradley-Terry model [16]. The probability that condition i defeats condition j, p_{ij}, is given by Eq. 3. A goodness-of-fit test was performed on the results, and the model was not rejected.

	A	B	C	D	Total
A		14	5	10	29
B	10		5	6	21
C	19	19		14	52
D	14	18	10		42

Fig. 16. Results of paired comparison of "Which corresponds to your movement" and estimation results of π.

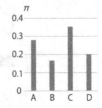

	A	B	C	D	Total
A		19	7	14	40
B	5		8	11	24
C	17	16		18	51
D	10	13	6		29

Fig. 17. Results of paired comparison of "Which one do you prefer" and estimation results of π.

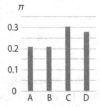

	A	B	C	D	Total
A		11	7	12	30
B	13		10	7	30
C	17	14		13	44
D	12	17	11		40

Fig. 18. Results of paired comparison of "Which is more natural" and estimation results of π.

$$p_{ij} = \frac{\pi_i}{\pi_i + \pi_j} \qquad (3)$$

The results showed that condition C with convergences angle and without user's shadows is the highest value. The user's shadows were not useful as the robot's expressions of "watching you." Sejima et al. [28] evaluated the attractiveness of human shadows on the eyes in a picture. According to their research, in the case of female photos, the evaluation was higher when there were human shadows in the eyes, and in the case of male photos, the evaluation was lower when there were human shadows in the eyes. This suggests that participants saw the KiroPi V2 as a male in this experiment.

5.2 Eyes Movement Bias

In experiments described in 4.4 and 5.1, the participants were constantly looking at the robot throughout the experiment. This situation is thought to be unnatural. So, another experiment in a more natural situation was conducted. In this experiment, experimental participants looked at the robot sideways or straight on.

Experimental conditions are 4° of horizontal movements of eyes. The degree of movements of both eyes determined in 4.4 was called as "1×" condition in this experiment. The degree of movement was doubled, tripled, or quadrupled from "1×" to "2×," "3×," or "4×", respectively.

The layout was the same as the experiment described in 4.4, except for new point E. Point E was located 50 cm to the left of the robot as shown in Fig. 14. Ten participants (5 males and 5 females) were asked to walk from point C through point A to point E. They were asked to look sideways at the robot when they walked towards A. They were asked to look straight at the robot when they walked towards E. Then the robot randomly showed two conditions in four conditions and paired comparisons of "which corresponds to your movement" were conducted.

Figure 19 shows the results of "which responds to your movement." Values in tables refer to selected numbers in the paired comparisons. Charts show π ("strength") of each condition, calculated using the Bradley-Terry model [16]. A goodness-of-fit test was performed on the results, and the model was not rejected. The results showed that evaluation of the "3×" condition was the highest.

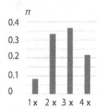

	1x	2x	3x	4x	Total
1x		1	3	1	5
2x	9		4	7	20
3x	7	6		9	22
4x	9	3	1		13

Fig. 19. Results of paired comparison of movement bias and estimation results of π.

6   Experiment 2: Shopping Scenario

6.1   Scenario

An experiment with a shopping scenario was conducted to evaluate the proposed interaction in a more realistic situation. In this scenario, a user was meant to see the robot while shopping and interact with it. Figure 20 shows the layout of the experiment. The user was aware that the robot was introducing a product at point (1). Next, she walked along, glancing slightly at the robot with concern, taking items from the shelves and putting them in her cart at point (2). Then, she walked a little past the robot, taking notice of the product introduced by the robot, and started to approach it at point (3). Finally, she approached the product (and the robot) and stops the point (4). There were pieces of tape on the floor indicating this route. The route from (3) to (4) is 20° from the front of the robot. On this route, a KiroPi v2 can estimate user's positions.

6.2   Method

Twenty-four participants (12 males and 12 females, aged 21 to 24 years) joined the experiment. Experimental conditions were the push-type interaction and the proposed eye-based interaction. Table 1 shows the speeches of the robot in each condition.

In the push-type interaction, the robot actively talked to a participant, spoke P1, P2, P3, and P4 between point (1) and point (2), and repeated all between point (3) and pint (4). Thesconvergence angles of eyes were fixed at the value corresponded to 2 m. In the eye-based interaction, the robot spoke E1 at point (2) and E1 and E2 at point (3). These convergence angles of eyes were moved as described in 4.3 and 4.4. In both conditions, the arms of the robot were moved based on speech using iRT [29]. Timing of speeches was controlled by experimenters. Figure 21 shows scenes of the experiment.

The participants engaged in experiments with two conditions in random order. After each experiment, they answered the questionnaire items shown in Fig. 22 using a 7-point Likert scale.

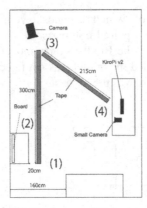

Fig. 20. The layout of Experiment 2.

Table 1. Translated speeches of each type of robots (originals are Japanese)

Push-type		Eye-based	
P1	I am KiroPi	E1	We sell gaufres here
P2	Do you like gaufres?	E2	The clock tower is printed on it
P3	Today is a sunny day		
P4	I can play a game with you		

Fig. 21. Scenes of Experiment 2.

6.3 Results

Figure 22 shows the results of the questionnaire. Bars show averages of answers, and error bars show standard deviations. The eye-based interaction received higher values on all items except for #7. A Wilcoxon signed-rank test detected significant differences between the push-type interaction and the eye-based interaction in item #1, #8, and #9 ($p < 0.01$) and #3 ($p < 0.05$). The eye-based interaction was natural (#1), declaring that the robot is watching participants (#3), enhancing the product (#8), and the participants felt that they wished to continue using it (#9). These results suggest that more modest and casual interaction than the push-type interaction was achieved.

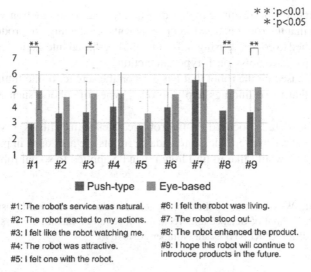

Fig. 22. Questionnaire items and results.

7 Discussion

The results of Experiment 1 revealed that people prefer the simple interaction with the convergence angle, and do not like the human shadows in eyes of the robot. It is thought to that they do not like the human shadows, because these are difficult to perceive in daily life. Some participants commented that the shadows are excessive. This suggests that they felt that there were too many visible elements of the robot.

Also, there was a large difference between the degree of eye movement desired when watching the robot while walking and when watching it constantly. Interestingly, this is the opposite result of the Mona Lisa effect. We would like to investigate this phenomenon in depth in the future.

The result of Experiment 2 shows that the eye-based interaction achieved modest and casual interaction compared to the traditional push-type interaction. The participants were not given any prior information about the robot's behavior, so this was the result of their first impression of the robot. Nevertheless, it is known that robots' impressions change through long-term use [30]. We wish to conduct a long-term field experiment to evaluate impression change in a real shopping context.

8 Conclusion

In this study, the authors develop and evaluate a robot that tells a user it is watching her/him with eyes in a shopping scenario. First, a concept of eye-based interaction advanced by social robots was proposed. Next, a method of user position estimation was developed for implementation of the eye-based interaction. Then, the eye-based interaction was completed through a parameter evaluation experiment. Finally, the eye-based interaction was compared to the traditional push-type interaction in a shopping scenario experiment. The results showed that the eye-based interaction was a way of naturally telling that the robot is watching participants, enhancing the product and users felt that they wished to continue using it. In sum, the eye-based interaction can be modest and casual, compared to noisy push-type interaction.

This study focused on the robot that has eyes on the screen. In the future, we would like to confirm that these findings apply to other types of robots, such as those with physical faces.

In addition, this study focused on the robotic sales staff. This is a typical role of robots in public spaces. Nevertheless, nowadays, robots are also used in private spaces, such as a home. We would like to find how it can be applied to social robots for home use.

Acknowledgment. We wish to thank the cooperation of Ryutaro Azuma and Ryosuke Ikeda who graduated from the School of Science and Technology, Kwansei Gakuin University. This work was supported by JSPS KAKENHI Grant Number 20H04096.

References

1. Kanda, T., Shiomi, M., Miyashita, Z., Ishiguro, H., Hagita, N.: An affective guide robot in a shopping mall. In: Proceedings of the 4th ACM/IEEE International Conference on Human Robot Interaction (HRI 2009), pp. 173–180, California, USA (2009).
2. Watabane, M., Ogawa, K., Ishiguro, H.: Minami-Chan: application and verification of androids to society through selling. J. Inform. Process. **57**(4), 1251–1261 (2016)
3. SoftBank Corp., https://www.softbank.jp/en/robot/. Accessed 12 Feb 2021
4. Nagao, Y., Umemura, H.: Elements constructing omotenashi and development of omotenashi evaluation tool (review and survey). J. Japan Indust. Manag. Assoc. **63**(3), 126–137 (2012)
5. Kuratomi, K., Kawahara, J.: The effect of facial attractiveness with catchligh in the eye, In: The 13th Conference of the Japanese Society for Cognitive Psychology, p. 147 (2015).
6. Kawamoto, C., Sejima, Y., Sato, Y., Watanabe, T.: Effects of difference in pupillary area on impressions in the pupil response interface. Correspond. Hum. Interf. **21**(7), 9–14 (2019)
7. Albert Mehrabian: Silent Messages: Implicit Communication of Emotions and Attitudes, Wadsworth Publishing Company (1972)
8. Abe, S., Fujii, S.: an examination on the effects of measures for restraining the illegal bicycle parking by using poster which has eye-spot designed to evoke presence of observers. J. City Plann. Inst. Japan. **50**(1), 37–45 (2015)
9. Bateson, M., Nettle, D., Roberts, G.: Cues of Being Watched Enhance Cooperation in a Real World Setting, biology letters, 2(3), 412–414 (2006).
10. Sekiyama, K.: Speech perception through auditory and visual modalities: linguistic/cultural differences and their developmental changes. Cogn. Stud. Bull. Japanese Cogn. Sci. Soc. **18**(3), 87–401 (2011)
11. Masaki, Y., William, M., Takahiko, M.: Are the windows to the soul the same in the East and West? Cultural differences in using the eyes and mouth as cues to recognize emotions in Japan and the United States. J. Exp. Soc. Psychol. **43**(2), 303–311 (2007)
12. Brooks, R.A., Breazearl, C., Marjanovic, M., Scassellati, B., Williamson, M.M.: The Cog Project: Building a Humanoid Robot, In: Computation for Metaphors, Analogy, and Agents, 52–87 (1998).
13. NEC Platforms Ltd., PaPeRo I, https://www.necplatforms.co.jp/solution/papero_i/. Accessed 12 Feb 2021

14. MJI Inc., Tapia, https://mjirobotics.co.jp/en/. Accessed 12 Feb 2021
15. Unirobot Corporation., Unirobot, https://www.unirobot.com. Accessed 12 Feb 2021
16. NTT Disruption Europe SLU, https://www.jibo.com/. Accessed 12 Feb 2021
17. Okuda, U., Aoyagi, S., Yamamoto, M., Satoshi, F., Watabane, T.: KiroPi: A tablet-based robot with arm-shaped hardware for personality. Trans. Hum. Interf. Soc. **20**(2), 209–220 (2018)
18. Azuma, R., Onishi, S., Fukumori, S., Aoyagi, S., Yamamoto, M.: Development of a communication rovot who "does" a bad thing. IEICE Tech. Rep. **119**(39), 79–80 (2019)
19. Takahashi, H., Komatsu, T.: Investigation of user's impression when they can establish eye-contact with a robot by chance, In: The 27th Conference of the Japanese Society for Cognitive Psycholog, pp.1–36 (2010).
20. Yonezawa, T., Yamazoe, H., Utsumi, A., Abe, S.: Verification of behavioral designs for gaze-communicative stuffed-toy robot. IEICE Trans. Inform. Syst. **92**(1), 81–92 (2009)
21. Kozima, H., Nakagawa, C., Yasuda, Y.: Interactive Robots for Communication-Care: A Case-Study in Autism Therapy, In: IEEE International Workshop on Robots and Human Interactive Communication, pp. 341–346 (2005).
22. Shi, C., Satake, S., Kanda, T., Ishiguro, H.: Field trial for social robots that invite visitors to stores. J. Robot. Soc. Japan **35**(4), 334–345 (2017)
23. Okada, M., Hoshi, Y., Yamazaki, K., Yamazaki, A., Kuno, Y., Kobayashi, Y.: Museum guide robot attracting visitors in a talk: synchronously coordination in verbal and bodily behaviors. Hum-Agent Interact. Sympos. **2008**, 2B–1 (2008)
24. Murakawa, Y., Totoki, S.: Evaluation of "behavior" of service robot "enon"-experimental operation of enon in a shopping center. Human-Agent Interact. Symposium **2008**, 2B–1 (2006)
25. Kouchi, M., Mochimaru, M.: Anthropometric Database of Japanese Head 2001, National Institute of Advanced Industrial Science and Technology, H16PRO-212, (2008).
26. Miyagawa, K., Beppu, S., Tanaka, Y., Takeda, T., Tomita, N., Yanagihara, Y.: A study of vergence effect on binocular-stereo-vision system. ITE Tech Rep **25**(38), 69–73 (2001)
27. Ralph, A.B., Milton, E.T.: Rank analysis of incomplete block designs: the method of paired comparisons. Biometrika **39**(3), 450–470 (1995)
28. Sejima, Y., Nishida, M., Watabane, T.: Development of an Expression Method of Twinkling Eyes that Superimposes Human Shadows on Attractive Pupils, In: Proceedings of the Human Interface Symposium, pp. 475–478, (2019).
29. Watanabe, T., Okubo, M., Ogawa, H.: An embodied interaction robots system based on speech. Transact. Japan Soc. Mech. Eng. Ser. C **66**(648), 2721–2728 (2000)
30. Saizo, A.., Satoshi, F., Michiya, Y.: A Long-term Evaluation of Social Robot Impression, In: Proc. 22nd International Conference on Human-Computer Interaction, pp.131–144 (2020)

Am I Conquering the Robot? the Impact of Personality on the Style of Cooperation with an Automatic System

Rou Hsiao and Wei-Chi Chien(✉)

National Cheng Kung University, No. 1, Dasyue Rd., Tainan 701, Taiwan, R.O.C.
{p36084051,10708041}@gs.ncku.edu.tw

Abstract. From washing machines, automatic doors, robot vacuum cleaners, to the self-driving system, or robot arms, automation has become common in modern life. The experience of using these products or systems depends on the performance quality and users' trust in the automation system. The experience can also differ from person to person since people have different desirability of control. This paper constructs a research framework and experiment design to explore the correlation between the humans' trust in robots, individual desirability of control, and their experiential quality in a human-robot cooperative task. When people can participate in a robot's task performance, our result suggests a positive correlation between trust and desirability of control.

Keywords: Human-Robot interaction · Humans' trust in robot · Desirability of control · User experience

1 Introduction

Nowadays, automation systems "live" everywhere in our daily lives. Things like robots have many benefits that human power cannot afford. However, Groom and Nass suggested to research robots by evaluating their potential to enhance humans' capability rather than robots' capability to replace humans [1]. Their perspective, therefore, also suggests studying cooperative work between humans and robots. The collaboration or interaction has been studied in the fields like HCI, HRI, CSCW. In such interdisciplinary research fields about automation, to explore possible positive applications of technology in humans' lives and understand their impacts, psychological studies on practical uses of the systems provide reflections on the design of technology. In this research, we are especially interested in humans' trust in the interaction with robots or automation systems. To the matter of trust, Lee and See found that improper trust can drive to abuse or misuse of automation devices [2]. However, humans' confidential experiences in cooperative tasks are psychologically proven to be related to the trust and controllability of the partners [3]. Therefore, from a user-centered perspective, users' desirability of control and the resulting trust in the automation system arises in cooperative using scenarios.

This research is a preliminary study focused on the correlations between humans' desirability of control, trust scores, and the subjective experience of the collaboration

M. Kurosu (Ed.): HCII 2021, LNCS 12763, pp. 216–227, 2021.
https://doi.org/10.1007/978-3-030-78465-2_16

with an automation system. We designed scenario with a small autonomous robot driving on an oval track, in which a remote control allows humans to manipulate the driving performance. In the experiment, we inquired the participants' controlling attitude, invited them to cooperate with the robot, observed their performance, and measured their subjective experiences of the tasks.

2 Humans' Trust in Robot: Review of Related Studies

Trust inevitably impact our interaction with people and things [4, 5]. Many researchers have set the role of humans' trust in robots [2, 6–8]. Sanders, et al. identified three categories of factors that affect trust in human-robot interaction, including robot-related, human-related, and environmental (contextual) factors [6]. Inspired by their framework, we first reviewed the related studies in humans' trust in the robot (**TR**) in the following.

The robot-related factors in TR include robots' performance, appearance, and types. When robots' attributions match users' expectation, TR may increase. For example, robots' behavior ("*robotiquette*" in Dautenhahn's term) should be considerate, active, non-disturbing, flexible, and capable of enhancing TR and users' confidence in their cooperative tasks [9]. Also, the perceived reliability, predictability, and dependability of robots are found to be influential in TR, for example, Ross found that participants changed their reliance on and trust in automation systems according to its perceived reliability of the systems [10]. Besides, Desai et al. found a significant correlation between the robot's reliability and TR in a cooperative scenario (a fire scene) [11]. In Lohani et al.' experiment (an emergency landing scene), they found the functional expertise and the "social skill" of the robots amplifies humans' motivation to work together with them and, therefore, the reliability and TR [12]. Other studies of robots' anthropomorphism, robots expressivity for social cues like emotions or dispositions are also found to be influential in TR [13–15].

It seems, therefore, that TR is not only a static status but dynamic and task-oriented reflection. Despite humans' reflection on automation systems, humans' capabilities, social values, and personality could also influence TR. For instance, researchers found different TR levels when users from different generations interact with automatic systems [16]. Besides, while gender difference is shown in the perceived anthropomorphism of robots [17], it is, interestingly, not significant in the evaluation of TR [18]. Also, novices and veterans of an automation system have significant differences in TR [19]. TR is also task-oriented. For example, in Chen and Terrence's experiment shows that participants' capability in task performance changes their experience with an automation system [20]. Besides, delivering TR is found to be easier when people consider tasks to be simple [21]. To observe TR, the proper set-up of the task difficulties is, therefore, essential in experiment design.

It seems that the TR, as an experiential component of human-robot interaction, is resulted by complex factors. A classical perspective on reliable the design of an automatic system is the controllability of the system [22]. However, the modern fashion of technology design tends to have things "smart" – the idea of "being able to control" is replaced by "do not need to control." However, the desirability of control is part of our personality and related to personal well-being [23]. Therefore, design researchers like Klapperich et al. discussed the experience design between automation and autonomy and brought the psychological issue of desirability to control back into discussion [24]. This preliminary experiment explored the correlation between humans' personality (desirability of control: **DC**), the performance qualities, TR, and the resulted experiential quality (**EQ**).

3   Experiment

3.1   Robot System

We built an automated robot (a small car) with a remote control (Fig. 1.) and set up an oval track with eight gates that regularly open and close (like traffic lamps; Fig. 2). The oval lane is about 12.6 meters in length and 1.8 meters in width. The gates are close and open by lifting and laying down a physical barrier. The gates switch in two different frequencies. While the gates 2, 5, and 7 switch in a shorter cycle (close 2 s and open 5 s in repeat: difficulty high), others in a longer cycle (close 2 s and open 10 s in repeat: difficulty low). The robot can run on the track autonomously. When engaging into a closed gate, the robot detects the barrier and stops. It goes again when the gate opens again. The joystick on the remote control provides the possibility to speed up (forward joystick) or slow down (backward joystick) the robot. The system is built with Arduino developer board, IR switches for tracking the driving lane, ultrasonic modules for detecting barriers (closed gates), and Blue-tooth modules for remote communication.

Fig. 1.   (left) the robotic car and (right) Remote control

3.2   Measurement Tools and Interview

Three types of scales were used in this experiment. The desirability of Control Scales (DC scales; see [23] for more details) was used to measure participants' desirability of control as a personality. The DC scales has 20 items. Participants score from 1 to 7 on a Likert scale (1 = the statement does not apply to me at all, 7 = the statement always applies to me) in response to their belief that the statement is applicable. The

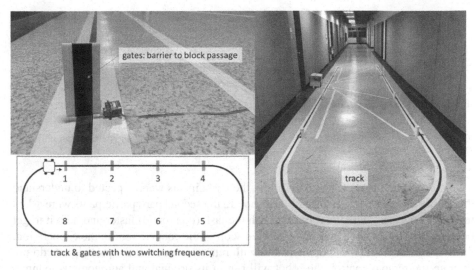

Fig. 2. set-up of the driving track

higher the total scores, the more desirability of controlling over everyday events. The participants reported their DC scale before the experiment. The TR was measured by the scales of Trust between People and Automation (see [25] for more details), a 7 points scale with 12 items inquiring people's trust feeling on an automation system. Finally, we designed a third questionnaire (scale of experiential qualities: EQ-scale) with four items for participants to report their subjective experience, including emotion, emotional fluctuation, control experience (from being fully controlled by the system to fully controlling the system), and evaluation (interpretation) of the robot's "happiness."

Besides, a short interview was conducted after each participant finished their experiment. This interview includes some simple questions about participants' feelings after the task performances, such as when they are motivated to accelerate or decelerate the robot, the change of trust feelings between the first and second experiment, and the emotional status in them during the interaction. The participants' controlling behavior of remote control, like speeding-up and slowing-down, is recorded in the device.

3.3 Task and Procedure

13 participants including 6 females and 7 males, aged from 20 to 30 (M = 24.7, σ = 1.65), participated in our experiment. They first reported their DC scales and were introduced to evaluate the system as the first part of the experiment. In the first part, participants had to observe the robot accomplish one round of the track by itself. As a motivation to observe the robot's performance, participants were asked to record the performance (time and number of failures) of the robot. Three types of failures were recorded (see Table 1), and minus points would be added (as a motivation to observe). After the observation, participants reported the TR-scales and EQ-scales (without the item of control experience).

Table 1. failure types and the observation task

Type	Failure situation	Assignments in observation task
A	There is a standing obstacle and the robot hit it without stop	Mark "×" and deduct two points
B	The obstacle stands up when the robot is passing it	Mark "△" and deduct one points
C	There is no obstacle but the robot stops	Mark "□" and deduct two points

After the first part of the observation, the participants were expected to understand the ability and task performance of the robot. In the second part, participants were asked to "work together" with the robot to finish the task (one round) faster and help it to get better scores. A research assistant was then scoring the cooperation. In the cooperation, participants brake or speed up the robot with remote control. If the participants do not operate the remote control, the robot will run in its original and autonomous manner. Finally, participants will be asked to fill the TR-scales and EQ-scales again. After that, a brief interview was conducted.

4   Results and Analysis

To better analyze our data, we categorized the participants into two groups based on their percentile of DC score: Participants with the first 54%ile DC score are categorized as high-DC (N = 7) and the last 46%ile low-DC (N = 6). The observation task took about 262 s (N = 13, SD = 17.16), and the number of failures is 6.85 times on average (N = 13, SD = 2.23). The cooperative task took 242 s on average (N = 13, SD = 12.44), and the failures were 3.15 times on average (N = 13, SD = 1.95). There was no perfect performance in each task.

4.1   Evaluation of the Performance and TR

In our experiment, all participants finished the tasks, but none of our participants made a perfect run (number of failures: M = 3.15, SD = 1.95). In the cooperative task, the average controlling time is 131.52 s (N = 13, SD = 74.83), average accelerating time 117.25 s (SD = 70.97), decelerating time 14.27 s (SD = 11.45), and count of activating manual control 62.85 times (SD = 29.31).

Paired-sample T-Test shows that the performance quality including time ($t[12] = 3.56, p = .004$) and the count of failures ($t[12] = 4.59, p = .001$) is significantly better in the cooperative task (see Fig. 3). Although the performance time and quality in the cooperative task are significantly better, both the time and count of using the remote control are not significantly correlated to the time and quality of performance. In our experiment scenario, the result implies that cooperation helps improve performance; however, more intensive control did not guarantee better performance.

To the performance quality and TR: Paired-samples T-Test shows that, overall, TR in the cooperative task is better than observation task ($t[12] = -2.64, p = .021$). Besides,

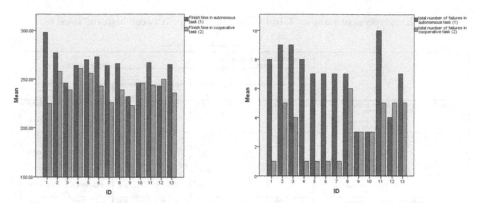

Fig. 3. performance time and count of failures in two tasks

when dividing participants into high and low DC groups, high-DCs made less type-A failure (running against the barrier) (M = 0.43, N = 7, SD = .79) than low-DCs (M = 1.33, N = 6, SD = 1.03); however, the difference is not significant (t[11] = −1.793, p = .10). Through Pearson's product-moment correlation coefficient, we did not find a significant correlation between the performance quality and TR in general. However, significant correlation between TR in task 1 and task 2 is significant (*Pearson's r* = .625, N = 13, p = .022). TR could, therefore, be more influenced by personal factors, rather than the factual situation. In a Pearson's correlation test with EQ, we only found a significant correlation between the number of failures in the cooperative task (r =−.594, N = 13, p = .032) and emotional positiveness, which is not surprising – if one makes fewer mistakes in the task, s/he feels happier. To the gender questions, we found no significant difference in DC, TR (in both tasks), or the performance quality in the cooperative task.

4.2 Evaluation of DC and TR

To the questions about humans' desirability of control (DC), we see a potential but not significant correlation between DC and participants' time using the remote control (*Pearson's r* = .455, N = 13, p = .118). In an independent-samples T-Test with the high and low DC groups, the high DC group significantly slows down the robot more often than low DC group (F[11] = 2.57, p = 0.026; Table 2 and Fig. 4). According to the interview, some high DC participants reported that they were very nervous and worried about the robot running against the barriers, and, therefore, they took over the control almost always to prevent the robot from driving too fast. Besides, gender difference is detected in an independent-samples T-Test, in which male participants (M = 103.43, N = 7, SD = 10.50) have higher DC than female (M = 90.33, N = 6, SD = 8.94).

The correlation between DC and TR in the observation task (task 1) is not significant. In fact, some participants reported their outsider feeling during the observation in the interview. However, in the cooperative task, we found a significant and positive correlation between DC and TR (*Pearson's r* = .629, N = 13, p = .021; see Fig. 5). While TR is not correlated to the performance quality of the robot (see 4.1) this result

Table 2. independent-samples T-Test of control behavior between high and low-DC

Independent Samples Test

		Levene's Test for Equality of Variances		t-test for Equality of Means				
		F	Sig.	t	df	Sig. (2-tailed)	Mean Difference	Std. Error Difference
Total participation control time in cooperative task (2)	Equal variances assumed	6.560	.026	1.863	11	.089	70635.66667	37909.53701
	Equal variances not assumed			1.772	7.121	.119	70635.66667	39866.04144
Control acceleration time in cooperative task (2)	Equal variances assumed	6.801	.024	1.525	11	.156	57130.97619	37467.31536
	Equal variances not assumed			1.453	7.284	.188	57130.97619	39314.45894
Control deceleration time in cooperative task (2)	Equal variances assumed	1.158	.305	2.567	11	.026	1.350469E4	5259.900121
	Equal variances not assumed			2.703	8.953	.024	1.350469E4	4995.321178
Switch time in cooperative task (2)	Equal variances assumed	.669	.431	.786	11	.449	13.024	16.572
	Equal variances not assumed			.819	9.819	.432	13.024	15.897

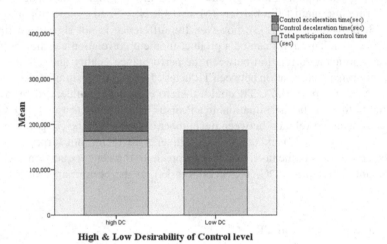

High & Low Desirability of Control level

Fig. 4. total control time of high/low DC participants

becomes inspiring. From an intuitive understanding, TR should be corresponding to the performance quality, especially in the high-DC group. However, the result is not consistent with this hypothesis. It could be the situation, that our participants accepted the robot to "make some mistakes" (or, to say, the robot in the experiment got "spoiled"). Therefore, TR becomes a judgement based on personal preference. High-DC participants tend to consider themselves to be responsible for the result. Therefore, the robot (system) become more reliable, when high-DCs feels that they "have their control" back. We do observe a higher TR in the cooperative task in the high DC group, although the difference is not significant in an independent-samples T-Test (t[11] = 1.649, p = .127; see Fig. 6).

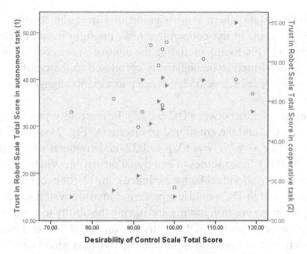

Fig. 5. desirability of control and TR in both tasks

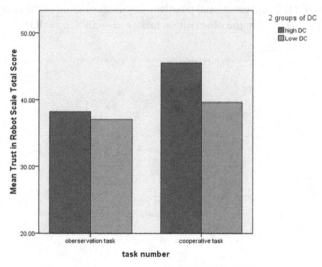

Fig. 6. TR in two tasks and two different DC groups

4.3 Evaluation of EQ, DC, and TR

In an independent-samples T-Test of EQ and two tasks, only the item of emotional fluctuation shows the significant difference (t[24] = -2.64, p = .014), which seems reasonable – when participants play a role in cooperation, they have stronger emotional arousal. However, the scores of emotional fluctuations in two tasks are significantly correlated with each other (*Pearson's* r = .58, N = 13, p = .0036), which implies a probability that, in our experiment, the score of emotional fluctuation might be more a personal emotional status and not influenced by the tasks.

In the observation task, there is no significant correlation between performance quality and any EQ item. In the cooperative task, no significant correlation between control behavior and EQ is found, including the control experience. However, the total number of failures are found to be negatively correlated to the emotional positiveness (*Pearson's r* = −.594, N = 13, *p* = .032) – When participants engaged into more failures, they were less happy.

We exams the correlation between DC and EQ. Interestingly, positive and significant correlation between DC and the emotional positiveness (Fig. 7) is found both in observation task (*Pearson's r* = .625, N = 13, *p* = .022) and cooperative task (*Pearson's r* = .795, N = 13, *p* = 0.001). Since scores of emotional positiveness in two tasks are not correlated with each other (individual factor excluded), the result becomes contradictive to our intuitive guess that high-DC would less prefer automation systems. Our explanation is that, for people preferring control, joining and having the ability to control artifacts dealing with the situation provides high-DC positive emotions. However, how do we explain that high-DC also have more positive emotions in the observation task? We consider the performance quality could mediate the result of emotional positiveness. In a partial correlation analysis of the high-DC group taking failure number as the controlling factor, the correlation between DC and emotional positives is still significant in the cooperative task (*r* = .91, *p* = .034) but not in the observation task (*r* = −.098, *p* = .85).

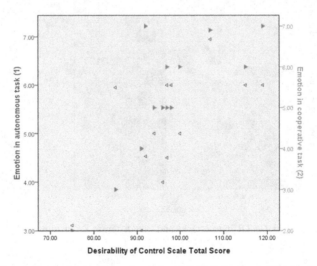

Fig. 7. Correlation between DC and emotion in two tasks ($r = .63$, $p = .021 < .05$)

To the gender issue, in an independent-samples T-Test, we found male participants significant feel emotionally more positive than female participants, especially in the cooperative task (t[11] = 2.968, N = 7, *p* = .013; female participants: M = 4.16, SD = 1.4; male: M = 6.13, SD = .88;). While this can be influenced by the cultural bias, in our experiment, gender difference does not lie in performance quality but their preference.

4.4 "Happiness" of the Robot

An item we added in our EQ questionnaire is the "happiness" of the robot (HR). Potential usage of this item is to the interpretation of robots' anthropomorphism. While robots do not really have emotions (at least, in our system design), we would like to know where the anthropomorphic experience could come from. First, we tested the items of performance quality and found a significant correlation between HR and the count of failures (*Pearson's r* $= -.458$, N $= 26$, $p = .019$). Besides, HR is significantly correlated to emotional positiveness (*Pearson's r* $= .386$, N $= 26$, $p = .008$), which implies the fact that the judgement of the robot's happiness is a subjective reflection on participants' experienced happiness. Although a positive correlation is detected between HR and DC, a partial correlation analysis clears it away. All in all, these results show that the anthropomorphic experience is both related to the robots' performance and humans' emotional quality in the interaction with the robot, but not to individual desirability of control.

5 Discussion and Conclusions

In this research, we design an experiment with two tasks to explore the correlation between many factors, including the performance quality of an automation system (a robot), humans' control behavior and desirability of control (DC), task-resulted human trust in the robot (TR), and experiential qualities (EQ), including emotional positiveness, emotional fluctuation, control experience, and the "happiness" of a robot.

As a preliminary exploration, a brief review of the actual experiment scenario would help clarify our contribution. The first task with observation and scoring was afforded to enhance participants' understanding of the system and its purpose. While the robot made a few failures in its solo work, the cooperative task introduced the participants a challenge to improve performance quality. The task of the robot to drive on a one-way track is symmetric to participants' in cooperation – they both process the information of the gates and react to the accessibility by speeding up or slowing down. The difficulty was set up at a relatively low level, by which cooperation did improve the quality of performance; however, more control did not contribute to the quality of performance. Evidence is that the performance quality was not correlated to TR. Therefore, the different attributions of participants' cooperation experience would more reflect their psychological status like DC or TR but less their operative skills.

Some limitation should be noted: An experiment with 13 participants could be biased in culture and age due to the small sample size. The cooperative task designed in the experiment is relatively simple. In actual scenario, human-robot cooperation could be much more complex and contextual. We categorized the participants into two groups according to their DC scores. While Burger and Cooper suggested the value 100.7 to separate high-DC, due to the small sample size, we strategically split our samples with a value between 92 and 98. The definition of high-DC can be not consistent with Burger and Cooper's concept.

Despite the limitation, we found several inspiring results. Desai et al.'s study [11] showed evidence that TR is a significant outcome of an automation system's reliability, which is contributed by subjective judgement rather than actual performance. Our study shows a consistent conclusion and provides a psychological explanation. First, through the set-up of the task difficulty, the presented TR reflect participants' psychological attribution but not their judgements of the robot. Under this condition, we further found that DC is positively correlated to TR in the cooperative task. Because we set up an automation task before, our explanation is that high DCs prefer handling the situation, and if the robot provides the opportunity for participation, high DCs show more trust in the system. Participants' desirability of control would be satisfied by taking over the authority in cooperative tasks. This idea also explains why high DCs show more positive emotions the cooperation. Therefore, we can assume that, if participants had finished a fully manual task first, and the automation function then joins into the second cooperative task, the resulted emotional positiveness and TR would be contrarily negatively correlated to DC.

Finally, we observed psychological projection by evaluating the robot's "happiness" and found a significant correlation to personal emotions. To study the experiential quality and the assumption of a reversed correlation between DC and TR will be our next research issue.

References

1. Groom, V., Nass, C.: Can robots be teammates? Benchmarks in human-robot teams. Interact. Stud. **8**(3), 483–500 (2007)
2. Lee, J.D., See, K.A.: Trust in automation: designing for appropriate reliance. Hum. Factors **46**(1), 50–80 (2004)
3. Das, T.K., Teng, B.S.: Between trust and control: developing confidence in partner cooperation in alliances. Acad. Manage. Rev. **23**(3), 491–512 (1998)
4. Dirks, K.T., Ferrin, D.L.: The role of trust in organizational settings. Organ. Sci. **12**(4), 450–467 (2001)
5. Muir, B.M.: Trust in automation: part I. Theoretical issues in the study of trust and human intervention in automated systems. Ergonomics **37**(11), 1905–1922 (1994)
6. Sanders, T., Oleson, K.E., Billings, D.R., Chen, J.Y.C., Hancock, P.A.: A model of human-robot trust: Theoretical model development. Proc. Hum. Factors Ergon. Soc. Annu. Meeting **55**(1), 1432–1436 (2011)
7. Billings, D.R., Schaefer, K.E., Chen, J.Y.C., Hancock, P.A.: Human-robot interaction: developing trust in robots. Int. Conf. Hum. Robot. Interact. **58**(4), 525–532 (2016)
8. Dzindolet, M.T., Peterson, S.A., Pomranky, R.A., Pierce, L.G., Beck, H.P.: The role of trust in automation reliance. Int. J. Hum. Comput. Stud. **58**(6), 697–718 (2003)
9. Dautenhahn, K.: Socially intelligent robots: Dimensions of human-robot interaction. Philos. Trans. R. Soc. B: Biol. Sci. **362**(1480), 679–704 (2007)
10. Ross, J.: Moderators of trust and reliance across multiple decision aids. Electronic Theses and Dissertations 2004–2019, 3754 (2008)
11. Desai, M., et al.: Effects of changing reliability on trust of robot systems. In: International Conference on Human-Robot Interaction, pp. 73–80 (2012)
12. Lohani, M., Stokes, C., McCoy, M., Bailey, C.A., Rivers, S.E.: Social interaction moderates human-robot trust-reliance relationship and improves stress coping. In: International Conference on Human Robot Interaction (2016)
13. Natarajan, M., Gombolay, M.: Effects of anthropomorphism and accountability on trust in human robot interaction. In: International Conference on Human-Robot Interaction, pp. 33–42 (2020)

14. Bartneck, C., Kulić, D., Croft, E., Zoghbi, S.: Measurement instruments for the anthropomorphism, animacy, likeability, perceived intelligence, and perceived safety of robots. Int. J. Soc. Robot. **1**(1), 71–81 (2009)
15. Duffy, B.R.: Anthropomorphism and the social robot. Robot. Auton. Syst. **42**(3–4), 177–190 (2003)
16. Scopelliti, M., Giuliani, M.V., Fornara, F.: Robots in a domestic setting: A psychological approach. Univ. Access Inf. Soc. **4**(2), 146–155 (2005)
17. Schermerhorn, P., Scheutz, M., Crowell, C. R.: Robot social presence and gender: Do females view robots differently than males?. In: International Conference on Human-Robot Interaction, 263–270 (2008)
18. Evers, V., Maldonado, H.C., Brodecki, T.L., Hinds, P.J.: Relational vs. group self-construal: Untangling the role of national culture in HRI. In: International Conference on Human-Robot Interaction, pp. 255–262 (2008)
19. Desai, M.: Sliding scale autonomy and trust in human-robot interaction. University of Massachusetts Lowell (2007)
20. Chen, J.Y.C., Terrence, P.I.: Effects of imperfect automation and individual differences on concurrent performance of military and robotics tasks in a simulated multitasking environment. Ergonomics **52**(8), 907–920 (2009)
21. Shu, P., Min, C., Bodala, I., Nikolaidis, S., Hsu, D., Soh, H.: Human trust in robot capabilities across tasks. In: International Conference on Human-Robot Interaction, pp. 241–242 (2018)
22. Shneiderman, B., Maes, P.: Direct manipulation vs. interface agents. Interactions **4**(6), 42–61 (1997)
23. Burger, J.M., Cooper, H.M.: The desirability of control. Motiv. Emot. **3**(4), 381–393 (1979)
24. Klapperich, H., Uhde, A., Hassenzahl, M.: Designing everyday automation with wellbeing in mind. Pers. Ubiquit. Comput. **24**, 763–779 (2020)
25. Jian, J., Bisantz, A., Drury, C.: Foundations for an empirically determined scale of trust in automated systems. Int. J. Cogn. Ergon. **4**(1), 53–71 (2000)

Kansei Evaluation of Robots in Virtual Space Considering Their Physical Attributes

Shun Imura$^{(\boxtimes)}$, Kento Murayama, Peeraya Sripian, Tipporn Laohakangvalvit, and Midori Sugaya

Shibaura Institute of Technology, 3-7-5 Toyosu, Koto-ku, Tokyo 135-8548, Japan
{ma20011,ma18100,peeraya,tipporn,doly}@shibaura-it.ac.jp

Abstract. In recent years, the demand for robots has increased, and their roles have changed. In other words, there are increasing opportunities for them to be used not only in industrial applications such as factories, but also in daily life. In order for users to continue using these robots, the impression they have towards the robots needs to be considered. However, at present in the new coronavirus disease, it is difficult to actually assemble a robot. Instead, designing and developing a robot in virtual space can be an alternative. In this study, we evaluated the affective values of robots in a virtual space. We created a virtual space as a university campus, along with three pairs of robots with different shapes. Then, we performed kansei evaluation of the robots employing Semantic Differential (SD) for questionnaire. The results show how the ratings differ for each of the robot pairs and adjective pairs. In particular, we found that some adjective pairs had higher ratings than other adjective pairs, suggesting different impressions on our designed robots.

Keywords: Virtual space · Robot · Kansei evaluation

1 Introduction

As robots are used in daily life, their impressions are important for users to continue to use them. Unlike industrial robots, in case of robots that we are interacting with on a daily basis, such as aibo [1] and PARO [2], having good impression will make users feel pleasant and want to use them actively. Therefore, an evaluation of the robot impressions is necessary. Knowing the difference in how physical attributes influenced the user impressions suggest how to create robots that contribute to continuous use.

Kansei engineering is defined as "a technology that translates and expresses the psychological image of a product into a concrete product design" [3]. It proposed a concept that various human psychological differences, such as diverse values and preferences, can be evaluated by evaluation method in kansei engineering. A study [4] per-formed kansei evaluation of robot impressions using facial photographs of 80 robots, and reported that the familiarity of the robots increased as their appearance changed from mechanical to human-like. However, in such comparative studies of robot impression evaluation, one

© Springer Nature Switzerland AG 2021
M. Kurosu (Ed.): HCII 2021, LNCS 12763, pp. 228–240, 2021.
https://doi.org/10.1007/978-3-030-78465-2_17

robot is compared to a completely different robot, making it difficult to evaluate how physical attributes of the robots affect to the impressions.

In this research, we proposed to design robots systematically by differing physical attributes and evaluate their impressions using kansei evaluation method. The purpose of this research is to clarify the similarities and differences of the affective values among our designed robots. The details of our robots, evaluation method, and evaluation results are presented in this paper.

2   Robot Pairs

Under a collaborative project with DePauw University [5], our team members including students from DePauw University designed and developed three types of robots (talking robots, floating guide robots, and vending machine robots) and a virtual space that mimics a university campus (Fig. 1). For each robot design, we made a pair by differing one physical attribute to differ "kawaii" degree using round and angular shapes for more and less "kawaii" degrees respectively. Based on the research that curved systems are cuter than straight systems, round shapes were set as the more kawaii ones [6]. The details of the three robot pairs are described in the following sections.

Fig. 1. Virtual space

2.1   Talking Robot (Robot Pair 1)

This robot (Fig. 2) usually walks around the campus. In addition, when people talk to it, it interacts by jumping, nodding, and chatting with them. The size of the robot is about the height of a person's knee.

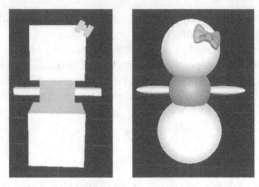

Fig. 2. Robot Pair 1 - Talking Robots

2.2 Floating Guide Robot (Robot Pair 2)

This robot (Fig. 3) floats at the eye level and keeps a certain distance from the visitor. It responds to voice commands, answers questions, and guides visitors to places they want to go. It is about the size of a human head.

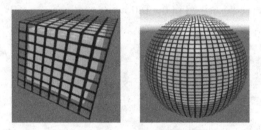

Fig. 3. Robot Pair 2 - Floating Guide Robots

2.3 Vending Machine Robot (Robot Pair 3)

This robot (Fig. 4) patrols the campus, detects people who enters a certain area around it, and approaches people to offer a drink. The size of the robot is about the same as human.

Fig. 4. Robot Pair 3 - Vending Machine Robots

3   Experiment Method

3.1   Questionnaire

In order to clarify the difference in the affective values given by the robots, we placed each pair of robots in the virtual space and performed affective evaluation using a questionnaire based on Semantic Differential (SD), that is, a questionnaire to rate on several adjective pairs using 5-point rating scale. The SD is used to measure the meaning or image of various events that a person makes a theoretical composition [7]. As shown in Table 1, we used 20 adjective pairs including "kawaii vs. not-kawaii." These adjective pairs were created in the project [5], with the last four items added. These adjective pairs were chosen based on how the robot's creators wanted the subjects to evaluate the robots. The adjectives on the left side of Table 1 were rated as 1, and those on the right side were rated as 5.

Table 1. Adjective pairs for evaluation of robot pairs

Adjective pairs
a: Unapproachable - Approachable
b: Ugly - Beautiful
c: Untrustworthy - Trustworthy
d: Uncool – Cool
e: Unfriendly - Friendly
f: Clumsy - Graceful
g: Scary - Unscary
h: Distressing - Comfortable
i: Rude - Respectful
j: Unenjoyable - Enjoyable
k: Unintelligent - Intelligent
l: Not kawaii - Kawaii
m: Not willing to use again - Willing to
n: Dislike - Like
o: No presence - Has a presence
p: Weird – Not weird
q: Disturbing - Not disturbing
r: Unsafe - Safe
s: Not kind - Kind
t: Untender - Tender

3.2   Experimental Procedure

In the experiment, we played pre-recorded videos of the robot pairs in the virtual space, and asked the participants to answer the questionnaire using Google Form (Fig. 5). For each robot pair, two videos were shown consecutively: one for square robots and one for round robots. The participants were asked to answer the questionnaire immediately after each robot pair's video was finished.

The robots were placed on the left and right sides of the video screen, and the robot on the left side was used as the evaluation standard (evaluation value: 3), in which one was expected to be more kawaii than the other. In order to prevent the bias in the evaluation, we did not explain to participants which robot was the one expected to be kawaii.

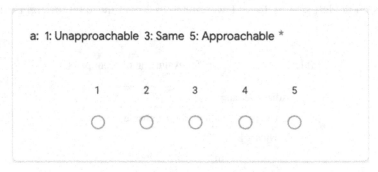

Fig. 5. Part of the Google Forms questionnaire

4   Experiment Results

A two-way analysis of variance was conducted to analyze the important perspectives in evaluating the affective values of the robots. As shown in Table 2, there are main effects of Robot Pairs ($p < 0.01$) and Adjective Pairs ($p < 0.01$), but no interaction effect between them.

Table 2. The result of two-way ANOVA

Source	Type III sum of squares	Df	Mean square	F	Sig.
Intercept	9010.001	1	9010.001	1480.108	0
Robot Pair	18.595	2	9.297	17.052	0
Adjective Pair	88.435	19	4.654	8.537	0
Robot Pair * Adjective Pair	20.892	38	0.55	1.008	0.458

Based on these results, we further performed multiple comparisons of Scheffe for each factor. The results are as follows:

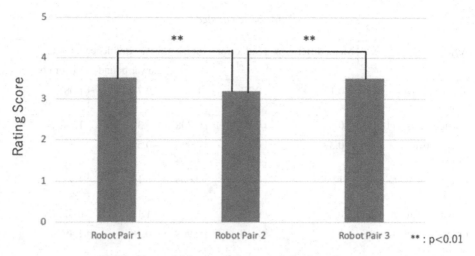

Fig. 6. The multiple comparison result for the robot pairs

- The multiple comparison result for the robot pairs (Fig. 6) shows that there are significant differences in overall rating scores between Robot Pairs 1 and 2 (p < 0.01) and Robot Pairs 2 and 3 (p < 0.01), but not between Robot Pairs 1 and 3, indicating the following tendency of scores: Robot pairs 1 = Robot pair 3 > Robot pair 2.
- The multiple comparison results for some adjective pairs (Tables 3, 4, 5, 6 and 7) show that there are significant differences between the following combinations: a and d, k; d and e, g, h, l, r, s, t; e and k; k and l, r, s, t; and l and o (p < 0.05 for every combinations).

Table 3. The multiple comparison result for "a: Unapproachable – Approachable"

Adjective pair	Mean difference	Std. error	Sig.	95% confidence interval	
				Lower bound	Upper bound
b: Ugly - Beautiful	0.46	0.17	0.99	−0.46	1.38
c: Untrustworthy - Trustworthy	0.41	0.17	0.998	−0.51	1.33
d: Uncool – Cool	1.13**	0.17	0.001	0.21	2.05
e: Unfriendly - Friendly	0.10	0.17	1	−0.82	1.02
f: Clumsy - Graceful	0.36	0.17	1	−0.56	1.28
g: Scary - Unscary	0.15	0.17	1	−0.77	1.08

(*continued*)

Table 3. (*continued*)

Adjective pair	Mean difference	Std. error	Sig.	95% confidence interval	
				Lower bound	Upper bound
h: Distressing - Comfortable	0.15	0.17	1	−0.77	1.08
i: Rude - Respectful	0.62	0.17	0.808	−0.31	1.54
j: Unenjoyable - Enjoyable	0.38	0.17	0.999	−0.54	1.31
k: Unintelligent - Intelligent	1.03[**]	0.17	0.008	0.10	1.95
l: Not kawaii - Kawaii	−0.26	0.17	1	−1.18	0.67
m: Not willing to use again - Willing to	0.56	0.17	0.909	−0.36	1.49
n: Dislike - Like	0.36	0.17	1	−0.56	1.28
o: No presence - Has a presence	0.69	0.17	0.58	−0.23	1.61
p: Weird – Not weird	0.36	0.17	1	−0.56	1.28
q: Disturbing - Not disturbing	0.31	0.17	1	−0.61	1.23
r: Unsafe - Safe	−0.03	0.17	1	−0.95	0.90
s: Not kind - Kind	0.10	0.17	1	−0.82	1.02
t: Untender - Tender	0.00	0.17	1	−0.92	0.92

**: $p < .01$

Table 4. The multiple comparison result for "d: Uncool – Cool"

Adjective pair	Mean difference	Std. error	Sig.	95% confidence interval	
				Lower bound	Upper bound
a: Unapproachable - Approachable	−1.13[**]	0.17	0.001	−2.05	−0.21
b: Ugly - Beautiful	−0.67	0.17	0.663	−1.59	0.26
c: Untrustworthy - Trustworthy	−0.72	0.17	0.495	−1.64	0.20
e: Unfriendly - Friendly	−1.03[**]	0.17	0.008	−1.95	−0.10
f: Clumsy - Graceful	−0.77	0.17	0.331	−1.69	0.15

(*continued*)

Table 4. (*continued*)

Adjective pair	Mean difference	Std. error	Sig.	95% confidence interval	
				Lower bound	Upper bound
g: Scary - Unscary	−0.97*	0.17	0.021	−1.90	−0.05
h: Distressing - Comfortable	−0.97*	0.17	0.021	−1.90	−0.05
i: Rude - Respectful	−0.51	0.17	0.965	−1.44	0.41
j: Unenjoyable - Enjoyable	−0.74	0.17	0.411	−1.67	0.18
k: Unintelligent - Intelligent	−0.10	0.17	1	−1.02	0.82
l: Not kawaii - Kawaii	−1.38**	0.17	0	−2.31	−0.46
m: Not willing to use again - Willing to	−0.56	0.17	0.909	−1.49	0.36
n: Dislike - Like	−0.77	0.17	0.331	−1.69	0.15
o: No presence - Has a presence	−0.44	0.17	0.995	−1.36	0.49
p: Weird – Not weird	−0.77	0.17	0.331	−1.69	0.15
q: Disturbing - Not disturbing	−0.82	0.17	0.198	−1.74	0.10
r: Unsafe - Safe	−1.15**	0.17	0	−2.08	−0.23
s: Not kind - Kind	−1.03**	0.17	0.008	−1.95	−0.10
t: Untender - Tender	−1.13**	0.17	0.001	−2.05	−0.21

*: $p < .05$, **: $p < .01$

Table 5. The multiple comparison result for "e: Unfriendly - Friendly"

Adjective pair	Mean difference	Std. error	Sig.	95% confidence interval	
				Lower bound	Upper bound
a: Unapproachable - Approachable	−0.10	0.17	1	−1.02	0.82
b: Ugly - Beautiful	0.36	0.17	1	−0.56	1.28
c: Untrustworthy - Trustworthy	0.31	0.17	1	−0.61	1.23
d: Uncool – Cool	1.03**	0.17	0.008	0.10	1.95
f: Clumsy - Graceful	0.26	0.17	1	−0.67	1.18

(*continued*)

Table 5. (*continued*)

Adjective pair	Mean difference	Std. error	Sig.	95% confidence interval	
				Lower bound	Upper bound
g: Scary - Unscary	0.05	0.17	1	−0.87	0.97
h: Distressing - Comfortable	0.05	0.17	1	−0.87	0.97
i: Rude - Respectful	0.51	0.17	0.965	−0.41	1.44
j: Unenjoyable - Enjoyable	0.28	0.17	1	−0.64	1.20
k: Unintelligent - Intelligent	0.92*	0.17	0.049	0.00	1.85
l: Not kawaii - Kawaii	−0.36	0.17	1	−1.28	0.56
m: Not willing to use again - Willing to	0.46	0.17	0.99	−0.46	1.38
n: Dislike - Like	0.26	0.17	1	−0.67	1.18
o: No presence - Has a presence	0.59	0.17	0.864	−0.33	1.51
p: Weird – Not weird	0.26	0.17	1	−0.67	1.18
q: Disturbing - Not disturbing	0.21	0.17	1	−0.72	1.13
r: Unsafe - Safe	−0.13	0.17	1	−1.05	0.79
s: Not kind - Kind	0.00	0.17	1	−0.92	0.92
t: Untender - Tender	−0.10	0.17	1	−1.02	0.82

*: $p < .05$, **: $p < .01$

Table 6. The multiple comparison result for "k: Unintelligent - Intelligent"

Adjective pair	Mean difference	Std. error	Sig.	95% confidence interval	
				Lower bound	Upper bound
a: Unapproachable - Approachable	−1.03**	0.17	0.008	−1.95	−0.10
b: Ugly - Beautiful	−0.56	0.17	0.909	−1.49	0.36
c: Untrustworthy - Trustworthy	−0.62	0.17	0.808	−1.54	0.31
d: Uncool – Cool	0.10	0.17	1	−0.82	1.02
e: Unfriendly - Friendly	−0.92*	0.17	0.049	−1.85	0.00

(*continued*)

Table 6. (*continued*)

Adjective pair	Mean difference	Std. error	Sig.	95% confidence interval	
				Lower bound	Upper bound
f: Clumsy - Graceful	−0.67	0.17	0.663	−1.59	0.26
g: Scary - Unscary	−0.87	0.17	0.105	−1.79	0.05
h: Distressing - Comfortable	−0.87	0.17	0.105	−1.79	0.05
i: Rude - Respectful	−0.41	0.17	0.998	−1.33	0.51
j: Unenjoyable - Enjoyable	−0.64	0.17	0.74	−1.56	0.28
l: Not kawaii - Kawaii	−1.28**	0.17	0	−2.20	−0.36
m: Not willing to use again - Willing to	−0.46	0.17	0.99	−1.38	0.46
n: Dislike - Like	−0.67	0.17	0.663	−1.59	0.26
o: No presence - Has a presence	−0.33	0.17	1	−1.26	0.59
p: Weird – Not weird	−0.67	0.17	0.663	−1.59	0.26
q: Disturbing - Not disturbing	−0.72	0.17	0.495	−1.64	0.20
r: Unsafe - Safe	−1.05**	0.17	0.005	−1.97	−0.13
s: Not kind - Kind	−0.92*	0.17	0.049	−1.85	0.00
t: Untender - Tender	−1.03**	0.17	0.008	−1.95	−0.10

*: $p < .05$, **: $p < .01$

Table 7. The multiple comparison result for "l: Not kawaii - Kawaii"

Adjective pair	Mean difference	Std. error	Sig.	95% confidence interval	
				Lower bound	Upper bound
a: Unapproachable - Approachable	0.26	0.17	1	−0.67	1.18
b: Ugly - Beautiful	0.72	0.17	0.495	−0.20	1.64
c: Untrustworthy - Trustworthy	0.67	0.17	0.663	−0.26	1.59
d: Uncool – Cool	1.38**	0.17	0	0.46	2.31
e: Unfriendly - Friendly	0.36	0.17	1	−0.56	1.28

(*continued*)

Table 7. (*continued*)

Adjective pair	Mean difference	Std. error	Sig.	95% confidence interval	
				Lower bound	Upper bound
f: Clumsy - Graceful	0.62	0.17	0.808	−0.31	1.54
g: Scary - Unscary	0.41	0.17	0.998	−0.51	1.33
h: Distressing - Comfortable	0.41	0.17	0.998	−0.51	1.33
i: Rude - Respectful	0.87	0.17	0.105	−0.05	1.79
j: Unenjoyable - Enjoyable	0.64	0.17	0.74	−0.28	1.56
k: Unintelligent - Intelligent	1.28**	0.17	0	0.36	2.20
m: Not willing to use again - Willing to	0.82	0.17	0.198	−0.10	1.74
n: Dislike - Like	0.62	0.17	0.808	−0.31	1.54
o: No presence - Has a presence	0.95*	0.17	0.032	0.03	1.87
p: Weird – Not weird	0.62	0.17	0.808	−0.31	1.54
q: Disturbing - Not disturbing	0.56	0.17	0.909	−0.36	1.49
r: Unsafe - Safe	0.23	0.17	1	−0.69	1.15
s: Not kind - Kind	0.36	0.17	1	−0.56	1.28
t: Untender - Tender	0.26	0.17	1	−0.67	1.18

*: $p < .05$, **: $p < .01$

5   Discussion

From Fig. 6, Robot Pair 2 was rated lower than Robot Pairs 1 and 3. This can be attributed to the simple shape of the robot. Tables 3, 4, 5, 6 and 7 also shows that there are differences in the rating scores among some adjective pairs, which can be interpreted as follows:

- The adjective pair "a. Unapproachable - Approachable" had significantly higher average score than the adjective pairs "d: Uncool - Cool" and "k: Unintelligent - Intelligent" (Table 3). This indicates that approachability is more important than coolness and intelligence.
- The adjective pair of "d: Uncool - Cool" had a significantly lower mean value than the adjective pairs of "e: Unfriendly – Friendly", "g: Scary – Unscary", "h: Distressing – Comfortable", "l: Not kawaii – Kawaii", "r: Unsafe – Safe", "s: Not kind – Kind", and "t: Untender – Tender" (Table 4). This indicates that evaluations such as friendly, unscary, comfortable, kawaii, safe, kind, and tender are more important than coolness.

- The adjective pair of "e: Unfriendly – Friendly" had a significantly higher mean value than the adjective pair of "k: Unintelligent – Intelligent" (Table 5). This indicates that friendliness is more important than intelligence. This is similar to the results in Table 3, showing that the evaluation value for familiarity is higher than that for intelligence.
- The adjective pairs of "k: Unintelligent – Intelligent" had significantly lower means than the adjective pairs of "l: Not kawaii – Kawaii", "r: Unsafe – Safe", "s: Not kind – Kind", and "t: Untender – Tender" (Table 6). This indicates that evaluations such as kawaii, safe, kind, and tender are more important than intellectuality.
- The adjective pair of "l: Not kawaii – Kawaii" had a significantly higher mean value than the adjective pair of "o: No presence - Has a presence" (Table 7). This indicates that kawaii is more important than presence.

These results indicate that among the adjective pairs used in this study, the kansei of approachable, friendly, not scary, pleasant, kawaii, safe, kind, and tender are important. They also show that the evaluation values for soft images such as "friendly," "kawaii," and "tender" tend to be significantly higher than those for hard images such as "intelligent" and "cool," indicating that round-shaped robots tend to give users soft images.

6 Conclusion and Future Works

By using adjective pairs for affective evaluation, we examined how the physical charac-teristics of the robots affect the affective values. In particular, kansei such as approach-able, friendly, not scary, comfortable, kawaii, safe, kind, and tender are important for round robots, and should be taken into consideration when creating robots that are involved in people's daily lives. In the future, it will be necessary to examine whether there is a difference in the affective values given by robots in virtual space and in real space.

Acknowledgement. This research was based on the results of a collaborative project [5] between Shibaura Institute of Technology, Japan and DePauw University, the United States. We would like to thank Prof. Michiko Ohkura, of Shibaura Institute of Technology, and Prof. Dave Berque and Prof. Hiroko Chiba of DePauw University for permission to use the results of the project and for their guidance. We would also like to express our sincere thanks to Cade Wright and Kevin Bautista for creating the virtual space and the robots.

References

1. Sony Corporation. https://us.aibo.com. Accessed 26 Feb 2021
2. Shibata, T., et al.: Emotional robot for intelligent system—artificial emotional creature project. In: Proceedings of 5th IEEE International Workshop on ROMAN, pp. 466–471 (1996)
3. Mitsuo, N.: What is Kansei engineering? Soc. Fiber Sci. Technol. **50**(8), 468–472 (1994)
4. Mathur, M.B., Reichling, D.B.: Navigating a social world with robot partners: a quantitative cartography of the Uncanny Valley. Cognition **146**, 22–32 (2016)
5. Berque, D. et al.: Cross-cultural design and evaluation of robot prototypes based on Kawaii (Cute) attributes. In: Proceedings of HCI International (2021, in press)

6. Shuto, M., Sayaka, G., Tetsuro, A., Michiko, O.: Systematic study for Kawaii products (3rd report) - comparison of Kawaii feeling in 3D and 2D. Virtual Real. Soc. Jpn. **13**, 2B5–2B6 (2008)
7. Ryo, K., Yuuta, H., Masanoei, K., Hirosi, T., Yukinobu, H.: Proposal construction system for a kansei evaluation approach using SD about the robots. Fuzzy Syst. Symp. **26**, 1278–1281 (2010)

The Use of a Sex Doll as Proxy Technology to Study Human-Robot Interaction

An Jacobs[1,2] (iD), Charlotte I. C. Jewell[1,2], and Shirley A. Elprama[1,2](✉) (iD)

[1] imec-SMIT-Vrije Universiteit Brussel, Pleinlaan 9, 1050 Brussels, Belgium
{an.jacobs,shirley.elprama}@vub.be
[2] BruBotics, Vrije Universiteit Brussel, Pleinlaan 2, 1050 Brussels, Belgium

Abstract. We studied via a survey (n = 187) how people think about the interaction with sex robots by using a sex doll as a proxy technology. An interactive public installation was created centered around a female sex doll. People passing by could participate in the survey while interacting with the installation and the doll. The findings suggest that no gender differences were found, but that we did find a successful way to study a sensitive and uncommon topic. Finally, we also propose alternative ways to elicit responses about sex robots in future research.

Keywords: Human-Robot interaction · Sex · Robots · Relationships · Sex doll · Proxy technology assessment

1 Introduction

In the past decade, sex toys, dolls and robots have become available for purchase [1]. A sex doll can be described as "*human-like, full-body, anatomically correct anthropomorphic doll*", while a sex robot can be described as "*human-like, full-body, anatomically correct humanoid service robot*" [2]. To date, however, little empirical research exists on sex dolls and sex robots [2]. While existing empirical research on sex dolls has mainly focused on sex doll users, by e.g. studying responses from a Real Dolls forum as done by Su and colleagues [3], the research on sex robots has mainly been conducted via online surveys on the acceptance of sex robots [4].

In their review on sex dolls and robots, Döring et al. [2] conclude that in sex doll research there has been described how people can have a meaningful relationship with the doll, while in sex robot research they focus only on sex and not on the other social and relational aspects. The authors of the review also remark that not a single study used a real sex doll or robot as stimulus material.

The purpose of our study was to give the participants an embodied experience with a technology that resembles a sex robot - a sex doll. We used a proxy technology assessment to study future technologies by studying existing technologies that resemble the future technologies as much as possible [5]. As we already pointed out in prior work [6] both sex dolls and sex robots are mainly modeled after women's bodies on categories matching the pornographically categories of the heterosexual male created by the porn industry. We purposively conducted this study in the public domain to encourage reflecting on a

© Springer Nature Switzerland AG 2021
M. Kurosu (Ed.): HCII 2021, LNCS 12763, pp. 241–250, 2021.
https://doi.org/10.1007/978-3-030-78465-2_18

subject that is considered taboo. We focused on the five senses since these are the first interaction points to trigger emotions and reflections on what we desire or revolt in daily life in intimate relations. We used a female sex doll as a proxy technology to answer the following research question: *How do people think and feel about the use of a sex robot, in particular with regard to the five human senses (see, smell, touch, hear and taste)?*

2   Method

An interactive public installation (see Fig. 1) was designed by the authors based on the five human senses. For each sense an experience stimulated the participants to reflect on their requirements for interacting intimately with a robot. During this experience, participants were asked to fill in a questionnaire via their smartphone or via tablet provided by the researchers. The installation was designed to include as many diverse participants as possible by creating a safe space to participate, using recognizable poles with rope like in a museum or a guided tour. To increase the accessibility and attraction of the installation, we also needed to limit the time spend visiting the installation, limiting the topics we could cover in the questionnaire. Next, we describe the flow of the interactive installation.

Fig. 1. The installation with the sex doll (left). The participants were guided through the installation via the questions about the female sex doll (right) in an online survey.

2.1   Procedure and Measures

The access to the installation was shielded by poles with rope, like you see at events or airports to guide the path of the public. The participant was invited to wait in line and check in via a QR code with their personal smart phone. After a general introduction to the installation, they were first asked to fill in three socio-demographic questions (age, gender and mother tongue) and to give consent to the use of their data. Next, they were asked what the word sex robot made them think of (Q1, see Table 1 for an overview of the questions). The first stop in the installation was the view on the female sex doll called Camila sitting in a chair (Q2). Subsequently, we showed a short clip of two commercially available sex robots (RealDoll, Harmony and Henry) to stimulate reflection on sound and voice (Q3). Then, the visitor was invited to sit next to the doll on a sofa and was questioned about the experience of touch (Q4–7). Finally, we provided five sample fragrance bottles (e.g. perfumes, silicone) and let the participants pick their preferred fragrances (Q8). We did not have the participants taste something, but we let them reflect on it (Q9). Finally, we asked whether using a sex robot is considered cheating (Q10).

Table 1. shows an overview of the questions that were posed in the survey

Question	Topic	Statement	Answering options
Q1	General	What is the first word you think of or thought of when you heard the word sex robot? Please write down one word in the box below	Open ended question
Q2	See	Do you think that people find Camila (sex doll) attractive?	Definitely yes – probably yes – might or might not – probably not – definitely not
Q3	Hear	In which language would you want Harmony/Henry (sex robot) to speak to you?	Multiple choice (one option): Dutch, Flemish, French, English, German, Could not hear any sound, Other
Q4	Touch	Did you touch Camila (sex doll)?	Yes – No
Q5	Touch	Which part(s) did you touch?	Multiple options: Fingers, arm, shoulder, breasts, neck, lips, cheek, nose, hair, thigh, lower leg, foot, other.
Q6	Touch	What do you think about the way Camila (sex doll) feels?	Open ended question
Q7	Touch	What was the reason(s) for not touching Camila?	Open ended question
Q8	Smell	How would you want a sex robot to smell?	The participants could blindly pick 1 out of 5 bottles of the same size and form. Each bottle contained a cotton ball with one scent: male perfume, female perfume, disinfectant, silicone and no scent
Q9	Taste	How, according to you, should taste be incorporated in future sex robots?	Open ended question
Q10	Cheating	I consider the use of a sex robot by my partner as cheating	Strongly agree – Somewhat agree – Somewhat disagree – Strongly disagree – I don't know

2.2 Data Collection and Analysis

Data was collected at a public event organized around a book launch on robotics and for two full days on the campus of our university. The quantitative analysis was done with IBM SPSS version 27. We used a Mann-Whitney U-Test or an independent t-test to compare differences between male and female respondents, and between younger and older participants. The data met the assumptions for a Mann-Whitley U-test as described in [7]. Some assumptions for the independent t-tests were violated but this is reported in more detail in the result section. The qualitative analysis was done with Microsoft Excel to support a thematic analysis of the open answers in the questionnaires.

2.3 Participants

187 participants filled in the questionnaire (50% was male; 49% female and 1% other). The participants ranged between 18 and 71 years old (mean = 26.1; SD = 10.2). The mother tongue of the participants was Dutch (64%), French (16%), English (4%), German (3%) and 14% selected other languages. We did not ask about their sexual orientation and relationship status since this was an exploratory study and we wanted to keep the barrier towards their participation as low as possible.

3 Results

The participants were asked what the first word was that came into their mind after reading the word 'sex robot'. The five most frequently mentioned words were *'weird'*, *'sex'*, *'technology'*, *'unnatural'*, *'interesting'* and *'fun'* as can be seen in Table 2.

Table 2. Shows the 5 most frequently mentioned words associated with sex robot

Word	Examples	Frequency (n = 183)
Weird	Weird, bizarre, strange	39 (21%)
Sex	Sex, blowjob, orgasm	20 (11%)
Technology		7 (4%)
Unnatural	Artificial	6 (3%)
Interesting		6 (3%)
Fun		6 (3%)

3.1 See

In response to the question "*Do you think that people find Camila attractive*", the participants answered definitely yes (10%), probably yes (29%), might or might not (32%), probably not (20%) and definitely not (10%). We also checked whether there were sex and age differences for this statement, but no significant differences were found.

For all comparisons in this paper between **gender**, we only included male and female participants. The Median attractiveness score was not statistically significant between males (3) and females (3), $U = 4139, z = -0.003, p = 0.998$. The score of 3 referred to the middle point in the scale and corresponded to the option "*might or might not*".

To compare the difference between **younger and older** participants we used the same test and we divided the participants in two groups: younger (aged 18–25 years old) and older (aged 26 years and older). We used 25 years old as the cut-off point since is this is considered the general age to end your university studies in Belgium. The Median attractiveness score was statistically significant between younger (3) and older participants (4), $U = 2514, z = -3.1, p = 0.002$. Older participants rated the doll to be more attractive to the public compared to students. The score of 3 referred to the middle point in the scale and corresponded to the option "*might or might not*" while 4 referred to "*probably yes*".

The sex doll, as also the existing sex robots, has visually all features of a classical porn stereotype (blond, slim, with big breasts). Our participants are rather equally distributed in their opinion on the perceived attractiveness of the doll for the general public. We did not ask about their own interpretation, but let people project on the expectation of the opinion of the general public. The dominance and internalization of the heteronormative male gaze can maybe be an explanation for the absence of a gender difference.

3.2 Hear

The participants were also asked in which language they would want to speak with a female or male sex robot. For the female robot, 57% of the participants preferred their mother tongue whereas 43% preferred another language than their mother tongue. For the male robot, 55% preferred their mother tongue and 46% preferred another language. The majority of the participants (81%) chose the same language for both robots.

The two venues where the data was collected are international environments where other languages than the own mother tongue are often used; this could explain the preference for other languages. The origin of the question about language was stimulated by the longstanding association of a foreign language with adultery and erotism [8]. This also seems to be reflected in the statistics.

3.3 Feel

The doll is made from high quality silicon, and when the skin is touched it is not rigid. We overheard many times people calling out that it felt so "real". The participants were asked whether they touched the sex doll and the majority (70%; n = 116) did touch the doll which indicates that we designed a safe space to explored touch in the installation. The most frequent reasons that were given why participants did not touch the doll were comments such as "*it's weird*" or "*uncomfortable*".

Those 116 people that touched the doll were asked which body parts they touched: arm (66%), fingers (45%), cheek (37%), breasts (24%), lower leg (22%), hair (22%), lips (21%), nose (20%), shoulder (16%), neck (16%), thigh (15%), foot (6%) and other (7%).

The researchers also saw a lot of times that the touch was more like squeezing the skin. Especially the flexibility of the doll's cheek was put to the test, which is a very intimate gesture we display often with children and relatives.

The average amount of body parts that was touched by the 116 respondents was 3.2 (SD = 2.8) with a minimum amount of touched body parts 1 and 12 as a maximum. Figure 2 show the percentage with which each body part was touched by male and female respondents.

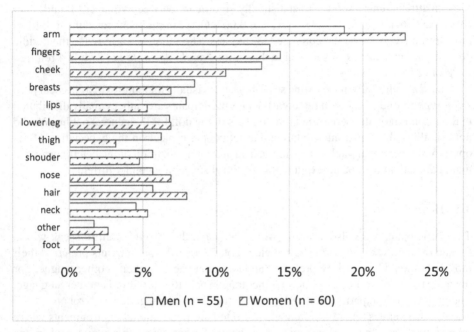

Fig. 2. Shows which body parts of the sex doll were touched by men and women (n = 115)

We investigated whether there was a difference in the number of body parts touched by male and female respondents with an independent-samples t-test. There were 55 males and 60 females. Although a Boxplot with gender and the number of body parts touched revealed 6 outliers, we decided to keep them in the data. While the data was not normally distributed, we decided to conduct an independent-samples t-test since the sample size was rather small and the data was fairly even skewed per gender. The number of body parts touched was approximately equal for both groups. Females touched the sex doll on average 3.2 times (SD = 3.0) while males touched the doll 3.3 times on average (SD = 2.7). The difference was not significant with (95% CI, −1.02 to 1.10), $t(113) = 0.071, p = 0.94$.

The same analysis was conducted to compare students and non-students and also no significant difference was found (95% CI, −1.34 to 0.91). $t(114) = -0.380, p =$

0.71. Students touched the sex doll on average 3.2 times (SD = 2.8) while non-students touched the doll 3.4 times (SD = 2.9).

3.4 Smell

How does a sex robot need to smell to appeal to a human? We know from prior research that fragrances - like perfumes and deodorants – are mainly designed and presented as female or male. They are seen - as other cosmetics - as means to enhance our biological traits, to be more attractive to a potential sexual partner. Is there this expectation that a sex robot mirrors our human-human expectations or are there other preferences [9]? The male deodorant was chosen by 38.4% of the participants as the most preferred scent for a sex robot and almost equally preferred was female floral perfume (37.8%). Other scents that were picked included silicone (11%), nothing but air (7%), sanitizer (3%) and other (2%). Silicone was chosen, because the doll was made of this material and sanitizer was picked, because this could be used to clean the doll after use.

A total of 124 participants (62 males and 62 females) picked either the male deodorant or the female floral perfume. 57% of the males preferred the female perfume, while 44% preferred the female perfume. For females, 57% picked the male perfume, while 44% picked the male perfume. This difference in proportions was 0.13 and it was not significant with $p = 0.15$.

A total of 125 participants (90 younger and 35 older participants) picked either the male deodorant or the female perfume. 51% of the younger participants preferred the male deodorant, while 49% preferred the female floral perfume. 49% of the older participants preferred the male deodorant, while 51% preferred the female floral perfume. The difference in proportions was 0.03 and the difference was not significant with $p = 0.8$.

3.5 Taste

For the topic of taste, we opted for an open question since we had very little cues to offer pre-structured choices from scientific literature like we did with the other senses.

The following question was posed about taste: *"How, according to you, should taste be incorporated in future sex robots?"* Most people answered that they didn't know (26%). Other examples of answers include that no taste was needed (15%), that a sex robot should taste realistically (like a human) (13%) or sweet (13%). Other categories that were identified can be found in Table 3. If a body part was mentioned that should have a taste, lips were mainly mentioned.

3.6 Moral Closing Question on Cheating

Since sexuality is still a taboo topic, it is also related to morality, how one should and should not behave to be accepted in society. The hetero normative dominant view on relationships in our Western society is that monogamous relationships are the norm. In the survey study of Scheutz and Arnold [10] one of the questions about acceptable behavior was if people agreed with the statement that sex robots could be appropriately

Table 3. Preferences relate to the taste of sex robots

Category	Examples	Frequency (N = 163) (100%)
Don't know	*"No idea"*, *"I'm not sure"*	42 (26%)
No taste	*"For me no taste"*, *"Tasteless"*	24 (15%)
Realistic (like a human)	*"like a human"*, *"skin"*,*"salty"*	22 (13%)
Sweet	"Like a strawberry", "Fruit", "Sweet"	21 (13%)
Did not answer the question	–	10 (6%)
Other	*"Not a lot* (taste)", *"Not silicone"*, *"A lot* (of taste)", *"Maybe"*	9 (6%)
Yes, taste	"Yes, it's good to have"	8 (5%)
Body part	*"A certain taste when you kiss the robot perhaps"*, *"around the lips"*	7 (4%)
Customizable	*"I don't think the robot should any like a human being. I could be like an electronic cigarette, choosing your taste in function of what you want."*	6 (4%)
Various food and drinks	*"When kissing at least a good taste like peppermint"*, *"Chocolate"*, *"Like a good glass of champagne"*	6 (4%)
Make up	*"Add high end perfume with a minor taste to it"*, *"Lip gloss"*	4 (2%)
Good	*"Good"*, *"Very tastefully"*	4 (2%)

used instead of cheating on their partner. Men agreed on average more with this statement than women. We reversed the moral problem by asking whether they agreed with the following statement: *"I consider the use of sex robots by my partner as cheating."* They answered the following: strongly agree (17%), somewhat agree (29%), somewhat disagree (14%), strongly disagree (27%) and I don't know (13%). Overall, more than half of the respondents agreed that they consider the use of sex robots by their partner as cheating. We also calculated whether there were gender or age differences for this statement. Although gender differences were close to being significant, we did not find gender or age differences for the statement on cheating.

We used a Mann-Whitney U-Test to compare **gender differences** for the statement on cheating. For this analysis, we considered the *"I don't know"* option as missing data. The Median score on cheating was not statistically significant between males (2) and females (3), $U = 2005.5$, $z = -1.9$, $p = 0.054$. The score of 2 referred to *"somewhat disagree"* while the score of 3 referred to *"somewhat agree"*.

We also investigated **age differences** with regard to the statement on cheating. The Median score on cheating was not statistically significant between younger (3) and older participants (2), $U = 1593, z = -1.5, p = 0.144$.

4 Conclusion and Discussion

All interaction with humans, and certainly intimate interactions are multisensorial. In this study, we stimulated people to think about these different sensing requirements in interacting with a robot marketed for intimate, sexual interactions. Sex with a doll or a robot, is a taboo subject, as we also noticed by the responses to the sex doll that included comments such as *"weird"*. However, we argue that more research is needed to investigate how a (sex) robot could contribute to interactions between or with people. Although previous research has found some gender differences, we did not find any gender differences in this study. Our research has some limitations such as only using a female sex doll as a stimulus and not a male sex doll. The research was conducted in a public place which might have influenced the more sensitive questions (e.g. touching a doll where more appropriate vs. where you might touch a doll when being more intimate), while other researchers have suggested that sex dolls or robots would be typically used in a home environment [2]. By conducting this research, we are (one of the firsts) to use a real sex doll as a stimulus for research on sex robots. Although it allowed to study the topic to some extent, future research might need to be conducted in a more private setting to elicit more open responses from the participants.

In future research, we will aim to collect more data from a larger sample size and include other relevant variables such as sexual orientation and relationship status. It is possible that few significant findings were found due to our small sample size. Also, we would like to collect more qualitative data which allow to inspire the formulation of design requirements of sex robots. One potential way to conduct this research is to organize a co-creation session after seeing our doll installation to inspire and encourage thinking out of the box about other body shapes that are not male heteronormative [cf. 6]. Another potential approach to discuss this subject with participants is by collecting data via an online chat bot, where participants can freely express their opinions on the topic of sex robots via open ended questions, or alternatively have participants talk in a photobooth like setup about sex robots. In future research, we would also want to include more qualitative research data and also more (open-ended) questions related to (relational) activities (dining, caressing, dressing the robot up) people would like to engage in with sex robots.

Our installation was also invited to an exhibition on robots which unfortunately was cancelled due to the COVID-19 pandemic. The nature of our exhibition would allow a corona proof experience if the doll would be disinfected regularly and if the visitors would disinfect their hands before participating in the experience, nonetheless it is not an ideal setup for current pandemic times.

In conclusion, we have developed a successful way and approach to question about and to involve in an uncommon and sensitive topic such as sex robots. Our approach can be reused and adapted to collect more data for future research.

References

1. Döring, N., Pöschl, S.: Sex toys, sex dolls, sex robots: our under-researched bed-fellows. Sexologies **27**(3), 51–55 (2018)
2. Döring, N., Rohangis Mohseni, M., Walter, R.: Design, use, and effects of sex dolls and sex robots: scoping review. J. Med. Internet Res. **22**(7) (2020).10.2196/18551
3. Su, N.M., Lazar, A., Bardzell, J., Bardzell, S.: Of dolls and men: anticipating sexual intimacy with robots. ACM Trans. Comput.-Hum. Interact. **26**(3) (2019). 10.1145/3301422
4. Szczuka, J., Krämer, N.: Influences on the intention to buy a sex robot: an empirical study on influences of personality traits and personal characteristics on the intention to buy a sex robot. In: Cheok, A.D., Devlin, K., Levy, D. (eds.) Love and Sex with Robots: Second International Conference, pp. 72–83. Springer, New York, USA (2017). https://doi.org/10.1007/978-3-319-57738-8_7
5. Pierson, J., Jacobs, A., Dreessen, K., Van den Broeck, I., Lievens, B.: Walking the interface: uncovering practices through 'proxy technology assessment'. In: Proceedings of EPIC 2006: The Second Annual Ethnographic Praxis in Industry Conference, pp. 40–54. National Association for the Practice of Anthropology; Portland, Oregon (2006)
6. Jewell, C.I.C., Jacobs, A.: Will you fall head over heels in love with a robot? In: Jacobs, A., Tytgat, L., Maus, M., Meeusen, R., Vanderborght, B. (eds.) 30 Questions and Answers on Man, Technology, Science & Art. VubPress (2019)
7. Laerd Statistics: Statistical tutorials and software guides. https://statistics.laerd.com/ (2015). Accessed 25 Feb 2021
8. Kellman, S.G.: Promiscuous tongues: erotics of translingualism and translation. Neohelicon **40**(1), 35–45 (2013)
9. Allen, C.: The artificially scented ape: investigating the role of fragrances and body odours in human interactions. University of Stirling (2015)
10. Scheutz, M., Arnold, T.: Are we ready for sex robots? In: 11th ACM/IEEE International Conference on Human-Robot Interaction (HRI), pp. 351–358. IEEE (2016)

Relationship Between Robot Designs and Preferences in Kawaii Attributes

Tipporn Laohakangvalvit[(⊠)], Peeraya Sripian, Midori Sugaya, and Michiko Ohkura

Shibaura Institute of Technology, 3-7-5, Toyosu, Koto-ku, Tokyo 135-8548, Japan
{tipporn,peeraya,doly}@shibaura-it.ac.jp,
ohkura@sic.shibaura-it.ac.jp

Abstract. As robots have been increasingly involved in human lives I modern society, it is necessary to further develop the robots that give positive impression to human. Therefore, we pursued a collaborative project in which Japanese and American university students designed and developed kawaii robots. Before and after the collaborative work, preferences of kawaii attributes were also evaluated by a questionnaire. As a result, we obtained eight different robot pairs. In addition, we performed cluster analysis using the questionnaires on kawaii preferences and obtained clusters of participants before and after the collaborative work. Finally, we analyzed the relationship between robot designs and the clustering results. The cluster analysis shows that more than half of the participants did not change their kawaii preferences, while some of them did especially those who did not have preconceived images of kawaii robots. Therefore, we concluded that participants developed a deeper understanding about kawaii after collaborating on this project about the diversity of opinions people have about the concept of kawaii.

Keywords: Virtual space · Kawaii · Robot

1 Introduction

In modern society, robots have been increasingly involved in human lives. Advancements in technology have been applied to robot development which enables them to effectively support human tasks in various scenarios, for example, service robots in public spots, companion robots for children and the elderly, and so on [1]. Because a future society with human-robot interaction is approaching, it is necessary to further develop the robots to give positive impressions to humans [2, 3].

Based on the Affective Engineering approach, affective values can strengthen the impact on the first impressions of products and services [4]. Kawaiiness is one affective values that denotes such positive connotations as cute, lovable, and charming, and plays a critical role in the worldwide success of many products such as Hello Kitty and Pokemon [5, 6]. Based on this success, we believe that kawaiiness will be a key factor for future product development.

Previous studies have examined the attributes that contribute to kawaiiness: shape, size, color, texture, and tactile sensation, for example [7]. By employing these kawaii

© Springer Nature Switzerland AG 2021
M. Kurosu (Ed.): HCII 2021, LNCS 12763, pp. 251–261, 2021.
https://doi.org/10.1007/978-3-030-78465-2_19

attributes to robot designs, we expected to improve human's impressions of robots by enabling robots to give more positive effect in human-robot interaction.

As kawaii products are increasingly popular not only in Japan but also worldwide, it will be useful to investigate people's preferences for kawaiiness by taking into account the diversity by nationalities, genders, and even individuals [8]. Various factors might impact the shifting of understanding and impression in kawaii products. Revealing the diversity of kawaii preferences will be useful to design future kawaii robots that provide emotional fulfilment for a variety of users.

Therefore, we carried out a collaborative project to design and develop kawaii robots [9]. This paper presents the analysis of results collected from the students participating the project. The purpose is to clarify the relationship between robot designs and preferences in kawaii attributes. This research result will be useful as evidence that participating students could develop deeper understanding about kawaii after collaborating on this project that explored the diversity of opinions people have about the concept of kawaii.

2   Robot Designs

In this project, we asked participants to collaborate online to design robots in virtual space. The participants were divided into two groups. Each group had four members: half of them live in Japan and the other half live in the United States. Each group first designed a virtual environment for the robots. Then, each participant designed one robot pair based on a requirement that one robot in the pair was more kawaii than the other one by changing one physical attribute. Finally, they developed the virtual space and robots using Unity as a development platform. The details of design and implementation of this collaborative project are described in [9].

Team A designed and developed four robot pairs in a train station as shown in Figs. 1, 2, 3 and 4. Team B designed and developed four robot pairs in a university (using our Toyosu campus of Shibaura Institute of Technology as a model) as shown in Figs. 5, 6, 7 and 8. For all figures, more-kawaii robots are shown on the left side and less-kawaii ones are shown on the right side.

Fig. 1. Robot pairs #A1 in train station by Team A, Participant P_A1

Fig. 2. Robot pairs #A2 in train station by Team A, Participant P_A2

Fig. 3. Robot pairs #A3 in train station by Team A, Participant P_A3

Fig. 4. Robot pairs #A4 in train station by Team A, Participant P_A4

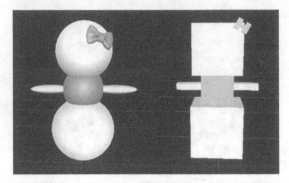

Fig. 5. Robot pairs #B1 in university by Team B, Participant P_B1

Fig. 6. Robot pairs #B2 in university by Team B, Participant P_B2

Fig. 7. Robot pairs #B3 in university by Team B, Participant P_B3

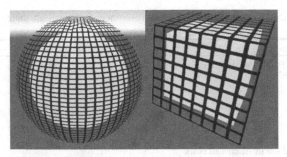

Fig. 8. Robot pairs #B4 in university by Team B, Participant P_B4

3   Questionnaire About Kawaii Preferences

We used a questionnaire about kawaii preferences to confirm similarities and differences of preferences in kawaii attributes such as color. As show in Table 1, the questionnaire consists of ten items: five items ask to choose the most kawaii colors (Q1 to Q5), one item ask to choose more kawaii characters (Q6), and four items ask to choose more kawaii dresses (Q7 to Q10). These questions were designed based on our previous studies on the kawaiiness of colors [10], characters [11], and dresses [12].

In addition, the participants answered this questionnaire two times, before and after working on the 1.5-month collaborative project (pre- and post-questionnaire), in order to observe any changes in the understanding and preferences about kawaii. The orders of colors, characters, and dresses are different between the two questionnaires.

4   Results

4.1   Result of Robot Designs

Based on the physical attributes and behaviors of all eight robot designs, we divided the robots into three groups as follows:

- **Group 1 (Living creatures)**: The robots look and behave similar to living creatures, i.e., having facial features like human, and moving like living animals. The robots in this group consist of #A3, #B1, and #B2.
- **Group 2 (Non-living creatures)**: The robots look and behave like machines. The robots in this group consist of #A1 and #A4.
- **Group 3 (Intermediate creatures)**: The robots look and behave like the mixture of living (Group 1) and non-living (Group 2) creatures. The robots in this group consist of #A2, #B3, and #B4.

Table 1. Questionnaire about preferences in kawaii attributes

ID	Question	Choices
Q1	Choose the most kawaii color	1A 1B 1C 1D 1E
Q2	Choose the most kawaii color	2A 2B 2C 2D 2E
Q3	Choose the most kawaii color	3A 3B 3C 3D 3E
Q4	Choose the most kawaii color	4A 4B 4C 4D 4E
Q5	Write the number of the most kawaii color from your choices in the previous 4 questions	-
Q6	Which is more kawaii?	A B
Q7	Which dress is more kawaii?	A B
Q8	Which dress is more kawaii?	A B
Q9	Which dress is more kawaii?	A B
Q10	Which dress is more kawaii?	A B

4.2   Results of Questionnaire About Kawaii Preferences

Pre-questionnaire Results. We obtained the pre-questionnaire results before starting the collaborative work (Table 2). We used a total of 10 parameters (i.e., Q1, Q2, Q3, Q4, Q5, Q6, Q8, Q10, gender, and country of residence; Note that Q7 and Q9 were excluded because all answers were the same.) as input of the cluster analysis using two-step clustering method with log-likelihood distance measure and Schwarz's Bayesian Criterion (BIC). As a result, the participants were divided into two clusters with the following cluster membership:

- Cluster #1: P_A3, P_B1, P_B2, P_B3
- Cluster #2: P_A1, P_A2, P_A4, P_B4

Table 2. Pre-questionnaire result and corresponding country of residence

Team	Participant	Q1	Q2	Q3	Q4	Q5	Q6	Q7	Q8	Q9	Q10	Country
A	P_A1	1A	2E	3B	4E	3B	A	A	B	A	B	US
A	P_A2	1E	2D	3A	4E	2D	B	A	B	A	B	Japan
A	P_A3	1E	2A	3C	4C	3C	B	A	B	A	B	US
A	P_A4	1D	2E	3E	4E	4E	A	A	B	A	A	Japan
B	P_B1	1D	2A	3C	4C	2A	B	A	A	A	B	US
B	P_B2	1C	2A	3C	4C	2A	B	A	B	A	A	US
B	P_B3	1B	2A	3C	4E	3C	B	A	B	A	B	Japan
B	P_B4	1C	2D	3B	4A	3B	B	A	B	A	B	Japan

Along with the clustering result, we obtained the result of input importance for the pre-questionnaire. Table 3 shows the distribution of parameters of each cluster ordered by the input importance. The percentages indicate the number of participants selecting the shown answer in each parameter.

Post-questionnaire Result. We obtained the post-questionnaire results after finishing the collaborative work (Table 4). We used a total of 10 parameters (i.e., Q1, Q2, Q3, Q4, Q5, Q6, Q7, Q10, gender, and country of residence; Note that Q8 and Q9 were excluded because all answers were the same.) as input of the cluster analysis using two-step clustering method with log-likelihood distance measure and a fixed number of clusters of two ($k = 2$). We changed the clustering criterion from the pre-questionnaire clustering analysis to observe the change of cluster membership while the number of clusters was still the same. As a result, the participants were divided into two clusters with the following cluster membership:

- Cluster #1: P_A2, P_A3, P_B1, P_B2, P_B4
- Cluster #2: P_A1, P_A4, P_B3

Table 3. Distribution of parameters from pre-questionnaire ordered by input importance

Input Parameter	Input Importance	Cluster #1 (P_A3, P_B1, P_B2, P_B3)		Cluster #2 (P_A1, P_A2, P_A4, P_B4)	
Q2	1.00		2A (100%)		2E (50%)
Q3	0.77		3C (100%)		3B (50%)
Q4	0.63		4C (75%)		4E (75%)
Q5	0.60		3C (50%)		3B (50%)
Q6	0.57		B (100%)		B (50%)
Country	0.46		US (75%)		Japan (75%)
Q8	0.31		B (75%)		B (100%)
Q1	0.08		1B (25%)		1A (25%)
Gender	0.00		Male (75%)		Male (75%)
Q10	0.00		B (75%)		B (75%)

Table 4. Post-questionnaire result and corresponding country of residence

Team	Participant	Q1	Q2	Q3	Q4	Q5	Q6	Q7	Q8	Q9	Q10	Country
A	P_A1	1A	2E	3B	4A	3B	A	A	B	A	B	US
A	P_A2	1E	2D	3E	4D	2D	B	A	B	A	B	Japan
A	P_A3	1D	2B	3E	4C	3E	B	A	B	A	B	US
A	P_A4	1C	2E	3B	4D	3B	A	A	B	A	B	Japan
B	P_B1	1C	2A	3C	4B	3C	B	A	B	A	B	US
B	P_B2	1A	2B	3C	4C	2B	B	B	B	A	B	US
B	P_B3	1B	2E	3C	4C	3C	A	B	B	A	A	Japan
B	P_B4	1C	2E	3C	4E	3C	B	A	B	A	B	Japan

Along with the clustering result, we obtained the result of input importance for the post-questionnaire. Table 5 shows the distribution of parameters of each cluster ordered by the input importance.

Table 5. Distribution of parameters from post-questionnaire ordered by input importance

Input Parameter	Input Importance	Cluster #1 (P_A2, P_A3, P_B1, P_B2, P_B4)		Cluster #2 (P_A1, P_A4, P_B3)	
Q6	1.00		B (100%)		A (100%)
Q3	0.45		3C (60%)		3B (66.7%)
Q10	0.33		B (100%)		B (66.7%)
Q2	0.31		2B (40%)		2E (100%)
Q5	0.24		3C (40%)		3B (66.7%)
Country	0.14		US (60%)		Japan (66.7%)
Q1	0.11		1C (40%)		1A (33.3%)
Q4	0.11		4C (40%)		4A (33.3%)
Gender	0.07		Male (80%)		Male (66.7%)
Q7	0.07		A (80%)		A (66.7%)

5   Discussion

A comparison between pre- and post-questionnaire clustering results is interpreted as follows:

- For both results, "gender" and "country" parameters have low importance, which indicate that the genders and countries of residence have less influence on the kawaii selection than the individual preference.
- From the distributions of parameters of post-questionnaire, the participants tend to change their answers after the collaborative work as shown by the changes of cluster memberships. In addition, the percentages of most parameters for both clusters are lower than 50%. These results indicate less robust and more diverse selections after the collaborative work.
- Though the post-questionnaire has greater diversity than the pre-questionnaire, there is a certain consistency in cluster membership: "P_A3, P_B1, P_B2" (Cluster #1) as well as "P_A1, P_A4" (Cluster #2) are in the same clusters as shown in Table 6.

Table 6. Comparison of cluster memberships between pre- and post-questionnaires

Cluster #	Pre-questionnaire	Post-questionnaire
1	**P_A3**, **P_B1**, **P_B2**, P_B3	P_A2, **P_A3**, **P_B1**, **P_B2**, P_B4
2	**P_A1**, P_A2, **P_A4**, P_B4	**P_A1**, **P_A4**, P_B3

We further considered the relationship between robot designs and kawaii preferences. More than half of the participants did not change their kawaii preferences, while some participants did. particularly P_A2, P_B3 and P_B4, all of whose robots are in Group 3 (Intermediate creatures). These three participants might not have preconceived images of kawaii, resulting in designing the robots as intermediate creatures and also changing their kawaii selections after being influenced and developing their understanding about kawaii by various images of kawaii robots of other participants. On the other hand, the rest of the participants tend to have preconceived images of kawaii. They designed the robots as either living or non-living creatures and also did not change their kawaii selections even after the collaborative work.

In summary, we obtained the following findings:

- Kawaii selection may change. However, there exists a certain consistency.
- Kawaii selection is not different between countries of residence and gender.
- The post-questionnaire results are more diverse, which may indicate that the participants developed deeper understanding about kawaii after joining this collaborative project for the diversity of kawaii concept.

6 Conclusion

This paper presents an affective evaluation of kawaii robot designs and their relationship with preferences in kawaii attributes from our collaborative project [9]. Two groups of participants collaborated to design and develop a virtual space. Then, each participant designed and developed their own robot pairs by changing one physical attribute to make one robot more kawaii than the other. In addition, they answered questionnaire on kawaii preferences before and after the collaborative work.

Based on the collaborative work, we obtained robots divided into three groups: living-creatures, non-living creatures, and intermediate creatures. Next, we performed cluster analysis of the participants using the pre- and post-questionnaires which show clusters of participants and important attributes of each cluster. Finally, we analyzed the relationship between robot designs and clustering results. The cluster analysis shows that more than half of the participants did not change their kawaii preferences, while some of them did. Therefore, we concluded that some participants developed a deeper understanding about the concept of kawaii through this collaborative project.

For future work, we will continue to analyze more data from the affective evaluation of the robot pairs to clarify the impressions of the robots in relation to the physical attributes.

Acknowledgment. We thank the following team members for participating in this collaborative project: Prof. Dave Berque, Prof. Hiroko Chiba, Kevin Bautista, Jordyn Blakey, Eric Spehlmann and Cade Wright of the DePauw University as well as Chen Feng, Shun Imura and Wenkang Huang and Kento Murayama of the Shibaura Institute of Technology.

References

1. Coronado, E., Venture, G., Yamanobe, N.: Applying Kansei/affective engineering methodologies in the design of social and service robots: a systematic review. Int. J. Soc. Rob., 1–11 (2020)
2. Pereira, A., Leite, I., Mascarenhas, S., Martinho, C., Paiva, A.: Using empathy to improve human-robot relationships. In: Lamers, M.H., Verbeek, F.J. (eds.) HRPR 2010. LNICST, vol. 59, pp. 130–138. Springer, Heidelberg (2011). https://doi.org/10.1007/978-3-642-19385-9_17
3. James, J., Watson, C.I., MacDonald, B.: Artificial empathy in social robots: an analysis of emotions in speech. In: 27th IEEE International Symposium on Robot and Human Interactive Communication (RO-MAN 2018), Nanjing, China, pp. 632–637. IEEE (2018)
4. Nagamachi, M.: Kansei engineering: a new ergonomic consumer-oriented technology for product development. Int. J. Ind. Ergon. 15(1), 3–11 (1995)
5. Kovarovic, S.: Hello kitty: a brand made of cuteness. J. Cult. Retail Image 4(1), 1–8 (2011)
6. Allison, A.: Portable monsters and commodity cuteness: Pokemon as Japan's new global power. Postcolonial Stud. 6(3), 381–395 (2003)
7. Ohkura, M., Komatsu, T., Aoto, T.: Kawaii rules: increasing affective value of industrial products. In: Watada, J., Shiizuka, H., Lee, K.-P., Otani, T., Lim, C.-P. (eds.) Industrial Applications of Affective Engineering, pp. 97–110. Springer, Cham (2014). https://doi.org/10.1007/978-3-319-04798-0_8
8. Lieber-Milo, S., Nittono, H.: How the Japanese term Kawaii is perceived outside of Japan: a study in Israel. SAGE Open 9(3), 1–7 (2019)
9. Ohkura, M., Sugaya, M., Sripian, P., Laohakangvalvit, T., Chiba, H., Berque, D.: Design and implementation of Kawaii robots by Japanese and American university students using remote collaboration. In: 7th International Symposium on Affective Science and Engineering (ISASE 2021). Japan Society of Kansei Engineering, Tokyo, Japan (2021, in press)
10. Komatsu, T., Ohkura, M.: Study on evaluation of Kawaii colors using visual analog scale. In: Smith, M.J., Salvendy, G. (eds.) Human Interface 2011. LNCS, vol. 6771, pp. 103–108. Springer, Heidelberg (2011). https://doi.org/10.1007/978-3-642-21793-7_12
11. Ohkura, M., Yamasaki, Y., Horie, R.: Evaluation of Kawaii objects in augmented reality by ECG. In: The 36th Annual International Conference of the IEEE Engineering in Medicine and Biology Society (EMBC 2014), FB14.12, Chicago, USA (2014)
12. Fukuoka, R., Tombe, T., Sripian, P., Ohkura, M.: Comparison of relations of Kawaii feelings and eye-tracking information between 3D and 2D images using HMD with eye-tracking. In: The 14th Spring Meeting of Japan Society of Kansei Engineering. Japan Society of Kansei Engineering, Nagano, Japan (2019). (in Japanese)

Perceived Robot Attitudes of Other People and Perceived Robot Use Self-efficacy as Determinants of Attitudes Toward Robots

Rita Latikka[1]([✉]) [ID], Nina Savela[1] [ID], Aki Koivula[2] [ID], and Atte Oksanen[1] [ID]

[1] Faculty of Social Sciences, Tampere University, Kalevantie 5, 33014 Tampere, Finland
{rita.latikka,nina.savela,atte.oksanen}@tuni.fi
[2] Faculty of Social Sciences, University of Turku, Assistentinkatu 7, 20014 Turku, Finland
akjeko@utu.fi

Abstract. The emergence of artificial intelligence and robotization is prospected to transform societies remarkably. This study examined the associations between perceived robot attitudes of other people, perceived robot use self-efficacy, and attitudes toward robots. An online survey was collected from respondents living in the United States ($N = 969$). Analyses were conducted using t-tests, linear regression models, and mediation analyses with bootstrapped estimates. Results showed that participants with prior robot use experience expressed more positive attitudes toward robots, more positive perceived robot attitudes of other people, higher robot use self-efficacy, and higher general interest in technology and its development compared to participants without prior robot use experience. Perceived positive robot attitudes of other people, perceived robot use self-efficacy, and general interest in technology correlated with more positive attitudes toward robots among all study participants. Further, results showed that the association between perceived robot use self-efficacy and attitudes toward robots was particularly strong among those without prior robot use experience, highlighting the importance of self-efficacy beliefs in the early stages of technology adoption. The mediation analysis showed that the association between perceived robot attitudes of other people and attitudes toward robots was indirect through perceived robot use self-efficacy. The association between perceived robot use self-efficacy and attitudes toward robots was indirect through general interest in technology. Results indicate the importance of social psychological aspects of robot use and their usefulness in professionals' implementation of new robot technologies.

Keywords: Robots · Attitudes · Social psychology · Social influence · Robot use self-efficacy

1 Introduction

The emergence of artificial intelligence and robotization is prospected to transform societies remarkably [26]. Different human characteristics predicting successful implementation of novel technologies have been a topic of researchers' interest for decades [25]. This line of research is relevant also today as robots become more familiar to people. Increasingly, scholars have been investigating attitudes toward robots and their acceptance in various fields and walks of life [6, 13, 28–30, 35]. However, more research is needed on the social psychological factors determining attitudes toward robots beyond the traditional technology acceptance models. Social psychological research has established that social factors and confidence in one's own abilities to successfully perform in certain tasks could influence people's thinking and behavior [2, 5, 8, 9]. Despite the possible high relevance of these factors in determining attitudes toward robots, they have been sporadically studied thus far in the context of robots and investigations have been limited to a specific field or a robot type.

Attitudes refer to relatively steady positive, negative, or neutral evaluations of the target [14]. They are formed, as suggested by attitude multicomponent theory, through three main components: cognitive, affective, and behavioral information [33]. Cognitive component mirrors one's beliefs and cognitive evaluations of the object, affective information considers feelings of and emotional responses to the object, and behavioral part refers to individuals' behavioral intentions and self-reported or observable behaviors [7, 28]. Treating dimensions as a single attitude construct has proven to be valid [1, 32], and together the dimensions can provide a comprehensive view on attitudes. Various widely used technology acceptance models have identified human attitude as determining factor of behavioral intention or actual use of novel technologies including social robots [10, 16, 39].

Social influence, drawing upon social information processing theory, suggests that information conveyed by the individual's own social network influences the way one views the target technology [34, 36]. In addition to information persuasion, social psychologists investigating conformity, compliance, and social norms have studied the idea that people's behavior and opinions are affected by social factors [8, 9]. In the context of technology, social norms have been adapted and further studied, extending the original technology acceptance model (TAM) to include social influence [11, 21]. Attitudes have been suggested to function socially – that is, attitudes are also affected by social influences, including adopting other peoples' attitudes [40].

Self-efficacy beliefs refer to one's perceptions of own capabilities to succeed in a specific situation or a task [2, 5]. Self-efficacy beliefs shape the way how individuals think, feel, behave, and motivate themselves [4]. The concept of perceived self-efficacy is based on social cognitive theory (STC) [3] which explains human activity through triadic reciprocal determinism among personal, environmental, and behavioral aspects bidirectionally affecting each other [37]. Self-efficacy beliefs have been explored yet only sporadically within the context of robots, even though it has a long history in technology acceptance research in general. In the context of robots, robot use self-efficacy has been identified as a separate construct from general self-efficacy beliefs [38], and to associate with higher acceptance of robots [24], and trust toward robots and artificial intelligence [31].

In the light of previous literature, the role of firsthand experiences of robots remains somewhat ambiguous. However, several studies have indicated that previous robot use experience predicts more positive attitudes toward robots [6, 16, 29]. In earlier technology research, it has been demonstrated that prior user experience of technology associates with stronger technology-specific self-efficacy beliefs [17, 20]. However, the net effect of positive self-efficacy beliefs has also found to decrease when one gains more user experience of the technology [18]. In addition to prior user experience and technological expertise, various sociodemographic factors may influence human attitudes toward robots, including gender, age, and educational background [12, 13, 19].

The aim of this survey study was to explore the associations between perceived robot attitudes of other people, perceived robot use self-efficacy, and attitudes toward robots. Differences between those with and without previous robot use experience were examined. Further, additional analyses were conducted to explore the role of perceived robot use self-efficacy and general interest in technology as potential mediators. Our hypotheses were:

H1: Perceived positive robot attitudes of other people associate with more positive attitudes toward robots.
H2: Perceived robot use self-efficacy associates with more positive attitudes toward robots.
H3: Participants with prior robot use experience express more positive attitudes toward robots than ones without.
H4: Participants with prior robot use experience express higher perceived robot use self-efficacy than ones without experience.

2 Methods and Materials

2.1 Participants

A survey was conducted online among American respondents in April 2019 ($N = 969$; 51.15% female, $M_{age} = 37.15$ years, $SD_{age} = 11.35$ years, *range* 15–94 years). Majority of respondents worked full or part time (86.58%), roughly ten percent (10.63%) were unemployed, and some of them were students (2.79%). More than half (65.53%) of the participants had achieved a college, a master's degree, professional degree, or higher. Approximately one-third of the study participants (33.23%) had previous experiences of interacting or using robots, while the majority (60.78%) reported not having any previous experiences, and some (5.99%) respondents were unsure if they had used or interacted with a robot previously.

2.2 Procedure

Amazon Mechanical Turk's pool of respondents was utilized for participant recruitment. The study applied the protocol offered by [22] to guarantee that the respondents were located in the United States. In the survey, respondents filled out their sociodemographic information, answered to psychological measures, views on robots, and previous user experiences. The academic ethics committee of Tampere region confirmed in December 2018 that the research project did not involve ethical problems.

2.3 Measures

Attitudes toward robots were measured applying its three dimensions: cognitive, affective, and behavioral information [33]. Question items utilized were: "How positive or negative is your view on robots if you think about your gut feeling?", "How positive or negative is your view on robots if you think about the facts you know about robots?", and "How positive or negative is your view on robots if you think about using or interacting with a robot?". Respondents answered on a scale from 1 (*very negative*) to 7 (*very positive*). Three statement items were used: "I would interact with a robot, if given the opportunity", "I feel excited when I think about robots of the future", and "Based on my knowledge about robots, I think they are a necessary part of the future". Answers were given on a scale from 1 (*strongly disagree*) to 7 (*strongly agree*). A six-item composite variable was created for analyses showing excellent reliability based on McDonald's omega coefficient ($\omega = .93$; $M = 4.83$; $SD = 1.30$).

Perceived robot attitudes of other people were measured with three questions and three statements. Questions utilized in this study were: "How positive or negative is the view on robots in general of the people that are close to you?", "How positive or negative is the view on robots in general of other people you know?", and "How positive or negative is the view on robots in general of the people that you respect?", to which respondents answered on a scale from 1 (*very negative*) to 7 (*very positive*). Statement measures were: "I know a lot of people who have a positive view on robots", "Most of the people who are close to me have a positive view on robots", and "Most of the people I respect have a positive view on robots" to which responses were given on a scale from 1 (*strongly disagree*) to 7 (*strongly agree*). A six-item composite variable was created showing excellent reliability ($\omega = .93$; $M = 4.64$; $SD = 1.16$).

Perceived robot use self-efficacy was measured with three items applied from the robot use self-efficacy scale (RUSH-3) [38]. The items used in this study were: "I'm confident in my ability to learn how to use robots", "I'm confident in my ability to learn simple programming of robots if I were provided the necessary training", and "I'm confident in my ability to learn how to use robots in order to guide others to do the same". Scale adjustment included dropping a word 'care' from the original scale. Answers were given on a scale from 1 (*strongly disagree*) to 7 (*strongly agree*). A three-item composite variable was coded showing good inter-item reliability ($\omega = .87$; $M = 5.38$; $SD = 1.19$).

As control variables, age was measured as continuous, and gender as a binary (0 = male, 1 = female) variable. A degree in engineering or technology was asked "Do you have a degree from the field of engineering or technology?", to which participants answered either no or yes (0 = no, 1 = yes). Prior robot use experience question was formed as "Have you ever used a robot or been in an interaction with a robot?", to which participants answered on a scale "Yes", "No", or "I don't know". For analysis, a dummy variable was created (0 = no/don't know, 1 = yes). General interest in technology and its development was asked: "I am interested in technology and its development", the answer options ranged from (*strongly disagree*) to 7 (*strongly agree*).

2.4 Statistical Techniques

All analyses were conducted with Stata 16 software. Beyond descriptive statistics, analyses included Welch two sample t-tests with unequal variances, ordinary least square

(OLS) regression. Mediation analyses were run with 2000-replication bootstrap [15, 27] using khb command [23]. The background assumptions of OLS models were tested with the correlation matrix, VIF values, and Breusch-Pagan test to detect drawbacks from multicollinearity and heteroscedasticity. Heteroscedasticity was detected in OLS models via significant results in the Breusch-Pagan test ($p < .001$). Hence, we report OLS regression models with robust Huber-White standard errors (*Robust SE B*), unstandardized (B) and standardized (β) regression coefficients, model goodness-of-fit measures (R^2), and model test (F) and p values.

3   Results

Results from t-test for two independent samples indicated that based on means, participants with prior robot use experience expressed significantly more positive attitudes toward robots ($M = 5.13$, $SD = 1.15$, $t[732.93] = -5.5513$, $p < .001$), and perceived robot attitudes of other people ($M = 4.98$, $SD = 1.06$, $t[706.63] = -6.6637$, $p < .001$), higher perceived robot use self-efficacy ($M = 5.59$, $SD = 1.04$, $t[755.32] = -4.2926$, $p < .001$), and more general interest in technology and its development ($M = 5.73$, $SD = 1.28$, $t[650.999] = -2.3281$, $p = .010$) compared to participants without prior robot use experience. Hence, respondents were divided into two groups for the regression models: those with ($n = 322$, 33.23%) and those without or not sure if they had previous robot use experience ($n = 647$, 66.77%). Table 1 shows the descriptive overview of the two sub-samples.

Table 1. Descriptive overview of two study samples.

Variables	Group 1: With prior robot use experience ($n = 322$)				Group 2: Without prior robot use experience ($n = 647$)			
	N	%	M	SD	N	%	M	SD
Attitudes	322		5.13	1.15	647		4.67	1.34
Attitudes of others	322		4.98	1.06	647		4.48	1.18
Self-efficacy	322		5.59	1.04	647		5.27	1.25
Technology interest	322		5.72	1.28	647		5.52	1.30
Age	322		35.80	10.92	647		37.83	11.51
Gender	318				636			
Female	143	44.97			345	54.25		
Male	175	55.03			291	45.75		
Degree in technology	322				647			
Yes	135	41.93			125	19.32		
No	187	59.07			522	80.68		

Note. Attitudes = Attitudes toward robots, Attitudes of others = Perceived positive robot attitudes of other people, Self-efficacy = Perceived robot use self-efficacy, Technology interest = General interest in technology and its developments

Table 2 shows the results of linear regression models for attitudes toward robots among participants with prior robot use experience. In model 1, perceived positive robot attitudes of others correlated positively with attitudes ($\beta = .76, p < .001$). In model 2, both perceived positive robot attitudes of other people ($\beta = .63, p < .001$), and perceived robot use self-efficacy ($\beta = .27, p < .001$) correlated with the attitudes. In model 3, in addition to perceived positive robot attitudes of other people ($\beta = .62, p < .001$), and perceived robot use self-efficacy ($\beta = .15, p = .025$), interest in technology ($\beta = .21, p = .001$) correlated with more positive attitudes. In the final model 4, all three positive correlates remained significant while controlling for age, female gender, and degree in technology or engineering. The final model explained 67% of the variance for attitudes toward robots ($R^2 = .67, F = 106.20, p < .001$).

Table 3 shows the results of linear regression for attitudes toward robots among participants without prior robot use experience. In model 1, perceived positive robot attitudes of other people correlated positively with more positive attitudes ($\beta = .78, p < .001$). In model 2, both perceived positive robot attitudes of other people ($\beta = .66, p < .001$), and perceived robot use self-efficacy ($\beta = .26, p < .001$) correlated with the attitudes. In model 3, perceived positive robot attitudes of other people ($\beta = .62, p < .001$), and perceived robot use self-efficacy ($\beta = .18, p < .001$), and interest in technology ($\beta = .16, p < .001$) correlated with more positive attitudes. In the final model 4, positive associations remained statistically significant while adjusting for background variables. The final model explained 67% of the variance for attitudes toward robots ($R^2 = .67, F = 301.71, p < .001$).

Given the observed changes in coefficients between different steps in both regression models, final part of the analyses focused on examining potential mediators with all study participants ($N = 969$). Two potential indirect effects were examined: 1) indirect effects of perceived robot use self-efficacy on the link between perceived positive robot attitudes of other people and attitude toward robots, and 2) indirect effects of general interest in technology on the link between perceived robot use self-efficacy and attitude toward robots.

Figure 1 illustrates the mediation analysis for perceived robot use self-efficacy. As expected, perceived positive robot attitudes of other people were found to directly associate with more positive attitudes toward robots ($B = .87, SE = .02, t = 42.06, \beta = 78, p < .001$), also when controlling perceived robot use self-efficacy ($B = .73, SE = .03, t = 25.17, \beta = 66, p < .001$). Further, perceived positive robot attitudes of others were directly associated with higher perceived robot use self-efficacy ($B = .48, SE = .03, t = 13.67, \beta = .47, p < .001$). Finally, perceived robot use self-efficacy affected significantly the link between perceived positive robot attitudes of others and attitudes toward robots, and the bootstrapped unstandardized indirect effect was .14 ($z = 7.16, p < .001, 95\% \text{ CI} = .098 - .172$).

Figure 2 illustrates the mediation analysis for general interest in technology. Perceived robot use self-efficacy associated directly with more positive attitudes toward robots ($B = .62, SE = .03, t = 20.15, \beta = .57, p < .001$), also when adjusting for interest in technology ($B = .42, SE = .04, t = 9.88, \beta = .39, p < .001$). Further, perceived robot use self-efficacy associated directly with interest in technology ($B = .66, SE = .03, t = 18.36, \beta = .61, p < .001$). Finally, interest in technology had an indirect effect

Table 2. Regression model for attitudes toward robots among participants with prior robot use experience in Study 1 ($n = 322$).

Measure	M1			M2			M3			M4		
	B	Rob SE B	β	B	Rob SE B	β	B	Rob SE B	β	B	Rob SE B	β
Attitudes of others	.83	.04	.76***	.69	.05	.63***	.67	.05	.62***	.66	.05	.61***
Self-efficacy				.30	.06	.27***	.16	.07	.15*	.15	.07	.13*
Technology interest							.19	.06	.21**	.19	.06	.22**
Age										.00	.00	−.02
Female										−.09	.07	−.04
Degree in technology										.11	.08	.05
Model R^2	.58			.64			.66			.67		
Model F	415.68			278.44			213.42			106.20		
Model p	***			***			***			***		

Note. Dependent variable: Attitudes toward robots
*$p < .05$. **$p < .01$. ***$p < .001$.

Table 3. Regression model for attitudes toward robots among participants without prior robot use experience in Study 2 ($n = 647$).

Measure	M1 B	M1 Rob SE B	M1 β	M2 B	M2 Rob SE B	M2 β	M3 B	M3 Rob SE B	M3 β	M4 B	M4 Rob SE B	M4 β
Attitudes of others	.88	.02	.78***	.75	.04	.66***	.71	.04	.62***	.70	.04	.62***
Self-efficacy				.28	.04	.26***	.20	.04	.18***	.20	.04	.18***
Technology interest							.16	.03	.15***	.16	.04	.16***
Age										.00	.00	−.01
Female										−.13	.06	−.05*
Degree in technology										.07	.06	.02
Model R^2	.60			.66			.67			.67		
Model F	1250.85			937.44			626.18			301.71		
Model p	***			***			***			***		

Note. Dependent variable: Attitudes toward robots
*$p < .05$. **$p < .01$. ***$p < .001$.

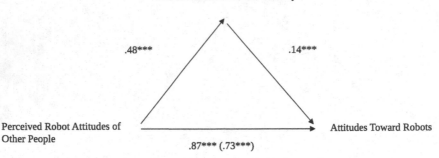

Fig. 1. Unstandardized regression coefficients for the relationship between perceived robot attitudes of other people and attitudes toward robots as mediated by perceived robot use self-efficacy among all study participants ($N = 969$). The unstandardized regression coefficients between perceived robot attitudes of others and attitudes toward robots controlling for perceived robot use self-efficacy is in parentheses. *** $p. < .001$.

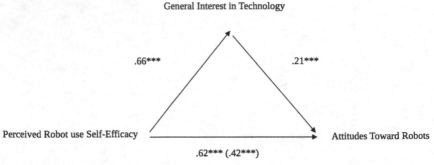

Fig. 2. Unstandardized regression coefficients for the relationship between perceived robot use self-efficacy and attitudes toward robots as mediated by interest in technology among all study participants ($N = 969$). The unstandardized regression coefficients between perceived robot use self-efficacy and attitudes toward robots controlling for general interest in technology is in parentheses. *** $p. < .001$.

on the link between perceived robot use self-efficacy and attitudes toward robots, and the bootstrapped unstandardized indirect effect was .21 ($z = 7.66, p < .001, 95\%$ CI $= .155 - .262$). Age, female gender, and degree in engineering or technology were used as control variables for both bootstrapped estimations.

4   Discussion

This study investigated the associations between perceived robot attitudes of others, perceived robot use self-efficacy, and attitudes toward robots. Perceived positive robot attitudes of other people were found to associate with more positive attitudes toward robots among those who had prior robot use experience and those who did not, thus confirming our first hypothesis. The findings support previous observations that attitudes can be influenced by others and ones' social environment to a certain extend [34, 36, 40].

To confirm our second hypothesis, results also showed that perceived robot use self-efficacy was associated with more positive attitudes toward robots in both models. Results support previous findings on the link between self-efficacy beliefs and robot acceptance in care work context [24, 38]. Results also showed that general interest in technology associated significantly with more positive attitudes toward robots among respondents with and without firsthand experiences of robots, stressing its important role in the formation of attitudes.

Differences between those with and without previous robot use experience were assessed. Results indicated that participants with prior robot use experience expressed significantly more positive attitudes toward robots (H3), higher robot use self-efficacy (H4), more positive perceived robot attitudes of others, and higher general interest in technology and its development compared to participants without prior robot use experience. However, in the regression models the differences remained limited in terms of significancy of associations. Female gender was negatively associated with attitudes toward robots among those without prior robot use experience only. The association between female gender and more negative attitudes toward robots has also been demonstrated in previous studies [12, 13, 19].

The results also showed that the association between perceived robot use self-efficacy and attitudes toward robots was especially strong among those without prior robot use experience. This finding supports the literature suggesting that prior user experience predicts higher technology-specific self-efficacy beliefs [17, 20], but the net effect of positive self-efficacy beliefs can decrease after gaining more user experience [18]. Finding highlights the importance of supporting individuals' self-efficacy beliefs in the early stages of technology adoption. Among participants with prior robot use experience, the association between general interest in technology and attitudes toward robots was notably strong, suggesting the importance of general technology interest in attitude formation after the first user experiences.

Additional mediation analyses examined the interrelations between the studied variables. Perceived robot use self-efficacy was found to have a significant indirect effect on the connection between perceived positive robot attitudes of other people and attitudes toward robots. General interest in technology had a significant indirect effect on the association between perceived robot use self-efficacy and attitudes toward robots, suggesting a partial mediation effect. Finding is understandable from the perspective that self-efficacy beliefs influence the way humans feel, think and motivate themselves [4], for example, in the form of increasing interest in target technology. Both indirect effects were significant but moderate, implying that the variables are related to each other only to some extent.

Our study has limitations in terms of its cross-sectional design and the fact that its only respondents were U.S. residents. However, our study is strengthened by the fact that the sample was relatively large and consisted of respondents who are geographically widespread and come from different sociodemographic backgrounds. We also adjusted for numerous factors in the models, including age, gender, and educational background. Future studies could continue investigating the potential long-term effects of perceived robot attitudes of other people, perceived robot use self-efficacy on the attitudes toward robots, and the actual use of robots. Further, as robots are becoming more familiar to humans, it is important to continue studying the role of user experiences from the perspective of the quality of such experiences and accumulation of experience after multiple uses and encounters.

Our results underline the importance of social psychological factors related to the formation of attitudes toward robots. People give high value to how their own social circles and salient others perceive robots. Attitudes toward robots are also connected to beliefs of own abilities to use such technology. General interest in technology and user experiences of robots both promote positive attitudes toward robots. Results stress the importance of social psychological aspects of robot use and their usefulness in professionals' implementation of new robot technologies.

Funding Acknowledgment. This work was supported by the Finnish Cultural Foundation (Robots and Us Project, 2018–2020, PIs Jari Hietanen, Atte Oksanen, and Veikko Sariola).

Disclosure statement. The authors report no conflict of interest.

References

1. Bagozzi, R.P., Burnkrant, R.E.: Single component versus multicomponent models of attitude: some cautions and contingencies for their use. In: Olson, J.C., Abor, A., MI: Association for Consumer Research (eds.) Advances in Consumer Research, vol. 7, pp. 339–344 (1980)
2. Bandura, A.: Self-efficacy: toward a unifying theory of behavioral change. Psychol. Rev. **84**(2), 191–215 (1977)
3. Bandura, A.: Social Foundations of Thought and Action: A Social Cognitive Theory. Prentice-Hall, Englewood Cliffs (1986)
4. Bandura, A.: Self-efficacy. In: Ramachaudran, V.S. (ed.) Encyclopedia of Human Behavior, vol. 4, pp. 71–81. Academic Press, New York (1994)
5. Bandura, A.: Self-Efficacy: The Exercise of Control. Freeman, New York (1997)
6. Bartneck, C., Suzuki, T., Kanda, T., Nomura, T.: The influence of people's culture and prior experiences with Aibo on their attitude towards robots. AI Soc. **21**(1–2), 217–230 (2007)
7. Breckler, S.J.: Empirical validation of affect, behavior, and cognition as distinct components of attitude. J. Pers. Soc. Psychol. **47**(6), 1191–1205 (1984)
8. Cialdini, R.B., Goldstein, N.J.: Social influence: compliance and conformity. Annu. Rev. Psychol. **55**, 591–621 (2004)
9. Cialdini, R.B., Trost, M.R.: Social influence: social norms, conformity and compliance. In: Gilbert, D.T., Fiske, S.T., Lindzey, G. (eds.) The Handbook of Social Psychology, pp. 151–192. McGraw-Hill (1998)
10. Davis, F.D., Bagozzi, R.P., Warshaw, P.R.: User acceptance of computer technology: a comparison of two theoretical models. Manage. Sci. **35**(8), 983–1003 (1989)
11. Dickinger, A., Arami, M., Meyer, D.: The role of perceived enjoyment and social norm in the adoption of technology with network externalities. Eur. J. Inf. Syst. **17**(1), 4–11 (2008)
12. Flandorfer, P.: Population ageing and socially assistive robots for elderly persons: the importance of sociodemographic factors for user acceptance. Int. J. Popul. Res. **2012**, article ID 829835 (2012). https://doi.org/10.1155/2012/829835
13. Gnambs, T., Appel, M.: Are robots becoming unpopular? Changes in attitudes towards autonomous robotic systems in Europe. Comput. Hum. Behav. **93**, 53–61 (2019)

14. Haddock, G., Maio, G.R.: Attitudes. In: Hewstone, M., Stroebe, W., Jonas, K. (eds.) Introduction to Social Psychology, 6th edn., pp. 171–200. Wiley (2015)
15. Hayes, A.F., Scharkow, M.: The relative trustworthiness of inferential tests of the indirect effect in statistical mediation analysis: does method really matter? Psychol. Sci. **24**(10), 1918–1927 (2013)
16. Heerink, M., Kröse, B., Evers, V., Wielinga, B.: Assessing acceptance of assistive social agent technology by older adults: the almere model. Int. J. Soc. Rob. **2**(4), 361–375 (2010)
17. Hill, T., Smith, N.D., Mann, M.F.: Role of efficacy expectations in predicting the decision to use advanced technologies: the case of computers. J. Appl. Psychol. **72**(2), 307–313 (1987)
18. Hu, P.J.H., Clark, T.H., Ma, W.W.: Examining technology acceptance by schoolteachers: a longitudinal study. Inf. Manage. **41**(2), 227–241 (2003)
19. Hudson, J., Orviska, M., Hunady, J.: People's attitudes to robots in caring for the elderly. Int. J. Soc. Rob. **9**(2), 199–210 (2017)
20. Igbaria, M., Iivari, J.: The effects of self-efficacy on computer usage. Omega **23**(6), 587–605 (1995)
21. Im, I., Hong, S., Kang, M.S.: An international comparison of technology adoption: testing the UTAUT model. Inf. Manage. **48**(1), 1–8 (2011)
22. Kennedy, R., Clifford, S., Burleigh, T., Waggoner, P.D., Jewell, R., Winter, N.J.: The shape of and solutions to the MTurk quality crisis. Polit. Sci. Res. Methods **8**(4), 614–629 (2020)
23. Kohler, U., Karlson, K.B., Holm, A.: Comparing coefficients of nested nonlinear probability models. Stata J. **11**(3), 420–438 (2011)
24. Latikka, R., Turja, T., Oksanen, A.: Self-efficacy and acceptance of robots. Comput. Hum. Behav. **93**, 157–163 (2019)
25. Lee, Y., Kozar, K.A., Larsen, K.R.: The technology acceptance model: past, present, and future. Commun. Assoc. Inf. Syst. **12**(1), 50 (2003)
26. Makridakis, S.: The forthcoming artificial intelligence (AI) revolution: its impact on society and firms. Futures **90**, 46–60 (2017)
27. MacKinnon, D.P., Lockwood, C.M., Williams, J.: Confidence limits for the indirect effect: distribution of the product and resampling methods. Multivar. Behav. Res. **39**(1), 99–128 (2004)
28. Naneva, S., Sarda Gou, M., Webb, T.L., Prescott, T.J.: A systematic review of attitudes, anxiety, acceptance, and trust towards social robots. Int. J. Soc. Rob. **12**, 1179–1201 (2020)
29. Nomura, T., Kanda, T., Suzuki, T.: Experimental investigation into influence of negative attitudes toward robots on human–robot interaction. AI Soc. **20**(2), 138–150 (2006)
30. Nomura, T., Suzuki, T., Kanda, T., Kato, K.: Measurement of negative attitudes toward robots. Inter. Stud. **7**(3), 437–454 (2006)
31. Oksanen, A., Savela, N., Latikka, R., Koivula, A.: Trust toward robots and artificial intelligence: an experimental approach to human-technology interactions online. Front. Psychol. **11**, 568256 (2020)
32. Ostrom, T.M.: The relationship between the affective, behavioral, and cognitive components of attitude. J. Exp. Soc. Psychol. **5**(1), 12–30 (1969)
33. Rosenberg, M.J., Hovland, C.I.: Cognitive, affective and behavioral components of attitudes. In: Rosenberg, M.J., Hovland, C.I. (eds.) Attitude Organization and Change: An Analysis of Consistency Among Attitude Components, pp. 1–14. Yale University Press (1960)
34. Salancik, G.R., Pfeffer, J.: A social information processing approach to job attitudes and task design. Adm. Sci. Q. **23**(2), 224–253 (1978)
35. Savela, N., Turja, T., Oksanen, A.: Social acceptance of robots in different occupational fields: a systematic review. Int. J. Soc. Rob. **10**(4), 493–502 (2018)
36. Schmitz, J., Fulk, J.: Organizational colleagues, media richness, and electronic mail: a test of the social influence model of technology use. Commun. Res. **18**(4), 487–523 (1991)

37. Stajkovic, A.D., Luthans, F.: Social cognitive theory and self-efficacy: going beyond traditional motivational and behavioral approaches. Organ. Dyn. 26(4), 62–74 (1998)
38. Turja, T., Rantanen, T., Oksanen, A.: Robot use self-efficacy in healthcare work (RUSH): development and validation of a new measure. AI Soc. 34, 137–143 (2019)
39. Venkatesh, V., Morris, M.G., Davis, G.B., Davis, F.D.: User acceptance of information technology: toward a unified view. MIS Q. 27(3), 425–478 (2003)
40. Yang, H.D., Yoo, Y.: It's all about attitude: revisiting the technology acceptance model. Decis. Support Syst. 38(1), 19–31 (2004)

Research on Interactive Experience Design of Peripheral Visual Interface of Unmanned Logistics Vehicle

Zehua Li and Qianwen Chen[✉]

Nanjing University of Science and Technology, Nanjing, China

Abstract. With the continuous development and maturity of autonomous driving systems, the huge demands of the logistics and distribution industry collide with autonomous driving systems, and the inspiration for intelligent logistics and distribution has been burst out, and driverless logistics vehicles have emerged as the times require. In order to improve the transportation safety, distribution efficiency, and interactive experience of unmanned logistics vehicles, the design of the peripheral visual interface of unmanned logistics vehicles is studied, and the application scenarios of unmanned logistics vehicles are analyzed at different levels. The logistics vehicle has conducted preliminary cognitive efficiency and psychological comfort research in the road transportation scene, providing a theoretical reference for the design of the peripheral visual interface of the unmanned logistics vehicle. It is believed that the design of the peripheral visual interface will be more perfect and promote unmanned the rapid development of driving logistics vehicles.

Keywords: Unmanned logistics vehicle · Interaction design · Human-machine interface · Interaction experience

1 Preface

In today's society, logistics and distribution have gradually become an indispensable service item in people's daily life. In order to pursue higher distribution speeds, major enterprises have begun to reform and innovate from aspects such as intelligence, unmanned, and big data. Moreover, with the continuous development of smart technology, the social demand for smart travel continues to increase. Automakers represented by Google and Tesla have successively introduced autonomous driving systems. It is believed that autonomous vehicles will replace traditional travel methods in the future cities. Mainstream. The huge demand of the logistics and distribution industry collided with the increasingly mature autonomous driving system, bursting out the inspiration of intelligent logistics and distribution, and unmanned logistics vehicles came into being. Unmanned logistics vehicles can reduce the time cost of delivery personnel, greatly improve the efficiency of logistics classification and distribution, and realize the industrialization upgrade of the logistics industry. At this stage, a small number of unmanned

© Springer Nature Switzerland AG 2021
M. Kurosu (Ed.): HCII 2021, LNCS 12763, pp. 275–287, 2021.
https://doi.org/10.1007/978-3-030-78465-2_21

logistics vehicles have been put into use, but they are all limited to the sorting and picking of logistics transfer stations. They have not yet reached the stage of intelligent distribution. However, with the maturity of autonomous driving system technology and the popularization of 5G technology, Unmanned logistics vehicles will soon be realized and put into the market for use.

During the work of unmanned logistics vehicles, there are still many complicated information exchange issues, such as: information exchange between unmanned logistics vehicles and other road users in the public road network, information exchange with users during delivery, etc., all need to be improved the most important feature of unmanned logistics vehicles is the use of big data for unmanned intelligent distribution. Whether on the public road network or direct interaction with users, it is carried out by itself, so traditional people are informal Communication methods will disappear, and interactive activities can only be conducted through formal communication methods such as signal lights, but this will increase the risk index to the public road network, challenge the psychological comfort of road users, and create a trust problem. Therefore, it is very necessary to find a way to interact with unmanned logistics vehicles, so that road users can understand the expected behavior of unmanned logistics vehicles, and improve the tolerance of unmanned logistics vehicles and traffic safety. The latest solution at this stage is to equip the vehicle body with a visual interface on the periphery of the unmanned logistics vehicle. The unmanned logistics vehicle transmits important driving information to road users through the visual interface on the periphery of the vehicle body, and the road users display the peripheral visual interface Identify and judge the information, understand the expected behavior of the unmanned logistics vehicle, and then perform the corresponding actions. Similarly, the interactive activities between the unmanned logistics vehicle and the user can also be carried out through the external visual interface to enhance the user's interactive experience.

This paper carries out research status based on the design of unmanned logistics vehicles and peripheral visual interface, and analyzes the application scenarios of unmanned logistics vehicles in a hierarchical manner, and conducts a preliminary cognitive efficiency of unmanned logistics vehicles in road transportation scenarios. And psychological comfort. The information exchange of unmanned logistics vehicles through the peripheral visual interface can improve road safety and the efficiency of logistics distribution, thereby promoting the development of unmanned logistics vehicles.

2   Analysis of the Interface Design Composition of Autonomous Vehicles

2.1   Research Status of Unmanned Logistics Vehicles

In the context of the rapid development of intelligent technology, autonomous driving technology has become increasingly mature and perfect. Many auto companies have launched their own autonomous vehicles, which has accelerated the commercialization of autonomous vehicles. However, due to policies, technology, and traffic safety, manned autonomous driving There are many restrictions on the actual operation of cars on the road. Under this premise, the realization of unmanned logistics vehicles carrying loads is relatively simple. The driving distance of unmanned logistics vehicles is relatively short, the coverage area is fixed, and it can carry out cargo transportation, monitoring and early warning, environmental sanitation, etc., saving labor costs. At the same time, Internet shopping has become the norm. Driverless logistics vehicles can provide faster and more efficient delivery services, improve the entire Internet shopping process, form a closed loop, and optimize the Internet shopping experience.

In recent years, China's logistics industry has developed rapidly. With the improvement of upstream and downstream logistics infrastructure, logistics costs are also decreasing year by year. However, there is still a gap with foreign developed countries. Intelligent logistics is a new opportunity to reduce costs. Many companies in China have already tested and practiced smart logistics, applying autonomous driving technology to unmanned logistics vehicles, and matching cameras, sensors and other equipment to deal with big data calculations in complex scenarios, and provide new smart distribution solutions, which can realize intelligent automatic logistics distribution. The driving of the unmanned logistics vehicle relies on the planned route of a fixed range. The principle is simple, but there are many problems in actual operation. There will be a large number of trees, grass, telephone poles, and optical cables on the roadside, which will cause satellite positioning. In order to cope with these problems, the algorithm research of autonomous driving systems is also constantly being developed and improved. In addition, the current situation of the social situation where shared bicycles is randomly placed may cause traffic problems at different levels.

China's Alibaba, JD, Didi, UISEE and other companies are actively developing and implementing driverless logistics vehicles, and are committed to creating a new logistics delivery experience. In May 2018, at the Alibaba CAINIAO Global Smart Logistics Summit, Alibaba and RoboSense jointly released the world's first unmanned logistics vehicle G Plus with solid-state lidar, which indicates that unmanned driving has entered the era of solid-state lidar. Ali's rookie unmanned logistics vehicle G Plus has stronger 3D environment awareness when driving, and can clearly predict the shape, distance, orientation, speed, and direction of obstacles such as pedestrians, cars, and trucks in the driving direction, and indicate the road Driving areas, etc., to ensure that unmanned logistics vehicles can pass smoothly in complex road environments. In March 2019, the new energy express unmanned vehicle independently developed by CAINIAO Network was put into use at the Hebei Xiong'an New Area Citizen Service Center. According to reports, the unmanned vehicle can load more than 200 small packages at a time, complete the express delivery connection from the station to the smart cabinet, can sense the surrounding environment, and avoid various dynamic and static obstacles such as pedestrians and vehicles (see Fig. 1). In 2019, the Hong Kong Airport Authority officially launched the L4 level unmanned logistics vehicle developed in cooperation with UISEE to transport luggage to the airport apron in the restricted area. This is the world's first unmanned logistics vehicle to be implemented in the actual airport operating environment. Compared with the previous driver-driven vehicle, the unmanned logistics vehicle does not need to consider manpower issues and can still operate under bad weather, thereby reducing human factors. Accident rate, ensure safe transportation, increase operation rate, and improve logistics reliability (see Fig. 2). The close integration

Fig. 1. Cainiao new energy express unmanned vehicle.

Fig. 2. UISEE driverless logistics vehicle.

of new autonomous driving technology and logistics distribution scenarios will promote the rapid development of "unmanned" in China's logistics industry.

2.2 Research Status of Peripheral Visual Interface Design

The "peripheral visual interface" is a visual human-computer interaction device located on the periphery of the car body. Autonomous driving technology is developing rapidly. After some institutions and automakers have carried out closed road tests on real vehicles, the state of California and others issued regulations allowing autonomous vehicles to be tested on public roads. Cities such as Beijing and Shanghai have also taken the lead in opening roads for autonomous vehicles. test. Although major automakers and governments have liberalized the testing of autonomous vehicles, pedestrians on some roads are still accustomed to cars operated by human drivers, creating trust issues on the roads for testing autonomous vehicles. The emergence of the "peripheral visual interface" can solve this problem with a high probability, allowing self-driving cars and pedestrians to have a good interactive experience, and improving the psychological comfort of pedestrians.

In recent years, there have been many experience programs for autonomous driving vehicles and pedestrian interaction activities. For example, Lex Fridman et al. provided subjects with relevant images to investigate the cognitive efficiency of subjects for different types of autonomous vehicle interface design; Lagstrom et al. studied the use of the LED display to indicate the mode of the vehicle in different states, such as the LED display making a gradual motion toward the center to indicate the start of the vehicle; the concept car of the Swedish car company Semcon will have a "smile" pattern Add to the interface; Mercedes-Benz Company proposed to project a crosswalk image on the road in front of the vehicle to inform pedestrians that it is safe to pass.

3 Analysis of Application Scenarios of Unmanned Logistics Vehicles

The workflow of unmanned logistics vehicles is similar to that of human delivery personnel, which can be roughly divided into four processes: 1. Sorting and picking goods at logistics storage bases or distribution sites, 2. Participating in public transportation networks for logistics transportation, 3. Reaching target users Address, notify users and interact with users, complete logistics distribution, 4. Conduct commercial advertising during the entire logistics distribution period. Therefore, when designing the peripheral visual interface, it is necessary to consider the interactive activities of the same scene at the same time. The most important thing is the four scenes of the work process: warehouse distribution, road transportation, logistics and distribution, and advertising (see Fig. 3).

3.1 Warehouse Distribution Scene

The starting point of the unmanned logistics vehicle should be at the logistics storage base or distribution site. Now the sorting and loading work of the logistics transfer center is manually completed by the express staff, which consumes a lot of time and cost, which is a traditional labor-intensive work. Long and stable output is required. When the number of logistics increases sharply, the courier staff's ability is limited, and

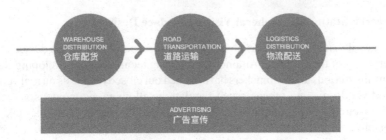

Fig. 3. Scenes work flow chart.

there will be lost parts, missing parts, and wrong parts, which will reduce the delivery efficiency. Unmanned logistics vehicles can solve this to a large extent. One problem. For the express delivery that has arrived at the express delivery site, the driverless logistics vehicle can read the order page or access the online data platform to obtain express delivery information, including the type of express delivery, package size, delivery area, recipient name, contact information, etc. Information, so as to automatically sort and load goods, forming a technology-intensive storage and distribution scene. At this time, the main work of the express staff is to cooperate with the unmanned logistics vehicle to perform simple operations and handle abnormal express delivery, reduce the labor consumption of repetitive simple tasks, and improve the efficiency and accuracy of sorting.

3.2 Road Transport Scene

Closed-field short-distance freight transportation is generally considered to be the first application scenario for autonomous driving technology. Unmanned logistics vehicles generally drive-in closed areas such as schools, residential communities, and industrial parks. Although there are fewer other vehicles in this physical scene, there are more other traffic participants such as pedestrians and bicycles. Human complexity and randomness make human behavior more complicated than vehicles, and because autonomous driving technology is still a new thing at present, pedestrians often cannot clearly understand unmanned logistics vehicles when facing unmanned vehicles on the road. As a result, pedestrians misjudge the driving path of the unmanned logistics vehicle, which affects the pedestrian's next behavior and leads to sudden collision accidents. Therefore, when interactively designing the peripheral visual interface of unmanned logistics vehicles, it is necessary to focus on the transportation scenarios of unmanned logistics vehicles to ensure the safety of road traffic participants.

3.3 Logistics Distribution Scene

The core function of unmanned logistics vehicles is logistics distribution, so it is of great significance to improve the efficiency of distribution and complete efficient distribution under the premise of ensuring safe driving. In the entire logistics distribution process, the unmanned logistics vehicle can complete basic functions such as dispatching and shipping, and can plan the route rationally through the big data platform, so that each logistics order can be delivered according to the optimal path, in the shortest the most distributed goods under time and path, to achieve efficient and punctual delivery of goods. Secondly, unmanned logistics vehicles can also complete additional functions such as packaging and recycling to achieve green and environmental protection and save resources.

3.4 Advertising Scene

The unmanned logistics vehicle itself is a kind of advertisement propaganda carrier, and can be used as a kind of communication medium in public places when it is distributed in schools, residential communities, industrial parks and other areas. The shape of the unmanned logistics vehicle can be used as a carrier of its company culture and expand its brand influence. In addition to conveying the operating status of the vehicle to the road users, the peripheral visual interface can also advertise the remaining part to form a mobile advertising board to expand commercial benefits.

4 Research on Cognitive Efficiency and Psychological Comfort in Road Transportation Scene

4.1 Experimental Design

Using eye tracking technology and Likert scale method to design an experimental study to test the cognitive efficiency and psychological comfort of different unmanned logistics vehicle peripheral visual interface design schemes in road transportation scenarios, and find the optimal design scheme. The data collection is divided into two groups: eye tracking technology-collecting pedestrian cognitive efficiency data, and Likert scale method-collecting pedestrian psychological comfort score data.

4.2 Participant

Thirty graduate students in Nanjing University of Science and Technology participated in this experimental study, and 30 valid subjects (15 males, 15 females) were tested. Their physical indicators are normal, the retina's ability to distinguish images is normal, there are no special conditions such as color blindness, and they can walk normally. The subjects were between 22 and 25 years old, with an average age of 23.5 years. The subject was consistent with the research investigating the behavior of public road network users, and before the experiment, none of the subjects had been exposed to the experimental materials used in this study.

4.3 Experimental Site and Equipment

This experiment was carried out in the laboratory of the School of Design, Art and Media, Nanjing University of Science and Technology. The experimental equipment used in the experiment was a Tobii T120 eye tracker and a Lenovo laptop. The analysis and reporting platform of the experiment was the supporting Tobii Studio software. The subject sits upright in front of the laptop, keeping a measurable distance between the eyes and the screen, about 50-80 cm. The device uses the corneal reflection pattern and other information to calculate the eye movement information such as the position and gaze of the eyeball, and then organizes the information through the software and processing, output related eye movement data.

4.4   Experimental Materials and Procedures

The experimental materials use text, graphics, colors and other visual elements to combine, and design 3 groups (4 in each group) of peripheral visual interface experimental materials to express the different states of unmanned logistics vehicles in road transportation scenes, and test pedestrians versus unmanned the cognitive efficiency and psychological comfort of driving a logistics vehicle are calculated based on the data to calculate the optimal set of solutions. Among them, the color information uses the red and green in the traditional public transportation system, and the blue in the visual interface of the existing unmanned logistics vehicle; the image information uses the "circle" and "arrow" graphics; the text information uses "Driving", "Turn Left", "Turn Right", "Please pick Up" to indicate different states. Then superimpose this visual information on the peripheral visual interface of the "Neolithic Unmanned Logistics Vehicle" and place it on the road of the residential area to determine the experimental scenario (see Fig. 4, Fig. 5, and Fig. 6).

Before the start of the experiment, the participants were explained to the participants the instructions and procedures of the experiment, and invited to fill in the informed consent form and the basic situation survey form. The whole experiment process was quiet, and the subjects were done independently.

(1) Instruct the subjects to sit within an effective distance range of about 60–70 cm before the test screen, maintain a comfortable sitting posture, and adjust the horizontal eye position to be the same height as the screen.
(2) The five-point method is used to calibrate the sight line of the subjects to ensure that the visual accuracy of each subject is within the range of $1.0°$ in both the horizontal and vertical directions.
(3) Start the experiment: the computer screen will play the image of the unmanned logistics vehicle on the road in the residential area. The subjects need to simulate and imagine that they are in this environment, and then proceed according to the information displayed on the external visual interface of the unmanned logistics vehicle. Determine what state the unmanned logistics vehicle is in and whether you are safe. During the whole process, the dominant hand is required to always hold the mouse lightly, so that it is convenient to react quickly after the judgment is completed.
(4) After the 3 groups of experimental materials have been played, score the 3 groups of experimental materials for their psychological comfort. The scoring method is based on the Likert scale scoring method: 5 points are very comfortable, 4 points are comfortable, 3 points are fair, 2 points are uncomfortable, and 1 point is very uncomfortable. Finally, the experiment ends.

Fig. 4. Experimental material group 1.

Fig. 5. Experimental material group 2.

4.5 Experimental Data Analysis

In the eye tracking experiment, through the analysis of the eye movement experiment data of 30 subjects, the total visit time of the first group was 5.15 s, and the average time was 1.2875 s, and the total visit time of the second group was 2.55 s, and the average time was 0.6375 s, the total visit time of the third group is 6.15 s, and the average time is 1.5375 s, that is, the second group has the shortest total visit time, the shortest average time, and the highest cognitive efficiency (Fig. 7).

Fig. 6. Experimental material group 3.

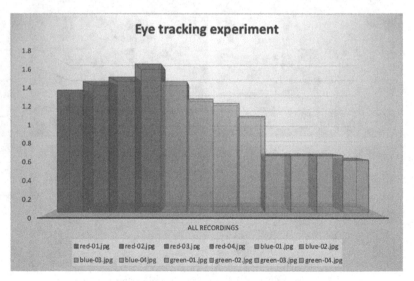

Fig. 7. Comparison chart of eye tracking experiment data.

Likert scale method, through the analysis of the score data of 30 subjects, the scores of the first group of programs are 4.0, 3.95, 3.9, 4.1, and the average score is 3.9875, and the scores of the second group of programs are 4.2, 4.23, 4.25 and 4.2, the average score is 4.22, the scores of the third group of programs are 2.7, 2.45, 2.4, 2.5, and the average is 2.5125, so the second group of programs has the best psychological comfort, then the first group of programs, and finally the third group of programs (Fig. 8).

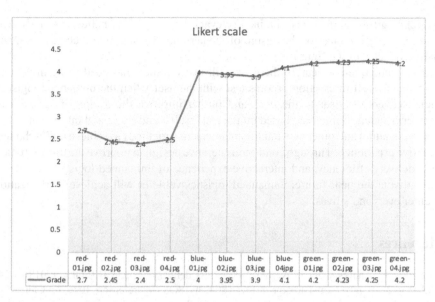

Fig. 8. Likert scale method scoring comparison chart.

4.6 Experimental Results

Among the 3 groups of peripheral visual interface solutions designed, the second group has the highest cognitive efficiency and the best psychological comfort, can convey information very accurately, and better interact with pedestrians. Through the conversation with the subjects, we found that everyone has a high degree of acceptance of unmanned logistics vehicles, and they are very much looking forward to the realization of unmanned logistics vehicles, but remain skeptical about safety and hope that the peripheral visual interface can provide more effective information, thereby enhancing the interactive experience.

Therefore, in the design of the peripheral visual interface of the unmanned logistics vehicle, for the key information, especially in the road transportation scene, the green and red in the traditional public transportation system should be used to express yes or no. For the secondary information, you can Use other colors for expression to meet different aesthetic needs. More use of a combination of text and image elements can improve the cognitive efficiency and psychological comfort of pedestrians, enable pedestrians to better communicate with unmanned logistics vehicles, and improve the safety index during transportation.

5 Conclusion

This paper carries out research status based on the design of unmanned logistics vehicles and peripheral visual interface, and analyzes the application scenarios of unmanned logistics vehicles in a hierarchical manner, and conducts a preliminary cognitive efficiency of unmanned logistics vehicles in road transportation scenarios. And the research on psychological comfort has obtained relevant data, which is believed to have certain guiding significance for the design of the peripheral visual interface of unmanned logistics vehicles in the future.

In the subsequent research, there are still many issues that need to be improved, such as the overall interaction process test with the user when the unmanned logistics vehicle delivers the user to the user, and further improve the design of the human-computer interaction interface based on the test results, and try to add intelligent voice, Facial recognition and other new intelligent interactive methods to achieve multi-channel interactive experience. Through continuous iterative design to improve the transportation safety, delivery efficiency, and interactive experience of unmanned logistics vehicles, I believe that in the near future, unmanned logistics vehicles will achieve marketization and enter everyone's lives.

References

1. Zhang, N.: Analysis of "Idriverplus" driverless delivery vehicle [EB/OL]. (2018-04-24) [2020-12-20]. http://kuaibao.qq.com/s/20180424G18OST00?refer=cp_1026. (in Chinese)
2. Chen, X.J.: What is the most amazing function about rookie driverless logistics vehicles. Automot. Obs. **7**, 99 (2018). (in Chinese)
3. Fridman, L., Mehler, B., Xia, L., et al.: To walk or not to walk: crowdsourced assessment of external vehicle-to-pedestrian displays. In: Proceedings of the Transportation Research Board 98th Annual Meeting, Washington (2019)
4. Lagstrom, T., Lundgren, V.M.: AVIP-Autonomous Vehicles Interaction with Pedestrians. Chalmers University of Technology, Goteborg (2015)
5. Snyder, J.B.: This Self-driving Car Smiles at Pedestrians [EB/OL]. (2016-09-16) [2020-11-11]. https://www.autoblog.com/2016/09/16/this-self-driving-car-smiles-atpedestrians/
6. Mercedes-Benz Company: The Mercedes-Benzes F 015 luxury in motion [EB/OL]. [2019-09-16]. https://www.mercedes-benz.com/en/mercedes-benz/innovation/research-vehicle-f-015-luxury-in-motion/
7. Kwasniowski, S., Zajac, M., Zajac, P.: Telematic problems of unmanned vehicles positioning at container terminals and warehouses. In: Mikulski, J. (ed.) TST 2010. CCIS, vol. 104, pp. 391–399. Springer, Heidelberg (2010). https://doi.org/10.1007/978-3-642-16472-9_43
8. Cheng, I.L,, Cheng, C.H., Liu, D.G.: A learnable unmanned smart logistics prototype system design and implementation. In: 2019 IEEE International Conference on Artificial Intelligence Circuits and Systems (AICAS), pp. 221–224. IEEE (2019)
9. Repin, S., Evtiukov, S., Maksimov, S.: A method for quantitative assessment of vehicle reliability impact on road safety. Transp. Res. Procedia **36**, 661–668 (2018). https://doi.org/10.1016/j.trpro.2018.12.128
10. Vorozheikin, I., Marusin, A., Brylev, I., Vinogradova, V.: Digital technologies and complexes for provision of vehicular traffic safety. In: International Conference on Digital Transformation in Logistics and Infrastructure (ICDTLI2019), vol. 1, pp. 385–389. Atlantis Highlights in Computer Sciences (2019). https://doi.org/10.2991/icdtli-19.2019.67
11. Butakov, V., Ioannou, P.: Driving autopilot with personalization feature for improved safety and comfort. In: 2015 IEEE 18th Conference on Intelligent Transportation Systems, Las Palmas, Spain, pp. 387–393 (2015). https://doi.org/10.1109/itsc.2015.72
12. Daziano, R.A., Sarrias, M., Leard, B.: Are consumers willing to pay to let cars drive for them? Analyzing response to autonomous vehicles. Transp. Res. Part C Emerg. Technol. **78**, 150–164 (2017). https://doi.org/10.1016/j.trc.2017.03.003

13. Kotte, J., Josten, J., Zlocki, A., Eckstein, L.: Impact of a visual and haptic driver advice and preview system on a range optimized way of driving in electric vehicles. Transp. Res. Procedia **14**, 1071–1079 (2016). https://doi.org/10.1016/j.trpro.2016.05.177
14. Kyriakidis, M., Happee, R., De Winter, J.C.F.: Public opinion on automated driving: results of an international questionnaire among 5000 respondents. Trans. Res. Part F Traffic Psychol. Behav. **32**, 127–140 (2015). https://doi.org/10.1016/j.trf.2015.04.014
15. Likert, R.: A Technique for the measurement of attitudes. Arch. Psychol. **22**(40), 1–55 (1932)

A Measurement of Attitude Toward Working with Robots (AWRO): A Compare and Contrast Study of AWRO with Negative Attitude Toward Robots (NARS)

Lionel P. Robert Jr.(✉) ⓘ

School of Information and Robotics Institute, University of Michigan,
Ann Arbor, MI 48109, USA
lprobert@umich.edu

Abstract. Organizations are increasingly relying on a workforce that includes humans and robots working collaboratively. Yet, many humans are reluctant to work with robots. To help identify and predict who is likely to want to work with a robot, this paper introduces a new scale called attitude toward working with a robot (AWRO). The author conducted a study to assess the AWRO scale's construct validity and reliability along with its predictive power in relation to NARS. The AWRO scale was administered to 220 restaurant employees. AWRO demonstrated good construct validity and reliability and was also much more predictive of worker outcomes than NARS. Results of this study have implications for a workforce that includes humans and robots working collaboratively.

Keywords: Negative attitude toward robots · Attitude toward working with a robot · NARS · AWRO · Working with robots

1 Introduction

Organizations are increasingly relying on a workforce that includes humans and robots working collaboratively. Yet, many humans are reluctant to work with robots [1]. Currently, the negative attitude toward robots (NARS) scale is often used to help assess an individual's attitude toward robots [2]. NARS is a general attitude measure designed to assess an individual's overall attitude toward robots [3]. Prior literature on attitudes suggests that the more specific an attitude measure, the more predictive it will be in assessing someone's future behavior [4, 5]. This suggests that a measure designed specifically to assess an individual attitude toward working with a robot would be better at assessing how likely it would be for someone to want to engage in collaborative work with the robot.

To address the problem of creating new scales that are more specific to a workplace setting, the author had several goals in this paper. First, this paper introduces a new set of scales to measure an individual's attitude toward working with a robot (AWRO). To test this measure, the author administered the AWRO scale to 220 restaurant employees.

© Springer Nature Switzerland AG 2021
M. Kurosu (Ed.): HCII 2021, LNCS 12763, pp. 288–299, 2021.
https://doi.org/10.1007/978-3-030-78465-2_22

Second, the study assessed the reliability and the discriminant and convergent validity of this new scale alongside the existing NARS scale. Finally, this study compared the predictive ability of this new scale on work outcomes against the existing NARS scale. In all, this study examined the impact of the AWRO scale to predict someone's willingness to work with a robotic co-worker.

This paper contributes to the human–robot interaction literature in several ways. First, it introduces a new measure that can help determine who is and who is not likely to want to work with a robot. Practically, this could aid in the selection, hiring and assigning of employees who are likely to enjoy and be successful working with robots. Theoretically, this new scale could help scholars better control for individual differences likely to impact human–robot interactions. Second, this study examined the incremental value of this new scale alongside NARS. This allowed for direct comparison with regard to predictability while also assessing measurement validity between the scales.

2 Background

2.1 Working with Robots

Humans are increasingly being asked to work collaboratively with robots. Human–robot work collaboration (HRWC), where humans and robots work side by side to complete work, is expected to increase [1]. This work arrangement allows repetitive and tedious tasks to be off-loaded to robots. This has the potential to help reduce the physical injuries associated with repetitive motion [6]. This also has the benefit of freeing humans to focus on other tasks that cannot be easily performed by robots [7]. This explains why robots are being deployed in assembly lines, order fulfillment centers, and product inspections service centers [8]. For example, Amazon is adding 15,000 robots a year to work with employees in its 20 fulfillment centers [9]. Robots are projected to replace as much as half the workforce in 10–20 years [7, 10, 11].

Organizations are left with the challenge of integrating humans and robots into a cohesive workforce. This challenge is made harder because some humans are reluctant to work with robots. This is, in part, because some workers are concerned about the loss of their future employment to robots [12]. In other cases, humans are just apprehensive or fearful of working with a robot [13]. Organizations are seeking ways to identify workers who might be more willing to work with robots. Considering the importance of human and robot work collaboration, more theoretical and empirical work is needed [1, 13].

2.2 Attitudes

Attitudes are an individual's predisposed favorable or unfavorable feelings about a particular person, place, thing, event or action [14]. As such, attitudes not only represent but also influence an individual's thoughts and behavior [14, 15]. This explains why attitudes feature prominently in many social–psychological theories, such as the Theory of Planned Behavior [14]. Generally, the more favorable an attitude an individual has toward another person, place, thing, event or action, the more likely that individual is to engage with the other person, place, thing, event or action.

2.3 Negative Attitudes Towards Robots Scale (NARS)

Nowhere has this been truer than in understanding human interactions with technology [15, 16]. Favorable attitudes toward a technology indicate that someone is more likely to use or accept that technology [15, 16]. Differences in individuals' attitudes regarding technology can be profound [17]. Several prominent technology acceptance models include attitude as a key construct [16].

NARS is one measure of a person's attitude toward robots used to predict when someone would prefer or not prefer to interact with robots [2, 18]. Nomura et al. [2] developed NARS in Japan to measure general human negative attitudes toward robots. Since then, NARS has been adapted and widely used to measure human attitudes toward robots [3]. In many studies, NARS has been employed as control variable to take into account that some individuals are more or less receptive to robots [13, 18].

2.4 Attitude Toward Working with Robots (AWRO)

Although attitude has been recognized as a key predictor of behavior, scholars have distinguished between general and specific attitudes [18]. General attitudes refer to favorable or unfavorable feelings toward a category of people, places, things, events or actions, whereas specific attitudes are more narrowly focused on favorable or unfavorable feelings toward a particular instance within a category of people, places, things, events or actions [19]. General attitudes are more predictive of general tendencies to engage in behaviors involving a broad category of people, places, things, events or actions, whereas specific attitudes are better predictors of behaviors involving a particular instance within one of those categories [see 4, 5].

The differences between general and specific attitudes are not absolute but are instead relative. For example, NARS can be considered a measure of an attitude toward a particular technology. In this way, NARS can be considered a specific measure of a general attitudinal measure of a specific technology. Yet, in another way, NARS could be viewed as a general measure of someone's attitude toward a robot. Attitude toward working with a robot represents a specific instance of a more general category of interacting with robots. A more specific measure of attitude toward working with a robot might provide a much predictive measure for organizations. To address this gap, the author proposes a specific measure of attitude toward robots in reference to work.

3   Method and Analysis

3.1   Participants

The participants were 220 restaurant employees. The participants' ages ranged from 18 to 67 years, with a mean of 36.8 years and a standard deviation of 12.3 years. The majority of the employees were females, 64.5%, followed by males, 34.5%, one transgender male, 0.5%, and one who preferred not to answer, 0.5%. The average restaurant employee worked 8.8 h per day, with a standard deviation of 2.5 h. The average restaurant employee had been working in the restaurant industry for 9.5 years.

3.2   Data Collection

This sample was obtained with the help of a panel service company via Qualtrics. The survey was administered online using a web-based platform and the participants were assured that their responses were confidential and that only the researcher would see their responses.

3.3   Measurements

Control Variables. There were five control variables: age, gender, marital status, work hours per day, and time in the profession. Gender and marital status were treated as categorical variables. The specific categories are listed in Table 1.

Table 1. Control variables.

	Label	N
Gender 1	Female	142
Gender 2	Male	76
Gender 3	Transgender female	0
Gender 4	Transgender male	1
Gender 5	Not listed	1
Gender 6	Prefer not to answer	1
Marital status 1	Single (never married)	89
Marital status 2	Married or domestic relationship	100
Marital status 3	Widowed	3
Marital status 4	Divorced	24
Marital status 5	Separated	4

Independent Variables. The two independent variables were AWRO and NARS. The items for both measures are shown in Table 2.

Table 2. Measurement Items for NARS and AWRO.

NARS	AWRO
I would feel uneasy if I were given a job where I had to use robots. (NARS 1)	I am someone who would enjoy working with a robot. (AWRO 1)
I would feel nervous operating a robot in front of other people. (NARS 2)	I am someone who would be happy to receive work from a robot. (AWRO 2)
I would hate the idea that robots or artificial intelligences were making judgments about things. (NARS 3)	I am someone who would find it fun to give work to a robot to perform. (AWRO 3)

(*continued*)

Table 2. (*continued*)

NARS	AWRO
I am concerned that robots would be a bad influence on children. (NARS 4)	I am someone who would like to collaborate with a robot to accomplish my work. (AWRO 4)
If robots had emotions, I would not be able to make friends with them. (NARS 5)	I am someone who find it fun to work with a robot. (AWRO 5)
I do not feel comforted being with robots that have emotions. (NARS 6)	I am someone who would prefer to work with a robot. (AWRO 6)

Dependent Variables. The two dependent variables were turnover intention from working with a robot and expected job satisfaction with working with a robot. Items for turnover intention were adapted from [20], while items for job satisfaction were adapted from [21] to represent the context of working with a robot. The items for both measures are shown in Table 3.

Table 3. Items for turnover intention and job satisfaction for working with a robot.

Turnover intention	Job satisfaction
Working with a robot would likely de/increase my intention to leave my organization in the future. (TO1)	If I had to work with a robot, I would still recommend this job to a good friend of mine. (JS1)
Working with a robot would likely de/increase my intention to seek another job in another organization. (TO2)	If I had to work with a robot, I would be satisfied with my job. (JS2)
Working with a robot would de/increase me considering leaving my organization. (TO3)	If I had to work with a robot, I would be generally happy with my job. (JS1)

Item Reliability. The AWRO multi-item measurement scale demonstrated high reliability with an alpha of .95. Each item was also reliable, as shown in Table 4. Dropping any item would not increase the overall construct reliability.

Table 4. AWRO measurement item reliability.

AWRO	Reliability if item deleted
AWRO 1	.93
AWRO 2	.94
AWRO 3	.94

(*continued*)

Table 4. (*continued*)

AWRO	Reliability if item deleted
AWRO 4	.93
AWRO 5	.93
AWRO 6	.94

Discriminant and Convergent Validity. Convergent and discriminant validity were assessed using factor analysis with a varimax rotation. Table 5 shows the factor loadings for each item. Values less than .40 are not shown in the table. Except for one item, all cross-loadings were less than .40, demonstrating discriminant validity [22]; two items had loadings less than .70, suggesting good although not great convergent validity. It should be noted that NARS demonstrated less convergent and discriminant validity than AWRO. More specifically, NARS had three items with factor loadings that fell below .60 and 1 item that fell below .70. NARS cross-loaded more with job satisfaction than AWRO.

Table 5. Factor loadings.

AWRO	AWRO	Turnover intention	Job satisfaction	NARS
AWRO 1	.70			.41
AWRO 2	.64			
AWRO 3	.80			
AWRO 4	.82			
AWRO 5	.76			
AWRO 6	.64			
TO1		.92		
TO2		.90		
TO3		.91		
JS1			.74	
JS2			.81	
JS3			.83	
NARS 1	.43			.49
NARS 2				.56
NARS 3				.63
NARS 4			.46	.70
NARS 5				.79
NARS 6				.71

Correlation Matrix. The correlation matrix is shown in Table 6. P value significance is shown by the number of asterisks, with * p < .05, ** p < .01 and ** p < .001. As expected, NARS and AWRO were correlated.

Table 6. Correlation matrix.

	Mean	Std	AWRO	Job satisfaction	NARS
AWRO	3.77	1.60			
Job satisfaction	3.50	1.46	.69**		
NARS	4.30	1.41	−.77**	−.57**	
Turnover intention	4.66	1.43	−.54**	−.60**	.50**

3.4 Results

To access the predictability of AWOR against NARS, the models were analyzed using General Linear Model (GLM) in SPSS 27. The sample size for the analysis was 220 and all betas represented unstandardized regression coefficients. P value significance is shown by the number of asterisks, with * p < .05, ** p < .01 and *** p < .001.

Model 1. The results in Table 7 reflect the analysis without AWRO. Results for this analysis, model 1, as shown in Table 7, explained 29% of the variance in turnover intention ($F_{10, 209} = 7.6, p < .001$) and 34% of job satisfaction ($F_{10, 209} = 9.7, p < .001$).

Table 7. General linear model 1 results.

	Turnover intention		Job satisfaction	
	Coef.	S.E.	Coef.	S.E.
Intercept	.85	1.5	6.02	1.5***
Gender = 1	1.85	1.26	−.303	1.24
Gender = 2	1.5	1.26	−.011	1.24
Gender = 4	−1.04	1.77	.91	1.74
Gender = 6	.00	.	.00	.
Marital status = 1	.61	.65	−.17	.64
Marital status = 2	.57	.65	−.23	.63
Marital status = 3	.27	.96	−.29	.95
Marital status = 4	.33	.68	−.05	.67

(*continued*)

Table 7. (*continued*)

	Turnover intention		Job satisfaction	
	Coef.	S.E.	Coef.	S.E.
Marital status = 5	.00	.	.00	.
Age	−.00	.01	−.00	.01
Work hours per day	−.04	.04	.04	.03
Time in the profession	−.01	.01	−.01	.01
NARS	.46	.06***	−.56	.06***
AWRO				
R-square	.29		.34	
Adjusted R-square	.25		.31	
F	7.6***		9.7***	

Model 2. The results in Table 8 reflect the analysis with AWRO. Results for the model 2 analysis are shown in Table 8 and explained 35% of the variance in turnover intention ($F_{11, 208} = 9.5$, $p < .001$) and 50% of job satisfaction ($F_{11, 208} = 17.7$, $p < .001$).

Table 8. General linear model 2 results.

	Turnover intention		Job satisfaction	
	Coef.	S.E.	Coef.	S.E.
Intercept	2.23	1.60	2.92	1.45*
Gender = 1	2.81	1.20*	−1.03	1.10
Gender = 2	2.64	1.22*	−.84	1.10
Gender = 4	.00	.	.00	.
Marital status = 1	.62	.62	−.31	.56
Marital status = 2	.58	.62	−.17	.56
Marital status = 3	.02	.92	.13	.83
Marital status = 4	.35	.65	−.09	.59
Marital status = 5	.00	.	.00	.
Age	.00	.01	−.01	.01
Work hours per day	−.05	.03	.05	.03

(*continued*)

Table 8. (*continued*)

	Turnover intention		Job satisfaction	
	Coef.	S.E.	Coef.	S.E.
Time in the profession	−.01	.01	−.01	.01
NARS	.19	.10*	−.08	.09
AWRO	−.33	.08***	.56	.07***
R-square	.35		.50	
Adjusted R-square	.31		.47	
F	9.5***		17.7***	

Incremental Value. To assess the incremental value of the addition of AWRO, we compared both model R-squares for each dependent variable. As seen in Table 9, the addition of AWRO significantly increased the variance explained for both turnover intention and job satisfaction over and above the model without AWRO. P value significance is shown by the number of asterisks, with * $p < .05$, ** $p < .01$ and *** $p < .001$.

Table 9. Incremental value.

	Turnover intention R-square	Job satisfaction R-square
Model 2 with AWRO	.35	.50
Model 1	.29	.34
Difference	.06	.16
F	19.57***	67.84***

Multicollinearity. Two linear regression analyses were conducted to test for possible multicollinearity between NARS and AWRO. In both models, the variance inflation factor (VIF) remained 2.5 or lower. VIF values of over 4 are considered to be an indication of a moderate multicollinearity, while values over 10 are considered to be severe multicollinearity. Therefore, multicollinearity does not appear to be a problem.

4   Discussion

4.1   Summary of Findings

The goal of this research was to introduce a new measure to help determine who is likely to want to work with a robot. To that end, the research findings can be organized into two overarching findings. One, the new measure AWRO demonstrated reliability as well as discriminant and convergent validity. Two, AWRO explained additional variances in both turnover intention and job satisfaction over and above NARS. Taken together, these findings highlight the potential importance of AWRO. Next, we detail contributions to the literature, theoretical implications and study limitations.

4.2 Contributions

This paper contributes to the HRI literature by helping to predict who is and who is not likely to want to work with a robot. AWRO provides a much more specific measure of attitudes toward working with robots, and this measure could be deployed alongside NARS if needed. Theoretically, this new scale is likely to better help scholars control for individual differences when empirically testing their theories of work-related human–robot interactions. This is likely to lead to better assessment of such theories by accounting for more relevant context-specific individual differences.

This study also contributes to the literature by demonstrating AWRO's incremental value in the presence of NARS. That said, there were cross-loadings between AWRO and NARS. This suggests that applying one or the other might be preferred. With that in mind, we conducted an additional analysis with just AWRO, without NARS, along with the control variables in Model 2, which predicted .33 of turnover intention and .49 of job satisfaction. Model 1 in Table 7, which had NARS and not AWRO, predicted .25 of turnover intention and .34 of job satisfaction. Therefore, AWRO had a higher predictive power when it came to explaining the two work outcomes in this study.

Finally, practically AWRO can aid in the selection, hiring and assigning of employees who are likely to enjoy and be successful working with robots. Currently, organizations that are struggling to determine whom to hire or assign to collaboratively work with robots have little guidance. AWRO provides one approach to assess an employee's readiness and willingness to work with a robotic co-worker.

4.3 Limitations

The paper has several limitations and opportunities for future research. The study employed a cross-sectional survey approach. This allowed the study to employ a highly generalizable sample. Unfortunately, like all cross-sectional survey approaches, it suffers from issues of internal validity. Future research could examine the predictive power of the AWRO scale in either an experimental setting or a survey study setting that separates via time the collection of the independent variables from the dependent variable. The study asked restaurant employees to anticipate how they might feel working with a robot with regard to their turnover intention and job satisfaction. This might have more accurately reflected their attitudes if they had worked with a robot. However, future studies could possibly ask restaurant employees who have worked with a robot about their experiences relative to turnover intention and job satisfaction.

5 Conclusion

Collaboration with others is at the heart of many productive work arrangements [23, 24]. Robots are increasingly becoming that collaborative work partner in many new work arrangements. Nonetheless, many humans are reluctant to work with robots. This paper introduced and tested AWRO, a new work-specific scale for assessing someone's willingness to work with a robot. However, there is much to learn regarding the use of AWRO. This study is an important start in our understanding of the usefulness of AWRO. Nonetheless, future research is needed to build and expand our understanding of AWRO.

References

1. You, S., Kim, J.H., Lee, S., Kamat, V., Robert Jr., L.P.: Enhancing perceived safety in human–robot collaborative construction using immersive virtual environments. Autom. Constr. **96**, 161–170 (2018)
2. Nomura, T., Suzuki, T., Kanda, T., Kato, K.: Measurement of negative attitudes toward robots. Interact. Stud. **7**(3), 437–454 (2006)
3. Xia, Y., LeTendre, G.: Robots for future classrooms: a cross-cultural validation study of negative attitudes toward robots scale in the U.S. context. Int. J. Soc. Rob. (2020). https://doi.org/10.1007/s12369-020-00669-2. Accessed 10 Feb 2021
4. Ajzen, I., Fishbein, M.: Attitude-behavior relations: a theoretical analysis and review of empirical research. Psychol. Bull. **84**(5), 888–918 (1977)
5. Eagly, A.H., Chaiken, S.: The Psychology of Attitudes. Harcourt Brace Jovanovich College Publishers, Fort Worth (1993)
6. Schneider, S., Susi, P.: Ergonomics and construction: a review of potential hazards in new construction. Am. Ind. Hyg. Assoc. J. **55**(7), 635–649 (1994)
7. Esterwood, C., Robert, L.: Robots and COVID-19: re-imagining human–robot collaborative work in terms of reducing risks to essential workers. SSRN 2021. SSRN. https://papers.ssrn.com/sol3/papers.cfm?abstract_id=3767609. Accessed 10 Feb 2021
8. Knight, W.: Are you ready for a robot colleague? MIT Technol. Rev. (2015). https://www.technologyreview.com/s/541676/are-you-ready-for-a-robot-colleague/. Accessed 6 Feb 2021
9. Clark, P., Bhasin, K.: Amazon's robot war is spreading. Bloomberg (2017). https://www.bloomberg.com/news/articles/2017-04-05/robots-enlist-humans-to-win-the-warehouse-war-amazon-started. Accessed 6 Feb 2021
10. Qureshi, M.O., Syed, R.S.: The impact of robotics on employment and motivation of employees in the service sector, with special reference to health care. Saf. Health Work **5**(4), 198–202 (2014)
11. Ackerman, E.: U.S. army considers replacing thousands of soldiers with robots. IEEE Spectr. (2014). https://spectrum.ieee.org/automaton/robotics/military-robots/army-considers-replacing-thousands-of-soldiers-with-robots. Accessed 6 Feb 2021
12. Webster, M.: Could a robot do your job? USA Today (2014). https://www.usatoday.com/story/news/nation/2014/10/28/low-skill-workers-face-mechanization-challenge/16392981/. Accessed 6 Feb 2021
13. You, S., Robert, L.: Emotional attachment, performance, and viability in teams collaborating with embodied physical action (EPA) robots. J. Assoc. Inf. Syst. **19**(5), 377–407 (2018)
14. Ajzen, I.: Attitudes, Personality, and Behavior, 2nd edn. McGraw Hill International, New York (2005)
15. Robert Jr., L.P., Sykes, T.A.: Extending the concept of control beliefs: integrating the role of advice networks. Inf. Syst. Res. **28**(1), 84–96 (2017)
16. Venkatesh, V., Morris, M.G., Davis, G.B., Davis, F.D.: User acceptance of information technology: toward a unified view. MIS Q. **27**(3), 425–478 (2003)

17. Robert, L.P., Alahmad, R., Kim, S., Esterwood, C., You, S., Zhang, Q.: A review of personality in human robot interactions. Found. Trends Inf. Syst. **4**(2), 107–210 (2020)
18. Smith, E.R., Sherrin, S., Fraune, M.R., Šabanović, S.: Positive emotions, more than anxiety or other negative emotions, predict willingness to interact with robots. Pers. Soc. Psychol. Bull. **46**(8), 1270–1283 (2020)
19. Vining, J., Ebreo, A.: Predicting recycling behavior from global and specific environmental attitudes and changes in recycling opportunities. J. Appl. Soc. Psychol. **22**(20), 1580–1607 (1992)
20. Irving, G.P., Coleman, D.F., Cooper, C.L.: Further assessments of a three-component model of organizational commitment: generalizability and differences across occupations. J. Appl. Psychol. **82**(3), 444–452 (1997)
21. Eisenberger, R., Cummings, J., Armeli, S., Lynch, P.: Perceived organizational support, discretionary treatment, and job satisfaction. J. Appl. Psychol. **82**(5), 812–820 (1997)
22. Fornell, C., Larcker, D.F.: Evaluating structural equation models with unobservable variables and measurement error. J. Mark. Res. **18**(1), 39–50 (1981)
23. Robert Jr., L.P., Dennis, A.R., Ahuja, M.K.: Differences are different: Examining the effects of communication media on the impacts of racial and gender diversity in decision-making teams. Inf. Syst. Res. **29**(3), 525–545 (2018)
24. Robert, L.P., You, S.: Are you satisfied yet? Shared leadership, trust and individual satisfaction in virtual teams. In: Proceedings of the 2013 iConference, pp. 461–466. IDEALS, Fort Worth (2013)

Service Sector Professionals' Perspective on Robots Doing Their Job in the Future

Nina Savela[✉] [iD], Rita Latikka[iD], Reetta Oksa[iD], and Atte Oksanen[iD]

Faculty of Social Sciences, Tampere University, Kalevantie 5, 33014 Tampere, Finland
nina.savela@tuni.fi

Abstract. After a long history of industrial automation, robots are entering service fields at an accelerating rate due to the recent technological advances in robotics. Understanding the acceptance and applicability of robots is essential for successful introduction, desired benefits, and well-managed transformation of the labor market. In this work, we investigated whether service sector professionals consider robots applicable to their field compared to professionals from other sectors. We collected survey data from Finnish ($N = 1817$) and U.S. participants ($N = 1740$) and analyzed them using ordinary least squares regression. Results showed that Finnish and U.S. participants from the service sector disclosed a less positive attitude toward robots' suitability to their own occupational field compared to participants from other fields. Younger age, technological expertise, prior experience interacting with robots at work, and positive attitude toward robots were associated with higher perceived robot suitability. Perceived robot suitability was also found to mediate the relationship between occupational sector and positive interaction attitudes. The results indicate that robots entering into service industries evokes some resistance and doubt in professionals of these fields. Increasing technological knowledge and prior experience with robots at work are central factors when introducing robots in a socially sustainable way.

Keywords: Robots · Work · Service sector · Perceived suitability · Social acceptance · Attitudes

1 Introduction

After a long history of industrial robots and automation, robots are entering service fields at an accelerating rate due to the recent technological advances in robotics and are expected to revolutionize the service sector [1]. The service sector consists of multiple fields, such as health care and education, ranging from service production to customer interaction. Designing new technology for humans to use in new domains of work involves factors such as user acceptance and intention to use [2]. The people working in the field decide whether or not they prefer to use or interact with a new technology, which may remain unactualized despite the original intention or plan of other stakeholders. Therefore, understanding the acceptance and applicability of robots is essential for successful introduction, desired benefits, and well-managed transformation of the labor market.

© Springer Nature Switzerland AG 2021
M. Kurosu (Ed.): HCII 2021, LNCS 12763, pp. 300–317, 2021.
https://doi.org/10.1007/978-3-030-78465-2_23

The consumption and use of service robots is rising rapidly [3]. Robots can be classified as service robots and further to personal and professional service robots, referring to a device designed for professional or nonprofessional use that performs functions that are useful to human beings and that are outside the scope of industry [4]. Thus, a robot is defined by the specific domain it is designed for, but its appearance and level of automation can vary from a robotic device to a humanoid robot and from teleoperated to autonomous robots. To give a few examples, the humanoid robots NAO [5, 6] and Pepper [7] were designed and optimized especially for human interaction. A telepresence robot, Double, is also intended to facilitate social interaction [8], and the more autonomous Paro is a seal-like robot designed to act as a therapeutic tool [9].

Designing robots for the service sector has raised some concerns among researchers and engineers regarding the successful interaction and acceptance of people with no technological expertise [10]. People have also been found to react unfavorably to working in close collaboration with robots instead of humans [11]. Previous studies comparing acceptance of robots in different jobs and life domains suggest that people could be more hesitant to accept and adapt robots in contexts in which close interaction with robots or creative abilities are required [12, 13]. Hence, these domains are suspected to be more resistant to robot deployment, particularly when substituting humans.

Research on social acceptance of robots working in different occupational fields has focused more on health and social services during recent decades [14]. Care work professionals have been found to be receptive to robot work, for example in surgery [15–17]. A study regarding psychology students' willingness to adopt humanoid robots in their work field showed that they had a positive attitude toward using robots; however, they felt like they did not have the needed abilities to utilize robots [18]. Adaptability of robots to education has also generated some research interest. Researchers have found robots suitable for teaching domains such as children's education, engineering, and mathematics [19–22]. Also, in surveillance and military, robots have been found be accepted for dangerous tasks, such as search and rescue activities [23]. Similarly, also used for defense, drones are examples of robots flying in a confined space [24].

Apart from the service sector, robots and automation have been used for years for tasks such as lifting and assembling objects in the manufacturing industry. In addition, robots have been gradually adopted in other fields, such as in agriculture for assisting with milking activities [25]. Industrial robots are the largest category of robots outside the scope of service robots. Industrial robots include similar type of devices than service robots but are defined as industrial robots based on the context in which they are used. Other than industrial and service robots, there is a lack of specific categories of robots, because service robots are sometimes defined to include all robots used outside of industrial context. However, if categorized based on the specific service fields, robots outside of service sector could include professional service robots, such as delivery robots or robotic storage systems [26, 27], and personal service robots in domestic use, such as vacuum cleaner robots [28]. Social acceptance of robots in occupational fields outside the service sector has been given far less attention in research [14].

Individual differences might also affect the acceptance of robots, but the results concerning sociodemographic factors have been mixed in previous studies. Some research teams have not found a statistically significant relationship between age and acceptance of robots [29, 30], and those who have, have suggested that future researchers consider the prior experience in technology as a control to account for the variance it potentially produces [31, 32]. Female gender has been found to be negatively connected to acceptance of robots [33, 34], but this has also been criticized and instead suspected to derive from females' lower technological competence and less prior experience with robots [31]. Income has not been found to affect robot acceptance, although the research literature on this matter is scarce [35].

Introducing new technology such as advanced robots affects society more broadly. For this reason, researchers have requested a broader examination of acceptance of and resistance to robots in new domains beyond a customer- and user-centered research approach [36]. In addition to customers, it is valuable to consider the perspectives of professionals' and employees' from the fields because they are competing with robots for the jobs and they hold the unique human abilities that advanced technology is not yet able to offer in work life [37]. Professionals are also key players in innovation spread and technology innovation adoption [38, 39] and are a valuable source of information regarding the applicable work domains that currently exist for robots and the current state of social acceptance of robots within these fields.

1.1 Perceived Suitability and Related Theories

Attitudes toward technology have previously been measured using the technology acceptance model (TAM) [40], which has been applied from the theory of reasoned action (TRA) [41]. The original TAM focused on predicting the actual usage behavior, including external variables as one aspect in the beginning of the model. More detailed external variables that take into account the subjective norm and prior experience of using the technology were added to the TAM2 [3].

The utility of the TAM and its extended versions for advanced technology such as robots has received some critique [42]. For example, the wide range of robotic technologies from fully teleoperated to highly autonomous devices raises questions regarding whether robots are being used by the user or if users are rather interacting with these technological entities. Some attempts at robot acceptance models have been made. For example, Heerink, Kröse, Evers, and Wielinga [43] validated the Almere model for assessing older adults' acceptance of assistive social agent technology. In addition to perceived usefulness and ease of use, the Almere model includes perceived adaptability, which is part of the instrumental aspect regarding the utility and gained benefits. However, the model has been mostly applied in eldercare research.

The unified theory of acceptance and use of technology (UTAUT) model, which has been widely used in studies regarding information technology acceptance and usage, is a combination of eight different models. In addition to the previously mentioned TAM [40] and TRA [41], the model consists of the theory of planned behavior [44], the innovation diffusion theory [45], the motivational model [46], the personal computer utilization model [47], social cognitive theory [48], and model that integrates TAM and theory of planned behavior [49]. The UTAUT model includes expected performance, effort expectancy, social influence, and facilitating conditions [50]. It has been utilized, for example, by Heerink et al. [43, 51] in eldercare and, more recently, in studies by Conti et al. [18, 20] on robot usage in children's education and psychology practice. In addition, the UTAUT has been used in studies measuring interaction experience with the NAO robot [52] and the acceptance and adoption of robotic surgery [53].

Attitude constructs have been discovered to play a crucial role in actual behavior also in the UTAUT model. Attitudinal beliefs and perceptions have been found to be directly associated with behavioral intention, which is in turn connected to use behavior [54]. Moreover, in the UTAUT model, behavioral intention mediates the relationship of performance expectancy, effort expectancy, social influence, and facilitating conditions to use behavior [54]. The UTAUT2 model was developed based on the UTAUT model but considering both the organizational and consumer usage contexts. The revised model includes hedonic motivation, price value, and habit [55]. Job fit is argued to be a part of performance expectancy in the UTAUT2 framework [56], and the model has been utilized, for example, in adaptation of mobile banking [57]. Thus far, research using the UTAUT2 model to examine robot acceptance remains scarce. However, in this study, we investigated the relationship between professionals' perspectives on job fit or suitability of robots and their comfortableness interacting with robots themselves. Thus, the original UTAUT model offered the most suitable theoretical framework for technology acceptance examination for the purpose of our study. Its constructs of perceived performance expectancy and behavioral intention offer an apt theoretical background for discovering the perceived suitability of robots in the service sector.

1.2 Research Overview

In this article, we report two studies that included participants from two different contexts: Finland and the United States. Both countries are highly technologically oriented, which is positively connected to robot acceptance at work [58]. The service sector's increasing trend is prominent in both countries and has been significant regarding employment for decades, especially in the United States, accounting for over 80% of the working population [59, 60]. Due to the similar key characteristics of technology orientation and structure and trend of the growing service sector, we examined participants from both countries to answer our research questions. In Study 1, our main interest was to find out if there is a connection between the service sector and perceived suitability by professionals in the Finnish context. In Study 2, we aimed to replicate the finding in the context of the United States and further investigate the factors contributing to this relationship and the mediating role of perceived robot suitability for interaction attitudes of the professionals.

The results will contribute to the understanding of how the introduction of robots in new occupational fields is received as applicable among the professionals of the field. In our studies, we considered that the service sector consists of multiple fields involving service production and customer interaction. Other sectors are classified apart from the service sector and include occupational fields such as manufacturing, agriculture, and transportation (see Appendix 1 for the full list of classifications). Considering the scarce research comparing different occupational fields on which to base hypotheses, we established research questions for our studies. Using the binary classification for the service sector, the aim of this article was to examine the following research questions:

- **H1:** How does perceived suitability of robots to one's own occupational field differ between service sector professionals and those from other fields?
- **H2:** How do the sociodemographic factors, prior experience, and attitude toward robots in general associate with perceived suitability of robots to one's field?
- **H3:** Does perceived suitability mediate the relationship between occupational sector and attitudes toward interaction with robots?

Based on technology acceptance models and previous research related to acceptance of robots, we proposed testing a short path model from the professionals' occupational field to professionals' perceptions of robot suitability to their field and further to their attitudes toward interacting with robots (see Fig. 1).

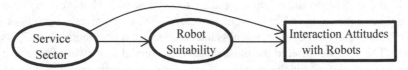

Fig. 1. Proposed path model based on research questions. Age, gender, income level, technology degree, prior interaction experience with robots, and general attitude toward robots in the model.

2   Methods and Materials

2.1   Study 1

Participants. A sample from the Finnish working population was collected in March 2019. The survey participants were aged between 18 and 65 ($N = 1817$, 46.84% female, $M_{age} = 41.75$ years, $SD_{age} = 12.19$ years). We recruited the participants via Norstat's pool of volunteers, with a response rate of 28.3%. We used a stratified sampling strategy to get a sample that would represent the Finnish workforce population in terms of age and gender. Participants were informed that by completing the survey they allow the reuse of the data for further research and that they may exit the survey at any time. The academic ethics committee of Tampere region confirmed in December 2018 that the research project did not involve ethical problems.

Measures. We measured participants' attitude toward robots working in their own field by asking them to rate the following statement on a scale from 1 to 7: "My current job could be done by a robot in the future." Participants were also asked to choose their occupational field from the International Standard Industrial Classification of All Economic Activities (ISIC) list [61]. This main independent variable was created by further categorizing I–S of the ISIC list into a dummy variable, in which service sector received a value of 1 and other sectors a value of 0 (see Appendix 1). Industries were classified as part of the service sector if they provided intangible goods, in other words services, and concerned interaction with customers [62]. Our categorization of service industries was similar to those of the World Bank [63], the U.S. Census Bureau [64], and

Official Statistics of Finland [65]. The same classification has also been used in other studies [66].

Sociodemographic background variables (age, gender, household's annual gross income level), were used as control variables. Age was used as a continuous variable and gender as a dummy variable. Income level was measured and used as a dummy variable by first asking about participants' monthly income in euros and then categorizing them as low- or high-income earners if they earned less than €2000 or €2000 and above, respectively. Descriptive statistics of the Study 1 variables are presented in Table 1.

Table 1. Summary of Descriptive Statistics of the Study 1 Variables ($N = 1817$).

Measure	n	%	M	SD	Range
Suitability of robots to one's own field	1817		2.10	1.54	1–7
Service sector	1817				0–1
1 = Service sector	1189	65.44			
0 = Other	628	34.56			
Age	1817		41.75	12.19	18–65
Gender	1817				0–1
1 = Female	851	46.84			
0 = Male	966	53.16			
Low-income earners	1817				0–1
1 = Under 2000 €	368	20.25			
0 = 2000 € and over	1449	79.75			

Statistical Analyses. We analyzed the data using ordinary least squares regression analysis using sequential models. Model 1 includes only the service sector as an independent variable, and the full Model 2 includes the sociodemographic variables. In the models, we report unstandardized regression coefficients (B), standard error of estimate ($SE\ B$), standardized coefficients (β), and p-values for statistical significance. We did not detect multicollinearity, but because of the heteroscedasticity of residuals, we ran the models using Huber-White standard errors (i.e., robust standard errors).

2.2 Study 2

Participants. We collected data from the U.S. participants via Amazon Mechanical Turk in January and April 2019 ($N = 2072$, 50.81% female, $M_{age} = 36.98$ years, $SD_{age} = 11.43$ years); participants' age ranged from 15 to 94 years old. In line with Study 1, only the working population was considered in the final sample ($N = 1740$, 49.53% female, $M_{age} = 36.87$ years, $SD_{age} = 10.81$ years). Participants were informed that by completing the survey they allow the reuse of the data for further research and that they may exit the survey at any time. The academic ethics committee of Tampere region confirmed in December 2018 that the research project did not involve ethical problems.

Measures. Suitability of robots to one's own field was measured with two questions on a scale from 1 to 7: "Robots suit my occupational field well" and "My current job could be done by a robot in the future." A sum variable created from these two statements was used as the dependent variable ($\alpha = .74$). Participants were also asked to choose an occupational field that was closest to their work or study from the ISIC list. This main independent variable was a dummy variable created from the ISIC categories in the same way as in Study 1. Participants from different service fields were given a value of 1 and other participants a value of 0.

Sociodemographic background variables (age, gender, household's annual gross income level) and other independent variables relevant to the robot context (a degree in technology or engineering, prior experience interacting with robots at work, attitude toward robots) were used as control variables. Age was used as a continuous variable and gender as a dummy variable. Income level was measured and used as a dummy variable by first asking about participants' households' gross annual income and then categorizing them as low- or high-income earners if their household earned less than $35,000 or $35,000 and above, respectively.

We measured prior interactional experience and technological expertise of the participants to account for the critique concerning the effects of sociodemographic factors in robot acceptance research [31]. This was also critical because of the hypothetical nature of our research and rating attitudes toward robots in general versus specific robots, hence helping to consider the different images of robots people have in mind when they are scoring their attitudes. Technological expertise was measured by asking whether participants had a degree in technology or engineering or not. They also responded regarding whether they had used or interacted with robots at work before or not. Both were used as dummy variables. We also asked the participants to rate their attitude toward robots in general on a scale from 1 to 7. Descriptive statistics of the Study 2 variables are presented in Table 2.

For additional path model analysis, we measured interactional attitude by asking about participants' perceived comfortableness with interacting with robots in various ways (see Appendix 2 for the full list of questions). For example, we asked, "How comfortable would you be about shaking hands with a robot?" and "How comfortable would you be about having a conversation with a robot?" We asked participants to score their responses to 12 questions on a 7-point Likert scale from *strongly disagree* to *strongly agree*.

Statistical Analyses. We analyzed data using ordinary least squares regression analysis using sequential models. Model 1 includes only the service sector as an independent variable; in Model 2, we added the sociodemographic variables; and Model 3 is a full model of all the variables used. In the models, we report unstandardized regression coefficients (B), standard error of estimate ($SE\ B$), standardized coefficients (β), and p-values for statistical significance. Multicollinearity or heteroscedasticity of residuals was not detected. For additional analysis, we used path regression modelling and a khb package [67] for mediation examination. All the statistical analyses were conducted with Stata 12 and Stata 16 programs.

Table 2. Summary of Descriptive Statistics of the Study 2 Variables ($N = 1740$).

Measure	n	%	M	SD	Range	n of items	α
Suitability of robots to one's own field	1740		7.39	3.35	2–14	2	.75
Service sector	1740				0–1		
1 = Service sector	1326	76.21					
0 = Other	414	23.79					
Age	1737		36.87	10.81	15–94		
Gender	1718				0–1		
1 = Female	851	49.53					
0 = Male	867	50.47					
Low annual income households	1740						
1 = Under $35,000	426	24.48					
0 = $35,000 and over	1314	75.52					
Degree in technology	1740				0–1		
1 = Yes	470	27.01					
0 = No	1270	72.99					
Interaction experience with robots at work	1740				0–1		
1 = Yes	250	14.37					
0 = No	1490	85.63					
Positive attitude toward robots	1740		4.96	1.35	1–7		

3 Results

3.1 Study 1

We present the results of linear regression models among Finnish participants in Table 3. Service sector professionals perceived robots as less suitable for their field ($\beta = -.08$, $p = .001$), as shown in Model 1. The negative connection remained after adding age, gender, and household's annual gross income as controls in Model 2 ($\beta = -.07$, $p = .002$). In Model 2, with sociodemographic control variables, older age predicted lower perceived suitability ($\beta = -.18$, $p < .001$). Gender was found to be unrelated to perceived suitability ($\beta = -.01$, $p = .752$). Higher income was found to be negatively connected to perceived suitability ($\beta = -.08$, $p < .001$). The final model was statistically significant ($p < .001$) and explained 6% of the variance.

Table 3. Suitability of Robots to One's Own Occupational Field in Study 1 ($N = 1817$).

Measure	Model 1 ROBUST			Model 2 ROBUST		
	B	SE B	β	B	SE B	β
Service sector	−.26	.08	−.08**	−.24	.08	−.07**
Age				− .02	.00	−.18***
Gender (female)				− 02	.07	−.01
Low-income earners				.48	.10	.13***
Model R^2		.01			.06	
Model F		11.53			26.51	
Model p		***			***	

Note. Dependent variable: Suitability of robots to one's own occupational field sum variable
$* p < .05. ** p < .01. *** p < .001$

3.2 Study 2

We present the results of linear regression models among U.S. participants in Table 4. As in Study 1, service sector professionals perceived robots as less suitable for their field (β $= - .06, p = .008$), as shown in Model 1. The negative connection remained after adding age, gender, and household's annual gross income as controls in Model 2 (β $= - .06, p = .013$). The relationship of the service sector and perceived suitability of robots in their own field was still statistically significant after adding strong predictor variables in Model 3 (β $= - .06, p = .011$).

Higher income was not found to be connected to perceived suitability, based on Model 2 (β $= - .01, p = .646$) and Model 3 (β $= - .03, p = .150$). Older age predicted lower perceived suitability in both Model 2 (β $= - .20, p < .001$) and Model 3 (β $= - .17, p < .001$). A negative connection between the female gender and lower perceived suitability was found in Model 2 (β $= - .07, p = .002$), but it disappeared after adding technology degree, prior interactional experience with robots at work, and attitude toward robots in Model 3 (β $= - .00, p = .910$). A degree in technology was the strongest predictor in Model 3, predicting higher perceived suitability (β $= .23, p < .001$). Prior interactional or user experience with robots at work predicted higher perceived suitability (β $= .12, p < .001$). Positive attitude toward robots was also connected to high perceived suitability (β $= .16, p < .001$). The final model was statistically significant ($p < .001$) and explained 17% of the variance in perceived suitability.

Results of the additional analyses are shown in a path model in Fig. 2. According to the path model, being in the service sector predicts lower perceived robot suitability ($B = - .44, SE = .17, β = - .06, p = .012$) and perceived suitability in turn predicts positive interaction attitudes ($B = .60, SE = .10, β = .12, p < .001$). Working in the service sector does not directly decrease the probability of positive interaction attitudes before or after

Table 4. Suitability of Robots to One's Own Occupational Field in Study 2 ($N = 1740$).

Measure	Model 1 ($N = 1740$) ROBUST			Model 2 ($N = 1715$) ROBUST			Model 3 ($N = 1715$) ROBUST		
	B	$SE\ B$	β	B	$SE\ B$	β	B	$SE\ B$	β
Service sector	−.50	.19	− .06**	− .46	.18	− .06*	− .44	.17	−.06*
Age				−.06	.01	− .20***	−.05	.01	− .17***
Gender (female)				−.49	.16	− .07**	−.02	.15	−.00
Low annual income households				.09	.19	.01	.25	.18	.03
Degree in technology							1.74	.18	.23***
Interaction experience with robots at work							1.12	.21	.12***
Positive attitude toward robots							.39	.06	.16***
Model R^2		.01			.05			.17	
Model F		10.99			24.28			57.34	
Model p		***			***			***	

Note. Dependent variable: Suitability of robots to one's own occupational field sum variable
$* p < .05. ** p < .01. *** p < .001$

controlling for perceived robot suitability to one's field. However, working in the service sector, or more accurately a standard-deviation increase in the service sector variable, leads to lower perceived robot suitability to one's own field, which is then translated into a lower probability of positive interaction attitudes of 26.44 percentage points, on average. The difference between the full and reduced model, hence the mediating effect of robot suitability, is statistically significant ($z = - .26, p = .021$), and the confounding percentage for the service sector variable is 36.79%.

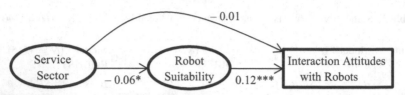

Fig. 2. The estimated path model in Sample 2 ($N = 1740$). Age, gender, income level, technology degree, prior interaction experience with robots, and general attitude toward robots in the model.

4 Discussion

In this work, we investigated whether service sector professionals consider robots as applicable to their own field as people from other sectors. We collected survey data from two countries, Finland and the United States. Based on both cultural backgrounds, service sector professionals perceived robots as less suitable to their own occupational field than did professionals from other fields. Young participants were more likely to consider robots suitable to their own field in both samples. Low-income was associated with perceived robot suitability only in Finnish working population, and no difference between genders was found in either cultural background. In addition, examination of U.S. respondents revealed that technology education, prior experience interacting with robots at work, and general positive attitude toward robots were positively connected with perceived suitability of robots to one's own occupational field. The path model analysis supports our proposed model in which service sector is negatively connected to attitude toward interacting with robots via perceived robot suitability (Fig. 2).

Our results indicate that robots entering the service sector evokes more negativity concerning suitability in associated professionals than in those of other occupational fields, which is in line with previous research results concerning lower perceived suitability of robots to social or artistic fields of work [12, 13]. Hesitant reception of robots in the service sector may derive from shorter history in utilizing robots in these fields compared to industries such as manufacturing. Furthermore, a lack of knowledge about the technological potential of advanced service robots and prior experience with robots in the work context contribute to perceived suitability of robots to one's occupational field.

In agreement with this, our analyses show that the relationship between occupational sector and perceived suitability is affected by age, technology expertise, prior interactional experience with robots at work, and attitudes toward robots. Older participants were less likely to consider robots suitable even after controlling for technological expertise and prior experience with robots at work, which somewhat contradicted previous research concerning domestic and eldercare robots, although the direction of the relationship remained the same [31, 32]. However, the effect of gender disappeared after controlling for technological expertise and prior robot experience, confirming the suspicions of previous researchers about the controlling effect of prior technological experience at least in the case of gender [32]. The association of income was not confirmed due to the mixed results regarding low-income respondents' positive response on robot suitability. Future researchers should investigate the income factor further, especially because research concerning sociodemographic factors behind acceptance of robots has produced mixed results in the literature also before. One reason for mixed result could also be cultural variation that has been noted previously [58].

Finally, the additional analysis of interactional attitudes highlights how the negative perceptions of the service sector professionals could impact their intention and actual use of and interaction with robots. According to the TAM, Almere model, and UTAUT model, attitudinal beliefs of perceived usefulness, adaptability, job fit, and performance expectancy play a key role in acceptance to use or interact with robots. In UTAUT model, for example, expectations also predict behavioral intention and actual behavior [49, 52]. Therefore, as our findings indicate, negative attitudes toward robot suitability can decrease both the intention and the actual use of robots in the service sector.

It has also been noted that the social acceptance of robot workers may be dependent on the characteristics of the robot, for example, appearance, level of autonomy, or task compatibleness. In addition to the comprehensive investigations of the factor of robot appearance [68–70], future studies should continue to investigate the impact of robot autonomy level on social acceptance and the sense of autonomy of the interacting human [71]. Future research should also investigate if online service context yields different results, as some evidence indicates trusting behavior when humans are replaced by robots and artificial intelligence in gamified online environment [72].

Our results contribute to the understanding of how the introduction of robots in new occupational fields is perceived by service sector professionals compared to professionals from other sectors. When developing new generations of service robots and planning to introduce them into new fields of work, it should be noted that the resistance might challenge the deployment of robots in the service field in particular. Although the service sector consists of multiple different occupational fields, these fields share similarities in customer interaction, uncertainty about the abilities of the new advanced robots, and possible fear of being replaced by robots. Therefore, sustainable policy and technology development should consider workers' and professionals' acceptance of deploying robots in their own field of work. Providing early technological education and interactional experience with robots and enhancing knowledge about the advancement and potential of technology are essential for the perceived suitability and acceptance of robots in the service sector.

Funding Acknowledgment. This Work Was Supported by the Finnish Cultural Foundation (Robots and Us Project, 2018–2020, PIs Jari Hietanen, Atte oksanen, and Veikko Sariola) and the Finnish Work Environment Fund (Professional Social Media Use and Work Engagement Among Young Adults Project, Project Number 118055 PI: Atte Oksanen).

Disclosure Statement.. The Authors Report no Conflict of Interest.

Appendix 1

The following is the International Standard Industrial Classification of All Economic Activities (ISIC) list. Industries included in the service sector are in *italics*.

A. Agriculture, forestry and fishing
B. Mining and quarrying
C. Manufacturing
D. Electricity, gas, steam and air conditioning supply
E. Water supply; sewerage, waste management and remediation activities
F. Construction
G. Wholesale and retail trade; repair of motor vehicles and motorcycles
H. Transportation and storage
I. *Accommodation and food service activities*
J. *Information and communication*
K. *Financial and insurance activities*
L. *Real estate activities*
M. *Professional, scientific and technical activities*
N. *Administrative and support service activities*
O. *Public administration and defense; compulsory social security*
P. *Education*
Q. *Human health and social work activities*
R. *Arts, entertainment and recreation*
S. *Other service activities*
T. Activities of households as employers; undifferentiated goods- and services-producing activities of households for own use
U. Activities of extraterritorial organizations and bodies

Appendix 2

The following questions were used in path analysis for measuring participants' perceived comfortableness with interacting with robots.

How comfortable would you be about.

... using a robot as equipment at work?
... having a robot as your co-worker?
... shaking hands with a robot?
... hugging a robot?
... robot giving you a pat on the back?
... giving a robot a pat on the back?
... robot's surface being hard when touching it?
... robot's surface being soft when touching it?
... having a conversation with a robot?
... asking robot a question?
... responding to robot's question?
... robot following your movements with its gaze?

References

1. Schwab, K.: The Fourth Industrial Revolution. Penguin Books, London, England (2017)
2. Venkatesh, V., Davis, F.D.: A theoretical extension of the technology acceptance model: four longitudinal field studies. Manage. Sci. **46**(2), 186–204 (2000). https://doi.org/10.1287/mnsc.46.2.186.11926
3. International Federation of Robotics: Executive Summary World Robotics 2018 Service Robots. World Robotics 2018 edition (2018). https://ifr.org/downloads/press2018/Executive_Summary_WR_Service_Robots_2018.pdf
4. International Organization for Standardization: Robots and robotic devices — Safety requirements for personal care robots (ISO Standard No. 13482:2014) (2014). https://www.iso.org/obp/ui/#iso:std:iso:13482:ed-1:v1:en
5. Gouaillier, D., et al.: Mechatronic design of NAO humanoid. In: IEEE International Conference on Robotics and Automation, Kobe, Japan, pp. 769–774. IEEE (2009). https://doi.org/10.1109/ROBOT.2009.5152516
6. Johnson, D.O., Cuijpers, R.H., Pollmann, K., van de Ven, A.A.J.: Exploring the entertainment value of playing games with a humanoid robot. Int. J. Soc. Robot. **8**(2), 247–269 (2015). https://doi.org/10.1007/s12369-015-0331-x
7. Tanaka, F., Isshiki, K., Takahashi, F., Uekusa, M., Sei, R., Hayashi, K.: Pepper learns together with children: development of an educational application. In: IEEE-RAS 15th International Conference on Humanoid Robots (Humanoids), Seoul, 2015, pp. 270–275 (2015). https://doi.org/10.1109/HUMANOIDS.2015.7363546
8. Aaltonen, I., Niemelä, M., Tammela, A.: Please call me? Calling practices with telepresence robots for the elderly. In: HRI 2017 - Companion of the 2017 ACM/IEEE International Conference on Human-Robot Interaction, pp. 55–56. ACM (2017). https://doi.org/10.1145/3029798.3038396
9. Shibata, T.: Therapeutic seal robot as biofeedback medical device: qualitative and quantitative evaluations of robot therapy in dementia care. Proc. IEEE **100**(8), 2527–2538 (2012). https://doi.org/10.1109/JPROC.2012.2200559
10. Ceccarelli, M.: Problems and issues for service robots in new applications. Int. J. Soc. Robot. **3**(3), 299–312 (2011). https://doi.org/10.1007/s12369-011-0097-8
11. Savela, N., Kaakinen, M., Ellonen, N., Oksanen, A.: Sharing a work team with robots: the negative effect of robot co-workers on in-group identification with the work team. Comput. Hum. Behav. **115**, 106585 (2021). https://doi.org/10.1016/j.chb.2020.106585
12. Taipale, S., de Luca, F., Sarrica, M., Fortunati, L.: Robot shift from industrial production to social reproduction. In: Vincent, J., Taipale, S., Sapio, B., Lugano, G., Fortunati, L. (eds.) Social Robots from a Human Perspective, pp. 11–24. Springer, Cham (2015). https://doi.org/10.1007/978-3-319-15672-9_2
13. Takayama, L., Ju, W., Nass, C.: Beyond dirty, dangerous and dull: What everyday people think robots should do. In: Proceedings of the Third ACM/IEEE International Conference on Human-Robot Interaction, 12–15 March 2008, Amsterdam, pp. 25–32. Curran Associates, Red Hook (2008). https://doi.org/10.1145/1349822.1349827
14. Savela, N., Turja, T., Oksanen, A.: Social acceptance of robots in different occupational fields: a systematic literature review. Int. J. Soc. Robot. **10**(4), 493–502 (2017). https://doi.org/10.1007/s12369-017-0452-5
15. Jones, V.S., Cohen, R.C.: Two decades of minimally invasive pediatric surgery-taking stock. J. Pediatr. Surg. **43**(9), 1653–1659 (2008). https://doi.org/10.1016/j.jpedsurg.2008.01.006
16. Palep, J.H.: Robotic assisted minimally invasive surgery. J. Minimal Access Surg. **5**(1), 1–7 (2009). https://doi.org/10.4103/0972-9941.51313

17. Wasen, K.: Replacement of highly educated surgical assistants by robot technology in working life: paradigm shift in the service sector. Int. J. Soc. Robot. **2**(4), 431–438 (2010). https://doi.org/10.1007/s12369-010-0062-y

18. Conti, D., Cattani, A., Di Nuovo, S., Di Nuovo, A.: Are future psychologists willing to accept and use a humanoid robot in their practice? Italian and English students' perspective. Front. Psychol. **10**2019https://doi.org/10.3389/fpsyg.2019.02138

19. Belpaeme, T., Kennedy, J., Ramachandran, A., Scassellati, B., Tanaka, F.: Social robots for education: a review. Sci. Robot. **3**(21), eaat5954 (2018). https://doi.org/10.1126/scirobotics.aat5954

20. Conti, D., Di Nuovo, S., Buono, S., Di Nuovo, A.: Robots in education and care of children with developmental disabilities: a study on acceptance by experienced and future professionals. Int. J. Soc. Robot. **9**(1), 51–62 (2016). https://doi.org/10.1007/s12369-016-0359-6

21. Mubin, O., Stevens, C.J., Shadid, S., Al Mahmud, A., Dong, J.J.: A review of the applicability of robots in education. Technol. Educ. Learn. **1**, 1–7 (2013). https://doi.org/10.2316/Journal.209.2013.1.209-0015

22. ReichStiebert, N., Eyssel, F.: Learning with educational companion robots? Toward attitudes on education robots, predictors of attitudes, and application potentials for education robots. Int. J. Soc. Robot. **7**(5), 875–888 (2015). https://doi.org/10.1007/s12369-015-0308-9

23. Katz, J.E., Halpern, D.: Attitudes towards robots suitability for various jobs as affected robot appearance. Behav. Inf. Technol. **33**(9), 941–953 (2014). https://doi.org/10.1080/0144929X.2013.783115

24. Floreano, D., Wood, R.J.: Science, technology and the future of small autonomous drones. Nature **521**, 460–466 (2015). https://doi.org/10.1038/nature14542

25. Hansen, B.G.: Robotic milking-farmer experiences and adoption rate in Jæren, Norway. J. Rural. Stud. **41**, 109–117 (2015). https://doi.org/10.1016/j.jrurstud.2015.08.004

26. Booth, S., Tompkin, J., Pfister, H., Waldo, J., Gajos, K., Nagpal, R.: Piggybacking robots: human-robot overtrust in university dormitory security. In: Proceedings of the 2017 ACM/IEEE International Conference on Human-Robot Interaction, pp. 426–434. ACM (2017). https://doi.org/10.1145/2909824.3020211

27. Lamballais, T., Roy, D., De Koster, M.B.M.: Estimating performance in a robotic mobile fulfillment system. Eur. J. Oper. Res. **256**(3), 976–990 (2017). https://doi.org/10.1016/j.ejor.2016.06.063

28. Hendriks, B., Meerbeek, B., Boess, S., Pauws, S., Sonneveld, M.: Robot vacuum cleaner personality and behavior. Int. J. Soc. Robot. **3**(2), 187–195 (2011). https://doi.org/10.1007/s12369-010-0084-5

29. Kuo, I.H., Rabindran, J.M., Broadbent, E., Lee, Y.I., Kerse, N., Stafford, R.M.Q., MacDonald, B.A.: Age and gender factors in user acceptance of healthcare robots. In: RO-MAN 2009-The 18th IEEE International Symposium on Robot and Human Interactive Communication, pp. 214–219. IEEE (2009). https://doi.org/10.1109/ROMAN.2009.5326292

30. Reich, N., Eyssel, F.: Attitudes towards service robots in domestic environments: the role of personality characteristics, individual interests, and demographic variables. Paladyn J. Behav. Robot. **4**(2), 123–130 (2013). https://doi.org/10.2478/pjbr-2013-0014

31. Flandorfer, P.: Population ageing and socially assistive robots for elderly persons: the importance of sociodemographic factors for user acceptance. Int. J. Popul. Res. **2012**(829835), 1–13 (2012). https://doi.org/10.1155/2012/829835

32. Ezer, N., Fisk, A.D., Rogers, W.A.: Attitudinal and intentional acceptance of domestic robots by younger and older adults. In: Stephanidis, C. (ed.) UAHCI. LNCS, vol. 5615, pp. 39–48. Springer, Heidelberg (2009). https://doi.org/10.1007/978-3-642-02710-9_5

33. de Graaf, M.M.A., Ben Allouch, S.: The relation between people's attitudes and anxiety toward robots in human-robot interaction. In: 2013 IEEE RO-MAN, pp. 632–637. IEEE (2013). https://doi.org/10.1109/ROMAN.2013.6628419

34. Halpern, D., Katz, J.E.: Unveiling robotophobia and cyber-dystopianism: The role of gender, technology and religion on attitudes towards robots. In: 2012 7th ACM/IEEE International Conference on Human-Robot Interaction (HRI), pp. 139–140. IEEE (2012). https://doi.org/10.1145/2157689.2157724

35. Giuliani, M.V., Scopelliti, M., Fornara, F.: Elderly people at home: Technological help in everyday activities. In: ROMAN 2005. IEEE International Workshop on Robot and Human Interactive Communication, 2005, pp. 365–370. IEEE (2005). https://doi.org/10.1109/ROMAN.2005.1513806

36. Salvini, P., Laschi, C., Dario, P.: Design for acceptability: Improving robots' coexistence in human society. Int. J. Soc. Robot. 2(4), 451–460 (2010). https://doi.org/10.1007/s12369-010-0079-2

37. Wirtz, J., et al.: Brave new world: service robots in the frontline. J. Serv. Manag. 29(5), 907–931 (2018). https://doi.org/10.1108/JOSM-04-2018-0119

38. Ferlie, E., Fitzgerald, L., Wood, M., Hawkins, C.: The nonspread of innovations: the mediating role of professionals. Acad. Manag. J. 48(1), 117–134 (2005). https://doi.org/10.5465/amj.2005.15993150

39. Badham, R., Ehn, P.: Tinkering with technology: human factors, work redesign, and professionals in workplace innovation. Hum. Fact. Ergon. Manuf. Serv. Ind. 10(1), 61–82 (2000). https://doi.org/10.1002/(SICI)1520-6564(200024)10:1%3c61::AID-HFM4%3e3.0.CO;2-O

40. Davis, F.D.: Perceived usefulness, perceived ease of use, and user acceptance of information technology. Manag. Inf. Syst. Q. 13(3), 319–340 (1989). https://doi.org/10.2307/249008

41. Fishbein, M., Ajzen, I.: Belief, Attitude, Intention and Behavior: An Introduction to Theory and Research. Addison-Wesley, Reading (1975)

42. Young, J.E., Hawkins, R., Sharlin, E., Igarashi, T.: Toward acceptable domestic robots: applying insights from social psychology. Int. J. Soc. Robot. 1(1), 95–108 (2009). https://doi.org/10.1007/s12369-008-0006-y

43. Heerink, M., Kröse, B., Evers, V., Wielinga, B.: Assessing acceptance of assistive social agent technology by older adults: the Almere model. Int. J. Soc. Robot. 2(4), 361–375 (2010). https://doi.org/10.1007/s12369-010-0068-5

44. Ajzen, I.: The theory of planned behavior. Organ. Behav. Hum. Decis. Processes 50(2), 179–211 (1991). https://doi.org/10.1016/0749-5978(91)90020-T

45. Rogers, E.M.: Diffusion of Innovations, 4th edn. The Free Press, New York (1995)

46. Davis, F.D., Bagozzi, R.P., Warshaw, P.R.: Extrinsic and intrinsic motivation to use computers in the workplace. J. Appl. Soc. Psychol. 22(14), 1111–1132 (1992). https://doi.org/10.1111/j.1559-1816.1992.tb00945.x

47. Thompson, R.L., Higgins, C.A., Howell, J.M.: Personal computing: toward a conceptual model of utilization. Manag. Inf. Syst. Q. 15(1), 125–143 (1991). https://doi.org/10.2307/249443

48. Bandura, A.: Social Foundations of Thought and Action: A Social Cognitive Theory. Prentice-Hall, Englewood Cliffs (1986)

49. Taylor, S., Todd, P.A.: Understanding information technology usage: a test of competing models. Inf. Syst. Res. 6(2), 144–176 (1995). https://doi.org/10.1287/isre.6.2.144

50. Venkatesh, V., Morris, M.G., Davis, G.B., Davis, F.D.: User acceptance of information technology: toward a unified view. Manag. Inf. Syst. Q. 27(3), 425–478 (2003). https://doi.org/10.2307/30036540

51. Heerink, M., Kröse, B., Evers, V., Wielinga, B.: Measuring acceptance of an assistive social robot: a suggested toolkit. In: Proceedings—IEEE International Workshop on Robot and Human Interactive Communication, pp. 528–533. IEEE (2009). https://doi.org/10.1109/ROMAN.2009.5326320

52. Vega, A., Ramírez-Benavidez, K., Guerrero, L.A.: Tool UTAUT applied to measure interaction experience with NAO robot. In: Kurosu, M. (ed.) HCII. LNCS, vol. 11568, pp. 501–512. Springer, Cham (2019). https://doi.org/10.1007/978-3-030-22636-7_38

53. Krishnan, G., Mintz, J., Foreman, A., Hodge, J.C., Krishnan, S.: The acceptance and adoption of transoral robotic surgery in Australia and New Zealand. J. Robot. Surg. **13**(2), 301–307 (2018). https://doi.org/10.1007/s11701-018-0856-8

54. Dwivedi, Y.K., Rana, N.P., Jeyaraj, A., Clement, M., Williams, M.D.: Re-examining the unified theory of acceptance and use of technology (UTAUT): towards a revised theoretical model. Inf. Syst. Front. **21**(3), 719–734 (2017). https://doi.org/10.1007/s10796-017-9774-y

55. Venkatesh, V., Thong, J., Xu, X.: Consumer acceptance and use of information technology: extending the unified theory of acceptance and use of technology. Manag. Inf. Syst. Q. **36**(1), 157–178 (2012). https://doi.org/10.2307/41410412

56. Molnar, A., Weerakkody, V., El-Haddadeh, R., Lee, H., Irani, Z.: A framework of reference for evaluating user experience when using high definition video to video to facilitate public services. In: Dwivedi, Y.K., Henriksen, H.Z., Wastell, D., De', R. (eds.) TDIT. IAICT, vol. 402, pp. 436–450. Springer, Heidelberg (2013). https://doi.org/10.1007/978-3-642-38862-0_27

57. Alalwan, A.A., Dwivedi, Y.K., Rana, N.P.: Factors influencing adoption of mobile banking by Jordanian bank customers: extending UTAUT2 with trust. Int. J. Inf. Manage. **37**(3), 99–110 (2017). https://doi.org/10.1016/j.ijinfomgt.2017.01.002

58. Turja, T., Oksanen, A.: Robot acceptance at work: a multilevel analysis based on 27 EU countries. Int. J. Soc. Robot. **11**(4), 679–689 (2019). https://doi.org/10.1007/s12369-019-00526-x

59. Official Statistics of Finland: Labour force survey. ISSN:1798–7857. Statistics Finland, Helsinki (2006). http://www.stat.fi/til/tyti/2006/tyti_2006_2007-06-20_tie_001_en.html

60. U.S. Bureau of Labor Statistics: Employment by major industry sector. Employment Projections (2017). https://www.bls.gov/emp/tables/employment-by-major-industry-sector.htm

61. United Nations: International Standard Industrial Classification of All Economic Activities (ISIC) Revision 4 (2008). https://unstats.un.org/unsd/classifications/Econ/isic

62. Fisher, A.G.: Production, primary, secondary and tertiary. Econ. Rec. **15**(1), 24–38 (1939). https://doi.org/10.1111/j.1475-4932.1939.tb01015.x

63. The World Bank (n.d.): Survey methodology. https://www.enterprisesurveys.org/methodology

64. The U.S. Census Bureau (n.d.): Services. https://www.census.gov/econ/services.html

65. Official Statistics of Finland: Turnover of service industries. Statistics Finland, Helsinki (2008). http://www.stat.fi/til/plv/plv_2008-09-26_luo_001_en.html. ISSN=1799–0998

66. Geum, Y., Kim, M.S., Lee, S.: Service technology: definition and characteristics based on a patent database. Serv. Sci. **9**(2), 147–166 (2017). https://doi.org/10.1287/serv.2016.0170

67. Kohler, U., Karlson, K.B., Holm, A.: Comparing coefficients of nested nonlinear probability models. Stand. Genomic Sci. **11**(3), 420–438 (2011). https://doi.org/10.1177/1536867X1101100306

68. Li, D., Rau, P.P., Li, Y.: A cross-cultural study: effect of robot appearance and task. Int. J. Soc. Robot. **2**(2), 175–186 (2010). https://doi.org/10.1007/s12369-010-0056-9

69. Mori, M., MacDorman, K.F., Kageki, N.: The uncanny valley [from the field]. IEEE Robot. Autom. Mag. **19**(2), 98–100 (2012). https://doi.org/10.1109/MRA.2012.2192811

70. Walters, M.L., Syrdal, D.S., Dautenhahn, K., Te. Boekhorst, R., Koay, K.L.: Avoiding the uncanny valley: robot appearance, personality and consistency of behavior in an attention-seeking home scenario for a robot companion. Auton. Robot. **24**(2), 159–178 (2008). https://doi.org/10.1007/s10514-007-9058-3

71. Latikka, R., Savela, N., Koivula, A., Oksanen, A.: Attitudes toward robots as equipment and coworkers and the impact of robot autonomy level. Int. J. Soc. Robot. (2021). https://doi.org/10.1007/s12369-020-00743-9
72. Oksanen, A., Savela, N., Latikka, R., Koivula, A.: Trust toward robots and artificial intelligence: an experimental approach to human-technology interactions online. Front. Psychol. **11**, 568256 (2020). https://doi.org/10.3389/fpsyg.2020.568256

User Experience Best Practices
for Human-Robot Interaction

Dorothy Shamonsky(✉) (iD)

Brandeis University, 415 South Street, Waltham, MA 02453, USA
dshamonsky@ics.com

Abstract. User experience (UX) design of human-robot interaction (HRI) is an emerging practice [1]. Best practices for this discipline are actively evolving as robotics expands into commercial markets. As is typical of emerging technologies, the technology itself takes center stage, continuing to present challenges to proper functioning as it is tested in real world applications. Also, deployment comes at a high price until the market is competitive enough to drive hardware and development prices down. All these aspects preclude an emphasis on UX design, until the technology and associated market reaches a tipping point and good user experience is in demand. If robots continue to be deployed at rates the industry currently predicts, the need for user experience design knowledge and best practices for HRI is eminent. Best practices are a collection of methods, specifically principles, heuristic evaluators and taxonomies [2]. Principles embody high level guidance for design direction and design processes [3]. Heuristics ensure measurable "must have" base-functionality [4–6]. Taxonomies provide a conceptual understanding of possible categories of interactivity [7–9]. This paper focuses on two aspects of best practices, 1.) proposing a robustly user-centric set of emerging technology principles for HRI, which is the area of best practices least explored by the literature, and 2.) proposing a design matrix as a beginning step in addressing the complexity of HRI.

Keywords: Human-robot interaction · HRI best practices · HRI heuristics · Emerging technology principles

1 Introduction

Emerging technologies, because they are still actively evolving, live in tech-centric cultures of engineering. In order to mature beyond R&D laboratories and become marketable, they need to transition to user-centered design cultures where HCI and UX professionals have the opportunity to increase their usability. Technologies like robotics present a challenge to HCI designers because best practices for creating highly usable and appealing user experiences are not fully realized. Developing the experience, knowledge and subsequent best practices for how to design a good user experience for a new technology take time, once a technology is sufficiently mature enough to deploy to real customers. First you must have a workable technology and then design professionals can use historical precedents, trial and error designs, and user testing to refine a set of best

© Springer Nature Switzerland AG 2021
M. Kurosu (Ed.): HCII 2021, LNCS 12763, pp. 318–328, 2021.
https://doi.org/10.1007/978-3-030-78465-2_24

practices. We are currently in the phase of refining best practices for HRI. This paper seeks to put forth a UX professional's methodology for advancing those best practices that includes ten UX Principles for HRI design, and a matrix showing how to break down the complexity of the design problem.

History is a good starting point for developing a design practice for an emerging technology. Thus, adapting practices from desktop, web, mobile, embedded and IoT is a logical starting point for robots. The common "computer interface" retains some similarities across technologies, even if it is embodied in the completely different physical form of a robot. Some practices carry over unchanged. For example, doing user research and following a standard design process remain keystones to any viable HCI practice regardless of the technology. User research is about people and people don't change compared to technology. User research is also technology agnostic even if there are some techniques specific to particular technologies, like eye-tracking on websites to trace user attention [10]. Similarly, the design process – discover, analyze, ideate, test – applies to any design activity.

But three distinct and significant differences are apparent between robotics and screen-based computer systems, and therefore deeply significant to the user: 1.) The variety of robot types and how they can be applied to tasks is immense, 2.) Robots will mature to be significantly more multimodal, intelligent and powerful than previous computers, and 3.) Robots are by nature anthropomorphic and humans react differently to them as a result; they elicit feelings of interacting with a living being. These three significant differences of robots compared to screen-based systems require a significantly fresh take on their design best practices. The concept of Natural User Interfaces (NUIs) is a viable path away from the historical framework to a new one [11].

The concept of NUIs was initially derived from the belief that computers should eventually be able to meet humans 100% on their level of interactivity, and that the human would need no special computer skills, but instead interact as they know how to interact in the physical world of humans, animals and artifacts. NUI principles have not been widely adopted by the HCI profession because they are not particularly relevant to legacy technology, but instead pertain to emerging technologies with multimodal interaction and non-screen interfaces. As such, NUI principles should prove valuable to HRI design.

2 Related Work

A common HRI evaluation approach in the literature is to present case studies of HRI systems in the field. A corresponding approach is to present controlled lab studies. Both of these types of studies offer lessons learned with users and are valuable in refining best practices, although they are too narrow focused and system-specific for the purposes of this paper. What is relevant are the efforts at creating new lists of heuristic evaluators [4–7]. Borrowing from legacy practice is the process commonly suggested and employed by these efforts, beginning from popular heuristic lists that were developed over the last couple of decades amid screen-based interfaces in [12–16]. The appeal of heuristics and particularly short lists of heuristics is that they enable quick, abbreviated evaluations that are still very effective in finding weaknesses in a system. The best results might occur from an HCI professional doing the heuristic evaluation, but even non-HCI professionals can use a list of heuristics and get good results [4].

Only a small number of novel heuristics have been suggested for robot evaluation beyond the legacy versions, and they pertain to using more natural forms of interaction including natural speech [4, 5], more direct interaction with the robot [4], the need for precise control [5], and the convenience value of autonomy [5].

Deriving robot taxonomies is also a technique to understand models of robot interaction [7–9]. The appeal of categorizing robots is that they are so diverse and varied. A robot taxonomy is useful in understanding and putting structure to the diversity of robots and tasks they might be applied to. Besides the types of robots and tasks, there can be different interaction configurations of users, for example, several users can interact with one robot or one user might manage a fleet of robots. [7–9]. Using classification to determine context of use resonates with UX design. Analysis of context of use is a typical and necessary first step in determining the exact scope and focus of a design effort. A concise analysis system such as taxonomies is a powerful tool [17].

Another evaluation technique is to create a set of evaluation factors that span a wider spectrum of emotional and social issues [18]. This is a more user-centered approach compared to straight taxonomies, which lean toward being technology centric. Evaluation factors are not prescriptive like heuristics, but takes into consideration user emotions, such as feelings of security or attitudes about technology.

3   Purpose and Scope of Best Practices

Best practices are methods and techniques that have proven to produce good results in a professional field [2]. They are a framework for success. Using best practices leads to better outcomes, with efficiency and with fewer mistakes. An important aspect of becoming a professional in your field is learning and integrating your professions best practices into your working methods and habits. However, best practices are generally large in volume and complicated in their details and require study and experience to make them organic to a profession. Usually there isn't one authoritative document describing a set of best practices, but many versions and opinions with some that stand out as having more popularity or authority. The exception is when a practice is regulated by a governing body for compliance or licensing.

In discussing or applying best practices, it is helpful and convenient to use abbreviated forms of the concepts. The problem with articulating best practices in a short format is boiling dense knowledge down to a size that is concise but still useful. In the field of HCI, that concise format takes on two primary forms: heuristic evaluators and principles of practice. These abbreviated forms will need to satisfy our purpose in this text. But keep in mind that they represent the tip of an iceberg of knowledge. As such, heuristics and principles work best for those trained in the HCI field, who are able to understand the meaning behind an abbreviated version.

3.1   Heuristic Evaluators

A heuristic is a rule of thumb. It's a quick means to test if a solution is sufficient. In the field of HCI heuristic evaluators are an abbreviated but powerful tool for checking a system and spotting weaknesses. They ensure that minimum standards are met. Designers and engineers both like heuristic evaluators because it's a concrete, simple method to ensure that no typical flaws are left in an interface. Heuristics can be applied using yes/no answers or grading on a simple scale of 1 to 5. As a result, heuristic evaluations can yield quantitative results.

3.2 Principles of Practice

Principles are fundamental truths and are often aspirational rather then rule-based. They might be perceived as almost the opposite of heuristics. Where heuristics insure at lease the minimum quality in a design, principles inspire the maximum or the best quality. They define what the designer hopes to accomplish under the best-case scenarios. As such, principles are more appropriate for qualitative evaluations.

4 Borrowing from Legacy Best Practices for HRI

Common sense dictates that one would first look to existing or legacy best practices as a starting point to develop best practices for a new technology. Digital technologies, although they can be very varied, have some consistent qualities embodied in the computer interface. Therefore, some practices continue to be valid even as hardware and software evolve. For instance, *providing feedback to input from a user* is a general practice that is valid for the foreseeable future, but the exact nature of the feedback is dependent on specific hardware and software attributes. On a screen-based interface, feedback would be visible as text, color, animation or a screen change, for example. With a robot that has no end user screen interface (or even if there was one) the feedback could be a physical response in the position of the robot or an aural response.

Technology evolves in a more or less incremental manner, so beginning from existing practices is a good starting point. As mentioned previously, many general practices will still apply. Knowledge and skills that relate to more specific technologies, like touch or voice interaction, only pertain to a system using that modality. What is new about robotics is not just the technology itself, but the potential complexity of the interface. It can be more multifaceted compared to PCs and smart phones, with mechanical moving parts, unique physical housing, multimodal interactions. AI, safety concerns and many context-of-use options. Achieving good usability is robotics is overall a huge design challenge.

To be an effective designer in HRI would ideally require one versed in a broad range of HCI subdisciplines or requires a team with a range of skills from Industrial Design to Artificial Intelligence. Previous authors, in attempts to propose HRI-specific practices, have drawn upon legacy practices and taken small steps away from that starting point. By analyzing the overall design problem, the complexity is more apparent and so too, is the need for new concepts about HRI.

5 Analyzing the Design Problem

Even considering robotics at a limited scope of current or near future technology, HRI presents more complexity to a designer than more mature technologies HCI professionals design for every day such as personal computers, mobile devices and embedded devices. Robots often are multimodal, have mechanical moving parts and mobility, and possess some level of AI, agency or autonomy. For the end user, they may have a screen or button interface to interact with, but they may simply interact with the robot directly. Robots are poised to become the most complex interfaces that HCI designers will design for because robots are moving us closer to interactions that mimic human or animal interactions. Robot interfaces will eventually be the most advanced *and* hopefully, the easiest to use.

How does a usability designer approach this problem? In analyzing any design problem, a common methodology is to break the problem into smaller chunks [10]. Those chunks represent logical buckets of design knowledge. Any design problem is multi-dimensional and can be sliced in different ways. For the purposes of this paper, here is a breakdown of the interaction design pieces that are necessary with a generalized robot. UX for a robot requires design skill in:

1 Context of use
2 Safety
3 Physical design and ergonomics
4 General interaction (heuristics and principles)
5 Interaction modalities
6 AI, agency and autonomy

The complexity suggests - and the above list represents only the large categories of a design breakdown - that the best practices for robotics will eventually have many facets and that the focus on taxonomies and heuristics evaluators in the literature is only the first steps in this process of developing best practices for HRI. Taking this list and turning it into a spatial configuration is potentially an even more helpful way to analyze the design problem.

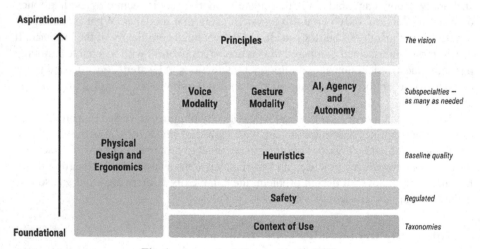

Fig. 1. A generic design matrix for HRI.

5.1 A Design Matrix

Figure 1 lays out the chunks of robot UX design in a spatial format. Reading from bottom to top roughly suggests order of consideration, although it also suggests that the lower down elements are foundational and necessary while the upper ones are aspirational and are what takes the user experience from workable to good or excellent.

Context of Use. Because the variety of robots is large and the ways robotics can be applied to tasks is so varied, context of use is the foundation of the matrix and first piece of the analysis. Determining the configuration of human to robot, (i.e., one human to one robot, one human to many robots, etc.) and determining the environment and tasks that will be performed, immediately serves to limit the scope of the problem. Taxonomies are helpful documents for this analysis [7–9].

Safety. As advocates for users, designers consider the users' safety of utmost importance. For that reason, safety is placed right after determining the context of use and before any interaction design. No one wants to be injured or perish in a robot accident due to careless design and no designer wants to be responsible for that. In the design of potentially harmful devices, regulations are already in place. Many safeguards against accidents with robots are considered and remedied at the engineering level. Use error is still the concern of the HCI professional who is qualified to meet design to the safety requirements.

Physical Design and Ergonomics. Physical design of a robot and the ergonomics of the physical interface fall into the realm of an Industrial Designer. For that reason, it is placed in the matrix to the side of the layers of UX design. However, the physical design and the UX design are closely intertwined. How a robot looks has a huge influence on how the user feels about the robot and how they perceive they should interact with it. The ergonomics of physical button controls is important for good usability but more particularly the ergonomics of an exoskeleton or robotic prosthetic limb is crucial to its usability.

General Interaction (Heuristic and Principles). The combined heuristics and principles constitute the general interaction best practices. Legacy heuristic evaluators that were developed for screen-based interactions still apply for the most part because they are very user-centric rather than technology-centric [19]. For instance, *support easy recovery from errors* is not a hardware or software-dependent rule. Also, as mentioned in the "Related Work" section, other authors have offered modified heuristic evaluators for HRI [4–7]. Heuristics constitute a baseline of good interaction behaviors and are a stopgap to typical design errors in usability design. Conversely, principles provide the vision and inspiration for a successful UX.

Interaction Modalities. Although most HCI professionals are skilled in screen-based interactions, other modalities such as gesture and voice are still considered a specialty until they become more widely used. Because of that, they are separated from the category of "General Interaction" and given their own space in the matrix [20–23].

AI. Still only well understood by a small subset of UX designers, and also evolving rapidly [24].

6 New UX Principles for HRI

As rich as the body of existing HCI expertise is, new ideas and practices are needed in HRI [25]. Does it require a major shift in how we conceive of interacting with digital artifacts? Probably so. The consistent thread in visions of the future of interface design is that it is always easier and more natural for humans to interact with technology. We can assume that future technology will be smarter and can address our natural ability to use multiple senses, facial expressions and body language to communicate. The sum total of robot technology will eventually add up to interfaces that feel convincingly like interacting with another living being. Does this require a paradigm shift in HCI thinking?

One compelling proposal that has been put forward and does require designers to reorient their thinking is the concept of a Natural User Interface (NUI) [26]. The most comprehensive explanation of NUIs was explained in the 2007 book, "Brave NUI World," by Wigdor and Wixon [11]. The primary goal of a NUI is to allow the user to feel that interacting with technology feels as natural as possible. "Natural" meaning how human interact with the world, with capabilities that humans are adapted for. Because the possibilities of a NUI are apparently limitless, it is easier to describe what it is not. It is not a standard GUI – a screen-based interface controlled by a pointing device – but it can be anything beyond the limitations of a GUI. Technically it does include mobile devices and touch screens, but NUIs are not limited to particular input or output technology. GUIs and CLUs are defined by the technology, while NUIs are defined by the experience.

To feel natural to humans, one might assume a NUI interface must mimic real-world interactions. That is an easy way to think about it. For example, voice interaction comes naturally to humans provided they can use language as they know it and not be forced to remember special commands in order to communicate. One might imagine a robot speaking back in a natural way, as C-3PO does in the movie "Star Wars." But in contrast, humans communicated with R2-D2 using natural language and R2-D2 responded with whistles and beeps, and yet the communication worked well. A modified version of "natural"?

The concept of natural is frequently misunderstood to mean that the technology should imitate humans or living beings as much as possible, implying that a robot should be designed to look and act indistinguishable from something truly alive. It's one of the main arguments against NUIs, implying that they demand a rigid end product. That is not the definition of a NUI. Instead, it simply enables a user to interact in a way that doesn't require them to learn new ways of communicating or interacting. They can talk, gesture and use facial expressions. It's the NUIs job to be able to interpret the human signals and respond in a way that the human is likely to understand. There is no requirement to literally imitate life as we know it.

A NUI offers limitless creative opportunities for interactions with technology, which is what makes it sustainable as a concept. It the short term, its value is getting designers beyond GUIs. The design goal of usability design is to keep making interactions with technology easier for users, and NUI is a concept that can advance the state of HCI design in that direction. The following set of ten proposed HRI principles draws upon the concepts embodied by NUIs and adapts them to robotics.

6.1 Usability Principles for HRI

Summary: These high-level principles are future-looking, and embrace natural, multimodal, screen-optional, tangible interaction.

1. Choose the robot type, and input and output modality that is right for the context of use.

   Opposite of PCs, robots are not general-purpose devices but instead are designed for a particular range of tasks, often very specific tasks. Having the right device for the context of use, that includes appropriate modalities for that context is key. For example, voice interaction is appropriate where hands and eyes are occupied with other tasks but would not work on a noise-filled manufacturing floor. Context of use also encompasses the configuration of the number of robots to humans.

2. Enable direct interaction with the robot as much as possible.

   Enable the user to interact directly with the robot rather than having mandatory separate apps and controllers, unless the context of use specifically requires it, as with remote control. Also, separate apps are appropriate for programming scripts and settings. Separate end user apps can be a convenience, particularly when remote control makes a task easier, but should be supplemental to direct interaction with the robot itself.

3. Make interacting with the robot natural by leveraging instinct and innate skills.

   Since humans have many innate physical and cognitive skills for interacting with physical reality, take advantage of those. Abilities such as motor memory and orienting in 2 and 3-D space can be utilized. Besides using language, sounds are able to elicit a range of emotions from alarm to calm universally in humans.

4. Utilize already learned behavior.

   Our learned behavior spans all of our senses and motor skills; it is not restricted to the eye-hand coordination that PCs have made use of. Learned behavior often uses multiple of our senses without our being aware that it does. Multimodal devices can tap into a wider spectrum of learned behavior than GUIs already do. For example, a device that captures air gestures can potentially use full body actions to interact with the device.

5. Have the robot help the user understand how to work with it.

   The less training needed the better. Using innate and learned behavior is valuable but only goes so far. The complexity of robotics requires another level of assistance to the user. Robots should be enabled to train users about themselves.

6. Make the robot highly responsive.

Responsive feedback has been a longstanding characteristic of a good user experience on GUIs. We expect robots to be equally iif not more responsive than GUIs. Robots have more of a relationship with anthropomorphism than GUIs do, so that suggests a personality. Consider designing robots with personality. Everyone likes an extrovert.

7. Give the robot visceral appeal.

Enjoyable and appealing is a part of any good user experience. The market demands it and that is the new normal.

8. Enable the robot to build trust in the user.

Robots that possess social intelligence not only feel more natural to us as humans, but they are also able to build trust in users to a greater degree. Seek to design social savvy robots, which can be enhanced by making the user experience personalized. A personalized user experience automatically makes it more valuable to the user.

9. Build in intelligence.

AI is a core necessity of almost all robots. In order to meet some of the above requirements and in order to have autonomy and decision-making ability robots need to have a level of intelligence.

10. Keep it simple and elegant.

Have nothing superfluous in the design, have no unnecessary complexity, and follow the above design principles.

7 Refining Practices

Although it has not been a topic in this paper, user research and testing are of utmost importance in the formation of best practices. Although this paper is a theoretical proposal focused on design principles, they do not come solely out of designers' imaginations. They come from experience designing and testing designs with users. Best practices, when they exist, allow a designer to shortcut a lot of experimentation. But when best practices do not exist or are still in a formative stage, then discovery of must actively go on in the form of iterative designing and user testing. User testing is fundamental to proving the value and viability of any practice before it can be deemed best.

8 Summary

For decades the HCI community have stated that computers should be *easy to use*. With robotics, easy to use sounds incorrect. With AI, mobility and anthropomorphism a new age of interaction design is upon us and we are no longer *using computers*. Instead, we are interacting, sharing and collaborating. It is now more appropriate to say robots should be useful, appealing and *easy to interact with*. We will be living and working with robots - that's a fact. As UX designers, our goal is to make that as good as possible for people. Designing highly usable robots requires skill, time, and effort. It requires a professional UX design practice that follows best practices for HRI.

References

1. Lindblom, J., Andreasson, R.: Current challenges for UX evaluation of human-robot inter-action. In: Schlick, C., Trzcieliński, S. (eds.) Advances in Ergonomics of Manufacturing: Managing the Enterprise of the Future. Advances in Intelligent Systems and Computing, vol. 490, pp. 267–77. Springer, Cham (2016). https://doi.org/10.1007/978-3-319-41697-7_24
2. Best Practice: https://en.wikipedia.org/wiki/Best_practice. Accessed 12 Feb 2021
3. Tognazzini, B.: First Principles, HCI Design, Human Computer Interaction (HCI), Principles of HCI Design, Usability Testing. https://asktog.com/atc/principles-of-interaction-design/. Accessed 12 Feb 2021
4. Clarkson, E., Arkin, R.: Applying heuristic evaluation to human-robot interaction systems. In: GVU Tech Report No. GIT-GVU-06–08 (2006). ftp://ftp.cc.gatech.edu/pub/gvu/tr/2006/06-08.pdf
5. Powers, A.: FEATURE, what robotics can learn from HCI. Interactions 15(2), 67–69 (2008). https://doi.org/10.1145/1340961.1340978
6. Weiss, A., Wurhofer, D., Bernhaupt, R., Altmaninger, M., Tscheligi, M.: A methodologi-cal adaptation for heuristic evaluation of HRI. In: 19th International Symposium in Robot and Human Interactive Communication, Viareggio, pp. 1–6 (2010). https://doi.org/10.1109/ROMAN.2010.5598735.
7. Malik, A.A., Bilberg, A.: Developing a reference model for human–robot interaction. Int. J. Interact. Des. Manufact. (IJIDeM) 13(4), 1541–1547 (2019). https://doi.org/10.1007/s12008-019-00591-6
8. Yanco, H.A., Drury, J.L.: Classifying human-robot interaction: an updated taxonomy. In: 2004 IEEE International Conference on Systems, Man and Cybernetics, The Hague, vol. 3, p. 2841 (2004). https://doi.org/10.1109/ICSMC.2004.1400763
9. Yanco, H.A, Drury, J.L.: A taxonomy for human-robot interaction. In: Proceedings of the AAAI Fall Symposium on Human-robot Interaction, pp. 111–119 (2002)
10. Rosenzweig, E.: Successful User Experience: Strategies and Roadmaps. Morgan Kaufmann Publishers Inc., San Francisco (2015). https://doi.org/10.1016/C2013-0-19353-1
11. Wigdor, D., Wixon, D.: Brave NUI World, Designing Natural User Interfaces for Touch and Gesture. Morgan Kaufman, Boston (2011)
12. Shneiderman, B.: Designing the User Interface: Strategies for Effective Human-Computer Interaction. Addison-Wesley Publishing Co., Reading (1987)
13. Scholtz, J.: Evaluation methods for human-system performance of intelligent systems. In: Proceedings of PERMIS'02 (2002)
14. Nielsen, J.: Finding usability problems through heuristic evaluation. In: Proceedings of the SIGCHI Conference on Human Factors in Computing Systems, pp. 373–380. Association for Computing Machinery, Monterey (1992). https://doi.org/10.1145/142750.142834
15. Nielsen, J.: Enhancing the explanatory power of usability heuristics. In: Proceedings of the SIGCHI Conference on Human Factors in Computing Systems, pp. 152–158. Association for Computing Machinery, Boston (1994). https://doi.org/10.1145/191666.191729

16. Mankoff, J., Dey, A.K., Hsieh, G., Kientz, J., Ames, M., Lederer, S.: Heuristic evaluation of ambient displays. In: Proceedings of CHI'03, pp. 169–176 (2003)
17. Onnasch, L., Roesler, E.: A taxonomy to structure and analyze human–robot interaction. Int. J. Soc. Robot. 1–17 (2020). https://doi.org/10.1007/s12369-020-00666-5
18. Weiss, A., Bernhaupt, R., Lankes, M., Tscheligi, M.: The USUS evaluation framework for human-robot interaction. Proc. AISB **09**(4), 11–26 (2009)
19. Nielsen, J.: 10 Usability Heuristics for Interface Design. https://www.nngroup.com/articles/ten-usability-heuristics/. Accessed 12 Feb 2021
20. Liu, H., Wang, L.: Gesture recognition for human-robot collaboration: a review. Int. J. Ind. Ergon. **68**, 355–367 (2018). https://doi.org/10.1016/j.ergon.2017.02.004
21. Sheikholeslami, S., Moon, A., Croft, E.A.: Cooperative gestures for industry: exploring the efficacy of robot hand configurations in expression of instructional gestures for human–robot interaction. Int. J. Robot. Res. **36**, 699–720 (2017). https://doi.org/10.1177/0278364491770 9941
22. Getting Started with the Guide | Alexa Skills Kit: https://developer.amazon.com/en-US/docs/alexa/alexa-design/get-started.html. Accessed 12 Feb 2021
23. Principles of Leap Motion Interaction Design: https://blog.leapmotion.com/6-principles-of-interaction-design/. Accessed 12 Feb 2021
24. Our Principles – Google AI: https://ai.google/principles/. Accessed 12 Feb 2021
25. Campana, J.R., Quaresma, M.: The importance of specific usability guidelines for robot user interfaces. In: Marcus, A., Wang, W. (eds.) DUXU 2017. LNCS, vol. 10289, pp. 471–483. Springer, Cham (2017). https://doi.org/10.1007/978-3-319-58637-3_37
26. Shamonsky, D.: User Experience Design Principles for a Natural User Interface (NUI). https://www.ics.com/blog/user-experience-design-principles-natural-user-interface-nui. Accessed 12 Feb 2021

Application for the Cooperative Control of Mobile Robots with Energy Optimization

José Varela-Aldás[1,2](✉) ⬤, Christian Ichina[1], Belén Ruales[1] ⬤,
and Víctor H. Andaluz[3] ⬤

[1] SISAu Research Group, Universidad Tecnológica Indoamérica, 180103 Ambato, Ecuador
{josevarela,belenruales}@uti.edu.ec
[2] Department of Electronic Engineering and Communications, University of Zaragoza,
44003 Teruel, Spain
[3] Department of Electrical and Electronics, University of the Armed Forces – ESPE,
171103 Sangolquí, Ecuador
vhandaluz1@espe.edu.ec

Abstract. Cooperative control of mobile robots allows to transport heavy loads collaboratively between 2 or more robots, these applications have motivated the development of new control strategies to coordinate multiple robots automatically. On the other hand, energy optimization in robotic systems is increasingly important to ensure autonomy and take care of resources. This article introduces an application for cooperative control of 3 mobile robots in open loop, the goal is to coordinate the position and parameters of the triangular shape created from the distances between robots. The control algorithm is designed using the Pontryagin principle, starting from the training model and solving differential equations with numerical methods. Mobile robots are built using 3D printing technology and free hardware with wireless Bluetooth communication to receive orders from the remote station. The application is implemented on a computer by inserting the developed algorithm and generating the control orders, this program is developed in Matlab through a main menu for user management. The results present the simulation and experimentation of the system, highlighting the positions and velocities generated by cooperative control with energy optimization, as well as the images of the movements made by the robots according to the orders sent. Finally, a usability score for the app that demonstrates high acceptance is obtained.

Keywords: Mobile robots · Cooperative control · Optimal Control · Energy Consumption · Human-machine interface

1 Introduction

1.1 Preliminary Information

The materialization of robots has had a great boost thanks to free access technologies such as 3D printing and Arduino that have been widely extended allowing the construction of robots quickly and easily [1, 2]. In addition, the development of human-machine

© Springer Nature Switzerland AG 2021
M. Kurosu (Ed.): HCII 2021, LNCS 12763, pp. 329–340, 2021.
https://doi.org/10.1007/978-3-030-78465-2_25

control interfaces has allowed the user to fully exploit the characteristics of the systems, controlling multiple robots from the same panel to direct autonomous tasks and configure parameters remotely [3]. These technology combined with robotics have resulted in new proposals that have increased due to the multiple applications of education, assistance, transport, logistics, among others [4–7].

In the industrial field, robotics provides solutions to the problems of productivity, inefficiency, prevents accidents that occur in the construction industry, as well as avoids occupational diseases such as musculoskeletal disorders that occur in workers for repetitive work, heavy loads, [8] Robots are also used in the industry to improve machining, welding, painting, transport and more [9].

In the internal logistics of the industries, mobile robots are applied for the transport of cargo, this is why they must ensure safe navigation, which entails proper planning of the routes so that they can meet the objective of displacement despite the obstacles encountered on the road [10]. Consequently, by optimally planning the movement of mobile robots with wheels [11], improves efficiency and increases autonomy by making good use of batteries [12].

This human-machine interaction is breaking the paradigm of artificial intelligence over man, because human intelligence is [13, 14], because of this, the study and development of prototypes from classrooms are important to generate proposals that strengthen production processes in a sustainable way.

The growing development of research that applies mobile robots in cooperative tasks opens up countless opportunities while showing the importance of optimizing energy consumption in the execution of collaborative operations [15, 16]. In this sense, optimal control is responsible for the study and implementation of algorithms that allow to reach the desired states and minimize an objective function in the process. The Pontryagin principle is a technique widely used in optimal control and allows to find control actions to solve optimization problems [17, 18].

1.2 Related Works

In relation to work related to this proposal, controllers have been developed for the cooperative control of multiple robots. In [15] two different techniques are presented for coordinated teams of multiple robots in people tracking, one based on a reinforced learning algorithm and the other based on a particle filter, coordinating the robots for a cooperative search from different positions, this proposal is validated by simulation. In [16] the control of a group of terrestrial robots with heterogeneous characteristics through linear algebra is implemented, considering primary and secondary objectivess for the monitoring of a path and in this process modifying the shape and orientation at any time, this proposal is validated by real experiments with different mobile robots. In [19] omni directional mobile robots are compared, experimenting on custom-made hardware to evaluate the performance of both controllers, resulting in better qualities for distributed optimization-based control.

In relation to cooperative mobile robotics and optimization, [20] features optimal transport control for a multi-robot cooperative system based on Voronoi tessellation-based coverage control and Lyapunov stability analysis, finding results that improve the original controller and avoid local optimal points. [21] tracking of autonomous vehicles, minimizing the difference between desired and actual outputs, the optimal control algorithm considers an objective function of minimum energy consumption, the proposal results in a consumption of 0.37% of the battery with 95% of the trajectory tracking.

This work features a computer application for cooperative control of three differential mobile robots with minimal power consumption, developed with low-cost technology. The control algorithm is developed based on the Pontryagin principle for a minimal energy problem. The results show the operation of the system implemented in both simulation and experimentation, evaluating the correct functioning of the proposal.

2   Proposal Design

2.1   Overview

The objective of the application is to control three mobile robots cooperatively optimizing energy consumption, where the operator enters the desired parameters and runs the controller. For this purpose, mobile robots are built using freely accessible technology, the user interface is developed, and the main computer communicates wirelessly with the robots. Figure 1 presents the general diagram of the proposal, where the computer contains the application developed in Matlab through a graphical interface to enter the parameters and visualize the results. Cooperative control has two main components; the characteristics of the formation of the robots such as mutual distance and angle of the shape, and the desired position data that locate the triangular shape according to the user's requirements. The results generated by the application are the positions and velocities of the robots that allow to reach the desired parameters. In addition, a usability test is applied to engineering students to analyze user interface acceptance.

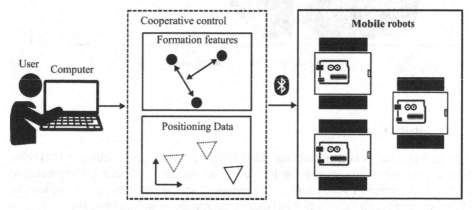

Fig. 1. General diagram of cooperative control of mobile robots.

2.2 3D Design of Robots

As for the mechanical structure of the robots, it is built by 3D printing; the 3D designs are presented in Fig. 2. The transfer of movement is performed by tracks providing better grip to the earth and greater stability. The robot has a compartment to install the electronic circuit and another container for the battery. The overall sizes of the robot are: 12 cm long, 10 cm wide and 8 cm high. The motion configuration is unicycle type, this involved one motor per track, giving two action velocities: linear velocity (forward-backward) and angular velocity around the center (right-left). The electronic circuit is modularly designed with main components: Arduino board, motor driver and Bluetooth communication module.

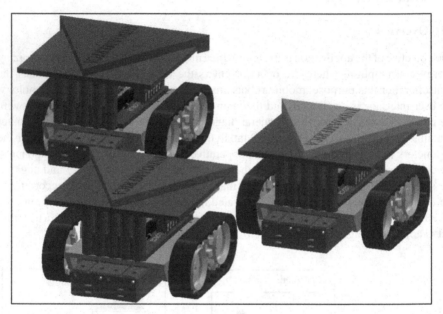

Fig. 2. 3D design of mobile robots.

2.3 Control Algorithm

The algorithm has been implemented following the 5 steps of the Pontryagin [18] combining two control objectives, robot formation and energy optimization. The procedure includes: deduction of state equations, definition of the target function to complete the Hamiltonian, finding the equations of the control variables, and applying the derivatives formulated for optimization. The system of differential equations resulting from this method considers boundary conditions and is resolved by numerical methods. Regarding the state equations, the model proposed in [16] is used, it relates the states of the robots with the states of the shape, for this, it creates 2 lines that form the base (v) and the height (o) of the triangle, and the tips are the robots positioned on the plane; where

(1) represents the positions of the robot (x_i, y_i) including a fictional robot located in the center of the base of the triangle; and (2) represents the characteristics of the shape, this includes the positions of the shape (x_j, y_j), the distances (d_j), and the angles (a_j). The training model is presented in (3), which relates states through a transformation matrix $(\boldsymbol{J})$.

$$X(t) = \begin{bmatrix} x_1 y_1 x_2 y_2 x_v y_v x_3 y_3 \end{bmatrix} \tag{1}$$

$$F(X(t))) = \begin{bmatrix} x_v y_v d_v a_v x_o y_o d_o a_o \end{bmatrix} \tag{2}$$

$$d(F(X(t)))/dt = J(X(t))\, d(X(t))/dt \tag{3}$$

Control variables are the velocities of robots defined by (4), these are obtained by deriving the positions of robots relative to time. On the other hand, the index of the target function (V) is defined, for the equation of energy menima defined in (5), which implies a direct relationship enters the velocities of the robots and the energy consumed.

$$u(t) = d(X(t))/dt \tag{4}$$

$$V(u(t)) = 1/2 u(t)^T u(t) \tag{5}$$

The first step is to find the Hamiltonian presented in (6), this contains the function at minimum (V), the equations of states (F), and the multipliers of Lagrange.

$$H(X(t), u(t)) = V(u(t)) + \Lambda(t)^T F(X(t)) \tag{6}$$

Step two requires the Hamiltonian derivative to control velocities and solve independent equations equal to zero, according to (7), this to determine the optimal solution of velocities in robots. The third step is to replace the solutions found in (7) in the Hamiltonian.

$$H(X(t), u(t))/d(u(t)) = 0 \tag{7}$$

The fourth step is to solve the differential equations obtained from applying the formulas (8) and (9), this allows to $\boldsymbol{\Lambda}s$ for the optimal solution of the control problem, including the control conditions for the outputs of the $\boldsymbol{F}s$ state equations. Contour conditions are the desired characteristics for the shape, i.e. the desired positions, distances and angles. This system of equations is solved using numerical methods and shooting method for final conditions, this with the help of mathematical software. The numerical results obtained are the Lagrange multipliers that determine the optimal control velocities for minimum power consumption.

$$d(F_s(X(t)))/d(t) = d(H(X(t), u(t)))/d(\Lambda(t)) \tag{8}$$

$$d(\Lambda_s(t))/d(t) = -d(H(X(t), u(t)))/d(X(t)) \tag{9}$$

3   System Implementation

3.1   Electronic Circuit

The electronic circuit has been implemented using free hardware, with the main processor being an Arduino mini to reduce the space required. Figure 3 features the printed circuit board and 3D circuit developed for mobile robots, the board contains tracks on both sides and holds the motors at the bottom. DC motors work with voltages from 6 to 12 V, with a TB6612FNG driver for both actuators. The HC-06 module provides Bluetooth communication to receive information sent by the remote application.

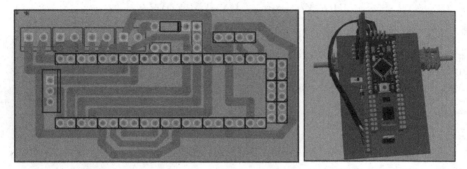

Fig. 3. Electronic circuit of mobile robots.

3.2   Robot Manufacturing

To proceed with the manufacture of the robots, the 3D components are printed, and the electronic circuit built. Figure 4 displays photos of mobile robots assembled and ready for operation. The operating tests fine-tune the velocities, checking the distances traveled because control is performed in an open loop.

3.3   User Interface Application

The application is developed in Matlab, it creates a main menu with user interface tools using structured programming language. Figure 5 displays the main menu window for cooperative control of robots, where several editable components containing the initial conditions and desired parameters of the control are evident. In addition, the menu contains the simulation and execution buttons, in both cases it is sent to run the optimization algorithm, the main functions used are "fsolve" for contour conditions (shooting method) and "ode45" to solve differential equations. The results are shown in the position plot and in the velocities plots that are displayed in new windows. In execution, robot velocities are sent through wireless communication, powering the engines to replicate cooperative control positions. On the other hand, communication is done by a single serial frame that contains the velocities for each engine in the order of the robots, in this way each robot understands which velocities to use, according to the assigned numbers.

Fig. 4. Assembled Mobile Robots.

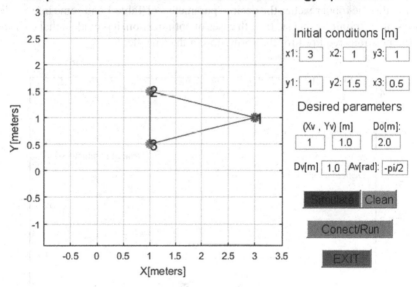

Fig. 5. Main menu of the cooperative control application.

4 Results

4.1 Simulation

The evaluation of the system is carried out by simulation and experimentation, obtaining the graphical results for cooperative control analysis. Table 1 presents the data for a simulation test, detailing the initial conditions and desired parameters, including 2 optimization sequences. The desired parameters do not include the position of the triangle height (x_{od}, y_{od}) or the angle of this segment (a_{od}) because this data is calculated to form an isosceles triangle.

Table 1. Simulation data for cooperative control.

Parameters desired	Optimization 1	Optimization 2	Initial conditions	
x_{vd} [m]	3	-5	x_1 [m]	0
y_{vd} [m]	3	4	y_1 [m]	0
d_{vd} [m]	1	3	x_2 [m]	0
a_{vd} [rad]	$\pi/2$	0	y_2 [m]	-1
d_{od} [m]	2	2	x_3 [m]	1
			y_3 [m]	-1

Figure 6 presents the positions generated in the simulation of the control algorithm, observing that the robot reaches the desired parameters of Table 1 and some intermediate positions of the training process. In both cases of optimization, it is evident that the robots reach the positions required for the formation of the triangle.

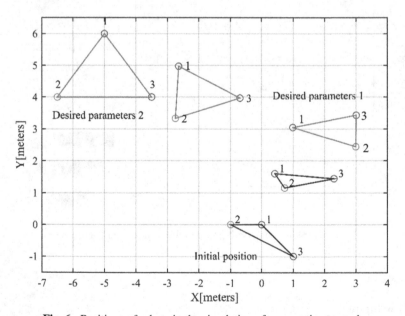

Fig. 6. Positions of robots in the simulation of cooperative control.

Figure 7 presents the control velocities for robots in both optimization cases, these velocities are the minimum to reach the desired target in the given time (8 s). By calculating the energy consumption index, V_1x30 [m^2/s^2] and V_2x 93 [m^2/s^2] are obtained,

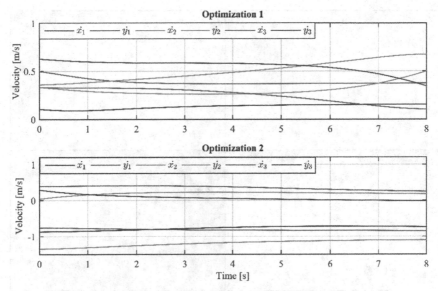

Fig. 7. Velocities of robots in the simulation of cooperative control.

which guarantees the minimum consumption according to the method used for the control algorithm.

4.2 Experimentation

Experimental tests are carried out on the built robots, linking the Bluetooth terminals to the computer and using the developed application. Figure 8 shows photos of the evolution of robots to experimental tests using Table 1 parameters, visually showing that robots reach positions close to expected positions (in reference to Fig. 6) by the open loop control algorithm.

4.3 Usability

In addition, the application is evaluated by means of a usability test with 21 senior students of Industrial Engineering and Systems, who used the application with mobile robots. The SUS test is used, which allows to know the acceptance of the system using different factors in software and hardware, including robotic systems [6]. Table 2 shows usability results, achieving 88.8% performance that ensures good user acceptance of application features, although item 7 has a low score, demonstrating that the system requires pre-use knowledge.

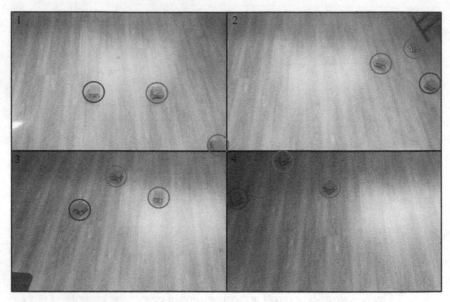

Fig. 8. Photos of robot cooperative control experimentation.

Table 2. Usability Test Results (SUS).

Question	Mean (N = 21)	Operation
1. I think I would like to use this system frequently	4.3	3.2
2. I find this system unnecessarily complex	**1.2**	**3.8**
3. I think the system is easy to use	4.5	3.5
4. I think you would need technical support to make use of the system	**1.3**	**3.7**
5. I find the various functions of the system quite well integrated	3. 9	2. 9
6. I have found too much inconsistency in this system	**1.8**	**3.2**
7. I think most people would learn to make use of the system quickly	3.3	2.3
8. I found the system quite uncomfortable to use	**1.5**	**3.5**
9. I have felt very safe using the system	3. 7	2. 7
10. I would need to learn a lot of things before I can manage the system	**1.5**	**3.5**
TOTAL		**35.5 (88.8%)**

5   Conclusions

The optimization of energy consumption in mobile robot allows greater autonomy in the execution of pre-programmed tasks, being important to develop applications that allow to execute cooperative positioning tasks with the minimum energy consumption. The system implemented in this work allows to control three mobile robots cooperatively through a computer application implemented in Matlab, for this a cooperative control scheme with energy optimization is developed. In addition, the use of low-cost technology facilitates the reproducibility of this proposal, using 3D printing and Arduino in the construction of robots.

The results show a correct functioning of the system, presenting graphs of the behavior of robots in simulation and experimentation. Simulation shows the robots in formation and the positions traveled in the process, also reviewing the control velocities and performance index that regulates the optimization algorithm. Experimentation shows images with moving robots according to remote orders sent by the application, although this component is limited because control is performed in open loop. Finally, the usability test determines an acceptance of 88.8%, validating the multidisciplinary tool that is implemented in this proposal.

References

1. Espera, A.H., Dizon, J.R.C., Chen, Q., Advincula, R.C.: 3D-printing and advanced manufacturing for electronics. Prog. Addit. Manufact. **4**(3), 245–267 (2019). https://doi.org/10.1007/s40964-019-00077-7
2. Buitrago, P.A., et al.: Mobile arduino robot programming using a remote laboratory in UNAD: pedagogic and technical aspects. In: Auer, M.E., May, D. (eds.) REV 2020. AISC, vol. 1231, pp. 171–183. Springer, Cham (2021). https://doi.org/10.1007/978-3-030-52575-0_14
3. Kassawat, M., Cervera, E., del Pobil, A.P.: Multi-robot user interface for cooperative transportation tasks. In: Ferrández Vicente, J.M., Álvarez-Sánchez, J.R., de la Paz López, F., Toledo Moreo, J., Adeli, H. (eds.) IWINAC 2019. LNCS, vol. 11487, pp. 77–81. Springer, Cham (2019). https://doi.org/10.1007/978-3-030-19651-6_8
4. Varela-Aldás, J., Miranda-Quintana, O., Guevara, C., Castillo, F., Palacios-Navarro, G.: Educational robot using lego mindstorms and mobile device. In: Advances and Applications in Computer Science, Electronics and Industrial Engineering. CSEI 2019. Advances in Intelligent Systems and Computing, pp. 71–82 (2019). https://doi.org/10.1007/978-3-030-33614-1_5.
5. Varela-Aldás, J., Buele, J., Jadan-Guerrero, J., Andaluz, V.H.: Teaching STEM competencies through an educational mobile robot. In: Zaphiris, P., Ioannou, A. (eds.) HCII 2020. LNCS, vol. 12206, pp. 560–573. Springer, Cham (2020). https://doi.org/10.1007/978-3-030-50506-6_38
6. Varela-Aldás, J., Guamán, J., Paredes, B., Chicaiza, F.A.: Robotic cane for the visually impaired. In: Antona, M., Stephanidis, C. (eds.) HCII 2020. LNCS, vol. 12188, pp. 506–517. Springer, Cham (2020). https://doi.org/10.1007/978-3-030-49282-3_36
7. Mantha, B.R.K., Jung, M.K., de Soto, B.G., Menassa, C.C., Kamat, V.R.: Generalized task allocation and route planning for robots with multiple depots in indoor building environments. Autom. Constr. **119**, 103359 (2020)
8. Follini, C., et al.: BIM-integrated collaborative robotics for application in building construction and maintenance (2021). https://doi.org/10.3390/robotics10010002

9. Bottin, M., Cocuzza, S., Comand, N., Doria, A.: Modeling and identification of an industrial robot with a selective modal approach (2020). https://doi.org/10.3390/app10134619

10. Huang, Y., Li, Z., Jiang, Y., Cheng, L.: Cooperative path planning for multiple mobile robots via HAFSA and an expansion logic strategy (2019). https://doi.org/10.3390/app9040672

11. Liu, S., Sun, D.: Modeling and experimental study for minimization of energy consumption of a mobile robot. In: 2012 IEEE/ASME International Conference on Advanced Intelligent Mechatronics (AIM), pp. 708–713 (2012) https://doi.org/10.1109/AIM.2012.6265887.

12. Verstraten, T., Furnémont, R., Mathijssen, G., Vanderborght, B., Lefeber, D.: Energy consumption of geared DC motors in dynamic applications: comparing modeling approaches. IEEE Robot. Autom. Lett. 1, 524–530 (2016). https://doi.org/10.1109/LRA.2016.2517820

13. Braga, A., Logan, R.K.: The emperor of strong AI has no clothes: limits to artificial intelligence2017https://doi.org/10.3390/info8040156

14. Varela-Aldás, J., Chávez-Ruiz, P., Buele, J.: Automation of a Lathe to increase productivity in the manufacture of stems of a metalworking company. In: Botto-Tobar, M., Zambrano Vizuete, M., Torres-Carrión, P., Montes León, S., Pizarro Vásquez, G., Durakovic, B. (eds.) ICAT 2019. CCIS, vol. 1195, pp. 244–254. Springer, Cham (2020). https://doi.org/10.1007/978-3-030-42531-9_20

15. Goldhoorn, A., Garrell, A., Alquézar, R., Sanfeliu, A.: Searching and tracking people with cooperative mobile robots. Auton. Robots. 42, 739–759 (2018)

16. Acosta, J.F., de Rivera, G.G., Andaluz, V.H., Garrido, J.: Multirobot Heterogeneous control considering secondary objectives. Sensors 19, 4367 (2019)

17. Asgari, M., Nikoobin, A.: Analysis of optimal dynamic manipulation for robotic manipulator based on Pontryagin's minimum principle. Arab. J. Sci. Eng. 45(11), 9159–9169 (2020). https://doi.org/10.1007/s13369-020-04663-8

18. Subbaram Naidu, D.: Optimal control systems (2002)

19. Ebel, H., Eberhard, P.: A comparative look at two formation control approaches based on optimization and algebraic graph theory. Rob. Auton. Syst. 136, 103686 (2020)

20. Inoue, D., Ito, Y., Yoshida, H.: Optimal transport-based coverage control for swarm robot systems: generalization of the voronoi tessellation-based method. IEEE Control Syst. Lett. 5, 1483–1488 (2020)

21. Holovatenko, I., Pysarenko, A.: Energy-efficient path-following control system of automated guided vehicles. J. Control. Autom. Electr. Syst. 32, 1–14 (2021)

Educational Robot European Cross-Cultural Design

Anna-Maria Velentza[1,2]([✉]) [iD], Stavros Ioannidis[1], Nefeli Georgakopoulou[2,3],
Mohammad Shidujaman[4,5], and Nikolaos Fachantidis[1,2] [iD]

[1] School of Educational and Social Policies, University of Macedonia, Thessaloniki, Greece
nfachantidis@uom.edu.gr
[2] LIRES Robotics Lab, University of Macedonia, Thessaloniki, Greece
[3] INREV Laboratory, Paris 8 University, Paris, France
[4] Academy of Arts and Design, Tsinghua University, Beijing, China
[5] Bangladesh Robotics Foundation, Dhaka, Bangladesh

Abstract. Educational robots have been used successfully in a variety of teaching applications and have been proven beneficial in teaching STEM studies. Although educational robots are already been using, it is important to identify the robot's characteristics -appearance, functionality, voice- that is closer to the users' needs. Our target is to use participatory design procedures to identify the users' attitudes and needs to construct an educational robot based on them. In this paper, we introduce the STIMEY Robot, which created through these procedures after a cross European study where five different countries participated. The robot evaluated in real classroom environment with students aged between 13 and 18 years old, who had a STEM les-son with the aid of the robot. Our results clearly suggest that students agreed with the robot's interactive skills and ability to provide feedback and also they statistically significantly changed their attitudes towards its usability after having a lesson with it.

Keywords: Educational robots · Cross-culture · Participatory design · Robot design · Real class evaluation · STEM

1 Introduction

Social robots are getting more involved in our everyday lives because of their ability to express verbal and nonverbal cues, conversation abilities, and emotional bonds that can be built in humans after human-robot interaction activities [1]. Those robots' characteristics have proven beneficial for their use in the educational field. One of the main challenges is to match their social behavior, style, appearance, and interaction with the educational demands and the actual users' needs. Social robots when teaching a lesson in typical education students, seem to accomplish similar tutoring skills with human teachers, especially when they perform controlled tasks and manage to enhance students' cognitive and affected outcomes [2]. There is also evidences that children- social robots' interaction can increase children's' communication and language performance [3]. More

© Springer Nature Switzerland AG 2021
M. Kurosu (Ed.): HCII 2021, LNCS 12763, pp. 341–353, 2021.
https://doi.org/10.1007/978-3-030-78465-2_26

specifically, social robots seem to be helpful in STEM studies. For example, the Cozmo robot can deliver exercises and engaging materials to students between 14 and 17 years old and they significantly improved their knowledge in mathematics [4]. Educational robots boost teamwork and problem-solving activities and thus, those engaged in STEM education are successful in a variety of learning scenarios [5].

Despite their usability and effectiveness through different learning activities, there is moral consideration regarding the use of social robots in education. Those considerations may vary across different educational cultures. Focus groups with Dutch Educational Policymakers Considerations revealed 15 theoretical values that vary from 'the robots' capability to lower teachers' workload' to 'matters about the escalating influence of commercial enterprises on the educational system' [6]. The different educational cultures are a view of the currency of general cultural differences between different countries, especially from different continents. There are cultural differences in people from Asian, American, African, European populations regarding their attitudes toward robots, their acceptance, and their usability [7]. On the other hand, countries in the same continents such as Europe, seem to have similar attitudes towards robots, despite some minor differences regarding the level of acceptance of robots in their every-day life [8].

Before being able to design efficient educational robots, there are still some answers about the users' attitudes towards robots' characteristics that are certainly missing. The stakeholders whose opinions we should take into consideration are primary the students but also the teachers and the parents. Also, before constructing an educational robot we should merge their learning and educational needs with their social and cultural habits.

There are four critical stages in the design procedure of a social robot· taking into consideration previous studies, the robot's impact on the target group's behavior, the stakeholders' attitudes towards robots, and their feedback and reaction regarding the robot's final appearance [9]. Augmented Reality (AR) and Virtual Reality (VR) technologies is an interactive way of engaging stakeholders in multiple human-robot interaction scenarios [10]. Although there are also other interactive design activities such as drawing or showing images of existing robots or robotics parts [11], the stakeholders need to collaborate with robots within the targeted operational environment [12].

In our study, under the Horizon 2020 funded project STIMEY [13] we conducted a cross- European user- centered design procedure in order to identify the ideal characteristics that an educational robots should have. For this purpose, we took into consideration the robot's appearance, usability, hardware, and software features. We collaborated with the stakeholders -teachers, students, parents- and based on them, we designed a robot prototype based on their needs and test it in a real school classroom environment. Our most important findings are that a) stakeholders from different European countries - Germany, Belarus, Greece, Finland, and Spain are having similar needs and ideas about the ideal educational robot and b) after testing the robot prototype in Greek schools we found out that the robot prototype was positively evaluated. c) Students aged between 13 and 18 years old, after having a lesson with the STIMEY robot teaching assistant, statistically significantly re-evaluated their opinion regarding the usefulness of a robot in the classroom in comparison with their opinion before having a lesson with it. The stakeholder who participated in the robot's design procedure were from both north and south European countries and thus the STIMEY robot prototype seems to be a representative educational robot for European stakeholders' needs. To the best of the authors' knowledge, there are no other studies actively involving the educational stakeholders in the development process of educational robots in a cross European study, while the stakeholders' opinions, as expressed in our experiments, are by themselves, valuable contributions for the development of efficient educational robots.

2 Related Work

Appearance and functionality are the more common robot characteristics that researchers typically focus on since they are the key factors that affect the human- robot interaction and can determine the time humans will spend with a robot performing a specific task [14]. Experience is a key factor for accepting technology and robots [15]. Moreover, humans prefer to collaborate with robots with characteristics that fit into their norms regarding the performed task, such as serious personality traits for serious activities and cheerful personality traits for cheerful activities [16, 17]. Li et al., performed multi- culture research between Korean, Chinese, and German populations regarding their attitudes about a robot's appearance and performed tasks. Results showed cultural differences in participants' engagement and likeability. Moreover, participants during the interview procedure, expected the robot appearance to match with the task that the robot was supposed to perform but that did not confirm during the subjective rating procedure [18].

The social educational robot Wolly is an example of a robot that designed through participatory designed procedures and constructed and implemented (software and hardware) based on the target group needs [19]. Bertel et al., suggested a semi-structured participatory design procedure for the children's' involvement in the designed procedure [20].

A user-centered design procedure in a sample of 116 university students indicated that they preferred to collaborate with a robot with both machinery and humanoid appearance and basic facial characteristics. Additionally, they suggested that an educational robot should provide user-centered support based on the students' learning needs [21, 22]. Velentza et al., shown that university students, pre-service teachers had statistically significant different opinions about the ideal characteristics that a robot- tutor should have before and after having a course with it [23]. Similarly, with [21], students before interacting with a social robot preferred to collaborate with a robot with machinery characteristics while after the interaction, they both preferred machinery and humanoid characteristics [23]. On the other hand, although younger adults are more familiar with robots than the previous generations, when a group of students instructed to draw a robot, the most frequent drawing stemmed from books' illustrations [24].

3 Present Study

Based on the research results described in the last section, it is very clear that it is important to investigate the impact of educational stakeholders' opinions about the ideal characteristics that a robot teaching assistant should have to efficiently interact with students and collaborate with teachers. It is also important to identify those characteristics after constructing a robot-prototype based on their needs and evaluate it in action in a real classroom environment, as suggested by [25], and not only by approaching the stakeholders' beliefs theoretically or via VR and AR technologies.

The current study, thus, explores whether there is any difference in the educational stakeholders -students, teachers, parents, school principals- attitudes and opinions regarding a teaching assistant educational robot based on their culture. All the participants were from European countries. Based on their needs and beliefs, the STIMEY consortium designed and constructed a robot prototype. After constructing the prototype, we tested and evaluated it in real school classrooms in order to identify:

1) What are the participants' positions, and attitudes towards STEM and STIMEY science before having a lesson with the STIMEY robot?
2) What is the effect of their demographic profile?
3) Did the lesson with the STIMEY robot reinforce students' positions, and attitudes towards STEM science and STIMEY?

3.1 Hypothesis

Based on [8] we expect that although there are cultural differences between European countries and their educational standards, they will have similar attitudes toward the appearance and the usability of an educational robot. Moreover, we expect that students after having a lesson with the robot will improve their attitudes toward STEM and educational robots. Finally, we believe that the robot prototype will be positively evaluated after its use, especially because of the user-centered design procedure followed by the STIMEY Project partners.

4 Participatory Design

4.1 Participants

In the study participated a total number of 132 stakeholders, (Finland n = 27, Greece n = 24, Spain, n = 24, Germany n = 30, Belarus n = 27) and among them were students between 10 and 18 years old, teachers and school directors from primary, lower secondary and upper secondary education, parents and professionals engaged in STEM related careers. A gender balance among participants was ensured (female n = 73, male n = 59).

4.2 Procedure

The procedure followed the participatory design standards and the stakeholders worked in close collaboration with expert groups in order to analyze their attitudes, consider their needs, evaluate the benefits and deficiencies of a products' design before, during, and after its development and implementation. There were five stages during the procedure· preliminary research, design, development and implementation, pilots, final implementations. For the data collection, we held focus group sessions for each country participating in the STIMEY consortium, following the same protocol in all the cases [26].

Robot. In the beginning, during the co-design focus groups, participants indicated their ideas regarding the ideal robot's appearance and the robot's voice commands. Based on them, 103 items/ideas were grouped based on their conceptual similarity at six groups of requirements· a) Appearance of the robot (32), b) Functionality of voice commands (27), c) voice of the robot (19), d) personality of the robot (6), e) language of the voice commands (2), f) voice commands' risks (2). Each group of requirements presented to the stakeholders followed by a short description. One of the participants' priorities when discussing the robot's appearance characteristics was its small size (n = 26). Then to be human-like/humanoid (n = 14), able to be customized/modified by students (n = 14), not human-like/not humanoid (n = 12), robot-like/ machine-like (n = 11) and easy to carry/portable (n = 10). The most common participants' requirements for the robot's voice commands were to be adjustable (n = 12) and simple/easy to understand (n = 11). More detailed information regarding the stakeholders' association in the different steps of the procedure can be found in Christodoulou et al., [27] accompanied by preliminary evaluation results of the robot prototype STEM-oriented robot-assisted collaborative online teaching-learning task.

4.3 STIMEY Robot Prototype

From the 103 items referring to the robot, 78 were adopted in the design procedure (78%), while 22 did not for various reasons (24%), such as the contradiction of one requirement with another, high costs, or time-consuming integration, technology limitations or technical restrictions.

The STIMEY robot, depicted in Fig. 1 was designed to encourage students to involve more actively during the learning process through the STIMEY Platform based on a variety of principles:

1. The STIMEY robot was able to talk, reply to students' questions based on a set of pre-programmed behaviors, provide them with feedback, evaluate their answers in given knowledge acquisition questions, change facial expressions, move its hands and head, move backward and forward through wheels. In its back, it has an embedded mobile phone, serve as the robot's 'brain', giving information to the students.
2. The STIMEY robot will accompany the students as a partner and will communicate with them (speech/listening, gesture, etc.) as a friend. Based on its feature to act as a friend makes it capable to help students with a variety of learning tasks through the online platform. The robot is also able to enhance communication between students (using video, speech, and gestures).
3. The STIMEY robot will be upgraded (software and hardware) to show cognitive, emotional, and physical development. The evolution of the robot will be based on the student's progress, as shown by their electronic profile, portfolio, and creativity curve (STEM progress) which are scored in the STIMEY Platform. In this way, the capabilities of any STIMEY robot will represent its owners.

4. The STIMEY robot will have a small size, enough to be carried in a bag or placed on a table. It will have some human characteristics (e.g. face, arms, torso) and will be customized in terms of adding or extracting parts on the robot. At the same time, its appearance will also have some machinery features and its general design will follow a cartoonish style. The robot will also have different forms based on the stakeholder's requirements, as shown in Fig. 1, left picture, and various color options.

The robot will be like a student pal, and it may vary according to students' creativity. Even though the torso will not be constructed with iron materials, it will be fall resistant.

Voice Commands. The voice commands of the robot will be adjustable and easy to use, will be functional, easy to control and they will support learning. Moreover, the user will be able to monitor the voice commands (also with a text application). The voice commands will be given gradually to the robot and the user will have a certain level of freedom in selecting them.

Robot's voice: human-like, friendly and clear, kind and joyful.

Fig. 1. The STIMEY Robot Prototype, left: two different versions of the robot, middle: happy facial expression, right: the robot's back with the embedded mobile phone device.

5   Evaluation- Experimental Design

5.1   Participants

The total number of participants was 92, 43 Boys 42 Girls, and seven who preferred not to mention their gender. 51 of them studied in junior high school, aged between 13 and 15 years old and 40 of them in senior high school aged between 16 and 18 years old. Only one student did not mention his/her age. They were all assigned to Greek schools and they all had normal or corrected to normal vision and hearing and their native language was the language of the lesson and the given questionnaires. They participated in the experiment after the principal of their school applied for participation through a project open invitation. The experiments lasted for one month and took place for every school classroom at the same hour in the morning in their school unit.

5.2 Design

In each school classroom, we conducted one lesson which lasted for two hours with the aid of the STIMEY Platform and Robot prototype. In this course, we first introduced the STIMEY platform and its capabilities to the students. The students then completed questionnaires related to their opinions regarding the hypothetical use of a robot during their courses. Then the lesson was implemented utilizing the STIMEY educational Platform, accompanied by the STIMEY Robot which was the tutor of the lesson in collaboration with a teacher with STEM studies expertise. Finally, after the end of the lesson, the students were asked to complete an online questionnaire regarding their Attitudes, Positions, and Behaviours towards STEM and STIMEY robot (STQ). The participants had as much time as they wanted to fill the questionnaire anonymously.

The given questionnaire, STQ was tailor-made, designed by the project partners based on the evaluation needs. There were three demographic, two close types, and 22 Likert scale questions (from 1–5, evaluated from totally agree to totally disagree with the questions' statement).

5.3 Procedure

In the beginning, all the students who participated in the lesson were informed about the STIMEY program and its actions, as well as about its online Platform and the STIMEY robot. Students were then asked to answer a 10 min pre-test questionnaire. The students then logged in to the STIMEY platform using their credentials. Before having the lesson with the robot, there was a familiarization phase where the students watched two videos (ten minutes duration) with the STIMEY Robot in action. After the end of the video, the robot stood in the middle of the class as shown in Fig. 2 and each student had access to one pc or tablet. The lesson that the robot taught to the students was about STEM and more specifically about the 'Dark Side of the Moon', explaining basic physics and astrophysics principles regarding the lighting conditions of the moon. The lesson was adapted based on their educational level. Our goal was to show as many robot's features and behaviors during the course about its appearance (i.e. different facial expressions) and usability (i.e. feedback, interconnectivity with the web- platform) before they evaluate it.

5.4 Data Analysis

Before the data analysis, we performed a Varimax factor analysis on the robot's characteristics and students- STIMEY robot interaction as well as a Cronbach's alpha reliability analysis on the dimensions of opinions, positions, and attitudes towards STEM sciences and the STIMEY robot.

For the analysis of the STQ, we calculated the Mean Value (MV) and Standard Deviation (SD) for each STQ question. To identify the effect of the students' demographical characteristics on their attitudes toward STEM studies and STIMEY robot, we applied a Kruskal Wallis test. Additionally, we conducted a paired-sample t-test to compare the differences in the students' attitudes before and after having a lesson with the robot.

Fig. 2. Classroom set up during the robot's evaluation

5.5 Results

The Varimax factor analysis on the Likert scale questions revealed three dimensions regarding the students' interaction with the robot with Kaiser-Meyer-Olkin (KMO) 0.7, and four regarding their attitudes before and after the lesson as shown in Table 1. The first factor includes 6 questions with $\alpha = 0.8$ and named after the context of the questions as 'Student Feedback'. The second factor (5 questions), named 'Student-Robot Interaction', with $\alpha = 0.66$ and the third one 'Non-interaction'.

Table 1. Cronbach's alpha dimensional analysis.

Dimensions	Questions	Cronbach's alpha
Positive Opinion about STEM and STIMEY before the lesson	3	0,684
Positive Behavior about STEM and STIMEY before the lesson	2	0,621
Positive Opinion about STEM and STIMEY after the lesson	3	0,713
Positive Behavior about STEM and STIMEY after the lesson	2	0,724
Student's Feedback	6	0,807
Student-Robot Interaction	5	0,661
Non interaction	1	-

According to the students' evaluations, they agreed that the robot should give them positive feedback ($MV = 4.18$, $SD = 0.66$), and they have positive attitudes about its interactive abilities ($MV = 4,01$, $SD = 0,62$), positive opinions towards STEM studies and STIMEY robot after having a lesson with it ($MV = 4,11$, $SD = 0,71$) and also positive behavior ($MV = 3,71$, $SD = 0,89$). On the other hand, the students' behavior towards STEM studies and STIMEY robot before having a lesson with the robot is neither positive nor negative ($MV = 3,51$, $SD = 0,91$), similarly with their attitudes toward the robot's non-interaction ($MV = 3,20$, $SD = 1,47$), as shown in Fig. 3.

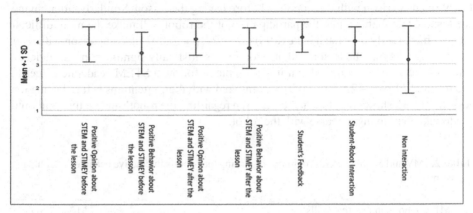

Fig. 3. MV and SD of the students' opinions, behaviour, attitudes towards STEM sciences and STIMEY Robot

The Kruskal Wallis measures indicated that there is a statistically significant difference regarding the students' gender and their attitudes toward STEM studies and STIMEY robot before having any lesson with it. More specifically, boys have more positive attitudes in comparison with others, girls and prefer not to say at H(2) = 8,69, p = 0,013 < 0,05. There were no statistically significant differences regarding students' age.

Most of the students, 32,97% (N = 30), indicated that Mathematics is the most difficult STEM course. Physics follows at 26,37% (N = 24) and then geography (10,99%, N = 10), biology, and the rest of them are split between chemistry, computer science, and engineering. It is worth mentioning that basic principles of computer science and engineering that are thought into school are theoretical without application and exercises.

Before having a lesson with the STIMEY robot, the students claimed that the use of the robot in the teaching procedure will make the most difficult STEM course (each student considered the one he/she declared at the beginning of the questionnaire) more pleasant (MV = 4.22, SD = 0.89), interesting (MV = 3.9, SD = 1.03) and more easily understandable (MV = 3.54, SD = 1.01). Moreover, they implied that the robot will help them focus more during the lesson on the difficult course (MV = 3.06, SD = 1.02) and that it will motivate them to follow an academic career in the future (MV = 3.38, SD = 1.11).

After having a lesson with the robot, the students claimed that the use of the robot in the teaching procedure will make the most difficult subject more pleasant (MV = 4.25, SD = 0.89), interesting (MV = 4.14, SD = 0.85), and more easily understandable (MV = 3.93, SD = 0.92). Moreover, they implied that the robot will help them focus more during the lesson on the difficult subject (MV = 3.75, SD = 0.95) and that it will motivate them to study from an academic perspective the more difficult subject in the future (MV = 3.67, SD = 1.05).

When comparing the two conditions, before and after having the lesson with the robot, students statistically significant improved their opinion that the robot will make the most difficult course more interesting, as shown by the t-test at t(90) = −2,23, p = 0,029 in comparison with their opinion before having the lesson. Similarly, after having the lesson, they believe that the participation of the robot will make the more difficult subject more easily understandable (t(90) = −3,27, p = 0,002) in comparison with their belief before having the lesson with it. Moreover, statistically significant more students, after the robot lesson, implied that it is possible to follow a STEM academic career in the future, (t(90) = −2,50, p = 0,014) compared with their intentions before having the lesson. Table 2 shows the students' evaluation regarding the robot's interactive skills and feedback after having a course with the robot.

Table 2. MV and *SD* of students' opinions regarding the robot's interactive behavior after having a lesson with it.

STIMEY robot's interactive skills	M.V	SD
After the end of the lesson, the STIMEY robot should give reward and positive feedback by using its facial expressions to the students based on their effort in the platform	4,37	0,77
During the lesson, STIMEY robot should ask questions to the students to provide them with additional information regarding the course	4,35	0,77
When the STIMEY robot provides additional information to the students, it should approach them and encourage them by using its facial expressions	4,34	0,88
When the STIMEY robot provides a quiz to the students, it should reward them for every correct answer by using body movements and facial expressions	4,21	0,86
When the lesson is over, STIMEY robot should verbally reward students about their effort (i.e. by saying 'congratulations')	4,14	0,86
When the STIMEY robot provides a quiz to the students, it should verbally reward them for every correct answer	4,13	0,96
When students post in the platform, STIMEY robot should verbally reward them by saying 'Well Done'	4,07	0,94
When the teacher prepares a lesson through the platform, STIMEY robot should send notifications to the students	4,00	0,93
When students post in the platform, STIMEY robot should not reward them verbally, but by using its body movements and facial expressions	3,91	1,02
When the STIMEY robot shows a video to the students, it should verbally comment on it (i.e. highlight the important parts of the video)	3,86	1,18

(*continued*)

Table 2. (*continued*)

STIMEY robot's interactive skills	M.V	SD
When the STIMEY robot shows a video to the students, it should look at them	3,45	1,14
When the STIMEY robot shows a video to the students, it should not show facial expressions such as surprize of close one eye, neither to intervene	3,20	1,47

Finally, students found that their favourite characteristic of the robot's appearance was its eyes (49,45%, N = 45), head (20,88%, N = 19), arms (14,29%, N = 13) and equally its torso and backpack at 7.69% (N = 7).

6 Discussion and Conclusions

Robots' characteristics such as their social behavior have been proven beneficial in educational and teaching tasks by strengthening student's cognitive and affective outcomes [2]. Educational robots also help students better understand and appreciate STEM studies [5]. It is important to identify the ideal robots' characteristics that enhance both students' learning outcomes and make them enjoy the lesson more, by taking into consideration among other factors, their culture. In the current study, we described the importance of designing and constructing educational robots based on the stakeholders' needs by conducting user-centred design procedures. The current robot design procedure took place during the HORIZON 2020 funded Project STIMEY. The educational stakeholders, students, teachers, school principals, parents, wherefrom five different European countries, giving a representative sample of the European population. They all had similar opinions regarding their attitudes about the ideal educational robot's appearance, voice, and functionality and we end up with six categories of recommendations. By following the majority of them (78%), we designed and constructed the STIMEY Robot prototype which was among others, portable, small-sized, a combination of humanoid, machinery, and cartoonish characteristics, able to change facial expressions, move parts of its body and give voice feedback and reward to the students.

In the present study, we consider the robot's evaluation in Greek schools, by 92 students aged between 13 and 18 years old who had a two hours STEM lesson instructed by the STIMEY Robot. Results showed that students after having a lesson with the robot had positive attitudes and behaviors towards its interactive skills and ability to give feedback. Moreover, after having a lesson with the robot, students statistically significantly improve their beliefs regarding the robot's ability to make even the most difficult course more interesting (p = .029) and more easily understandable (p = .002). Furthermore, students believe that it is possible to follow a future carrier in STEM studies, in comparison with their beliefs before having a lesson with the robot (p = .014).

As future work, we plan to evaluate the robot with students and stakeholders in more European countries and for others abroad in Europe to find out if we can generalize our principles regarding the educational robot characteristics.

References

1. Onyeulo, E.B., Gandhi, V.: What makes a social robot good at interacting with humans? Information **11**(1), Art. no. 1 (2020). https://doi.org/10.3390/info11010043
2. Belpaeme, T., Kennedy, J., Ramachandran, A., Scassellati, B., Tanaka, F.: Social robots for education: a review. Sci. Robot. **3**(21) (2018). https://doi.org/10.1126/scirobotics.aat5954
3. Neumann, M.M.: Social robots and young children's early language and literacy learning. Early Childhood Educ. J. **48**(2), 157–170 (2019). https://doi.org/10.1007/s10643-019-009 97-7
4. Ahmad, M.I., Khordi-moodi, M., Lohan, K.S.: Social robot for STEM education. In: Companion of the 2020 ACM/IEEE International Conference on Human-Robot Interaction, New York, NY, USA, pp. 90–92, March 2020. https://doi.org/10.1145/3371382.3378291
5. Benitti, F.B.V., Spolaôr, N.: How have robots supported STEM teaching? In: Khine, M.S. (ed.) Robotics in STEM Education, pp. 103–129. Springer, Cham (2017). https://doi.org/10. 1007/978-3-319-57786-9_5
6. Smakman, M., Berket, J., Konijn, E.A.: The impact of social robots in education: moral considerations of dutch educational policymakers. In: 2020 29th IEEE International Conference on Robot and Human Interactive Communication (RO-MAN), August 2020, pp. 647–652 https://doi.org/10.1109/RO-MAN47096.2020.9223582.
7. Nomura, T.: Cultural differences in social acceptance of robots. In: 2017 26th IEEE International Symposium on Robot and Human Interactive Communication (RO-MAN), pp. 534–538, August 2017. https://doi.org/10.1109/ROMAN.2017.8172354
8. Gnambs, T., Appel, M.: Are robots becoming unpopular? changes in attitudes towards autonomous robotic systems in Europe. Comput. Hum. Behav. **93**, 53–61 (2019). https://doi.org/10.1016/j.chb.2018.11.045
9. A framework for organizing the tools and techniques of participatory design|Proceedings of the 11th Biennial Participatory Design Conference. https://dl.acm.org/doi/abs/10.1145/190 0441.1900476?casa_token=3HZNgr5FT1QAAAAA:9mHWxUIh_7fQkLbi4qE4Fn-hNlI5S tbwQu4H3K9igIzZjyQ4AnSLsE6fGy4IgO3hSDpJd3WEJNgAccessed 19 Mar 2020
10. Jalowski, M., Fritzsche, A., Möslein, K.M.: Applications for persuasive technologies in participatory design processes. In: Oinas-Kukkonen, H., Win, K.T., Karapanos, E., Karppinen, P., Kyza, E. (eds.) PERSUASIVE 2019. LNCS, vol. 11433, pp. 74–86. Springer, Cham (2019). https://doi.org/10.1007/978-3-030-17287-9_7
11. Rose, E.J., Björling, E.A.: Designing for engagement: using participatory design to develop a social robot to measure teen stress. In: Proceedings of the 35th ACM International Conference on the Design of Communication, Halifax, Nova Scotia, Canada, pp. 1–10, August 2017. https://doi.org/10.1145/3121113.3121212
12. Salter, T., Werry, I., Michaud, F.: Going into the wild in child–robot interaction studies: issues in social robotic development. Intell. Serv. Robot. **1**(2), 93–108 (2008). https://doi.org/10. 1007/s11370-007-0009-9
13. 'STIMEY'. https://www.stimey.eu/home. Accessed 27 Apr 2020
14. Faccio, M., Minto, R., Rosati, G., Bottin, M.: The influence of the product characteristics on human-robot collaboration: a model for the performance of collaborative robotic assembly. Int. J. Adv. Manuf. Technol. **106**(5–6), 2317–2331 (2019). https://doi.org/10.1007/s00170-019-04670-6
15. Heerink, M.: Exploring the influence of age, gender, education and computer experience on robot acceptance by older adults. In: 2011 6th ACM/IEEE International Conference on Human-Robot Interaction (HRI), pp. 147–148, March 2011. https://doi.org/10.1145/1957656. 1957704

16. Goetz, J., Kiesler, S., Powers, A.: Matching robot appearance and behavior to tasks to improve human-robot cooperation. In: The 12th IEEE International Workshop on Robot and Human Interactive Communication, 2003. Proceedings. ROMAN 2003, pp. 55–60, November 2003. https://doi.org/10.1109/ROMAN.2003.1251796

17. Velentza, A.-M., Heinke, D., Wyatt, J.: Museum robot guides or conventional audio guides? an experimental study. Adv. Robot. **34**(24), 1571–1580 (2020). https://doi.org/10.1080/016 91864.2020.1854113

18. Li, D., Rau, P.L.P., Li, Y.: A cross-cultural study: effect of robot appearance and task. Int. J. Soc. Robot. **2**(2), 175–186 (2010). https://doi.org/10.1007/s12369-010-0056-9

19. Gena, C., Mattutino, C., Perosino, G., Trainito, M., Vaudano, C., Cellie, D.: Design and development of a social, educational and affective robot. In: 2020 IEEE Conference on Evolving and Adaptive Intelligent Systems (EAIS), May 2020, pp. 1–8. https://doi.org/10.1109/EAI S48028.2020.9122778.

20. Bertel, L.B., Rasmussen, D.M., Christiansen, E.: Robots for real: developing a participatory design framework for implementing educational robots in real-world learning environments. In: Kotzé, P., Marsden, G., Lindgaard, G., Wesson, J., Winckler, M. (eds.) INTERACT 2013. LNCS, vol. 8118, pp. 437–444. Springer, Heidelberg (2013). https://doi.org/10.1007/978-3-642-40480-1_29

21. Reich-Stiebert, N., Eyssel, F., Hohnemann, C.: Exploring university students' preferences for educational robot design by means of a user-centered design approach. Int. J. Soc. Robot. **12**(1), 227–237 (2019). https://doi.org/10.1007/s12369-019-00554-7

22. Reich-Stiebert, N., Eyssel, F.: Robots in the classroom: what teachers think about teaching and learning with education robots. In: Agah, A., Cabibihan, J.-J., Howard, A.M., Salichs, M.A., He, H. (eds.) ICSR 2016. LNCS (LNAI), vol. 9979, pp. 671–680. Springer, Cham (2016). https://doi.org/10.1007/978-3-319-47437-3_66

23. Velentza, A.-M., Pliasa, S., Fachantidis, N.: Future Teachers choose ideal characteristics for robot peer-tutor in real class environment. In: presented at the International Conference on Technology and Innovation in Learning, Teaching and Education, TECHEDU2020 (2020)

24. Höflich, J.R., El Bayed, A.: Perception, acceptance, and the social construction of robots—exploratory studies. In: Vincent, J., Taipale, S., Sapio, B., Lugano, G., Fortunati, L. (eds.) Social Robots from a Human Perspective, pp. 39–51. Springer, Cham (2015). https://doi.org/ 10.1007/978-3-319-15672-9_4

25. Darriba Frederiks, A., Octavia, J.R., Vandevelde, C., Saldien, J.: Towards participatory design of social robots. In: Lamas, D., Loizides, F., Nacke, L., Petrie, H., Winckler, M., Zaphiris, P. (eds.) INTERACT 2019. LNCS, vol. 11747, pp. 527–535. Springer, Cham (2019). https:// doi.org/10.1007/978-3-030-29384-0_32

26. Pnevmatikos, D., Christodoulou, P., Fachantidis, N.: Designing a socially assistive robot for education through a participatory design approach: Guiding principles for the developers. Int. J. Soc. Robot.

27. Christodoulou, P., Reid, A.A.M., Pnevmatikos, D., del Rio, C.R., Fachantidis, N.: Students participate and evaluate the design and development of a social robot. In: 2020 29th IEEE International Conference on Robot and Human Interactive Communication (RO-MAN), pp. 739–744, August 2020. https://doi.org/10.1109/RO-MAN47096.2020.9223490

Digital Wellbeing

Designing for Self-awareness: Evidence-Based Explorations of Multimodal Stress-Tracking Wearables

Riccardo Chianella[1] ⓘ, Marco Mandolfo[2](✉) ⓘ, Riccardo Lolatto[3] ⓘ,
and Margherita Pillan[1] ⓘ

[1] Department of Design, Politecnico di Milano, Via Durando 38, 20158 Milan, Italy
riccardo.chianella@asp-poli.it, margherita.pillan@polimi.it
[2] Department of Management, Economics and Industrial Engineering, Politecnico di Milano,
Via Lambruschini 4/B, 20156 Milan, Italy
marco.mandolfo@polimi.it
[3] Department of Electronics, Informatics and Bioengineering, Politecnico di Milano, Via Ponzio
34/5, 20133 Milan, Italy
riccardo.lolatto@polimi.it

Abstract. Early wearable devices using multimodal data to promote stress-awareness are emerging on the consumer market. They prove to be effective tools to support users in tracking their daily activities, yet their potential still needs to be further explored. From a user experience design perspective, such wearable devices could help users understand how they feel stress and ultimately shed light on its psychophysiological bases. Based on this rationale, this paper reports the results of evidence-based explorations aimed at formalizing knowledge regarding the use of multimodal stress-tracking wearables. Following a human-centered design process, we design an interactive prototype that tracks two stress-related parameters, namely physiological and perceived stress. We employ a smartwatch to track blood volume pulse and heart rate variability to assess physiological stress, whereas we rely on self-reports gathered through a smartphone to assess perceived stress. We then test the prototype in a controlled setting with 16 end-users. Tests combine qualitative and quantitative research methods, including in-depth interviews, eye-tracking, and surveys encompassing a Kano model-based and AttrakDiff questionnaires. In-depth interviews reveal insights about the type and quantity of information users expect. Ocular scanpaths provide directions to leverage the cognitive effort required by users when interacting with multiple devices. Lastly, evidence from surveys highlights the features and functions that multimodal stress-tracking apps should include. Based on our findings, we create a set of considerations on personal informatics promoting stress awareness from a user experience design perspective. Lastly, we outline future directions for the research design of wearable solutions to promote self-awareness.

Keywords: Stress monitoring · User experience · Personal wellbeing ·
Multimodal research · Interaction design · Evidence-based design

© Springer Nature Switzerland AG 2021
M. Kurosu (Ed.): HCII 2021, LNCS 12763, pp. 357–371, 2021.
https://doi.org/10.1007/978-3-030-78465-2_27

1 Introduction

We live in a world dominated by what Weiser once defined as "calm technology" [1]. We surround ourselves with devices designed to silently keep track of our behavior and to reduce our efforts in continuously interacting with them. Locations, formats or supports do not represent a boundary anymore. It is the rise of ubiquitous computing [2], where computers become core components of everyday objects, from smart home assistants to wearable devices. As the work of computers is receding to the background, collected data is brought to the center of attention of users. Data can generate relevant information which users could never access on their own. The increasingly relevance of data in information consumption led to a whole new class of self-tracking-oriented systems, namely "personal informatics" [3].

Self-tracking covers various domains, spanning from physical and mental health [4], finance [5], productivity [6], to even energy consumption [7]. Self-tracking devices reduce the amount of effort and cognitive load necessary to keep track of personal activities and habits. Self-tracked data often reveals behavioral patterns that may be adjusted or that can stimulate reflection. This holds the potential of creating feedback loops [8]. Varisco provided a framework showing how visualizations of self-tracked data allow people to mirror themselves [9]. Users become more aware of their habits, as they compare self-tracked data with actual events in their lives. This comparison might prompt users to reflect upon the relationship between a quantitative measure and their subjective experiences, thus fostering self-awareness.

Wearable devices have been adopted to raise awareness on users' health [10]. A portion of these systems focuses on measuring stress, a critical element hindering human health and well-being [11]. In fact, stress can have negative effects on the basic dimensions of mental and physical health. For example, uncontrolled stress levels can raise individuals' chance of developing cardiovascular diseases [12]. Moreover, the effects of stress-related well-being issues have an enormous impact on an organizational [13] and societal level [14]. Hence, stress tracking retains the potential of making people better understand their stress levels by increasing self-awareness and foster appropriating coping strategies. Furthermore, stress-tracking devices can help reducing barriers to help seeking. Indeed, even when people are aware of their stress-related issues, support and assistance may not always be easily accessible (e.g., economically, geographically, or socially).

Early wearable devices using multimodal data gathering are emerging on the market [15, 16]. These devices collect data via multiple channels (e.g., physical movements, physiological activations, self-reports) to provide richer information to users about their behavior. To date, prototypes of multimodal wearable devices for stress-tracking have been proposed [17]. However, the potential for these devices to successfully promote awareness must still be released. In fact, given the complexity of the definition, quantification and perception users have about stress, these devices could play a crucial role in connecting correlated information in a more explicit way. Moreover, by providing a more systematic view on the different types of stress, users can prioritize a specific datum and retrieve the information they need. These considerations open up different opportunities to explore how stress-tracking experiences should be designed.

Based on this rationale, this paper reports the results of evidence-based explorations aimed at formalizing knowledge regarding the use of multimodal stress-tracking wearables. With this end, we first design an interactive prototype following a human-centered design process. Our prototype intends to assess stress levels combining physiological activations and self-reports. Next, we test the prototype through a series of exploratory individual tests with end-users. This principle derives from Don Norman's view on user-centered systems design, where the users' feedback is considered as the main driving factor of the design process [18]. In our user tests, we combine qualitative and quantitative research methods, including eye-tracking, surveys, and in-depth interviews. This multimethod research approach aims at supporting awareness and responsibility within the design processes [19]. Lastly, we advance a set of suggestions stemming from evidence-based tests.

2 Designing the Experience

2.1 Design Concept

We followed a mixed design process which was functional to our goal: generate and prototype a set of UX explorations to ultimately discuss with our end-users. To ensure that our explorations reflected the best options of the solution space, we followed the innovation-oriented British Design Council's Double Diamond model [20], which stresses the importance of alternating divergent and convergent phases for developing ideas. In terms of UX methodology we considered Preece, Sharp & Rogers' interaction design process [21], which is built on four pillars: establishing requirements, designing alternatives, prototyping, and evaluating. The prototype was iterated multiple times stepping from a low-fidelity model (paper prototype, wireframe) to a high-fidelity model (final interactive prototype).

The experience was designed for users who are willing to assess their stress levels in relation to two parameters: physiological stress and perceived stress. Indeed, the concept of stress has different exteriorizations, which include neurophysiological and psychological responses [22]. Despite being closely interconnected, evidence shows that these can be measured separately [23]. Given the current state-of-the-art of personal informatics systems operating in the field of mental health awareness, our approach was to differentiate the collection of data depending on each individual type of stress by designing two complementary segments for a single experience.

To quantify physiological stress, we employed a smartwatch able to acquire physiological signals such as blood volume pulse (BVP) and compute the heart rate variability (HRV) during a Sit-To-Stand protocol. As described by Lucini et al. [24] the task consists in a phase of 5 min in which the subject must stay still on a chair followed by a phase of 3 min of active orthostatism, inducing a sympathetic activation easily identifiable in the HRV signal. Therefore, the segment of the experience related to physiological stress measurement was designed to work on a smartwatch. To quantify perceived stress, we considered a device where users could report their answers in a written form. Therefore, we employed a smartphone, due to its greater display. In conclusion, the interactive system was ideated to include two complementary software applications running on two

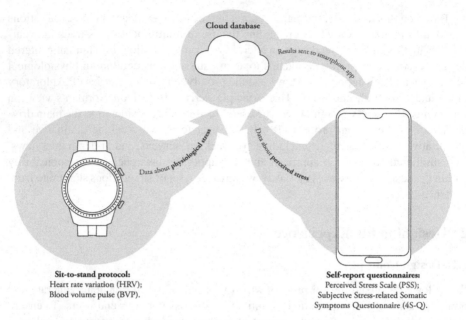

Fig. 1. Multi device system for physiological and perceived stress measurement

different pieces of hardware, namely a smartwatch and a smartphone. A visualization of the interaction between the devices and their respective collected data is visualized in Fig. 1.

2.2 UX Prototyping

Following Buchenau & Suri's view on experience prototyping as an opportunity to understand existing experiences and to explore design ideas [25], we built an interactive prototype to test the impact it would generate on users. The final prototype consisted of a series of interfaces guiding users in measuring the two types of stress, visualizing collected data, comparing results over time, evaluating discrepancies between physiological and perceived stress, and providing links to external sources for stress management. The main steps of the user interface flow are visualized in Fig. 2a and b.

Given our goal to raise our users' self-awareness in relation to their stress levels, stronger attention was given to those segments showing the comparison between perceived and physiological stress. As shown in the last two interfaces of Fig. 2b, the two parameters have always been kept separate, both in the test results and in the stress history sections. To facilitate the comparison, stress parameters from each category were classified on a 0–100% scale, where 0% means "fully relaxed" and 100% means "highly stressed". A color labeling system was implemented to guide the user's understanding of "good" and "bad" results.

All the interfaces were made responsive using Figma [26], a collaborative interface design tool. The system allows the creation of vector-based graphics and the import of additional graphics in various media formats. Most of the interactive elements (buttons, sliders, windows, and toolbars) were prototyped directly on Figma, while illustrations, animations and icons were prototyped using Adobe Illustrator, Adobe Photoshop and Blender. Figma is online and desktop-based, yet it can connect to a device (e.g. smartphone) for testing. Therefore, a mirroring software application, namely "Figma Mirror", was installed in the devices used for the experiment. One of the features of the experience included the temporal evolution of the user's stress results. Since subjects did not have access to the application prior to the experiment, we included a fake data set containing results over 8 weeks before the date of the experiment. Subjects were told about this at the beginning of the experiment, before exploring the applications.

Fig. 2a. Core user interfaces of the smartphone segment, where users can answer self-report questionnaires (PSS and 4S-Q) as well as compare test results.

Fig. 2b. Core user interfaces of the smartwatch segment, where users are guided through a Sit-To-Stand protocol to measure their physiological stress levels.

3   Experience Testing

3.1 Participants

16 subjects took part in individual testing sessions. The average age was 24.4 years old (8 females). We did not filter participants based on a specific profession, background, or information literacy. All subjects owned a smartphone and had basic digital skills.

3.2 Procedure

The user tests took place in a controlled laboratory setting. The test room had as few stimulus-eliciting objects as possible to ensure that subjects could be free from any distraction that could have biased their stress levels. Upon arrival, a laboratory assistant briefed the participants about the objective of the study and written consent was obtained. Subsequently, the test equipment was set up and each subject was invited to sit in front of a desk. Subjects wore a pair of eye-tracking glasses and were guided through the eye-tracking calibration. Next, the prototypes were set up. We simulated the smartwatch by tying a second phone to the subject's wrist. The choice was motivated by the fact that smartwatches available in the market do not support any mirroring application. As visualized in Fig. 3, the device displayed the image of a smartwatch running the interactive prototype. Throughout the whole duration of the experiment, a facilitator was present in the room. The role of the facilitator was to introduce the subject to the experiment, assign him/her a set of tasks to test the prototype, provide technical assistance and lead the semi-structured interview.

The approximate duration of each user test was of 40 min. Each experimental session involved four sequential phases. First, each subject went through a 2-min free exploration phase. Once subjects understood that they could interact with two different prototypes, they were given some time to spontaneously explore them. For this phase of free exploration, they could navigate through the prototypes, yet they were not allowed to start any measurement. Subjects became familiar with the application's main features and with the name of the sections. During this phase, the facilitator remained silent.

Second, the assessment of perceived and physiological stress was carried out. Subjects were given a set of five tasks, each one of them regarding a specific feature. For the whole duration of this phase, the facilitator asked the subject to think out loud. The first task was to *take a stress test* to measure the subject's physiological stress and to *answer a questionnaire* to measure the subject's perceived stress. Subjects were asked to perform both tasks simultaneously. Since physiological stress measurement was performed through a Sit-to-Stand protocol, subjects were asked by the smartwatch application to stand up half-way through the test. In the meantime, they were guided through a section of a PSS and a 4S-Q questionnaires. The facilitator moved onto the next task only after subjects completed the tests and read their results. The second task aimed to *retrieve temporal information about stress levels*. The facilitator asked the subject to indicate the moment in which they were least stressed over the last two months by interacting with one or both the prototypes. No additional information was given, and subjects had to perform the task autonomously. The facilitator moved onto the next task only when the given answer was correct. The third task aimed to *understand the definition of stress*. Subjects were asked to use the applications to learn more about stress, and specifically about perceived and physiological stress. To complete the task, they had to orally report this definition to the facilitator. This allowed us not only to understand whether the section containing this information was easily accessible, but also to assess the quality of the textual information. The facilitator moved onto the next task only after a definition to stress was given. The fourth task aimed to *retrieve external sources for stress management*. The facilitator asked the subjects to interact with the prototypes and report the names of a few stress management applications. Similarly to the previous task, this allowed to understand both the levels of accessibility and comprehensibility of information. The facilitator moved onto the next task only after subjects could read out loud the names of the listed stress management applications. The fifth and last task aimed to *retrieve information about the frequency of the stress tests*. Just for this task, participants were asked to interact only with the smartwatch prototype. This constraint was given to simulate a situation in which users wanted to retrieve the information as quickly as possible, thereby without having to look for their smartphones or go through numerous steps. The facilitator moved onto the next phase only when users reported when the next stress test was scheduled for.

For the last section of the user test, subjects wore the pair of eye-tracking glasses and the wrist-worn device off. Subsequently, they were asked a set of questions by the facilitator. The questions were prepared in advance and their purpose was to guide the conversation as well as to ensure that subjects expressed their view on all the sections of the application. Subjects were asked if they understood the purpose of each task, if the displayed information was accessible (and if they found it clear, misleading, essential or superfluous), if they understood something new about themselves and if they believed that the experience was accurate, trustworthy, and privacy-concerning. Lastly, an interview was carried out followed by two online surveys.

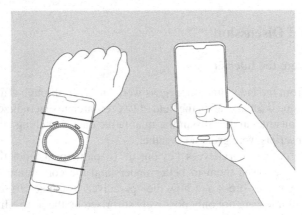

Fig. 3. Right-handed subjects were tied a device running the smartwatch prototype on the left wrist, while they could still interact with the smartphone prototype using either both hands or just their right one.

3.3 Measures

Throughout the experiment, we collected both qualitative and quantitative data through a multimodal approach. Collected data included a transcript of an interview regarding their thoughts on the experience, answers to a pair of digital questionnaires and a video recording of the session.

In UX design, qualitative research methods can help define whether subjects find an experience comprehensive and accessible [27]. If our designed experience met these qualities, subjects would spontaneously start reflecting about their stress-awareness. Therefore, to validate the impact generated by comparing the subject's levels of physiological and perceived stress, we conducted individual semi-structured interviews.

On the other hand, quantitative research methods allow access to more specific information about measurable qualities of an experience [27]. First, we wanted to know whether the experience was able to stimulate interest in the users. We quantified the level of engagement and the usability of the interactive prototype by measuring its hedonic, aesthetic, and pragmatic qualities. To do so, subjects were asked to answer Hassenzahl et al.'s AttrakDiff questionnaire [28] after testing the prototype. The questionnaire asks users to indicate their opinion on the overall system relative to a pair of contrasting adjectives (e.g., technical-human). Once an overall impression was given, we measured how subjects perceived each main function of the experience. Function-specific data was collected by giving an additional questionnaire, namely Kano et al.'s model [29]. This model is used in UX research to classify those features that are perceived as essential for a product to create meaning and those features who are just attractive add-ons. Finally, we wanted to understand whether users could successfully navigate through both prototypes while measuring their perceived and physiological stress simultaneously. Therefore, we measured the subjects' cognitive effort by recording their gaze throughout the whole session with eye-tracking glasses.

4 Results and Discussion

4.1 Findings from the Interviews

The transcripts from the individual interviews were analyzed through affinity diagramming. This technique is often used in the field of UX research to externalize and organize large amounts of unstructured or dissimilar qualitative data. Matching comments from the interview transcripts were grouped together.

Overall, most of the interviewees (15 out of 16 participants) positively reported that the experience allowed them to better understand the correlation between their physiological response to stress and how they perceived it. Quotes from some of our subjects show that they were not only positively surprised by the possibility to compare the two types of stress, but also to have an objective measure to indicate it.

> "Sometimes I feel stressed, but I notice that it's just because I have an upcoming exam to take. My body is healthy, but I tend to overthink and I get worried about being sick. This app could give me an objective perspective, and it could help me chill about it".

> "I know myself. I think I'm already aware of my stress levels. However, I can't quantify this level exactly like this app does. In my opinion, this would be a useful supporting tool".

Interviewees perceived the moment in which they saw the results of the simultaneous measurements as a wake-up call for reflecting about the current state. Some of them even described the application as a powerful tool for working on their own mental health, to the point where "*it could be very helpful for those who are seeing a therapist and want to keep focusing on their stress during their treatment*".

Furthermore, a very important aspect that emerged from the interviews is linked to data privacy. All subjects understood that our proposed system relies on distributed sensing to track data about physiological and perceived stress, and that collected data is then stored and elaborated in a cloud-based database. Regardless of the level of security of the cloud, some concerns about data privacy were raised during the individual interviews. Most smartphone-owners are already aware of the way their phones constantly collect and send data to external databases, especially with applications that can track sports. This was reflected by the answers given by most subjects, who stated that they "*did not care about knowing if this data is shared with a third-party*" since they "*do not find this data sensitive*". However, some of our participants expressly described feeling skeptical about having their stress levels tracked through an app. To quote two of them:

> "*This seems to me like something quite personal. This information is not about a vital parameter, yet it is still extremely personal. This is something more personal than my running time. If someone could get their hands on this data, I feel like they would use it for marketing purposes, and I would feel uncomfortable*".

> "*All I care about is that, regardless of where they are stored, this information would not be shared with people that I know. There, that would irritate me*".

Although subjects who shared this opinion are in a minority (2 out of 16 participants), their perspective is still extremely relevant to the matter. To some users, personal stress levels seem to be considered as sensitive data. This raises some important considerations on the notion of trust.

Overall, we can confirm that our experience successfully managed to generate a feedback loop among all the subjects. As a suggestion for the development systems with the aim of improving the user's self-awareness, we thereby defend that these should:

A. Let users see the results for both stress types together and have a direct comparison.
B. Actively guide users through the measurement, regardless of the type of commitment required by the data collection protocol.
C. Prioritize transparency. The more (relevant) information users see, the more reliable and valuable the experience will feel.
D. Share how data is handled and make sure that users know about their data privacy.

4.2 Findings from the Eye-Tracking Recordings

By observing the videos recorded from the eye-tracking glasses, we also retrieved some useful insights regarding the cognitive effort required by users when measuring the level of both their stress types. Some participants had no issues interacting with both devices or with shifting their attention from one to the other in a relatively short time period. However, other subjects were unable to do so. The most common case was the one in which they did not notice the smartwatch interface telling them to stand up because they were too focused on answering a PSS questionnaire. An example of this can be seen by comparing the two subjects in Fig. 4 and 5.

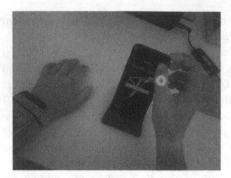 

Fig. 4. Scanpath (2-s interval) from one of the evaluations. This subject noticed the watch telling her to stand up to finish the Sit-To-Stand protocol while answering the PSS questionnaire.

Fig. 5. Scanpath (2-s interval) from one of the evaluations. This subject was so focused answering the PSS questionnaire, he did not notice the watch telling him to stand up to start the second part of the Sit-To-Stand protocol. He only noticed the message once the questionnaire was over.

The scanpaths revealed that not all users were able to follow two applications running on both devices. Hence, we defend that measuring simultaneously both types of stress might lead to a cognitive overload. This should be an important consideration because it introduces the limitation of interacting in a system including distributed sensors. Therefore, systems aiming at raising self-awareness should:

E. Avoid or limit simultaneous interactions with multiple devices.
F. When this cannot be limited, we suggest the implementation of different stimuli, such as haptic or aural stimuli. By associating each stimulus to a certain device, users could be better guided throughout the experience.

4.3 Findings from the Questionnaires

The answers from the questionnaires provided further feedback regarding the experience. Moreover, it contributed to identifying a hierarchy of the most important features that users expect in devices aiming at generating the same feedback loop. Results from the *AttrakDiff* questionnaire are shown in Fig. 6, 7 and 8. These prove that the prototype generated a positive reaction, receiving particularly high scores regarding its pragmatic quality (*PQ*) and attractiveness (*ATT*) (Fig. 7). Overall, the experience is positioned in the "desired" level of perception (Fig. 8). This means that the attributes of the prototype can be considered as a guideline for systems with a similar scope.

Second, results from Kano's model-based questionnaire revealed the importance of each of the complementing features of the system. We performed a discrete analysis with the dataset and thus considered the mode of the subjects' responses. Scores are reported in Table 1. Based on the results, each feature was classified either as *nonsense* (without a purpose), indifferent (feature with a low impact on the overall user experience), *attractive* (the feature was unexpected yet appreciated), *must-be* (this function answers some basic

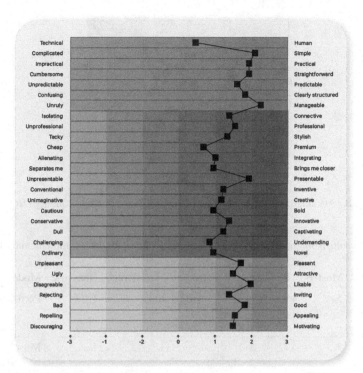

Fig. 6. AttrakDiff questionnaire results. Among the pairs of adjectives subjects were shown to describe the experience, most of them agreed on the words "manageable", "presentable" and "likable".

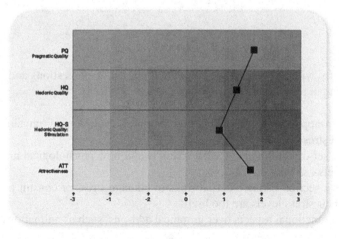

Fig. 7. AttrakDiff results by category.

needs users feel are the minimum requirement to enjoy the experience) and *performance* (core features that directly impact the perceived quality of the experience) [27].

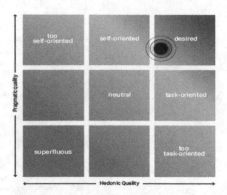

Fig. 8. AttrakDiff results: pragmatic quality (*PQ*) over hedonic quality (*HQ*).

Table 1. Results from the Kano model-based questionnaire for each complementary feature.

	Must-Be	Performance	Attractive	Indifferent	Nonsense	Mode
Temporal evolution of stress	5	9		1	1	Performance
Explanation of stress	7	7			1	Must be/Performance
Stress management sections	2	2	5	4	3	Attractive
Animations and visual effects	2	1	2	11		Indifferent

Consistently with our results, we can enrich our set of suggestions and defend that systems aiming at measuring stress should also:

G. Include in-app sections showing the temporal evolution of physiological and perceived stress.

H. Include a set of definitions of what stress is and how physiological and perceived stress levels can vary.

I. Consider a section listing external links to manage stress or consult professionals in case their stress levels are too high.

J. Prioritize functional aspects over graphical add-ons, such as animations and visual effects.

5 Conclusions and Further Development

Through an evidence-based exploratory test, we were able to gather insights about how users interact with multimodal stress-tracking wearables. Insights about the type and quantity of information users expect to see in the experience were retrieved from qualitative research by directly interviewing the subjects. Moreover, a scanpath analysis through eye-tracking glasses provided directions to leverage the cognitive effort required by users when interacting with multiple devices. Finally, the consideration of the results of two evaluating questionnaires supported the definition of some exemplary user interfaces and generated additional suggestions on the most important functions stress-awareness-rising apps should include.

Our contribution expands how user experience design can be applied to multimodal stress-tracking wearables to eventually promote self-awareness, formalizing the knowledge regarding the use of such devices. Our explorations can thus become a starting point for designing new forms of personal informatics systems based on self-tracking and evidence-based comparisons of personal data. Further developments of this study could investigate how the generation of feedback loops can support psychological therapy. For example, by revealing how stressed users feel over time could help individuate or cope with chronic stress. Therefore, further developments of this study could show how to adopt UX design to support medical services. Moreover, we believe that additional research could address how to create feedback loops around other physiological or psychological responses. For example, similar experiences could increase awareness around hunger or tiredness. By expanding the notion of self-tracking to unexplored fields of human emotions, UX design could become a fundamental pillar among all the existing approaches to self-tracking and ubiquitous computing.

Nonetheless, we must still reflect upon the ethical implications of a dystopian world where humans can self-track everything about themselves. Our study only represents the beginning of a trajectory which is destined to grow, yet it already showed some concerns about data privacy. To this moment, we are unable to predict how dynamics will evolve and what policies will emerge to avoid this, yet we know that as designers we have the possibility to control this. More specifically, UX designers share the power and the responsibility to craft meaningful experiences that should be perceived both as objective and as transparent with their end-users as possible.

The generalizability of these results is subject to certain limitations. First, we acknowledge the limited sample size related to our exploratory study. While qualitative research can ensure the generation of useful insights even with the involvement of only a few subjects, we believe that a natural progression of the work should involve a greater number of participants to advance sound quantitative analyses. Second, we acknowledge that our prototype displayed only fictious physiological data, thus we only simulated the real experience. Accordingly, we cannot rule out that interacting with actual physiological responses may determine a broader spectrum of user responses. For instance, changing breathing patterns to modulate the heart rate may have a direct impact on the physiological measure of stress, which can in turn alter user's stress perceptions. Along this line of thinking, future work may explore real-time interactions between stress measures.

Acknowledgments. This research was developed with the support of Huawei Technologies Co., Ltd. as part of a research project investigating possible stress monitoring techniques. The sponsor did not play any role in the data collection and analysis. Hence, we hereby declare that we have no conflict of interest.

References

1. Weiser, M., Brown, J.S.: Designing calm technology. PowerGrid J. **1**(1), 75–85 (1996)
2. Weiser, M.: The computer for the 21st century. ACM SIGMOBILE Mob. Comput. Commun. Rev. **3**, 3–11 (1999)
3. Li, I., Dey, A., Forlizzi, J.: A stage-based model of personal informatics systems. In: Proceedings of the SIGCHI Conference on Human Factors in Computing Systems, pp. 557–566 (2010)
4. DiClemente, C.C., Marinilli, A.S., Singh, M., Bellino, L.E.: The role of feedback in the process of health behavior change. Am. J. Health Behav. **25**(3), 217–227 (2001)
5. Rapp, A., Cena, F.: Personal informatics for everyday life: How users without prior self-tracking experience engage with personal data. Int. J. Hum. Comput. Stud. **94**, 1–17 (2016)
6. Moore, P., Piwek, L., Roper, I.: The quantified workplace: A study in self-tracking, agility and change management. In: Ajana B. (eds) Self-Tracking. Palgrave Macmillan, Cham (2018).
7. Seligman, C., Darley, J.M.: Feedback as a means of decreasing residential energy consumption. J. Appl. Psychol. **62**(4), 363 (1977)
8. Young, N.: The virtual self: how our digital lives are altering the world around us. McClelland & Stewart Limited (2012)
9. Varisco, L., Colombo, S., Casalegno, F.: Designing with data. Anticipating the impact of personal data usage on individuals and society. In: Advances in Intelligent Systems and Computing, pp. 870–876. Springer (2019)
10. Gastaldi, L., Lettieri, E., Mandolfo, M.: Consumer adoption of digital technologies for lifestyle monitoring. In: 2019 IEEE 23rd International Symposium on Consumer Technologies, pp. 11–16. IEEE (2019)
11. Siirtola, P.: Continuous stress detection using the sensors of commercial smartwatch. In: Adjunct Proceedings of the 2019 ACM International Joint Conference on Pervasive and Ubiquitous Computing and Proceedings of the 2019 ACM International Symposium on Wearable Computers, pp. 1198–1201 (2019)
12. Steptoe, A., Kivimäki, M.: Stress and cardiovascular disease. Nature Rev. Cardiol. **9**, 360–370 (2020)
13. Arroba, T., James, K.: Reducing the cost of stress: an organisational model. Personnel Rev. **19**, 21–27 (1990)
14. Hassard, J., Teoh, K.R.H., Visockaite, G., Dewe, P., Cox, T.: The cost of work-related stress to society: A systematic review. J. Occup. Health Psychol. **23**, 1–17 (2018)
15. Timmons, A.C., Chaspari, T., Han, S.C., Perrone, L., Narayanan, S.S., Margolin, G.: Using multimodal wearable technology to detect conflict among couples. Computer **50**(3), 50–59 (2017)
16. Qi, W., Aliverti, A.: A multimodal wearable system for continuous and real-time breathing pattern monitoring during daily activity. IEEE J. Biomed. Health Inf. **24**(8), 2199–2207 (2019)
17. Indikawati, F.I., Winiarti, S.: Stress detection from multimodal wearable sensor data. In: IOP Conference Series: Materials Science and Engineering, vol. 771, p. 012028 (2020).
18. Pea, R.D.: User centered system design: new perspectives on human-computer interaction. J. Educ. Comput. Res. **3**(1), 129–134 (1987)

19. Mandolfo, M., Pavlovic, M., Pillan, M., Lamberti, L.: Ambient UX research: user experience investigation through multimodal quadrangulation. In: Streitz, N., Konomi, S. (eds.) HCII 2020. LNCS, vol. 12203, pp. 305–321. Springer, Cham (2020). https://doi.org/10.1007/978-3-030-50344-4_22
20. Design Council: The Design Process: The 'double diamond' design process model (2005)
21. Preece, J., Sharp, H., Rogers, Y.: Interaction Design: Beyond Human-Computer Interaction. Wiley (2015)
22. Ursin, H., Eriksen, H.R.: The cognitive activation theory of stress. Psychoneuroendocrinology **29**(5), 567–592 (2004)
23. Brosschot, J.F., Pieper, S., Thayer, J.F.: Expanding stress theory: prolonged activation and perseverative cognition. Psychoneuroendocrinology **30**(10), 1043–1049 (2005)
24. Lucini, D., Norbiato, G., Clerici, M., Pagani, M.: Hemodynamic and autonomic adjustments to real life stress conditions in humans. Hypertension **39**(1), 184–188 (2002)
25. Buchenau, M., Suri, J. F.: Experience prototyping. In: Proceedings of the 3rd conference on Designing interactive systems: processes, practices, methods, and techniques, pp. 424–433 (2000).
26. Figma. https://www.figma.com. Accessed 11 Feb 2021
27. Nunnally, B., Farkas, D.: UX Research: PRACTICAL Techniques for Designing Better Products. O'Reilly (2016)
28. Hassenzahl, M., Platz, A., Burmester, M. Lehner, K.: Hedonic and ergonomic quality aspects determine a software's appeal. In: Proceedings of the CHI 2000 Conference on Human Factors in Computing, pp. 201–208 (2000)
29. Kano, N., Nobuhiku, S., Fumio, T., Shinichi, T.: Attractive quality and must-be quality. J. Japanese Soc. Q. Control **14**(2), 39–48 (1984)

Annoyed to Discontinue: Factors Influencing (Dis)Continuance of Using Activity Tracking Wearables

Kaja J. Fietkiewicz[(✉)] and Aylin Ilhan

Heinrich Heine University, Universitätsstr. 1, 40225 Düsseldorf, Germany
{kaja.fietkiewicz,aylin.ilhan}@hhu.de

Abstract. What influences the continued usage of activity tracking wearables? Several studies investigated the acceptance of activity tracking technologies, but the reasons for a continued usage or abandonment of this technology are rarely addressed. This study is focusing on current and former users of activity tracking wearables and their different perceptions of the technology. For this purpose, an online survey was conducted and a convenience sample of 235 valid cases was obtained. Factors potentially influencing the continued usage included age, gender, community feeling, motivation, design, or perceived data sensitivity.

Keywords: Activity tracking wearables · Abandonment · Continuance · Discontinuance

1 Introduction

The technological development and digitization overtake all spheres of our lives. The shift towards increased application of digital goods and services, including the wellness and healthcare domain, appears omnipresent. The COVID-19 pandemic seems to have accelerated the acceptance and implementation of digital and mobile alternatives. Due to lockdowns and social distancing regulations, it became somewhat encouraged to switch from cash to mobile payment methods, from personal meetings to virtual conferences, and from social meetups in person to conversations through instant messaging and other mobile apps. According to IDC [1], "the spread of COVID-19 also had adverse effects on the supply of smart and basic watches […]" and further "given the hyper focus on overall health and fitness in today's climate, vendors would do well to […] provide guidance on how to live healthier lives." Because of the pandemic, many people needed to stay at home and, consequently, remain seated for a prolonged period of time. The World Health Organization (WHO) warned about the negative effects of such sedentary daily routine and encouraged everyone to implement at least some physical activity and exercises at home (#HealthAtHome[1]). Indeed, the providers of different fitness tracking applications saw the opportunity for growth. For many fitness applications, extended free

---

[1] https://www.who.int/news-room/campaigns/connecting-the-world-to-combat-coronavirus/healthyathome/healthyathome---physical-activity.

© Springer Nature Switzerland AG 2021
M. Kurosu (Ed.): HCII 2021, LNCS 12763, pp. 372–389, 2021.
https://doi.org/10.1007/978-3-030-78465-2_28

trials have been offered, whereas many gyms needed to close and started offering online courses for home workouts instead.[2] Even if the sales of activity tracking technologies steadily increase [1–3], only time will tell if this trend will maintain after the pandemic. Furthermore, an increased usage of fitness applications does not necessarily go with increased acceptance and adoption of activity tracking wearables like fitness wristbands.

The term activity tracking technologies (ATTs) refers to smart watches (e.g., Apple Watch, Samsung Gear), fitness trackers (e.g., Fitbit, Garmin, Xiaomi) as well as mobile applications (e.g., Strava, DownDog). These ATTs do not only track the vitals but can send different reminders and be a constant motivator for the users to stand up and move, or to take a mindful moment. In this study, however, we focus on the activity tracking wearables, including smart watches and fitness trackers.

ATTs were investigated for some time now, however, most studies focused on the accuracy of the trackers (see, e.g., [4, 5]) or usability, engagement, adoption, and acceptance (see, e.g., [6–12]). According to Shin et al. [13], who conducted a systematic literature review from 2013 until 2017, the number of studies on activity tracking technologies increased over the last years. Some studies investigated why and to what extent users of these technologies engage, adapt and use the devices [7, 8, 10–12]. Even if there is a trend of fitness tracking wearables' adoption and increased number of investigations on activity tracking technologies, one critical question remains open: Does this lead to a sustainable and continuous usage?

The adoption of a new trend (adoption being the first step before continued usage of ICT [14]), can be influenced by many different factors. It might be based on a genuine interest or gained benefits, but also on social pressure or the need to belong [15]. Even though the usage might bear many benefits, sometimes some (partially unforeseen) risks can arise. Users of fitness tracking wearables often apply the new technology even when having concerns about privacy risks [15]. This seemingly contradictory behavior might be attributed to the so-called privacy paradox [16–18]. In order to profit from the fitness and health benefits coming from the new technology, users need to wear it regularly and face the potential challenges and privacy threats [15]. Activity- and health-related data might give the consumer more power to control, monitor, analyze and improve his or her health, fitness and/or physique. Still, different privacy risks arise and lead to concerns regarding adoption or continued usage [15, 19, 20]. Lidynia, Schomakers, and Ziefle [20] identified several privacy and data security barriers. For example, the non-users of their study were somewhat more concerned than the active users of fitness tracking applications about data misuse, forwarding data to third parties, or not having any control over own data [20].

Activity tracking wearables are quite a new trend predominantly used for leisure [20], which might lead to somewhat different factors influencing the adoption, use, and especially, its continuance [21]. Apparently about half of the consumers abandon their wearables within the first six months after adoption [21–24]. This would indicate that the usage of ATTs is not sustainable, at least when it comes to wearables. It seems that at some point this, sometimes expensive, tool is either not needed anymore, or its usage becomes unprofitable. Even though the abandonment of information systems within the domain of health is nothing new, there are only few studies investigating the factors

---

[2] https://www.mobihealthnews.com/news/europe/fitness-goes-digital-during-covid-19-crisis.

behind it, even less focusing on ATTs in the consumer context [25, 26]. Prior studies mainly address factors that drive users to adopt a new wearable, rather than the ones influencing them to continue the usage. However, the true success of Information and Communication Technology (ICT) is more dependent on the users' continued usage [27–29].

This study will draw on the insights of several investigations and expand them by looking at further challenges for continued usage of wearable ATTs. As the next paragraphs will demonstrate, there are already few studies that investigated, e.g., older adults' adoption and usage behavior [30], where apart from traditional acceptance models, aspects such as design, community, and self-efficacy were given attention. Meyer et al. [31] identified a total of six different usage patterns for activity tracker users, whereas Hermsen et al. [32] identified age and user experience as factors contributing to a sustained use of this technology. The next sections will give an overview of the existing theories and models for investigation of ICT or Information System (IS) adoption and usage, followed by a short overview of theories and studies specifically addressing the activity tracking wearables. This investigation contributes to previous research in several ways. The theoretical contribution lies in the extension of commonly applied factors seen as contributors to prolonged usage of ICT, here, specifically fitted to the activity tracking wearables domain. These theoretical implications are gained from the study's empirical contribution. For the investigation, a unique data set was collected through an online survey of current as well as former users of ATTs.

2   Theoretical Background

2.1   Adoption and Continued Usage of ICT

Beyond the domain of activity tracking technology, there is a vast research on factors influencing adoption and usage of ICT. By now, there are several established models and theories applied to investigate this human-computer interaction (HCI) domain. One example is the Technology Acceptance Model (TAM, [33]), which considers why and how people accept and use a particular technological innovation [21], and which was further extended to TAM2 [34] and TAM3 [35]. The Unified Theory of Acceptance and Use of Technology (UTAUT, [36]) focuses on individual users and the adoption and usage of ICT in the workplace. UTAUT was further adjusted for the consumer context into UTAUT2 [37]. In the UTAUT2 proposed by Venkatesh et al. [37], incorporated were three additional constructs: hedonic motivation (e.g., enjoyment [38–42]), price value (e.g., higher costs can influence consumer adoption decision), and habit [37]. This shows that the newer models do not investigate perceived usefulness and technical understanding alone, but incorporate further aspects directly influencing users' motivation.

The adoption of ICT is only the first step towards the technology's success, which can be measured based on the post-implementation user behavior, also called post-adoption [29, 43, 44]. How can this post-adoption user behavior be described? According to Limayem [29], "[u]nlike the initial adoption decision, continuance is not a one-time event, but may better be envisioned as the result of a series of individual decisions to continue using a particular IS, thereby reflecting its longitudinal nature. The decisions to continue to use an IS follow an initial adoption decision. As the same decision is made repeatedly in response to the same recurring situation, IS continuance behavior tends to take on an increasingly habitualized (automatic) nature [45], [which] ends with the users' final decision to discontinue [27]". In the case of ATTs, this could indicate that the wearables might be perceived as useful to become physically more active and/or to change some health-related routines. In this case, the wearable is more of a facilitator (means to an end), rather than primary motivator for the behavior change [46]. Therefore, the question arises whether the decision to discontinue appears once the "new" behavior has been habitualized.

Apart from the intended behavior change, which factors might influence the adoption and continued usage of ICT? Some of the frequently mentioned aspects are the utilitarian benefits, hedonic needs such as fun, excitement and pleasure, as well as the feeling of being in control [21, 47–50]. All these beneficial factors need to be weighed against costs and possible efforts [21, 36, 37, 51]. Another important notion is the one that with regular and frequent application of ICT, the user behavior becomes habitual or automatic over time [29]. The creation of habit through motivating nudges can be supported by implementation of gamification elements, which are quite popular within fitness tracking applications (such as step challenges, leaderboards, or collection of badges) [52]. Hong et al. [28] compared the explanatory power of different models (ECM-IT by Bhattacherjee [27], TAM by Davis [33] and a hybrid ECM-IT comprised of the prior two model) in order to find the one most effective in predicting users' continued usage behavior. The factors that were worked out included perceived ease of use, perceived usefulness, confirmation, and satisfaction.

2.2 Adoption, Continued and Discontinued Usage of Fitness Tracking Wearables

What are the factors influencing adoption and usage of fitness tracking technology in particular? In their study, Meyer et al. [31] identified and classified several patterns of activity tracker use such as try-and-drop, slow-starter, experimenter, hop-on hop-off, intermittent and power user. Such differentiation can support successful design of effective technology and long-term health applications. Even though the most common use for activity trackers is usually a behavior change intervention, the potential of behavior change based on a long-term use is receiving more and more attention [31]. This can be attributed to the fact that in the long term not the thoughts about the behavior are driving the decision to continue but, e.g., the improved physical health [31]. Hermsen et al. [32] confirmed earlier findings that habitual use of an activity tracker tends to decline at a slow exponential pace. Most users of activity trackers in their study continued to use them for at least half a year and around 12% still used it after 300 days. The predictors for a sustained use were the age of the participant and user experience [32]. Karapanos et al. [53] differentiated between purposive (with a specific motivational goal) and explorative (not seeking any particular information or feedback) users, and emphasize the importance of self-set goals prior to the usage of an activity tracker. Explorative users might get discouraged from using a tracker if the feedback they receive is not what they have expected, so that the initial experience turns out to be negative. For example, learning that one does not walk enough, but not receiving any feedback on how to change this status quo, might constitute a barrier to adoption of the tracker. On the other hand, a purposive user intentionally searching for this kind of information, will not be discouraged by such feedback [53].

According to Pfeiffer et al. [54], the strongest drivers for the intention to use activity tracking technologies include the perceived usefulness, perceived enjoyment, social influence, trust, personal innovativeness, and perceived support of well-being. In the context of activity tracking, the users' trust plays a very crucial role since the usage usually involves collection and analysis of personal data. The aspect of trust might be particularly important in the pre-adoption phase [54]. However, the adoption and continued (or discontinued) usage of fitness tracking wearables could be influenced by different factors. Some of them are user-specific personal factors, which influence the consumer behavior and include not only personal characteristics (like age or gender), but also experience with the technology [21, 36, 37, 55, 56]. Many models explain technology adoption in the customer context, however, to better understand the adoption of activity trackers, also the technology-specific characteristics need to be accounted for. These can include "the demand for data security, an aesthetic appearance of the device as well as the specific intended purpose for the usage of such devices" [54].

Lidynia et al. [20] found out that one motivation to use ATTs was the possibility to improve or maintain well-being, to stick to routines, and to achieve goals faster (which might indicate higher task-orientation). This would mean that ATTs are used for specific goals such as being physically more active and maintaining this habit. Regarding the influence of the goal-setting and initial motivation to adopt the technology, Canhoto et al. [21] explained that "general fitness goals (e.g. moving more) was associated with sustained and stable use," "specific fitness goals (e.g. prepare for marathon) [...] with loyalty but changing patterns of use," and "nutrition related goals (e.g. lose weight) was associated with product switching and irregular use." Hermsen [32] also mentions goal-related factors as being influential to sustained usage. Frie et al. [70] investigated patterns in behavior of people before they stopped tracking their weight. Apparently, their physical activity (monitoring) frequency declined and their weight increased, which is "suggesting that declining motivation for weight control and difficulties with making use of negative weight feedback might explain why people stop tracking their weight. The increase in daily steps but decrease in physical activity tracking frequency post-stop might result from selective measurement of more active days" [70].

Even when the consumers are interested in the technology, studies have shown that the duration of use remains limited to less than a year [20], sometimes the abandonment occurs after only few weeks [69]. Lidynia et al. [20] explain that some arguments for abandonment might be the "mismatch in expectation [...], a change in health status that no longer necessitates the use, as well as technology complexity or failure."

Previous research investigated diverse factors as possible contributors to continued usage of tracking technology. In the focus of this study are the user's age, gender, social influence, design and privacy perception, all addressed in more detail in the following.

Age. According to Hermsen [32], one of the most important determinants for sustained use of ATTs is the user's age. Investigations of age-related factors showed that younger users are in general more willing to embrace innovation, they tend to be more task-oriented as well as more susceptible to peer influence [21, 36, 57, 58]. Several studies focused on older adults and their intention to use ATTs [30, 59, 60]. The investigation by Lee, Xie et al. [30] showed that older participants recognized several benefits of the technology, e.g., seeing health information, managing own health, but the actual use of the provided information decreased over weeks and so did the application of ATTs during exercise. One of the mentioned reasons for this development was the aspect of novelty. Furthermore, the studies by Lee, Ajisafe, et al. [59] and Lee, Xie, et al. [30], indicated that the perceived benefits, such as informativeness, decreased over time.

Gender. Another factor influencing adoption and usage of a new technology is gender. Even though some studies indicated that men are usually more willing to embrace new technology than women [61], or that there is a gender-dependent difference in choosing utilitarian or hedonic features [36], Canhoto and Arp [21, 36] could not detect any noticeable differences in terms of actual products used by each gender. The authors elaborated that gender might not play as significant role in the use of technology as previously thought.

Social Influence. Further contributing factors are social influence and community. With "social influence" meant is the consumer's perception of how important his/her adoption and usage of new technology is to others (e.g., family and friends) [37], or "the extent to which consumers perceive that important others (e.g., family and friends) believe they should use a particular technology" [64]. The so-called "social context" shows what is acceptable in a particular social system [21, 62]. Regarding the aspect of "community," Canhuto et al. [21] indicated that for many users factors like fun and enjoyable experience were important, and could be achieved "through the community of users around the application or device". Furthermore, Clawson et al. [26] show the importance of community proceeding from theories on health behavior change. For example, "a health tracker can enable interpersonal interactions to facilitate observational learning" (Social Cognitive Theory) [26, 63]. Canhoto and Arp [21] made a recommendation for product manufacturers by indicating the importance of an easy way to share users' activities within the relevant communities. Finally, consumer technology might "be regarded as a symbol for fashion and wealth [...]. Individuals therefore adopt the technology to increase their self-importance" [64].

Privacy. Lidynia et al. [20] conducted a study with 166 participants from Germany and compared users and non-users of fitness tracking wearables and applications in order to analyze chances and barriers to adoption of this technology. The investigated barriers included privacy and security concerns. In result, even though the technology is met with approval, one of the biggest barriers is the concern for one's privacy, since the collected data is perceived as rather sensitive [20]. The perceived sensitivity of collected data, however, does not necessarily influence the willingness to adopt and use the technology [15]. At first sight, the voices in the literature seems to be divided—privacy and data security are a prominent concern of the (potential) users [65, 66], but it does not seem to be an ultimate barrier to adoption. The concerns include "the lack of transparency about how personal information will be used, and the uncertainty about which other third parties data might be transferred to" [21, 67]. Stock et al. [68] postulated that the "perceived privacy risk" has a negative influence on behavioral intention to use activity trackers, however, no significant influence could be confirmed. The authors concluded that it is not necessary to address consumers' potential negative perception of data privacy risks, and instead the hedonic benefits of the devices should be more emphasized [68]. This discrepancy between the data privacy concern and actual user behavior can be explained with the so-called privacy paradox [16, 18]. Vital et al. [66] explain that even when users engage in privacy-protective behaviors, they see them as likely insufficient (and the privacy violations as inevitable).

Design. As in any other application and ICT, the user experience (UX) is a very important factor deciding about the products' success, also for fitness tracking technology [30, 32]. It is critical to design the ATTs in a way that helps users to "interpret, understand, gain motivation and act on their data" [69]. In contrast to a mobile application, wearables are an object worn on the body (usually wrist) and is visible to others. Canhoto et al. [21] stress the importance of "designing distinctive devices that consumers feel proud to wear, and which are also ergonomic and comfortable, so that the consumers do not feel compelled to take it off." Pfeiffer et al. [54] did not identify perceived aesthetics as an influential factor for adoption of the technology.

Further Factors. There are studies implicating different correlations between the usage of a fitness tracking wearable and of an app. According to Lidynia [20], for their participants "there was not a clear separation between health and fitness devices and applications," and the use of a wearable "changes the perception and intention to use a fitness app" [20]. According to Canhoto and Arp [21], both are perceived as part of an ecosystem helping them to achieve a goal. Canhoto and Arp [21] emphasize the importance of data accuracy and usefulness, since their interviewees "valued infrastructure that enable wearables to capture data anywhere and anytime and facilitate data aggregation." All in all, previous studies focused on mainly interviewing and/or investigating users of activity technology and their intentions to potentially discontinue the use of tracking technology. This study makes use of data sample of users and former users of activity trackers.

2.3 Research Questions

Based on the insights gathered from the literature review on factors influencing the adoption and continued use of ICT, we formulated research questions for the current study. The study aims at answering what are the differences between current and former users of activity tracking wearables, in order to identify possible factors influencing sustained or continuous use of ATT. Here, we first focus on personal characteristics of the users like age, gender, origin, and fitness routine: (**RQ1**) What are the differences between the two groups regarding personal characteristics, e.g., age, fitness routine or origin? Subsequently, we focus on factors related to the technology, like data accuracy, privacy concerns, design or factors related to its usage, like community: (**RQ2**) What are the differences between these two groups regarding the perception of wearables (e.g., design)?

3   Methods

3.1   Survey Structure

The conducted online survey included different blocks of questions. After asking about usage of fitness tracking application and wearable (yes, no, not anymore), the fitness and activity levels of the participants (active daily routine vs. sedentary routine; exercising daily vs. not exercising at all), the survey included several questions about chances and barriers to adoption of wearables investigated by Lidynia et al. [19], which are factors such as design ('Have an unappealing design', is too expensive), privacy concerns and perceived sensitivity of information, or motivation. Finally, socio-demographic data (age, gender, origin) was collected.

3.2   Data Collection

This investigation is part of a bigger research investigation on fitness tracking applications and wearables with focus on data privacy and sensitivity as influential factor [15]. The data collection included users, non-users, and former users of fitness/activity tracking wearables and mobile applications. For this investigation, the focus is set on current and former users of wearables to better understand and detect possible reasons that impact sustainable continuance of usage. This survey was conducted from February 26, 2019, until May 28, 2019. We did a convenience sample as it is not possible to reach out to all former users as well as current users of wearables. We distributed the survey within health- and fitness-related Facebook groups and other social media channels. Based on author's language skills the survey was available in English, German and Polish. Overall, the sample includes 235 valid respondents (see Table 2).

3.3   Data Preparation and Analysis

For the data analysis we used SPSS Statistics 26. Among active users (continuing to use wearables) excluded were participants who used the wearable for less than a year (the avg. duration of wearable usage by former users were several months; "at least 1 year" makes the sample comparable, since the active users apparently overcame the threshold of several months). Furthermore, previous research showed that users abandon wearables (and often the applications) between 2 weeks to 6 months after the initial adoption.

Regarding the age of the participants, for further analysis a categorization into four generations, based on research on inter-generational differences in digital media usage [71], was conducted. The four generations include: Silver Surfers (at least 60 years old), Gen X (40–59 years old), Gen Y (between 24 and 39 years old), and finally, Gen Z (up to 23 years old). As for this sample, the biggest age group is Gen Y (63.5%) and Gen X (21%).

In order to investigate the influence of perceived data sensitivity, three different user groups were estimated based on perceived sensitivity of data pieces (several types of data pieces collected by ATT, like burned calories, gender, weight, steps, or GPS) similarly to [15]. For this purpose a k-means cluster analysis (k = 3) was conducted, which yield the clusters CL1 (n = 35; most data pieces perceived as "very sensitive", therefore the

Table 1. List of variables used for the investigation.

Variable	Description
APP	Usage of activity tracking application
WEARABLE	Usage of activity tracking wearable
ACTIVITY_LV	Non-exercise activity ("not active" to "very active")
FITNESS_LV	Exercise activity ("never" to "every day")
DUMMY_SILVER	Dummy variable for "Silver Surfers"
DUMMY_GENX	Dummy variable for "Gen X"
DUMMY_GENY	Dummy variable for "Gen Y"
DUMMY_GENZ	Dummy variable for "Gen Z"
DUMMY_USA	Participants from the USA
DUMMY_EU	Participants from Europe
DUMMY_CONCERNED	Dummy variables for three user types estimated based on their perceived sensitivity of data pieces collected by activity tracking technology (clusters 1–3)
DUMMY_NEUTRAL	
DUMMY_UNCONCERNED	
DUMMY_FEMALE	Dummy variable for gender
FUN*	Activity tracking wearables make exercising more fun
ANNOYING*	Activity tracking wearables are annoying in day to day life
DISTRACTION*	Activity tracking wearables are too much distraction (e.g. at work)
ACCURATE*	Activity tracking wearables make the measured data more accurate
SENSITIVE_DATA*	Activity tracking wearables collect data that is much more sensitive
USEFUL_FUNCT*	Activity tracking wearables have useful additional functions
DATA_SECURITY*	Activity tracking wearables make me more concerned about data security
MOTIVATION*	Activity tracking wearables are a better motivation (due to instant feedback and reminders)
TECH_SURVEIL*	Activity tracking wearables lead to too much technical surveillance
BETTER_CONTROL*	Activity tracking wearables give me better control over health
EXPENSIVE*	Activity tracking wearables are too expensive
STATUS_SYMBOL*	Activity tracking wearables are a status symbol
UNAPPEALING*	Activity tracking wearables have an unappealing design

(*continued*)

Table 1. (*continued*)

Variable	Description
COMMUNITY*	Activity tracking wearables make me feel included in the fitness community

* These variables regard participants' agreement with statements about wearables (5-point Likert scale, "strongly disagree" to "strongly agree").

user group was defined as "concerned"), CL2 (n = 82 most data pieces perceived as "sensitive" or "neutral", hence, the user group was defined as "neutral") and CL3 (n = 28 most data pieces perceived as "natural" or "not sensitive", hence, the user group was defined as "unconcerned"). All variables included in the investigation are listed in Table 1 with the respective description.

For the final analysis, the Person's Chi-squared test for personal characteristics described with nominal or ordinal variables and Mann-Whitney U Test for technology-related perception and ordinal variables were applied.

4 Results

In total 621 participants completed the online survey, however, only 294 were currently using an activity tracking wearable, whereas 43 were former users of such a device. For the investigation only participants who continued the usage for at least one year were included for further investigation. Only participants from the EU and USA were included. These restrictions led to the final sample of N = 235. Table 2 shows the description of the collected data.

To answer the first research question (RQ1), what are the differences between current and former users of activity tracking wearables, with focus on personal characteristics (e.g., age, fitness routine or origin), Person's Chi-squared test was conducted. Table 3 shows the results in a cross table. When considering our sample and the usage of fitness tracking applications, more than half of the users who discontinued using a wearable also discontinued using the fitness tracking application (n = 22, 51.2%). Still, over 30% continued to use the application (n = 15, 24.9%). Interestingly, 6 participants claimed not to be using an application, even though they have been using a wearable (this could be either a mistake in survey completion or they did not see the necessity of actively using an app). Related to this "inconsistency", within the sample of participants who continued the usage of wearables, 4.2% (n = 2) claim not to use an app, and another 4.2% not to use it anymore. Here, again the question arises whether they completed the survey incorrectly or do not see the necessity of a fitness tracking application. Still, there is a significant difference between the participants who continued and the ones who discontinued the usage of wearables ($X^2(2) = 80.367$, Phi = 0.585, p < .001), since most people abandoning wearables also discontinue using the application, whereas active wearable users still apply it.

Another significant difference within our sample could be detected between the different generations ($X^2(3) = 18.609$, Phi = 0.283, p < .001). The results, however,

Table 2. Description of collected data sample (N = 235).

Application	Yes	191 (81.3%)
	No	13 (6%)
	Not anymore	30 (12.8%)
Wearable	Usage > 1 year	192 (81.7%)
	Discontinued	43 (18.3%)
Avg. usage duration before discontinuance		3 ("several months")
Gender	Female	127 (54%)
	Male	107 (45.5%)
Origin	Europe	148 (63%)
	USA	68 (28.9%)
Generations	Silver Surfer	16 (6.8%)
	Gen X	75 (31.9%)
	Gen Y	126 (53.6%)
	Gen Z	16 (6.8%)
Avg. activity level		3 "moderately active"
Avg. fitness level		6 "exercising 3 or more times per week"

need to be interpreted cautiously, because the sample is quite small (especially for the oldest, Silver Surfers, and the youngest, Gen Z, user groups). The results indicate that the older generations are more likely to continue the usage of wearable devices, since within our sample 93.8% of Silver Surfers, 85.3% of Gen X and 84.1% of Gen Y continued the usage for at least a year. In contrast, only 43.8% of this sample's Gen Z continued using the wearable.

The final significant differences are given between the different everyday activity types that the participants demonstrate ($X^2(2) = 8.638$, Phi = 0.192, p = .013). With daily "activity" meant is sedentary vs. active lifestyle during the day (e.g., office/desk job or one requiring more mobility), which is not related to a fitness or exercising routine. Here, over 90% of participants with "active" lifestyle continued to use the wearable after 1 year. Considering the "moderately" active and the "barely moving" participants, around 75% within both groups continued the usage of the wearable. Finally, there were no significant differences between the different fitness types (fitness or exercising routine), the perceived sensitivity of fitness tracking data by the participants, or the origin of the users (Table 3).

To answer the RQ2 focusing on the technology, a Mann-Whitney U Test was conducted. Table 4 shows the results of the U Test between users who continued and the ones who discontinued usage of fitness tracking wearables. The dependent variables are several statements about wearables as explained in methods section. The statements were valued on a 5-point Likert scale. Interestingly most of the differences are significant. There were no significant differences in the distribution of the answers for the statements about the accuracy and sensitivity of collected data (both groups rather agree), the questionable data security (both groups have a neutral perception), and the statement about wearables being a status symbol (here, again, both groups have a "neutral" perception). The participants who continued using the wearable find them to be fun and to have useful functions, to be motivating and giving them a better control over their health. In contrast to users who discontinued the usage, they do not agree that wearables are annoying, a distraction in everyday life and have an unappealing design. They are also more neutral than users who abandoned the wearables regarding the fear of technical surveillance and the costs of the technology ("too expensive").

Table 3. Results of the Person's Chi-squared test (personal characteristics x continued use of wearables).

		Discontinued	Continued	Significance tests
Using application	No	6 (14%)	8 (4.2%)	$X^2(2) = 80.367, p < .001$
	Yes	15 (34.9%)	176 (91.7%)	Phi $= 0.585, p < .001$
	Not anymore	22 (51.2%)	8 (4.2%)	
Generations	Silver surfers	1 (6.3%)	15 (93.8%)	$X^2(3) = 18.609, p < .001$
	Gen X	11 (14.7%)	64 (85.3%)	Phi $= 0.283, p < .001$
	Gen Y	20 (15.9%)	106 (84.1%)	
	Gen Z	9 (56.3%)	7 (43.8%)	
Activity type	Barely moving	13 (24.1%)	41 (75.9%)	$X^2(2) = 8.638, p = .013$
	Moderate	22 (24.2%)	69 (75.8%)	Phi $= 0.192, p = .013$
	Active	8 (8.9%)	82 (91.1%)	
Fitness type	Not very active	4 (26.7%)	11 (5.9%)	$X^2(2) = 1.053, p = .591$
	Moderate	2 (13.3%)	12 (7.0%)	Phi $= .068, p = .591$
	Active	34 (17.3%)	163 (87.2%)	
Perceived data sensitivity	Concerned	12 (34.3%)	23 (65.7%)	$X^2(2) = 3.981, p = .137$
	Neutral	17 (20.7%)	65 (79.3%)	Phi $= 0.166, p = .137$
	Unconcerned	4 (14.3%)	24 (85.7%)	
Gender	Male	19 (44.2%)	88 (46.1%)	$X^2(2) = 0.050, p = .822$
	Female	24 (55.8%)	103 (53.9%)	Phi $= -.015, p = .822$

Table 4. Results of Mann-Whitney U Test (technology-related features and perceptions); measured on a 5-point Likert scale.

	Discontinued usage (median)	Continued usage (median)	Test statistics
FUN	4	4	U $= 2627.500$ p $= .003$
ANNOYING	3	2	U $= 1743.500$ p $< .001$
DISTRACTION	3	2	U $= 2145.000$ p $< .001$
ACCURATE	4	4	U $= 3008.000$ p $= .072$

(continued)

Table 4. (*continued*)

	Discontinued usage (median)	Continued usage (median)	Test statistics
SENSITIVE_DATA	4	4	U = 3415.000 p = .533
USEFUL_FUNCT	4	4	U = 2276.500 p = .001
DATA_SECURITY	3	3	U = 2965.000 p = .169
MOTIVATION	4	4	U = 2909.000 p = .006
TECH_SURVEIL	4	3	U = 2186.500 p < .001
BETTER_CONTROL	4	4	U = 2713.500 p = .001
EXPENSIVE	4	3	U = 2716.000 p = .005
STATUS_SYMBOL	3	3	U = 3386.500 p = .264
UNAPPEALING	3	2	U = 2501.500 p < .001
COMMUNITY	3	3	U = 3138.500 p = .071

5 Discussion

What are the differences between current and former users of activity tracking wearables? First, we focused on personal characteristics that went beyond age and gender. We included activity type in everyday life (sedentary vs. active daily routine), fitness type (regular exercise vs. no exercise), the simultaneous use of fitness tracking activity application and perception of data sensitivity. We could confirm that age appears to be an influencing factor, whereas gender (as confirmed by previous research does not). Interestingly, the activity type had a significant influence in contrast to the fitness activity type. This would indicate that these two characteristics need to be investigated separately in the future. Finally, there was a correlation between usage of the wearable and an application. There appear to be no significant influences of the users' perception of data sensitivity (this could again indicate the privacy paradox; however, this investigation did not include non-users who might have higher data privacy concerns preventing them to adopt the technology in the first place).

Secondly, we turned to technology-related perceptions of the former and current users. There appear to be several significant factors differentiating users who continue the usage of wearables. The positive factors included fun, data accuracy, additional useful functions provided by the wearable, motivating effect of the wearable, and better control over one's health and fitness. Interestingly, there were no significant differences regarding the community feeling or seeing the wearable as a status symbol. Regarding the negative factors or barriers, the significant differences were given for annoyance, distraction, feeling of increased technical surveillance, the high costs of the wearable (too expensive), and unappealing design. This indicates again that data security or privacy related concerns do not seem to distinguish users who abandoned the wearable and the ones who continued to use it for at least one year. It appears that users abandoning the technology see some functionalities as annoying and distracting or leading to technological surveillance. In contrast, users not abandoning the technology see the functionality of a wearable as a useful addition, giving them more control over their health and fitness as well as motivating them.

6 Conclusion and Limitations

Based on previous studies, the discontinued usage of wearables might be influenced by achieving a habitualized behavior and the desired goals (especially for more task-oriented users). The questions for future investigations are: What happens after the behavior has been habitualized? It is interesting to investigate the changes in behavioral patterns after reaching a specific goal—why would consumers still be using wearables and applications? What features could influence their willingness to continue the usage for task-oriented people? As the investigation showed, the participants were already moderately active. This means that the wearables' use might support being more active or at least to maintain their activity level. In this context, it would be interesting to investigate the goals of users with different daily activity levels and if the information and features provided by the ATT is perceived as continually informative and needed.

The results showed that it is also crucial to understand users' circumstances, the environment and situation in which they are using wearables and mobile applications. Here factors like feeling annoyed or getting distracted, might lead to a discontinuance. Another factor might be the age of the user. More insights into the personal characteristics (like task-orientation or ego-orientation [52]) would be a helpful addition in the future research. Finally, constant reminders send by the wearable to be physically active (or "move") must not necessarily help to change the behavior long-term. For some people it can even lead to annoyance and abandonment of the technology. A solution could be a more informative and tailored guidance through the process and personalized feedback loops for the user together with understandable and useful insights.

This study has some limitations. One is the sample size, especially regarding the former users and the older generation. Therefore, the results need to be interpreted cautiously. Furthermore, the survey distribution leads to limitations regarding the country representatives as the participants in this sample are mainly from Germany. The role of habit (e.g., daily usage over prolonged period of time) and its antecedents in the context of continued usage might influence the results but was not considered at this stage of the investigation.

References

1. IDC: Earwear and Wristbands Drive First Quarter Growth in the Worldwide Wearables Market, Says IDC. https://www.idc.com/getdoc.jsp?containerId=prUS46432620. Accessed 15 June 2020
2. IDC: IDC Reports Strong Growth in the Worldwide Wearables Market, Led by Holiday Shipments of Smartwatches, Wrist Band, and Ear-Worn Devices. https://www.idc.com/getdoc.jsp?containerId=prUS44901819
3. Statista: Absatz von Wearables weltweit nach führenden Herstellern im 1. Quartal der Jahre 2019 und 2020. https://de.statista.com/statistik/daten/studie/433019/umfrage/quartalsabsatz-von-wearables-weltweit-nach-hersteller/

4. Evenson, K.R., Goto, M.M., Furberg, R.D.: Systematic review of the validity and reliability of consumer-wearable activity trackers. Int. J. Behav. Nutr. Phys. Act. **12** (2015). https://doi.org/10.1186/s12966-015-0314-1

5. Rosenberger, M.E., Buman, M.P., Haskell, W.L., McConnell, M.V., Carstensen, L.L.: Twenty-four hours of sleep, sedentary behavior, and physical activity with nine wearable devices. Med. Sci. Sports Exerc. **48**, 457–465 (2016). https://doi.org/10.1249/MSS.0000000000000778

6. Feng, Y., Li, K., Agosto, D.E.: Healthy users' personal health information management from activity trackers: the perspective of gym-goers. Proc. Assoc. Inf. Sci. Technol. **54**, 71–81 (2017). https://doi.org/10.1002/pra2.2017.14505401009

7. Fritz, T., Huang, E.M., Murphy, G.C.: Persuasive technology in the real world: a study of long-term use of activity sensing devices for fitness. In: CHI 2014: Proceedings of the SIGCHI Conference on Human Factors in Computing Systems, pp. 487–496 (2014)

8. Gouveia, R., Karapanos, E., Hassenzahl, M.: How do we engage with activity trackers? a longitudinal study of habito. In: UbiComp 2015 – Proceedings of the 2015 ACM International Joint Conference Pervasive Ubiquitous Computing, pp. 1305–1316 (2015). https://doi.org/10.1145/2750858.2804290

9. Ilhan, A., Henkel, M.: 10,000 steps a day for health? user-based evaluation of wearable activity trackers. In: Proceedings 51st Hawaii International Conference System Science, pp. 3376–3385 (2018). https://doi.org/10.24251/hicss.2018.428.

10. Lyall, B., Robards, B.: Tool, toy and tutor: Subjective experiences of digital self-tracking. J. Sociol. **54**, 108–124 (2018). https://doi.org/10.1177/1440783317722854

11. Nelson, E.C., Verhagen, T., Noordzij, M.L.: Health empowerment through activity trackers: an empirical smart wristband study. Comput. Human Behav. **62**, 364–374 (2016). https://doi.org/10.1016/j.chb.2016.03.065

12. Rooksby, J., Rost, M., Morrison, A., Chalmers, M.: Personal tracking as lived informatics. In: Conf. Hum. Factors Comput. Syst. - Proc. 1163–1172 (2014). https://doi.org/10.1145/2556288.2557039

13. Shin, G., Jarrahi, M.H., Fei, Y., Karami, A., Gafinowitz, N., Byun, A., Lu, X.: Wearable activity trackers, accuracy, adoption, acceptance and health impact: A systematic literature review. J. Biomed. Inform. **93**, 103153 (2019). https://doi.org/10.1016/j.jbi.2019.103153

14. Schumann, L., Stock, W.G.: The Information Service Evaluation (ISE) model. Webology. **11**, 1–20 (2014)

15. Fietkiewicz, K.J., Ilhan, A.: Fitness tracking technologies: data privacy doesn't matter? the (Un)Concerns of users, former users, and non-users. In: Proceedings of the 53rd Hawaii International Conference System Science, vol. 3, pp. 3439–3448 (2020). https://doi.org/10.24251/hicss.2020.421.

16. Norberg, P.A., Horne, D.R., Horne, D.A.: The privacy paradox: personal information disclosure intentions versus behaviors. J. Consum. Aff. **41**, 100–126 (2007). https://doi.org/10.1111/j.1745-6606.2006.00070.x

17. Taddicken, M.: The "privacy paradox" in the social web: the impact of privacy concerns, individual characteristics, and the perceived social relevance on different forms of self-disclosure1. J. Comput. Commun. **19**, 248–273 (2014). https://doi.org/10.1111/jcc4.12052

18. Hargittai, E., Marwick, A.: "What can i really do?" explaining the privacy paradox with online apathy. Int. J. Commun. **10**, 3737–3757 (2016)

19. Lidynia, C., Brauner, P., Ziefle, M.: A step in the right direction – understanding privacy concerns and perceived sensitivity of fitness trackers. In: Ahram, T., Falcão, C. (eds.) AHFE 2017. AISC, vol. 608, pp. 42–53. Springer, Cham (2018). https://doi.org/10.1007/978-3-319-60639-2_5

20. Lidynia, C., Schomakers, E.-M., Ziefle, M.: What are you waiting for? – perceived barriers to the adoption of fitness-applications and wearables. In: Ahram, T.Z. (ed.) AHFE 2018. AISC, vol. 795, pp. 41–52. Springer, Cham (2019). https://doi.org/10.1007/978-3-319-94619-1_5
21. Canhoto, A.I., Arp, S.: Exploring the factors that support adoption and sustained use of health and fitness wearables. J. Mark. Manag. **33**, 32–60 (2017). https://doi.org/10.1080/0267257X.2016.1234505
22. Junaeus, S.: The Rise of Fitness Wearables. https://www.centercode.com/blog/2015/10/the-rise-of-fitness-wearables. Accessed 15 June 2020
23. Endeavour Partners: Inside Wearables Part 2: Key developments for adoption and engagement. https://medium.com/@endeavourprtnrs/inside-wearables-part-2-july-2014-ef301d425cdd
24. Levy, D.: Emerging mHealth: Paths for growth (2014)
25. Ledger, D., McCaffrey, D.: Inside wearables: how the science of human behavior change offers the secret to long-term engagement (2014)
26. Clawson, J., Pater, J.A., Miller, A.D., Mynatt, E.D., Mamykina, L.: No longer wearing: Investigating the abandonment of personal health-Tracking technologies on craigslist. In: UbiComp 2015 - Proceedings 2015 ACM International Joint Conference Pervasive Ubiquitous Computing, pp. 647–658 (2015). https://doi.org/10.1145/2750858.2807554.
27. Bhattacherjee, A.: Understanding information systems continuance: an expectation-confirmation model. MIS Q. **34**, 567–594 (2001)
28. Hong, S.J., Thong, J.Y.L., Tam, K.Y.: Understanding continued information technology usage behavior: a comparison of three models in the context of mobile internet. Decis. Support Syst. **42**, 1819–1834 (2006). https://doi.org/10.1016/j.dss.2006.03.009
29. Limayem, M., Hirt, S.G., Cheung, C.M.K.: How habit limits the predictive power of intention: the case of information systems continuance. MIS Q. **31**, 705–737 (2007)
30. Lee, B.C., Xie, J., Ajisafe, T., Kim, S.H.: How are wearable activity trackers adopted in older adults? comparison between subjective adoption attitudes and physical activity performance. Int. J. Environ. Res. Public Health. **17**, 1–14 (2020). https://doi.org/10.3390/ijerph17103461
31. Meyer, J., Wasmann, M., Heuten, W., El Ali, A., Boll, S.C.J.: Identification and classification of usage patterns in long-term activity tracking. In: Conference Humam Factors Computing System - Proc. 2017-May, pp. 667–678 (2017). https://doi.org/10.1145/3025453.3025690
32. Hermsen, S., Moons, J., Kerkhof, P., Wiekens, C., De Groot, M.: Determinants for sustained use of an activity tracker: Observational study. JMIR mHealth uHealth 5 (2017). https://doi.org/10.2196/mhealth.7311
33. Davis, F.D.: Perceived usefulness, perceived ease of use, and user acceptance of information technology. MIS Q. Manag. Inf. Syst. **13**, 319–339 (1989). https://doi.org/10.2307/249008
34. Venkatesh, V., Davis, F.D.: Theoretical extension of the technology acceptance model: four longitudinal field studies. Manage. Sci. **46**, 186–204 (2000). https://doi.org/10.1287/mnsc.46.2.186.11926
35. Venkatesh, V., Bala, H.: Technology acceptance model 3 and a research agenda on interventions. Decis. Sci. **39**, 273–315 (2008). https://doi.org/10.1111/j.1540-5915.2008.00192.x
36. Venkatesh, V., Morris, M.G., Davis, G.B., Davis, F.D.: User acceptance of information technology: toward a unified view. MIS Q. **27**, 425–478 (2003)
37. Venkatesh, V., Thong, J.Y.L., Xu, X.: Consumer acceptance and use of information technology: extending the unified theory of acceptance and use of technology. MIS Q. **34**, 567–594 (2012)
38. Thong, J.Y.L., Hong, S.-J., Tam, K.Y.: The effects of post-adoption beliefs on the expectation-confirmation model for information technology continuance. Int. J. Hum. Comput. Stud. **64**, 799–810 (2006). https://doi.org/10.1016/j.ijhcs.2006.05.001
39. van der Heijden, H.: User acceptance of hedonic information systems. MIS Q. **28**, 695–704 (2004)

40. Brown, S.A., Venkatesh, V.: Model of adoption of technology in households: a baseline model test and extension incorporating household life cycle. MIS Q. **29**, 399–426 (2005)
41. Holbrook, M.B., Hirschman, E.C.: The experiential aspects of consumption: consumer fantasies, feelings, and fun. J. Consum. Res. **9**, 132 (1982). https://doi.org/10.1086/208906
42. Nysveen, H., Pedersen, P.E., Thorbjørnsen, H.: Intentions to use mobile services: antecedents and cross-service comparisons. J. Acad. Mark. Sci. **33**, 330–346 (2005). https://doi.org/10.1177/0092070305276149
43. Saga, V.L., Zmud, R.W.: The nature and determinants of it acceptance, routinization, and infusion. In: Levine, L. (ed.) Diffusion, Transfer and Implementation of Information Technology, pp. 67–86. Elsevier Science, Amsterdam (1994)
44. Jasperson, J., Carter, P.E., Zmud, R.W.: A comprehensive conceptualization of post-adoptive behaviors associated with information technology enabled work systems. MIS Q. Manag. Inf. Syst. **29**, 525–557 (2005). https://doi.org/10.2307/25148694
45. Limayem, M., Hirt, S.G., Chin, W.W.: Intention does not always matter: the contingency role of habit on IT usage behavior. In: Proccedings of the 9th European Conference on Information Systems, pp. 274–286 (2011)
46. Angulo, G., Brogan, D., Martini, A., Wang, J., Clevenger, L.A.: Health features of activity trackers: motivation, goal achievement, and usability. In: Conf. Proceeding Michael L. Gargano 14th Annu. Res. Day. A5–1 (2016)
47. Hew, J.J., Lee, V.H., Ooi, K.B., Wei, J.: What catalyses mobile apps usage intention: an empirical analysis. Ind. Manag. Data Syst. **115**, 1269–1291 (2015)
48. Holbrook, M.B., Batra, R.: Assessing the role of emotions as mediators of consumer responses to advertising. J. Consum. Res. **14**, 404 (1987). https://doi.org/10.1086/209123
49. Turel, O., Serenko, A., Bontis, N.: User acceptance of hedonic digital artifacts: a theory of consumption values perspective. Inf. Manag. **47**, 53–59 (2010). https://doi.org/10.1016/j.im.2009.10.002
50. Meuter, M.L., Ostrom, A.L., Bitner, M.J., Roundtree, R.: The influence of technology anxiety on consumer use and experiences with self-service technologies. J. Bus. Res. **56**, 899–906 (2003). https://doi.org/10.1016/S0148-2963(01)00276-4.
51. Seddon, P.B.: A respecification and extension of the DeLone and McLean model of IS success. Inf. Syst. Res. **8**, 240 (1997)
52. Ilhan, A., Fietkiewicz, K.J.: Learning for a healthier lifestyle through gamification: a case study of fitness tracker applications. In: Buchem, I., Klamma, R., Wild, F. (eds.) Perspectives on Wearable Enhanced Learning (WELL), pp. 333–364. Springer, Cham (2019). https://doi.org/10.1007/978-3-319-64301-4_16
53. Karapanos, E., Gouveia, R., Hassenzahl, M., Forlizzi, J.: Wellbeing in the making: peoples' experiences with wearable activity trackers. Psychol. Well-Being **6**(1), 1–17 (2016). https://doi.org/10.1186/s13612-016-0042-6
54. Pfeiffer, J., Von Entress-Fürsteneck, M., Urbach, N., Buchwald, A.: Quantify-ME: Consumer acceptance of wearable self-tracking devices. In: 24th Eur. Conf. Inf. Syst. ECIS 2016 (2016)
55. Lancelot Miltgen, C., Popovič, A., Oliveira, T.: Determinants of end-user acceptance of biometrics: Integrating the "big 3" of technology acceptance with privacy context. Decis. Support Syst. **56**, 103–114 (2013). https://doi.org/10.1016/j.dss.2013.05.010
56. Rogers, E.M.: Diffusion of innovations. Simon & Schuster International, London (2003)
57. Dickinger, A., Arami, M., Meyer, D.: The role of perceived enjoyment and social norm in the adoption of technology with network externalities. Eur. J. Inf. Syst. **17**, 4–11 (2008). https://doi.org/10.1057/palgrave.ejis.3000726
58. Yi, M.Y., Jackson, J.D., Park, J.S., Probst, J.C.: Understanding information technology acceptance by individual professionals: Toward an integrative view. Inf. Manag. **43**, 350–363 (2006). https://doi.org/10.1016/j.im.2005.08.006.

59. Zhou, J., Salvendy, G. (eds.): ITAP 2015. LNCS, vol. 9193. Springer, Cham (2015). https://doi.org/10.1007/978-3-319-20892-3
60. Abouzahra, M., Ghasemaghaei, M.: The antecedents and results of seniors' use of activity tracking wearable devices. Heal. Policy Technol. **9**, 213–217 (2019). https://doi.org/10.1016/j.hlpt.2019.11.002
61. Hasan, B.: Exploring gender differences in online shopping attitude. Comput. Human Behav. **26**, 597–601 (2010). https://doi.org/10.1016/j.chb.2009.12.012.
62. Liebenau, J., Harindranath, G.: Organizational reconciliation and its implications for organizational decision support systems: a semiotic approach. Decis. Support Syst. **33**, 389–398 (2002). https://doi.org/10.1016/S0167-9236(02)00007-6.
63. Bandura, A.: Health promotion by social cognitive means. Heal. Educ. Behav. **31**, 143–164 (2004)
64. Buchwald, A., Letner, A., Urbach, N., Von Entreß-Fürsteneck, M.: Insights into personal ICT use: Understanding continuance and discontinuance of wearable self-tracking devices. In: 26th Eur. Conf. Inf. Syst. Beyond Digit. - Facet. Socio-Technical Chang. ECIS 2018 (2018)
65. Motti, V.G., Caine, K.: Users' privacy concerns about wearables. In: Brenner, M., Christin, N., Johnson, B., Rohloff, K. (eds.) FC 2015. LNCS, vol. 8976, pp. 231–244. Springer, Heidelberg (2015). https://doi.org/10.1007/978-3-662-48051-9_17
66. Vitak, J., Liao, Y., Kumar, P., Zimmer, M., Kritikos, K.: Privacy attitudes and data valuation among fitness tracker users. In: Chowdhury, G., McLeod, J., Gillet, V., Willett, P. (eds.) iConference 2018. LNCS, vol. 10766, pp. 229–239. Springer, Cham (2018). https://doi.org/10.1007/978-3-319-78105-1_27
67. Lupton, D.: Apps as artefacts: towards a critical perspective on mobile health and medical apps. Societies. **4**, 606–622 (2014). https://doi.org/10.3390/soc4040606
68. Ernst, C.-P. (ed.): The drivers of wearable device usage. PI, Springer, Cham (2016). https://doi.org/10.1007/978-3-319-30376-5
69. Asimakopoulos, S., Asimakopoulos, G., Spillers, F.: Motivation and user engagement in fitness tracking: heuristics for mobile healthcare wearables. Informatics **4**, 5 (2017). https://doi.org/10.3390/informatics4010005
70. Frie, K., Hartmann-Boyce, J., Jebb, S., Oke, J., Aveyard, P.: Patterns in weight and physical activity tracking data preceding a stop in weight monitoring: observational analysis. J. Med. Internet Res. **22**, 1–14 (2020). https://doi.org/10.2196/15790
71. Fietkiewicz, K.J., Lins, E., Baran, K., Stock, W.G.: Inter-Generational comparison of social media use: investigating the online behavior of different generational cohorts. In: 2016 49th Hawaii International Conference on System Sciences (HICSS), pp. 3829–3838. IEEE Computer Society (2016). https://doi.org/10.1109/HICSS.2016.477

Human Computer Interaction Challenges in Designing Pandemic Trace Application for the Effective Knowledge Transfer Between Science and Society Inside the Quadruple Helix Collaboration

A. Gallego[1] , E. Gaeta[1] , A. Karinsalo[2], V. Ollikainen[2], P. Koskela[2] ,
L. Peschke[3] , F. Folkvord[4,6] , E. Kaldoudi[7] , T. Jämsä[7] ,
F. Lupiáñez-Villanueva[4,5] , L. Pecchia[7] , and G. Fico[1(✉)]

[1] Universidad Politécnica de Madrid, Madrid, Spain
gfico@lst.tfo.upm.es
[2] VTT Technical Research Centre of Finland, Espoo, Finland
[3] Bilkent University, Ankara, Turkey
[4] Open Evidence Research, Universitat Oberta de Catalunya, Barcelona, Spain
[5] Department of Information and Communication Sciences, Universitat Oberta de Catalunya, Barcelona, Spain
[6] Tilburg School of Humanities and Digital Sciences, Tilburg University, Tilburg, The Netherlands
[7] The European Alliance for Medical and Biological Engineering and Science, Heverlee, Belgium

Abstract. In the last decade, smartphone users grown from 2.8 billion worldwide in 2018 to 3.8 billion in 2021. This fact associates with greater ease of publishing and accessing fake news. This is a particularly concerning issue in a global crisis situation such as the COVID-19 pandemic. As stated by the WHO, this is a global health crisis and the spread of fake information could have a direct impact on people's wellbeing.

Due to this situation, all systems which compose the quadruple helix (i.e., science, economy, politics and media and culture-based public) are under great pressure. On the one hand, citizens demand fast and trusted information, and on the other hand, the scientific community is pushed to publish, resulting in scientific papers published very fast and, sometimes, without adequate peer review processes, as reflected by the unprecedented number of retreats.

The PandeVITA ecosystem will contribute to offering a better understanding of how societal actors' behave, understanding their reaction to and interaction with science and health developments in the context of pandemics, with the aim to encourage citizens to contribute to scientific research with different kinds of data.

This paper describes a novel approach to citizen science interventions and user engagement based on motivational theory and behavioral science, aiming to provide a set of architectural components, technologies, tools and analytics to assess citizens' activities, system performance and stakeholders-related key performance indicators (KPIs) in an observatory fashion, allowing to investigate the motivation of the target participants, user engagement and long-term retention.

M. Kurosu (Ed.): HCII 2021, LNCS 12763, pp. 390–401, 2021.
https://doi.org/10.1007/978-3-030-78465-2_29

Keywords: Quadruple helix · Knowledge circulation · RRI · SSH · Pandemic crisis · Citizen science · HCI · Behavioural change techniques

1 Introduction

Throughout history, people have experienced the emergence of many infectious diseases that have killed millions of people. This has happened when viruses spread much fast than the human capability to develop natural defences necessary to prevent the disease onset. The World Health Organization (WHO) defines a pandemic as "an epidemic occurring worldwide, or over a very wide area, crossing international boundaries and usually affecting a large number of people" [1]. In 2020, in response to the COVID-19 outbreak, the WHO declared first the Public Health Emergency of International Concern (January 2020) and then a pandemic (March 2020), which is still ongoing while we write this paper.

Since the first case identified in December 2019, there has been an increasing spread of the SARS-CoV-2 virus across continents, facilitated probably also by the unprecedented amount of global travellers and movements of goods.

Given the fluidity of the global situation, the lack of knowledge and the late reaction of policy-makers, the immediate response to the pandemic has not been able to prevent the spreading of the disease. Yet, the mid-term reaction seems to be outstanding, with human beings establishing many historical records such as starting the administration of a safe and effective vaccination campaign in less than 10 months from the virus identification.

Since the very first months of this pandemic, despite the lack of evidence and global guidance, governments of different countries have focused their efforts on implementing numerous non-pharmaceutical measures to contain the virus such as (1) closing the borders of countries; (2) defining a curfew; (3) closing non-essential establishments and ultimately regional or national lockdowns. Although some of these measures appears to have helped in reducing the rate of infection and patients' mortality, they have also had negative consequences, leading to a socio-economic crisis. Moreover, this situation has been aggravated by the lack of a common super-national plans, which has made decision-making within the quadruple helix (science, economy, politics and media and culture-based public) difficult as Anna Glaser states in the study "How COVID-19 reshuffles the European innovation ecosystem" [2]. Finally, the current pandemic has demonstrated that European regulatory frameworks for strategic elements, such are personal protective equipment and medical devices, are inadequate to respond to the crisis [3].

A major difference compared to previous pandemics, such as the H1N1 pandemic in 2009, is the wide smartphone penetration in worldwide societies nowadays. Finances Online estimated that 3.5 billion people had their own smartphone by 2020, meaning a smartphone penetration of 44.91% [4]. This means that an unprecedented number of citizens have easy access to news, including fake news, if compared to previous pandemics and global disasters. Therefore, the spreading of fake news has a great and unprecedented impact, affecting the well-being of citizens around the globe. This translates into concerns from citizens who are not able to distinguish which news are truthful, and which not. Therefore, citizens are demanding more support from the scientific community in the dissemination of data and news directly with no economic or political biases.

While the virus is still present, most economic sectors are being damaged and the population is becoming confused by the spectrum of measures at the local, regional, and national level not always linked to the epidemiology of the pandemic situation, it is necessary to develop solutions that facilitate communication inside the quadruple helix at the European level and beyond.

Exploiting the high penetration of smartphones and their growing trend, in this study we have identified an ecosystem framework that will allow us to use mobile applications and a dashboard as tools to facilitate access to reliable information endorsed by health authorities, health professionals and scientists while promoting teamwork, collaboration and the exchange of ideas inside the quadruple helix to improve the decision-making process.

2 State of the Art

The current COVID-19 pandemic context differs from that of previous pandemics for many reasons, including the high penetration of smartphones, used by up to 70% in Europe in 2017 [5]. For this reason, during the whole span of this pandemic, efforts have been focused on developing different services and applications to support control of the COVID-19 spread.

Contact tracing, along with robust testing, isolation and care of cases, is a key strategy for interrupting chains of transmission of SARS-CoV-2 and reducing COVID-19-associated mortality [6]. Contact tracing aims at identifying individuals who have been in contact with people who are infected with SARS-CoV-2 and provide them supported quarantine. Contact tracing can be used to find a source of infection by identifying settings or events where infection may have occurred, allowing for targeted public health and social measures. Although this technique was unknown to a large share of the population before the SARS-COV2 virus appeared, it is indeed not new. Contact-tracing has been used throughout history to fight and control pandemics, such as smallpox in India. Larry Brilliant, who was part of a World Health Organization team in the 1970s that helped eradicate smallpox, described this experience during his interview "My wish: Help me stop pandemics" [7]. In the interview, he expressed the need for early detection and early response to reduce the quick spread of the virus. In the fight against smallpox, the steps adopted were to (1) identify each case as early as possible, (2) start treating the patient immediately and isolate them, (3) identify all last contacts and (4) isolate them. In those days, when smartphones did not exist, the way to trace contacts was to go from house to house to find out if a person had been in contact with a positive. As a result of this rudimentary technique, smallpox was reduced in India within four years and subsequently eradicated. Making contact tracing the main weapon against a pandemic. Nevertheless, SARS-CoV-2 is spreading too fast to be contained by manual contact tracing so, to be controlled, this process should be faster, more efficient, and at a larger scale [8]. In order to meet this objective and benefit from the growing use of smartphones, numerous contact-tracing applications have been developed since 2020, such as Aarogya Setu [9] from India, TraceTogether [10] from Singapore, Private Kit

[11] from the United States, Stop-Covid19 [12] from Italy or COVID Radar [13] from the Netherlands, among others.

Most of these applications follow a common strategy: contact-tracing, i.e. they use Bluetooth and/or GPS technologies embedded in mobile phones to collect information on the places visited and the people with whom users have been in close contact, which is also known as contact tracing. If positive to SARS-CoV-2, the user can (or must in some counties) indicate this in the application, so that all users who have been in contact with this person and have the application installed will be alerted (without revealing personal details). Although all these applications share a common approach, some of them include specific features:

- Aarogya Setu will include educational content to determine what to do in case the user has been in contact with a COVID-19 positive or has been infected by the COVID-19 disease.
- TraceTogether provides users with a Bluetooth device, with the same functionality as the application, but without the need for a mobile phone. In this case, the data will be downloaded only if the user tests positive, in which case the health authorities will notify users who came into contact.
- COVID Radar, following a different approach, aims to collect different information from citizens through surveys to provide data for scientific research. With this data, the app displays maps showing the areas of greatest risk or areas where the virus is spreading faster.

These are just some of the applications available today, as numerous applications have been rapidly developed since the COVID-19 pandemic started. In order to be successful, those Apps have to reach a significant percentage of the population. Unfortunately, although these applications were initially well received by the public and were presented as a great solution for controlling the pandemic, the adoption of most of these applications is under 30% [14].

Deciding whether to use or not a tracking App is based on both intrinsic and extrinsic motivations, according to the Self Determination Theory [15] and Nudge Theory [16]. These theories are designed to reach a mental state, in agreement with the Flow Theory [17], that can keep users engaged in expected behaviours. As Stavros A. Nikou [18] stated, intrinsic motivation is driven by personal rewards as inherent satisfaction, enjoyment, or challenge for the individual. On the other hand, extrinsic motivation is based on the use of external factors such as incentives or punishments to increase or decrease the likelihood that a user will perform a given action again.

Other studies, such as the one conducted by Gaston Antezana et al. [19], suggest the implementation of Behaviour Change Techniques (BCT) to foster the adoption and adherence to the solutions offered in the areas of health, education, criminology, energy, and international development. These types of methodologies are often used in conjunction with gamification techniques (e.g., rewards, classification table, levelling and avatars) to encourage user behaviour change. This same study analysed more than 30 mobile applications in the health area and affirmed that all the applications considered included at least one BCT. The study also concluded that the most widely used techniques are the establishment of objectives, the existence of programmed consequences and the use of associations (prompts/cues).

In addition to these methodologies, there are usability requirements that have been shown to improve user adherence. For example, in the study conducted by L.C. Ming [20], where 223 COVID-19 applications were reviewed, some features that could improve users' adherence have been defined. Firstly, they should include the contact-tracing service along with educational content on prevention, detection and monitoring of COVID-19 to be a complete COVID-19 application. On the other hand, the app should be available at the supranational level (e.g., European level) and contain different updated statistical analyses on COVID-19 incidence by zones, most crowded areas and other information of interest supported by scientific evidence. Finally, although not indispensable, it would be interesting and helpful for clinicians and citizens alike if these applications could integrate different health monitoring functions communicating with portable medical devices.

Although these proposals would result in a complete application focused on meeting users' needs and encouraging adherence, issues related to privacy and data acquisition remain a major concern. This is evidenced in the survey conducted in United Kingdom in May 2020 [21], where it is found that one of the main concerns of users is the purpose for which their data is collected and who will have access to it.

The mistrust perceived in society is mainly because these solutions are not always clearly endorsed by the scientific community and health authorities. It is important to note that this situation of mistrust stems from an ecosystem in which the transparent exchange of information among the different members of the quadruple helix and political decision-making processes does not exist [22].

Given the fact that in pandemic situations, such as the one we are currently experiencing, the collaboration of citizens is a major requirement, it is essential to work on acquiring the trust of citizens by providing privacy-preserving tools. Thus, the 'citizens science' paradigm, through which citizens contribute actively to science providing Real World Data (RWD), will be strengthened by conducting co-creation and design thinking methodologies.

In this context, the EU Funded PandeVITA project has been conceived. One of the main objectives of PandeVITA is to facilitate the knowledge transfer between the members of the quadruple helix at the European level. For this purpose, a mobile application and a platform that will act as a single official, secure, and reliable communication channel will be developed, allowing to:

• Collect data about citizens' contacts.
• Provide citizens with real and clear information about the COVID-19 situation endorsed by scientists.
• Engage citizens to provide data for scientific and health purposes following the responsible research and innovation (RRI) approach.
• Increase social awareness and responsibility by implementing behavioural change techniques.
• Ensure coherence between public authorities and reduce information overload.
• Ensure full protection of privacy and personal rights.

Finally, using these data, various scientists will study how the pandemic situation affects different parameters such as mobility and will help them define indicators and decision criteria, harmonized among the actors of the quadruple helix, together with the users following co-creation. The proposed solution aims to go further by developing a tool to guarantee the correct flow of information among quadruple helix members securely.

3 Methodology

The methodology applied in this project is composed of a set of activities that will enable to develops criteria and indicators for more efficient interaction between science and society in times of pandemic crises and the creation of a theoretical framework that allows an effective information flow for collaborations between science and society inside of the quadruple helix at the European level.

The information flow that we used as reference for our study is shown in Fig. 1 and based on [23] and [24].

Once the criteria, indicators, and theoretical framework for effective communication is identified in the first phase, we have focused our attention on the creation of the Pande-VITA ecosystem. Via this ecosystem, citizens should be able to gather data for scientific experts. This data would be very useful to achieve accurate and efficient research to combat pandemics, granting responsible usage and handling personal data according to European ethical standards and regulations. Furthermore, the ecosystem will:

- supply citizens with specific, accurate and effective recommendations and advice generated by politicians and based on evidence coming from scientists,
- motivate citizens to use the applications by offering them in return trust and transparency in data management,
- generate social awareness and responsible behavior among citizen in the context of user-generated content enabling an effective traceback of a pandemic situation,
- provide relevant information about mobility impact and communication patterns for present and future measures and sustainable developments by collecting Real World Data (RWD) via a citizen science-based approach.

The methodology we have proposed includes four sequential phases:

1. An analysis of the type of contact-tracing technologies used, standards and interoperable services selected, protocols created, and model of communication (centralized or federated) has been carried out. Furthermore, horizontal, and vertical scalability are discussed based on the exploitation of containerization, orchestration, and sidecar technologies. The analysis addresses how citizens have received this type of application and the reasons for the current low adherence despite the high smartphone penetration. Finally, current facilitators and barriers of adherence to social distancing in pandemic situations and how these types of applications can help increase social distancing compliance are defined [23]. This phase identifies the needs, limitations, and expectations of citizens.

Circulation of knowledge

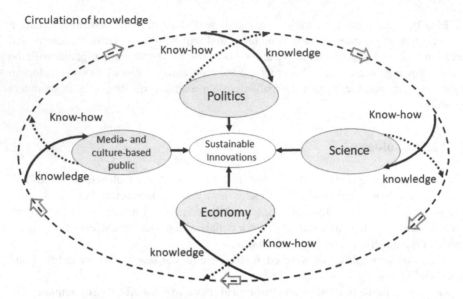

Fig. 1. Quadruple Helix circulation of information [23, 24]

2. A first approach of the PandeVITA theoretical framework, based on the Real-World Data (RWD) line of action, enabling the circulation of knowledge within the quadruple helix is shown in Fig. 1. This relies on a validated loop between science and society where citizens will be able to contribute with their activities and knowledge to scientific research while the science community will provide more accurate recommendations to the public, politics, and employers based also on RWD.

3. The next phase involves the description of the data lake integration plan life cycle including all RWD data sets to be collected, processed or generated during and after the execution of the project. Within this phase, standards and organizational interoperability will drive the process of the theoretical model formalization to provide a general scalable solution.

4. In the last phase, a preliminary version of the implementation of the PandeVITA ecosystem based on the PandeVITA theoretical framework is defined. In the PandeVITA ecosystem, a platform, a dashboard and an application will enable citizens to contribute with their own knowledge (e.g., collecting data, etc.) to scientific research under the framework and guidance of RRI and Society for Simulation in Healthcare (SSH). As the majority of citizens have a smartphone, it is justifiable to implement a mobile application for the use of citizens to collect data. These inputs are needed to develop criteria and indicators for more efficient interaction between science and society in times of pandemic crises. Besides, these data help to better understand knowledge gaps and identify activities to recommend more specific and efficient measures. Based on the results obtained during the first phase of the study 'investigation of currently available COVID-19 solutions', this first version of the PandeVITA Platform and application has been designed. Among the main problems that have been detected in the use of contact-tracing applications are the low adherence of

users and the great concern for privacy and data protection. This requires designing a platform that includes modules that promote PandeVITA application adherence, while ensuring privacy and the correct data management by governments and health authorities.

4 Results

From a Human Computer Interaction perspective, the main result is a set of models of behaviour and a theory of change, implemented as a nudge strategy including game elements within the PandeVITA ecosystem. This will result in an improved engagement from citizen with respect to previous experiences.

From a technological perspective, the PandeVITA ecosystem is implemented on a 3-layer architecture [25] based on a DEV-OPS culture, shown in Fig. 2. In a classical 3-layer architecture we have a data layer, a service layer on the top of the data layer and an application on top of the data layer. In the 3D layered architecture that we propose, we have also a vertical layer devote to scaling and deploying the components of each layer.

From a service perspective, we have identified a common layer, called Open API service descriptions, where services are described, also shown in Fig. 2. This has a direct interface with the PandeVITA API gateway that is the entry point to the services of the ecosystem. Within the ecosystem services, we can find several infrastructure services: security & privacy, authorization & authentication, event stream and data lake infrastructure. The data lake infrastructure is connected through an event stream, used for synchronization, with the data source connectors services. These services are dedicated to the integration and harmonization of data coming from different sources in a common and standard data model. On top of this data model several core ecosystem services are provided: Content Management service (CMS), analytics and DSS, location-based service, data sharing and dynamic consent management and nudge strategy service.

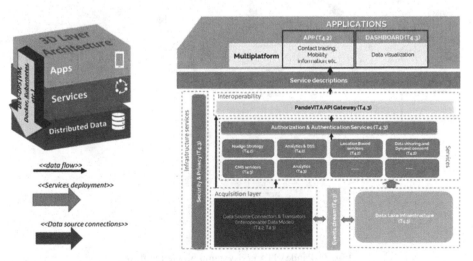

Fig. 2. PandeVITA ecosystem architecture [25]

Of major importance is the nudge strategy service as it is designed to implement a citizen motivation strategy. This motivation strategy will consider the interaction among the ecosystem stakeholder to trigger behavioral changes in citizens. Via an effective data flow, citizens and stakeholders are engaged in a loop, thus benefiting all. The main idea behind the motivation strategy that will be implemented in the nudge strategy service is to connect intrinsic and extrinsic motivation with the actors of the quadruple helix. Intrinsic motivations [26] are related to behaviors that cause an inherent satisfaction of the user, without external rewarding properties, for instance studying a subject because you find it fascinating or playing sports or a game that you want to do because you like the feeling this gives you and you want to become better in doing it. The behavior itself is a reward, this is when motivation comes from "internal" factors to meet personal needs. On the other hand, extrinsic motivations [27] are related to external rewards, for example, pay users for maintaining a certain behavior or punish a user when he engages in improper behavior. Within PandeVITA our idea is to create a dynamic motivation strategy (based on nudge technologies and self-determination theory) that applies:

- Intrinsic motivation to the citizen that has an internal feeling of collaboration with science and society, giving them the opportunity to explore, learn, and actively collaborate to the management of pandemics. This kind of user will use the PandeVITA without any obvious external rewards. They use it just for interest, rather than because of an outside incentive, such as a reward. We will associate intrinsic motivation with the

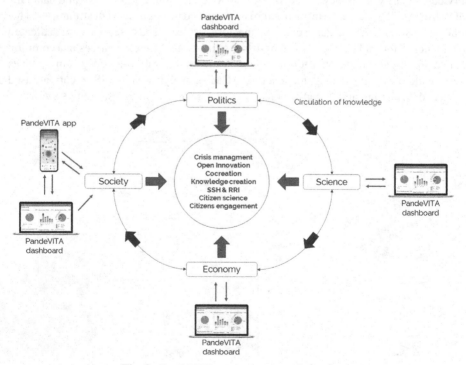

Fig. 3. PandeVITA ecosystem knowledge flow

civic sense of the citizens' and ethical recommendations, mainly driven by scientists and social actors.

- Extrinsic motivation to physical and monetary rewards mainly driven, for instance, by incentives that a particular city, town or region could offer.

The PandeVITA dashboard defines and propagates these motivations to the citizens' PandeVITA app. Users stratification will be used to optimize the motivations strategy and maximize the probabilities of creating flow and minimize the effect of demotivating users.

Figure 3 shows the first design of knowledge transfer integrating the PandeVITA dashboard and PandeVITA app. Using the PandeVITA app, citizens will produce anonymized data for health and scientific purpose. This data will be able to be consulted by all members of the quadruple helix in the dashboard. The dashboard will present all the information gathered about the last COVID-19 situation at the European level. Thus, a decision-making process between Politics, Science, Economy and Society could be established and eventually enable the creation of reliable and valid input for the PandeVITA app, providing behavioural changes mechanics in agreement with the decision taken to achieve effective management of the crisis.

Finally, all these results will be quantitatively and qualitatively evaluated against specific KPI that have already been defined. Table 1 shows the KPIs and expected values.

Table 1. KPI description and expected values.

KPI#	KPI description	Expected KPI value
KPI 1	The PandeVITA platform enables citizen science with the co-operation between science and society	At least 500 participants use the PandeVITA ecosystem and collaborate with scientists generating data
KPI 2	Users stay on the platform and engage with researchers and developers	Over 90% of the users stay active on the app and platform after 6 months. The users have provided feedback to researchers in all the use case studies. The users have sent at least 70 feature requests, bug reports and other feedback to the development team during the project lifetime
KPI 3	PandeVITA platform trace back the mobility of citizens	PandeVITA data enables to define at least 5 different categories of mobility behavior
KPI 4	PandeVITA platform provides data for more specific categories	PandeVITA data enables to define of at least 5 different categories to measure the impact of scientific recommendations on social awareness
KPI 7	PandeVITA app and platform fulfil the framework and guidance of RRI	All relevant stakeholders are involved in the definition of the platform and the evaluation process
KP 8	During data transfer via the PandeVITA app and platform, the privacy and personality rights are fully protected	The technical side of data transfer will be fully documented. The technical documentation will be open access on the PandeVITA website

5 Conclusion

In this paper, we have presented the first version of the PandeVITA ecosystem. The aim is to set-up an ICT ecosystem designed to help citizens and actors of the quadruple helix for better management and effective communication during crisis derived from pandemic events. At the same time, behavioural change methodologies will be applied to promote the fulfilment of restrictions and to accelerate crisis resolution. Our goal is to describe how human-machine interaction is used to foster data acquisition and data sharing between members of the quadruple helix under the RRI and SSH framework.

The importance of the development of the PandeVITA ecosystem lies in these knowledge circulations that can help to mitigate the economics, healthcare and social drawbacks associated with lockdown and misinformation we are observing during the COVID-19 crisis.

Our main proposal addresses these drawbacks by building an effective motivation strategy based on the Self Determination Theory to keep different user types engaged with the ecosystem. Effective classification of user types will be a key aspect of the success of PandeVITA. By using a motivation strategy with the wrong user type could have the adversarial effect of demotivating them.

Anyway, an important limitation to this approach is related to the digital divide, whenever a country or a region is digitally isolated, they are not able to access the solution.

The result of these four phases is the first release of the PandeVITA platform, app and dashboard. In the PandeVITA platform, one of the main goals is to contribute to a better understanding of how societal actors behave and how they react to and interact with science and health in the context of pandemics. The PandeVITA platform offers new opportunities to contribute to scientific research. The tools aim to encourage citizens to contribute to scientific research with different kinds of data.

References

1. World Health Organization (WHO). https://www.who.int/csr/disease/swineflu/frequently_asked_questions/pandemic/en/. Accessed 15 Jan 2021
2. Glaser, A., de Géry, C.: How COVID-19 reshuffles the European innovation ecosystem. ESCP Business school (2020)
3. Pecchia, L., et al.: The inadequacy of regulatory frameworks in time of crisis and in low-resource settings: personal protective equipment and COVID-19. Health Technol. **10**(6), 1375–1383 (2020)
4. Finances Online. https://financesonline.com/number-of-smartphone-users-worldwide/. Accessed 15 Jan 2021
5. GSMA. https://www.gsma.com/mobileeconomy/wp-content/uploads/2020/03/GSMA_MobileEconomy2020_Europe.pdf. Accessed 17 Jan 2021
6. World Health Organization: digital tools for COVID-19 contact tracing: annex: contact tracing in the context of COVID-19. World Health Organization (2020)
7. Brilliant, L.: My wish: help me stop pandemics, TED Talk. https://www.ted.com/talks/larry_brilliant_my_wish_help_me_stop_pandemics. Accessed 15 Jan 2021
8. Ferretti, L., Wymant, C., Kendall, M., et al.: Quantifying SARS-CoV-2 transmission suggests epidemic control with digital contact tracing. Science **368**(6491), 1–9 (2020)

9. Government of India. Aarogya Setu Mobile App. https://www.mygov.in/aarogya-Setu-app/. Accessed 17 Jan 2021
10. Government of Singapore. Trace Together Mobile App. https://www.tracetogether.gov.sg/. Accessed 17 Jan 2021
11. MIT. Private Kit Mobile App. https://safepaths.mit.edu/. Accessed 17 Jan 2021
12. Webtek. STOP COVID19 Mobile App. https://www.stopcovid19.it/en/. Accessed 17 Jan 2021
13. LUMC. COVID Radar Mobile App. https://www.covid-radar.nl/en/. Accessed 17 Jan 2021
14. Naous, D., Bonner, M., Humbert, M., Legner, C.: Towards mass adoption of contact tracing apps -- learning from users' preferences to improve app design. arXiv (2020)
15. Ryan, R.M., Deci, E.L.: Self-determination theory: basic psychological needs in motivation, development, and wellness. Guilford Publishing (2017)
16. Thaler, R.H., Sunstein, C.R.: Nudge: improving decisions about health, wealth, and happiness. Yale University Press (2008)
17. Csikszentmihalyi, M.: Flow: the psychology of optimal experience. J. Leis. Res. **24**(1), 93–94 (1990)
18. Nikou, S.A., Economides, A.A.: Mobile-based assessment: integrating acceptance and motivational factors into a combined model of self-determination theory and technology acceptance. Comput. Hum. Behav. **68**, 83–95 (2017)
19. Antezana, G., et al.: An evaluation of behaviour change techniques in health and lifestyle mobile applications. Health Inform. J. **26**, 104–113 (2020)
20. Ming, L.C., Untong, N., et al.: Mobile health apps on COVID-19 launched in the early days of the pandemic: content analysis and review. JMIR mHealth and UHealth **8**(9), e19796. National Library of Medicine (2020)
21. Ipsos MORI. The health foundation COVID-19 survey a report of survey findings on public attitudes towards a potential smartphone app to 'track and trace' Coronavirus outbreaks. https://www.health.org.uk/sites/default/files/2020-06/Health-Foundation-polling-contact-tracing-app-May-2020.pdf. Accessed 19 Jan 2021
22. Enria, L., Waterlow, N., et al.: Trust and transparency in times of crisis: results from an online survey during the first Wave (April 2020) of the COVID-19. medRxiv (2020)
23. Coroiu, A., Moran, C., Campbell, T., Geller, A.C.: Barriers and facilitators of adherence to social distancing recommendations during COVID-19 among a large international sample of adults. PLoS ONE **15**(10), e0239795 (2020)
24. Carayannis, E., Barth, T., Campbell, D.F.J.: The Quintuple Helix innovation model: global warming as a challenge and driver for innovation. J. Innov. Entrepreneurship **1**(2), 1–12 (2012)
25. 3-Tier architecture: a complete overview. https://www.jinfonet.com/resources/bi-defined/3-tier-architecture-complete-overview/. Accessed 22 Jan 2021
26. Lee, W., Reeve, J., Xue, Y., Xiong, J.: Neural differences between intrinsic reasons for doing versus extrinsic reasons for doing: an fMRI study. Neurosci. Res. **73**(1), 68–72 (2012)
27. Tranquillo, J., Stecker, M.: Using intrinsic and extrinsic motivation in continuing professional education. Surg. Neurol. Int. **7**(7), S197–S199 (2016)

A Study on the Usability of Different Age Groups to the Interface of Smart Bands

Xiao-Yu Jia$^{(\boxtimes)}$ (iD) and Chien-Hsiung Chen (iD)

National Taiwan University of Science and Technology,
No. 43, Keelung Road, Section 4, Da'an District, Taipei City 10607, Taiwan
{D10810805,cchen}@mail.ntust.edu.tw

Abstract. The usability of smart band interface is very important to the user experience. The purpose of this research study was to explore the usability of different age groups in the operation of different smart band interfaces. The experiment was carried out by using a 3 × 2 mixed two-factor design. The experimental factors were the smart band style and the participants' age. The conclusions are as follows: (1) Clear, simple, and consistent operation logic should be established for the interface interaction of smart band products to prevent users from being confused. (2) The combination of visual and tactile sensation and timely and effective feedback are beneficial to enhance the interactive experience of smart band interface based on small screen interaction. The form of touch screen in addition to touch buttons is easier to be accepted by users. (3) The designers should try to meet the needs of various consumer groups, or make choices based on the characteristics of the target consumer groups. Younger people usually hope to get faster feedback, for the older people, on the contrary, too many freedom of operation will reduce usability and cause confusion. (4) Faster operation efficiency may not lead to users' better system usability evaluation, and the number of misoperations in interaction should be minimized to avoid the frustration and loss of patience.

Keywords: Interactive design · Interface usability · Smart band · Older people · System Usability Scale (SUS)

1 Introduction

According to the quarterly tracking report of China's wearable device market, in the third quarter of 2019 [1], China's wearable device market shipped nearly 200 million units by 2023. As a wearable device, the interface usability [2] of smart bands is very important to the users' experience, and five commonly principles in interaction design include Visibility, Feedback, Constraints, Consistency and Affordance [3].

Besides, with the progress of medical treatment and living standards, the proportion of the global older population is increasing year by year. The older group is different from the younger group in physiology and psychology. Because of sensory, motor, and cognitive changes due to ageing, older people may need more time to learn, be more error-prone, and need more steps to operate the system [4].

© Springer Nature Switzerland AG 2021
M. Kurosu (Ed.): HCII 2021, LNCS 12763, pp. 402–414, 2021.
https://doi.org/10.1007/978-3-030-78465-2_30

Due to its wearable properties, the small interface size of the smart band, and the wide age distribution of users, the interface of smart band has higher requirements for usability. Therefore, the purpose of this research study is to compare three hot-selling smart band products on the market and explore the usability problems of different age groups in the operation of the smart band interface.

2 Related Work

2.1 Design Principles in Human-Computer Interaction (HCI)

Design principles can assist designers in thinking and design to enhance user experience. Five common principles in interactive design include: Visibility, Feedback, Constraints, Consistency and Affordance [3]. Specific explanations are listed as follows:

Visibility. The visibility of the function allows the user to know what to do next. Control devices with high visibility, such as handles, buttons or switches, allow people to intuitively know how to use them.

Feedback. Feedback includes returning the information of the end of the behavior to the user, and prompting the user which operations have been completed and can continue. The feedback types in interactive design include audio, tactile, verbal, visual, and a combination of these. Giving back in an appropriate way can also provide the necessary visibility for interaction.

Constraints. Restriction refers to the design of restrictive methods that produce various user interactions in a given situation. The use of different types of graphical representations can also limit the user's interpretation of a certain question or information space.

Consistency. Consistency refers to designing interfaces with similar operating modes and using similar elements to achieve similar tasks. The highly consistent interface follows similar rules for selecting objects using the same operation method. The advantage of having a highly consistent interface is that it is easy to learn and use. Users only need to learn a simple operation mode to be suitable for operating all objects.

Affordance. Predictiveness refers to the properties of an object that can prompt the user how to use it. There are two types of predictability: perceivable and real [2]. In the screen-based graphical interface, the designer can control mainly the perceptible predictability.

2.2 Usability Issues of the Older People in the Smart Bands Interface

Smart bands acquire a wide range of users as they have formed an affordable price by focusing on specific sensing technologies [5]. The current smart band product functions mainly include basic data viewing (time and date, weather, etc.), exercise (real-time recording of various exercise data), health (heart rhythm monitoring, sleep, blood oxygen level, etc.), payment (offline payment, card package, etc.), information reminder (call reminder, short message reminder, etc.) and other functions (intelligent voice control, music, clock, stopwatch, etc.).

The interactive area of the smart band interface is small and the information display is limited. The display screen is usually between 0.95 in. and 1.4 in. The screen operation method is mainly full-screen touch plus the "home button" or "sliding touch" operation. With the continuous improvement of consumer demand, more and more smart bands are designed with larger-size color displays and the screens are turned into full touch screens. In addition, personalized settings (such as setting the main menu background image by consumers) are becoming more and more popular among consumers. In addition, the interface of existing smart band products on the market generally adopts a "shallow and broad" information architecture method.

Usability is not a single, one-dimensional property of a user interface and is traditionally associated with learnability, efficiency, memorability, errors and satisfaction attributes [6]. With the advancement of medical care and living standards, the proportion of the global older population is increasing year by year. As people get older, various physical and psychological functions are significantly reduced, so the usability of the interface for the elderly is more demanding.

The mental model is a concept derived from cognitive psychology. It is a dynamic internal representation of the external world or events [7–9]. Studies have shown that the user's age and experience have a significant impact on the mental model [10]. Fang et al. [11] compare the perceived usability and emotional response of younger and older users to the health information display form of wearable interface.

Regarding smart band products, whether the difference between the older and the younger is significant, and whether the interface of different age groups needs to be designed specifically, it is worthy of further research and discussion.

3   Methods

The purpose of this study was to explore the usability of different age groups in the operation of smart bands interface by comparing three hot-selling smart bands in the Chinese market. The experiment was mainly in quantitative way, supplemented by qualitative method. The quantitative part included basic information, operational task performance test, and System Usability Scale (SUS) [12].

3.1   Participants

A total of 24 participants were invited by convenience sampling, including 12 younger participants (M = 24.42, SD = 3.78) and 12 older participants (M = 56.25, SD = 6.34). The sex ratios of the younger group and the older group were 7 males (52.3%) and 5 females (41.7%); the number of participants with smart bracelet experience of the two groups was both 16.7%; in addition, the ratio of the younger group with a bachelor degree or above was 33.3%, and the older group was 16.7%.

3.2 Materials

The experiment was conducted with a 3×2 two-factor mixed design, the research variables were smart bands style (i.e., Xiaomi, Huawei, and Lifesense) and the age of the participants (i.e., older versus younger).

There were two reasons for choosing the above three smart bands in this study: Firstly, in the "2020Q1 China Smart Bracelet Brand Ranking TOP15" report [13], Xiaomi, Huawei and Lifesense were ranked in the TOP4 respectively, and the three selected smart bands were one of the company's best-selling models. Secondly, the selected three smart bands were very close in screen size, which also avoided the influence of some potential confusion variables on the experimental results to a certain extent.

The basic information of the experimental samples of the three is shown in Table 1, They were Sample 1- Xiaomi Mi Smart Band 4 (NFC) (hereinafter referred to as Xiaomi), Sample 2- Huawei HONOR Band 5 (NFC) (hereinafter referred to as Huawei) and Sample 3- Lifesense Band 5S (hereinafter referred to as Lifesense).

Table 1. Description of experimental samples.

Sample images			
Sample names	Sample 1: Xiaomi Mi Smart Band 4 (NFC)	Sample 2: Huawei HONOR Band 5 (NFC)	Sample 3: Lifesense Band 5S
Screen size	0.95 inch	0.95 inch	0.96 inch
Screen resolution	240*120 pixels	240*120 pixels	160*80 pixels

3.3 Procedure

All the participants completed the experiment without compensation. The experiment was carried out in a fixed site, and the experiment time of each participant was about 30 min. The experimental process of this study was as follows:

Fill in Basic Personal Information. The content included the gender, age, education level and the use experience of smart band products.

Task Operation and Fill in the System Usability Scale (SUS). The experimenter introduced the content and task of the experiment to the participants, and had made sure they know the task clearly. Then the experimenter recorded the time (seconds) of each task and observed the problems of the participants during their operation. After each task was completed, the participants were asked to fill in the System Usability Scale (SUS).

In the operation task, two factors were used in the experiment. Each participant operated three samples in turn. The control of sample test sequence aimed to offset the errors that might be caused by sequence and continuity effect. The operation tasks mainly focused on the usability of the basic functions of the smart bands interface, which were shown in Table 2.

Personal Interview. The participants were asked to briefly describe their feelings during the operation process, discussed the advantages and disadvantages and put forward suggestions.

Table 2. Contents of the operation tasks.

Task	Content	Purpose
1	Check "the current number of steps" and "movement distance" and read out the numbers	The easy-to-use interface for viewing basic data with the smart band
2	Click "Alipay" to display the QR code	Find the efficiency of the payment function entrance
3	Measure the "heart rate" and read the numbers	The ease of use of the heart rhythm measurement function
4	Click on the "indoor run" to start the exercise, and then finish the exercise	The search difficulty and ease of use of the sports function entrance, test the ease of use of the smart band interface for complex task operations
5	Use the "stopwatch" for 8 s and then stop. Then click exit	The search difficulty and ease of use of secondary functions

4   Results

The collected data were analyzed using a mixed two-way analysis of variance (ANOVA) in SPSS with the three smart bands style as the within-subjects factor, and the participants' age as the between-subjects factor. The significant value α was set to 0.05. In addition, the results with significant main effect were further analyzed by the LSD post hoc tests to help address the differences among the factor levels.

4.1   Operation Time of the Tasks

Task 1: Check "the Current Number of Steps" and "Movement Distance". Based on the mixed two-way ANOVA results in Table 3 regarding the operation time in Task 1, the main effect of participants' age was significant ($F = 7.604$, $P = 0.011 < 0.05$). The operating time of the younger group ($M = 41.25$, $SD = 34.79$) was significantly shorter than that of the older group ($M = 56.75$, $SD = 31.34$).

In addition, the main effect of the smart bands style regarding the operation time in Task 1 was significant (F = 9.543, P = 0.000 < 0.05). The Post Hoc test (LSD) results showed that the operation time of the Lifesense smart band (M = 30.29, SD = 20.23) was significantly shorter than the Xiaomi smart band (M = 68.00, SD = 35.03), and the operation time of Lifesense smart band (M = 30.29, SD = 20.23) was significantly shorter than that of Huawei smart band (M = 55.42, SD = 37.07).

Table 3. The mixed two-way ANOVA of operation time (Task 1)

Source	SS	df	MS	F	P	Post Hoc
Age	7180.014	1	7180.014	7.604	0.011*	Young < Old
Style	17692.194	2	8846.097	9.543	0.000**	Lifesense < Xiaomi; Lifesense < Huawei
Age × Style	499.528	2	249.764	0.269	0.765	

* Significantly different at $\alpha = 0.05$ level (*P < 0.05).
** Significantly different at $\alpha = 0.01$ level (**P < 0.01).

Task 2: Click "Alipay" to Display the QR Code. Based on the mixed two-way ANOVA results in Table 4 regarding the operation time in Task 2, the main effect of the smart bands style was significant (F = 3.283, P = 0.047 < 0.05). The Post Hoc test (LSD) results showed that the operating time of Huawei smart band (M = 11.46, SD = 13.81) was significantly shorter than that of Lifesense smart band (M = 19.37, SD = 9.71).

Table 4. The mixed two-way ANOVA of operation time (Task 2)

Source	SS	df	MS	F	P	Post Hoc
Age	741.125	1	741.125	3.883	0.061	
Style	798.778	2	399.389	3.283	0.047*	Huawei < Lifesense
Age × Style	457.000	2	228.500	1.878	0.165	

* Significantly different at $\alpha = 0.05$ level (*P < 0.05).
** Significantly different at $\alpha = 0.01$ level (**P < 0.01).

Task 3: Measure the "Heart Rate". Based on the mixed two-way ANOVA results in Table 5 regarding the operation time in Task 3, the main effect of the smart bands style was significant (F = 3.782, P = 0.031 < 0.05). The Post Hoc test (LSD) results showed that the operation time of the Xiaomi smart band (M = 8.83, SD = 9.21) was significantly shorter than that of the Huawei (M = 13.71, SD = 5.13). The operating time (M = 10.25, SD = 5.60) of Lifesense was significantly shorter than that of the Huawei smart band (M = 13.71, SD = 5.13).

Table 5. The mixed two-way ANOVA of operation time (Task 3)

Source	SS	df	MS	F	P	Post Hoc
Age	110.014	1	110.014	1.774	0.197	
Style	301.861	2	150.931	3.782	0.031*	Xiaomi < Huawei; Lifesense < Huawei
Age × Style	48.028	2	24.014	0.602	0.552	

* Significantly different at $\alpha = 0.05$ level (*P < 0.05).
** Significantly different at $\alpha = 0.01$ level (**P < 0.01).

Task 4: Click on the "Indoor Run" to Start the Exercise, and Then Finish the Exercise. Based on the mixed two-way ANOVA results in Table 6 regarding the operation time in Task 4, the main effect of the participants' age was significant (F = 15.698, P = 0.001 < 0.05). The Post Hoc test (LSD) results showed that the operation time of the younger group (M = 30.03, SD = 17.21) was significantly shorter than that of the older group (M = 45.72, SD = 23.21).

Table 6. The mixed two-way ANOVA of operation time (Task 4)

Source	SS	df	MS	F	P	Post Hoc
Age	4480.889	1	4480.889	15.698	0.001**	Young < Old
Style	10745.583	2	5372.792	24.047	0.000**	Xiaomi < Huawei; Lifesense < Huawei
Age × Style	2286.194	2	1143.097	5.116	0.010*	

* Significantly different at $\alpha = 0.05$ level (*P < 0.05).
** Significantly different at $\alpha = 0.01$ level (**P < 0.01).

The main effect of the smart bands style regarding the operation time in Task 4 was significant (F = 24.047, P = 0.000 < 0.05). The Post Hoc test (LSD) results showed that the operation time of the Xiaomi smart band (M = 33.04, SD = 15.96) was significantly shorter than the Huawei smart band (M = 54.71, SD = 23.23), and the operation time of the Lifesense smart band (M = 26.00, SD = 14.15) was significantly shorter than that of the Huawei smart band (M = 54.71, SD = 23.23).

In addition, there was a significant interaction between the participants' age and the smart bands style in Task 4 (F = 5.116, P = 0.010 < 0.05). In combination with Fig. 1, it can be seen that when using the Xiaomi smart band to operate, the time used by the younger group of participants (M = 24.83) was shorter than that of the older group (M = 41.25). When using the Huawei smart band to operate, the operation time of the younger group (M = 40.08) was shorter than that of the older group (M = 69.33). When using the Lifesense smart band to operate, the time (M = 25.17) used by the younger group was slightly shorter than that of the older group (M = 26.83).

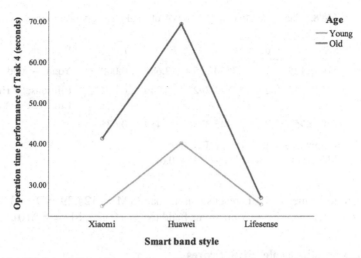

Fig. 1. The interaction of age and smart band style on the operation time of Task 4

Task 5: Use the "Stopwatch" for 8 s and Then Stop. Based on the mixed two-way ANOVA results in Table 7 regarding the operation time in Task 5, the main effect of the smart bands style was significant (F = 14.253, P = 0.001 < 0.05). The Post Hoc test (LSD) results showed that the operation time of the younger group (M = 29.64, SD = 8.13) was significantly shorter than that of the old group (M = 40.19, SD = 14.29).

Table 7. The mixed two-way ANOVA of operation time (Task 5)

Source	SS	df	MS	F	P	Post Hoc
Age	2233.347	1	2233.347	14.253	0.001**	Young < Old
Style	486.083	2	243.042	1.898	0.162	Lifesense < Huawei
Age × Style	55.028	2	27.514	0.215	0.807	

* Significantly different at α = 0.05 level (*P < 0.05).
** Significantly different at α = 0.01 level (**P < 0.01).

Analysis of Total Task Operation Time. Based on the mixed two-way ANOVA results in Table 8 regarding the total tasks operation time, the main effect of the participants' age was significant (F = 22.686, P = 0.000 < 0.05). The Post Hoc test (LSD) results showed that the total operation time of the younger group (M = 122.58, SD = 47.39) was significantly shorter than that of the old group (M = 179.17, SD = 52.27).

In addition, the main effect of the smart bands style regarding the total tasks operation time was significant (F = 6.346, P = 0.004 < 0.05). The Post Hoc test (LSD) results showed that the total operation time of the Lifesense smart band (M = 124.29, SD = 37.21) was significant shorter than the Huawei smart band (M = 168.00, SD = 65.68),

Table 8. The mixed two-way ANOVA of total tasks operation time

Source	SS	df	MS	F	P	Post Hoc
Age	57630.125	1	57630.125	22.686	0.000**	Young < Old
Style	26145.583	2	13072.792	6.346	0.004**	Lifesense < Huawei; Lifesense < Xiaomi
Age × Style	1890.750	2	945.375	0.459	0.635	

* Significantly different at $\alpha = 0.05$ level (*$P < 0.05$).
** Significantly different at $\alpha = 0.01$ level (**$P < 0.01$).

the total operation time of the Lifesense smart band (M = 124.29, SD = 37.21) was significantly shorter than the Xiaomi smart band (M = 160.33, SD = 57.10).

4.2 System Usability Scale (SUS) Scores

Table 9 summarizes the descriptive statistics of "smart bands style" on System Usability Scale (SUS) scores of the three smart bands.

Table 9. Descriptive statistics of "smart bands style" on System Usability Scale (SUS) scores

	Xiaomi	Lifesense	Huawei
M	61.14	65.31	55.42
SD	13.17	13.95	13.94
N	24	24	24

* Significantly different at $\alpha = 0.05$ level (*$P < 0.05$).
** Significantly different at $\alpha = 0.01$ level (**$P < 0.01$).

Based on the mixed two-way ANOVA results in Table 10 regarding the SUS scores, the main effect of the participants' age was significant (F = 4.281, P = 0.020 < 0.05). The Post Hoc test (LSD) results showed that the SUS score of Huawei smart band (M = 65.31, SD = 13.95) was significantly higher than that of Lifesense smart band (M = 55.42, SD = 13.94). Figure 2 showed the relationship between the SUS interval and the scores of the three samples [12].

In addition, there was a significant interaction between participants' age and the smart bands style on the SUS scores (F = 3.286, P = 0.047 < 0.05). Combined with Fig. 3, it could be seen that the SUS scores of the Xiaomi smart band in the younger group (M = 63.12) was higher than that of the older group (M = 59.17), and the older group (M = 68.54) had a higher score for the Huawei smart band. The score of the Xiaomi smart band was higher than that of the younger group (M = 62.08), and the score of the Lifesense smart band in the older group (M = 62.08) was higher than the younger group (M = 48.75).

Table 10. The mixed two-way ANOVA of the System Usability Scale (SUS) scores

Source	SS	df	MS	F	P	Post Hoc
Age	501.389	1	501.389	2.029	0.168	
Style	1184.896	2	592.448	4.281	0.020*	Huawei > Lifesense
Age × Style	909.549	2	454.774	3.286	0.047*	

* Significantly different at $\alpha = 0.05$ level (*P < 0.05).
** Significantly different at $\alpha = 0.01$ level (**P < 0.01).

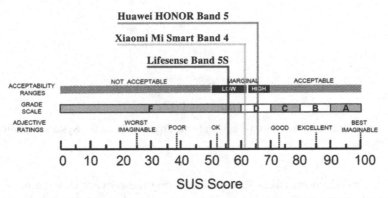

Fig. 2. The relationship between the interval of the System Usability Scale (SUS) and the scores of three samples

4.3 Discussions

Based on the above quantitative data together with the experimenter's observation and interview part, around the five principles of interactive design summarized by Preece et al. [3], the research results were analyzed as follows:

Insufficient visibility lead to multiple wrong clicks. The visibility of the function should help users to intuitively know how to operate: The location of the physical touch buttons of the smart band was not obvious (Table 11(a)), the corresponding functions expressed by icons was unclear (Table 11(b)), and the visual hierarchy in the interface were unreasonable (in Task 1). In addition, the older people showed a low sensitivity to visibility and couldn't understand the functions represented by certain icons. This might be one of the reasons why the younger group used significantly shorter time to search for specific functions than the older group.

Rich visual feedback is the key to successful direct manipulation [14]. The three target samples were mainly based on the feedback type that combined tactile and visual. Among them, in the operation that required a long press of the touch key to exit a certain function (in Task 4), the feedback including animation and text sometimes brought operational misunderstandings to the participants (Table 11(c)), especially for the older group, in this type of operation, showed significant learning difficulties compared to younger group.

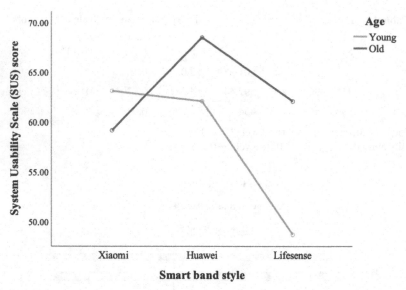

Fig. 3. The interaction of participants' age and smart band style on the System Usability Scale (SUS) scores

Device-embedded interfaces should considering the coexists with the noise, combined with the typically limited screen and computational resources needed to render it [14]. Both graphical interface [3] or physical interface should make the constraints for the user's operations. First of all, the older participants showed difficulties in the operation of Sample 1 (Xiaomi 4 NFC version) which could not only swipe up and down, but also swipe right. Combining the results of interviews and SUS scores also showed that older participants preferred more restricted but simpler styles (like Sample 3, Lifesense 5s), while younger participants preferred styles with higher operating freedom.

The consistency of the icon design or text description of the function caused a certain degree of distress to the participants (Table 11(d)). User interfaces should be based on user mental models rather than implementation models [14]. The users' natural usage habits and mental model might also be the reason for the overall low subjective evaluation of Sample 3 (Lifesense 5s) smart band although it was the most efficient in the operation of multiple tasks.

The misleading prophecy caused great distress to the participants: when a triangular arrow indicating "start" appeared on the non-touchable screen, the participants would repeatedly try to click, and tend to classified the cause as "insensitive system response" (Table 11(e)). In Task 4, when the participants tried to quit the exercise, due to the insufficient predictive combination of the interface icons, color and spacial positions (Table 11(f)), attempted to quit but failed repeatedly and brought users' negative emotions finally.

Table 11. Example pictures of the experimental interface

Example pictures of the experimental interface		
	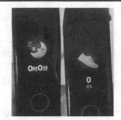	
(a) Examples of visibility issues (From left to right: Sample 1, Sample 3)	(b) Examples of visibility issues (Sample 2)	(c) Examples of feedback issues (From left to right: Sample 2, Sample 1)

(d) Examples of consistency issues (From left to right: Sample 3, Sample 1)	(e) Examples of affordance issues (Sample 3)	(f) Examples of affordance issues (From left to right: Sample 2, Sample 1, Sample 1)

5   Conclusions and Future Implications

Based on the quantitative and qualitative research results, the following suggestions were initially proposed:

Clear, simple, and consistent operation logic should be established for the interface interaction of smart band products to prevent users from being confused.

The combination of visual and tactile sensation and timely and effective feedback are beneficial to enhance the interactive experience of smart band interface based on small screen interaction. The form of touch screen in addition to touch buttons is easier to be accepted by users.

The designers should try to meet the needs of various consumer groups, or make choices based on the characteristics of the target consumer groups; Younger people usually hope to get faster feedback, for the older people, on the contrary, too many freedom of operation will reduce usability and cause confusion.

Faster operation efficiency may not lead to users' better system usability evaluation, and the number of misoperations in interaction should be minimized to avoid the frustration and loss of patience.

Since the samples in this study were products that had been sold on the market, independent variables could not be fully controlled. In future experiments, strict variable control will be carried out based on the results of this study in order to obtain more objective and convincing conclusions.

References

1. IDC China. Q3 China wearable device Market quarterly tracking report in 2019 (2019). https://news.znds.com/article/42860.html
2. Norman, D.A.: Affordance, conventions, and design. Interactions **6**(3), 38–43 (1999). https://doi.org/10.1145/301153.301168
3. Preece, J., Sharp, H., Rogers, Y.: Interaction Design: Beyond Human-Computer Interaction, 4th edn. Wiley, West Sussex (2015)
4. Conci, M., Pianesi, F., Zancanaro, M.: Useful, social and enjoyable: mobile phone adoption by older people. In: Gross, T., et al. (eds.) INTERACT 2009. LNCS, vol. 5726, pp. 63–76. Springer, Heidelberg (2009). https://doi.org/10.1007/978-3-642-03655-2_7
5. He, Z.L., Kim, S.H., Du, H.G.: The influence of consumer and product characteristics on intention to repurchase of smart band. Int. J. Asia Digital Art Des. Assoc. **21**(1), 13–18 (2017). https://doi.org/10.20668/adada.21.1_13
6. Nielsen, J.: Usability Engineering. Morgan Kaufmann, Burlington (1994)
7. Johnson-Laird, P.N.: Mental Models: Towards a Cognitive Science of Language, Inference, and Consciousness, no. 6. Harvard University Press, Cambridge (1983)
8. Craik, K.J.W.: The Nature of Explanation, vol. 445. CUP Archive (1952)
9. Sifaqui, C.: Structuring user interfaces with a meta-model of mental models. Comput. Graph. **23**(3), 323–330 (1999). https://doi.org/10.1016/S0097-8493(99)00041-2
10. Ziefle, M., Bay, S.: Mental models of a cellular phone menu. Comparing older and younger novice users. In: Brewster, S., Dunlop, M. (eds.) Mobile HCI 2004. LNCS, vol. 3160, pp. 25–37. Springer, Heidelberg (2004). https://doi.org/10.1007/978-3-540-28637-0_3
11. Fang, Y.M., Chun, L., Chu, B.C.: Older adults' usability and emotional reactions toward text, diagram, image, and animation interfaces for displaying health information. Appl. Sci. **9**(6), 1058 (2019). https://doi.org/10.3390/app9061058
12. Bangor, A., Kortum, P., Miller, J.: Determining what individual SUS scores mean: adding an adjective rating scale. J. Usability Stud. **4**(3), 114–123 (2009)
13. iiMedia Research. "2020Q1 China Smart Bracelet Brand Ranking TOP15" report (2020). https://www.iimedia.cn/c880/70727.html
14. Cooper, A., Reimann, R., Cronin, D., Noessel, C.: About Face: The Essentials of Interaction Design. Wiley, Hoboken (2014)

Attention to Breathing in Response to Vibrational and Verbal Cues in Mindfulness Meditation Mediated by Wearable Devices

Eunseong Kim, Jeongyun Heo$^{(\boxtimes)}$, and Jeongmin Han

Kookmin University, Seoul, South Korea
{g2020010,yuniheo,jeongminhan}@kookmin.ac.kr

Abstract. As mental healthcare services such as digital mindfulness meditation spread, research to improve user experience is expected to become increasingly important. Thus, this study investigated user perception when a guide for breathing awareness during digital mindfulness meditation is provided through a vibration cue. Focusing on the breath during mindfulness meditation is important, but beginner and intermediate meditators find it difficult due to inner and outer distractions. For this reason, we propose a design guideline for an intervention method that allows the user to concentrate on breathing without disturbing the surrounding environment. In particular, vibration cues can be effective for breathing awareness, because they induce positive neurophysiological changes in the brain, allowing for improved focus and attention. In addition, we measured EEG and HRV to compare changes in user perception. The experiment was designed as within-subjects, and 12 beginner meditators participated. Results of EEG and HRV analysis showed that when verbal and vibration cues were provided at the same time, positive neurological changes were induced and that the user could focus on breathing most effectively. This study's results provide insights on the design of mindfulness wearable-vibration applications in practical terms, along with expanded knowledge of digital mental healthcare and HCI research.

Keywords: Digital mindfulness meditation · Vibration cue · Neuroscience

1 Introduction

The increasing use of digital mental healthcare services has been accompanied by greater public interest in pursuing emotional well-being. Due to the recent pandemic, attention has turned to the accessibility and quality of digitization (here, remote systems) related to mental health, leading to improvements [1]. It is becoming more important to create digital services that improve user experience and promote mental well-being [2]. Mindfulness meditation has become a central and representative example of this [3].

Meditation comes in a range of forms, but most begin with attention training. In general, meditation is divided into the following groups. Concentration meditation (e.g., transcendental meditation) focuses attention on a specific object, such as the breath. Mindfulness meditation emphasizes receptive attention, which accepts all kinds of stimuli

© Springer Nature Switzerland AG 2021
M. Kurosu (Ed.): HCII 2021, LNCS 12763, pp. 415–431, 2021.
https://doi.org/10.1007/978-3-030-78465-2_31

without judgment including thoughts, emotions, sensations, and images [4, 5]. Mindfulness meditation seeks to achieve a comfortable state by focusing on the present moment for short periods of time [6]. It also helps to reduce stress and treat psychological disorders, such as borderline personality disorder, recurrent depression, and anxiety disorder [7–9]. Mindfulness meditation is often presented to users through the use of digital software, such as applications that use verbal cues [3].

Over the past several years, Human-Computer Interaction (HCI) researchers have explored factors that positively influence the user experience and the meditation effect of technology, focusing on the mindfulness program [10]. They proved the utility of providing mindfulness meditation services based on advanced digital technologies, such as Embodied Conversational Agent [11], application [12], and virtual reality [13]. Among them, digital mindfulness meditation is useful for steadily performing meditation for a short period of time without time and space constraints [11].

The essence of meditation has traditionally been considered qualitative and spiritual. Most studies to demonstrate a quantitatively beneficial effect from meditation have been conducted with scientific tools, such as neurology [14, 15]. Use of electroencephalogram (EEG) and measures of heart rate variability (HRV) have demonstrated that positive neurophysiological changes are induced by practicing mindfulness meditation [15, 16]. Among specific factors, meditation may significantly improve attention, emotional regulation, and self-aware processing [17, 18].

The main factor that influences how meditation induces neurological changes is breathing. Breathing is considered the basic and most important factor in mindfulness meditation. In addition, prior studies have established proved the importance of breathing during meditation. For example, in people suffering from mental illness and stress, the consistent practice of breathing exercises has been shown to influence positive emotions [19, 20]. In particular, novices and intermediate users in mindfulness meditation have difficulty concentrating on their breathing because they are not skilled at meditation. It is natural for people to become drowsy or be unable to concentrate during meditation, especially when it is digitally mediated. However, if it persists, it may be difficult to reach the necessary state of interest and comfort for meditation; this may hinder continuous performance. In digital mindfulness meditation, breathing guides are provided primarily as verbal cues through the voice user interfaces. This may be because the breathing guidance provided in digital mindfulness meditation is mainly expressed in verbal cues. A verbal cue may effectively guide the meditator to focus on breathing, but if it is repeated, it may distract and disturb the meditator's inner self [11]. That is, novice meditators may not be aware of when they breathe. A message about relaxation (e.g., "Keep a calm mind") and a cue about breathing (e.g., "inhale" or "exhale") are provided alternately through verbal cues only. By guiding the concentration toward breathing, the meditator can feel comfortable and stable during short breaks, thereby increasing the level of immersion in the mindfulness meditation [13]. It is necessary to seek an intervention method that can help the meditator concentrate on breathing and meditation more fully without disturbing the direction of the attention. Here, it should be noted that physical and visual feedback have a positive effect on the meditator's perception and focus when breathing [21–23]. In particular, it has been proven that physical feedback, such as a vibration cue, can help improve concentration and cognitive ability [24]. The physical feedback, such as a vibration cue, is an effective intervention method that can assist breathing awareness by inducing a momentary focus on human cognitive ability. Previous studies have found that whole body vibration (WBV) can help relieve arousal states by improving brain function, concentration, and cognitive ability [24]. For example, the results of a Stroop Color-Word Interference showed that WBV contributed to the increase of attention and cognition of healthy adults and ADHD patients [25].

The above stated does not mean that the verbal cues provided by the existing digital mindfulness meditation service should be replaced with vibration cues. If only the vibration cue is provided in response to the meditator's breathing during meditation, the user may find it difficult to interpret the meaning of the vibration, and there is a possibility that it will reduce concentration due to the unexpected physical stimulation. Therefore, the vibration cue can be supplemented by the verbal cue (i.e., "inhale" and "exhale") to clearly remind the meditator when to breathe.

This study investigated the effect of breathing guidance provided as a vibration cue during meditation. To this end, a vibration intervention system (VIS) as a band-type device was developed, and evaluation of the vibration cue's effectiveness was conducted based on EEG and HRV values. In Sect. 1 (i.e., Related Work), we investigate the reasons why wearable devices are effective in providing specific messages, as well as the basis that EEG and HRV are indicators for evaluating meditation effects. Section 2 (i.e., Method) defines the overall experimental design for evaluating vibration cue's utility. In addition, we introduce our intervention system based on previous studies that proved the effect of vibration in the human cognitive aspect. Section 3 (i.e., Results) compares experimental results of three breathing guide conditions (verbal, vibration, verbal and vibration) from a statistical viewpoint. The last section (i.e., Conclusion and Discussion) defines the vibration cue's utility. In addition, the section suggests directions for further study based on prior research that has investigated physical signals for breathing.

2 Background

2.1 Wearable Devices for Providing a Vibration Cue

The advance of technology in the field of digital healthcare services has led to the active use of wearable devices. Wearable technology tracks data on location, interaction, and physical activity to quantify a user's behavioral patterns [26]. Thus, wearable devices are being used to provide feedback (e.g., the visual notification or vibration cues) to promote positive behavioral changes in users through the collection of personal information [27, 28]. Cases of its use in daily life are increasing, and such as in healthcare contexts such as exercise [29], mindfulness [30], and breath detection [31].

In particular, the vibration cue provided through a band-type device can function as a message with various meanings, depending on the design. For example, a vibration can be used as a navigation element to guide the user in the direction of the road by providing a vibration to the left or to the right of the wrist [32], or it can be used to regularly remind the user to drink water [33].

A band-type device can be used to effectively provide a vibration cue that can aid in breathing awareness due to its familiarity to the user and can efficiently communicate intention [3]. Using Arduino, we developed a vibration cue for a band-type device (i.e., VIS) to convey information on the timing and method of breathing during mindfulness meditation and investigated its utility.

2.2 EEG and HRV Measurements During Digital Mindfulness Meditation

Recent scientific studies have quantitatively shown the benefits of mindfulness meditation for psychological, neurological, and cardiovascular areas [34, 35]. In particular, mindfulness meditation induces changes in the readout of an EEG, which is related to the central nervous system (CNS), and HRV, which is related to the autonomic nervous system (ANS) [15].

EEG studies of meditation have shown increases in theta power due to psychophysiological changes that take place during meditation [36, 37]. Increased theta power is associated with the changes in CNS arousal that are routinely seen in meditators [38]. Another brain phenomenon resulting from meditation is the transient and sudden oscillation of brain waves and increases in the overall frontocentral coherence. These changes mainly occur in the low frequencies (i.e., alpha, theta) [36]. The activation of alpha and theta waves during meditation occurs when attention is paid, and this change is associated with improved overall cognitive function. Prior studies support our hypothesis that higher activation of alpha and theta waves has a significant effect on breathing awareness and mindfulness experience.

HRV indicates a change in value for the HR, or heartbeat interval, and it is a physiological index for the ANS, which plays a role in the maintenance and regulation of the organs [39]. In particular, HRV is used to analyze chronic diseases, psychopathology, and stress. Recently, it has been used to investigate attention control processes, including mindfulness meditation [40]. The ANS is divided into the sympathetic nervous system (SNS) and the parasympathetic nervous system (PNS) [41]. Cardiac stress response is closely related to the activation of SNS. When SNS is activated relatively much, it is close to an unstable state, because it accelerates HR [42]. Conversely, when the PNS is activated, it can slow down HR to maintain a stable heart state [43]. That is, changes to the HRV value can be applied to evaluate the performance effect of Mindfulness Meditation [15]. In summary, in that mindfulness meditation has a bidirectional effect between CNS and ANS, it is important to observe the changes in EEG (i.e., related to CNS) and HRV (i.e., related to ANS) during mindfulness meditation [15].

For these reasons, we tried to measure the effect of the vibration cue. In addition, breathing guides provided during mindfulness meditation were presented under three conditions (i.e., verbal fade, vibration fade, and verbal and vibration fade), and these were compared and analyzed by EEG and HRV values.

3   Method

3.1   Procedure

A total of 12 university students and office workers aged from 20 to 40 (mean = 27.92, SD = 4.25) years were recruited through a mobile announcement. Of the participants,

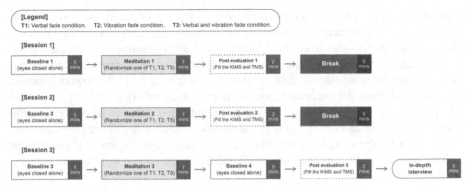

Fig. 1. Experimental procedure.

8 (66.7%) were women. All participants were healthy adults. They self-report without anxiety disorders, cardiovascular disease, depression, neurological and pulmonary disease, and alcoholism. In addition, the participants included novice meditators without experience in digital mindfulness meditation. This was a within-subjects experiment, so all participants were exposed to all three meditation conditions. After the experiment was over, each participant received $15 compensation. This experiment was approved by the Institutional Review Board (IRB) of the Life Research Committee in Kookmin University.

Data for three participants were deleted, for the following reasons: sudden utterances occurred during the experiment and data measurement; some data were not saved due to errors in the EEG and HRV software; and the time allotted for the participant was exceeded, causing a trial to be stopped halfway. Therefore, for hypothesis testing and data analysis, data from nine participants were used.

The experiment was conducted in three sessions, where each session consisted of the sections establishment of a baseline (eyes closed alone), breathing meditation task, and post evaluation (see Fig. 1). Only in the final session, after the breathing meditation task was completed, were additional baseline measurements were performed. In the verbal fade condition, breathing guidance was provided in a basic meditation narration and played through a Bluetooth connection with a Smart Voice Speaker (Nugu by SK Telecom) and a laptop. Each digital mindfulness meditation program was controlled through Adobe Premiere Pro 2020. In the vibration condition and the verbal and vibration condition, the vibration cue was provided to prompt the meditator to follow the breathing guidance of the narration. The vibration cue was controlled via a button at a location far from the participant (i.e., connected to the Arduino Uno board).

The participants were asked to sign a consent form after taking their assigned seats and receiving an explanation of the experimental outline. Then, VIS, HRV, and EEG equipment put on, in that order. Because the HRV equipment must be placed on the bare skin close to the heart, a human body model image with the appropriate heart position marked was provided. The VIS and EEG equipment were placed by the experimenter on the participant during 10-min break for this purpose. Because the experiment was designed as a within-subjects study, participants measurements were taken for each of the three conditions. To this end, the experimenter provided the participants an explanation of how the breathing guide would be provided for each condition. In addition, because was expected to experience some difficulty in breathing according to the vibration cue, a short practice period was given. Meditations under all conditions were conducted for 7 min each. In the verbal fade condition, breathing guidance were provided only by the voice. In addition, as air circulated in the sinuses through the nose, this lowers pressure in the brain and stabilizes the brain waves, more effectively relaxing the body and mind, so the participants were encouraged to breathe through their noses while performing the breathing meditation tasks [44]. In the vibration fade condition, breathing guidance were provided only by the vibration cue without a voice guide. Finally, under the condition of verbal and vibration fade, the same voice and the vibration cue were simultaneously provided.

Fig. 2. Participants in the experiment and their surroundings.

The participants conducted the experiment individually in a room that created a comfortable atmosphere with simple interior pieces and soft, ambient lighting (see Fig. 2). In the first session, the participant rested with eyes closed for 5 min to measure the ordinary waves, followed immediately by breathing meditation for 7 min. Each participant conducted experiments on all three conditions. Distribution of the breathing guidance conditions was assigned using Latin Square Design to avoid sequential learning effects.

After the meditation was over, post-evaluation was conducted on the KIMS to measure breathing awareness and the TMS to measure mindfulness experience. After each evaluation, the participants were given a break for 5 min, during which they were prohibited to use their cell phones. Because, the EEG equipment had to be worn for a long period, it was loosened before the breaks. The second session was conducted in the same way, and with only the experimental condition differing. During the third session, the participants closed their eyes for 5 min, took a break, performed mindfulness meditation for 7 min, and then closed their eyes for an additional 5 min. An additional baseline measurement task was conducted to obtain data on any neurophysiological changes in the participants after the meditation in the three conditions.

The post-evaluations were conducted at the end of the session to avoid potential memory loss of the earliest sessions. After all sessions were complete, the participants participated a 5-min in-depth interview. In addition, recording was conducted to collect qualitative data on breathing awareness and the mindfulness experience. In this experiment, objective data were secured through EEG and HRV equipment, and subjective data were obtained on the KIMS and the TMS (for post-evaluation), and in-depth interviews. Both types of data make it easy to gain additional insights, and measurements of the two types of data were performed because of their potential advantage for securing additional insight and producing validity by investigating the consistency of the results.

3.2 Vibration Intervention System (VIS)

We investigated whether the vibration cue would be an intervention that did not disturb the meditator's attention. Thus, we developed the vibration cue VIS in the form of a band-type device (see Fig. 3A), because wearable devices, such as bands, can effectively provide breathing feedback to users during digital mindfulness meditation [3]. The basic hardware was made by modifying the silicone strap of Xiaomi Mi Band Series 3. The micro-vibration motor (i.e., 8000RPM, 133.33 Hz) was attached. In addition, the VIS was connected using a 5M wire because it was controlled directly using a controller (i.e., button) that was far from the participant. Components such as micro-vibration motors and buttons were connected to the Arduino Uno Board via USB 2.0 (see Fig. 3B).

The software was programmed through Arduino IDE 1.8.13. We used a fade in/fade out style for the vibration to match the rhythm of breathing. That is, when the participant inhaled, it increased from a low vibration value to a high value (with a fade in from a vibration value of 0 to 255), and at exhale, it decreased from a high vibration to a low one (fade out: 255 to 0). In the highest value of 255, for example, the fade in/fade out was similar to the median vibration value of a typical smartphone. The vibration signal was activated only when the breathing guide was provided, so the signal was controlled through the switch case statement. Therefore, when the button is pressed once (i.e., button value of 0 to 1), the vibration cue is played (i.e., vibration value of 0 to 255, 255 to 0), and when the experimenter presses the button again (i.e., button value of 1 to 0), the vibration cue's playback stops.

Participants were asked to wear the VIS in the form of a band-type device during the experiment. The vibration cue was activated only in the vibration fade condition and in the verbal and fade condition.

(A)   **(B)**

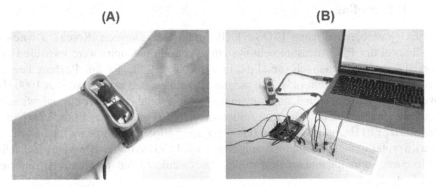

Fig. 3. (A) Wearing the VIS and (B) circuit connection.

3.3 Digital Mindfulness Meditation

The script for mindfulness meditation narration used in our experiment was a reconstitution of a script provided by UCLA Health ("Breathing Meditation," 5 min). The revised narration was a 7-min course. The script provided by UCLA Health basically consisted of sentences for emotional relaxation (e.g., "Your mind will be calm"). A total of five pairs of breathing sentences, one for inhalation and one for exhalation, were inserted (i.e., reconstitution).

The first completed meditation script was verified by two experts who have been practicing meditation and teaching for 20 years. The experts were men and women in their 50s, and they participated in for 30-min interviews through the Zoom online video conferencing tool. These interviews produced the following insights: because frequent breathing instructions can burden the user, a total of three reminders is appropriate, at 1-min intervals; (2) providing natural sounds as background can help novice meditators focus on the meditation, and the interval between narration sentences should be 3–5 s. The two meditation experts were given $25 each to compensate them for their time.

The digital mindfulness meditation script was recorded by a professional freelance announcer (a woman in her 30 s). She was asked to record with a constant, calm tone, volume constant, and was provided $135 after recording.

The completed digital mindfulness meditation sound was designed in Adobe Premiere Pro 2020 to be used in each of the three meditation conditions. In the verbal fade condition, the original voice was used without any separate editing. As an additional explanation, "fade" means that breathing guidance is used from only the beginning to the middle of meditation. The concept of fade was applied to induce participants to breathe on their own even in the second half of meditation. In the vibration fade condition, the breathing reminder guide was given only as a vibration cue. The VIS was activated only when breathing was needed and was controlled via the Arduino's remote device. The verbal and vibration fade condition uses the original sound because the breathing guide is provided simultaneously with voice and vibration. Therefore, the vibration cue was provided identically to the vibration fade condition.

3.4 EEG Recording

The EEG was recorded using BIOS-ST (BioBrain Inc., Daejeon, Korea), a wireless eight-channel dry EEG measurement system. Electrode positions were measured and analyzed across eight channels (i.e., Fp1, Fp2, T3, T4, O1, O2, Fz, and Pz) based on the International 10–20 System [45]. The measured analog signal was sampled at 1000 Hz, converted into a digital signal, and transmitted to a personal computer through wireless Bluetooth communication. The transmitted digital EEG signal was filtered by Notch Filter 60 Hz, 120 Hz, and Band Pass 0.5–5-Hz using BioScan (BioBrain Inc., Daejeon, Korea), a professional EEG analysis program. Then, EEG rhythmic data were created for each frequency domain, and spectral values were calculated that quantitatively reflected the EEG rhythm.   .

3.5 Extraction of HRV from ECG Signal

The ECG signal was measured using a wireless ECG system BIOS-EP200 (BioBrain Inc., Daejeon, Korea) in a standard limb lead method. The measured analog ECG signal was sampled at 250 Hz, converted to a digital signal, and then transmitted to a personal computer through a wireless Bluetooth communication. The transmitted digital ECG signal was filtered through a Notch Filter 60 Hz, 120 Hz, and Band Pass 0.5–100 Hz, using BioScan (BioBrain, Daejeon, Korea), an ECG analysis program, and RRV tachogram data was created by detecting the ECG peak. LF, HF, and TP were calculated for frequency domain analysis, and RMSSD, SDNN, and pNN50 were calculated for the time domain analysis.

3.6 Measures of Subjective Experiences

We reconstituted certain items on the KIMS for use in evaluating the breathing awareness [46]. The KIMS is used to evaluate the psychological characteristics of mindfulness and reflects four mindfulness evaluation skills (i.e., observing, describing, acting with awareness, and accepting without judgement). Among these, acting with awareness includes items to evaluate the state of attention and concentration for the practice of mindfulness meditation. In these questions (i.e., to assess items on the attention and concentration status), keywords (i.e., as a noun) for breathing awareness were inserted that centered on items with unclear nouns, and six items were selected.

The state version of the TMS was used to assess the Mindfulness experience for each of the three meditation conditions [47]. The participants were novice meditators who were unfamiliar with mindfulness meditation, so the intuitive items that were easy to understand were selected from the TMS. The TMS items were grouped into Curiosity (factor 1, six items), which evaluates the meditator's perception of the current situation, and Decentering (factor 2, seven items), which reflects inner awareness. All items were measured on a 5-point Likert scale.

4   Results

4.1 EEG Data Analysis of Relative Theta and Alpha Powers

One-way ANOVA was performed to compare the means for relative theta and alpha power according the breathing guidance conditions. The mean for relative theta power was better for the verbal and vibration fade condition (M = .25, SD = .08) than in the verbal fade condition (M = .18, SD = .04) or the vibration fade condition (M = .18, SD = .04), F (2) = 3.44, p = .04 (see Fig. 4A).

Likewise, the mean for the relative alpha power was highest in the verbal and vibration fade condition (M = .39, SD = .09). This was statistically significantly higher than the means for the vibration fade condition (M = .29, SD = .07) and the verbal fade condition (M = .27, SD = .08), F (2) = 4.6, p = .02 (see Fig. 4B).

The Tukey post-hoc test shows the significantly different results for the verbal fade condition and the verbal and vibration fade conditions show significant differences

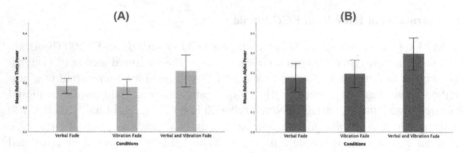

Fig. 4. (A) Theta power and (B) alpha power in the three conditions.

(p = .03). These results support our hypothesis that the relative theta and alpha powers for the verbal and vibration fade condition are higher than for the other conditions.

The paired-sample t test indicates no significant difference in the relative theta power for the baseline and meditation conditions (see Fig. 5A). In the verbal and vibration fade condition (M = .25, SD = .08), the mean of relative theta power increased by about .04 in the frontal lobe area (Fp1, Fp2, and Fz) compared to the baseline (M = .21, SD = .09), p = .09 (see Fig. 5B). This marked an increase in the relatively high average value relative to other conditions. The mean for relative theta power increased by about .01 in the verbal fade condition (M = .19, SD = .04) relative to baseline (M = .18, SD = .06), p = .82.

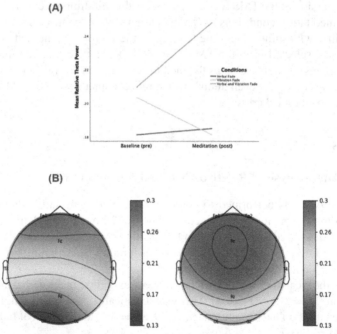

Fig. 5. (A) Comparison of the baseline (pre) and the meditation (post) and (B) mapping of theta power (baseline about the eyes closed and meditation for the verbal and vibration fade condition).

Compared to the baseline (M = .2, SD = .08), the mean of the relative theta power in the vibration fade condition (M = .18, SD = .06) decreased by about .02, p = .27.

4.2 HRV Data Analysis

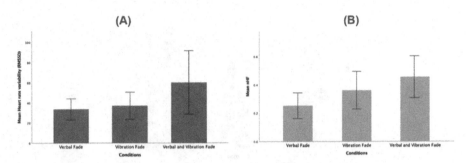

Fig. 6. Comparison of (A) RMSSD and (B) nHF.

One-way ANOVA showed the difference in the means between RMSSD and normalized HF (nHF) for the three conditions. RMSSD was analyzed to determine the short-term variability of the heart rate (see Fig. 6A). The mean for RMSSD was highest in the verbal and vibration fade condition (M = 59.92, SD = 24.38). The vibration fade condition (M = 36.92, SD = 14.56) and the verbal fade condition (M = 33.45, SD = 11.29) showed relatively low mean values. However, the difference was not significant F (2) = 2.89, p = .08.

nHF was analyzed to investigate the activation of the parasympathetic nerve (see Fig. 6B). The mean for nHF was significantly higher in the verbal and vibration fade condition (M = .45, SD = .18), F (2) = 3.6, p = .04, than vibration fade condition (M = .36, SD = .16) and the verbal fade condition (M = .25, SD = .11). In addition, the Tukey post-hoc test found significant differences between the verbal fade condition and the verbal and vibration fade condition (p = .04).

4.3 Data Analysis of Subjective Experiences

MANOVA was performed to test the hypotheses with reference to two dependent variables (breathing awareness and mindfulness experience) (see Fig. 7). The mean for breathing awareness was significantly higher in the verbal and vibration fade condition (M = 4.11, SD = .62) than in the vibration fade condition (M = 2.93, SD = .6) and than in the verbal fade condition (M = 3.13, SD = .57), which confirms H1, F (2) = 8.72, p = .002.

The mean for the mindfulness experience was significantly higher in the verbal and vibration fade condition (M = 3.9, SD = .68). This showed higher results than in the verbal fade condition (M = 3.31, SD = .55) and in the vibration fade condition (M = 2.9, SD = .58), supporting H2, F (2) = 6.48, p = .006.

A Tukey post-hoc test showed that both the verbal fade condition (p = .00) and the vibration fade condition (p = .01) showed significant differences from the verbal and vibration fade condition in terms of the mean for breathing awareness. On the other hand, the mean for the mindfulness experience was only significantly different between the verbal and vibration fade condition and the vibration fade condition (p = .01).

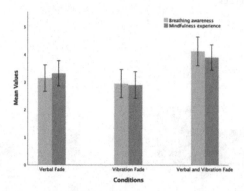

Fig. 7. Differences in mean values for breathing awareness and mindfulness experience.

5 Conclusion and Discussion

The main purpose of this study was to investigate whether there was a positive result on user perception under the condition that the guidance for breathing during mindfulness meditation was provided as verbal and vibration cues.

The findings of this study fall into five main groups. (1) The means for the relative theta and alpha powers were the highest in the verbal and vibration fade condition. (2) The mean value of the relative theta power in the verbal and vibration fade condition was about .04 greater than the baseline, the largest increase compared to other conditions. This value was most increased around the frontal lobe (Fp1, Fp2, and Fz). (3) The highest mean value for RMSSD was shown in the verbal and vibration fade condition, The results for (2) and (3) were not statistically significant, but the verbal and vibration condition showed a relatively high mean value for RMSSD and compared with the baseline (i.e., before meditation). The mean value of the relative theta power was greater than for other conditions. This indicated breathing intervention for the digital mindfulness meditation can be effectively provided through the verbal and vibration cue. In addition, the fact that the statistical results for (2) and (3) were significant at the 10% level can be interpreted as providing partial support for this aspect (i.e., p = .09, .08, respectively). Greater likelihood of statistical significance may come from expansion of the study to more participants. (4) The mean for nHF was highest in the verbal and vibration fade condition. This condition, therefore, contributed to the activation of the participant's parasympathetic nerve. (5) The results of the subjective assessment of breathing awareness and the mindfulness experience produced the highest mean values in the verbal and vibration fade condition.

Thus, our study indicated that breathing guides in digital mindfulness meditation that are simultaneously given as the verbal cue and a vibration cue induce positive emotional experiences, along with awareness of and focus on breathing. Thus, our findings make several contributions. First, we proposed a VIS to support concentration and awareness of breathing for mindfulness meditation. Second, the vibration cue we provided induced a positive effect on overall meditation satisfaction and breathing awareness in the digital mindfulness program. This suggests that the use of a digital mindfulness meditation service allows vibration intervention to be effectively utilized as a means of maximizing the efficiency of the user's meditation and breathing performance. Furthermore, added vibration cues can improve immersion in digital mindfulness meditation and have a strong influence on skills development in novice meditators. From a practical point of view, the approach developed here it can be commercialized as a wearable-only application. Third, our intervention, which enables internalization that does not alter the meditator's surroundings, can help habituation users to mindfulness meditation through breathing in daily life. Finally, we proved through a quantitative experiment that the vibration cue had a significant effect on neurological changes during digital mindfulness meditation. This constitutes a contribution to knowledge of meditation [12, 15]. This work will support effective digital mindfulness meditation services in practical terms and will provide insights into how users can use such services efficiently.

This study has found positive effects in the use of the vibration cue, but some limitations appear as well. EEG and HRV measures were chosen to reflect the interior state of the meditator. Short-term measurement of neurological data has been adopted by many studies to allow comparison between before and after meditation [15, 39]. Our results, however, are thus unable to predict effects of the use of a vibration cue in digital mindfulness meditation over the long term. Therefore, a long-term investigation into vibration cues' effects will be needed. For example, investigating the increased meditation effect through the vibration cue is expected in response to the spread of Mindfulness Based Stress Reduction (MBSR) in daily life or in panic disorder. This requires sufficient knowledge about the vibration cue and can be meaningful further research. In an in-depth interview, three participants responded that they changed their breathing patterns due to sudden vibrations. Changing the breathing pattern according to the vibration fade in/out can potentially trigger negative emotions depending on subjectivity and context. One counter-direction is to proceed with sufficient prior explanation and knowledge about the vibration cue. Another direction is to induce participants to follow the breath when they want. For example, in a mindfulness meditation, continuously providing vibration fade in/out until the meditation is over can be effective [21–23, 48]. In particular, the advantage is that the vibration process can induce participants to breathe according to the vibration cue when they wish.

Finally, because this study showed the usefulness of providing both a verbal cue and the vibration cue at the same time, we concluded that the vibration cue could guide the user's breathing during mindfulness meditation. However, depending on the situation, the verbal cue can distract the user's attention. To compensate for this, we considered a method of providing verbal and vibration cues at the beginning of meditation and only vibration cues from the middle. In this case, the verbal cue helps understand the meaning of the vibration cue. As a result, the participant is expected to be effective in inducing comfortable breathing, because it is possible to grasp the meaning smoothly (i.e., learning effect) even if only the vibration cue is provided (i.e., in the latter part).

Acknowledgments. The authors thank Kiseong Kim, Ph.D., and Daeyong Shin, Mr. (BioBrain Inc., Daejeon, Korea) for the analysis of the electroencephalograms.

References

1. Torous, J., Myrick, K.J., Rauseo-Ricupero, N., Firth, J.: Digital mental health and COVID-19: using technology today to accelerate the curve on access and quality tomorrow. JMIR Mental Health **7**, e18848 (2020). https://doi.org/10.2196/18848
2. Alexopoulos, A.R., Hudson, J.G., Otenigbagbe, O.: The use of digital applications and COVID-19. Community Ment. Health J. **56**, 1202–1203 (2020). https://doi.org/10.1007/s10 597-020-00689-2
3. Zhu, B., Hedman, A., Li, H.: Design digital mindfulness for personal wellbeing. In: Proceedings of the 28th Australian Conference on Computer-Human Interaction - OzCHI 2016, Launceston, Tasmania, Australia, pp. 626–627. ACM Press (2016). https://doi.org/10.1145/3010915.3011841
4. Kristeller, J.L., Hallett, C.B.: An exploratory study of a meditation-based intervention for binge eating disorder. J. Health Psychol. **4**(3), 357–363 (1999). https://doi.org/10.1177/135 910539900400305
5. Mar Jha, A.P., Krompinger, J., Baime, M.J.: Mindfulness training modifies subsystems of attention. Cogn. Affect. Behav. Neurosci. **7**, 109–119 (2007). https://doi.org/10.3758/CABN. 7.2.109
6. Bishop, S.R., et al.: Mindfulness: a proposed operational definition. Clin. Psychol. Sci. Pract. **11**, 230–241 (2004). https://doi.org/10.1093/clipsy.bph077
7. Shorey, R.C., Elmquist, J., Wolford-Clevenger, C., Gawrysiak, M.J., Anderson, S., Stuart, G.L.: The relationship between dispositional mindfulness, borderline personality features, and suicidal ideation in a sample of women in residential substance use treatment. Psychiatry Res. **238**, 122–128 (2016). https://doi.org/10.1016/j.psychres.2016.02.040
8. Soler, J., et al.: Effects of the dialectical behavioral therapy-mindfulness module on attention in patients with borderline personality disorder. Behav. Res. Ther. **50**(2), 150–157 (2012). https://doi.org/10.1016/j.brat.2011.12.002
9. Goldin, P.R., Gross, J.J.: Effects of mindfulness-based stress reduction (MBSR) on emotion regulation in social anxiety disorder. Emotion **10**(1), 83 (2010). https://doi.org/10.1037/a00 18441
10. Kosunen, I., Salminen, M., Järvelä, S., Ruonala, A., Ravaja, N., Jacucci, G.: RelaWorld: neuroadaptive and immersive virtual reality meditation system. In: Proceedings of the 21st International Conference on Intelligent User Interfaces, Sonoma California, USA, pp. 208–217. ACM (2016). https://doi.org/10.1145/2856767.2856796
11. Shamekhi, A., Bickmore, T.: Breathe deep: a breath-sensitive interactive meditation coach. In: Proceedings of the 12th EAI International Conference on Pervasive Computing Technologies for Healthcare, pp. 108–117. ACM, New York (2018). https://doi.org/10.1145/3240925.324 0940
12. Salehzadeh Niksirat, K., Silpasuwanchai, C., Mohamed Hussien Ahmed, M., Cheng, P., Ren, X.: A framework for interactive mindfulness meditation using attention-regulation process. In: Proceedings of the 2017 CHI Conference on Human Factors in Computing Systems, Denver Colorado USA, pp. 2672–2684. ACM (2017). https://doi.org/10.1145/3025453.302 5914

13. Prpa, M., Tatar, K., Françoise, J., Riecke, B., Schiphorst, T., Pasquier, P.: Attending to breath: exploring how the cues in a virtual environment guide the attention to breath and shape the quality of experience to support mindfulness. In: Proceedings of the 2018 Designing Interactive Systems Conference, Hong Kong China, pp. 71–84. ACM (2018). https://doi.org/10.1145/3196709.3196765

14. Harne, B.P., Hiwale, A.S.: EEG spectral analysis on OM mantra meditation: a pilot study. Appl. Psychophysiol. Biofeedback **43**(2), 123–129 (2018). https://doi.org/10.1007/s10484-018-9391-7

15. Tinga, A.M., Nyklíček, I., Jansen, M.P., de Back, T.T., Louwerse, M.M.: Respiratory biofeedback does not facilitate lowering arousal in meditation through virtual reality. Appl. Psychophysiol. Biofeedback **44**(1), 51–59 (2018). https://doi.org/10.1007/s10484-018-9421-5

16. Mankus, A.M., Aldao, A., Kerns, C., Mayville, E.W., Mennin, D.S.: Mindfulness and heart rate variability in individuals with high and low generalized anxiety symptoms. Behav. Res. Ther. **51**(7), 386–391 (2013). https://doi.org/10.1016/j.brat.2013.03.005

17. Hernández, S.E., Barros-Loscertales, A., Xiao, Y., Gonzalez-Mora, J.L., Rubia, K.: Gray matter and functional connectivity in anterior cingulate cortex are associated with the state of mental silence during Sahaja yoga meditation. Neuroscience **371**, 395–406 (2018). https://doi.org/10.1016/j.neuroscience.2017.12.017

18. Tang, Y.-Y., Tang, R., Rothbart, M.K., Posner, M.I.: Frontal theta activity and white matter plasticity following mindfulness meditation. Curr. Opin. Psychol. **28**, 294–297 (2019). https://doi.org/10.1016/j.copsyc.2019.04.004

19. Silverman, W.K., Pina, A.A., Viswesvaran, C.: Evidence-based psychosocial treatments for phobic and anxiety disorders in children and adolescents. J. Clin. Child Adolesc. Psychol. **37**, 105–130 (2008). https://doi.org/10.1080/15374410701817907

20. van der Zwan, J.E., de Vente, W., Huizink, A.C., Bögels, S.M., de Bruin, E.I.: Physical activity, mindfulness meditation, or heart rate variability biofeedback for stress reduction: a randomized controlled trial. Appl. Psychophysiol. Biofeedback **40**(4), 257–268 (2015). https://doi.org/10.1007/s10484-015-9293-x

21. Yu, M.M., Wu, H., Lee, M., Hung, Y.: Multimedia-assisted breathwalk-aware system. IEEE Trans. Biomed. Eng. **59**(12), 3276–3282 (2012). https://doi.org/10.1109/TBME.2012.2208747

22. Van Rooij, M., Lobel, A., Harris, O., Smit, N., Granic, I.: DEEP: a biofeedback virtual reality game for children at-risk for anxiety. In: Proceedings of the 2016 CHI Conference Extended Abstracts on Human Factors in Computing Systems, pp. 1989–1997 (2016). https://doi.org/10.1145/2851581.2892452

23. Kaushik, R., Kaushik, R.M., Mahajan, S.K., Rajesh, V.: Biofeedback assisted diaphragmatic breathing and systematic relaxation versus propranolol in long term prophylaxis of migraine. Complement. Ther. Med. **13**, 165–174 (2005). https://doi.org/10.1016/j.ctim.2005.04.004

24. Boerema, A.S., et al.: Beneficial effects of whole body vibration on brain functions in mice and humans. Dose-Response **16**, 1559325818811756 (2018). https://doi.org/10.1177/1559325818811756

25. Fuermaier, A.B.M., Tucha, L., Koerts, J., van Heuvelen, M.J.G., van der Zee, E.A., Lange, K.W.: Good vibrations – effects of whole body vibration on attention in healthy individuals and individuals with ADHD. PLoS ONE **9**(2), e90747 (2014). https://doi.org/10.1371/journal.pone.0090747

26. Zhao, Z., Arya, A., Whitehead, A., Chan, G., Etemad, S.A.: Keeping users engaged through feature updates: a long-term study of using wearable-based exergames. In: CHI, pp. 1053–1064 (2017). https://doi.org/10.1145/3025453.3025982

27. Rapp, A., Cena, F.: Affordances for self-tracking wearable devices. In: Proceedings of the 2015 ACM International Symposium on Wearable Computers - ISWC 2015, Osaka, Japan, pp. 141–142. ACM Press (2015). https://doi.org/10.1145/2802083.2802090

28. Li, I., Dey, A., Forlizzi, J.: A stage-based model of personal informatics systems (2010). https://doi.org/10.1145/1753326.1753409

29. Kim, S., Lee, S., Han, J.: StretchArms: promoting stretching exercise with a smartwatch. Int. J. Hum.-Comput. Interact. **34**, 218–225 (2018). https://doi.org/10.1080/10447318.2017.134 2408

30. Hao, T., Bi, C., Xing, G., Chan, R., Tu, L.: MindfulWatch: a smartwatch-based system for real-time respiration monitoring during meditation. In: Proceedings of the ACM Interactive, Mobile, Wearable and Ubiquitous Technology, vol. 1, pp. 1–19 (2017). https://doi.org/10.1145/3130922

31. Corbishley, P., Rodriguez-Villegas, E.: Breathing detection: towards a miniaturized, wearable, battery-operated monitoring system. IEEE Trans. Biomed. Eng. **55**, 196–204 (2008). https://doi.org/10.1109/TBME.2007.910679

32. Dobbelstein, D., Henzler, P., Rukzio, E.: Unconstrained pedestrian navigation based on vibrotactile feedback around the wristband of a smartwatch. In: Proceedings of the 2016 CHI Conference Extended Abstracts on Human Factors in Computing Systems, San Jose, California, USA, pp. 2439–2445. ACM (2016). https://doi.org/10.1145/2851581.2892292

33. Fortmann, J., Cobus, V., Heuten, W., Boll, S.: WaterJewel: design and evaluation of a bracelet to promote a better drinking behaviour. In: Proceedings of the 13th International Conference on Mobile and Ubiquitous Multimedia, pp. 58–67 (2014). https://doi.org/10.1145/2677972.2677976

34. Rubia, K.: The neurobiology of meditation and its clinical effectiveness in psychiatric disorders. Biol. Psychol. **82**, 1–11 (2009). https://doi.org/10.1016/j.biopsycho.2009.04.003

35. Xue, S.-W., Tang, Y.-Y., Tang, R., Posner, M.I.: Short-term meditation induces changes in brain resting EEG theta networks. Brain Cogn. **87**, 1–6 (2014). https://doi.org/10.1016/j.bandc.2014.02.008

36. Aftanas, L.I., Golosheikin, S.A.: Changes in cortical activity in altered states of consciousness: the study of meditation by high-resolution EEG. Hum. Physiol. **29**(2), 143–151 (2003). https://doi.org/10.1023/A:1022986308931

37. Lomas, T., Ivtzan, I., Fu, C.H.Y.: A systematic review of the neurophysiology of mindfulness on EEG oscillations. Neurosci. Biobehav. Rev. **57**, 401–410 (2015). https://doi.org/10.1016/j.neubiorev.2015.09.018

38. Jacobs, G.D., Friedman, R.: EEG spectral analysis of relaxation techniques. Appl. Psychophysiol. Biofeedback **29**(4), 245–254 (2004). https://doi.org/10.1007/s10484-004-0385-2

39. Christodoulou, G., Salami, N., Black, D.S.: The utility of heart rate variability in mindfulness research. Mindfulness **11**(3), 554–570 (2020). https://doi.org/10.1007/s12671-019-01296-3

40. Azam, M.A., Katz, J., Fashler, S.R., Changoor, T., Azargive, S., Ritvo, P.: Heart rate variability is enhanced in controls but not maladaptive perfectionists during brief mindfulness meditation following stress-induction: a stratified-randomized trial. Int. J. Psychophysiol. **98**, 27–34 (2015). https://doi.org/10.1016/j.ijpsycho.2015.06.005

41. Koopman, F.A., Stoof, S.P., Straub, R.H., van Maanen, M.A., Vervoordeldonk, M.J., Tak, P.P.: Restoring the balance of the autonomic nervous system as an innovative approach to the treatment of rheumatoid arthritis. Mol. Med. **17**, 937–948 (2011). https://doi.org/10.2119/molmed.2011.00065

42. Esler, M., et al.: Effects of aging on epinephrine secretion and regional release of epinephrine from the human heart. J. Clin. Endocrinol. Metab. **80**, 435–442 (1995). https://doi.org/10.1210/jcem.80.2.7852502

43. Schwerdtfeger, A.R., Schwarz, G., Pfurtscheller, K., Thayer, J.F., Jarczok, M.N., Pfurtscheller, G.: Heart rate variability (HRV): from brain death to resonance breathing at 6 breaths per minute. Clin. Neurophysiol. **131**, 676–693 (2020). https://doi.org/10.1016/j.clinph.2019.11.013

44. Lee, K.-J., Park, C.-A., Lee, Y.-B., Kim, H.-K., Kang, C.-K.: EEG signals during mouth breathing in a working memory task. Int. J. Neurosci. **130**, 425–434 (2020). https://doi.org/10.1080/00207454.2019.1667787

45. Jasper, H.H.: The ten-twenty electrode system of the International Federation. Electroencephalogr. Clin. Neurophysiol. **10**, 370–375 (1958)

46. Baer, R., Smith, G., Allen, K.: Assessment of mindfulness by self-report: the Kentucky Inventory of Mindfulness Skills. Assessment **11**, 191–206 (2004). https://doi.org/10.1177/1073191104268029

47. Lau, M.A., et al.: The Toronto mindfulness scale: development and validation. J. Clin. Psychol. **62**, 1445–1467 (2006). https://doi.org/10.1002/jclp.20326

48. Giggins, O.M., Persson, U.M., Caulfield, B.: Biofeedback in rehabilitation. J. NeuroEngineering Rehabil. **10**, 60 (2013). https://doi.org/10.1186/1743-0003-10-60

CHIAPON: An Anthropomorphic Character Notification System that Discourages Their Excessive Smartphone Use

Kazuyoshi Murata[✉]

Aoyama Gakuin University, Sagamihara, Kanagawa 2525258, Japan
kmurata@si.aoyama.ac.jp

Abstract. Smartphones have become a central part of information processing devices. Smartphones are used for information searching, taking photographs, listening to music, and socializing. However, as the number of smartphone users continues to expand, a number of problems related to smartphone overuse have emerged. Smartphone overuse is most commonly discouraged by issuing warnings to users or imposing a time limit on usage. However, although these methods discourage smartphone use at the time of issue, simple warnings are ineffective and excessively severe restrictions can frustrate users. This paper proposes a system that messages users through an anthropomorphic character when their smartphone has been overused. The system, called "CHIAPON", was experimentally evaluated on 25 college students. The results showed that message notification by an anthropomorphic character can improve users' motivation to reduce their smartphone use, but the extent of this reduction was not clarified. However, the participants using CHIAPON perceived the system positively, suggesting that the effect of the system can increase with long-term use.

Keywords: Smartphone users' motivation · Excessive smartphone use · Message notification system

1 Introduction

Smartphones are rapidly spreading worldwide and have become a central part of information processing devices. In Japan, smartphone ownership has reportedly surpassed personal computer ownership since 2018[1]. Smartphones are beneficial in various situations, such as searching for information, taking photographs, listening to music, and socializing. However, as the number of smartphone users continues to rise, various problems related to smartphone overuse have also emerged.

For example, habitual smartphone use can lead to smartphone addiction [19]. Many smartphone users often check their smartphones while working, studying, walking, and performing their daily life activities. One cause of this excessive smartphone use is the fear of being judged or missed by others [20]. Such excessive smartphone use has

---

[1] https://www.soumu.go.jp/johotsusintokei/whitepaper/eng/WP2019/2019-index.html.

© Springer Nature Switzerland AG 2021
M. Kurosu (Ed.): HCII 2021, LNCS 12763, pp. 432–445, 2021.
https://doi.org/10.1007/978-3-030-78465-2_32

been linked to reduced productivity [5] and affected learning. A study on college students reported a negative relationship between smartphone use and grades [7, 13]. Smartphone and social media use during study has also been associated with smartphone interference in life [4]. Risks associated with the blue light of smartphone screens [16] and health effects such as neck pain from smartphone use [1, 2] have also been reported. Another study reported a relationship between smartphone use and depression and anxiety [6]. Furthermore, the increased use of smartphones has increased the number of smartphone-related accidents during walking. Smartphones use distracts pedestrians [15] and reduces their awareness of the immediate environment [14]. Experiments in a virtual environment have shown that talking, texting, listening to music, and using the Internet on a cell phone or using a cell phone while crossing the street reduces pedestrian safety [3, 18]. Solving the social problems caused by inappropriate smartphone use has attracted much interest. Conscious efforts by individuals to change their smartphone-usage habits often fail [17]. For this reason, a mechanism that discourage excessive use of smartphones is demanded.

Smartphone usage is most commonly discouraged by issuing warnings or prohibiting usage beyond a specified amount of time on the phone, such as Screen Time feature on an iPhone. Other methods include changing the screen to grayscale, which reduces users' satisfaction [9], or increasing the usage cost by enforcing additional tasks on users [11]. However, although these methods discourage smartphone use at the time of issue, simple warnings are ineffective and excessively severe restrictions tend to frustrate users [10].

There are two problems with these systems. First, users wish to continue using their smartphones, despite the opposing notifications and usage restrictions. Users may become annoyed with these mechanisms, ignore them, and eventually cease using them. If users were not forcibly restricted using their smartphones but were instead made to feel that they should not overuse them, they might mitigate their smartphone use without becoming dissatisfied.

The second problem is the smartphone-user relationship. Smartphones and users generally share a property-owner relationship. If some action from the property inhibits the behavior of the user, for example, if the system issues a warning, the user will likely become annoyed and frustrated by the warning. However, if the smartphone-user relationship is equal or intimate, the user may be more receptive to the encouragement.

The study proposes a system that encourages users to moderate their smartphone use without forcibly restraining their behavior with usage restrictions and warnings. Users of this system receive messages from an anthropomorphic character that discourage the excessive use of smartphones. This system, called CHIAPON, replaces smartphone-user (property-owner) relationship with a relationship between an anthropomorphic character and the user, which is intended to improve the acceptance rate of users. Specifically, the anthropomorphic character sends message notifications to the user. Whether message notification by the anthropomorphic character actually motivates users to discourage their excessive smartphone use was evaluated in an experiment.

This study targeted university students who often use smartphones. Under restrictions imposed by COVID-19, online lectures have become the mainstream in universities. Particularly in Japan, many students attend online lectures through their smartphones, which has dramatically increased the number of opportunities for smartphone use by university students. Therefore, smartphone dependence is expected to increase in this group.

However, conventional warnings and forced restrictions on use may reduce the number of opportunities for online education. Therefore, a system that discourages smartphone users from unnecessary use only is urgently demanded. This study is expected to make an effective contribution to the overuse problem.

2 Overview of CHIAPON

Our CHIAPON application notifies the user through an anthropomorphic character installed in the user's smartphone, which sends messages to discourage excessive use of the smartphone. CHIAPON is implemented as an application on the iPhone. When CHIAPON is started, the screen shown in Fig. 1 is displayed. In this example, the message is delivered by a penguin-like anthropomorphic character.

CHIAPON presents users with different messages and smartphone usages at specific times. To imbue the character with personality and increase its sense of intimacy with the user, messages such as "Hang in there," which encourage moderate use of the smartphone, are complemented with messages of sympathy for the situation, suggestions for other actions, reprimands for overuse, and utterances about the character itself. The content of the message is shown in Table 1, Table 2 and Table 3, and an example of the message display is shown in Fig. 2. Notifications are issued under three conditions as listed below.

– When the screen of the smartphone is lit
– When the smartphone is used for a certain amount of time
– At scheduled times

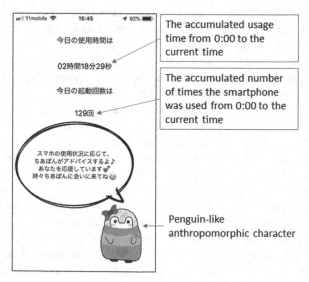

Fig. 1. The launch screen of CHIAPON.

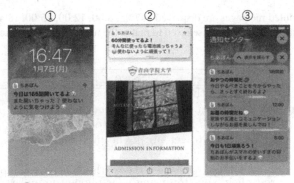

① When the screen of the smartphone is lit
② When the smartphone is used for a certain amount of time
③ At scheduled times

Fig. 2. Examples of messages displayed on the smartphone screen.

Table 1. The message notification when the screen lights up is randomly selected at the notification time.

Time	Message
4:00-21:59	– You've opened it again? Be careful not to overuse it! – I'm so surprised to be called so many times! – Let's try to reduce the number of times we open our phones to reduce overuse. – I'm watching you open your phone. – Before you use your phone, do something else first!
22:00-23:59	– We're almost done for the day! Is there anything left to do? – Have you checked your schedule for tomorrow? Can we have a good rest tomorrow? – It's getting late already, isn't it? Have you taken a bath yet? – Is there anything else to do today? – I'm getting ready for bed. - Don't you have anything else to do? – It's almost the end of the day. Try your best not to use your phone.
0:00-3:59	– I fell asleep. What's wrong? Let's go to bed. – You're still awake? Let's go to bed. – Close your phone and get some rest. – I was just dreaming... It was full of food... – The rhythm of early to bed and early to rise is important.

Table 2. When the smartphone is used continuously over a certain period of time, a notification message and the usage status are issued at 30-min intervals.

Message
– If you use your smartphone too much, the battery will run down. Try not to use it!

Table 3. The scheduled messages are displayed at 7:00, 8:00, 12:00, 15:00, 18:48, 22:00, 23:50, and 0:00. The messages are randomly selected to match the notification time, except at 22:00 and 0:00.

Time	Message
7:00	– Early bird catches the worm! I got up early for you, too! – Why don't you start exercising this morning? – Are you still sleepy? I want to sleep too. – It's cold and hard to get up in the morning, but let's make it a good day! – Why don't you try to make a day without using your phone?
8:00	– I'm here to help you stop using your phone too much. – Let's start the day by opening CHIAPON! Good luck today! – Good luck today! Come and see me sometimes! – Don't use your smartphone too much, I'm rooting for you! – Come see me and you'll see how much you use your phone!
12:00	– Are you using your phone too much in the morning? – Try not to use your phone too much in the afternoon! – What's for lunch today? Get off your phone and enjoy your lunch. – Enjoy your lunch while communicating with your family and friends! – Let's try not to look at your phones during lunchtime!
15:00	– Let's take a break from your phones! – If you do what you have to do today, you'll be done with it in no time. – The afternoon has just begun!Don't let your phone run out of battery! – Yum-yum... – Let's take a break and rest your phone along with your body!
18:48	– I'm hungry. Have you had dinner today? – We're almost done for the day. Try not to use your phone! – One more step and you'll be fine! – Dinner with the family is fun! – Try to talk to the people around you, maybe something good will come out of it.
22:00	– Today's usage status resets at midnight, so check it out.
23:50	– Look at how much you used your smartphone today. – Take a break tomorrow. – Be careful not to use your smartphone too much! – Try not to use your smartphone too much tomorrow. – I'm glad you're using your phone less!
0:00	– The usage status has been reset. Please reopen the screen of your smartphone and check it with CHIAPON.

2.1 Notification Timing: When the Screen of the Smartphone is Lit

When the screen of the smartphone lights, CHIAPON provides the user with a message and the usage status of the smartphone. The usage status is the accumulated number of times the smartphone was used on that day. Under the condition, the user will always see the messages when it appears. This timing is expected to discourage users from starting to use their smartphones, but will likely become annoying if the message appears every time the screen lights up. To avoid this problem, the frequency of the message notification was set to once per five light-up times of the screen between 4:00 am and 10:00 pm, and once per three light-up times between 10:00 pm and 4:00 am. These timing differ because the negative effects of smartphone use are probably greater at night than during the daytime. The number of times of smartphone use was measured as the number of light-up times of the screen.

2.2 Notification Timing: When the Smartphone Is Used for a Certain Amount of Time

When the smartphone is used continuously over a certain period of time, CHIAPON issues a notification message and the usage status at 30-min intervals. The continuous usage time was defined as the elapsed time since the smartphone screen was turned on. At this time, the usage status is the continuous usage time. This timing is expected to encourage users who are addicted to smartphones to discontinue their use.

2.3 Notification Timing: At Scheduled Times

Scheduled messages are displayed at 7:00, 8:00, 12:00, 15:00, 18:48, 22:00, 23:50, and 0:00. The anthropomorphic character of the smartphone is expected to interact proactively with the user, regardless of the smartphone usage. These interactions will strengthen and maintain the anthropomorphic character-user relationship.

2.4 Measuring the Number of Light-Up Screen Times and the Length of the Smartphone Use

The CHIAPON system measures the number of light-up times of the smartphone screen. It also measured the usage time, defined as the duration of the lit-up. The number of light-up times in one day and the total usage times can be checked on the display when CHIAPON is activated (similarly to Fig. 1).

3 Experiment

This experiment examined whether message notifications from smartphones can improve users' motivation to discourage and reduce excessive smartphone use. The hypotheses of the experiment are stated as follows:

- H1: Message notifications from a smartphone will reduce the smartphone-usage time.
- H2: Message notifications from a smartphone will improve users' motivation to discourage excessive smartphone use.

3.1 Methods

The results of CHIAPON were compared with those of a usage notification system that presents only the status of the smartphone usage. The comparison system was equivalent to a CHIAPON system with its anthropomorphic characters and message notifications removed. Figure 3 shows the start-up screen of the usage notification system and a notification example. The notification timing of this system was that of CHIAPON, but the notification content excluded the messages from the anthropomorphic character, and users were notified only of the usage status. The scheduled messages included the time and an instruction to "Open the app to see today's usage" only.

To test Hypothesis 1 (H1), the changes in the participants' smartphone-usage times before and after using CHIAPON and the usage status notification system were determined. To test hypothesis 2 (H2), whether the participants were more motivated to reduce their smartphone use after using CHIAPON and the usage notification system were determined. The results of the two notification systems were acquired and compared through the questionnaire described below.

The participants were 25 college students (20–24 y; 12 males, 13 females) divided into two groups: the CHIAPON group (6 males, 7 females) and the usage notification group (6 males,6 females).

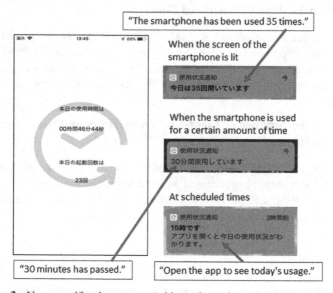

Fig. 3. Usage notification system (without the anthropomorphic character).

3.2 Procedure

The experiment was conducted as follows.

1. The experiment was explained to all participants. The participants were asked to use their smartphone for one week without using CHIAPON or the usage notification system.
2. The participants were asked to report their daily smartphone-usage time (displayed by the iPhone Screen time feature) on each day throughout the first week.
3. At the beginning of the second week, the system was installed on the participants' smartphones, the participants were instructed to the system for one week.
4. The participants were asked to report their daily smartphone-usage time (displayed by the iPhone Screen Time feature) on each day during the second week.
5. At the end of the experiment, the participants answered the following questionnaire.

[Q1] Have you thought about reducing your excessive smartphone use while using the CHIAPON or usage notification system? (1: disagree, 5: agree)
[Q2] This system sent notifications. Did you feel that the notifications were annoying? (Yes or no) If yes, what made you feel annoyed? Multiple answers are allowed.

"The form of the notification itself is annoying."
"The content displayed in the notifications is annoying."
"The tone of the notifications is annoying."
"The notifications interfered with smartphone use."
"The frequency of notifications was high."
"Other."

[Q3] Did you like about CHIAPON? (CHIAPON group only: free description)

Both systems were uninstalled after the experiment.

3.3 Results

One male participant in the CHIAPON group and one female participant in the usage notification group failed to measure the data of the screen time function. The results of both participants were omitted and the results from the remaining 12 members of the CHIAPON group (5 males, 7 females) and 11 members of the usage notification group (6 males, 5 females) were analyzed. On any day, the Screen Time feature displays the accumulated usage time from 0:00 to the time of checking the usage time. Therefore, the usage time cannot be accurately determined on the reporting date because it is affected by the timing of the checks. To reduce this uncertainty, the daily smartphone-usage time was calculated from the data of five days on each week (excluding the reporting day).

Figure 4 and Fig. 5 show the rates of decrease in daily smartphone-usage time before and after running the CHIAPON and user notification system, respectively. On average, the CHIAPON and user notification groups reduced their smartphone uses by 5.0[%] and 3.4[%], respectively. The smartphone-usage times before and after the system use in each group were not significantly different (t-test: CHIAPON group: $t_{(22)} = 0.580$, $p = 0.567$; usage notification group: $t_{(20)} = 0.300$, $p = 0.766$). In the CHIAPON group, seven of the 12 participants reduced their daily smartphone-usage time. The remaining four participants conversely increased their usage time, and one participant reported no change in usage time. In the usage notification group, eight of the 11 participants reduced their usage time and three participants increased their usage time. Moreover, the decrease rates in smartphone-usage times did not significantly differ between the CHIAPON and usage notification groups (t-test: $t_{(21)} = 0.298, p = 0.769$).

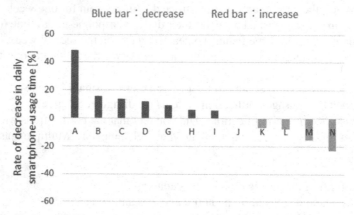

Fig. 4. Rate of decrease in daily smartphone-usage time (CHIAPON group).

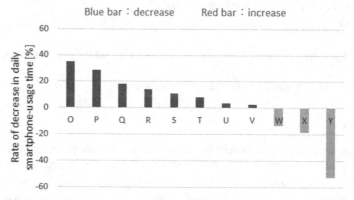

Fig. 5. Rate of decrease in daily smartphone-usage time (usage notification group).

Figure 6 shows the result of Q1 in the post-use questionnaire: "Have you thought about reducing your excessive smartphone use while using the CHIAPON or usage notification system?" The mean score was 3.4 in the CHIAPON group and 2.6 in the usage notification group, but the results of the two groups were not statistically different (t-test: $t_{(21)} = 1.698, p = 0.104$). However, focusing on the individual participants, seven out of 12 participants in the CHIAPON group reported a score of 4 or higher, indicating that more than half of the participants wanted to lower their smartphone use. In contrast, seven of the 11 participants in the usage notification group reported a score of 2 or lower.

Figure 7 shows the results of Q2 in the post-use questionnaire, phrased as "This system sent notifications. Did you feel that the notifications were annoying?" The number

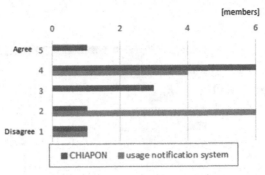

Fig. 6. Result of Q1: Have you thought about reducing your excessive smartphone use while using the CHIAPON or usage notification system?

of "yes" responses was eight out of 12 in the CHIAPON group and seven out of 11 in the usage notification group. When asked why the notifications were annoying, the most common answer among the participants of the CHIAPON group was "the frequency of notifications was high." Meanwhile, the participants in usage notification group reported "the form of notification itself is annoying," "the content displayed in notifications is annoying," and "the frequency of the notifications was high" in equal numbers. These findings suggest that the participants in the usage notification group were annoyed by the notification itself, but the participants in the CHIAPON group were annoyed only by the frequency of the notifications; the notifications themselves did not leave an unfavorable impression.

The opinions obtained from Q3 of the post-use questionnaire: "What did you like about CHIAPON (CHIAPON group only: free description)" were categorized into two groups: those who decreased their daily smartphone-usage time and those who increased their daily smartphone-usage time (see Fig. 8). The participants who decreased their usage time referred to the appearance and tone of the messages delivered by the anthropomorphic character. In contrast, participants who increased their usage time mentioned their own usage behaviors.

To investigate whether the results differed between males and females, the results of Q1 in the post-use questionnaire: "Have you thought about reducing your excessive smartphone use while using the CHIAPON or the usage notification system?" are categorized by gender in Table 4. The females gave higher ratings than males in the CHIAPON group, but no gender difference in the usage notification group.

4 Discussion

Many of the participants in both groups decreased their smartphone-usage time while adopting the systems. However, there was no significant difference between the CHIAPON and usage notification group, indicating that the decision to reduce smartphone-usage time was influenced not by the messages delivered through the anthropomorphic character, but by the notifications themselves. Based on these results, H1 "Message notifications from a smartphone will reduce smartphone-usage time" must be rejected.

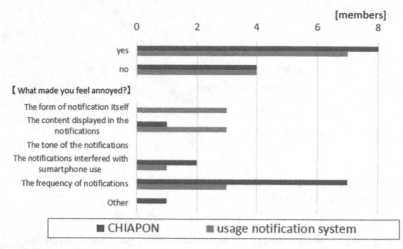

Fig. 7. Result of Q2: Did you feel that the notifications were annoying?

Participants who reduced their daily smartphone-usage time	Participant who increased their daily smartphone-usage time
• The character was cute and motivated me to use the iPhone less often. • The tone of message is gentle, so there is no sense of being coerced. • The tone of message is cute and therefore approachable. • The characters are cute. • I thought I should pay a little attention to the time of use of the smartphone. • I like the fact that it's an app that, while depressing, interferes with me in a good way, and it made me want to stop using my smartphone. • The character was cute and the message was soothing.	• I was able to remind myself that I was using my smartphone too much. • I thought I would do my best to reduce my smartphone usage. • I tried to get a good night's sleep. • As I became more aware of how much of my day I was using my smartphone, I decided to reduce my smartphone use. • I like the fact that it tells me how much time I have on my smartphone and the characters are cute.

Fig. 8. Result of Q3: What did you like about CHIAPON?

The results of Q1 in the post-use questionnaire: "Have you thought about reducing your excessive smartphone use while using the CHIAPON or usage notification system?" showed that more than half of the participants in the usage notification group were unmotivated to lower their excessive smartphone use. Furthermore, the results of Q2: "This system sent notifications. Did you feel that the notifications were annoying?" showed that irritated participants in the usage notification group were annoyed by both the contents and their frequency. That is, frequent usage notifications tend to irritate users. In this experiment, the usage period was one week, but over a longer period of time, the notifications might eventually be ignored or discontinued. In contrast, more than half of the participants in the CHIAPON group wanted to lower their excessive

Table 4. Gender differences in the results of Q1 (scored on a scale of 1–5).

CHIAPON group				Usage notification group			
male	Q1	female	Q1	male	Q1	female	Q1
M1	4	F1	4	M6	2	F8	2
M2	4	F2	3	M7	4	F9	1
M3	1	F3	4	M8	2	F10	4
M4	2	F4	4	M9	4	F11	2
M5	3	F5	5	M10	2	F12	4
		F6	3	M11	2		
		F7	4				
Ave.	2.8	Ave.	3.9	Ave.	2.7	Ave.	2.6

smartphone use. Although some participants in this group were annoyed by the notifications, the annoyance was mainly related to the frequency of the notifications, not the notifications themselves. The results Q3: "What did you like about CHIAPON?" showed that participants who decreased their smartphone-usage time paid more attention to CHIAPON character than to the usage situation or their own behaviour. These results suggest that participants who became intimate with the CHIAPON system were likely to reap its benefits. In addition, because the notifications delivered by the character were liked by the users, continuous use of the CHIAPON system can be expected when the frequency and timing of the notifications are appropriately adjusted. Based on these results, H2: "Message notifications from a smartphone will improve users' motivation to reduce their excessive smartphone use" is accepted.

The gender study revealed a likely difference in the effect of notifications between males and females. Participants in this experiment emphasized the cute appearance of the anthropomorphic character. This perception of the character might explain why the female participants were more motivated than male participants. Therefore, the anthropomorphic characters and messages delivered should be adapted to suit the gender or preferences of users.

This experiment demonstrated that participants were motivated to reduce their smartphone usage, but the extent of this reduction was not clarified. However, the participants in the CHIAPON group perceived the system positively, suggesting that the effect of the system can increase with long-term use. This expectation must be confirmed in long-term experiments. The pattern, frequency, and timing of the CHIAPON notifications must also be adjusted, as users might become habituated to the messages.

5 Related Works

Instead of warning against or prohibiting the use of smartphone, several methods have focused on improving users' motivation to reduce their smartphone use. For example, users of the MyTime [8] system enter a daily goal time limit on each of their installed app. The system displays the time remaining and suggests goals that can be accomplished without using the smartphone. This system encourages users to compete with their peers on refraining from smartphone use, and is intended for continuous use [12]. Such systems motivate users by allowing them to proactively input their own information into the smartphone, and by presenting obtained information. In contrast, CHIAPON approaches the user from the smartphone side. Whereas the existing systems focus on smartphone-usage information, CHIAPON conveys the messages through an anthropomorphic character. As CHIAPON is not incompatible with the existing systems, the two approaches might be combined into a more effective system.

6   Conclusion

To overcome the various problems caused by excessive smartphone use, many systems impose limits on smartphone usage. In this paper, a system that notifies excessive smartphone uses through an anthropomorphic character was proposed. This system, called "CHIAPON" was evaluated in an experiment on college students. The messages output from the CHIAPON system can potentially discourage users from excessive smartphone use. In future work, the pattern, frequency, and timing of the messages output by CHIAPON should be adjusted, and the effectiveness of the messages must be confirmed in long-term usage experiments.

Acknowledgements. This work was supported by JSPS KAKENHI Grant Number JP 20K11909. I would like to thank R. Yako and S. Yoshida for useful discussions.

References

1. AlAbdulwahab, S.S., Kachanathu, S.J., AlMotairi, M.S.: Smartphone use addiction can cause neck disability. Musculoskelet. Care **15**(1), 10–12 (2017)
2. Berolo, S., Wells, R.P., Amick, B.C.: Musculoskeletal symptoms among mobile hand-held device users and their relationship to device use: a preliminary study in a Canadian university population. Appl. Ergon. **42**(2), 371–378 (2011)
3. Byington, K.W., Schwebel, D.C.: Effects of mobile Internet use on college student pedestrian injury risk. Accid. Anal. Prev. **51**, 78–83 (2013)
4. David, P., Kim, J.H., Brickman, J.S., Ran, W., Curtis, C.M.: Mobile phone distraction while studying. New Media Soc. **17**(10), 1661–1679 (2015)
5. Duke, É., Montag, C.: Smartphone addiction, daily interruptions and self-reported productivity. Addict. Behav. Rep. **6**, 90–95 (2017)
6. Elhai, J.D., Levine, J.C., Dvorak, R.D., Hall, B.J.: Fear of missing out, need for touch, anxiety and depression are related to problematic smartphone use. Comput. Hum. Behav. **63**, 509–516 (2016)
7. Felisoni, D.D., Godoi, A.S.: Cell phone usage and academic performance: an experiment. Comput. Educ. **117**, 175–187 (2018)
8. Hiniker, A., Hong, S., Kohno, T., Kientz, J.A.: MyTime: designing and evaluating an intervention for smartphone non-use. In: Proceedings of the 2016 CHI Conference on Human Factors in Computing Systems, pp. 4746–4757 (2016)
9. Holte, A.J., Ferraro, F.R.: True colors: grayscale setting reduces screen time in college students. Soc. Sci. J. 1–17 (2020). https://doi.org/10.1080/03623319.2020.1737461
10. Kim, J., Jung, H., Ko, M., Lee, U.: GoalKeeper: exploring interaction lockout mechanisms for regulating smartphone use. Proc. ACM Interact. Mobile Wearable Ubiquitous Technol. **3**(1), 1–29 (2019)

11. Kim, J., Park, J., Lee, H., Ko, M., Lee, U.: LocknType: lockout task intervention for discouraging smartphone app use. In: Proceedings of the 2019 CHI Conference on Human Factors in Computing Systems, pp. 1–12 (2019)
12. Ko, M., et al.: NUGU: a group-based intervention app for improving self-regulation of limiting Smartphone use. In: CSCW 2015 - Proceedings of the 2015 ACM International Conference on Computer-Supported Cooperative Work and Social Computing, pp. 1235–1245 (2015)
13. Lepp, A., Barkley, J.E., Karpinski, A.C.: The relationship between cell phone use, academic performance, anxiety, and satisfaction with life in college students. Comput. Hum. Behav. 31(1), 343–350 (2014)
14. Lin, M.I., Huang, Y.P.: The impact of walking while using a smartphone on pedestrians' awareness of roadside events. Accid. Anal. Prev. 101, 87–96 (2017)
15. Nasar, J., Hecht, P., Wener, R.: Mobile telephones, distracted attention, and pedestrian safety. Accid. Anal. Prev. 40(1), 69–75 (2008)
16. Oh, J.H., Yoo, H., Park, H.K., Do, Y.R.: Analysis of circadian properties and healthy levels of blue light from smartphones at night. Sci. Rep. 5, 11325 (2015)
17. Schoenebeck, S.Y.: Giving up Twitter for lent: how and why we take breaks from social media. In: Proceedings of the SIGCHI Conference on Human Factors in Computing Systems, pp. 773–782 (2014)
18. Schwebel, D.C., Stavrinos, D., Byington, K.W., Davis, T., O'Neal, E.E., De Jong, D.: Distraction and pedestrian safety: how talking on the phone, texting, and listening to music impact crossing the street. Accid. Anal. Prev. 45, 266–271 (2012)
19. Van Deursen, A.J., Bolle, C.L., Hegner, S.M., Kommers, P.A.: Modeling habitual and addictive smartphone behavior: the role of smartphone usage types, emotional intelligence, social stress, self-regulation, age, and gender. Comput. Hum. Behav. 45, 411–420 (2015)
20. Wolniewicz, C.A., Tiamiyu, M.F., Weeks, J.W., Elhai, J.D.: Problematic smart-phone use and relations with negative affect, fear of missing out, and fear of negative and positive evaluation. Psychiatry Res. 262, 618–623 (2018)

Designing for App Usage Motivation to Support a Gluten-Free Diet by Comparing Various Persuasive Feedback Elements

Katrin Paldán[1]([⊠]), Andreas Künz[1], Walter Ritter[1], and Daire O. Broin[2]

[1] UCT Research, Vorarlberg University of Applied Sciences, Dornbirn, Austria
katrin.paldan@fhv.at
[2] Institute of Technology Carlow, Carlow, Ireland

Abstract. A gluten-free diet (GFD) is critical for people who are affected by celiac disease. To understand how to support people affected by celiac disease through persuasive technology, two apps called Snackfinder and CeliApp were designed within the EU-funded Erasmus + project DESQOL. While Snackfinder is based on the persuasive principle of social support and the CeliApp on self-monitoring, both applications require user entries to be effective. Therefore, various persuasive design elements were implemented in both applications to motivate users to make entries. The extent to which these persuasive design elements contributed to app usage motivation was evaluated in two comparative quasi-experimental user studies.

A significant difference in the motivation to make further entries in the Snackfinder App was found for positive versus negative feedback. No significant difference was found for the comparison of the two rating systems (Star rating versus Like rating) or the comparison of the two variants of color-based feedback in the CeliGear (a physical computing object) connected to the CeliApp. The evaluation of the social feedback in two rating systems and of two variants of the color-based feedback showed a high variance in the respondents' answers. To increase the persuasiveness of the apps presented, user- and context-adaptive design elements seem to be more promising compared to a one-size-fits-all approach.

Keywords: App usage · Motivation · Persuasion · User engagement · Self-monitoring · Social support · Feedback · User test · Evaluation · Health · Gluten-free diet

1 Introduction

Persuasive applications on mobile devices are promising for health-related behavioral support [1]. Self-monitoring of data can be easily implemented via smartphone apps. Analyses can be carried out on the basis of the data entered, which in turn can be visualized for the user. Mobile health applications aim to motivate users to minimize various risk factors or to promote protective factors that are considered effective for the management or treatment of chronic diseases or for a health-promoting lifestyle [2].

© Springer Nature Switzerland AG 2021
M. Kurosu (Ed.): HCII 2021, LNCS 12763, pp. 446–462, 2021.
https://doi.org/10.1007/978-3-030-78465-2_33

Some mobile health apps have shown promising results in randomized trials to support smoking cessation [3], to increase physical activity [4, 5], to support healthy sleep [6] or dietary compliance [7]. A characteristic of persuasive applications is that the supported target behavior (for example to be physical more active) is known to the user and the user has already formed the intention to achieve it.

In these examples, the communication is made with a purpose known to the user and can be described as persuasive according to the definition by Torning and Oinas-Kukkonen [8].This is also the case for applications that aim to make guideline-based dietary recommendations for a gluten-free diet (GFD) more likely for people affected by celiac disease. For example, MyHealthyGut developed in the US is an evidence-based app with the aim to empower users to effectively self-manage celiac disease and promote general good health [9]. Nikniaz et al. [10] conclude that their Persian-language smartphone application for celiac patients had a significant effect on celiac patients' knowledge about gluten-free foods and adherence to GFD. These results suggest that smartphone apps can increase awareness of food intake.

Persuasive elements on mobile applications can form the user experience and influence what people think and how they behave [11]. Reviews on strategies, techniques or principles of persuasion in mobile applications are presented by several authors [12–17]. Conscious self-monitoring and keeping wellbeing and nutrition diaries lead to raised awareness and constitutes a persuasive strategy in its own right [13, 16].

Although there is promising evidence of the benefits of mobile health apps for behavioral support, various reviews show that the scientific foundation and persuasive concepts based on theories of behavior change are addressed to varying degrees in apps [3, 7, 15]. So far, there are no generally valid statements about which persuasive strategies are particularly suitable for given target groups that need to maintain the behavior over a longer period of time and which design elements in the app make a long-term effect of persuasive technologies (PT) particularly likely.

There are various reasons why hardly any long-term effects of PT have been shown so far. The rather short study periods do not allow any statements about the long-term effects [15]. Moreover, studies on the technology adoption process have repeatedly found that the novelty effect and the interest in the technology wears off after about 2 weeks to 2 months and that there are high drop-out rates if no benefit is recognized in the functionality [18]. Encouraging mobile user engagement remains a challenge [19].

One sticking point, addressed in this paper, is motivating users to make data entries regularly and over a longer period of time. Kim et al. [20] define engagement motivation as user's motivation to engage in activities using their smartphones. Participants prefer applications that are quick and easy to administer [7]. This highlights the need for research in this direction to learn more about isolated persuasive design elements motivating users to make further entries in the app. Orji and Moffatt [15] recommend that future research should focus on establishing the interactions between individual strategies and the success of PT by examining the effectiveness of the persuasive strategies in isolation.

The aim of this work is to investigate the subjectively expressed motivation of users to different persuasive design elements in two applications supporting a gluten-free diet. Therefore, two prototypical applications and their persuasive elements are described, and the results of the user tests are presented. The overall objective for both apps is to provide mobile support for a gluten-free diet. Table 1 gives an overview of the persuasive strategies and evaluates design elements of both apps.

Table 1. Overview about the persuasive principles, the evaluated persuasive design elements and the primary outcomes in the two user tests presented in this paper.

Applications	Persuasive strategy	Evaluated persuasive design element (independent variable)		Primary outcome (dependent variable)
Snackfinder	Social support/ Social feedback	Star rating with positive or negative feedback	Like rating with positive or negative feedback	Motivation to make another snack entry after receiving social feedback about the previous snack entry
CeliApp with CeliGear	Self-monitoring/ color-based feedback in an ambient technology	LED color transition from red to green	LED color transition from green to red	Motivation to make another meal/symptom entry after receiving a color-based feedback from the CeliGear

The concept of the apps in both cases is to encourage users to make entries in the apps such as meals consumed, symptoms, or the entry of gluten-free snacks and where to get them. Without the user input, the application would not be effective and could not contribute to behavioral change. Therefore, persuasive design elements were implemented in both applications to increase the motivation to make entries. To what extent these persuasive design elements actually contribute to the motivation to make entries was evaluated in two quasi-experimental studies.

In application 1, called "Snackfinder", rating systems (star rating versus like/dislike rating) in combination with positive or negative feedback were implemented and tested. In application 2, called "CeliApp", the color transition of a physical computing object (CeliGear) in the form of an LED sphere is intended to motivate people to make entries by a color-based feedback.

The question to be investigated in this paper is to what extent the persuasive elements implemented and tested in the two applications Snackfinder and CeliApp can actually motivate users to make more entries in the app and to what extent the motivation of participating users differs between the individuals in the sample sizes. The results of the quasi-experimental user tests are then summarized descriptively and discussed with regard to the motivation to make more entries and the variance between the participating individuals. Finally, the findings as well as the future development of persuasive applications to support engagement motivation [20] are discussed.

2 Design Process for the Prototypical Development of Applications to Support a Gluten-Free Diet

For celiac disease a gluten-free diet is the only effective treatment, but it is difficult to adhere to a gluten-free diet [21]. Noncompliance with a gluten-free diet is often reported among teenagers affected by coeliac disease [22]. In the European project DESQOL, persuasive technologies to support adolescent to adhere to a gluten-free diet in everyday life are to be prototypically developed and tested with the target group of teenagers in Ireland, the Netherlands, Spain and Austria. The goal of the project is to create low-barrier mobile applications that support young people in their everyday life, make them aware of the possible complications coming from the disease, and to help them to follow a gluten-free diet.

Based on interviews and prototype tests, the mobile applications CeliApp and Snack-finder turned out to be the most promising tools so they were developed and tested in more detail as described in the upcoming section. The Snackfinder and CeliApp applications aimed to motivate the user to make entries in the app. The DESQOL project adopted a user-centered approach and involved users at different stages of the project (Fig. 1).

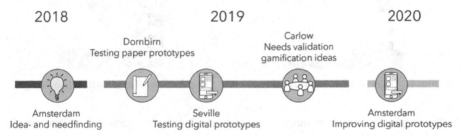

Fig. 1. Timeline for user-centered approach in the European Erasmus DESQOL Project

3   Applications 1: Snackfinder

3.1   App Description, Experimental Design and Procedure

App Description. The aim of the mobile application is to make it easier for people suffering from coeliac disease to find meals or snacks in their environment that suit their dietary preferences. Four main pages were implemented to operate the mobile application: the user profile, the snack list page, the snack map and the snack details page. These allow the user to find, create and rate snacks and meals. The user profile displays the user's data and provides access to the list of snacks created by that user.

Two different presentation methods were implemented to display the snacks. The first presentation method is a snack list that shows available snacks for the selected city. The other presentation method is a snack map based on Google Maps to show exact locations where snacks are available. By applying various filters such as "vegan", "gluten-free!", "low-fat", "vegetarian", "low-sugar" and "low-calorie", the snacks can be filtered by the user according to their preferences.

The fourth main component besides the snack list, the snack map, and the user profile is the snack detail page. The detail page (see Fig. 2 and Fig. 3) of a snack contains information about the individual snack, such as the creator of the snack entry, which tags the snack has received and how other users of the application have rated this snack. In addition, there is the possibility to leave a rating for the snack and thus let other users know how recommendable one thinks the snack is.

Fig. 2. Snack details with a star rating   **Fig. 3.** Snack details with a like rating

To compare two different rating systems, the following two variants for rating snacks were implemented:

- Rating component with a multi-level star rating (Fig. 4)
- Rating component with a two-stage like/dislike scale (Fig. 5)

Fig. 4. Star rating   **Fig. 5.** Like rating

The decision to implement these two rating systems was based on a review of various social media, e-commerce and gaming platforms such as Amazon, Facebook, Instagram, Netflix, Steam and Reddit. It became apparent that these platforms predominantly use like rating systems or have switched to them.

Experimental Design and Procedure. The aim of the study is to make statements about the perceived motivation for further entries from the user's point of view after they have received feedback. The feedback could have four characteristics: (1) Positive star rating, (2) negative star rating, (3) positive like rating, and (4) negative like rating. The feedback as a central point of interaction should thus be realized as optimally as possible from the user's point of view in future applications.

The hypotheses to be investigated are:

- Hypothesis 1: The motivation to create entries is higher with a two-level Like/Dislike rating of entries than with a five-level star scale.
- Hypothesis 2: There is a difference between positively and negatively worded feedback on the motivation to make further entries regardless of whether it is a star rating or a like/dislike rating.

In an experimental within-subjects design, the two different rating systems were tested.

The test subjects were recruited from the students' social environment in Austria. Since it was irrelevant for answering the research question, the test persons did not necessarily have to be affected by coeliac disease. Due to the timeline in the study semester, the application was only implemented for Android devices. The inclusion criterion was the ownership and use of an Android smartphone.

The gender distribution was relatively balanced in all 4 groups, with a slight majority of females in groups 2, 3 and 4. The age group of participants ranged from early 20s to mid 50s. It was determined that approx. 95% of the 30 respondents have already had experiences with different rating systems. The exact number of previous experiences per platform are shown as absolute numbers in Fig. 6. The category "other" includes, for example, hotel booking sites that use a star rating.

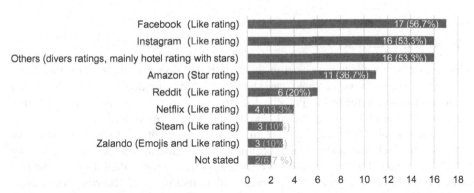

Fig. 6. Respondents' previous experience with rating systems on social media, E-commerce and gaming platforms in absolute numbers (percentage)

In the experiment, each test person tested both rating systems (stars, likes) by creating four snacks and evaluating two snacks with a predefined procedure depending on the group of the test person. The grouping of the individual test subjects to different sequences of given feedback was randomized. All test subjects (N = 30) were shown all four combinations of feedback variants, but in different order to avoid sequence effects. The test subjects received positive or negative ratings for the snacks they had prepared, depending on how they were divided into groups. Table 2 shows the group distribution and experimental conditions and sequence per group.

Table 2. Groups, sampling distribution and sequence per group

Sequence Group 1 (N = 8):	Sequence Group 2 (N = 8):
1. Snack 1: Star rating with positive feedback	1. Snack 1: Like rating with positive feedback
2. Snack 2: Star rating with negative feedback	2. Snack 2: Like rating with negative feedback
3. Snack 3: Like rating with positive feedback	3. Snack 3: Star rating with positive feedback
4. Snack 4: Like rating with negative feedback	4. Snack 4: Star rating with negative feedback
Sequence Group 3 (N = 7):	**Sequence Group 4 (N = 7):**
1. Snack 1: Star rating with negative feedback	1. Snack 1: Like rating with negative feedback
2. Snack 2: Star rating with positive feedback	2. Snack 2: Like rating with positive feedback
3. Snack 3: Like rating with negative feedback	3. Snack 3: Star rating with negative feedback
4. Snack 4: Like rating with positive feedback	4. Snack 4: Star rating with positive feedback

The data collection and testing of the hypotheses was done through an interview with the subjects. An online questionnaire via Google Forms was used to collect the data and IBM SPSS Statistics 26 was used for the statistical analysis. The raw data were analyzed descriptively, and, after checking the test prerequisites, the Wilcoxon test for paired samples was carried out for the comparison of the ratings.

3.2   Results of the User Tests

The descriptive results to the question "how motivated do you feel after receiving feedback about the snack you created" are shown in Table 3 divided by rating system and positive or negative feedback. Perceived motivation was recorded and mapped with a three-point scale of 1 = demotivated, 2 = neutral and 3 = motivated.

The mean value between the two rating systems (regardless of whether positive or negative feedback was given) is identical at 2.18 and the standard deviation differs by 0.105. The values for the star rating are somewhat less variable than those for the like rating. It could not be shown that the perceived motivation after receiving feedback is related to the rating system used.

The descriptive results to the second question "Based on the feedback received, would you make another entry for a snack in the app?" are shown in Table 4 divided by rating system and positive or negative feedback. The motivation to make another entry for a snack was recorded and mapped with a five-point scale of 1 = unmotivated, 2 = somewhat unmotivated 3 = neutral, 4 = rather motivated, and 5 = very motivated). The

Table 3. Comparison of the perceived motivation after receiving feedback between star rating and like rating on an answer scale of 1 = demotivated, 2 = neutral and 3 = motivated (N = 30)

Question: How motivated do you feel after receiving feedback about the snack you have created? Answer scale of 1 = demotivated, 2 = neutral and 3 = motivated *(N = 30)*			
Star rating Positive and negative feedback mixed		Like rating Positive and negative feedback mixed	
Mean (SD) 2.18 (±0.359)		Mean (SD) 2.18 (±0.464)	
Feedback positive	Feedback negative	Feedback positive	Feedback negative
Mean (SD) 2.80 (± 0.407)	Mean (SD) 1.57 (±0.626)	Mean (SD) 2.73 (±0.521)	Mean (SD) 1.63 (±0.615)

mean value between the two rating systems (regardless of whether positive or negative feedback was given) is very close at 3.68 for the star rating and 3.51 for the like rating. Also, the standard deviation hardly differs from each other by 0.17. The values for the star rating are somewhat less variable than those for the like rating.

Table 4. Comparison of the motivation to make another entry for a snack after receiving feedback between star rating and like rating on an answer scale of 1 = unmotivated, 2 = somewhat unmotivated, 3 = neutral, 4 = rather motivated and 5 = very motivated (N = 30)

Question: How motivated are you to make another snack entry in the app after receiving feedback? Answer scale of 1 = unmotivated, 2 = somewhat motivated, 3 = neutral, 4 = rather motivated and 5 = very motivated *(N = 30)*			
Star rating Positive and negative feedback mixed		Like rating Positive and negative feedback mixed	
Mean (SD) 3.68 (±0.932)		Mean (SD) 3.51 (±1.110)	
Feedback positive	Feedback negative	Feedback positive	Feedback negative
Mean (SD) 4.27 (± 0.944)	Mean (SD) 3.10 (±1.373)	Mean (SD) 4.10(±1.125)	Mean (SD) 2.93(±1.530)

In the investigated user group, there is no noticeable difference in the motivation to make a new entry depending on whether the test person receives feedback via the star rating or the like rating (Asymptotic Wilcoxon test: $z = -1.118$, $p = 0.264$, $n = 30$. Hypothesis, that the motivation to make another entry after receiving feedback is related to the rating system used could not be accepted.

In the two rating systems, receiving positive feedback had a more motivating effect than negative feedback. This is also confirmed by the test statistics. Regardless of the rating system, the means of the positive and negative ratings differ significantly from each other. This applies both to the question of how motivated they feel (asymptotic Wilcoxon test: z = −4.683, p = .000, n = 30) and to the question of whether the subjects would make further entries based on the feedback (asymptotic Wilcoxon test: z = −3.729, p = .000, n = 30). In terms of perceived motivation, the effect size according to Cohen (1992) is r = .85 and corresponds to a strong effect of positive feedback on motivation. In terms of motivation to make another entry, the effect size of r = .68 also corresponds to a strong effect. The differences in the mean values between positive and negative feedback determined with the Wilcoxon test can thus be classified as significant. Hypothesis 2 is therefore supported.

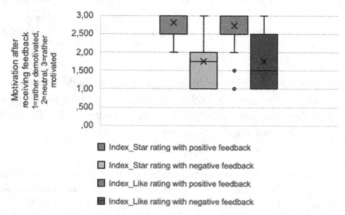

Fig. 7. Motivation index to make another snack entry after receiving social feedback about the foreign snack entry (N = 30; Whiskers in the boxplot represent the minimum and maximum)

Figure 7 shows the data collected on the Snackfinder app for the 30 participants on the perceived motivation to make further entries in the app after receiving feedback from the two items asked (Item 1: How motivated do you feel after receiving feedback about the snack you have created? Item 2: How motivated are you to make another snack entry in the app after receiving feedback?). It is presented as an index on a scale of 1 = rather demotivated, 2 = neutral and 3 = rather motivated. Figure 7 shows that participants found positive feedback (mean star rating = 2.8; median star rating = 3; mean like rating = 2,73; median like rating = 3) more motivating than negative feedback (mean star rating = 1.75; median star rating = 1.75; mean like rating = 1.75; median like rating = 1.5). In the case of positive feedback, the dispersion was also lower, although this can be seen in particular for positive star rating (SD positive star rating = 0.3619) whereas a positive like rating was perceived as rather demotivating by two participants. In the case of negative feedback, a wide spread of data can be found across rather demotivating, neutral and rather motivating, regardless of the rating system (SD positive like rating = 0.5040; SD = negative star rating = 0.6123; SD negative like rating = 0.6532). The motivation after receiving feedback of participating users differs between the individuals in the sample sizes.

4   Application 2: CeliApp with CeliGear

4.1   App Description, Experimental Design and Procedure

Since a gluten free diet is of enormous importance for coeliac patients, the users of the app should regularly monitor their meals and symptoms. The CeliApp is a nutrition and symptom diary app that rewards the user for entries.

The user of the app is reminded to provide entries into the app by an external "physical computing" object, which is stationary at the user's home. This object is equipped with an LED and communicates with the smartphone via WLAN. It lights up in five different colors, depending on the number of entries made on a given day (see Fig. 8). The colors red, yellow and green are used, as well as mixtures of these as intermediate steps. The color transition via the physical computing object (CeliGear) is intended to motivate people to make entries.

Fig. 8. CeliGear: a physical computing object showing five different colors as feedback element to motivate entries in the CeliApp (Color figure online)

Experimental Design and Procedure. The aim of the study is to investigate the effect of two color transitions on the motivation to make entries in the CeliApp.

The hypothesis to be investigated was:

• The motivation to make entries differs between the two variants of the color transition

To test the hypothesis, two variants of color transitions were compared: variant 1 and variant 2. With variant 1, the light of the LED starts with red in the morning and develops towards green with each entry. In variant 2, the light of the LED starts with the color green in the morning and turns more and more towards red during the day if no entries are made. The course of the day was simulated within a 20 min timeframe during the test. With continuous entries, the light retains the color green.

The motivation to make entries in the CeliApp for the Vorarlberg University of Applied Sciences and at the students' working environment (IMA-SystemsInformation-Technology GmbH). Since it was irrelevant for answering the research question, the test persons did not necessarily have to be affected by coeliac disease.

The assignment to the groups (see Table 5) with color gradient variant 1 (red to green) and color gradient variant 2 (green to red) was randomized. None of the participants suffered from red-green weakness.

The experiment was carried out according to the same scheme in both groups and differed only in the color transition of the LED. The lighting conditions were standardized

Table 5. Sample size, gender distribution and age distribution per variant

Variant 1 (Color transition red to green)	Variant 2 (Color transition green to red)
N = 14 (4 females, 10 males, mean age 34, range from age 16 to age 85)	N = 12 (2 females, 10 males, mean age 25, range from age 21 to age 32)

in all tests so that the light from the CeliGear was easy to see. After test persons had familiarized themselves with the CeliApp, the test started. The test persons then had to make entries in the CeliApp and answer the interview questions posed. By making entries in the app the color of the CeliGear changed according to the variant tested. For the interview, a questionnaire that was pretested beforehand was used to document the answers that subjects gave in the study run. In this questionnaire also confounding variables like red-green deficiency or a participant's favorite color were asked.

4.2   Results of the User Tests

The descriptive results to the question "How motivated are you to make further entries in the CeliApp?", which the users was asked several times in a simulated day after a color transition of the CeliGear occurred, are illustrated in Fig. 9 after color transition variant 1 (red to green) and variant 2 (green to red). Perceived motivation was recorded and mapped with a six-point scale of 1 = unmotivated at all to 6 = very motivated. The mean value and standard deviation for variant 1 overall measuring points is 4,04 (SD 1,39) and therefore hardly differs from the mean value and standard deviation for variant 2 over all measuring points with 3,98 (SD 1.24). Based on the descriptive evaluation, the hypothesis that the motivation of entries differs depending on the color transition was not supported.

Figure 9 shows the mean values and confidence intervals of the two variants per measurement time. Although the mean values per measurement time and current coloring differ, the noticeable overlap of the confidence intervals indicates a random difference. A more detailed examination also indicates a non-significant difference between variant 1 and variant 2.

Figure 10 shows the data collected for variant 1 of the color transitions in CeliGear on the perceived motivation to make further entries in the app after receiving feedback on a scale of 1 = not motivated at all to 6 = very motivated for the 14 participants. Mean and median in Fig. 10 show that participants found the colors differently motivating depending on the (simulated) time of day. The measures of dispersion indicate interpersonal differences in perceived motivation in relation to coloring. Both the color green and the color red are perceived very differently by users in the evening, which is indicated by the high dispersion in the answers (SD Day 1: Just before the LED switches off in the evening = 1,6919; Day 2: Just before the LED switches off in the evening = 1,9499). The color orange is perceived as motivating in different ways depending on the time of day, whereby the variance is higher in the evening as well (SD Day 2: Just before the LED switches off in the evening = 1,2157).

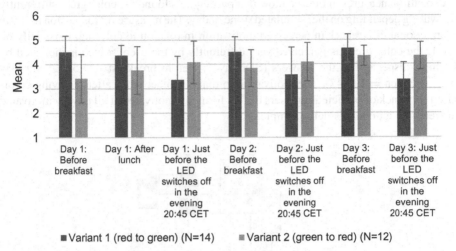

Fig. 9. Mean values and confidence intervals per measurement time point in the 3-day simulation of CeliApp and CeliGear usage shown by variant 1 (red to green) and variant 2 (green to red) (Color figure online)

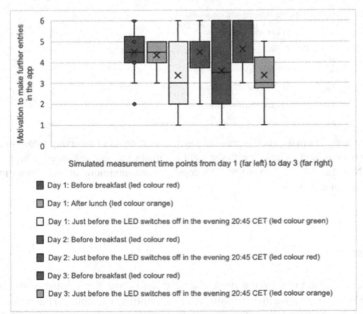

Fig. 10. Motivation to make another meal and symptom entry after receiving a color-based feedback from red to green (variant 1) with the CeliGear from 1 = not motivated at all to 6 = very motivated (N = 14; Whiskers in the boxplot represent the minimum and maximum) (Color figure online)

Figure 11 shows the data collected for variant 2 of the color transitions in the CeliGear on the perceived motivation to make further entries in the app after receiving feedback on a scale of 1 = not motivated at all to 6 = very motivated for the 12 participants. The location measures in Fig. 11 show that participants found the color green differently motivating depending on the (simulated) time of day. The measures of dispersion indicate interpersonal differences in perceived motivation in relation to coloring. Especially on day 1, the color green is perceived very differently by the users, which is indicated by the high dispersion in the answers (SD Day 1: Before breakfast = 1,5642; SD Day 1: After lunch = 1,5447). The motivation to make another entry after receiving color-based feedback of participating users differs form not motivated at all to very motivated between the individuals in the sample.

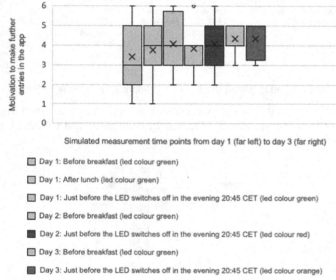

Fig. 11. Motivation to make another meal and symptom entry after receiving a color-based feedback from green to red (variant 2) with the CeliGear from 1 = not motivated at all to 6 = very motivated (N = 12; Whiskers in the boxplot represent the minimum and maximum motivation levels) (Color figure online)

5   Discussion

The user tests carried out have a pilot character and have some limitations, such as a small sample size, no uniform distribution of confounding variables in the randomization process, thereby an imbalance of gender and age distribution in the testing of the color-based feedback, acquisition of the study groups in the social environment of the test coordinators, sample composition, and artificially generated input situations due to the experimental setting. The results must therefore be interpreted with extreme caution. However, the tests do provide initial indications of the extent to which users found the implemented persuasive design elements motivating or demotivating. The results also indicate that the subjectively expressed motivation to make further entries in the app varies greatly between users.

For the development of persuasive technologies, the question therefore arises to what extent it is at all predictable for the creator of the PT, whether the persuasive strategy or the implemented persuasive concept will lead to the desired behavior, and whether the individuality of preferences (e.g. with regard to colors) or previous experiences (e.g. with regard to rating systems) can be taken more into account in personalized design and adaptation of persuasive elements. This is in line with Berkovsky et al. [23], who postulate that personalized technologies aim to enhance user experience by taking into account users' interests, preferences, and other relevant information and that "the persuasive power of a one-size-fits-all persuasive intervention could be enhanced by considering the users being influenced and their susceptibility to the persuasion being offered" [23, p. 9].

Personalization Through Context- and User-Adaptive System Design. The variance in the user reactions described above indicates, that a coupling of personalization and persuasion has the potential to enhance the impact of encouraging health apps, while addressing individual preferences more precisely.

In addition to personal preferences, the context in which a persuasive design element is presented and interpreted plays a role. Lu et al. give "insight into the psychological mechanisms of ambient persuasive technology by making clear that ambient stimuli (e.g., color) are part of a broader context that influences user's interpretation and the effectiveness of these stimuli" [24, p. 303].

One starting point would be the personalization of the application through a context- and user-adaptive system design, where the preferences and data entered by the user are integrated into the design of the persuasive concept. The design, such as the rating system (stars versus like/dislikes) or the color gradient of the LED display, could thus be better adapted to the user, which is also suggested by one user. For example, the CeliGear could be configured according to personal preferences (e.g. selectable color scheme, adjustable to getting up and going to bed times). In further field studies the context of the ambient stimuli should also be taken into account.

Making Users to Co-designers of the App Customization. For an optimal acceptance of the technology by all user groups it is important to involve the users in the decision process which design elements should be implemented. In this way, a better interaction between technology and the way users work can be guaranteed [25]. Participatory Design (PD) is a design method that involves all stakeholders [26]. However, the challenge here is that designers often have limited time resources available for development [27]. Methods and techniques need to be established that involve users in the adaptation of the app over a longer period of time and make them co-designers. A starting point could be the critical observation and evaluation of the mobile user engagement in the first period of use in the field. If defined goals are not achieved (e.g. hardly any entries are made in the diary), the possible reasons should be identified and discussed in a dialogue with the users that is triggered by the application. Based on these statements, alternative persuasive concepts and designs could be proposed.

The motivation to use the apps presented here will probably be higher for people affected by celiac disease. Therefore, a field study (21 day challenge) is planned in the further course of the project, in which a variant of the app will be used and tested by people suffering from celiac disease.

Engagement Motivation After Positive and Negative Social Feedback. Only for the positive feedback in the Snackfinder less variance in the user responses can be recognized. Even though positive social feedback is not something that app developers can directly control, providing social feedback seems to be important for motivating entries, independent of the rating system. The role of feedback to encourage users to stay in the community and to post entries are shown by Cheng et al. [28]. However, in the user tests presented here it was found that the motivation to make further entries was significantly higher with positive feedback than with negative feedback. However, this observation may be due to the data collection of the dependent variable by means of conducting interviews in the experimental setting. An objective measurement of actually made entries in a field study could come to a different result and show that negative feedback leads to more (but qualitatively worse) entries, which would be in line with other studies [28, 29].

6 Conclusion

Targeting behavior change through persuasive strategies such as self-monitoring and social support on smartphones require that the users interact with their devices. Without user interaction and data input, persuasive technologies (PT) will hardly identify the appropriate trigger to change or influence the behavior, beliefs or attitudes of their users [16]. However, motivating users to make entries in an app is still a challenge. With the user tests described in this paper we face this challenge with an isolated evaluation of persuasive design elements. The evaluation of social feedback in two rating systems and color-based feedback through a color transition indicates high variance in the respondents' answers. The findings suggest that in future more attention in development projects should be paid to identifying those design elements that make mobile user engagement more likely for individual users and their context.

Acknowledgements. This work was carried out as part of the DESQOL project. The DESQOL project was co-funded by the Erasmus + programme of the European Union (2018-1-IE02-KA203-000613).

We thank all the project partners in the DESQOL project for there expertise and their contribution to the user-centred design process to conceptualize the applications Snackfinder and CeliApp: The consortium lead partner Institute of Technology Carlow (Ireland), the lead medical partner St. Lukes Hospital in Kilkenny (Ireland), the Stitching Hogeschool van Amsterdam (The Netherlands), Universidad de Seville and Foundation IHP Seville (Spain) and the University of Applied Sciences Vorarlberg (Austria).

Our special thanks to the students in the computer science master program at the Vorarlberg University of Applied Sciences who developed the apps Snackfinder and CeliApp und conducted the user tests in their third semester (WS 2019/20).

The Snackfinder App was developed and tested by Christina Tschol, Christoph Fabian Rheinberger, Florian Sebastian Bechtold and Jan Fleisch.

The CeliApp was developed and tested by Anna Malena Rauch, Florian Richter, Gerhard Stark and Simeon Bösch.

References

1. Burke, L.E., et al.: Current science on consumer use of mobile health for cardiovascular disease prevention: a scientific statement from the American Heart Association. Circulation **132**, 1157–1213 (2015). https://doi.org/10.1161/CIR.0000000000000232
2. Zhang, X., Deng, Z., Parvinzamir, F., Dong, F.: MyHealthAvatar lifestyle management support for cancer patients. Ecancermedicalscience **12** (2018).https://doi.org/10.3332/ecancer.2018.849
3. Haskins, B.L., Lesperance, D., Gibbons, P., Boudreaux, E.D.: A systematic review of smartphone applications for smoking cessation. Transl. Behav. Med. **7**(2), 292–299 (2017). https://doi.org/10.1007/s13142-017-0492-2
4. Gal, R., May, A.M., van Overmeeren, E.J., Simons, M., Monninkhof, E.M.: The effect of physical activity interventions comprising wearables and smartphone applications on physical activity: a systematic review and meta-analysis. Sports Med. Open **4**(1), 1–15 (2018). https://doi.org/10.1186/s40798-018-0157-9
5. Coughlin, S.S., Whitehead, M., Sheats, J.Q., Mastromonico, J., Smith, S.: A review of smartphone applications for promoting physical activity. Jacobs J. Commun. Med. **2**(1) (2016). http://www.ncbi.nlm.nih.gov/pubmed/27034992
6. Shin, J.C., Kim, J., Grigsby-Toussaint, D.: Mobile phone interventions for sleep disorders and sleep quality: Systematic review. JMIR mHealth uHealth **5**(9), e131 (2017). https://doi.org/10.2196/mhealth.7244
7. Coughlin, S.S., Whitehead, M., Sheats, J.Q., Mastromonico, J., Hardy, D., Smith, S.A.: Smartphone applications for promoting healthy diet and nutrition: a literature review. Jacobs J. Food Nutr. **2**(3), 021 (2015). http://www.ncbi.nlm.nih.gov/pubmed/26819969
8. Torning, K., Oinas-Kukkonen, H.: Persuasive system design: state of the art and future directions. ACM Int. Conf. Proc. Ser. **350**, 1–8 (2009). https://doi.org/10.1145/1541948.154 1989
9. Justine Dowd, A., Jackson, C., Tang, K.T.Y., Nielsen, D., Clarkin, D.H., Nicole Culos-Reed, S.: MyHealthyGut: development of a theory-based self-regulatory app to effectively manage Celiac disease. mHealth **4**, 19–19 (2018). https://doi.org/10.21037/mhealth.2018.05.05
10. Nikniaz, Z., Shirmohammadi, M., Akbari Namvar, Z.: Development and effectiveness assessment of a Persian-language smartphone application for celiac patients: a randomized controlled clinical trial. Patient Educ. Couns. (2020). https://doi.org/10.1016/j.pec.2020.08.014
11. Lindemann, P., Koelle, M., Kranz, M.: Persuasive technologies and applications. Adv. Embed. Interact. Syst. **3**(2), 46 (2015). http://www.eislab.fim.uni-passau.de/files/publications/2015/TR2015-PersuasiveTechnologies.pdf
12. Cialdini, R.: Harnessing the science of persuasion. Harv. Bus. Rev. **79**(9), 72–81 (2001)
13. King, P., Tester, J.: The landscape of persuasive technologies. Commun. ACM **42**(5), 31–38 (1999). https://doi.org/10.1145/301353.301398
14. Halko, S., Kientz, J.A.: Personality and persuasive technology: an exploratory study on health-promoting mobile applications. In: Ploug, T., Hasle, P., Oinas-Kukkonen, H. (eds.) PERSUASIVE 2010. LNCS, vol. 6137, pp. 150–161. Springer, Heidelberg (2010). https://doi.org/10.1007/978-3-642-13226-1_16

15. Orji, R., Moffatt, K.: Persuasive technology for health and wellness: state-of-the-art and emerging trends. Health Inf. J. **24**(1), 66–91 (2018). https://doi.org/10.1177/146045821665 0979

16. Fogg, B.J.: Persuasive Technology: Using Computers to Change What We Think and Do. Morgan Kaufmann Publishers Inc., San Francisco (2003)

17. Oinas-Kukkonen, H., Harjumaa, M.: A systematic framework for designing and evaluating persuasive systems. In: Oinas-Kukkonen, H., Hasle, P., Harjumaa, M., Segerståhl, K., Øhrstrøm, P. (eds.) PERSUASIVE 2008. LNCS, vol. 5033, pp. 164–176. Springer, Heidelberg (2008). https://doi.org/10.1007/978-3-540-68504-3_15

18. de Graaf, M.M.A., Allouch, S.B., van Dijk, J.A.G.M.: Long-term evaluation of a social robot in real homes. Interaction Studies. Social Behaviour and Communication in Biological and Artificial Systems **17**(3), 461–490 (2016). https://doi.org/10.1075/is.17.3.08deg

19. Saksono, H., Castaneda-Sceppa, C., Hoffman, J., Morris, V., Seif El-Nasr, M., Parker, A. G.: Storywell: designing for family fitness app motivation by using social rewards and reflection. In: Proceedings of the 2020 CHI Conference on Human Factors in Computing Systems, pp. 1–13 (2020). https://doi.org/10.1145/3313831.3376686.

20. Kim, Y.H., Kim, D.J., Wachter, K.: A study of mobile user engagement (MoEN): engagement motivations, perceived value, satisfaction, and continued engagement intention. Decis. Support Syst. **56**(1), 361–370 (2013). https://doi.org/10.1016/j.dss.2013.07.002

21. Itzlinger, A., Branchi, F., Elli, L., Schumann, M.: Gluten-free diet in celiac disease—forever and for all? Nutrients **10**, 1796 (2018). https://doi.org/10.3390/nu10111796

22. Olsson, C., Hrnell, A., Ivarsson, A., Sydner, Y.M.: The everyday life of adolescent coeliacs: issues of importance for compliance with the gluten-free diet. J. Hum. Nutr. Diet. **21**(4), 359–367 (2008). https://doi.org/10.1111/j.1365-277X.2008.00867.x

23. Berkovsky, S., Freyne, J., Oinas-Kukkonen, H.: Influencing individually: fusing personalization and persuasion. ACM Trans. Interact. Intell. Syst. **2**(2), 1–8 (2012). https://doi.org/10.1145/2209310.2209312

24. Lu, S., Ham, J., Midden, C.: Red radiators versus red tulips: the influence of context on the interpretation and effectiveness of color-based ambient persuasive technology. In: Meschtscherjakov, A., De. Ruyter, B., Fuchsberger, V., Murer, M., Tscheligi, M. (eds.) PERSUASIVE 2016. LNCS, vol. 9638, pp. 303–314. Springer, Cham (2016). https://doi.org/10.1007/978-3-319-31510-2_26

25. Kensing, F., Blomberg, J.: Participatory design: issues and concerns. Comput. Support. Coop. Work **7**(3–4), 167–185 (1998). https://doi.org/10.1023/A:1008689307411

26. Davis, J.: Design methods for ethical persuasive computing. ACM Int. Conf. Proc. Ser. **350**, 1 (2009). https://doi.org/10.1145/1541948.1541957

27. Karppinen, P., Oinas-Kukkonen, H.: Three approaches to ethical considerations in the design of behavior change support systems. In: Berkovsky, S., Freyne, J. (eds.) PERSUASIVE 2013. LNCS, vol. 7822, pp. 87–98. Springer, Heidelberg (2013). https://doi.org/10.1007/978-3-642-37157-8_12

28. Cheng, J., Danescu-Niculescu-Mizil, C., Leskovec, J.: How community feedback shapes user behavior. In: Proceedings of the 8th International Conference on Weblogs and Social Media, ICWSM 2014, pp. 41–50 (2014)

29. Midden, C., Ham, J.: Using negative and positive social feedback from a robotic agent to save energy. In: Proceedings of the 4th International Conference on Persuasive Technology (2009). https://doi.org/10.1145/1541948.1541966.

Better Performance Through Mindfulness: Mobile Application Design for Mindfulness Training to Improve Performance in College Athletes

Félicia Roger-Hogan[✉], Tayler Wullenweber[✉], and Jung Joo Sohn[✉]

Purdue University, West Lafayette, IN 47907, USA
{frogerho,twullenw,jjsohn}@purdue.edu

Abstract. Collegiate student athletes commit almost all of their time and energy to extremely demanding and competing pressures as both a full-time student and athlete. With very limited time for self-care or mindfulness practices, athletes are restricted to their exhausting schedules that are set for them each and every day. In this paper, we introduce an application design named Muses which facilitates the coordination between coaches/trainers and student-athletes with their mindfulness training. Through a complementing two-faced interface design approach, we began our process by researching current competing mindfulness applications along with the NCAA guidelines to required participation hours each week as well as current programs' mindfulness practices. With two questionnaire surveys completed and a second round of research, we were able to obtain key insights from both general and collegiate athlete mindfulness surveys. This enabled us to begin and determine the final design direction and methods. The personal progress tracking and customization strategies were chosen as the primary features of the application motivating collegiate athletes and programs to practice mindfulness more often.

Keywords: Mindfulness · Social application · Improved athletic performance

1 Introduction

Being able to perform as a collegiate student athlete is a rewarding achievement that many young athletes dream about as they grow up and fans of the school praise as they watch them perform. What most do not understand is the extremely high time demanding and overwhelming pressures to compete at such a prestige stage. Not only are collegiate athletes required to participate in 20 h of countable athletic related activities (CARA) each week during their season, but to be enrolled as full-time students at 12 credit hours a semester as well [1]. Although athletes are limited to only 20 h of athletic related activity a week, most athletes have reported well over that amount claiming to spend almost 36 h a week on their specific sport and at least another 24–36 h on schoolwork outside the classroom [2]. On top of this, college athletes are still required to

© Springer Nature Switzerland AG 2021
M. Kurosu (Ed.): HCII 2021, LNCS 12763, pp. 463–475, 2021.
https://doi.org/10.1007/978-3-030-78465-2_34

attend academic, compliance, and other mandatory meetings as well as injury prevention treatment, sports psychologists' sessions, nutritionist meetings, prospective athlete host duties, team fundraising, media-related activities, and community service [2]. These mandatory team requirements do not count towards the athletes' 20 h weekly athletic practice and training schedule, therefore adding to the amount of time they have to set aside and are required to spend as a collegiate student athlete. With very limited time for athletes to relax and take time for themselves, they are at major risk for physical and emotional exhaustion resulting in major negative impacts on athletic performance and training abilities causing them to burn out.

As a result of such high degrees of stress, some college athletic programs and teams incorporate mental training and mindfulness exercises in their in-season and off-season schedules. By practicing and including more mental training into college athletes' schedules, they would lower their chances of burnout and stress allowing them to perform at the highest level they can on and off the field. In recent years, studies have shown that athletes' overall well-being improved after multiple sessions along with a decrease in anxiety [4]. With the limited time that athletes are already given for themselves, it becomes a challenge to understand when it is best to include mental training and mindfulness sessions into their schedules without adding to their current stress and anxiety levels.

In our research, we utilize a tracking and points reward system to design a mobile mental training application for college athletes. The athletes will be able to customize and track their own progress of the sessions they complete throughout the week. Points are rewarded for the performance and completion of the sessions. These points will then be displayed on the scoreboard within the app for the athlete and coaches to review at the end of each week. The application will allow for athletes to best utilize their limited time to incorporate short mindfulness sessions that are custom to their specific schedules. With a comprehensive mindfulness exercise library database full of sessions to choose from, not only will coaches and trainers have a wide variety of exercises to assign to their athletes, but for the athletes to also explore themselves on their own time to help achieve their goals. Coaches and trainers will also be able to create the best possible training schedules for their athletes in order for them to perform at their best based on how they are doing in their mental training sessions.

2 Related Studies

2.1 Existing Mindfulness Applications

We selected a few mindfulness and meditation apps to compare what features were available to users and what content and capabilities were preferred (Fig. 1).

Existing Apps	Headspace	Calm	MindSport	10% Happier	Balance	Apple Watch Breathing App	Breethe
Timer	x	x		x	x	x	
Guided Meditation	x	x	x	x	x		x
Motion		x					
Sounds	x	x			x		x
Visuals	x	x	x	x		x	x
Music		x	x	x	x		x
Reward System							
Analytics	x	x			x	x	
Interactive					x		
Gamification							
Social Media	x		x				
Notifications	x	x	x	x	x	x	
Reminders	x	x	x	x	x	x	x
Multiple Categories of Exercises	x	x	x	x	x		x

Fig. 1. Mindfulness and meditation comparison chart

2.2 Research and Analysis

Activities that count toward 20-h Rule: Competition, Practice, Strength and Conditioning, Supplemental Workouts, Film Review. Obligatory activities, but do NOT count toward the rule: Academic Meetings, Injury Treatment/Prevention, Sports Psychologist sessions, Nutritionist sessions, Prospective Student-Athlete Host duties, Team fundraising, Media Activities, Community Service, Compliance Meetings [5].

This time accounted for academics, athletics, other extracurriculars, socializing and sleeping. Per week, Division I reported their time as 24% Athletics, 25% Academics, 14% Socializing/Relaxing/Family, 29% Sleeping, 5% Other Extracurriculars, 2% Job. Division II reported their time as 23% Athletics, 24% Academics, 15% Socializing/Relaxing/Family, 29% Sleeping, 6% Other Extracurriculars, 4% Job. Division III reported 20% Athletics, 26% Academics, 15% Socializing/Relaxing/Family, 30% Sleeping, 5% Other Extracurriculars, 4% Job. (Participants in study were not asked to do any accounting toward the 20-h rule.) [1].

2.3 Design Goals

The Muses application features a two-sided interface, one for trainer use and one for athletes. One of our most important design goals for the Muses application is to ensure and increase student-athlete participation in mindfulness sessions. Per our research, athletes saw greater benefits after 5 or more sessions a week for multiple consecutive weeks [4]. In order to reinforce this important goal, we determined some important factors for our application design and content: motivation, convenience, time, and relevance. First, for the factor of motivation we decided to include reminders and notifications. We also determined that our users would feel more inclined to participate in sessions if they were customizable to their individual needs and schedules. A secondary motivator is that sessions can be assigned by trainers and coaches and added as individual goals. The most important criteria in deciding our mindfulness sessions and content on the Muses mobile application are time, relevance and convenience.

Mindfulness sessions need to be efficient and both times and formats of each session should be customizable to fit with individual needs and schedules. Second, our app will have a variety of content and sessions categorized clearly to help users, coaches and athletes alike, sort through content relevant to their sport and team. Our third factor of convenience is also important in supporting user motivation. All features within the Muses app will be easily accessible and navigation throughout the app intuitive.

3   Methods

To begin our research methods and key findings, we started by conducting a primary search to gain a better understanding of NCAA rules and regulations when it came to how many hours were required by athletes to participate in each week along with any possible schedules athletes or programs had reported. We also researched any existing mindfulness apps that were used in a general sense as well as what college athletic programs currently use for mental training with their athletes. Two rounds of surveys were then sent out followed by a secondary research based on our insights from the second survey.

3.1   First Round Survey

Our first survey was conducted to determine what programs or applications athletic teams currently use and what they find most beneficial for their athletes. We were able to obtain athlete's answers regarding which applications they currently use and how long and often they practice mindfulness. Athletes were able to provide written answers explaining how much improvement they have seen in their performance in their specific sport along with how helpful mindfulness exercises manage stress and anxiety levels. Participants were asked at the end of the questionnaire if they would be willing to participate in a follow up survey which would be sent out according to the participant's athletic status.

3.2   Second Round Survey

We conducted two questionnaire surveys to gain a better understanding of what athletes currently do for mindfulness training and what key features would be valued the most within the application. The first survey targeted those who are non-college athletes, but still practice mindfulness as a source of reducing stress and anxiety while the second survey was designed to specifically target current college athletes ranging from levels of NAIA up to NCAA D1. A total of 40 participants recorded their answers through the survey allowing us to obtain raw data and written testimonies from current college athletes on what motivates them to practice mindfulness and what limits them from spending more time on it.

3.3 Secondary Research

The main insights are listed below:

NCAA Countable Athletic Related Activities. While athletes are considered in-season, they are limited to 20 h a week with a max of 4 h a day of countable athletic related activities. Although this number is required by the NCAA, most athletes report spending more than 20 h a week on their specific sport. Activities that count towards the 20-h Rule include:

- Competitions
- Practice
- Strength and Conditioning
- Supplemental workouts
- Film review

Out of season, athletes are still required up to 8 h a week including lifting sessions, short film review, and individual practices with the coaching staff. Any athletic related activity during the 8-h week period that is under coach's supervision allows only 4 athletes per session. Most mandatory activities that are usually required by coaches, but don't count towards their countable hours include:

- Academic meetings
- Injury treatment/prevention
- Sports psychologist sessions
- Nutritionist meetings
- Prospective student athlete host duties
- Team fundraising
- Media activities
- Community service
- Compliance meetings

Increased Percentages in Mental Health Issues on Campus. Within recent years, studies have been done to observe the increase in mental health issues such as anxiety, stress, and depression. 30% of student athletes have claimed to experience overwhelming levels of stress with an increase of more than 5% since 2010 [4]. At the University of Southern California, a five-week program was conducted that included two-hour meetings which promoted psychological health and self-compassion. A three-session model with 45 min of body scans that were associated with the decrease of anxiety and allowed stress control were also included in the program [4].

F. Roger-Hogan et al.

Sessions were designed to involve focus on specific actions or experiences felt throughout the body within the present moment called Mindful Walking and Mindful Breathing. The program also included sessions called STOP which connected the individual's emotions and thoughts to the body when experiencing high levels of stress. Body Scans and Loving Kindness sessions were also included that concentrated on different areas of the body and mediation on one's positive intentions [4].

A typical Day of a Collegiate Student Athlete. A study done by the NCAA from 2005–2006 called the GOALS and SCORE study recorded how athletes spend their time during a typical in-season weekday and weekend. This time that was accounted for included academics, athletics, and other extracurriculars. Participants within this study were not asked to record activities towards the 20-h Rule [2]. Division I athletes reported spending their time per week as the following percentages (Figs. 2, 3, 4, 5):

- Athletics - 24%
- Academics - 25%
- Socializing/Relaxing/Family - 14%
- Sleeping - 29%
- Extracurriculars - 5%
- Jobs - 2%

Division II athletes reported their time as the following:

- Athletics - 23%
- Academics - 24%
- Socializing/Relaxing/Family - 15%
- Sleeping - 29%
- Extracurriculars - 6%
- Jobs - 4%

Division III athletes reported their time as the following:

- Athletics - 20%
- Academics - 26%
- Socializing/Relaxing/Family - 15%
- Sleeping - 30%
- Extracurriculars - 5%
- Jobs - 4%

3.4 Findings

What all, if anything, has prevented you from participating or practicing mindfulness training and exercises?

20 responses

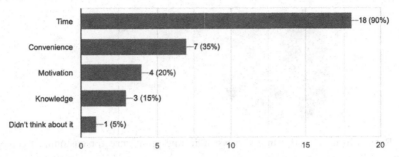

Fig. 2. Time, convenience and motivation as major factors that affect participation.

If you had the option and time, what would be the amount of time you would like to spend on mental training?

20 responses

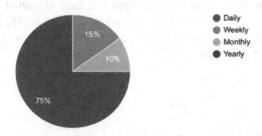

Fig. 3. Survey replies indicating desire to participate in regular mindfulness sessions.

What is your most likely preference for a timed session?

20 responses

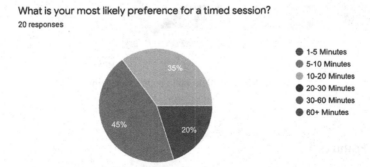

Fig. 4. Results from second round surveys indicating preference for shorter session duration.

Would you be inclined to participate in or incorporate more mindfulness training into practices or daily routines if you had the option to customize the timing and format to fit your individual schedule?
20 responses

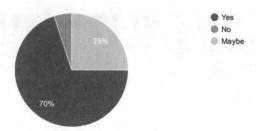

Fig. 5. Results from second round surveys indicating preference for customized content and participation.

4   Design Process

We went through several rounds of brainstorming and ideation to determine what features were needed and useful in the application. We then began to work on the information structure. We started with the design of the wireframe then identified work flows and finally began the design of the user interface. In the last step, we highlighted and refined key task flows and made an interactive prototype with animations, which enabled us to see and test our final design (Figs. 6 and 7).

Fig. 6. Muses athlete main pages wireframe

4.1   Key Features

Per our research and our responses during both rounds of surveys we were able to come up with three key features to showcase in our mobile application.

Fig. 7. Muses coach main pages wireframe

Exercise Library and Customizable Sessions

Muses' database of all mindful training sessions. Content will be categorized by type and sport. Coaches will use this feature to view and assign sessions to their athletes. Athletes will use this to view and add mindful sessions as goals alongside their assigned sessions. New content and recommendations added to the Library will populate on the coach's dashboard, while assigned sessions and added goals will be featured on the athlete's dashboard. Within the library, the default list will populate with sport specific and relevant sessions based on previous selected sessions.

Data and Mood Tracker

Shows athlete's progress in completing sessions as well as overall tracking of mood and wellbeing throughout usage of the mobile application. Our users are also able to use the journaling feature to record events and thoughts along with the mood tracker to better connect their feelings and how daily events can affect them.

Assigning/Goal Setting

This feature will allow coaches to assign sessions to their athletes and allow athletes to add sessions as goals to supplement their existing assignments from the Library.

4.2 Logo and Branding

Athlete is an ancient Greek word that means "one who competes for a prize" and was related to two other Greek words, athlos meaning "contest" and athlon meaning "prize."

The Greek word for meditation is melete. Melete was a term referring to disciplined study, a mental exercise or an exercise in thought. In Greek mythology, they often referred to the three Muses, Melete being one of them, the other two, Mneme (memory) and Aoide (song, voice).

These three muses represent the three gifts of the human mind — that of mental exercise, reflection, and vocalization. We want to encourage our users to discipline themselves by committing to mindfulness sessions, reflecting, and sharing their progress and custom sessions with others.

Teal, aqua, gold and orange were chosen for the branding and app colors largely due to their perception and meaning. Teal is a combination of the calming qualities of blue and the renewing qualities of green. It is perceived as reviving and rejuvenating and is known to represent clarity of thought. Aqua is the lighter variation and represents much of the same but also denotes inner peace, healing and empathy. Goldenrod yellow is associated with illumination, compassion and wisdom. Finally, orange enthusiasm, success, encouragement, health and balance.

5 Final Design

5.1 Home

The athlete side of the Muses application features a homepage that showcases the users progress, assigned sessions from their coaches and featured sessions based on the users favorites and recent activity. The coach side of the Muses application features a homepage that showcases recommended mindfulness sessions and their athlete's activities as they complete sessions assigned (Fig. 8).

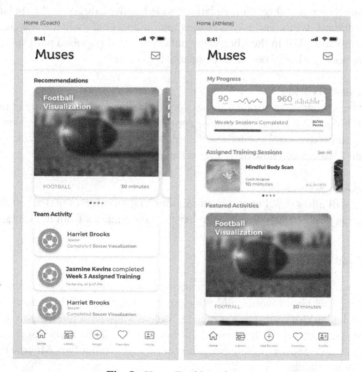

Fig. 8. Home/Dashboard pages

5.2   Library and Mindfulness Sessions

The library is easily accessible from the navigation at the bottom of the screen, users can start sessions from the assigned sessions on the homepage or from selecting individual sessions from the library. Users can favorite sessions from the library to save them for easy access at later times (Fig. 9).

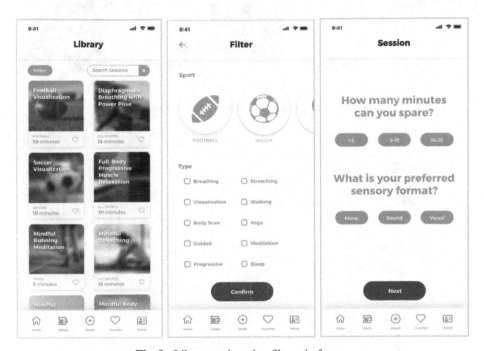

Fig. 9. Library and session filter wireframes

5.3   Assigning and Goal Adding

Athletes are also able to add additional sessions to their assigned sessions from their coaches by selecting 'Add Session'. Coaches are able to assign sessions to individuals or groups of athletes as well as entire teams by using the 'Assign' feature (Fig. 10).

5.4   Athlete Profile, Mood Tracking and Journaling

From the users' profile, athletes can view their progress and access settings as well as the journaling and mood tracking features of the Muses application. From the coaches' profile, users can view their teams and athletes as well as access settings (Fig. 11).

Fig. 10. Assigning and goal adding page wireframes

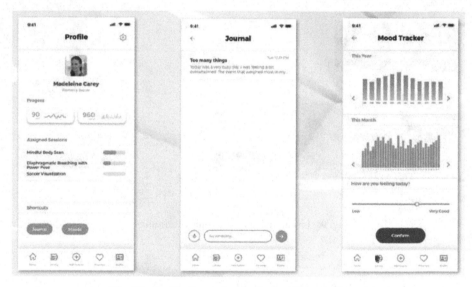

Fig. 11. Profile, journal and mood tracker wireframes

6 Application Evaluation and User Testing

To evaluate the effectiveness of our design we contacted a few participants to test out the Muses application. We asked our participants about the overall look and feel of the design and clarity of the user interface. Secondly, we asked their opinions about what features they favored and what features they did not like. Determining the usefulness of customized sessions was also a priority and we wanted to ensure that the time options we provided were sufficient to cover a variety of individuals needs and schedules. All of our participants approved of the design and navigation.

One of the preferred features of the Muses application was the ability to favorite sessions to be able to build their own personal library. Some of our interviewees mentioned wanting the journaling feature as a more prominent part of the application, but others felt that it was not a necessary feature. Ultimately our interviewees were happy with the final design and content intended for our coaches and athlete users.

7 Conclusion

To encourage athletes and college athletic programs to participate in mindfulness practices more often, we designed a two-faced interface mobile application for athletes and coaches to effectively take advantage of mental training based on the athletes' schedules. We began with conducting a primary research along with sending out a first survey to better understand NCAA rules and regulations along with what mindfulness applications athletes currently use. This was then followed up by a second round of surveys to gain insightful data on how exactly we can cater to coaches and their athlete's schedules. We collected athletes' answers on questions based on the amount of time they would be able commit to mindfulness sessions and what main reasons were limiting them from doing it now. Thus, a comprehensive mindfulness exercise library database with customizable sessions, long term data and progress tracking, and the ability for coaches to assign sessions to their athletes along with athletes setting their own goals became our key main features. Other features such as a weekly scoreboard for the athletes to keep track of their progress in completing sessions throughout the week, viewing feedback from trainers/coaches, and a personal chat feature will keep the athletes motivated to participate in mindfulness training more often resulting in enhanced performance in their specific sport.

References

1. The 20 Hour Rule, National Collegiate Athletic Association (2017). https://www.ncaa.org/sites/default/files/20-Hour-Rule-Document.pdf
2. Goals and Time Demands, National Collegiate Athletic Association (2017). https://www.ncaa.org/sites/default/files/2017GOALS_Time_demands_20170628.pdf
3. Furrer, P., Moen, Dr. F, Firing, Dr. K.: How Mindfulness Training may mediate Stress, Performance and Burnout. Sports J. (2015). https://thesportjournal.org/article/how-mindfulness-training-may-mediate-stress-performance-and-burnout/
4. Scholefield, R.M., Firsick, DM.: University of Southern California. "Athlete Mindfulness: The Development and Evaluation of a Mindfulness Based Training Program for Promoting Mental Health and Wellbeing in Student Athletes," National Collegiate Athletic Association (2017). https://www.ncaa.org/sites/default/files/2018RES_InnoGrant_USC_FinalReport_20180122.pdf
5. 2020–21 Guide for the College-Bound Athlete, National Collegiate Athletic Association (2020). http://fs.ncaa.org/Docs/eligibility_center/Student_Resources/CBSA.pdf

Holdable Devices: Supporting Mindfulness, Psychological Autonomy and Self-Regulation During Smartphone Use

Federico Julien Tiersen$^{(\boxtimes)}$ (iD) and Rafael Alejandro Calvo (iD)

Dyson School of Design Engineering, Imperial College London, London SW7 2DB, UK
`federico.tiersen16@imperial.ac.uk`

Abstract. It has been argued that consuming social and micro-targeted digital content rapidly and continuously arouses the brain into an impulsive, dopamine-fueled, 'automatic' flow state that leads to excessive and unhealthy smartphone use. The ubiquity of advertising-based products that exploit users' vulnerabilities to maximize engagement is leading to detrimental impacts on well-being and widespread addiction symptoms. In the UK, about 40% of adults think they spend too much time online, 60% consider themselves 'hooked' and 33% find disconnecting difficult.

The current digital solutions quantify and block app usage. However, guilt and self-coercion are unhealthy motivators, digital interventions rapidly desensitize users, and experiences of varying quality may occur on one app.

Here we introduce Holdable devices, biofeedback-based tangible interfaces that sense when smartphones are used inattentively or compulsively from the motion of the hand behind the phone and gently alert users to regain mindfulness through haptic feedback and abstract visualization. We describe our design process and a pilot study with three prototypes that evaluated user preferences and the intervention's impact on psychological factors related to problematic smartphone use. Results reveal the potential for beneficial impacts on cognitive and behavioral metrics and inform scopes for future designs.

Keywords: Design thinking · Emotions in HCI and design · Haptic user interface · Human-robot interaction · Psychology · Cognition and social sciences · Design for well-being

1 Introduction

Digital products with advertising-based or 'freemium' business models are primarily designed to maximise engagement. To this end, they harness micro-targeted emotionally-stimulating content, the illusion of connection (see social snacking [1]), social reciprocity and validation [2], gamification [3], and interface elements such as unlimited automatic content loading, manual refreshing followed by intermittent variable rewards, and the lack of visual cues of consumption. The ubiquity of such features has led to widespread problematic smartphone use (PSU) that some have labelled "behavioural addiction" [4],

© Springer Nature Switzerland AG 2021
M. Kurosu (Ed.): HCII 2021, LNCS 12763, pp. 476–495, 2021.
https://doi.org/10.1007/978-3-030-78465-2_35

causing tolerance increase, withdrawal symptoms, functional impairment [5], and short-ened attention spans [6]. Smartphones can increase multitasking, task switching and the expectation of being interrupted, leading to lower productivity [7] and reduced quality of in-person conversations [8]. Additionally, smartphones facilitate the formation of habits as users repeatedly associate dopamine-releasing events with a single source of sensory stimuli [9] and this conditioning results in the stimuli's source independently causing pleasure [10]. This environment leads to checking and using smartphones compulsively, violating end users' autonomy as experiences may not be volitional and reflectively self-endorsed [11].

While over half of Americans [12] recognise that media use often conflicts with personal goals or obligations, this is not sufficient to self-regulate and causes negative emotions of 'guilty pleasure' [13]. In the UK, about 40% of adults think they spend too much time online, 60% consider themselves 'hooked' and 33% find disconnecting difficult. Fifteen million UK internet users had undertaken digital detoxes in 2016 [14]. Lacking impulse control [15], children and teenagers are even more vulnerable.

Amount of use should be distinguished from the psychological relationship with the phone [16], which may be affected by both phone-related habits and social attachment styles [17]. A review by Elhai and colleagues [18] found relationships between PSU and anxiety, chronic stress, depression severity, and low self-esteem. The problem is multidimensional as different types of experiences may occur on the same platform [19]. For example, while active engagement with real-life peers on social media has benefits comparable to offline interactions, passive consumption of content can undermine life satisfaction [20] and affective wellbeing [21].

In this context, supporting *mindfulness* can empower users to mitigate such threats: "defined as the open and receptive awareness of what is occurring both within people and within their context, [mindfulness] facilitates greater autonomy and integrated self-regulation" [22]. In turn, autonomy is a crucial determinant of well-being [11]. Mind-fulness' attentional (present moment awareness) and attitudinal (non-judgement and unconditional acceptance [23]) components make it ideal to rethink ubiquitous com-puting experiences in a *positive computing* environment [24] where *calm technologies* leverage well-timed switches between the centre and periphery of attention to induce mindfulness and learning with minimal intrusion and frustration [25].

This study explores how a platform-agnostic product can enhance autonomy over all digital experiences and help prevent problematic habits. We report the design and pilot validation of Holdable devices (Fig. 1) that infer the *quality* of phone use from physiological markers and support mindfulness and self-reflection through biofeedback interventions and bidirectional interactions on tangible user interfaces (TUI).

Section 2 reviews multidisciplinary literature to identify design and research oppor-tunities. Section 3 explains the product development process, Sect. 4 its validation, and Sect. 5 discusses the study's outcomes, limitations, and implications.

Fig. 1. First generation prototypes of Holdable devices

2 Contextual Investigation and Related Work

2.1 Digital Environments that Hinder Mindfulness

Mindfulness can decrease PSU [18] and the emotional exhaustion that can be caused by social media [26], particularly benefitting individuals who overuse their smartphone [4] and often experience increased time distortion and underestimate their usage [27]. Conversely, smartphone use, involvement, vigilance, and problematic use are associated with lower trait mindfulness [28, 29].

In addition to emotionally-triggering content, engagement-based products compromise mindfulness by inducing immersion, temporal dissociation [30], repeated impulsive actions [9] and multitasking. This results in flow states of high positive valence and arousal (e.g., on Facebook [31]) and prolonged engagement after task completion. Regulating mind wandering and autonomously engaging with stimuli with a rational, values-led, non-compulsive approach requires executive control [32] through the brain's System 2 [33]. System 2 processing is slow, volatile, and subject to conscious judgments and attitudes [33]. In this state, stimuli are elaborated under a *central route* and decisions are taken through a thoughtful consideration and development of logical arguments that involves a high amount of cognition [34]. Conversely, in contexts where information is processed through the intuitive, automatic System 1 [33], such as social media, the person's attitudes are affected by *peripheral* processing [34]. Here, persuasion results from associations and simple, non-logical inferences about emotional cues in the stimulus [34]. This makes decision-making dependent on impulsive emotional bonds and formed habits and hence harder to manipulate [33].

Reflective thought processes can be inhibited by regular, cognitively-engaging stimuli [35] and experiences in which cognition is driven by the impulsive, subconscious System 1 [33]. Interfaces faster than mindful thought are ubiquitous (e.g., [36]) and induce System 1-driven flow [37]. Also, users seek psychological balance through extended experiences of an attentional state [38]: self-interrupting phone use requires great willpower as stable and prolonged arousal and engagement increase receptivity to similar stimuli [38] and result in flow states [31].

2.2 Related Products: Designing for Mindfulness and Self-regulation

Numerous software products promote self-surveillance through monitoring and limiting application usage [39–41]. Despite the value of insight-informed self-regulation [42], these products have potential for improvement. First, some platforms (e.g., social media, email) may impact users in nuanced ways depending on their habits and the environment of use. App usage timings are therefore insufficient to indicate nor quantify unhealthy use [17, 43]. Second, this approach relies on quantification and self-coercion, which are dysfunctional relative to intrinsic motivation and self-compassion [11, 24]. A review [44] highlights a lack of theoretical basis and empirical validation of PSU apps resulting in an excessive reliance on one-size-fits-all functionality blocking instead of understanding and challenging the underlying motivators for use. In 2018, none of them had scientific evidence for their effectiveness or acknowledged that there are problematic users with different traits and willingness and readiness to change [44]. Since then, app use tracking and limiting has been centralized into mobile operating systems [39, 40] and third parties have been banned from iOS [45].

Meanwhile, affective computing researchers developed models to predict stress [46], personality [47], emotion [48], sleep, and social interactions [49] from digital footprints. Bypassing content analysis, interaction patterns (e.g., typing, scrolling) can predict neurocognitive function with clinical accuracy [50]. These technologies, however, are yet to be implemented in mass-market products, where mindfulness interventions are not context-aware and are limited to repetitive prescheduled reminders to which users are rapidly desensitised [51]. These range from breathing exercises directed by haptic signals (e.g., Apple Watch Breathe [52]) to voice-guided meditations aimed at promoting mindfulness in different aspects of everyday life (e.g., sleep, eating, relationships) through relaxation, contemplation, self-reflection, and acceptance (e.g., Headspace [53]). While beneficial, such products have limitations.

First, they quantify mindful time, progress, and accomplishments and employ gamification tactics to encourage repeated engagement. For example, Apple Health users can count 'mindful minutes', Headspace users need to complete simpler meditations or to buy a premium subscription to access more advanced levels, and Calm users can grow 'streaks' by practicing for multiple consecutive days [54]. As unconditional acceptance is antithetical to quantification and goal-oriented striving, mindfulness interventions should instead promote momentarily dropping expectations and aspirations [55] by avoiding quantification, gamification and social comparison [24].

Second, they are feedforward-only systems that do not sense the user's psychological state or their current behaviour. They intervene at predetermined times through push notification reminders or when the user proactively engages with their app. Commercial neurofeedback products such as Muse headbands [56] seek to address this shortcoming by inferring mindfulness levels through electroencephalography (EEG) and heart rate sensors. The Muse app provides near real-time feedback on whether the mind is 'active' or 'calm' by playing, respectively, sounds of rain and bird chirpings. After meditation sessions, users are presented a graph of their brain activity levels and the number of 'birds' (deeply mindful moments) achieved in the past session, week or month. This reliance on quantification, gamification, and a single 'focus' metric that does not capture mindfulness' attitudinal qualities (the open, unconditional acceptance of one's internal state and external situation) may hinder an otherwise effective system. Moreover, EEG headbands are invasive devices that require high levels of stillness to provide reliable data. They therefore share the limitations of PSU and meditation apps of relying on extrinsic motivators and of being unsuitable for some of the scenarios in which phones can be (ab)used.

2.3 Contextual Mindfulness Interventions

The PSU and guided meditation apps reviewed above are limited to promoting reflection outside of the activity in which the user desires higher levels of mindfulness. Alternatively, reflection can happen during activities without sacrificing usability [57]. Compulsive behaviors induced by rapid stimuli and interface dark patterns (e.g., [58]) can be counteracted by short task lockouts [59] induced by 'microboundaries' [60]. Small, sporadic time or interaction costs such as content loading, unconventional interface designs or, in Cox and colleagues' study, smaller text size prompt users to switch to System 2. Keeping interventions subtle avoids causing frustration, interrupts passive flow states without requiring willpower, supports value-aligned behaviors, and increases task performance [60].

Similarly, extensive evidence suggests that external reminders to enter a state of deliberate present-moment awareness can prevent mind-wandering, multitasking and impulsive actions while awareness lasts and train the mindfulness trait, enhancing self-regulation feedback loops [61, 62]. Interventions should be meaningful, minimalistic, and aligned with the person's motivation levels, providing simple guidance rather than additional goal-oriented striving, distraction, or frustration [24].

External signals can be used to gauge the state of one's awareness and redirect attention through *biofeedback*, bypassing active cognitive regulation to regulate psychophysiological states such as breathing awareness [63], stress [64], mind-wandering, and anxiety [65]. Communicating one's psychological state through abstract, partially ambiguous representations instead of quantitative metrics can induce a curious, open, and intense introspection as the user needs to observe their internal states to try to understand what the feedback is indicating [66].

Associated with consistency of movement [67], *flow* is suitable for sensing and biofeedback. There is an opportunity in using haptic biofeedback, which has shown to support mindfulness in automatic, compulsive behaviours such as chewing [68] and walking [69] by increasing sensory-motor awareness [70]. During smartphone use, bidirectional TUIs with dynamic affordance (e.g., [71]) can stimulate the hand's unutilised psychophysical perception more than traditional vibrotactile means [72]. More generally, TUIs can directly support mindfulness during human-computer interaction (HCI) by remedying for the touch-deprivation, sensory impoverishment and loss of physicality associated with the digital age [73], and further enhance positive behaviour change by recreating affective touch (e.g., [74]) and social agency [75].

Based on the research described above we developed a biofeedback-based, multimodal intervention for PSU self-regulation. Unlike existing software solutions based on time tracking and app blocking, Holdables aim to intervene on the quality of cognition and behaviour to support mindfulness and self-reflection, directly diminishing vulnerability to PSU when users enter psychological states in which they are more susceptible. These include flow states of high valence and arousal induced by the prolonged, passive browsing of social content [31] in which peripheral thinking elaborates stimuli and leads to impulsive, non-reflective decision-making [34].

3 Design Engineering Process

3.1 Interaction Design

Compulsive smartphone usage could be argued to happen in two types of behaviours:

(1) *Prolonged task immersion*, reflecting flow states fuelled by passive content consumption (e.g., scrolling feeds, watching videos). Steadier, more subtle movement of the phone and hand distinguishes passive absorption of content from proactive activities that involve user input and result in task completion or social communication (e.g., texting or searching for information). Importantly, proactive use is not considered as problematic and should not trigger interventions: mindfulness interventions will target only *immersed* use.
(2) *High frequency of pick-ups*, reflecting multitasking and withdrawal symptoms.

Inferring these states from physiological markers can inform the timing of mindfulness interventions. Accuracy of compulsion detection is secondary due to privacy concerns and PSU's multidimensionality. The intervention was therefore designed to be subtle and gentle enough to avoid frustration at false positives and to be effective for users unable to distinguish between screen time and compulsive behaviour.

We designed touchpoints (Fig. 2) that were expected to promote autonomy and mindfulness at all levels of experience (see [76]) via desirable stickers and cases that gently nudge users through tactile feedback to effortlessly regain mindfulness when using their smartphone compulsively. While intervention thresholds can be personalised in later iterations, this study defines problematic frequency and task immersion times from averages of a population with PSU [77]. Crucially, proactive use resets the immersion timers so that Holdables only intervene when the phone is used passively.

3.2 Sensing and Inferring Frequency of Use, Prolonged Task Immersion, and User Input

Edge Computing for Privacy. Users consulted during the scoping phase of this study were reluctant to give access to smartphone sensors by downloading and running an app in the background, or to upload sensitive data to cloud servers. Moreover, relying on mobile operating systems puts PSU products at risk of extinction [45]. The device was therefore designed to host all sensing, processing, and actuation. This simplicity and transparency make its functioning more tangible and less surveillance-like.

Sensing Interface. System 1-driven flow is characterised by consistency of movement [67]. Experimenting with a BNO055 inertia measurement unit, however, revealed errors due to users' movement (e.g., walking, being in a vehicle) and sensor drift: measuring changes in motion between the hand and the phone is more reliable. Sensing touch location through mutual capacitance also allows to detect pickups for frequency inference and multi-touch input for bidirectional interactions.

Embedding conductive material into silicone rubber creates a multi-touch surface with affordance for complex interactions [78] while providing shock protection for internal components and the phone. A grid of stretchable conductive yarn [79] was placed

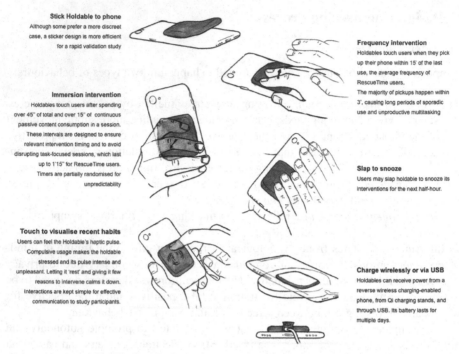

Stick Holdable to phone
Although some prefer a more discreet case, a sticker design is more efficient for a rapid validation study

Immersion intervention
Holdables touch users after spending over 45' of total and over 15' of continuous passive content consumption in a session. These intervals are designed to ensure relevant intervention timing and to avoid disrupting task-focused sessions, which last up to 1'15" for RescueTime users. Timers are partially randomised for unpredictability

Touch to visualise recent habits
Users can feel the Holdable's haptic pulse. Compulsive usage makes the holdable stressed and its pulse intense and unpleasant. Letting it 'rest' and giving it few reasons to intervene calms it down. Interactions are kept simple for effective communication to study participants.

Frequency intervention
Holdables touch users when they pick up their phone within 15' of the last use, the average frequency of RescueTime users.
The majority of pickups happen within 3', causing long periods of sporadic use and unproductive multitasking

Slap to snooze
Users may slap holdable to snooze its interventions for the next half-hour.

Charge wirelessly or via USB
Holdables can receive power from a reverse wireless charging-enabled phone, from Qi charging stands, and through USB. Its battery lasts for multiple days.

Fig. 2. Touchpoints of minimum viable Holdable devices

between two silicone rubber layers and connected to a FT5406EE8 controller via the MuCa breakout board [80] (Fig. 3) as suggested by Teyssier and colleagues [78]. DragonSkin FX-Pro 2A silicone layers of shore hardness and thickness similar to human epidermis (skin) and dermis (fat) tissue and the grid's 2–5 mm spatial acuity make affective interactions intuitive by recreating the affordance of human skin [78].

Fig. 3. Sensing interface iterations

Threads act as receiving and transmitting electrodes and mutual capacitance is created at their intersections, measured by electrode scanning, and sent to a master microcontroller via an I^2C bus at 10 Hz.

Pre-processing. Mutual capacitance increases with the proximity of charge-holding fingers, but variations are non-monotonic and hardware-dependent. Data was sent to a computer via serial communication for real-time visualisation in Processing [81] as RGB pixels to develop a process pipeline that accurately extracts the location and intensity of touch. The ControlP5 [82], MuCa [83] and OpenCV [84] libraries enabled the visualisation of outputs and the real-time tuning of gain, calibration, and artefact rejection parameters. Figure 4 displays the approaches tested: binary raw data thresholds, reading pre-processed touchpoint coordinates, 'blob' and touchpoint detection, and mapping the intensity of touch as RGB pixels. The latter was the most sensitive and least noisy and could be ran locally on M0/M4 microcontrollers (e.g., Arduino Nano IoT, Adafruit Feather M0).

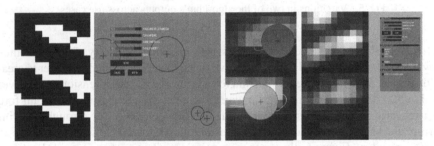

Fig. 4. Pre-processing methods tested.

Feature Extraction and Use Case Inference. A proprietary process pipeline and algorithm was programmed in microcontroller sketches to locally extract motion outcome measures. 32-bit controllers with ARM-SAMD processors allowed 10 Hz processing.

Tests were conducted with each prototype to uncover associations between motion metrics and the product's use cases and to define thresholds for the classification tree. Figure 5 illustrates visible variations in two metrics across all use cases: across the device's five use cases: 1) picking a phone up, 2) passively consuming content (e.g., watching videos, scrolling down feeds, swiping through stories), 3) proactive use with frequent user input (e.g., texting, looking up people or information, searching locations on a map), 4) slapping the interface to snooze its touches, 5) touching the interface with one or two fingers to visualize the quality of recent use.

3.3 Actuation

Changes in sensory stimulus induce sensory-motor awareness [70] and, subsequently, mindfulness. The device combines vibrotactile and mechanical feedback to stimulate all of the hand's mechanoreceptors [85]. Moreover, the presence of social agents, including robots [86], increases user's willingness to perform tasks. This phenomenon is enhanced when the robot *initiates* physical contact [75], with calming effects enhanced by human-like gesture dynamics and user expectations [87].

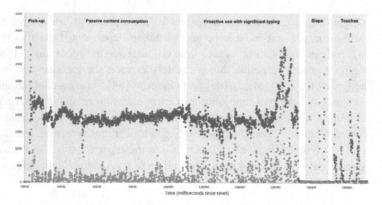

Fig. 5. Variations in two of the algorithm's outputs across use cases.

To achieve large mechanical movements, the active shape memory of Shape Memory Alloys (SMA) was combined with the passive shape memory of silicone rubber to create kinetic organic interfaces (see [88]) in thin form factors (e.g., [86]). Tension springs were baked at 500 °C from 0.5 mm NiTiCu wire to achieve enough elasticity and pull force when reheated to 45 °C to significantly displace the sensing layer through buckling. At 1mm thickness, the silicone layer's tension allows for 100% spring compression and 80% recovery. Figure 6 illustrates the system's mechanics, Fig. 7 its application in prototypes. Running 1.7 A through the spring completes this motion in 0.3 s, achieving a 3 cm/s velocity which maximizes pleasantness perceptions [89]. This design ensures Holdable's touches always reach users' fingers.

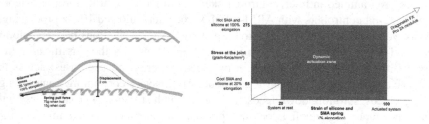

Fig. 6. Dynamic actuation mechanics.

Fig. 7. SMA springs in prototypes (left, center) and the actuation motion (right).

The brain perceives vibration stimuli as touch, and variations in speed, intensity and amplitude communicate affective states [74] despite limited degrees of freedom [90]. An external haptic system is the only way to intervene during the use of any app as the built-in vibration engines of commodity smartphones only allow apps running in the background to use standard notification haptics. Holdables' haptics should be distinct from smartphone vibration to prevent the frustration that can arise when people mistaking interventions for social notifications (see [91]). Haptic waveforms (Fig. 8) were designed in Macaron [92] and implemented via a DRV2605L breakout board and eccentric rotating mass actuators to complement mindfulness interventions and create pleasant or unpleasant sensations, discreetly, in visualisation interactions.

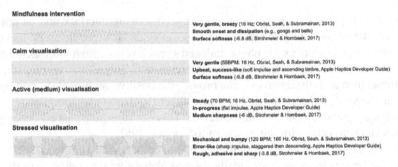

Fig. 8. Haptic waveforms used and their qualitative characteristics [85, 93, 94].

3.4 Power Management

Wireless charging was implemented through BH2001110010 and BQ51013B receiver modules adjacent to the phone. This also allows reverse charging from enabled smartphones. TP4056 modules regulated charging and protected components from short circuits. High-discharge (>5 C) LiPo batteries provide enough current to actuate the SMA through a IRLB8743PBF transistor switch. The system's average discharge rate of 11 mA guarantees 54.5 h of continuous usage with a 600 mAh battery, removing the need to switch the Holdable on and off so it does not miss any usage.

3.5 First Generation of Working Prototypes

Three devices (Fig. 9) were designed and built to broadly cover the spectrum of design opportunities identified in a morphological analysis and enable the investigations of user preferences and reactions.

These prototypes share the same functionalities but differ in form, meaning and user-device relationship: a discreet device, a visible accessory, and the phone's skin. This approach allows testing the core functionality while exploring the impact of different design decisions. Users develop (often anxious) social attachment *to* their phones [17]. As Holdables are inherently positioned as intermediate agents, the three designs tackle maladaptive co-dependency by leveraging *attachment theory* strategies.

Fig. 9. The first three embodiments of working Holdable devices. From left to right: *Holdable Original and Cover, Wave Up, Skinterface.*

Holdable Original and its cover are a high-tech-looking interface and an optional suede case-like sleeve to target more technology-savvy and low-profile users. Its visualisation interaction mirrors users' phone-induced stress levels through vibrotactile pulse. Its condition improves through rest, conveying resilience. This affiliative, empathic and secure rather than assertive approach can provide the positive emotional support needed to treat anxious attachment [95] and promote affect regulation and compliance, adherence, intimacy, and relatedness with the device. This can substitute past co-dependency dynamics and help cope with initial separation anxiety [95].

Wave Up has organic and asymmetric forms and colours with a granular, soft texture and stratified edges to provide an ideally located alternative for coping with the anxiety that may have led the user to reach to their phone through stress-relieving tactile stimulation, fidgeting, or visual engagement. Its representation of superficial, transient perturbations on a vast natural entity is aligned with the state Holdables aim to induce. Wave Up represents accessory-like Holdables. Such neutral but expressive products would target users that seek fashionable, gadgets, those with low awareness of their PSU, and those seeking avoidance of medical or moral connotations. Its vibrotactile waveforms are elongated and connected to express waves instead of pulse.

Skinterface was inspired by Teyssier et al.'s Skin-On interfaces [78]. This conceptual design intervenes to thank (rather than alert) users for frequent and immersed use, and its haptic and LED pulse is calmed when use becomes problematic. Exposing the phone as the *helper-abuser* makes the user aware of its tactics and places responsibility of addiction on the phone while new assertiveness and self-efficacy arise (traditional co-dependency psychotherapy strategies; [96]) from its uncanny, surrealist effect. Designed for temporary use, its unconventional aspect and its (unexpected, see [97]) hostility conflict with existing mental models and thus triggers System 2 [33]. Realistic anthropomorphism (e.g., [78]) may make the device uncanny [98] and, from a philosophical and psychoanalytical perspective, induce mindfulness by bringing users beyond the sense-perception-contingent, ego-driven Symbolic and into the Real [99]. Its grey colour transcends human race and denotes ubiquitous devices' role as extensions of our individual and societal organisms (see extended mind thesis; [100]).

4 Evaluation

A mixed-methods pilot study evaluated the prototypes' impact as interventions, their touchpoints' appropriateness, and their desirability. Although functional, these prototypes are still too bulky to be given to many participants for extended periods. As quantitatively evaluating within-participant psychometric changes on traits mindfulness, perceived autonomy and PSU would require at least two weeks of use [101], we opted for a more qualitative pilot to validate the product's efficiency and its psychological validation procedure and to inform further iterations.

An effective procedure must involve using a prototype in one's private daily routine, when they are not engaged in social interactions nor observed by an interviewer, to avoid the bias of feeling observed and capture moments in which PSU is more likely. After briefing, participants were left alone with their chosen prototype and made aware that usage data is not recorded. After minimum 12 h of use, their experience and desires were investigated in semi-structured interviews. Participants then evaluated their experience and perceptions about the product's impact on their psychological attachment to their smartphone and on their behaviours on a printed or digital questionnaire. Questions were adapted from the *Mindful Attention Awareness Scale* [102], *Motivation, Engagement and Thriving in User Experiences* [76], *Problematic Use of Mobile Phones* [103], *Smartphone Addiction Scale* [104], *Social Media Disorder Scale* [105], *Psychological Empowerment on Social Media* [106] to increase relevance in the study's context and evaluate Holdables' medium-term potential beyond the direct interactions of the last 12 h. Some questions were generated from Personas' needs. 5-point Likert scales were used to quantify the intensity of self-reported beliefs, with some reversely worded items to minimise bias.

Participants (n = 10, 6M/4F, aged 13–74) were recruited in person in Brussels, Belgium. Care was taken to cover a wide range of personas, and the sample includes potential users with PSU from mild to very high (Q1: $\mu = 3.3$, SD $= 1.06$; Q2: $\mu = 3.3$, SD $= 0.68$). Participants were not remunerated, and quantitative measurements were obtained anonymously and remotely to prevent bias.

4.1 Results

This section merges insights from questionnaire results (Q) and interviews [P]. Q scores of 1 (minimum) to 5 (maximum) indicate validation of the construct.

Participants' choices between prototypes showed differences in gender preferences. Only females chose Wave Up [P1, P5, P6, P9] and expressed fondness in Holdables as "decorative" accessories with metaphorical meaning [P1, P9], while men sought "minimalist design" and chose Original [P2, P7, P10], or "case-like invisibility" and chose the Cover [P3, P4, P8]. Females appreciated the silicone's softness for spontaneous stress-relieving interactions [P1, P5, P9].

Holdables have good usability (Q3: $\mu = 3.2$, SD $= 0.92$; Q4: $\mu = 3$, SD $= 1.25$). Feedback is neither intrusive (Q5: $\mu = 3.9$, SD $= 1.29$) nor forceful (Q6: $\mu = 3.2$, SD $= 1.22$) but made some feel guilt (Q7: $\mu = 2.2$, SD $= 1.03$). Guilt was mostly experienced "at the beginning while still discovering one's habits" [P1]. Whether users would feel stigmatized as problematic is highly attitude-dependent (Q8: $\mu = 3.7$, SD $= 1.57$). Participants felt confused until they understood what the device actually senses [P1–10] and were relieved by the lack of access to the phone's screen [P1, P2, P5, P6, P7, P9, P10] and impressed by its "cleverness" in detecting immersed use [P3, P4, P5, P7, P9] and distinguishing hands from things [P1, P2, P5, P7, P9]. The communication of these aspects will be crucial to incentivise adoption. Teenagers particularly valued not saving data [P2, P7, P10] and being able to take it off [P7, P10] to avoid parental control, and would embrace the device if it "replaced direct parental surveillance" [P7, P10]. All users wanted a much smaller form factor.

Touches induced mindful attention awareness (Q9: $\mu = 3.5$, SD $= 0.53$) and pulsing effectively informed of recent usage (Q10: $\mu = 3.4$, SD $= 0.84$). Although discovering one's compulsive habits was "useful and interesting" (Q11: $\mu = 3.3$, SD $= 0.67$), participants were divided in their appreciation of their abstract representation as a pulse. Females enjoyed a more personified device [P1, P6, P9] and teenagers suggested further interactions or complexity of feedback [P2, P7], while adult males were generally unimpressed [P4, P8].

Immersion interventions were well-timed (Q12: $\mu = 3.1$, SD $= 0.74$) and distinguishable from notifications (Q13: $\mu = 3.7$, SD $= 0.67$). Touches were soft (Q14: $\mu = 2.1$, SD $= 0.88$) and could be more noticeable [P2, P3, P5, P8]. Skinterface's movement was "strange" [P3] or felt like a "baby in the womb" [P1] that invited touch [P1, P5]. Variations between calm, active and stressed pulses were confusing for some (Q15: $\mu = 2.4$, SD $= 1.17$) [P2, P3, P8]. More complex, varied interactions [P1, P4, P7, P9] or being able to alternate [P1, P3, P6, P9] or personalize [P1, P7] shape, colour and function would help "preserve novelty", which induces mindfulness [36, 63].

All participants agreed that Holdables raised their awareness of how addictive apps can be (Q16: $\mu = 3.6$, SD $= 0.52$) and 80% realised to be using their phone more than they thought (Q17: $\mu = 3.2$, SD $= 0.79$). Reported new awareness of specific compulsive behaviours includes "cannot stop scrolling feeds" [P3], "TikTok videos on Instagram Explore" [P5], "turning into a zombie" [P4], "forgetting why I picked up my phone and doing something else" [P1] and "always, always using it when bored" [P1, P6].

There was consensus that Holdables can help not using phones when people know they should not (Q18: $\mu = 3.5$, SD $= 0.53$), and less perceived control from the phone (Q19: $\mu = 3.1$, SD $= 0.57$) makes general time management easier (Q20: $\mu = 3.2$, SD $= 0.79$). There was more division in its benefits for online and offline social life (Q21: $\mu = 2.9$, SD $= 1.29$) with users with less PSU and attachment anxiety unsurprisingly seeing less macro-scale benefits [P1, P3, P5, P8].

Holdables reduce impulsive (Q22: $\mu = 3.3$, SD $= 0.67$) and "automatic" use (Q23: $\mu = 3.3$, SD $= 0.48$; Q24: $\mu = 3.2$, SD $= 0.79$), but there was neither effectiveness (Q25: $\mu = 2.7$, SD $= 0.82$) nor a particular desire [P1–10] to pay more attention to one's surroundings while on the phone. While Holdables helped regulate passive social media use (e.g., scrolling, watching, swiping) [P1, P3, P4, P5, P6, P7, P9], they may not increase active use (e.g., talking to people and sharing content; Q26: $\mu = 2.3$, SD $= 0.82$) as engagement style is engrained within users' attitudes [P1, P2, P4, P8, P10].

5 Discussion and Conclusions

5.1 Implications and Limitations of Findings

This mixed-methods study design informed design developments through its broad qualitative insights and gave encouraging preliminary evidence for the product's potential as a behavioural intervention, serving as a pilot for a within-participant investigation with longer time windows and more desirable devices. Although the sample size is too small for a statistical analysis of the impact of personal traits and demographics on results, the range of demographics and personas covered was wide, and the emerging and distinct impact of gender on preferences highlights the opportunity for a more targeted recruitment (e.g., including children and teenage girls).

The chosen cognitive and behavioural metrics were appropriate and can be evaluated empirically through repeated measures in a within-participant longitudinal study with a larger sample and precisely targeted demographics, controlling for the use of the interface in different social contexts. Administering full questionnaires would guarantee psychometric validity and reliability and giving 'placebo' products with arbitrary actuation and visualization outputs to a randomized portion of the sample would reveal whether biofeedback-based interventions are truly beneficial. Future validations studies should compare the effects of this intervention to those of existing 'Screen Time' products, for example in a cross-over study. Usage data (the device's algorithm's outputs) over two weeks would reflect trait changes [101] and could be analysed in relation to experience sampling reports to quantify the immediate impact of its interventions on behaviour, the perceived and objective accuracy of the classification of user states, and medium-term behaviour change.

Research and Design Opportunities. All users demanded significantly smaller form factors for Holdable devices to be viable. Thinner devices with soft or printed electronics can have more degrees of freedom, better classification accuracy, and the ability to remember individuals' habits to further personalise the timing of interventions. Alternatively, for users that would compromise intervention precision and secondary functionalities for lower prices and novelty, a simple case without electronics can use low temperature SMA to perform intricate, organic motions when the hand is in prolonged contact with the same area of the case, or when the phone heats up with use.

Hardware developments will enable more organic and controllable actuation movements and more complex and localized multi-touch gestures for more novel interventions and more insightful visualisations. The resulting higher perceived empathy, social agency, and affordance for reciprocation of favours can contribute to effective persuasion [107]. Printed circuit boards, thinner silicone movable by thinner shape memory alloy wires, and film-thin haptic actuators would dramatically reduce form factors. Otherwise, components and sensors can be embedded into the silicone with a laser-cutter. Designing for assembly and manufacture rather than lockdown-imposed home fabrication was beyond this pilot study's scope, but will drastically optimize the layout, cost, and reliability of internal components.

While not saving data is valuable for teenagers and to make the devices non-intrusive, the most technology-savvy users requested more personalised and accurate inference of state and usage data. Further separating the Holdable range into high-precision and simple products could reach more users. For all users, adapting frequency and immersion thresholds and intervals automatically or manually to their behaviour can make interventions and visualisations more relevant and positive behaviour change more attainable. For example, teenagers may move their hands faster and more often than other demographics but may need more frequent interventions.

Benchmarking. The interface's multimodality and the novelty of interactions that can be achieved through the aforementioned design opportunities can be expected to prevent desensitization to interventions, a common shortcoming of digital behavioural interventions based solely on graphical user interfaces [51]. Moreover, participants were not users of Screen Time and app blockers and positively embraced the device's lack of coercion and intrusion. Future studies should compare biofeedback-based, multimodal interventions to digital, time-based interventions to evaluate the appropriateness, desirability, and effectiveness of Holdables in relation to existing systems.

5.2   Conclusions

Combining user-centred design, positive psychology, HCI and engineering methodologies resulted in the development of Holdables and a proposed paradigm shift in PSU interventions. Contrary to currently available software solutions, Holdables do not survey nor judge app usage but focus on the quality of fundamental cognitive and behavioural processes. Their interventions offer platform-agnostic support by gently inducing mindful attention awareness in moments of unplanned, inattentive behaviour, and by promoting compassionate self-reflection about one's dysfunctional habits through non-quantified visualisations. Tactile stimuli empower users to effortlessly self-regulate, and the TUI was perceived as intimate and non-invasive.

Preliminary data validates acceptability and potential benefits on user autonomy and mindfulness during phone use. Qualitative insights evaluated design decisions and features to inform further development opportunities, value propositions, and empirical validation procedures. Participant engagement is encouraging, and findings indicate that achieving smaller form factors while continuing to tailor different Holdables to different user attitudes and demographics can fulfil the device's potential as a widely accessible PSU solution. Further development and validation can then naturally extend Holdables into accessories for wearable and immersive technologies.

References

1. Gardner, W.L., Pickett, C.L., Knowles, M.: Social snacking and shielding: using social symbols, selves, and surrogates in the service of belonging needs. In: The Social Outcast: Ostracism, Social Exclusion, Rejection, and Bullying. Sydney Symposium of Social Psychology Series, pp. 227–241. Psychology Press, New York (2005)
2. Lanier, J.: Ten Arguments for Deleting your Social Media Accounts Right Now. The Bodley Head, London (2015)

3. Xi, N., Hamari, J.: Does gamification satisfy needs? A study on the relationship between gamification features and intrinsic need satisfaction. Int. J. Inf. Manage. **46**, 210–221 (2019). https://doi.org/10.1016/j.ijinfomgt.2018.12.002

4. Griffiths, M.D.K., Daria, J., Billieux, J., Pontes, H.M.: The evolution of Internet addiction: a global perspective. Addict. Behav. **53**, 193–195 (2016). https://doi.org/10.1016/j.addbeh.2015.11.001

5. Billieux, J., Maurage, P., Lopez-Fernandez, O., Kuss, D.J., Griffiths, M.D.: Can disordered mobile phone use be considered a behavioral addiction? An update on current evidence and a comprehensive model for future research. Curr. Addict. Rep. **2**(2), 156–162 (2015). https://doi.org/10.1007/s40429-015-0054-y

6. Lorenz-Spreen, P., Mønsted, B.M., Hövel, P., Lehmann, S.: Accelerating dynamics of collective attention. Nat. Commun. **10**(1), 1759 (2019). https://doi.org/10.1038/s41467-019-09311-w

7. Brumby, D.P., Cox, A.L., Back, J., Gould, S.J.J.: Recovering from an interruption: investigating speed–accuracy trade-offs in task resumption behavior. J. Exp. Psychol. Appl. **19**(2), 95–107 (2013). https://doi.org/10.1037/a0032696

8. Ward, A.F., Duke, K., Gneezy, A., Bos, M.W.: Brain drain: the mere presence of one's own smartphone reduces available cognitive capacity. J. Assoc. Consum. Res. **2**(2), 140–154 (2017). https://doi.org/10.1086/691462

9. Oulasvirta, A., Rattenbury, T., Ma, L., Raita, E.: Habits make smartphone use more pervasive. Pers. Ubiquit. Comput. **16**(1), 105–114 (2012). https://doi.org/10.1007/s00779-011-0412-2

10. Holmes, N.M., Marchand, A.R., Coutureau, E.: Pavlovian to instrumental transfer: a neurobehavioural perspective. Neurosci. Biobehav. Rev. **34**(8), 1277–1295 (2010). https://doi.org/10.1016/j.neubiorev.2010.03.007

11. Ryan, R.M., Deci, E.L.: Self-determination theory and the facilitation of intrinsic motivation, social development, and well-being. Am. Psychol. **55**(1), 68–78 (2000). https://doi.org/10.1037/0003-066X.55.1.68

12. Reinecke, L., Hofmann, W.: Slacking off or winding down? An experience sampling study on the drivers and consequences of media use for recovery versus procrastination. Hum. Commun. Res. **42**(3), 441–461 (2016). https://doi.org/10.1111/hcre.12082

13. Panek, E.: Left to their own devices: college students' "guilty pleasure" media use and time management. Commun. Res. **41**, 561–577 (2013). https://doi.org/10.1177/0093650213499657

14. Ofcom: The Communications Market Report 2016

15. Piaget, J.: Piaget's theory. In: Inhelder, B., Chipman, H.H., Zwingmann, C. (eds.) Piaget and His School. Springer Study Edition. Springer, Heidelberg (1976). https://doi.org/10.1007/978-3-642-46323-5_2

16. Walsh, S.P., White, K.M., Young, R.M.: Needing to connect: the effect of self and others on young people's involvement with their mobile phones. Aust. J. Psychol. (2010). https://doi.org/10.1080/00049530903567229

17. Konok, V., Gigler, D., Bereczky, B., Miklosi, A.: Humans' attachment to their mobile phones and its relationship with interpersonal attachment style. Comput. Hum. Behav. **61**, 537–547 (2016). https://doi.org/10.1016/j.chb.2016.03.062

18. Elhai, J.D., Levine, J.C., O'Brien, K.D., Armour, C.: Distress tolerance and mindfulness mediate relations between depression and anxiety sensitivity with problematic smartphone use. Comput. Hum. Behav. **84**, 477–484 (2018). https://doi.org/10.1016/j.chb.2018.03.026

19. Van Zalk, N.: Online peer engagement in adolescence. In: Van Zalk, N., Monks, C.P. (eds.) Online Peer Engagement in Adolescence: Positive and Negative Aspects of Online Social Interaction, pp. 1–17. Routledge (2020). https://doi.org/10.4324/9780429468360-1

20. Krasnova, H., Wenninger, H.E., Widjaja, T., Buxmann, P.: Envy on Facebook: a hidden threat to users' life satisfaction? In: 2013 International Conference on Wirtschaftsinformatik, Leipzig, Germany, pp. 1–17 (2013)
21. Verduyn, P., et al.: Passive Facebook usage undermines affective well-being: experimental and longitudinal evidence. J. Exp. Psychol. Gen. **144**(2), 480–488 (2015). https://doi.org/10.1037/xge0000057
22. Ryan, R.M., Deci, E.L. (eds.): Self-determination Theory: Basic Psychological Needs in Motivation, Development, and Wellness. Guilford Press, New York (2017). https://doi.org/10.1521/978.14625/28806
23. Bishop, S.R., et al.: Mindfulness: a proposed operational definition. Clin. Psychol. Sci. Pract. **11**(3), 230–241 (2004). https://doi.org/10.1093/clipsy.bph077
24. Calvo, R.A., Peters, D.: Positive Computing: Technology for Wellbeing and Human Potential. The MIT Press, Cambridge (2014). https://doi.org/10.7551/mitpress/9764.001.0001
25. Bakker, S., van den Hoven, E., Eggen, B.: Peripheral interaction: characteristics and considerations. Pers. Ubiquit. Comput. **19**(1), 239–254 (2014). https://doi.org/10.1007/s00779-014-0775-2
26. Charoensukmongkol, P.: Mindful Facebooking: The moderating role of mindfulness on the relationship between social media use intensity at work and burnout. J Health Psychol. **21**(9), 1966–1980 (2016). https://doi.org/10.1177/1359105315569096
27. Lin, Y.-H., et al.: Time distortion associated with smartphone addiction: identifying smartphone addiction via a mobile application (App). J. Psychiatr. Res. **65**, 139–145 (2015). https://doi.org/10.1016/j.jpsychires.2015.04.003
28. Woodlief, D.T.: Smartphone Use and Mindfulness: Empirical Tests of a Hypothesized Connection. University of South Carolina (2017)
29. Owen, B., Heisterkamp, B., Halfmann, A., Vorderer, P.: Trait mindfulness and problematic smartphone use, pp. 181–206 (2018)
30. Tan, W.-K., Lee, P.-W., Hsu, C.-W.: Investigation of temporal dissociation and focused immersion as moderators of satisfaction–continuance intention relationship: smartphone as an example. Telematics Inform. **32**(4), 745–754 (2015). https://doi.org/10.1016/j.tele.2015.03.007
31. Mauri, M., Cipresso, P., Balgera, A., Villamira, M., Riva, G.: Why is Facebook so successful? Psychophysiological measures describe a core flow state while using Facebook. Cyberpsychol. Behav. Soc. Netw. **14**(12), 723–731 (2011). https://doi.org/10.1089/cyber.2010.0377
32. Smallwood, J., Schooler, J.W.: The science of mind wandering: empirically navigating the stream of consciousness. Annu. Rev. Psychol. **66**, 487–518 (2015). https://doi.org/10.1146/annurev-psych-010814-015331
33. Kahneman, D.: Thinking, Fast and Slow. Farrar, Straus and Giroux (2011)
34. Petty, R.E., Cacioppo, J.T.: The Elaboration Likelihood Model of Persuasion, pp. 123–205. Elsevier, Amsterdam (1986).https://doi.org/10.1016/S0065-2601(08)60214-2
35. Lavie, N.: Distracted and confused?: selective attention under load. Trends Cogn. Sci. **9**(2), 75–82 (2005). https://doi.org/10.1016/j.tics.2004.12.004
36. Google UI Speed Guide. https://material.io/design/motion/speed.html. Accessed 23 Sept 2020
37. Doherty, W., Thadhani-Zugriff, A.: The economic value of rapid response time. IBM Technical Report GE20-0752-0 (1982)
38. Mark, G., Iqbal, S., Czerwinski, M., Johns, P.: Focused, aroused, but so distractible: temporal perspectives on multitasking and communications. In: Proceedings of the 18th ACM Conference on Computer Supported Cooperative Work & Social Computing, pp. 903–916. ACM (2015)

39. Use Screen Time on your iPhone, iPad, or iPod touch. https://support.apple.com/en-us/HT2 08982 (2019). Accessed 23 Sept 2020
40. Digital Wellbeing - Google (2020). https://wellbeing.google. Accessed 23 Sept 2020
41. AppBlock - Stay focused (2019). https://www.appblock.app/. Accessed 23 Sept 2020
42. Hiniker, A., Hong, S.R., Kohno, T., Kientz, J.A.: MyTime: designing and evaluating an intervention for smartphone non-use. In: Proceedings of the 2016 CHI Conference on Human Factors in Computing Systems, pp. 4746–4757. ACM (2016)
43. Shin, C., Dey, A.K.: Automatically detecting problematic use of smartphones. In: The 2013 ACM International Joint Conference on Pervasive and Ubiquitous Computing, pp. 335–344. ACM (2013)
44. Van Velthoven, M., Powell, J., Powell, G.: Problematic smartphone use: digital approaches to an emerging public health problem. Digit. Health 4, 1–9 (2018). https://doi.org/10.1177/2055207618759167
45. Nicas, J.: Apple Cracks Down on Apps That Fight iPhone Addiction. https://www.nytimes.com/2019/04/27/technology/apple-screen-time-trackers.html. Accessed 14 Dec 2019
46. Ciman, M., Wac, K.: Individuals' stress assessment using human-smartphone interaction analysis. IEEE Trans. Affect. Comput. 9(1), 51–65 (2018). https://doi.org/10.1109/TAFFC.2016.2592504
47. Kambham, N.K., Stanley, K.G., Bell, S.: Predicting personality traits using smartphone sensor data and app usage data. In: IEEE 9th Annual Information Technology, Electronics and Mobile Communication Conference (IEMCON) (2018)
48. Alibasa, M.J., Calvo, R.A.: Supporting mood introspection from digital footprints. In: 2019 8th International Conference on Affective Computing and Intelligent Interaction (ACII). IEEE Conference Publication. IEEE, Cambridge, United Kingdom (2019)
49. Lane, N.D., et al.: BeWell: sensing sleep, physical activities and social interactions to promote wellbeing. Mob. Netw. Appl. 19(3), 345–359 (2014). https://doi.org/10.1007/s11036-013-0484-5
50. Dagum, P.: Digital biomarkers of cognitive function. npj Digit. Med. 1, 10 (2018). https://doi.org/10.1038/s41746-018-0018-4
51. Yardley, L., et al.: Understanding and promoting effective engagement with digital behavior change interventions. Am. J. Prev. Med. 51(5), 833–842 (2016). https://doi.org/10.1016/j.amepre.2016.06.015
52. Use the Breathe App. https://support.apple.com/en-us/HT206999. Accessed 23 Sept 2020
53. Headspace - Be Kind to Your Mind. https://www.headspace.com/. Accessed 10 Feb 2021
54. Calm App. https://apps.apple.com/us/app/calm/id571800810. Accessed 10 Feb 2021
55. Kabat-Zinn, J.: Mindfulness-based interventions in context: past, present, and future. Clin. Psychol. Sci. Pract. 10, 125–143 (2006). https://doi.org/10.1093/clipsy.bpg016
56. Muse - Meditation Made Easy (2020). https://choosemuse.com/
57. McCarthy, J., Wright, P.C.: Technology as Experience. MIT Press, Cambridge, MA (2004)
58. Hooked, E.N.: How to Build Habit-Forming Products. Penguin, New York (2014)
59. Gould, S.J.J., Cox, A.L., Brumby, D.P., Wickersham, A.: Now check your input: brief task lockouts encourage checking, longer lockouts encourage task switching. In: Proceedings of the 2016 CHI Conference on Human Factors in Computing Systems, pp. 3311–323. ACM (2016)
60. Cox, A.L., Gould, S.J.J., Cecchinato, M.E., Iacovides, I., Renfree, I.: Design frictions for mindful interactions: the case for microboundaries. In: Proceedings of the 2016 CHI Conference Extended Abstracts on Human Factors in Computing Systems, pp. 1389–1397. ACM (2016)
61. Shapiro, S.L.S., Gary, E.R.: Intentional systemic mindfulness: an integrative model for self-regulation and health. Adv. Mind Body Med. 16(2), 128–134 (2000)

62. Chödrön, P.: How to Meditate: A Practical Guide to Making Friends with Your Mind. Sounds True, Boulder, CO (2007)

63. Yu, M.C., Wu, H., Lee, M.S., Hung, Y.P.: Multimedia-assisted breathwalk-aware system. IEEE Trans. Biomed. Eng. **59**(12), 3276–3282 (2012). https://doi.org/10.1109/tbme.2012.2208747

64. Prinsloo, G.E., Laurie Rauch, H.G., Lambert, M.I., Muench, F., Noakes, T.D., Derman, W.E.: The effect of short duration heart rate variability (HRV) biofeedback on cognitive performance during laboratory induced cognitive stress. Appl. Cogn. Psychol. **25**(5), 792–801 (2010). https://doi.org/10.1002/acp.1750

65. Khazan, I.Z.: The Clinical Handbook of Biofeedback: A Step-by-Step Guide for Training and Practice with Mindfulness (2013)

66. Long, K., Vines, J.: Mind pool. In: Extended Abstracts on Human Factors in Computing Systems on CHI EA 2013, CHI 2013. ACM Press (2013)

67. Yano, K., Lyubomirsky, S., Chancellor, J.: Sensing happiness. IEEE Spectr. **49**(12), 32–37 (2012). https://doi.org/10.1109/MSPEC.2012.6361760

68. Nicholls, B., Ang, C.S., Kanjo, E., Siriararya, P., Yeo, W.-H., Tsanas, A.: An EMG-based eating behaviour monitoring system with haptic feedback to promote mindful eating (2019)

69. Pryss, R., Reichert, M., John, D., Frank, J., Schlee, W., Probst, T.: A personalized sensor support tool for the training of mindful walking. In: IEEE 15th International Conference on Wearable and Implantable Body Sensor Networks (BSN). IEEE (2018)

70. Wang, D., Xu, M., Zhanq, Y., Xiao, J.: Preliminary study on haptic-stimulation based brainwave entrainment. In: IEEE Conference Publication. IEEE (2013)

71. Leithinger, D., Olwal, A., Hogge, A.G., Ishii, H., Follmer, S.W., Laboratory MIoTM, et al.: inFORM: dynamic physical affordances and constraints through shape and object actuation. In: Proceedings of the 26th Annual ACM Symposium on User Interface Software and Technology, UIST 2013 (2013).

72. Jang, S., Kim, L.H., Tanner, K., Ishii, H., Follmer, S.: Haptic edge display for mobile tactile interaction. In: CHI 2016 (2016)

73. Teyssier, M., Bailly, G., Lecolinet, É., Pelachaud, C.: Survey and perspectives of social touch in HCI. In: Proceedings of the 29th Conference on l'Interaction Homme-Machine, pp. 93–104. Association for Computing Machinery, Poitiers, France (2017)

74. Huisman, G.F., Darriba, A., Heylen, D.K.J. . Affective touch at a distance. In: Conference on Affective Computing and Intelligent Interaction, ACII 2013, pp. 701–702 (2013)

75. Shiomi, M., Nakagawa, K., Shinozawa, K., Matsumura, R., Ishiguro, H., Hagita, N.: Does a robot's touch encourage human effort? Int. J. Soc. Robot. **9**(1), 5–15 (2016). https://doi.org/10.1007/s12369-016-0339-x

76. Peters, D., Calvo, R.A., Ryan, R.M.: Designing for motivation, engagement and wellbeing in digital experience. Front. Psychol. **9**, 797 (2018). https://doi.org/10.3389/fpsyg.2018.00797

77. RescueTime (2019). https://www.rescuetime.com. Accessed 17 Dec 2019

78. Teyssier, M., Bailly, G., Pelachaud, C., Lecolinet, E., Conn, A., Roudaut, A.: Skin-on interfaces: a bio-driven approach for artificial skin design to cover interactive devices. In: Proceedings of the 32nd Annual ACM Symposium on User Interface Software and Technology, pp. 307–322. Association for Computing Machinery, New Orleans, LA, USA (2019)

79. DATASTRETCH: Elastic conductive yarn. https://www.tibtech.com/smartshop/index.php?id_product=157&controller=product&id_lang=1. Accessed 10 Feb 2021

80. Teyssier, M.: Muca: Multi Touch for Arduino (2020). https://muca.cc/. Accessed 10 Feb 2021

81. Processing (2020). https://processing.org/. Accessed 10 Feb 2021

82. Schlegel A: ControlP5 (2020). https://github.com/sojamo/controlp5. Accessed 10 Feb 2021

83. Teyssier, M.: Muca-board (2020). https://github.com/muca-board. Accessed 10 Feb 2021

84. OpenCV (2020). https://opencv.org Accessed 10 Feb 2021

85. Obrist, M., Seah, S.A., Subramanian, S.: Talking about tactile experiences. In: Proceedings of the SIGCHI Conference on Human Factors in Computing Systems, pp. 1659–1668. Association for Computing Machinery, Paris, France (2013)

86. Dautenhahn, K, Woods, S., Kaouri, C., Walters, M., Koay, K., Werry, I.: What is a robot companion - Friend, assistant or butler? (2005)

87. Teyssier, M., Bailly, G., Pelachaud, C., Lecolinet, E.: Conveying emotions through device-initiated touch. IEEE Trans. Affect. Comput. (2020). https://doi.org/10.1109/TAFFC.2020.3008693

88. Parkes, A., Poupyrev, I., Ishii, H.: Designing kinetic interactions for organic user interfaces. Commun. ACM **51**(6), 58–65 (2008). https://doi.org/10.1145/1349026.1349039

89. Morrison, I., Loken, L., Olausson, H.: The skin as a social organ. Exp. Brain Res. **204**, 305–314 (2009)

90. Bailenson, J.N., Yee, N., Brave, S., Merget, D., Koslow, D.: Virtual interpersonal touch: expressing and recognizing emotions through haptic devices. Hum. Comput. Interact. **22**(3), 325–353 (2007). https://doi.org/10.1080/07370020701493509

91. Twitter Search: Apple Watch Vibrates Breathe (2021). https://twitter.com/search?q=Apple%20Watch%20Vibrates%20Breathe&src=typed_query&f=live. Accessed 10 Feb 2021

92. Macaron v1.1.0. https://hapticdesign.github.io/macaron/ Accessed 18 May 2020

93. Strohmeier, P., Hornbæk, K.: Generating Haptic Textures with a Vibrotactile Actuator (2017)

94. Human Interface Guidelines: Haptics. https://developer.apple.com/design/human-interface-guidelines/ios/user-interaction/haptics/. Accessed 10 Feb 2021

95. Pistole, M.C., Watkins, C.E.: Attachment theory, counseling process, and supervision. Couns. Psychol. **23**(3), 457–478 (1995). https://doi.org/10.1177/0011000095233004

96. Moos, R.H., Finney, J.W., Cronkite, R.C.: Alcoholism Treatment: Context, Process and Outcome. Oxford University Press, New York (1990)

97. Yohanan, S., MacLean, K.E.: The role of affective touch in human-robot interaction: human intent and expectations in touching the haptic creature. Int. J. Soc. Robot. **4**(2), 163–180 (2012). https://doi.org/10.1007/s12369-011-0126-7

98. Mori, M.: The Uncanny Valley (2012). Translated by Karl F. MacDorman and Norri Kageki

99. Lacan, J.: Le seminaire - X - L'angoisse (1963)

100. Foglia, L., Wilson, R.: Embodied Cognition. Wiley Interdisciplinary Reviews: Cognitive Science (2017). Revision 4. https://doi.org/10.1002/wcs.1226

101. Voils, C.I., King, H.A., Maciejewski, M.L., Allen, K.D., Yancy, W.S., Shaffer, J.A.: Approaches for informing optimal dose of behavioral interventions. Ann. Behav. Med. **48**(3), 392–401 (2014). https://doi.org/10.1007/s12160-014-9618-7

102. Brown, K.W., Ryan, R.M.: The benefits of being present: mindfulness and its role in psychological well-being. J. Pers. Soc. Psychol. **84**(4), 822–848 (2003). https://doi.org/10.1037/0022-3514.84.4.822

103. Merlo, L.J., Stone, A.M., Bibbey, A.: Measuring problematic mobile phone use: development and preliminary psychometric properties of the PUMP scale. J. Addict. **2013**, 1–7 (2013). https://doi.org/10.1155/2013/912807

104. Kwon, M., et al.: Development and validation of a smartphone addiction scale (SAS). PLOS ONE **8**(2), e56936 (2013)

105. van den Eijnden, R.J.J.M., Lemmens, J.S., Valkenburg, P.M.: The social media disorder scale. Comput. Hum. Behav. **61**, 478–487 (2016). https://doi.org/10.1016/j.chb.2016.03.038

106. Li, Z.: Psychological empowerment on social media: who are the empowered users? Pub. Relat. Rev. **42**(1), 49–59 (2016). https://doi.org/10.1016/j.pubrev.2015.09.001

107. Fogg, B.J.: Persuasive technology: using computers to change what we think and do. Ubiquity **2002**, 2 (2002). https://doi.org/10.1145/764008.763957

Measurement and Analysis of Body Movements in Playing Futsal Using Smartphones

Tomohito Yamamoto(✉), Kento Sugiyama, and Ryohei Fukushima

Department of Information and Computer Science, College of Engineering, Kanazawa Institute of Technology, 7–1 Oogigaoka, Nonoichi, Ishikawa 921-8501, Japan
tyama@neptune.kanazawa-it.ac.jp,
b1701618@planet.kanazawa-it.ac.jp

Abstract. Sport activities have been analyzed using an Information Technology measuring system to improve players' performances in recent years. However, such approaches tend to require expensive systems, and, as a result, most users are professional players. In this study, to expand this approach to amateur players, we investigated the possibility of evaluating sport activities, particularly futsal, using only sensors on smartphones. It was possible to evaluate the activity of the team using an accelerometer sensor, which decreased as the game progressed. The activity increased after a sufficient rest. In addition, the degree of synchronization between body movements reflected the important situation of the game. For example, when the degree of synchronization was high, a change from defense to offense was often observed. On the other hand, when the degree of synchronization was low, the team was mostly pushed by the opponent team. Using the measurement results, it is possible to evaluate various activities during sports by sensors on smartphones.

Keywords: Sport · Body movement · Smartphone · Accelerometer sensor · Frequency analysis

1 Introduction

The body movements of players during various sport activities have been measured and analyzed in recent years to improve their performances. For example, leg trajectories of running or kicking movements of soccer have been analyzed to understand more efficient running forms or type of joint angle leading to obstacles from the perspective of biomechanics [1–4]. In addition to the analysis of individual players, the performances of team sports have also been evaluated using multiple sensor units. For example, the Rugby World Cup was held in Japan in 2019, where many teams used the Catapult system [5]. In this system, small sensor units were introduced and players of each team wore it on their backs with a "Digital Bra". Each team analyzed the values from these sensors to evaluate the exercise intensity and playing movements during practice and improve the team performance. In the future, this type of Internet of Things approach is expected to be more widespread. The accuracy of analysis will determine the game results, particularly in popular professional sports such as baseball and soccer.

© Springer Nature Switzerland AG 2021
M. Kurosu (Ed.): HCII 2021, LNCS 12763, pp. 496–506, 2021.
https://doi.org/10.1007/978-3-030-78465-2_36

Measurements by such devices have recently been spreading to the amateur level. For example, in marathons where the population already increases, an increasing number of users use Garmin or Apple's portable devices to record their daily training and improve their running performances. On the other hand, in team sports such as soccer at the amateur level, the introduction of the system has not progressed because the measuring system is still expensive. For example, the Catapult's measurement system costs thousands of dollars, so that most of the users are professional teams. Smartphones, which are now widely used, are almost equipped with sensors used in pro rugby or soccer teams. If such smartphone can be used, the cost of measurement can be significantly reduced, which can enable the use in various amateur sports.

Our research group has used smartphones to evaluate the group work, which is a typical method of "active learning", which has recently been introduced in numerous educational institutions [6, 7]. The amount of communication during group work and outcomes could be predicted from body movements measured by a smartphone. In this study, we introduce this system to the measurement of sport activities, particularly futsal. Smartphones have been used to evaluate sport activities, but they can be used for image acquisition or evaluation of basic solo sport activities [8, 9]. Few approaches have been proposed to evaluate the activities of team sports using sensors on smartphones.

Therefore, in this study, we prepared multiple smartphones and used them to measure and analyze sport activities performed by the team. Specifically, we measured a futsal game played by five players against five players and analyzed the state of the player using the acceleration sensor of the smartphone.

2 Methods

2.1 Measurements and Subjects

In this study, to clarify whether sport activities can be evaluated using the sensors on the smartphone, the body movements of the players during futsal performed by five players against five players were measured and analyzed. Eighteen subjects (teenagers to 50s years old) participated in the measurement. The participants were randomly divided into three teams consisting of five people (the remaining participants had a break) in one set. Those three teams played the match in a round-robin manner. Thus, one set consisted of three games. The time per game was 5 min. A total of five sets and 15 games were played with a measurement time of approximately 2 h. Figure 1 shows the actual measurement scene.

2.2 Measurement Equipment and Data Acquisition

In this study, body movements while playing futsal were measured using a smartphone (ASUS Zenfone 2). As shown in Fig. 2, the smartphone was inserted into the bibs with pockets so that it was in close contact with the player's body. The bibs for five players were prepared and one of the two teams wore them.

Fig. 1. Picture of the measurement.

In this measurement, the values of the three-axis accelerometer and geomagnetic sensor were continuously acquired at a sampling frequency of 60 Hz. The values from each sensor were saved in the smartphone and saved while monitoring on a notebook personal computer through Wi-Fi. In addition, 15 games were recorded using a video camera and analyzed together with the data obtained from the smartphone.

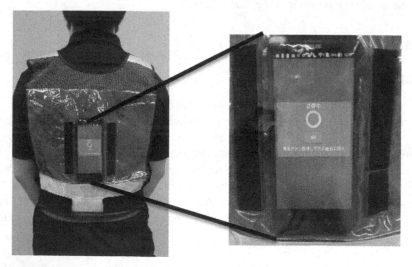

Fig. 2. Smartphone for the measurement.

2.3 Data Analysis

In this measurement, the values of the accelerometer and geomagnetic sensor were acquired using a smartphone. However, in this study, only those of the accelerometer sensor were analyzed.

As a procedure for the analysis, the norm value shown in Fig. 3 was calculated by the square root of squaring and adding the obtained values of the three axes. In the measurement, the acceleration obtained from the smartphone sometimes became larger than the actual measured value, and thus the amplitude value was cut by $\pm 2g$. The amplitude of this time-series data increases as the body movements during the play become more intense and the waveform cycle becomes shorter as the play speed increases.

Subsequently, the Fourier transform was applied to the time-series data to obtain the frequency distribution shown in Fig. 4. In this study, the amount of activity during the play was calculated by adding the amplitude values for this frequency. In addition, to facilitate the understanding of the obtained values, each value was divided by the value of the player with the highest amount of activity in all games. In addition to this frequency analysis, to investigate changes in body movements during the game, a sonogram that visualizes the frequency distribution changes over time is introduced. Figure 5 shows the results of the players, where blue indicates a low power, while yellow indicates a high power. According to this figure and recorded video, we analyzed the types of body movements performed during the playing time.

Finally, the degree of team synchronization was analyzed by calculating the correlation between the sonograms. Specifically, the correlations (10 ways) between the sonograms of each player were calculated every 2 s and their average values were calculated to analyze the similarity of the body movements of each player.

This measurement was approved by the ethics review committee of Kanazawa Institute of Technology. All participants consented to the use of the measurement data on the day.

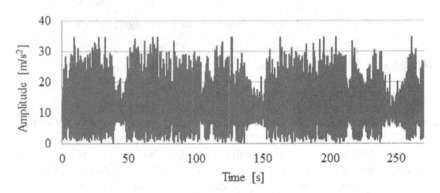

Fig. 3. Time series of the measured accelerometer sensor value.

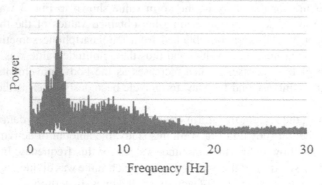

Fig. 4. Frequency data of the measured accelerometer value.

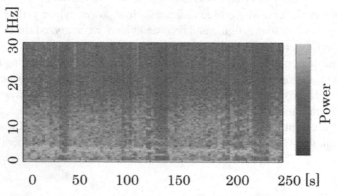

Fig. 5. Sonogram of the frequency data. (Color figure online)

3 Results

3.1 Activity of the Players in Playing Futsal

The change in activity through games was investigated. Figure 6 shows the sum of the activities of the five players in each match. The activities tend to gradually decrease from the first to the 15th game. This implies that each player gradually gets tired and stuck as the game progresses. It is possible to detect the significant value change from the 6th game to the 7th game. As shown in Fig. 7, during the measurement, the subjects had a break between games for approximately 2 min. However, at the 6th game after the end of two sets, each player's fatigue level became quite high and the subjects had a break of approximately 15 min before the 7th game. This effect is clearly presented as a change in activity.

These results indicate that the activity of the player during futsal can be properly evaluated using the acceleration sensor on the smartphone.

In this study, the differences in sonogram patterns were investigated to clarify the changes in the activities of individual players during the match. Figure 8 shows the sonograms of the five players in games 1, 6, 8, and 14 (the player numbers in the figure

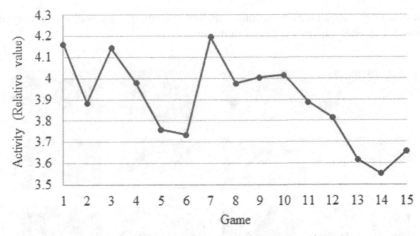

Fig. 6. Time series of activity of all team members.

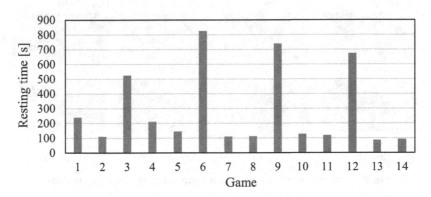

Fig. 7. Rest time of 15 games.

do not necessarily refer to the same player). The comparison of the first and sixth games shows that all players were moving actively in the first game because the yellow color of the figure is dominant, except for Player 1, who was the keeper in the first game. On the other hand, many blue streaks are observed in the 6th game when the activity decreases. These results indicate that each player was unable to run in the game because of fatigue. In addition, the yellow color in the high-frequency band slightly fades, which implies that quick operation was not possible for each player. In addition, each player was the keeper and had a rest during the game, which appears as a change in the blue band section of Players 1, 2, and 3 in the figure.

Subsequently, in match 8, the yellow area in the figure increased compared to the sixth match. The sonogram shows that the fatigue is relieved by such a proper rest. On the other hand, in the 14th game, the streaky blue color became conspicuous again in all figures, while the yellow color in the high-frequency band became lighter. At this moment, the sonogram shows that no player can run continuously and cannot move quickly.

By observing the changes in the sonogram in this manner, it is possible to understand, to some extent, each player's behavior in the match.

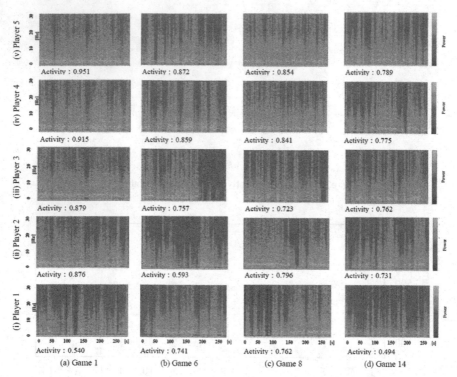

Fig. 8. Sonograms of five members in each game. (Color figure online)

3.2 Number and Synchronization of Body Movements in Playing Futsal

Figure 9 and 10 show the changes in the gap statistics obtained by a cluster analysis on the sonogram data of games 8 and 14. The results suggest that the frequency distribution can be classified into approximately 6–8 clusters. The analysis of the movements with the recorded video suggests that they can be roughly classified into 1: standing, 2: small ball handling, 3: passing, 4: running, 5: stop and kicking, 6: tapping, 7: walking, and 8: jogging in game 8 and 1: stop and kicking, 2: running, 3: jogging, 4: walking, 5: matching with other players, and 6: kicking in game 14. Figure 11(a) and (b) show the time series of the clustered body movements. The numbers of the figures show each body movement. In Game 8, eight movements are observed quickly and widely through the game. On the other hand, in Game 14, flat lines are sometimes observed and the variation of movements is relatively small because of fatigue.

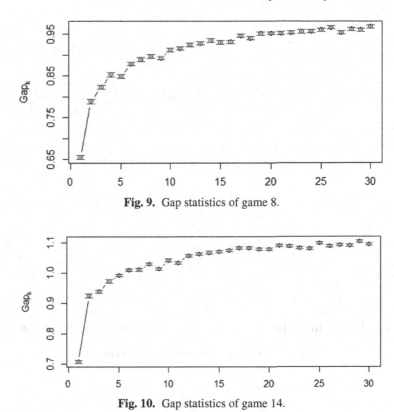

Fig. 9. Gap statistics of game 8.

Fig. 10. Gap statistics of game 14.

Finally, the synchronization of players in the team was analyzed. Figure 12 shows the time series data of the degree of synchronization between players in Game 1. The solid red circles indicate places with high correlation coefficients (top nine during the match). By checking the recorded video to detect the types of play in the place where this correlation coefficient is high, it is confirmed that the change from defense to offense occurs in seven out of nine places.

On the other hand, the blue dashed circles indicate the places where the degree of synchronization was low in the whole game (bottom seven during the match). Similarly, the recorded play in these sections in the video shows that the opponent's team hits a shot or the ball is taken out of the field. Moreover, the team was strongly pushed by the opponent team or made a big mistake.

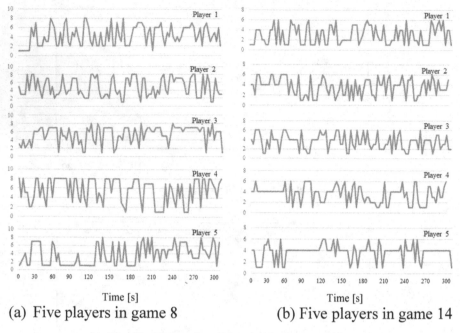

(a) Five players in game 8   (b) Five players in game 14

Fig. 11. Time series of clustered body movements.

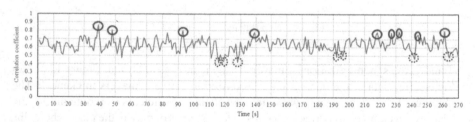

Fig. 12. Synchronization of the sonogram between players. (Color figure online)

4 Discussion

In this study, we investigated whether the activities of sports, particularly futsal, can be evaluated using sensors on smartphones. The activity of the team decreased as the game progressed, but increased as the physical strength was recovered by resting. In addition, through the sonogram of each player, the strength change of the player's body movement and its role in the play can be detected. Moreover, the results of the degree of synchronization between body movements during the game showed that, when the degree of synchronization is high, the change from defense to offense often occurs. However, when the degree of synchronization is low, the team is mostly pushed by the opponent team.

According to the measurement results, it is possible to evaluate various activities during sports using sensors on smartphones, particularly acceleration sensors. In the future, it may be possible to evaluate the performance of the entire team and performances of individual players at a low cost using this type of measurement and analysis. In particular, if the temporal change of the sonogram was quantified and the activity of the entire team was calculated, it could be easily evaluated whether each player got tired or whether the team played with a sufficient amount of exercise.

In addition, the analysis of the degree of synchronization of body movements during the play suggested that the degree of coordination between players changed during the game phase. In particular, a high degree of synchronization was often observed when the entire team changed to the attack phase. This synchronization occurred as the players' behaviors became similar when the entire team runs in the same way when heading for an attack and when passing the pass in a timely manner. On the other hand, a low synchronization was often observed when the team was pushed by the opponent team. One possible reason for this result is that the opponent team attacks when the team is disjointed, and, as a result, the movement of the team is further disjointed. Considering this situation, it is important to improve the team cooperation to prevent points from being scored.

5 Conclusions

In this study, we investigated whether sport activities can be evaluated using smartphone sensors. The activity of the team decreased as the game progressed, but increased as the physical strength was recovered by resting. In addition, the degree of synchronization between body movements during the game showed that, when the degree of synchronization was high, the change from defense to offense was often observed. However, when the degree of synchronization was low, the team was mostly pushed by the opponent team.

In future studies, we will evaluate sport activities by further analyses based on the basic obtained data. For example, we will improve the accuracy of estimating body movements from the frequency distribution using a deep learning approach. By integrating these results, we will realize an artificial intelligence coaching system that can be applied to various sports.

References

1. Gabbett, J.T.: The training - injury prevention paradox: should athletes be training smarter and harder? Br. J. Sports Med. **50**, 273–280 (2016)
2. Hashizume, S., Hobara, H., Kobayashi, Y.: Between-limb differences in running technique induces asymmetric negative joint work during running. Eur. J. Sport Sci. **19**(6), 757–764 (2019)
3. Barfield, W.R.: The biomechanics of kicking in soccer. Clin. Sports Med. **17**(4), 711–728 (1998)
4. Shinkai, H., Nunome, H., Isokawa, M., Ikegami, Y.: Ball impact dynamics of instep soccer kicking. Med. Sci. Sports Exer. **41**(4), 889–897 (2009)
5. Catapult. https://www.catapultsports.com/. Accessed 21 Dec 2020

6. Harada, N., Kimura, M., Yamamoto, T., Miyake, Y.: System for measuring teacher–student communication in the classroom using smartphone accelerometer sensors. In: Kurosu, M. (ed.) HCI 2017. LNCS, vol. 10272, pp. 309–318. Springer, Cham (2017). https://doi.org/10.1007/978-3-319-58077-7_24

7. Sakon, H., Yamamoto, T.: Body movements for communication in group work classified by deep learning. In: Kurosu, M. (ed.) HCII 2019. LNCS, vol. 11567, pp. 388–396. Springer, Cham (2019). https://doi.org/10.1007/978-3-030-22643-5_30

8. Olmedo, J., Tomás, A., Lamberto, V., Pueo, B.: Validity and reliability of smartphone high-speed camera and Kinovea for velocity-based training measurement. J. Hum. Sport Exerc. **16**, 1–11 (2020)

9. Roig, J., Gilson, N., Ribera, A., Contreras, R., Trost, S.: Measuring and influencing physical activity with smartphone technology: a systematic review. Sports Med. **44**(5), 671–686 (2014)

Using e-Health in the Prevention Against Covid-19: An Approach Based on the Theory of Planned Behavior

Meryem Zoghlami[✉], Salma Ayeb, and Kaouther Saied Ben Rached

Faculty of Economics and Management of Tunis, Research Laboratory: Business and Marketing Research (ERMA), University of Tunis El Manar, Tunis, Tunisia
{meryem.zoghlami,kaouther.benrached}@fsegt.utm.tn

Abstract. The development of Information and Communication Technologies (ICTs) has encouraged the introduction of many innovations in healthcare services, including a new form of health management. This study applies the Theory of Planned Behavior (TPB) in order to explain e-health use behavior to prevent Covid19. The research has used an internet based-survey in which 180 people took part. The results indicate that the attitude towards behavior, subjective norms as well as perceived control increase the intention to use e-health to prevent against Covid-19.

Keywords: e-health use · Internet · Covid 19 · Theory of Planned Behavior · Subjective norms

1 Introduction

Nowadays, e-health is considered as one of the most important manifestations of new practices in the health area [1, 2]. In January 2020, the World Health Organization included new technologies in generally, and e-health in particularly, as one of the "13 global health challenges of this decade" (ONU, 2020)[1]. According to Hage et al. [3] "E-Health services refers to any interactive communication and information technology aimed to improve community quality of life and/or individual health outcomes".

With the widespread use of the Internet, healthy individuals as well as patients have become more autonomous [4]. By checking for their symptoms and understanding their illnesses, they take precautionary measures to protect themselves and to prevent their symptoms from deteriorating.

With the quick spread of the pandemic and the dearth of information about its behavior, health management has become a daily concern for both public and health experts and professionals. Researchers from all over the world are sharing knowledge about the virus in an attempt to better understand its behavior, track its spread, and contain

---

[1] United Nations (2020), The 13 global health challenges of this decade. https://news.un.org/es/story/2020/01/1467872.

© Springer Nature Switzerland AG 2021
M. Kurosu (Ed.): HCII 2021, LNCS 12763, pp. 507–517, 2021.
https://doi.org/10.1007/978-3-030-78465-2_37

its virulence. Information about health protocols and the prevention of frontline health professionals is also exchanged to a large extent.

The study of the determinants of Internet users' behavior can potentially help us respond to the most important issues and suggest health protocols that involve interaction among health professionals and interaction between the public [5].

Therefore, in a context where the pandemic continues to cause uncertainty and anxiety, it seems interesting to work on this issue by analyzing the intention to use e-health in the prevention against Covid-19.

Ajzen's Theory of Planned Behavior – TPB [6, 7] served as the background's theoretical framework for this study. This theory takes into account the attitude towards the behavior, the subjective norms, and the intention as behavior adoption predictors of internet health use, to prevent against Covid-19. The main contribution of TPB lies in taking into account behavioral and social control factors [7, 8].

Firstly, this article, in the literature review section, presents the theoretical model retained from psychosocial theories, namely the Theory of Planned Behavior. In a second phase, we present the empirical test of the model in order to measure the impact of the selected variables on the use of e-health to prevent Covid19.

In the third part, we test structural models using the Partial Least Squares (PLS) structural equation modeling technique and discuss the obtained results.

2 Literature Review

Abundant literature has emerged around theoretical models to analyze the process of behavioral change in the health area [9]. Among them, the theories of reasoned action and planned behavior [10] are still the most successful causal models for accounting for behavioral change [11, 12].

Many studies have tried to test TPB to explore different types of behaviors: Addictive behaviors (smoking, alcohol, drugs, etc.), driving behaviors (driving, seatbelt use, etc.), medical supervision behaviors (mammograms, medical checkups, etc.), nutritional behaviors (consumption of sugar, vegetables, caffeine, etc.), sports behaviors (jogging, regular exercise, cycling, etc.), HIV-related behaviors (use of condoms, abstinence, etc.) and, finally, oral hygiene behaviors (tooth brushing) [13, 14]. These different illustrations prove the pertinence of the choice of this theory, particularly in the field of health education.

Based on this model, the best predictor of behavior is the behavioral intention that results from a combination of individual factors and normative or social factors. The individual factor represents the attitude towards the behavior, resulting from beliefs about the behavior and associated positive or negative consequences. The normative factor refers to the dependence on subjective norms. Many studies have shown that peers have the strongest normative influence among youth, particularly in the health field [15, 16].

Normative beliefs reflect how much importance a person attaches to the opinions of the people around him or her regarding the adoption of a new behavior [17]. In fact, people are only more likely to develop a strong intention to act if they think that family and friends would approve the behavior.

In view of completing and perfecting the theory of reasoned action, Ajzen and Fishbein have modified it by adding a third element: Perceived behavioral control, in order to take into account some constraints to the adoption of behavior not completely under individual control. This factor is intended to balance situations in which people have limited control (or believe they have limited control) over their behaviors and attitudes [18]. Ajzen is referring to every type of constraint, both internal (skills, knowledge, motivation) and external (time, money, opportunities), that an individual is exposed to when he intends to engage in a specific action. According to Ajzen [19], the presence of these constraints reduces individuals' control over behavior.

Thus, the TPB model states that attitude, subjective norms and perception of control over behavior are direct determinants of behavioral intention, which in turn has a direct influence on the actual behavior [19, 20].

The Theory of Planned Behavior consequently suggests the following hypotheses (Fig. 1):

- H1: Attitude towards behavior has a positive effect on the intention to use e-Health to prevent Covid19.
- H2: Subjective norms have a positive effect on the intention to use e-Health to prevent Covid19.
- H3: Perception of behavioral control has a positive effect on the intention to use e-Health to prevent Covid19.
- H4: Person's intention to use e-health to prevent Covid 19 has a positive effect on the use behavior.

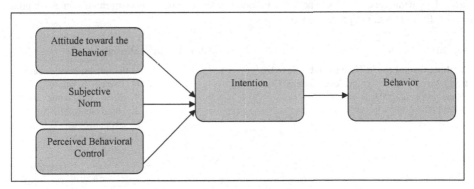

Fig. 1. The theory of Planned Behavior [8, 10–19]

3 Methodology

A questionnaire was posted online using Google's online survey software. Question-naires were circulated via online health discussion forums with a summary presenta-tion of the study's objective. We received 180 responses (after elimination of aberrant answers and incomplete questionnaires) with more than 83.3% of women and a mean age of 20–29 years.

In order to operationalize the research constructs, we used measurement scales from the literature. These are items taken from studies conducted by Godin et al. [21] and are based on the research of Ajzen et Fishbein [22, 23].

Ajzen and Fishbein [24] postulate that the intention to adopt or not a behavior is a direct result of a systematic analysis of three types of information:

- The "Attitudinal Dimension", can be defined as a global feeling (positive or negative) towards the behavior. The attitude scale used was measured using a 5-point differential semantic scale of pairs of adjectives.
- "The Subjective Norm", according to Ajzen, is defined as "the perceived social pres-sure to engage or not to engage in a behavior". To measure it we used four items on a five-point likert scale in a translated version adapted to our field.
- "Perceived behavioral control" is measured directly using three questions on a 5-point semantic scale as recommended by Ajzen [6].

The use of e-health is a variable consisting of 7 elements. Each of the first 6 elements has a specific objective, namely the use of the Internet to search for health services and information. More specifically, each element refers to the frequency of use of health sites to achieve one of these objectives [25].

Different measurement scales used are presented in Table 1.

Table 1. Characteristics of the Theory of Planned Behavior Theory measurement scales adapted to e-health use for covid prevention 19

Variables	Items	Number of items	Measuring scales
Attitude toward the Behavior *(Venketesh et al. 2003, Ajzen [7])*	The use e-health to be prevented against Covid 19 would be	4	Differential semantic scale (1: Useless–5: helpful; 1: Stress–5: relaxing; 1: Disadvantageous–5: advantageous 1: Unsatisfactory–5: satisfactory)

(continued)

Table 1. (*continued*)

Variables	Items	Number of items	Measuring scales
Subjective Norms *Fishbein and Ajzen* [24,36]	- Your doctor approves of you using e-Health to prevent covid19 - Your family approves of you using e-Health to prevent covid19 - Do your friends recommend you to use the internet to search for information about Covid 19? - Your work colleagues recommend you to use the internet to search for information on Covid 19	4	Likert scale (1: strongly disagree–5: strongly agree)
Perceived Behavioral Control *Ajzen* [6]	- Searching for information about covid 19 via internet is - If I wish, I could easily search for information about covid 19 via internet - In general, what degree of control do you feel you have over the search for information on the Covid19?	3	Differential semantic scale (1: difficult–5: easy; 1: unlikely–5: likely; 1: no control–5: full control)
Intention *Ajzen* [6]	- I intend to use e-Health to prevent covid19 - If the opportunity arises i will use e-Health to prevent covid19 - I am going to use e-Health to prevent covid19	3	Likert scale (1: stronglydisagree–5: strongly agree)
Use of e-health *Lemire et al.* [25]	- Understand a health problem or a disease of covid 19 - Look for a second medical opinion - Find a specific solution or a particular treatment to covid 19 - Prevent covid 19 by adopting a healthy lifestyle - Contact my doctor - Participate in forums and discussion groups - How often you consult health websites related to covid19 per month	7	Likert scale (1: never-5very often)

As regards data treatment, we used two statistical software programs: IBM SPSS Statistics for the purification of the measurement scales through an exploratory factor analysis (EFA) and SmartPLS for the evaluation of the internal and external model and the testing of hypotheses through a Confirmatory Factor Analysis (CFA).

4   Results and Interpretation

The questionnaires obtained were submitted to exploratory analysis at two levels:

At the first level, a Principal Component Factor Analysis (PCA) was conducted, using SPSS 18 software to test the validity of the chosen scale, its dimensionality, as also the reliability of the dimensions.

As reported in Table 2, PCA results indicate that Cronbach's Alpha values exceeded the 0.70 level for all variables. In addition, the KMO (Kaiser-Meyer-Olkin) presents good factor solutions and Bartlett's test is significant ($p = 0.000$). These results attest to the good reliability of our measurement scales.

Table 2. Results of exploratory studies

Constructs	KMO	Bartlett	Cronbach's α
Attitude toward the behavior	0.716	0.000	0.826
Subjective norm	0.762	0.000	0.870
Perceived behavioral control	0.696	0.000	0.763
Intention	0.584	0.000	0.915
Behavior	0.614	0.000	0.703

A second verification of the reliability of the measuring instruments was done by conducting a Confirmatory Factor Analysis using PLS2 software.

In order to test the research hypotheses, we have opted for structural equation modeling. We have chosen to use the Partial Last Square (PLS) approach which allows the analysis of complex models with a relatively limited sample size [26]. This method is applied in case of non-normality resulting from the heterogeneity of the observation groups [27].

The results obtained regarding the reliability and validity conditions of our model constructs are guaranteed. Indeed, the reliability coefficients obtained values are greater than the required thresholds (0.6).

The convergent validity of the model is supported by the fact that the values of the extracted mean variance (EVA) are higher than the recommended value of 0.5 [28]. In additional, the unidimensionality and reliability of all constructs were validated with high cronbach's alpha (Table 3).

The discriminant validity of each construct is verified by comparing the square roots of the AVE of the latent variables with the correlation of the other latent variables [28, 29].

Table 3. The convergent validity of constructs

Constructs	AVE	CR	Alpha Cronbach
Subjective norms	0.7356	0.9173	0.8807
Control	0.6905	0.8697	0.7775
Attitude	0.6976	0.9011	0.8555
Intention	0.8577	0.9475	0.9170
Behavior	0.6004	0.8177	0.6647

Table 4. The discriminant validity.

Constructs	Attitude	Use of e-health	Control	Intention	Subjective Norms
Attitude	**0.8352**				
Behavior	0.4834	**0.7748**			
Control	0.4408	0.3470	**0.8309**		
Intention	0.6741	0.6438	0.5418	**0.9261**	
Subjective norms	0.6571	0.4456	0.4198	0.8136	**0.8576**

As shown in Table 4 below, the discriminant validity of this study is ensured.

Thus, the results obtained regarding the conditions of reliability and validity of the constructs of the model are confirmed. In fact, the values of the reliability coefficients obtained are higher than the required thresholds (0.7), the convergent validity (assessed by the factorial contributions and the extracted mean variance) are satisfactory and the discriminant validity (assessed by the examination of the correlations between constructs and by the cross contributions) are acceptable. The results show that the model tested satisfies all the criteria required to proceed with the evaluation of the structural model.

The Table 5 shows that all R2s are greater than 0.1 and thus attest to the significance of the model. R2 values are 0.7292 for the intention to use the Internet and 0.4145 for the behavior. The analysis of Q2 for all constructs reveals positive values that lead to conclude on the predictive validity of our model.

Table 5. Quality of structural model

Constructs	Evaluation criteria		
	R2	Communality > 0.5: Good quality model fit	Cross-validation redundancy index (Q2) Q2 > 0: model predictive validity
Intention	0.7292	0.8577	0.1838
Behavior	0.4145	0.6004	0.2470

The GOF that we obtain is 0.64, which, based on the values reported by Fernandes [30], indicates a good general quality of the model.

The correlation relationships between constructs are estimated by verifying the standardized correlation coefficients (path coefficients) and Student's t-values obtained from the bootstrapping analyses. A correlation relationship is significant if the t-value is higher than the 1.96 threshold. The Table 6 presents the regression coefficients and Student's t-significance coefficients.

Table 6. The result of the hypothesis test

Causal relationship	Coefficients β	T of Student	Validation status of hypothesis
H1: Attitude → intention	0.1857	2.7329	Validated
H2: Subjective beliefs → intention	0.6052	8.2448	Validated
H3: Perceived control of behavior → intention	0.2059	2.8703	Validated
H4: Intention → Behavior	0.6438	9.0310	Validated

In the study, all research hypotheses are confirmed at the 5% threshold. The results show that subjective beliefs, attitude towards behavior and perceived control of behavior have a positive impact on the intention to use the Internet to prevent against covid19. In addition, the intention to use e-health to prevent covid19 has a positive impact on individuals' behavior, which in turn confirms the research hypotheses H1, H2, H3 and H4.

The results of the study showed that subjective attitudes and norms are powerful predictors of behavioral intention. The results are in agreement with previous studies based on the theory of interpersonal behavior [31]. Often, in the population, the adoption, maintaining, or abandonment of many behaviors are not only motivated by health reasons, but also reveal social and personal reasons.

Personal considerations determine the intention to use the Internet for health reasons. The subjective norm variable is found to be relevant and plays an important role on the intention to use e-health (beta = 0.6052; t = 8.2448). This suggests that consumers seek fulfillment in the sharing of common values.

According to Jeng and Tzeng [32]; Venkatesh et al. [33], the feeling of membership in the group may lead the individual to acting according to the group's norms in order to enhance his or her commitment to the group or just to become a member of the group. Thus, the social environment may indeed have an influence on the individual's behavior and on his intention to do or not a specific act.

Attitudes toward behavior are also a predictor of intention ($\beta = 0.187$; p $= 0.000$). These results show that positive attitudes developed during the use of e-health services are associated with the relationship between the patient and the health sites in issue. Congruence between service and site evaluation is highly envisageable. The positive perception formed on a health site can make the Internet user a regular consumer.

Using e-health generates a certain number of constraints that are challenging for everyone. Anticipating the ability to accept these constraints naturally has a significant influence on perceived control, and in turn affects the intention to use (beta = 0.207; p < 0.001).

5 Conclusion

With the increasing spread of Covid-19, the implications of these models for health promotion are important. The results give credence to the idea that health-related behaviors should be perceived from a social perspective rather than through the exclusive lens of their links to health issues. This presupposes the creation of reliable and secure medical sites, the enhancement of content quality, the presence and relevance of doctors, the promotion of exchange, and mutual support.

As we have seen that perceived control of behavior positively affects the intention to use e-health to prevent Covid19, we suggest that health professionals, governments, and reference groups should capitalize strongly on the benefits of the technological tools provided to citizens. It would be pertinent that the population be educated on the effectiveness and usefulness of the medical Internet in managing health and prevention.

These technologies must be considered as smoothing access to medical services and information necessary for prevention (such as barrier gestures, medications to avoid, etc.), facilitating and coordinating contact with health professionals [34].

In addition, we consider important to educate consumers about the use of technology in the health domain. In fact, a person who is well supported and supervised by a health care professional will have more important intentions of use towards health technology tools [35].

From a relational perspective, this research highlighted the importance of designing information and communication programs geared towards not only the prevention against the virus but also towards empowering citizens. The content of e-health must provide the appropriate information to the current situation. This is the case today of the collaboration initiated between WHO and Wikimedia aiming to facilitate and expand free access to reliable and truthful information on covid 19 (WHO, 2020)[2]. The objective, here, is to maintain direct and continuous contact with the individual as well as to predict and understand the subjective and contextual attitudinal factors of individual behavior.

References

1. Gabarron, E., et al.: Social media for health promotion in diabetes: study protocol for a participatory public health intervention design. BMC Health Serv. Res. **18**(1), 414 (2018). https://doi.org/10.1186/s12913-018-3178-7
2. Cases, A.S.: E-health: empowering the connected patient. J. Med. Manage. Econ. **35**, 137–158 (2017)

---

[2] World Health Organization (2020) the world health organization and Wikimedia foundation expand access to trusted information about covid 19 on Wikipedia. https://www.who.int/es/news/item/22-10-2020/22-10-2020.

3. Hage, E., Roo, J.P., Offenbeek, M., Boonstra, A.: Implementation factors and their effect on e-Health service adoption in rural communities: a systematic literature review. BMC Health Serv. Res. **13**, 19 (2013)

4. Ćwiklicki, M., Schiavoni, F., Klich, J., Plich, K.: Antecedents of use of e-health services in Central Eastern Europe: a qualitative comparative analysis. Health Serv. Res. (2020). https://doi.org/10.1186/s12913-020-5034-9

5. Li, J., Theng, Y., Foo, S.: Predictors of online health information seeking behavior: changes between 2002 and 2012. Health Inf. J. **22**(4), 804–814 (2015)

6. Ajzen, I.: Perceived behavioral control, self-efficacy, locus of control, and the theory of planned behavior. J. Appl. Soc. Psychol. **32**(4), 665–683 (2002). https://doi.org/10.1111/j.1559-1816.2002.tb00236.x

7. Ajzen, I.: The theory of planned behavior: reactions and reflections. Psychol. Health **26**(9), 1113–1127 (2011). https://doi.org/10.1080/08870446.2011.613995

8. Cousson-Gélie, F., Irachabal, S., Bruchon-Schweitzer, M., Dilhuydy, J.M., Lakdja, F.: Dimensions of cancer locus of control scale as predictors of psychological adjustment and survival in breast cancer patients. Psychol. Rep. **97**(3), 699–711 (2005). https://doi.org/10.2466/pr0.97.3.699-711

9. Armitage, C.J., Conner, M.: Social cognition models and health behaviour: a structured review. Psychol. Health **15**(2), 173–189 (2000). https://doi.org/10.1080/08870440008400299

10. Ajzen, I.: From intentions to actions: a theory of planned behavior. In: Kuhl, J., Beckmann, J. (eds.) Action Control. SSSSP, pp. 11–39. Springer, Heidelberg (1985). https://doi.org/10.1007/978-3-642-69746-3_2

11. Conner, M., Armitage, C.J.: Extending the theory of planned behavior: a review and avenues for further research. J. Appl. Soc. Psychol. **28**(15), 1429–1464 (1998). https://doi.org/10.1111/j.1559-1816.1998.tb01685.x

12. Hale, J., Brian, H., Green, H.K.: The theory of reasoned action. In: The Persuasion Handbook: Developments in Theory and Practice (2002). https://doi.org/10.4135/9781412976046.n14

13. Godin, G., Maticka-Tyndale, E., Adrien, A., Manson-Singer, S., Willms, D., Cappon, P.: Cross-cultural testing of three social cognitive theories: an application to condom use. J. Appl. Soc. Psychol. **26**, 1556–1586 (1996)

14. Godin, G., Vezina, L., Leclerc, O.: Factors influencing intentions of pregnant women to exercise after giving birth. Public Health Rep. **104**, 188–195 (1989)

15. Powell, W.W., Douglas, R.W., Kenneth, W.K., Owen-Smith, J.: Network dynamics and field evolution: the growth of interorganizational collaboration in the life sciences. Am. J. Sociol. **110**(4), 1132–1205 (2005). https://doi.org/10.1086/421508

16. Urberg, K.A., Degirmencioglu, S.M., Pilgrim, C.: Close friend and group influence on adolescent cigarette smoking and alcohol use. Dev. Psychol. **33**(5), 834–844 (1997). https://doi.org/10.1037/0012-1649.33.5.834

17. Schepers, J., Wetzels, M.: A meta-analysis of the technology acceptance model: investigating subjective norm and moderation effects. Inf. Manage. **44**, 90–103 (2007). https://doi.org/10.1016/j.im.2006.10.007

18. Mc Cormack Brown, K.: Theory of Reasoned Action/Theory of Planned Behavior (1999). http://hsc.usf.edu/~kmbrown/TRA_TPB.htm

19. Ajzen, I.: The theory of planned behaviour. Organ. Behav. Hum. Decis. Process. **50**(2), 179–211 (1991)

20. Taylor, S., Todd, A.P.: Understanding information technology usage: a test of competing models. Inf. Syst. Res. **6**(2), 144–176 (1995)

21. Godin, I., Garcia-Porrero, J.A., Dieterlen-Lievre, F., Cumano, A.: Stem cell emergence and hemopoietic activity are incompatible in mouse intraembryonic sites. J. Exp. Med. **190**(1), 43–52 (1999). https://doi.org/10.1084/jem.190.1.43

22. Ajzen, I., Fishbein, M.: Understanding Attitudes and Predicting Social Behavior. Prentice-Hall, Englewood Cliffs, NJ (1980)
23. Triandis, H.C.: Values, attitudes and interpersonal behavior. In: Page, M.M. (ed.) Nebraska Symposium on Motivation, 1979: Beliefs, Attitudes and Values. University of Nebraska Press, Lincoln (1980)
24. Fishbein, M., Ajzen, I.: Belief, Attitude, Intention and Behavior: An Introduction to Theory and Research. Addison-Wesley, Reading, MA (1975)
25. Lemire, M., Sicotte, C., Paré, G.: Internet use and the logics of personal empowerment in health. Health Policy 88(1), 130–140 (2008). https://doi.org/10.1016/j.healthpol.2008.03.006
26. Cassel, C.M., Hackl, P., Westlund, A.H.: On measurement of intangible assets: a study of robustness of partial least squares. Total Qual. Manage. 11(7) (2000). https://doi.org/10.1080/09544120050135443
27. Streukens, S., Wetzels, M., Daryanto, A., de Ruyter, K.: Analyzing factorial data using PLS: application in an online complaining context. In: Vinzi, V.E., Chin, W.W., Henseler, J., Wang, H. (eds.) Handbook of Partial Least Squares, pp. 567–587. Springer, Heidelberg (2010). https://doi.org/10.1007/978-3-540-32827-8_25
28. Fornell, C., Larcker, D.F.: Evaluating structural equation models with unobservable variables and measurement error. J. Mark. Res. 18(3), 39–50 (1981)
29. Wetzels, M., Odekerken-Schröder, G., Van Oppen, C.: Using pls path modeling for assessing hierarchical construct models: guidelines and empirical illustration. MIS Q. 33(1), 177–195 (2009)
30. Fernandes, V.: En quoi l'approche PLS est-elle une méthode a (re)-découvrir pour les chercheurs en management? M@n@gement 15(1), 102–123 (2012). https://doi.org/10.3917/mana.151.0102
31. Bergeron, F., Raymond, L., Rivard, S., Gara, M.F.: Determinants of EIS use: testing a behavioral model. Psychol. Comput. Sci. 14(2), 131–146 (1995)
32. Jeng, D.J-F., Tzeng, G.H.: Social influence on the use of clinical decision support systems: revisiting the unified theory of acceptance and use of technology by the fuzzy DEMATEL technique. Comput. Ind. Eng. 62(3), 819–828 (2012). https://doi.org/10.1016/j.cie.2011.12.016
33. Venkatesh, V., Morris, M.G., Davis, G.B., Davis, F.D.: User acceptance of information technology: toward a unified view. MIS Q. 27(3), 425–478 (2003). https://doi.org/10.2307/30036540
34. Salmon, F.D., Le Tallec, L.: La e-santé : de nouveaux usages pour les technologies individuelles en santé publique. Annales des Mines - Réalités industrielles 2014(4), 70 (2014). https://doi.org/10.3917/rindu.144.0070
35. Kailas, A., Chong, C.-C., Watanabe, F.: From mobile phones to personal wellness dashboards. IEEE Pulse 1(1), 57–63 (2010). https://doi.org/10.1109/MPUL.2010.937244
36. Fishbein, M., Ajzen, I.: Predicting and changing behavior: The reasoned action approach. Psychology Press (2010)

HCI in Surgery

Construction of a Knowledge Base for Empirical Knowledge in Neurosurgery

Ayuki Joto[1]([✉]), Takahiro Fuchi[1], Hiroshi Noborio[1], Katsuhiko Onishi[1], Masahiro Nonaka[2], and Tsuneo Jozen[1]

[1] Osaka Electro-Communication University, 1130-70 Kiyotaki, Shijonawate, Osaka 5750063, Japan
{mw19a003,mw20a008,nobori,onishi,jozen}@oecu.jp
[2] Department of Neurosurgery, National Hospital Organization Osaka National Hospital, Osaka, Japan

Abstract. Neurosurgeons accumulate a variety of empirical knowledge through surgeries. Post-operative reports, incident reports, and accident reports are effective means of recording and sharing empirical knowledge, but they are costly to analyze them, and new methods of sharing knowledge are needed. In addition, the interface using CG technology, which is used in surgical planning, is actively used as a means for doctors to easily obtain information, but it is not widely used for knowledge sharing. In this research, we aim to build a knowledge base to convey and utilize physicians' know-how, which is difficult to convey, by accurately expressing empirical knowledge using CG technology. One of the challenges in sharing empirical knowledge is the difficulty of handling medical information from the viewpoint of personal information protection. Medical information is data that can easily identify individuals and that has a very high importance of rare data. Therefore, we examined the environment for using medical information and appropriate anonymization. First, we proposed a method for constructing an ontology for neurosurgery based on the medical ontology that has been studied in the medical field by organizing the structure of empirical knowledge of doctors. In addition, we designed and fabricated a prototype interface using 3D models as a system for data input and search display. We selected the glTF format as the 3D model format to be used in this study. In this paper, we report on the construction of a knowledge base for sharing empirical knowledge of neurosurgery, and the evaluation of the ontology constructed by the proposed method.

Keywords: Neurosurgery · Ontology · glTF

1 Introduction

Neurosurgeons accumulate a wide range of empirical knowledge through surgeries. Post-operative reports and incident reports are effective means of recording and sharing the empirical knowledge of doctors. However, obtaining accurate

© Springer Nature Switzerland AG 2021
M. Kurosu (Ed.): HCII 2021, LNCS 12763, pp. 521–537, 2021.
https://doi.org/10.1007/978-3-030-78465-2_38

empirical knowledge from these reports is costly, and new methods of knowledge sharing are required.

On the other hand, StealthStation [1], an intraoperative navigation system used in surgical planning, integrates images from CT, MRI, CTA, MRA, fMRI, PET and SPECT, and provides an interface where detailed data and subtle representations can be represented by 3D models. The 3D model-based interface is easily informative if reviewed by a physician with specialized knowledge. However, the purpose of this system is to confirm the sensed data, not to share empirical knowledge during actual surgeries.

The 3D representation of medical information allows for the accurate representation of complex structures, which can be easily obtained by a physician with expert knowledge, but this technology is not widely used for sharing empirical knowledge. If we can combine these technologies to make empirical knowledge easier to understand and share, we can effectively improve the skills and knowledge of doctors. This research uses 3DCG models to accurately represent the details of the brain and blood vessels, which are important in expressing the empirical knowledge of neurosurgeons, and to build a knowledge base for communicating and using the knowledge of doctors that is difficult to convey.

One of the challenges in sharing this empirical knowledge is the difficulty of handling medical information from the perspective of personal data protection. Medical information is easily identifiable due to the nature of the data. Therefore, in order to share the information, it is necessary to limit the scope of data publication and to anonymize the data according to the scope of each data publication.

Minimising the scope of information sharing is a good first step, for example by considering the scope of data disclosure to include the doctor in charge, within their own departments, within their own hospitals, across hospitals in the same field of medicine, and to all healthcare professionals. At this stage, the medical data to be used are assumed to be electronic medical records, incident reports, accident reports, MRI images, CT images, and the empirical knowledge of physicians, and in this report we assume that the data will be used mainly by the doctor in charge.

In order to share empirical knowledge in neurosurgery, it is necessary to accurately represent the positional relationships of the brain and brain blood vessels, which are composed of complex structures. In this research, we assume that the 3D model is used, and the system is constructed by the Web application which has low implementation cost. For the 3D model format, we chose the JSON-based glTF format [2], which is suitable for use in web applications and has excellent scalability. The 3D model is based on the BodyParts3D [3] model, and where a particularly precise representation is required, a model based on DICOM data is used.

In this report, we describe the construction of a knowledge base for accumulating and utilizing the empirical knowledge of doctors in neurosurgery (called as BrainCGpedia). In order to construct BrainCGpedia, we first organized the structure of the empirical knowledge of doctors and proposed a method of constructing an ontology for neurosurgery with reference to medical ontology [4]. In addition, we designed and fabricated an interface using a 3D model as a system for data input and search display of empirical knowledge. Also, the proposed ontology construction method was used to represent actual case reports of doctors, and it was evaluated whether the reports of doctors could be represented.

2   Research Background

2.1   Information Sharing Methods for Neurosurgeons

Incident reports are effective in preventing medical accidents, but they are not fully utilized because doctors and nurses are very busy and do not have enough time to analyze them. As a result, the valuable empirical knowledge of physicians in incident reports may not be accurately obtained and may be overlooked. In addition, these reports are being digitized and various methods of analysis, such as text mining, are being tested. For the sharing of empirical knowledge among physicians, efforts are being made to use these reports and to develop new methods. This shows that while the effectiveness of existing reports is acknowledged, there is a need for new methods of sharing empirical knowledge of doctors due to the cost of analysis.

2.2   Neurosurgery Support System

At Kansai Medical University, where we are collaborating in this research, the StealthStation (Fig. 1) is used for surgical planning.

The StealthStation is an intraoperative navigation system marketed by Medtronic, which integrates CT, MRI, CTA, MRI, fMRI, PET, and SPECT images to provide detailed data and subtle representations in a 3D model.

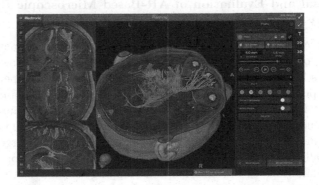

Fig. 1. StealthStation [5]

StealthStation is an interface that allows non-expert users to understand the location of the tumor using 3D models. However, the purpose of this system is to confirm the sensed data, not to share empirical knowledge during actual surgeries. Therefore, in order to include detailed shared information in surgical planning and postoperative follow-up, it is necessary to output the data to electronic medical records and to collaborate with them. In the human brain, it is difficult to distinguish visually whether a tumor should be removed or an important nerve that should not be damaged, and even doctors with specialist knowledge have difficulty performing surgery without careful advance surgical planning, simulations, and various instruments to support surgery. In recent years, using CG and VR technology, it has become possible to perform surgery after obtaining MRI data of the brain in advance and understanding the location of the tumor using CG and VR, as in the case of the aforementioned Stealth-Station.

However, there are still numerous research projects on the intraoperative determination of tumours due to problems such as dealing with brain shift [6]. In such a surgical environment, the empirical knowledge of the physician is important to help make objective intraoperative decisions. Thus, CG and VR technologies can be used to represent medical information to build very easy-to-understand interfaces that can be understood even by those who do not have specialized knowledge, but they are not widely used for the empirical knowledge of doctors. In addition, existing methods of sharing empirical knowledge of doctors are effective but too costly to analyze, so a new method of sharing is required. Therefore, this study aims to construct a knowledge base to convey and utilize the knowledge of doctors that is difficult to be conveyed by using CG technology to accurately represent empirical knowledge.

3   Related Research

3.1   Proposal and Evaluation of AR-Based Microscopic Brain Surgery Support System

In their research, Koeda et al. proposed an AR surgery support system using simultaneous localization and mapping (SLAM) by superimposing a 3D computer graphics brain model image on the intraoperative microscope image.

In the proposed system, a 3DCG model in STL (stand-ard triangulated language) format is created from DICOM data obtained from CT and MRI of a real patient, and the 3D model is superimposed on the microscope image in real time to confirm the position of blood vessels and tumors during surgery. In order to automatically update the 3D model according to the microscope image, we use SLAM (Simultaneous Localization and Mapping) to analyze the image and obtain the movement of the camera.

Together with these mechanisms, we are conducting this research in order to make it part of a system that supports medical practice.

In this paper, we use some of the 3D models based on the DICOM data created and used by the research team for the vascular parts of the brain, which need to be represented in more detail than the 3D models distributed in Body-Parts3D.

4   BrainCGpedia's Proposal

In this research, we investigate a system that enables doctors who have accumulated a lot of empirical knowledge to use it like their own memos, and to construct linked data that links the input empirical knowledge together, so that other medical professionals can search the data efficiently. In this chapter, we propose the assumption of the user and the use scene of BrainCGpedis, the confidentiality of the data used, the linkage with 3DCG model data for medical use, the empirical knowledge sharing method, the study of the interface for registration and retrieval, and the construction method of the ontology which constructs the linked data for efficient retrieval.

4.1   Assumptions About Users and Usage Scenarios

The users of BrainCGpedia are expected to be skilled neurosurgeons who share their empirical knowledge and other medical professionals who search and browse the shared empirical knowledge. We envisage that the users of the system will be skilled neurosurgeons who share their empirical knowledge and other healthcare professionals who search and browse the shared empirical knowledge.

When recording and sharing their own empirical knowledge, neurosurgeons are expected to use the system to record their intraoperative experiences as notes and to share them with other medical professionals.

For intraoperative use, the system is intended to be used when new metastases are discovered, or when other complications arise, such as ruptured blood vessels.

In the postoperative period, the system is intended to be used for investigating past postoperative complications and sequelae.

4.2   Data Confidentiality

BrainCGpedia deals with medical information as a supplement to the empirical knowledge of doctors. We also aim to make this data available to the public, not for personal use, but for eventual use by the general public. For this reason, the data to be used will be made anonymous. Therefore, it is necessary to anonymize each of the data to be used. At the present stage, we assume that the medical data to be used are electronic medical records, incident reports, accident reports, MRI images, CT images, and empirical knowledge of doctors.

In addition to the anonymisation of the data, there are other ways of maintaining the confidentiality of the data by limiting the scope of use. In our research, we divide the publication phase of the data as shown in the following Fig. 2.

Fig. 2. Scopes of disclosure

The minimum range is the doctor in charge, followed by in a medical office, in a hospital, and the maximum range is all medical professionals. The wider the range of disclosure, the more the data needs to be restricted, for example, by processing the information of the injured person, or by not disclosing the information of past medical history and chronic diseases. In this paper, we set the scope of data disclosure to [the doctors in charge]. We do not need to anonymize the data if it is intended to be used only by the doctor in charge. If the data is to be used only by the doctor in charge, anonymization is not necessary. Also, if the data is to be used within the same medical department or hospital, simple anonymization is not necessary for the same reason, because it is assumed that the data will be shared in situations such as surgery. In addition, we can consider a policy of open handling of data such as cases in articles, provided that the appropriate medical data usage permission flow is followed and personal information is encrypted. In addition, the accumulation of a history of data browsing can be expected to deter users from unauthorized use. In such a situation, the system can be considered for use by medical offices in other hospitals in the same medical field, and by medical professionals in general.

4.3   Setting up the Base 3D Brain Model

In order to share empirical knowledge in neurosurgery, we need an accurate representation of the complex structure of the brain and the location of the brain's blood vessels. Brain structures are generally classified in a hierarchical manner. Therefore, in this study, we define and use the hierarchical structure of the brain as well. In addition, there are various representations of the vascular structure of the brain, but in this paper, we refer to the predefined structure as the basic data.

The model format to be used in this study should be able to manage the model for each part by connecting it with the defined structure, be easy to handle on the Web, and be scalable for connecting the model with empirical knowledge. Therefore, the glTF format is chosen as the target format in this research.

BrainCGpedia uses the 3D model from BodyParts3D [3] as the base 3D model. Since the models distributed by BodyParts3D are in OBJ format, we convert them to glTF format and use them. For the models of blood vessels in the brain, which require particularly accurate representation, we use 3D models based on DICOM data created by Koeda et al. in the same research team using [6].

Since the models of BodyParts3D are created separately for each part of the body, it is necessary to consider an interface that can be decomposed and selected in the interface as well, assuming that it can be manipulated by decomposing each part of the hospital bed as shown in Fig. 3.

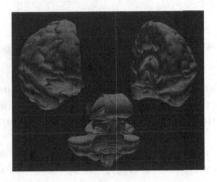

Fig. 3. Decomposed brain model

In the research of Koeda et al. neurosurgeons actually provided us with DICOM data of patients' examination results and microscopic data during neurosurgical operations, and based on these data, we have created highly accurate vascular models of the brain as shown in Fig. 4. In this report, these models are converted to glTF format as well and used.

4.4   Linked Data Structures for Efficient Searching

In this study, we use the glTF format as a model format to represent the hierarchical structure of the brain in the model file itself. By preparing models for each part of the brain, we can link shared empirical knowledge to each part of the brain, and the models themselves can have a semantic structure.

In addition, by creating ontologies from neurosurgical procedures and linking them together, we are able to link empirical knowledge and site-specific data in a complex way as linked data. The ontology that supports the structure of such specific linked data is described in the next chapter.

4.5   Ontology Construction Methods for Linked Data

In this research, it is necessary to construct an ontology for neurosurgery, not only to link models and empirical knowledge, but also to link empirical knowledge to each other and to create linked data. The construction of the ontology is

Fig. 4. Major vascular part of the brain model

carried out in two phases: an initial phase and a continuous phase. In the initial phase, the basic part of the ontology is created based on the medical ontology that has been studied in the medical field, and the ontology is constructed based on interviews with medical professionals, mainly active neurosurgeons, and surveys of books. In the continuation phase, we analyze the input empirical knowledge based on the created ontology, and optimize the ontology accordingly.

Figure 5 defines the minimum elements required for the construction of an ontology. The node representing the site of injury or disease includes parts of the human body indicated by anatomical terms, blood vessels, gray matter, etc. The disease node is represented by a general name, such as "cerebral infarction". A symptom node indicates the symptoms of the injured person. A technique node indicates the name of the surgical procedure. A severity node expresses the severity or progression of the disease in relation to a disease node. A result node indicates "death", "complete recovery", etc.

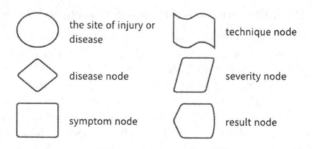

Fig. 5. Nodes in the ontology

Figure 6 show type of arrows that defines the elements that are considered necessary to represent the connection relationship between each node in Fig. 5 with reference to the medical ontology.

An arrow representing a structural child relationship represents a *part-of* relationship. The arrows extend from the parent node in the direction of the child node. An arrow representing a causal relation expresses a relation of axioms. The arrows extend in the direction of the node of the result arising from the node of the cause. The arrow representing the subordinate conceptual relationships expresses the *is-a* relation. The arrows extend from the higher concept to the lower concept. An arrow representing the passage of time represents the passage of time. The arrows extend from the past to the future. An arrow representing an attribute relationship represents an *attribute-of* relationship. Arrows representing arbitrary relationships are assumed to be set by the user. As an example of the representation, we can connect a disease node and a symptom node, and consider the aftereffects and complications. In the medical ontology, the passage of time is represented by information such as labels, In this research, however, because we are dealing with the empirical knowledge of doctors, the information about the time leading to recurrence and cure is very important.

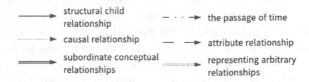

Fig. 6. Arrows showing the relationship between nodes

Each node is associated with a label representing the attribute, cause, site, chronic disease, symptom, type and frequency. The attribute label gives information about the injured person. The cause label indicates the specific cause. The part label is a label used to link the parts of the body. The pre-existing disease label indicates the pre-existing disease that the injured person has. Symptom labels are used to describe specific symptoms. The type label indicates the type of disease or symptom. Frequency label. The frequency label expresses the frequency with which the symptom occurs. The attribute label, the chronic disease label and the type label defined in this study are not used in the ontology. However, we use these information as labels in this research because they are important for expressing the empirical knowledge of doctors and for using them in the system as linked data.

These nodes, arrows and labels could be used to describe the onset of the disease, what symptoms occurred, what treatment was given and what the outcome was.

4.6   Interface for Registration and Reference

The registration interface for neurosurgeons to enter their empirical knowledge needs to allow them to enter data by linking their knowledge to the location of accurately represented blood vessels in the brain. Therefore, we need an interface that allows the user to enter empirical knowledge by specifying an accurately represented blood vessel in the brain. CT and MRI images should also be attached to the data input as additional information.

In order to search the shared empirical knowledge of neurosurgeons, we envisioned two search interfaces: one for the name of the disease or affected area, and the other for the area to be operated on. Therefore, it is necessary to prepare two interfaces: one is a keyword search, and the other is a search by specifying the target area from a 3D brain model. In addition, the system displays related links from the search results at the same time, so that the user can obtain knowledge efficiently in a limited time.

A neurosurgeon may encounter an unexpected event during an operation. If the surgeon can find the solution to the unexpected event in the operating room, it is possible to solve the problem. Therefore, in this research, we consider an interface that can be used from the operating room. In the case of using the interface from the operating room, it is assumed to be used in an emergency, and it is difficult to operate a keyboard and a mouse by taking off surgical gloves. Therefore, it is necessary to have an interface that can be operated without contact, such as motion capture. In the operating room, the motion controller should be smaller due to the high concentration of equipment and people [7]. Therefore, in this study, we investigated an interface using the Leap Motion Controller, which is small, inexpensive, and available for purchase.

5   Building BrainCGpedia

5.1   Registration Process for Making Empirical Knowledge Base

Figure 7 shows an overview of the BrainCGpediasystem. The flow of the system is as follows: First, an experienced neurosurgeon inputs empirical knowledge data into BrainCGpedia. In order to accurately link the empirical knowledge data to the parts of the brain model, a 3D brain model is used to specify the parts of the brain for inputting the empirical knowledge data. This empirical knowledge data can be freely retrieved and viewed by other healthcare professionals. The BrainCGpediawill consist of a web-based system with relatively low implementation cost. The 3D part of the input interface extends the annotation function of the Surface Viewer of the BrainBrowser, so that the server side holds the coordinate information on the model, the structural information of the model and the empirical knowledge data (textual knowledge, images, tags related to the disease and attribute information of the injured person). The 3D model used is a glTF transformation of each brain model obtained from BodyParts3D using obj2gltf [8]. Each part of this model is associated with an ID to be handled by the system. The granularity of this ID is based on the anatomical classification as in BodyParts3D.

The user can specify the name of the disease, the name of the procedure, the relevant label, and the empirical knowledge for the specified region.

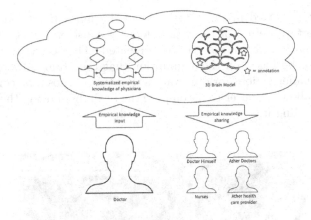

Fig. 7. Overview of the system

Fig. 8. An example of input form for empirical knowledge with 3D model interface

5.2 Empirical Knowledge Search and Browsing Interface Construction

We prepared two types of empirical knowledge search interfaces: a keyword search interface and a search interface by injury site. The search interface from the site of injury or disease uses a 3D model such as Fig. 9, and when an arbitrary part or blood vessel is selected, only the parts of the lower level are displayed. The user then selects the part of the body that he or she wants to know about and is presented with a list of cases associated with the relevant part of the body.

Figure 9 shows an example of the interface used in an operating room during surgery. When using the interface from the operating room, the aforementioned search interface operation using the 3D model is replaced with an arbitrary operation detected by the Leap Motion Controller. The model is manipulated by making a pinching hand shape with the index finger and the thumb, and the model is rotated when it is moved in the x- and y-axes, and the model is scaled when it is moved in the z-axes. When the index finger touches the 3D model for a certain period of time, the model is considered to be selected and detailed information about the part is presented. The selection of the model category should be based on the assumption that the brain is decomposed and divided into smaller regions for observation. For this purpose, we constructed an interface that allows the user to decompose the brain by moving the hand in the z-axis while holding it.

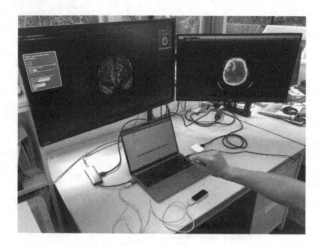

Fig. 9. Searching the knowledge base in a non-contact method

5.3   Ontology for the Construction of Linked Data of Empirical Knowledge to Support Neurosurgery

As indicated in Sect. 4.5, the construction of the ontology is divided into two phases: an initial phase and an ongoing phase. Figure 10 and Fig. 11 are part of the structure of the ontology created. Figure 12 shows the structure of the proposed ontology in RDBMS. The technique table represents the technique nodes; the ID column is the primary key of the technique table and the name column represents the name of the technique. The patients table is a table representing attribute labels: the ID column is the primary key of the patients table, the age column represents the age information of the injured person, the gender column represents the gender information of the injured person, and the chronic_condition column represents the chronic disease information of the injured person.

The ID column represents the primary key of the symptoms table, the name column represents the content of the symptom, the reason column represents the information of the cause label, the frequency column represents the information of the frequency label, and the type column represents the information of the type label.

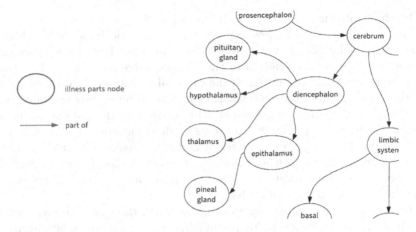

Fig. 10. Initial phase: part of a basic ontology focusing on the hierarchical structure of brain regions

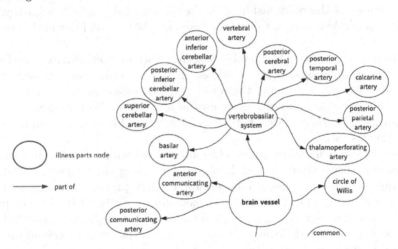

Fig. 11. Initial phase: part of a basic ontology focusing on the hierarchical structure of cerebral blood vessels

The parts table is a table representing the nodes of the injured or diseased part: the ID column is the primary key of the parts table, the name column is the name of the injured or diseased part, the model_id is the ID of each specific model part set in the gltf format, and the parent_part_id is the ID of the part. The part_id is assumed to be the id information of the record of the part which is the parent to express the *part-of* information.

The diseases table is a table representing disease nodes, where the ID column is the primary key of the diseases table and the name column contains the name of the disease.

The cases table is a table of case information. A case expresses an *is-a* relationship to a disease, and cases expresses more specific information than the diseases table. The ID column represents the primary key of the cases table, diseases_id represents the relation to the diseases table as a foreign key, reason column represents the information of the cause label, elapsed_time column represents the information of the time lapse, type column represents the information of the type label, patient_id represents the relation to the patients table as a foreign key, and severity column represents the information of the severity node.

The results table represents the result nodes: the name column contains specific result information such as complete recovery or death, the elapsed_time column contains information about the time lapse, and the case_id column is a foreign key related to the cases table.

There is a many-to-many relationship between the site of injury and disease information. In order to represent this many-to-many relationship, the part_disease table is prepared as an intermediate table. The part_id column expresses the relationship with the parts table as a foreign key, and the disease_id column expresses the relationship with the diseases table as a foreign key. The relationship between the part of the disease and the disease information records is traced via this table.

Similarly, the case_technique table is prepared as an intermediate table for the many-to-many relationship between case information and surgical techniques. The case_id column represents the relation to the cases table as a foreign key, and the technique_id column represents the relation to the techniques table as a foreign key. The relationship between case information and surgical records is traced via this table.

There is also a many-to-many relationship between symptoms and surgical procedures or disease information. In order to represent the relationship between symptoms and the two types of information, we have prepared a symptom table. The column "symptom_id" is a foreign key which is related to the Symptoms table, the column "symptom_type" is the information of the table to which the foreign key refers, and the column "symptom_id" is the primary key information of the table in the "symptom_type" column.

By using this structure, the relationship between the nodes expressed in the ontology is retained and can be used in the system.

The proposed ontology structure is embedded in the system to build the linked data.

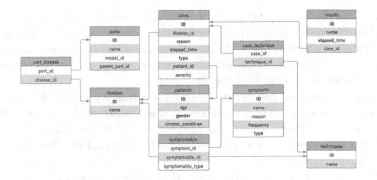

Fig. 12. Database structure of the ontology

6   Evaluation and Future Work

6.1   Construction of an Ontology on Pituitary Tumors

In the study report by Nakano et al. [9], a report of surgery for pituitary tumors is summarized. This report describes a 32p insertion procedure in an inpatient with two previous pituitary tumors that had been treated by craniotomy (transfrontal).

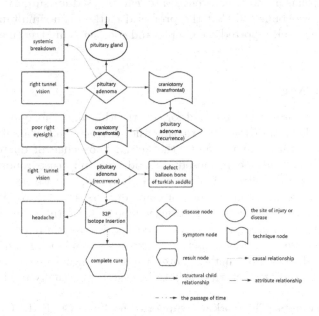

Fig. 13. Example of a pituitary tumor ontology

Figure 13 summarizes the report by Nakamura et al. into an ontology using our proposed method. First, we connected the brain injury site node and the disease node of the initial pituitary tumor with arrows to represent the attribute relationship. We also connected the reported symptoms caused by the pituitary tumor with arrows representing the causal relationship. Next, we connected the transfrontal surgery node to the pituitary tumor node with arrows representing causal relationships to represent the first surgery.

A node representing the recurrence of the pituitary tumor was connected to the node representing the procedure of this transfrontal surgery. The node of the recurrent pituitary tumor was also connected to the node of the second craniotomy (Transfrontal) by a causal arrow. The recurrent pituitary tumor node was also connected to the second surgery node, and the symptoms caused by the recurrent pituitary tumor were represented by similar arrows.

Finally, the 32P insertion technique node was connected to the recurrent pituitary tumour node with an arrow representing causality, and the complete cure node was connected to the recurrence node with an arrow representing the passage of time, as there was no recurrence for 10 years.

By creating such a structure, it is possible to obtain knowledge of related symptoms when searching for empirical knowledge of pituitary tumors. For example, we found that recurrent pituitary tumors were associated with headache, right visual field deprivation, and decreased right visual acuity. In addition, Nakamura et al. reported that recurrence of pituitary tumors is more frequent with the Tansfrontal method, and at the same time, the 32P insertion method, which has a lower recurrence rate, can be used for surgery.

Therefore, we confirmed that the proposed method can simultaneously represent symptoms and reported recurrence and complete cure treatments in pituitary tumors.

6.2　Future Work

In this paper, we proposed a method for constructing an ontology by considering the use of medical data for constructing the system, and evaluated whether the proposed method can represent the actual knowledge of doctors. In this evaluation, we applied the proposed method to public case reports, but the number of cases we verified this time was only a few, and we need to verify it by applying the empirical knowledge of many doctors. In addition, it is possible that more labels and node representations will be required than the current form. Specifically, the severity expressed as a node in this case is a node that depends on the disease node, so it may be better to express it as a label. In addition, since we were only able to construct the interface at the initial image level, we will need to further study the interface when the system is actually used by doctors.

Acknowledgements. This work was supported by JSPS KAKENHI Grant Number JP20K12086.

References

1. Gonçalves, J.M., et al.: Neuronavigation software to visualize and surgically approach brain structures. In: Proceedings of the Sixth International Conference on Technological Ecosystems for Enhancing Multiculturality (2018)
2. Khronos Group: gLTF Specification and Homepage. https://www.khronos.org/gltf/
3. Mitsuhashi, N., et al.: BodyParts3D: 3D structure database for anatomical concepts. Nucleic Acids Res. **37**(suppl_1), D782–D785 (2009)
4. Scheuermann, R.H., Ceusters, W., Smith, B.: Toward an ontological treatment of disease and diagnosis. Summit Transl. Bioinform. **2009**, 116 (2009)
5. StealthStation. https://www.medtronic.com/jpja/healthcareprofessionals/products/neurological/surgicalnavigationsystems/stealthstation/cranialneurosurgerynavigation.html
6. Koeda, M., Nishimoto, S., Noborio, H., Watanabe, K.: Proposal and evaluation of AR-based microscopic brain surgery support system. In: Kurosu, M. (ed.) HCII 2019. LNCS, vol. 11567, pp. 458–468. Springer, Cham (2019). https://doi.org/10.1007/978-3-030-22643-5_36
7. Afkari, H., et al.: The potentials for hands-free interaction in micro-neurosurgery. In: Proceedings of the 8th Nordic Conference on Human-Computer Interaction: Fun, Fast, Foundational (2014)
8. CesiumGS/obj2gltf: https://github.com/CesiumGS/obj2gltf
9. Nakano, T.: Therapy of the insert32P into the pituitary tumor. J. Jpn. Soc. Head Neck Surg. **4**(2), 123–127 (1994)

VR-Based Surgery Navigation System with 3D User Interface for Robot-Assisted Laparoscopic Partial Nephrectomy

Masanao Koeda[1(✉)], Akihiro Hamada[2], Atsuro Sawada[2], Katsuhiko Onishi[3],
Hiroshi Noborio[3], and Osamu Ogawa[2]

[1] Department of Human Information Engineering, Faculty of Computer Science and Systems Engineering, Okayama Prefectural University, 111 Kuboki, Soja-shi, Okayama 719-1197, Japan
koeda@ss.oka-pu.ac.jp
[2] Department of Urology, Graduate School of Medicine, Kyoto University, Yoshida-Konoe-cho, Sakyo-ku, Kyoto 606-8501, Japan
[3] Department of Computer Science, Osaka Electro-Communication University, Kiyotaki 1130-70 Shijonawate-shi, Osaka 575-0063, Japan

Abstract. We have been developing a surgical support system for Robot-Assisted Laparoscopic Partial Nephrectomy (RAPN) using augmented reality (AR) technology since April 2014. In our system, three-dimensional computer graphics (3DCG) models including kidneys, arteries, veins, tumors, and urinary tracts are generated from tomographic images (DICOM) preoperatively. The 3DCG models are superimposed on the endoscopic images and projected onto the operator's console and the operating room monitor. The position and orientation of the 3DCG models are automatically controlled in real-time according to the movement of the endoscope camera image, and the display position and transparency of the 3DCG models can be changed manually by the assistant if necessary. Now, we are developing a VR system that can manually control the 3DCG intuitively. In this paper, we describe the details of this system.

Keywords: Surgery navigation · VR · Head mounted display · User interface

1 Introduction

Partial nephrectomy is recommended because of the preservation of postoperative renal function. Robotic-assisted laparoscopic partial nephrectomy (RAPN) is a procedure that allows for the removal of cancer and keeps renal function. In the partial nephrectomy, the achievement of Trifecta (negative surgical margins, short renal warm ischemia time less than 25 min, and perioperative progress without complication) is required. The surgeon needs to distinguish the boundary between the tumor and normal tissue and quickly determine the area to be partially resected. The position of tumor is measured with the ultrasonography probe. However, it is insufficient when the tumor is totally endophytic or relatively isoechoic. There is a problem of misunderstanding the location and size of the tumor and the long determination time of the resection area. Appropriate guidance

© Springer Nature Switzerland AG 2021
M. Kurosu (Ed.): HCII 2021, LNCS 12763, pp. 538–550, 2021.
https://doi.org/10.1007/978-3-030-78465-2_39

on endoscopic images can assist in tumor discrimination and contribute to safe and rapid surgery.

We have been developing a surgical support system for RAPN using augmented reality (AR) technology since April 2014. In our system, three-dimensional computer graphics (3DCG) models including kidneys, arteries, veins, tumors, and urinary tracts are generated from tomographic images (DICOM) acquired from CT and/or MRI using the commercial software (SYNAPSE VINCENT, FUJIFILM Holdings Corporation, Tokyo, Japan) preoperatively. The 3DCG models are superimposed on the endoscopic images and projected onto the operator's console and the operating room monitor. The position and orientation of the 3DCG models are automatically controlled in real-time according to the movement of the endoscope camera image. The display position and transparency of the 3DCG models can be also controlled manually using a mouse or rotary controllers by the assistant if necessary. We have operated about 40 RAPNs with our navigation system.

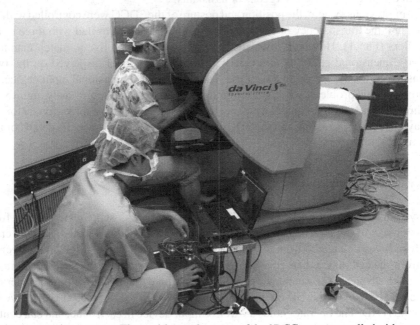

Fig. 1. Our previous system. The position and posture of the 3DCG were controlled with a mouse, and the transparency of each part of the 3DCG was controlled with three rotary controllers.

In the initial system, the position and posture of the 3DCG model were calculated by the optical flow of the endoscopic camera images [1, 2]. Since April 2018, we have introduced the feature point-based monocular SLAM (Simultaneous Localization and Mapping) for high accuracy tracking for the endoscopic camera position and posture estimation. By using SLAM technology, the tracking accuracy of 3DCG was improved in some situations, and malfunctions of tracking due to the movement of forceps and other objects moving in front of the endoscopic camera were greatly reduced [3]. Recently, we introduced multi-camera SLAM. This improved the speed of tracking start and greatly reduced the recovery time from tracking failure [4].

However, there are still discrepancies between the model and reality, which makes it impractical. The reason for this is,

1. The SLAM takes unnecessary feature points and makes a mistake in estimating the position and orientation of the endoscope camera.
2. The 3DCG model does not reflect the deformation of the organ.
3. The actual situation differs from the preoperative tomographic images.

To solve the first problem, we will apply the selection of feature points by machine learning and/or deep learning technology. As a solution to the second problem, we are considering implementing the point cloud matching using, for example, the Iterative Closest Point (ICP) algorithm. The third problem is difficult to solve fundamentally and requires the judgment of the surgeons or assistants.

In our previous system, the position and posture of the 3DCG were controlled with the mouse, and the transparency of each part of the 3DCG was controlled with three rotary controllers (Fig. 1). However, it was quite difficult and unintuitive to match manually the two-dimensional endoscopic image with the 3DCG model displayed on the two-dimensional PC monitor using the mouse, which is a two-dimensional input device.

To solve this problem, we are developing a system that can more easily, intuitively, and three-dimensionally manipulate manually in VR space with the three-dimensionally displayed endoscopic image and the 3DCG. In this paper, we describe the details of this system.

2   System Overview

The system configuration is shown in Fig. 2. The stereo endoscope video output from the vision cart of the da Vinci system is captured on a PC via an HDMI-USB converter. The disparity is calculated from the captured stereo images, and a point cloud is generated from the calculated disparity. Various camera parameters of the stereo camera are obtained in advance. The operator wears a head mounted display (HMD). The generated point cloud is displayed in 3D on the HMD. The 3DCG of the organ is also displayed in 3D on the HMD. The operator holds a wireless input device in each hand, and can control his/her viewpoint position and posture in the VR space with the joystick of the input device. The position and posture of the 3DCG can be controlled by grabbing (holding the appropriate button on the input device while moving the operator's hand close to the 3DCG in the VR space). At present, we have not implemented a function to adjust the transparency of the 3DCG. However, this implementation is not very difficult. Besides, we do not capture stereo images from the da Vinci but use pre-recorded movie files instead, because we cannot conduct experiments in the surgical field frequently.

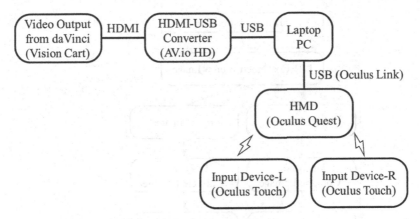

Fig. 2. System overview.

3   Process Flow

The flow of image processing is as shown in Fig. 3. The vision cart of the da Vinci outputs a single image which laterally combined the left and right camera images side by side. First, the left and right images are separated. Then, undistorted images and rectified images are generated using the previously measured camera parameters. Using these images, a disparity map is generated by SGBM (Semi-Global Block Matching) algorithm. The point cloud is generated from the obtained disparity map, the focal length of the camera, the baseline length of the stereo camera, and the coordinate of the principal point of the camera.

At present, we are developing two separate programs, A and B, for this process. Program A generates a disparity map from the captured stereo images. Program B displays the loaded point cloud and 3DCG model in the VR space and provides a user interface for intuitive control of the user's viewpoint and 3DCG of the organ. The point cloud can be loaded from the PLY file format. The 3DCG model was generated from a set of tomographic images taken preoperatively by CT and/or MRI. We use commercial software, SYNAPSE VINCENT to generate the 3DCG models. The 3DCG model consists of five parts: renal parenchyma, artery, vein, ureter, and tumor. Both programs are developed in C# using Unity [5].

In the following, we describe the details and status of these two programs.

4   Program A: Generating a Disparity Map

4.1   Stereo Camera Calibration

The calibration of the da Vinci stereo endoscope camera was conducted using checker pattern with 7×10 squares, 8 [mm] on a side (Fig. 4). The calibration pattern was printed by a laser printer on thick paper and pasted on a flat aluminum plate of 3 mm thickness. Selected 20 images (10 left and 10 right camera images each) shown in Fig. 5

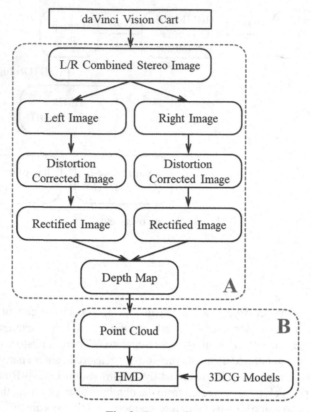

Fig. 3. Process flow.

were used for the calibration. The function findChessboardCorners, stereoCalibrate and stereoRectify in OpenCV (Ver. 3.4.6) were mainly used for the calibration. The estimated camera parameters are output.json file shown in Fig. 6.

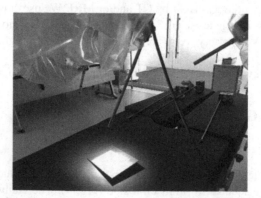

Fig. 4. A view of the calibration of the da Vinci stereo endoscope camera.

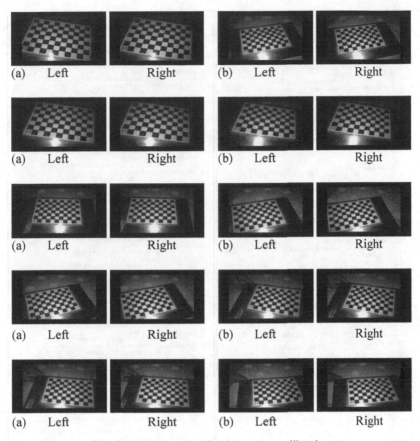

Fig. 5. 20 images used for the camera calibration.

4.2 Computing Disparity from Undistort and Rectified Stereo Image Pair

Consider the situation as shown in Fig. 7. B is the distance between the cameras (baseline length), f is the focal length, Z is the distance from the stereo camera center to the target object P, and u_L, u_R are the pixel distance from the left and right image centers, respectively.

Based on the similarity of the two rectangular triangles,

$$\frac{u_L}{f} = \frac{B + \alpha}{Z}$$

$$\frac{u_R}{f} = \frac{\alpha}{Z}$$

Eliminating α from these two equations, we obtain the following equation and the disparity d.

$$u_L - u_R = \frac{Bf}{Z} \equiv d$$

```
{
    "cameraMatrixL": {
        "type_id": "opencv-matrix",
        "rows": 3,
        "cols": 3,
        "dt": "d",
        "data": [ 6.6158544411377477e+02, 0.0,
5.3227234388154443e+02,
            0.0, 6.6158544411377477e+02,
7.0187055213007750e+02, 0.0,
            0.0, 1.0 ]
    },
    "distCoeffsL": {
        "type_id": "opencv-matrix",
        "rows": 1,
        "cols": 5,
        "dt": "d",
        "data": [ 3.2819405753342058e-02, -
7.8151779755825310e-02, 0.0,
            0.0, 5.0913705176298438e-02 ]
    },
    "cameraMatrixR": {
        "type_id": "opencv-matrix",
        "rows": 3,
        "cols": 3,
        "dt": "d",
        "data": [ 6.6158544411377477e+02, 0.0,
5.9067483518475831e+02,
            0.0, 6.6158544411377477e+02,
7.0086802487351110e+02, 0.0,
            0.0, 1.0 ]
    },
    "distCoeffsR": {
        "type_id": "opencv-matrix",
        "rows": 1,
        "cols": 5,
        "dt": "d",
        "data": [ 2.5989258512878192e-02, -
6.1120060584449520e-02, 0.0,
            0.0, 3.9436453959391861e-02 ]
    },
    "R": {
        "type_id": "opencv-matrix",
        "rows": 3,
        "cols": 3,
        "dt": "d",
        "data": [ 9.9999973631603545e-01,
5.0419218930792024e-04,
            -5.2264528684506947e-04, -
5.0311459123553116e-04,
            9.9999775184051465e-01,
2.0599003919061810e-03,
            5.2368269754344860e-04, -
2.0596368982736301e-03,
            9.9999774182359014e-01 ]
    },
    "T": {
        "type_id": "opencv-matrix",
        "rows": 3,
        "cols": 1,
        "dt": "d",
        "data": [ -4.4628028716208359e+00,
1.3297862627437707e-01,
            -2.3881676963759030e-01 ]
    },
    "E": {
        "type_id": "opencv-matrix",
        "rows": 3,
        "cols": 3,
        "dt": "d",
        "data": [ -5.0513595713418355e-05,
2.3854234505404795e-01,
            1.3347026474255044e-01, -
2.3647961401902262e-01,
            -9.3121630140388101e-03,
4.4629176102837400e+00,
            -1.3073328996752542e-01, -
4.4628598853129411e+00,
            -9.1234287319783558e-03 ]
    },
    "F": {
        "type_id": "opencv-matrix",
        "rows": 3,
        "cols": 3,
        "dt": "d",
        "data": [ 4.5808563719230326e-08, -
2.1632358692375318e-04,
            7.1729577291906807e-02,
2.1445298664834076e-04,
            8.4447920756340374e-06, -
2.7976591478054114e+00,
            -7.1895186761605237e-02,
2.7994081845473460e+00, 1.0 ]
    },
    "Rot_L": {
        "type_id": "opencv-matrix",
        "rows": 3,
        "cols": 3,
        "dt": "d",
        "data": [ 9.9817219249812505e-01, -
2.9348069397158349e-02,
            5.2829584005040689e-02,
2.9335064873576826e-02,
            9.9956911218465538e-01,
1.0217314925887119e-03,
            -5.2836806227752948e-02,
5.2989530993028788e-04,
            9.9860301978244170e-01 ]
    },
    "Prj_L": {
        "type_id": "opencv-matrix",
        "rows": 3,
        "cols": 4,
        "dt": "d",
        "data": [ 7.5496846641717934e+02, 0.0,
4.9100273895263672e+02,
            0.0, 0.0, 7.5496846641717934e+02,
6.8684198570251465e+02,
            0.0, 0.0, 0.0, 1.0, 0.0 ]
    },
    "Rot_R": {
        "type_id": "opencv-matrix",
        "rows": 3,
        "cols": 3,
        "dt": "d",
        "data": [ 9.9812952109567565e-01, -
2.9741374731839524e-02,
            5.3412636579533962e-02,
2.9838498074287071e-02,
            9.9955421075980355e-01, -
1.0216579746202682e-03,
            -5.3358440288185330e-02,
2.6134998386523247e-03,
            9.9857200364751153e-01 ]
    },
    "Prj_R": {
        "type_id": "opencv-matrix",
        "rows": 3,
        "cols": 4,
        "dt": "d",
        "data": [ 7.5496846641717934e+02, 0.0,
4.9100273895263672e+02,
            -3.3755894086883782e+03, 0.0,
7.5496846641717934e+02,
            6.8684198570251465e+02, 0.0, 0.0,
0.0, 1.0, 0.0 ]
    },
    "Q": {
        "type_id": "opencv-matrix",
        "rows": 4,
        "cols": 4,
        "dt": "d",
        "data": [ 1.0, 0.0, 0.0, -
4.9100273895263672e+02, 0.0, 1.0, 0.0,
            -6.8684198570251465e+02, 0.0, 0.0,
0.0,
            7.5496846641717934e+02, 0.0, 0.0,
2.2365530134499695e-01,
            0.0 ]
    }
}
```

Fig. 6. Camera parameters of the da Vinci stereo endoscope camera.

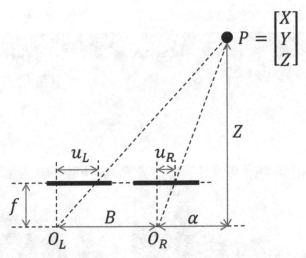

Fig. 7. Parallel image planes of left and right camera.

4.3 Generating Disparity Map

A disparity map generation program was created using Unity (Ver. 2019.4.9f1) and OpenCV for Unity (Ver. 2.3.9). An output example is shown in Fig. 8. The upper part of the figure is the disparity map and the lower part is undistorted and rectified left and right camera images. The disparity map is normalized from 0 to 255 using the function normalize, and then colored with COLORMAP_JET (Fig. 9) using the function applyColorMap. In the disparity map, the blue color indicates that the object is closer to the camera. On the other hand, the red color indicates that the object is far away from the camera.

The disparity map was obtained using the SGBM algorithm, and the parameters for SGBM are as follows. The computation time per frame was about 250 [ms].

```
mindisparity = 4;
numdisparities = 8;
blocksize = 2;
sadwindowsize = 4;
p1 = 1;
p2 = 100;
disp12maxdiff = 10;
prefiltercap = 1;
uniquenessratio = 2;
specklewindowsize = 1;
specklerange = 100;
```

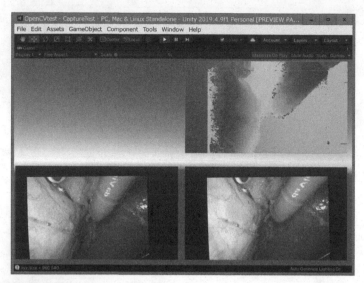

Fig. 8. Calculated disparity map. (Upper image: disparity map, Lower images: undistorted and rectified left and right image)

Fig. 9. Color gradation of COLORMAP_JET.

5   Program B: Displaying Point Cloud and 3DCG in VR Space

5.1   Convert Disparity Map to Point Cloud

Q matrix is used to estimate the 3D coordinate of the target point from disparity.

$$
Q\begin{bmatrix} u \\ v \\ d \\ 1 \end{bmatrix} = \begin{bmatrix} X' \\ Y' \\ Z' \\ W' \end{bmatrix}, \; Q = \begin{bmatrix} 1 & 0 & 0 & -c_x \\ 0 & 1 & 0 & -c_y \\ 0 & 0 & 0 & f \\ 0 & 0 & 1/B & 0 \end{bmatrix}
$$

where u, v, d are coordinate and disparity of the disparity map, c_x and c_y are the coordinates of the principal point in the left camera (the left camera dominant when stereo matching), f is the focal length and B is the baseline length of the stereo camera pair.

3D coordinate of the target point in real world $(XYZ)^T$ is calculated with

$$
\begin{bmatrix} X \\ Y \\ Z \end{bmatrix} = \begin{bmatrix} X'/W \\ Y'/W \\ Z'/W \end{bmatrix} = \begin{bmatrix} \frac{u-c_x}{d/B} \\ \frac{u-c_y}{d/B} \\ \frac{f}{d/B} \end{bmatrix}
$$

From the camera parameters shown in Fig. 6, f and B can be obtained as follows.

$$
f = 754.968, B = \frac{1}{0.224} = 4.464
$$

For example, if $d = 50$ [pixel],

$$Z = 67.41 \text{ [mm]}$$

Figure 10 is a graph showing the relationship between disparity and distance.

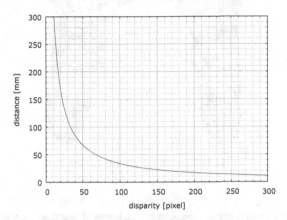

Fig. 10. Disparity and distance curve of our system

5.2 User Interface

The user's viewpoint in the VR space can be controlled with the controllers held in both hands. At present, the operations are assigned as shown in Fig. 11. Tilting the left-hand joystick back and forth, the user can move the viewpoint back and forth. Tilting the left-hand joystick to the left or right, the user can move the viewpoint in parallel to the left or right. Tilting the right-hand joystick back and forth, the user can move the viewpoint up and down. Tilting the right-hand joystick to the left or right, the user can rotate the viewpoint to the left or right.

The position and posture of the 3DCG can be controlled by grabbing (holding the middle finger button by close to the operator's hand to the 3DCG in the VR space).

5.3 Implementation

We used Oculus Integration [7] of Unity asset, which provides the core functionally for using the HMD (Oculus Quest) with Unity. Pcx [8] of Unity asset was used to read and display the point cloud data in PLY format. In this implementation, the number of loaded point clouds was 417519 points. Examples of the development environment of Unity, the user with the HMD and the controller, and the user's view through the HMD are shown in Figs. 12 and 13. The frame rate of this program was about 75 [fps].

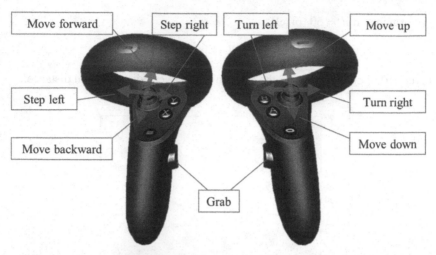

Fig. 11. Button mapping for the controllers

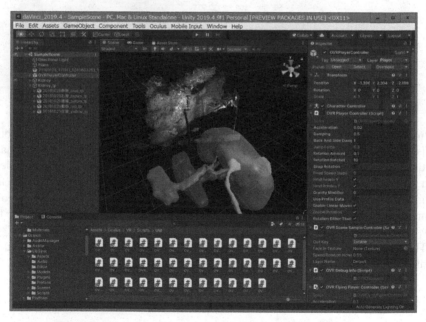

Fig. 12. Examples of the development environment using Unity.

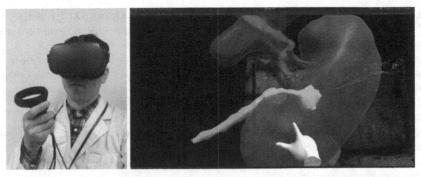

Fig. 13. User with the HMD and the controller and the example of user's view through HMD

6 Conclusion

In this paper, we presented the new VR system for handling 3DCG model intuitively in an endoscopic surgery support system. First, we obtained a disparity map from stereo endoscope camera images using Unity and OpenCV for Unity [6]. Then, the point cloud generated from the disparity map and the 3DCG of organs are displayed in the VR space through the HMD, and it was confirmed that the operation could be performed intuitively.

Currently, these processes are separated. However, we have confirmed that they do not work practically even if they are integrated. The reasons for this are as follows.

- The disparity image generation process is heavy.
- Asynchronous processing of point cloud generation and display is not implemented.
- The data transfer to the shader is slow.

The following are the possible solutions to these problems, and we are planning to work on these issues in the future.

- Implement GPU-based high-speed disparity image generation using a library such as [9].
- Implement asynchronous processing of point cloud generation and display.
- Shrink input images and thinning out point clouds.

References

1. Koeda, M., et al.: Image overlay support with 3DCG organ model for robot-assisted laparoscopic partial nephrectomy. In: Stephanidis, C. (ed.) HCI 2016. CCIS, vol. 617, pp. 508–513. Springer, Cham (2016). https://doi.org/10.1007/978-3-319-40548-3_84
2. Sengiku, A., et al.: Augmented Reality Navigation System for Robot-Assisted Laparoscopic Partial Nephrectomy. Springer International Publishing, Design, User Experience, and Usability: Designing Pleasurable Experiences, Part II. Lecture Notes in Computer Science, vol. 10289, pp. 575–584, 2017. https://doi.org/10.1007/978-3-319-58637-3_45

3. Sawada, A., Hamada, A., Sengiku, A., Koeda, M., Onishi, K., Ogawa, O.: The development of a 3D navigation system for robot-assisted partial nephrectomy using augmented reality technology. In: Proceedings of The 2019 Annual EAU Congress, vol. 18(1) (2019)
4. Hamada, A., et al.: The Current Status and Challenges in Augmented Reality Navigation System for Robot-Assisted Laparoscopic Partial Nephrectomy. Springer, Cham, Human-Computer Interaction. Design and User Experience. HCII2020. Lecture Notes in Computer Science, vol. 12182, pp. 620–629 (2020). https://doi.org/10.1007/978-3-319-58637-3_45
5. Unity Real-Time Development Platform|3D, 2D VR & AR Engine https://unity.com/
6. OpenCV for Unity|Integration|Unity Asset Store https://assetstore.unity.com/packages/tools/integration/opencv-for-unity-21088
7. Oculus Integration|Integration|Unity Asset Store https://assetstore.unity.com/packages/tools/integration/oculus-integration-82022
8. keijiro/Pcx: Point cloud importer & renderer for Unity https://github.com/keijiro/Pcx
9. fixstars/libSGM: Stereo Semi Global Matching by cuda https://github.com/fixstars/libSGM

Comparative Study of Potential-Based and Sensor-Based Surgical Navigation in Several Liver Environments

Takahiro Kunii[1]([⊠]), Miho Asano[2], Kanako Fujita[3], Katsunori Tachibana[4], and Hiroshi Noborio[3]

[1] Kashina System Co., Hikone, Japan
kunii@tetera.co.jp
[2] Preemptive Medicine and Lifestyle-Related Disease Research Center,
Kyoto University Hospital, Kyoto, Japan
[3] Department of Computer Science, Osaka Electro-Communication University,
Shijonawate, Japan
[4] Department of Biomedical Engineering, Osaka Electro-Communication University,
Shijonawate, Japan

Abstract. Medical navigators have gained recent attention for application in surgery to provide the surgeon with the position and orientation of malignant tumors as accurately as possible. Currently, extensive research is being conducted on producing surgical navigators; however, their practical application is difficult in the case of organ deformation. This study presents a medical navigation system using two types of algorithms to select a pathway from the scalpel tip near a malignant tumor in a 3D liver environment, which avoids blood vessels (arteries, veins, and portal veins) and the malignant tumor when they are regionally segmented inside the liver. The first algorithm involves potential-based navigation, in which the scalpel tip reaches its destination by adjusting the attraction to the destination (currently the malignant tumor) and the repulsion from the blood vessels. The second algorithm involves sensor-based navigation where the surgeon moves the scalpel in a straight line in the direction of the malignant tumor. When a blood vessel is encountered, the scalpel is moved in a clockwise or counterclockwise direction in a certain plane over a certain distance to avoid the blood vessel. It is then moved in a straight line in the direction of the malignant tumor again after approaching the malignant tumor monotonically or asymptotically.

In this study, both navigation algorithms select a path near the malignant tumor in the 3D liver environments with diverse shapes and arrangements of blood vessels and malignant tumors. The potential-based navigation algorithm then selects a shorter straight path near the malignancy, but the direction of the incision varies in a complex manner. Lastly, the sensor-based navigation algorithm selects a longer circuitous path near the malignancy, but the incision direction is uniform.

Keywords: Potential-based navigation · Sensor-based navigation · Surgical navigation · Collision-free and deadlock-free path · Path length and shape

© Springer Nature Switzerland AG 2021
M. Kurosu (Ed.): HCII 2021, LNCS 12763, pp. 551–565, 2021.
https://doi.org/10.1007/978-3-030-78465-2_40

1 Introduction

Navigation is generally used in automobiles (conditional 2D) [1], in airplanes (conditional 3D) [2, 3], and more recently, in robots (2D to 6DOF) [4]. Medical navigators are mainly utilized to provide the surgeon with the position and orientation of malignant tumors as accurately as possible (brain navigation) [5]. Currently, extensive research is being conducted on producing surgical navigators (plastic, brain, kidney, liver, etc.), but their practical application is difficult in the case of organ deformation. Pre- and post-operative brain digital imaging and communications in medicine (DICOM) feature point acquisition and mapping is being studied, along with the deformation modeling of the liver. With continued research and analysis, the physical parameters of the various regions of the organ can be obtained, and the actual deformation modeling can be achieved. This study presents a medical navigation system that guides a scalpel tip inside an organ near a malignant tumor. With the organ model proposed in this study, the deformation of the blood vessels and malignant tumors inside the organ can be achieved by intraoperatively measuring the deformation of the organ surface.

The research on an AR-based liver simulator for this study was started approximately 5 years ago [6]. Haptic devices were then used to deform and incise the liver, allowing for the free manipulation of the VR liver in an AR space [7]. In addition, the position and orientation of the scalpel were accurately measured in real space, and the scalpel was incorporated into the AR space along with the liver to build a liver navigation system [8].

Conversely, a fast algorithm was also proposed to calculate the Euclidean shortest distance between the scalpel tip and blood vessels using multiple cores of a general-purpose graphics processing unit (GPGPU) [9]. The algorithm was redesigned for omni-directional coverage in 3D space [10, 11]. The potential-based navigation algorithm was incorporated into the AR liver surgery by applying this 3D shortest distance calculation to the tip of the scalpel to guide the scalpel around the malignant tumor with appropriate attraction, while avoiding the blood vessels with appropriate repulsion [12].

The sensor-based navigation algorithm was proposed in this case, as the potential-based navigation algorithm involves the risk of bleeding owing to the scalpel being placed in a region with intricate blood vessels. When a group of blood vessels is detected, the scalpel avoids it by deviating in a large circle, approaching the malignant tumor from the starting point of the deviation, and then, moving straight toward the malignant tumor again from the point where it finishes avoiding the group of blood vessels. The avoidance motion of the blood vessel group is smooth with a constant curvature, and the rest of the motion is linear, making the chosen path easy to operate. Essentially, although a longer path is selected, it avoids regions with intricate blood vessels [13].

In this study, the two proposed types of navigation algorithms were applied to various vascular and malignant tumor environments in the liver, and the produced paths were compared to avoid contact between the blood vessels and scalpel tip near the malignant tumor. Consequently, the pathway produced by the sensor-based navigation algorithm was generally long with some trial and error, as it often involved a large detour to avoid regions with intricate blood vessels. Conversely, the path produced by potential-based navigation is generally short and involves considerable trial and error, because it selects a straightforward path that passes through the region with intricate blood vessels.

Because the above results were obtained in diverse environments, the aforementioned characteristics are concluded to be universal.

Section 2 briefly explains the two types of navigations methods. Section 3 discusses the deformation, addition, and migration of the blood vessels and the malignant tumors in the liver. In Sect. 3, the two types of navigation algorithms are used to generate different paths. The characteristics of the paths, such as their length, shape, and curvature are compared only if the paths are collision-free and deadlock-free. Section 4 provides the conclusion; lastly, Sect. 5 discusses the future implications of the study.

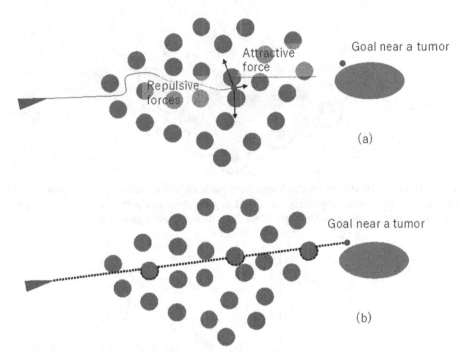

Fig. 1. (a) Deadlock among two circular obstacles in the potential-based navigation. (b) Deadlock-free path made by the sensor-based navigation exactly explained in [13].

2 Potential-Based Navigation and Sensor-Based Navigation Algorithms

The potential-based navigation algorithm is briefly described as follows. A scalpel primarily advances toward a tumor due to its attractive force. When the scalpel approaches a blood vessel, it is affected by its repulsive force and avoids it (Fig. 1(a), (b)). The magnitude of this repulsive force increases with the decrease in the distance to the nearest blood vessel. Occasionally, these attractive and repulsive forces balance each other, and the scalpel stops moving. This is called a deadlock (Fig. 1(c), (d)).

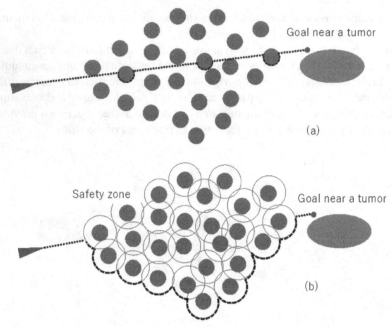

Fig. 2. (a) Straightly shorter deadlock-free path made by the sensor-based navigation around multiple obstacles without any safety zone. (b) Long deadlock-free path of detours made by the sensor-based navigation around multiple obstacles with safety zone precisely mentioned in [13].

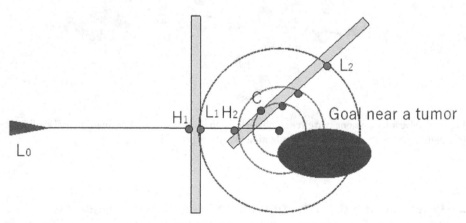

Fig. 3. Monotonous convergence of hit (H1, H2, …) or leave (L0, L1, …) points in sensor-based navigation which is deeply described in [13].

The sensor-based navigation algorithm is used to overcome the deadlock, as shown below. In this case, the scalpel advances directly toward the final position (Fig. 2(a), (b)). When the scalpel encounters a blood vessel, it traces the vessel while maintaining a certain distance (Fig. 2(b), (c)). Then, when the scalpel encounters a point that is closer to the goal than the initial point where it encountered the blood vessel, it leaves

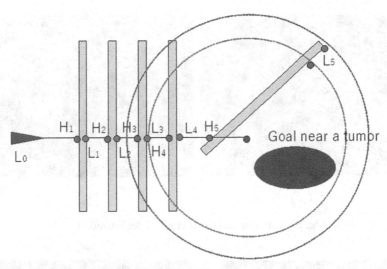

Fig. 4. Asymptotical convergence of hit (H1, H2, …) or leave (L0, L1, …) in sensor-based navigation exactly explained in [13].

Fig. 5. Original state of blood vessels.

the vessel and moves directly toward the goal again. Subsequently, different types of algorithms have been developed to determine whether the scalpel approaches the goal monotonically or asymptotically (Fig. 3 and 4).

All the explanations and diagrams in this section are presented in a 2D space. However, they can be easily extended to a 3D space. In potential-based navigation, all the attractive and repulsive forces are represented in the liver space as 3D vectors. In sensor-based navigation, a 3D vector is used in the liver space to trace a blood vessel, while

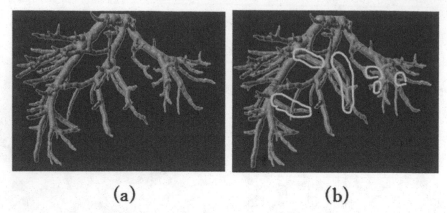

(a)   (b)

Fig. 6. (a) Before and (b) after blood deformation 1.

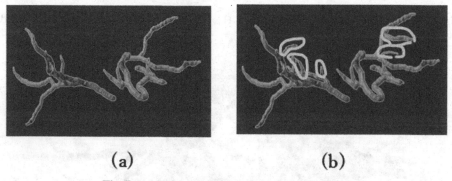

(a)   (b)

Fig. 7. (a) Before and (b) after blood deformation 2.

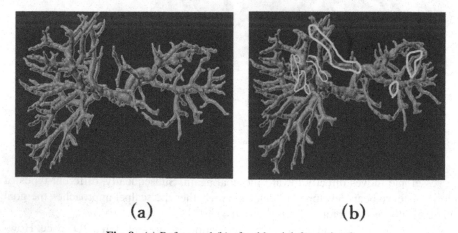

(a)   (b)

Fig. 8. (a) Before and (b) after blood deformation 3.

maintaining a certain distance. The direction of this vector can be chosen arbitrarily (e.g., by varying it to follow the perimeter of a 2D vessel cut by a fixed 2D plane). The sensor-based navigation algorithm always finds a take-off point around the vessel to approach the tumor without any deadlock because the take-off point is selected either monotonically or asymptotically.

3   Deformation and Migration of Liver Vessels and Malignant Tumors

In this section, a group of blood vessels and a malignant tumor of the liver are moved and deformed using Blender [14], which is a free and open source 3D computer graphics software toolset used to create animated films, visual effects, art, 3D printed models, motion graphics, interactive 3D applications, virtual reality applications, and computer games. The 3D modeling capabilities of Blender are used to move and deform a group of blood vessels and a malignant tumor in the liver. This allows us to evaluate whether

Fig. 9. Shrinkage of the tumor colored by green (upper left). (Color figure online)

Fig. 10. Green tumor moved to lower left.

Fig. 11. Green tumor moved to upper right. (Color figure online)

Fig. 12. Tumor moved to lower right. (Color figure online)

sensor-based navigation and potential navigation always choose a collision-free and deadlock-free path toward the tumor. Furthermore, if both are able to select different paths, the characteristics of each (e.g., changes in length, shape, and curvature) can be evaluated.

The vessels used in this study are mainly arteries, veins, and portal veins. By deforming the blood vessels, the distance between the vessels becomes closer, and the potential navigation algorithm may not be able to generate a pathway.

Figure 5 shows the initial state of the group of blood vessels used in this study. The growth and deformation of the vessels using Blender are shown in Figs. 6, 7, and 8. Here, the locations of the blood vessels that have been multiplied or deformed are circled. Furthermore, Figs. 9, 10, 11, 12 show how the malignant tumor mass is reduced in size and moved to the upper left, lower left, upper right, and lower right sides. In the above figures, the arteries are shown in red, the veins in blue, the portal vein in yellow, and the cancer cells (malignant tumor) are shown in green.

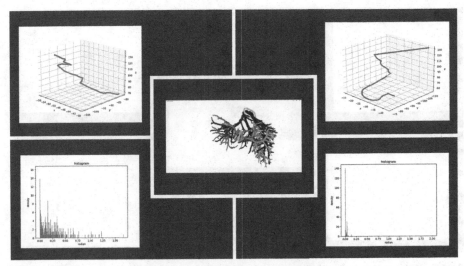

Fig. 13. (Center) Result 1 with the tumor model in the upper left corner. (Upper left and right) Collision-free and deadlock-free paths selected by the potential-based and sensor-based navigations. (Lower left and right) Histogram of path direction based on the potential-based and sensor-based navigations.

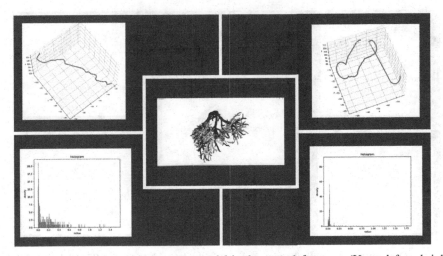

Fig. 14. (Center) Result 2 with the tumor model in the upper left corner. (Upper left and right) Collision-free and deadlock-free paths selected by the potential-based and sensor-based navigations. (Lower left and right) Histogram of path direction based on the potential-based and sensor-based navigations.

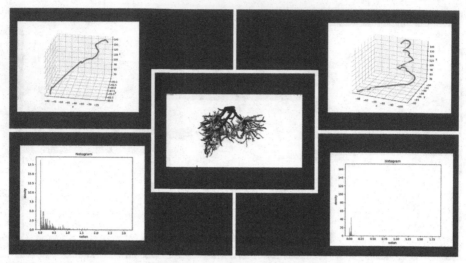

Fig. 15. (Center) Result 1 with the tumor model in the lower left corner. (Upper left and right) Collision-free and deadlock-free paths selected by the potential-based and sensor-based navigation algorithms. (Lower left and right) Histogram of path direction based on the potential-based and sensor-based navigation algorithms.

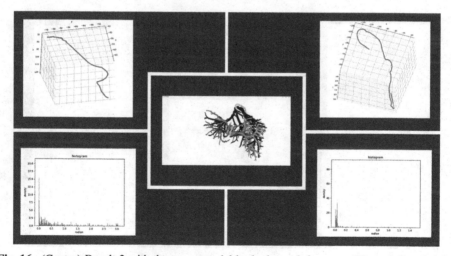

Fig. 16. (Center) Result 2 with the tumor model in the lower left corner. (Upper left and right) Collision-free and deadlock-free paths selected by the potential-based and sensor-based navigation algorithms. (Lower left and right) Histogram of path direction based on the potential-based and sensor-based navigation algorithms.

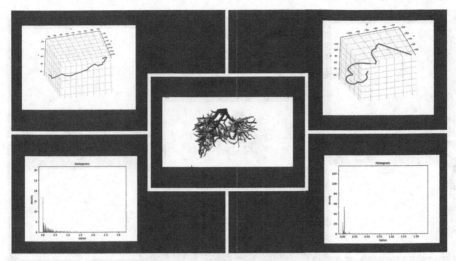

Fig. 17. (Center) Result 1 with the tumor model in the upper right corner. (Upper left and right) Collision-free and deadlock-free paths selected by the potential-based and sensor-based navigations. (Lower left and right) Histogram of path direction based on the potential-based and sensor-based navigations.

4   Experimental Results

This section explains the selection of the path for the liver models (with different malignancies) using potential-based and sensor-based navigation, along with their features (shapes, etc.) that are suitable for surgery.

As there are four tumor model patterns, two results are listed for each of the tumor model positions. The images of the navigation runs are shown in Figs. 13, 14, 15, 16, 17, 18, 19, 20.

It is observed that the sensor-based and potential methods work well by starting from different positions using the deformable models of the blood vessels and cancer cells. For the sensor-based method, some of the distance thresholds were exceeded, owing to which the paths did not reach the cancer cells; however, this was resolved by adjusting the thresholds. Conversely, the navigation using the potential method was not restricted in the blood vessels, which was a concern, and reached the area around the cancer cells.

In general, the navigation using the potential method selects a path with a relatively short distance from the tip of the scalpel to the malignant tumor. However, a significant amount of trial and error is required to determine the direction of the incision; moreover, this method is not preferable as it leads to bleeding. The upper left figures show the path length of the potential-based navigation and its shape, and the lower left figure shows the distribution of the incision direction of the scalpel in the potential-based navigation. It can observed that, although the selected path is linear and short in all the liver environments, the variation of its incision direction is large.

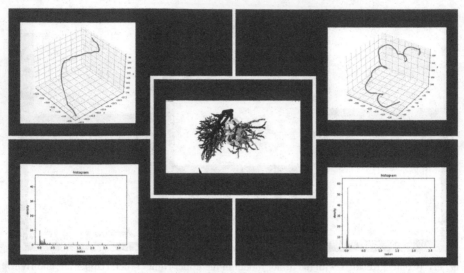

Fig. 18. (Center) Result 2 with the tumor model in the upper right corner. (Upper left and right) Collision-free and deadlock-free paths selected by the potential-based and sensor-based navigations. (Lower left and right) Histogram of path direction based on the potential-based and sensor-based navigations.

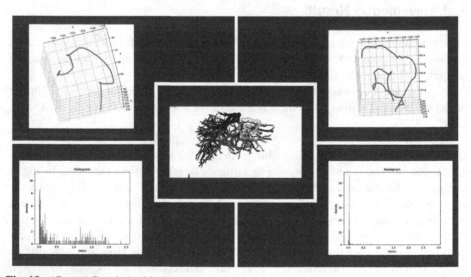

Fig. 19. (Center) Result 1 with the tumor model in the lower right corner. (Upper left and right) Collision-free and deadlock-free paths selected by the potential-based and sensor-based navigations. (Lower left and right) Histogram of path direction based on the potential-based and sensor-based navigations.

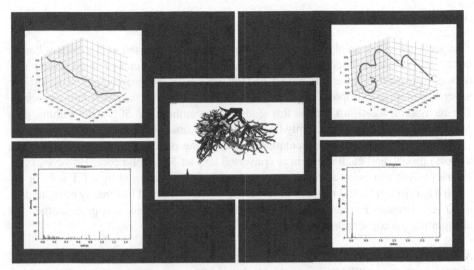

Fig. 20. (Center) Result 2 with the tumor model in the lower right corner. (Upper left and right) Collision-free and deadlock-free paths selected by the potential-based and sensor-based navigations. (Lower left and right) Histogram of path direction based on the potential-based and sensor-based navigations.

Conversely, the sensor-based navigation algorithm follows a relatively long route from the tip of the scalpel to the malignancy. However, this process does not involve trial and error to determine the direction of the incision, which reduces the risk of bleeding. The top-right figure shows the path length and shape of the sensor-based navigation algorithm, and the bottom right figure shows the distribution of the incision direction of sensor-based navigation.

5   Conclusion

In this study, various liver environments were created by deforming a patient liver model to determine whether the potential-based and sensor-based navigation algorithms can reliably select a path from the scalpel tip to the malignant tumor. In this process, the complexity of the vascular network is deliberately increased, and the distances between the vessels are decreased; however, both the navigation algorithms are able to select the path reliably. Therefore, it can be concluded that the sensor-based navigation algorithm must be used if the potential-based navigation algorithm fails to find the path, and then, switched back to the sensor-based navigation algorithm if the environment around the scalpel becomes too complex for the potential-based navigation algorithm to find the path. This study aimed to evaluate the characteristics of the paths selected by the two navigation algorithms. The results demonstrate that the path produced by the potential-based navigation algorithm is short and linear, but varies significantly in the incision direction; meanwhile, the path produced by the sensor-based navigation algorithm is long and curvilinear, but shows a small variance in the incision direction.

6 Future Research Implications

This study proposes an algorithm that combines the sensor-based and potential- based methods to simulate a liver surgery navigator. Several environments of blood vessels and tumors were created in the liver model, and the function of the two navigation algorithms is verified, aiming to improve the accuracy and performance of the path finding process. The navigation algorithm used in this study was a combination of two algorithms, and both of which were able to reliably find a path to the final destination.

In this study, DICOM segmentation is used as the patient liver (blood vessels and tumors) model, and each segment is converted into an STL polyhedra. However, considerable time and effort is required after the DICOM is captured by a CT scan or an MRI. Therefore, it would be more efficient if the DICOM could be directly navigated as a 3D environment. Further research can be conducted to achieve this process, thereby eliminating the conversion to STL.

Acknowledgements. This study was supported partly by the 2020 Grants-in-Aid for Scientific Research (No. 20K04407) from the Ministry of Education, Culture, Sports, Science and Technology, Japan.

References

1. https://en.wikipedia.org/wiki/Automotive_navigation_system
2. https://en.wikipedia.org/wiki/Inertial_navigation_system
3. https://en.wikipedia.org/wiki/Motion_planning
4. https://en.wikipedia.org/wiki/Robot_navigation
5. StealthStation ™ S8 surgical navigation system at Rambam Medical Center. https://www.you tube.com/watch?v=tUtuPIIO7DY
6. Onishi, K., et al.: Virtual liver surgical simulator by using Z-buffer for object deformation. In: Antona, Margherita, Stephanidis, Constantine (eds.) UAHCI 2015. LNCS, vol. 9177, pp. 345–351. Springer, Cham (2015). https://doi.org/10.1007/978-3-319-20684-4_34
7. Noborio, H., et al.: Fast surgical algorithm for cutting with liver standard triangulation language format using Z-buffers in graphics processing unit. In: Fujie, Masakatsu G. (ed.) Computer Aided Surgery, pp. 127–140. Springer, Tokyo (2016). https://doi.org/10.1007/978-4-431-55810-1_11
8. Koeda, M., et al.: Depth camera calibration and knife tip position estimation for liver surgery support system. In: Stephanidis, C. (ed.) HCI 2015. CCIS, vol. 528, pp. 496–502. Springer, Cham (2015). https://doi.org/10.1007/978-3-319-21380-4_84
9. Noborio, H., Kunii, T., Mizushino, K.: Comparison of GPU-based and CPU-based algorithms for determining the minimum distance between a CUSA Scalper and blood vessels, pp. 128–136, The SCITEPRESS Digital Library (Science and Technology Publications, Lda) (2016). https://doi.org/10.5220/0005634801280136. ISBN 978-989-758-170-0
10. Noborio, H., Kunii, T., Mizushino, K.: GPU-based omnidirectional shortest distance algorithm and its evaluation by changing GPU cores. In: Proceedings of the 13th International Conference of Computational Intelligence methods for Bioinformatics and Biostatistics (CIBB2016), The University of Stirling, Scotland, UK, pp. 76–81 (Sept 2016)
11. Noborio, H., Kunii, T., Mizushino, K.: Omni-directional shortest distance algorithm by complete parallel-processing based on GPU cores. Int. J. Biosci. Biochem. Bioinf. 8(2), 79–88 (2018). https://doi.org/10.17706/ijbbb.2018.8.2.79-88. ISSN 2010-3638

12. Noborio, H., Aoki, K., Kunii, T., Mizushino, K.: A potential function-based scalpel navigation method that avoids blood vessel groups during excision of cancerous tissue. In: Proceedings of the 38th Annual International Conference of the IEEE Engineering in Medicine and Biology Society (EMBC2016), Orlando Florida USA, pp. 6106–6112 (Aug 2016)
13. Noborio, H., Kawai, K., Watanabe, K., Tachibana, K., Kunii, T., Mizushino, K.: Deadlock-free and collision-free liver surgical navigation by switching potential-based and sensor-based functions. In: Kurosu, M. (ed.) HCII 2020. LNCS, vol. 12183, pp. 604–622. Springer, Cham (2020). https://doi.org/10.1007/978-3-030-49065-2_42
14. https://www.blender.org/

Voxel-Based Route-Search Algorithm for Tumor Navigation and Blood Vessel Avoidance

Takahiro Kunii[1]($\boxtimes$), Miho Asano[2], and Hiroshi Noborio[3]

[1] Kashina System Co., Hikone, Japan
kunii@tetera.jp
[2] Preemptive Medicine and Lifestyle-Related Disease Research Center, Kyoto University Hospital, Kyoto-shi, Japan
[3] Department of Computer Science, Osaka Electro-Communication University, Shijo-Nawate, Japan

Abstract. In this study, we propose an algorithm that determines a simple-shaped surgical path from the liver surface to its malignant tumor in 3D voxel space. The method has a good affinity with DICOM (Digital Imaging and Communications in Medicine standards) captured by MRI (Magnetic Resonance Imaging) or CT (computed tomography). It also accounts for voxel density, which reflects the probability of the existence of blood vessels along the cutting path. The algorithm selects a path that avoids high-density voxels and the entangled blood vessels that spawn them.

Keywords: Surgical path · Navigation · 3D voxel space

1 Introduction

In this study, we produce a medical navigation system that guides the scalpel tip inside an organ to its malignant tumor. The technology invoked for this task is generally used for automobiles (e.g., conditional 2D) [1], airplanes (e.g., conditional 3D) [2, 3], and robots (2D to six degrees of freedom) [4]. In the medical field, the capability is leveraged to provide surgeons with the position and orientation of malignant tumors as accurately as possible (e.g., brain navigation) [5].

Our research began with an augmented-reality (AR) liver simulator [6], for which we later applied haptic devices to simulate deformations and incisions, allowing us to freely manipulate the virtual organ in the AR space [7]. To build a liver navigation system, the position and orientation of the scalpel were accurately measured in real space, and the scalpel was incorporated into the AR space with the liver [8]. We later proposed a fast algorithm to calculate the Euclidean shortest distance between the scalpel tip and blood vessels using multiple graphical processing cores [9]. The algorithm was modified to cover all directions in 3D space [10, 11]. By applying this shortest-distance calculation to the tip of the scalpel, potential-based navigation was incorporated into a liver-surgery AR tool to guide the scalpel around the malignant tumor with appropriate attraction

© Springer Nature Switzerland AG 2021
M. Kurosu (Ed.): HCII 2021, LNCS 12763, pp. 566–581, 2021.
https://doi.org/10.1007/978-3-030-78465-2_41

while avoiding blood vessels with appropriate repulsion [12]. Because the potential-based navigation system guides the scalpel into a region having intricate blood vessels, sensor-based navigation was proposed subsequently. When a group of blood vessels is detected, the scalpel avoids it via a large circular path from the starting point of the avoidance and navigates straight to the tumor after group of blood vessels is avoided. The avoidance motion is smooth with a constant curvature, and the remaining motion is straight. Thus, the chosen path is easy to operate. Although the path is longer, it avoids areas having intricate blood vessels [13, 14].

The current method has drawbacks in that it is yet to support Digital Imaging and Communications in Medicine (DICOM) standardized region segmentation [15]. Additionally, stereolithography (STL) file conversions must be performed separately. The technique is not yet suitable for preoperative conferences where liver-cutting decisions are made. Furthermore, the system does not guarantee that an untangled pathway free of blood vessels will be found. Figure 1 shows example computer-assisted design imagery of intricate and simple paths, as provided by our method.

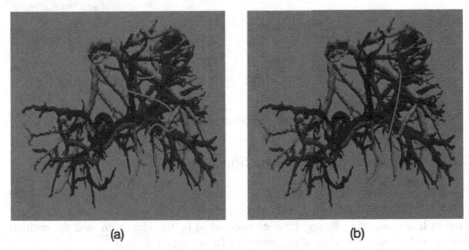

(a)   **(b)**

Fig. 1. (a) Intricate and (b) simple paths for obstacle (i.e., blood vessel) avoidance.

In view of these limitations and with the motivation to resolve them, we have added new capability to the potential and sensor-based methods. In the space along the z-axis that passes through an object to be avoided (Fig. 2(a)), the surgeon determines the starting point, Pe, and the location of the tumor, Pc. Because the goal is to avoid cutting the blocking object (e.g., blood vessel), the potential and sensor-based methods now allow backward and outside circular movement (Fig. 2(b)). It searches the generated voxel field of arbitrary size to navigate around the object (Fig. 2(c)).

Voxels of arbitrary size may be directly produced using DICOM standards, and there is now the possibility of providing DICOM region segmentation and its STL conversion. Our proposed algorithm is further explained in Sect. 2. In Sect. 3, we evaluate the algorithm via parameter manipulation and discuss the findings. In Sect. 4, we conclude and provide recommended future works.

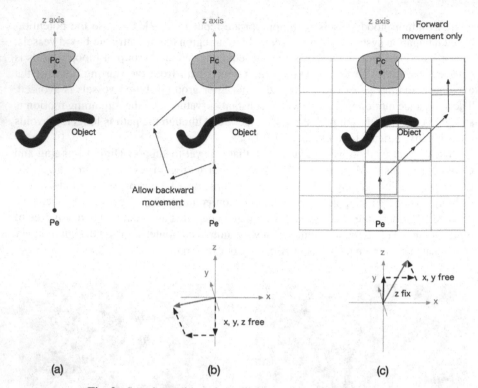

Fig. 2. Search conditions for collision- and deadlock-free paths.

2   Novel Search in the 3D Voxel Space

There are an infinite number of paths that can be taken to reach the periphery of the tumor. Therefore, we need guidelines to select from among them. The aforementioned straight line connecting Pe and Pc is considered to be the ideal path, and the optimal cutting path is obtained while considering the following conditions:

- Select a path that keeps the line as straight as possible.
- Select a path around blood vessels and bile ducts.

No recession of the z-axis is allowed. Therefore, if we perform the search from Pe to Pc, we may reach Pc', which is far away from Pc (Fig. 3).

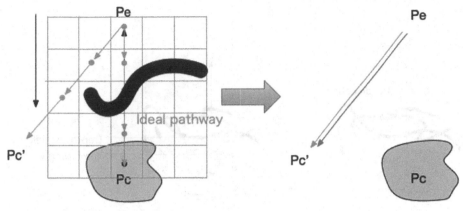

Fig. 3. Search from Pe to Pc.

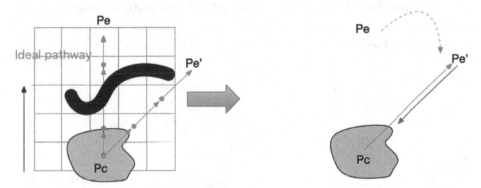

Fig. 4. Search from Pc to Pe.

To solve this problem, we instead start the search from center of the tumor, Pc, to give us the best and safest surgical incision from Pe' (Fig. 4).

2.1 Voxel Creation

To create a voxel in the on-line manner, the following steps are followed.

- Step 1: Determine the line of sight for Pe using Pc as the viewpoint.
- -Step 2: Render the STL models of blood and lymph vessels as obstacles using the determined line of sight in a parallel projection.
- -Step 3: The depth of the field of view during rendering is limited to the voxel width (Fig. 5), and the information of one layer of voxels is generated from the image rendered under this limitation.

Most renderers do not draw the backside of the polygon by default. Because the backside of the blood vessel is important to the procedure, (Fig. 6) we set the software to render the backside of the polygons.

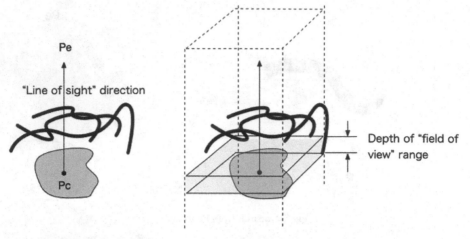

Fig. 5. Determination of the "Line of sight" and generation of the image.

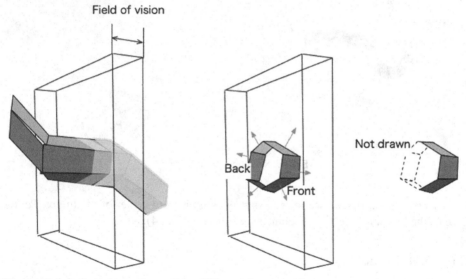

Fig. 6. Unless the polygon faces of the STL model are specified to be drawn on both sides, the backside will not be drawn.

While advancing the viewpoint by voxel width, Steps 2 and 3 are carried out to generate each voxel layer group sequentially (Fig. 7).

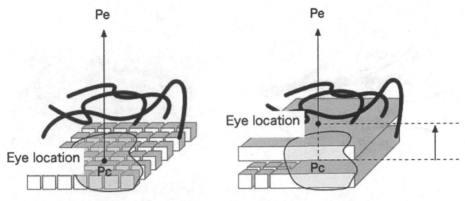

Fig. 7. Generating layers of voxels by moving the viewpoint.

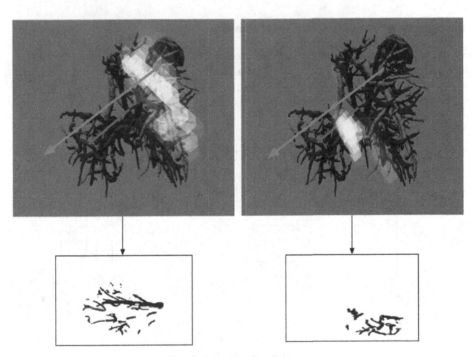

Fig. 8. Images of each layer.

2.2 Density of Each Voxel

For each voxel, the percentage of the voxel's interior (i.e., density) occupied by obstacles (e.g., blood vessels) is calculated based on the images generated for each layer (Figs. 8 and 9). Density = 0 means that there is no obstacle in the voxel, and density = 1 means that the entire voxel is filled with obstacles.

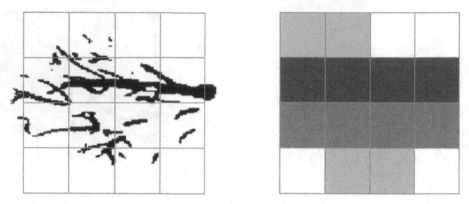

Fig. 9. Calculating density from layer images.

2.3 Searching 3D Space Using Voxel Density

For the search, we use the density of each voxel. First, the voxel containing Pc is set as the starting point, V0. Next, we search for a voxel to be advanced from the voxel layer by one voxel width in the line-of-sight direction. Then, a new voxel is set as the starting point, V0. Then, the process repeats (Fig. 10).

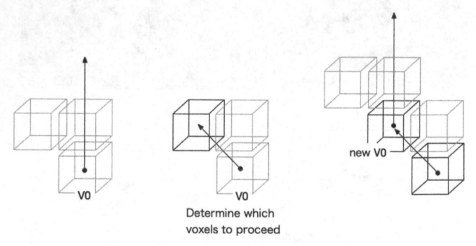

Determine which
voxels to proceed

Fig. 10. Advancing layers in the line-of-sight direction.

Voxel Group to Be Searched
The search target is the voxel-group layer that is one voxel ahead of V0 in the line-of-sight direction (z-axis). The cutoff path to be searched depends on the voxels in this layer being surveyed. In this system, there are nine adjacent voxels to be investigated centered on V1, which is one voxel ahead in the line-of-sight direction from V0 (Fig. 11).

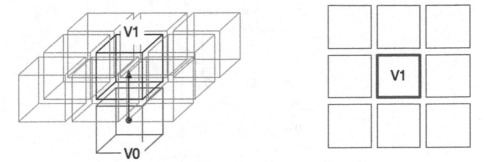

Fig. 11. Voxels to be surveyed.

Then, from the group of voxels to be investigated, the voxel having a density value less than the threshold and the lowest density value is determined to be the next voxel.

Preparation of the Position-Dependent Adjustment Function
The density value to be compared with the threshold is not the density value of the voxel as it is. We must instead consider the positional relationship dx and dy from V1 (Fig. 12). This allows us to account for the direction of the voxel when determining where to proceed. This lends itself to becoming our adjustment function.

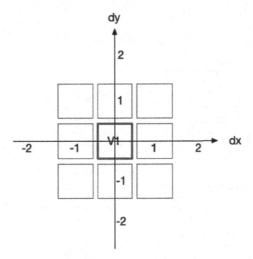

Fig. 12. Positional relationship from V1, dx, and dy.

For example, for a group of 3×3 voxels having density values shown in Fig. 13, if no adjustment is made, the first voxel candidate to be advanced will be the one having density $= 0.3$, and the second voxel candidate will be the one having density $= 0.4$.

As shown in Fig. 13, if an adjustment function is applied to a group of dense voxels such that the density value of all except the central voxel will be uniformly doubled, the voxel that is finally selected as the new V0 will be the central voxel (Fig. 14(a)). If we

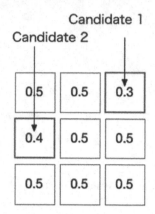

Fig. 13. Density values of a group of voxels.

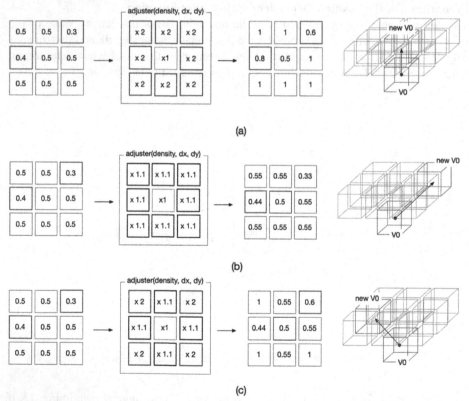

(a)

(b)

(c)

Fig. 14. Changes in the voxels selected by the adjuster function: (a) Multiply the density value of voxels other than the center by two; (b) Multiply the density value of voxels other than the center by 1.1; (c) Multiply the density value of voxels vertically or horizontally adjacent to the center voxel by 1.1, and multiplying the density value of other voxels by 2.

apply an adjustment function that multiplies this value by 1.1 instead of two, the voxel that is finally selected will be the first candidate (Fig. 14(b)). If the adjustment function is applied so that the voxels vertically or horizontally adjacent to the center voxel are multiplied by 1.1, and the other voxels are multiplied by two, the voxel to be selected becomes the second candidate (Fig. 14(c)).

For the evaluation test, the following function (Eq. (1)) is prepared as the adjuster function:

$$adjuster(density,\ dx,\ dy) = density + C\sqrt{dx^2 + dy^2}^{-3} \tag{1}$$

where C is an arbitrarily determined coefficient (Fig. 15).

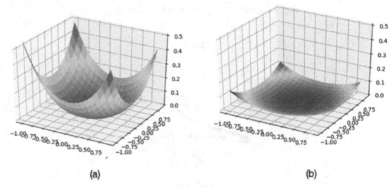

Fig. 15. Distribution of values added to the density value: (a) $C = 0.2$, (b) $C = 0.05$.

Dealing with Impassibility via Backtracking

As we proceed with the voxel layers (Fig. 16), it is possible that all voxels under investigation will become impassable. If so, the density value of the V0 voxel is set to one, and the level is searched again (Fig. 17).

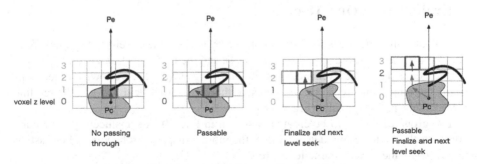

Fig. 16. Advancing the layer under investigation.

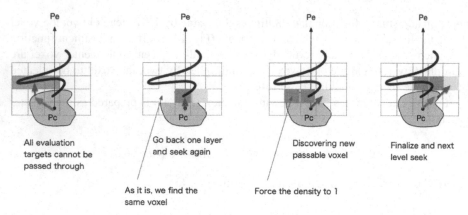

Fig. 17. Searching one level back again.

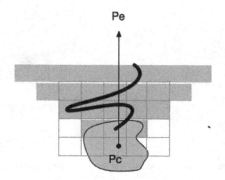

Fig. 18. Search area.

If it the path returns to the voxel containing the starting point, Pc, it is judged to be impassible. Via this backtracking operation, the entire region now extends in an inverted cone from the voxel containing Pc (Fig. 18) to become the new search target.

3   Evaluation of Our Algorithm

We evaluated the actual effect of our algorithm by varying the voxel-width values (5, 7, and 10 mm), the threshold values (0.6 and 0.4), and the C values (0.05, 0.2, and 0.4).

The geometry of the liver model is shown in Fig. 19(a). The yellowish object represents the tumor, the green arrows represent the vector from Pc to Pe, and the red line represents the pathway found (Fig. 19(b)).

The group of voxels to be created is shown in Fig. 20. A translucent yellow cube is one voxel. The lower the density value, the more transparent it becomes. For ease of viewing, only the voxels of one level are shown.

Figure 21 shows the results of the run by changing the voxel width, threshold, and C-value without changing the liver model and the vector from Pc to Pe.

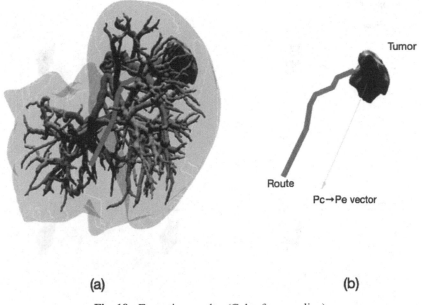

(a)   (b)

Fig. 19. Execution results. (Color figure online)

4mm   7mm   10mm

Fig. 20. Voxel groups created (voxel widths of 5, 7, and 10 mm).

The voxel width corresponds to the path resolution. Thus, the larger the width, the coarser the path detection. The value of C can be used to control the straightness, and the straightness increases with the value. However, if too much priority is given to straightness, detection becomes impossible. It can be seen that the threshold value has more to do with whether a path can be detected or not than with the shape of the path.

[Voxel wide:5]

Threshold:0.6

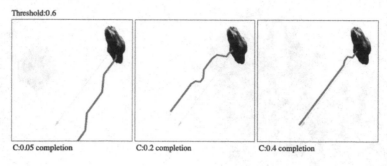

C:0.05 completion   C:0.2 completion   C:0.4 completion

Threshold:0.4

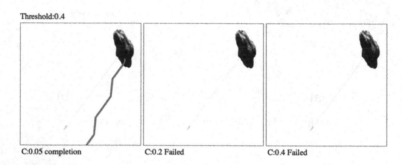

C:0.05 completion   C:0.2 Failed   C:0.4 Failed

[Voxel wide:7]

Threshold:0.6

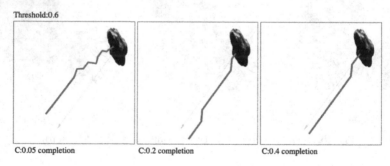

C:0.05 completion   C:0.2 completion   C:0.4 completion

Threshold:0.4

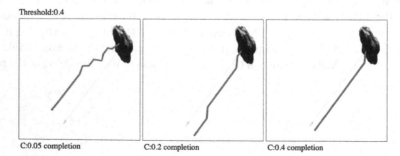

C:0.05 completion   C:0.2 completion   C:0.4 completion

Fig. 21. Execution results

[Voxel wide:10]

Threshold:0.6

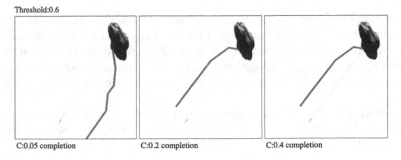

C:0.05 completion   C:0.2 completion   C:0.4 completion

Threshold:0.4

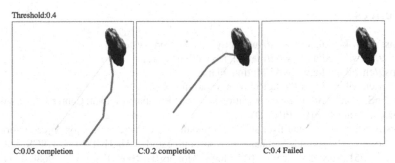

C:0.05 completion   C:0.2 completion   C:0.4 Failed

Fig. 21. (*continued*)

4 Conclusion

With our path-search method, we found that the surgical straightness and obstacle avoidance of the selected path could be adjusted by voxel width, threshold, and C value. The number of voxels to be investigated when searching for V0 in the next layer was fixed in this study at nine. However, by making this range adjustable, a more flexible path may be found.

In the human body, the importance of arteries, veins, nerves, and lymphatic system components varies depending on the type and thickness of their passages. By considering the type and thickness of the tubes in the calculation of density value, a more detailed control mechanism becomes possible.

In this study, we used STL as a model for arteries, veins, and malignant tumors, but by generating voxel groups from DICOM data at an arbitrary line of sight, it will become possible to perform pathfinding directly from the DICOM data structure [15].

Additionally, instead of searching along the Pc–Pe line, if voxels were to be considered as nodes and if the ease of movement between nodes were to be regarded as a distance, a path connecting Pc to Pe could be determined using a graph search (e.g., A* or Dijkstra [16, 17]). Then, the algorithm would find a path as long as it exists.

5 Furure Works

First, we compare the paths generated by this algorithm with those generated by conventional potential and sensor-based algorithms, and evaluate their strengths and weaknesses. Second, we build software to create flexible resolution 3D voxel maps from DICOM to speed up surgical navigation. Finally, we will represent brain shifts triggered by deformations of the brain surface taken under shadow-free light in its voxel map.

Acknowledgements. This study was supported partly by the 2020 Grants-in-Aid for Scientific Research (No. 20K04407) from the Ministry of Education, Culture, Sports, Science and Technology, Japan.

References

1. https://en.wikipedia.org/wiki/Automotive_navigation_system
2. https://en.wikipedia.org/wiki/Inertial_navigation_system
3. https://en.wikipedia.org/wiki/Motion_planning
4. https://en.wikipedia.org/wiki/Robot_navigation
5. StealthStation ™ S8 surgical navigation system at Rambam Medical Center. https://www.you tube.com/watch?v=tUtuPIIO7DY
6. Onishi, K., et al.: Virtual liver surgical simulator by using Z-buffer for object deformation. In: Antona, Margherita, Stephanidis,.Constantine (eds.) UAHCI 2015. LNCS, vol. 9177, pp. 345–351. Springer, Cham (2015). https://doi.org/10.1007/978-3-319-20684-4_34
7. Noborio, H., et al.: Fast surgical algorithm for cutting with liver standard triangulation language format using Z-buffers in graphics processing unit. In: Fujie, M.G. (ed.) Computer Aided Surgery, pp. 127–140. Springer, Tokyo (2016). https://doi.org/10.1007/978-4-431-55810-1_11
8. Koeda, M., et al.: Depth camera calibration and knife tip position estimation for liver surgery support system. In: Stephanidis, C. (ed.) HCI 2015. CCIS, vol. 528, pp. 496–502. Springer, Cham (2015). https://doi.org/10.1007/978-3-319-21380-4_84
9. Noborio, H., Kunii, T., Mizushino, K.: Comparison of GPU-based and CPU-based algorithms for determining the minimum distance between a CUSA scalper and blood vessels, pp. 128–136. The SCITEPRESS Digital Library (Science and Technology Publications, Lda) (2016). https://doi.org/10.5220/0005634801280136. ISBN 978-989-758-170-0
10. Noborio, H., Kunii, T., Mizushino, K.: GPU-based omnidirectional shortest distance algorithm and its evaluation by changing GPU cores. In: Proceedings of the 13th International Conference of Computational Intelligence methods for Bioinformatics and Biostatistics (CIBB2016), The University of Stirling, Scotland, UK, pp. 76–81 (Sept 2016)
11. Noborio, H., Kunii, T., Mizushino, K.: Omni-directional shortest distance algorithm by complete parallel-processing based on GPU cores. Int. J. Biosci. Biochem. Bioinf. **8**(2), 79–88 (2018). https://doi.org/10.17706/ijbbb.2018.8.2.79-88. ISSN 2010-3638
12. Noborio, H., Aoki, K., Kunii, T., Mizushino, K.: A potential function-based scalpel navigation method that avoids blood vessel groups during excision of cancerous tissue. In: Proceedings of the 38th Annual International Conference of the IEEE Engineering in Medicine and Biology Society (EMBC2016), Orlando, FL, USA, pp. 6106–6112 (Aug 2016)
13. Noborio, H., Kawai, K., Watanabe, K., Tachibana, K., Kunii, T., Mizushino, K.: Deadlock-free and collision-free liver surgical navigation by switching potential-based and sensor-based functions. In: Kurosu, M. (ed.) HCII 2020. LNCS, vol. 12183, pp. 604–622. Springer, Cham (2020). https://doi.org/10.1007/978-3-030-49065-2_42

14. Kunii, T., Asano, M., Fujita, K., Tachibana, K., Noborio, H.: Comparative study of potential-based and sensor-based surgical navigation in several liver environments. In: Kurosu, M. (ed.) Human-Computer Interaction. Human Values and Quality of Life. HCII 2021. Lecture Notes in Computer Science, Springer (2021, to appear)
15. https://en.wikipedia.org/wiki/DICOM#Data_format
16. Hart, P.E., Nilsson, N.J., Raphael, B.: A formal basis for the heuristic determination of minimal cost paths. IEEE Trans. Syst. Sci. Cybern. **4**(2), 100–107 (1968)
17. Dijkstra, E.W.: A note on two problems in connexion with graphs. Numer. Math. **1**, 269–271 (1959)

Development of a VR/HMD System for Simulating Several Scenarios of Post-Operative Delirium

Jumpei Matsuura[1], Takahiro Kunii[2(✉)], Hiroshi Noborio[3(✉)], Kaoru Watanabe[3(✉)], Katsuhiko Onishi[3(✉)], and Hideo Nakamura[4(✉)]

[1] Naragakuen University, Nara, Nara Prefecture, Japan
jmatsuura@nara-su.ac.jp
[2] Kashina System Co., Hikone, Shiga Prefecture, Japan
kunii@tetera.jp
[3] Department of Computer Science, OECU, Neyagawa, Osaka Prefecture, Japan
{nobori,kaoru,onishi}@osakac.ac.jp
[4] Department of Health-Promotion and Sports Science, OECU, Neyagawa, Osaka Prefecture, Japan
h-nakamu@osakac.ac.jp

Abstract. In this study, we used a virtual reality system, referred to as Unity, to simulate the world of the onset of postoperative delirium, as observed by patients with postoperative delirium, which cannot be realized in the real world. Here, we had the subject view the data created with Unity by connecting it to Oculus Quest 2 (head mounted display, HMD). Subsequently, we asked the participants to simulate the onset of delirium in two ways: by connecting the data created by Unity to Oculus Quest 2 (HMD) and by watching the video created by Unity on the display. We allowed nursing students to evaluate whether the system was highly realistic and convenient based on subjective data (i.e., questionnaire survey form) and objective data (i.e., physiological data, such as an autonomic nervous system).

Keywords: VR/HMD · Post-operative delirium · Hallucination · Simulating

1 Introduction

Delirium is a syndrome based on clouded consciousness with attention deficits that are caused by a temporary loss of brain functions. Its symptoms include restlessness disorientation hallucinations violent behavior and other symptoms that appear rapidly and fluctuate throughout the day [1]. According to the diagnostic criteria of the American Psychiatric Association (DSM-5) [2], delirium is diagnosed when all of the following symptoms are present: impaired consciousness, impaired cognitive functions, diurnal fluctuations, and causative physical factors or medications [3]. Owing to the aging of patients eligible for surgery, increasing severity of the disorder, and rising incidence of health-related complications, the prevalence of postoperative delirium is not expected to decrease in the future [4].

© Springer Nature Switzerland AG 2021
M. Kurosu (Ed.): HCII 2021, LNCS 12763, pp. 582–600, 2021.
https://doi.org/10.1007/978-3-030-78465-2_42

Intervention of postoperative delirium by nurses is also difficult as the onset of delirium occurs during the night when fewer medical personnel are present; hence, the detection of the onset of delirium is delayed. Although postoperative delirium is more likely to occur in elderly patients in acute cases after surgery, risk assessment and preventive care is dependent on the experience of each nurse. In addition, 95.7% of clinical nurses are aware of the difficulties in delirium care, but effective nursing care is not established to date [5]. Previous studies have reported that nurses who have not acquired sufficient knowledge on how to handle delirium cases are more likely to experience negative emotions such as anger and fear toward patients who develop delirium [6].

The three factors that contribute to the development of delirium are as follows: preparatory, direct, and inducing factors. Preparatory factors are the chronic central nervous system vulnerabilities of the patient, such as old age, dementia, and chronic cerebrovascular disease. Direct factors include drug addiction, central nervous system disease, metabolic disorders that affect the brain, and alcohol withdrawal. Meanwhile, inducing factors include psychological and social stress, sleep disturbance, sensory deprivation or sensory overload, and physical restraint or forced beum has three types: hypoactive type, which is characterized by depression and somnolence; hyperactive type, which is characterized by psychomotor agitation, such as verbal abuse of nurses, violent behaviors, and attempts to self-remove intravenous (IV) tubing; and mixed type, which is a combination of the hypoactive and hyperactive types.

Nurses cannot realistically see the world of postoperative delirium as patients are experiencing this condition. However, if nurses can experience postoperative delirium that the patients are experiencing, they will be able to relate to the thoughts and feelings of postoperative delirium patients. This case might change their treatment toward those patients and might be able to provide effective nursing care for postoperative delirium patients.

The greatest advantage of conducting research using virtual reality (VR) is that it can reproduce and simulate in VR, which is impossible or difficult to perform in reality.

Regarding research in the field of nursing using VR, Shimogawara [7] reported that a developed VR dementia experience program that simulates the world experienced by dementia patients has been effective for determining how dementia patients feel and to be closer to hearts. In addition, there have been studies on the world experienced by patients with schizophrenia [8]. However, research that internationally simulates postoperative delirium in three dimensions using VR is not available thus far.

In this study, we conduct basic research to develop a program to simulate the onset of postoperative delirium through VR to simulate the world of postoperative delirium patients so that effective future nursing care can be determined.

2   Method

2.1   Postoperative Delirium VR Video Creation

All ICU. Postoperative delirium often occurs in ICUs. To simulate delirium in VR, we used the hospital ward asset in Unity's Asset Store and Used the Intensive Care Unit (ICU) room (Fig. 1).

Fig. 1. Overall view of the ICU.

This asset has a hospital bed and equipment, such as IVs and monitors (Fig. 2).

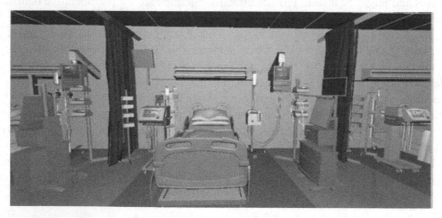

Fig. 2. Bed and peripheral equipment.

As the onset of postoperative delirium occurs at night, we recreated a dark hospital room (Figs. 3 and 4).

Fig. 3. ICU at night.

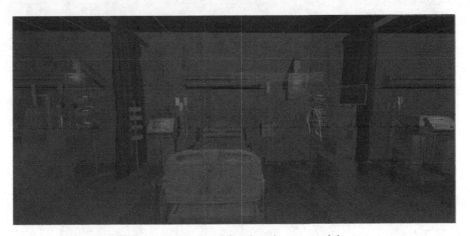

Fig. 4. Beds and peripheral equipment at night.

Audio in the ICU. The monitoring sound of the heart rate monitor and horror-like background music were implemented on Unity for the VR video.

In an actual ICU, the monitoring sound of the heart rate monitor is played 24 h a day. Thus, we created an empty game object to monitor the real-world heart rate in the hospital room. Further, we selected the Audio Source in the Add Component section, which allows me to add sound to the Audio Clip. The heart rate monitor sound we used was 65627300 from PIXTA. We added the Audio Source and used PIXTA's 65627300 for the heart-rate monitor sound and PIXTA's 37370267 for the horror-style background music. We used.wav as the audio file format to play the audio in Unity and enabled Play On Awake and Loop in Audio Source (Figs. 5 and 6).

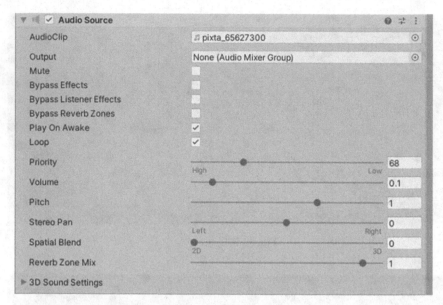

Fig. 5. Sound setting of heart rate monitor.

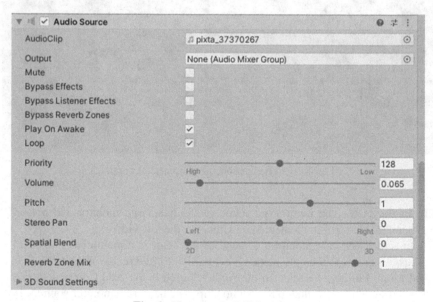

Fig. 6. Horror-style BGM settings.

Hallucinations: Appearance of Small Insects. One of the symptoms of postoperative delirium is hallucination of seeing small insects, such as cockroaches, that do not actually exist. Hence, we used Unity to recreate this hallucination: seven cockroaches suddenly appeared on the ceiling, moved horizontally and vertically for 3 min, and then disappeared (Figs. 7 and 8).

Fig. 7. Before the appearance of insects on the ceiling.

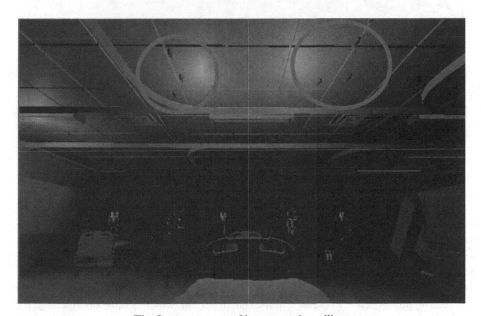

Fig. 8. Appearance of insects on the ceiling.

We created a phenomenon in which a cockroach suddenly appeared and disappeared from the ceiling. The program for creating this phenomenon is presented in Fig. 9.

```
1.          var pos=new Vector3(-2.356f,3.37f,-2.151f);
2.            var pos1=new Vector3(-2.356f,30.03f,-2.151f);
3.          timer1 += Time.deltaTime;
4.
5.          if(timer1 >= 180.0f)
6.          {
7.              // Put it on the ceiling
8.              if(timer1 <= 180.2f){
9.                  transform.position = pos;
10.             }
11.
12.             timer += Time.deltaTime;
13.             if(timer >=time){
14.             timer=0.0f;
15.             }
16.             else if(timer >= time/2){
17.             float z =  -1*speed;
18.             rb.AddForce(z, 0, 0);
19.             }else{
20.             float z =  speed;
21.             rb.AddForce(z, 0, 0);
22.             }
23.         }
24.         if(timer1 >= 360.0f){
25.             // Move it out of sight
26.             if(timer1 <=360.2f){
27.                 transform.position = pos1;
28.             }
29.         }
```

Fig. 9. Part of the script for the appearance and disappearance of cockroaches.

Hallucinations: Appearance of a Person Wearing a Protective Suit. The appearance of a person wearing a protective suit is one of the symptoms of postoperative delirium. When a non-existent person appears in front of the patient, the patient may experience psychomotor agitation. Therefore, we created hallucination in Unity. We used "The Scientist" from the Asset Store as the person who appeared wearing a protective suit. Further, we used this asset and placed it on the left side of the VR image from where the patient was sleeping. Then, we used the Shader function of Unity to add transparency to the whole body (Figs. 10 and 11). The reason for this was to create a sense of fear by creating transparency to create a non-existent person, which is only a hallucinogenic symptom.

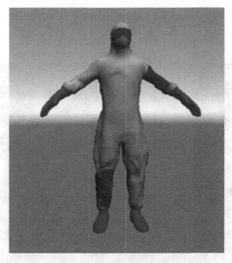

Fig. 10. Person in protective clothing (before Shader).

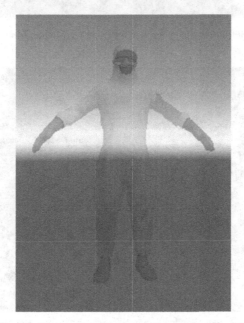

Fig. 11. Person in protective clothing (after Shader).

Hallucination: Setting Up a Phenomenon of Appearance and Disappearance of a Person Wearing a Protective Suit. We created a phenomenon wherein a person wearing protective clothing suddenly appeared in front of the left side of the bed and then disappeared. We set up the system in Unity so that the person will suddenly appear on the left side of the bed (Fig. 13) from nowhere (Fig. 12). This phenomenon was set to occur repeatedly to induce the hallucination symptom of a person suddenly appearing and disappearing.

Fig. 12. Before the appearance of a person wearing a protective suit.

Fig. 13. Appearance of a person wearing a protective suit.

The program for creating this hallucination is presented in Fig. 14. In the program for the appearance and disappearance of a person, a new variable was placed in line 4. This variable was set to move to a position 4 m up in the y direction from the initial value (i.e., the coordinates of the place where the asset was placed). Then, in line 7, we used Time.deltaTime to measure the time. Lines 9–21 use conditional expressions, of which line 12 is the process of moving the asset with a 4 m distance from the set location in the y-direction until 10 s have passed. In lines 13–21, there is a conditional expression, and in line 14, the conditional expression is set to appear at the set location after 10 s have elapsed. In lines 16–21, when 15 s have elapsed, the timer is moved to a location with a 4 m distance from the y-direction. In lines 16–21, when 15 s have passed, the object is moved to a distance 4 away from the y-direction, and the timer is reset. Therefore, the timer is set to 0, and a new count is started to ensure that this process works repeatedly.

```
1.      void Update()

2.         {

3.              // Move in the y direction from the initial value

4.              var pos = new Vector3(Sposi.x, Sposi.y + 4.0f, Sposi.z);

5.

6.              // measurement of time

7.              timer += Time.deltaTime;

8.

9.              if(timer <= 10.0f){

10.             // 10s Move in the y direction from the initial value until
it elapses

11.                 transform.position = pos;

12.             }

13.             else{

14.                 // 10s If it exceeds, it will move to the initial value

15.                 transform.position = Sposi;

16.                 if(timer >= 15.0f){

17.                 // 15s After that, move the object in the y direction and reset
the timer.

18.                     transform.position = pos;

19.                     timer = 0;

20.                 }

21.             }

22.         }
```

Fig. 14. Part of the script for the appearance/disappearance phenomenon of a person wearing a protective suit.

Hallucination: Reproduction of a Looming Ceiling. We used Unity to recreate the hallucinations of the ceiling as a symptom of delirium because the onset of delirium leads to a state of confusion and excitement due to fear.

Initially, the ceiling is observed in Unity (Fig. 15), but after 2 min, the ceiling starts to loom (Fig. 16). After another 2 min, the ceiling will close in on itself (Fig. 16), and when it reaches a certain point, it will return to its initial position, and then we set the repetition of this process.

Fig. 15. Before the ceiling approaches.

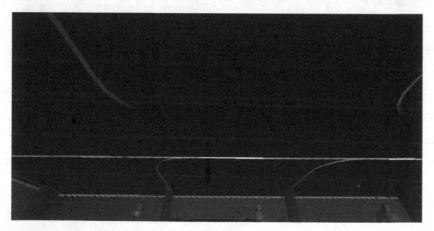

Fig. 16. Hallucinatory script approaching the ceiling.

Figure 17 shows part of the script used to create the looming ceiling phenomenon in Unity. In this program, the fourth line takes the current coordinate and treats it as the initial value, and the sixth line sets the position to be 0.1 m/s down in the y-direction from the initial position. Finally, in lines 8–10, a conditional expression was used to set the position to return to the initial position when it exceeded the 2.5 m coordinate in the y-direction. This process was set to occur repeatedly.

```
1.      void Update()↵
2.          {↵
3.              // Get the position of an object↵
4.              Vector3 Posi = this.gameObject.transform.position;↵
5.              // Move in the y direction from the acquired position↵
6.              this.gameObject.transform.position = new Vector3(Posi.x,
Posi.y - 0.1f * Time.deltaTime, Posi.z);↵
7.              // If the y direction exceeds 2.5f, it returns to the initial
position.↵
8.              if(Posi.y < 2.5f){↵
9.                  transform.position = Sposi;↵
10.             }↵
11.         }↵
```

Fig. 17. Part of a hallucinatory script approaching the ceiling.

Hallucination: Reproduction of the Appearance of Soldiers. We created a phenomenon wherein a soldier suddenly appeared in front of the left side of the bed, and in Unity, the soldier appeared on the left side of the bed (Fig. 19) from an empty space (Fig. 18). By setting this phenomenon repeatedly, we were able to recreate the hallucination of a soldier suddenly appearing.

Fig. 18. Before the appearance of soldiers.

Fig. 19. Soldier appearance.

In this program, the first line specified the coordinates where the soldier would come out, and the second line specified the coordinates where the soldier would be invisible to the subject. The time was set in the third line. The appearance of the soldier, as shown

```
1.      var pos=new Vector3(-4.66f,0.03f,-2.25f);
2.      var pos1=new Vector3(-4.66f,30.03f,-2.25f);
3.      timer += Time.deltaTime;
4.
5.      if(timer >= 420.0f)
6.      {
7.      // Put next to the bet
8.      if(timer <= 420.2f){
9.      transform.position = pos;
10.     }
11.     }
12.     if(timer >= 600.0f){
13.     transform.position = pos1;
14.     }
```

Fig. 20. Part of the soldier appearance script.

in Fig. 19, was set in line 9; the coordinates of pos1 were obtained in line 13, and the soldier was set to appear at those coordinates (Fig. 20).

2.2 Data Collection Method

The subjects were third- and fourth-year students enrolled in a nursing college (seven male and seven female).

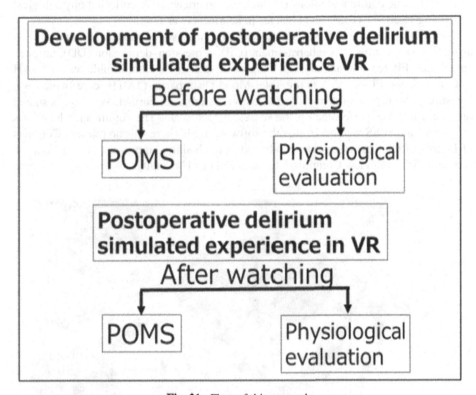

Fig. 21. Flow of this research.

This study was conducted using the following procedures (Fig. 21):

(1) A virtual reality system (Unity) was used to create a 12-min video of a postoperative delirium patient's view of the world, which is unrealizable in the real world.
   The contents of the videos were in the following order at 2-min intervals: no change, cockroaches appear, ceiling falls, people in protective clothing appear, soldiers attack, and no change.
(2) The data created by Unity were connected to the Oculus Quest 2 (head mounted display, HMD) (Fig. 22) to be viewed (Fig. 23).
(3) A video of the world of postoperative delirium created by Unity was played on a display (ASUS VX239).

The above two methods (HMD and display) were used to simulate the onset of delirium. We collected and analyzed subjective data (i.e., questionnaire survey form) and objective data (i.e., physiological data, such as an autonomic nervous system) as evaluation items. We asked the participants whether they felt more immersed in the HMD or the display used to view the images of the world of postoperative delirium.

For the subjective and objective data, we created a simulated postoperative delirium experience using Unity to recreate the postoperative state in the ICU ward, and then we measured the mood of the subjects using the Profile of Mood States (POMS II) mood evaluation scale before and after the simulated experience. We collected physiological data using HeartBIT (IBM) and changes in heartbeat over time.

The POMS II scale assesses a wide range of mood states with seven items: anger–hostility (AH), confusion–embarrassment (CB), depression–depression (DD), fatigue–anhedonia (FI), tension–anxiety (TA), vigor–energetic (VA), and friendliness (F). -AH + CB + DD + FI + TAVA is the Total Mood Disturbance (TMD) score, which is a measure of the degree of distress and affective disturbance. Further, Wilcoxon's signed rank sum test was performed on the scores of each scale. The significance level was set to 5%, and SPSS version 26 was the software used. There was no relevant Conflicts of Interest: COI. This study was conducted after obtaining approval (2–001) from the Research Ethics Review Committee of Nara Gakuen University.

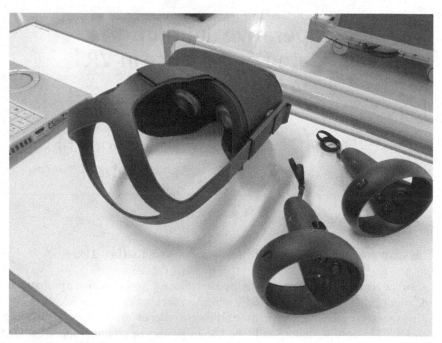

Fig. 22. Oculus Quest 2 (head mount display: HMD).

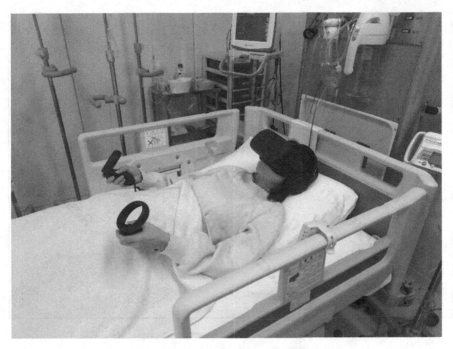

Fig. 23. Subject wearing an HMD.

3 Result

The stress level of the participants was measured from the autonomic nervous system during their viewing of the images of the world of the onset of postoperative delirium using an HMD (no change → cockroaches appear → ceiling falls → people in protective clothing appear → soldiers attack → no change). The results were compared between the groups (no change, cockroaches appear, ceiling falls, people in protective clothing appear, soldiers attack, no change), but no significant differences were found (Fig. 24).

Each mean value of POMS2 is shown as pre- and post-event. AH: 3.6 ± 5.16 and 5.7 ± 5.68. CB: 4.7 ± 6.26 and 12.0 ± 4.51. DD: 3.9 ± 4.85 and 7.7 ± 3.64. FI: 4.7 ± 6.18 and 11.7 ± 5.47. TA: 6.9 ± 6.47 and 16.0 ± 2.89. VA: 9.1 ± 7.22 and 3.4 ± 3.36. F: 15.3 ± 3.09, 8.6 ± 3.36; TMD: 38.0 ± 4.04, 46.3 ± 2.56. The p-values are as follows: AH: $p = 0.172$, CB: $p = 0.018$, DD: $p = 0.028$, FI: $p = 0.018$, TA: $p = 0.028$, VA. The test results showed significant differences in CB, DD, FI, TA, F, and TMD, except for AH and VA (Figs. 25 and 26).

Seven out of seven participants reported that the experience was more realistic when viewed via Oculus Quest 2 (HMD) and when viewed using the display (ASUS VX239).

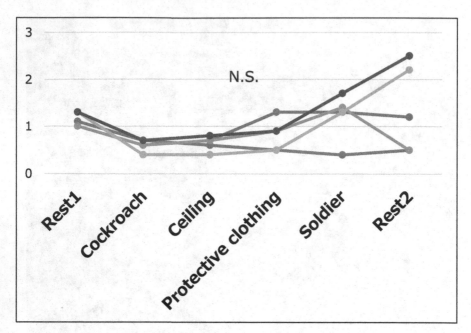

Fig. 24. LF/HF autonomic nerves.

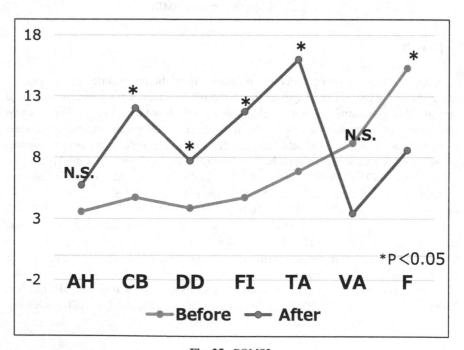

Fig. 25. POMS2.

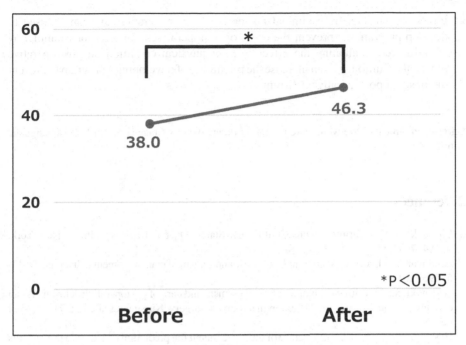

Fig. 26. TMD.

4 Discussion

This study revealed the following two points:

(1) By simulating the world of postoperative delirium in VR using an HMD, we found that mood and emotional states became unfavorable even in healthy subjects.
(2) The simulated experience using the HMD was more realistic than the simulated experience using the display (ASUS VX239).

5 Future Works

In this study, we created a virtual reality monitor and HMD platform that allows users to view video content on postoperative delirium. This makes it easy for anyone, anywhere to simulate the experience postoperative delirium.

However, the following three issues must be addressed in the future:

1. By allowing nurses and nursing students to easily simulate the world of postoperative delirium patients, we hope that they are able to understand the feelings of patients with postoperative delirium.
2. Based on the impressions and comments of postoperative delirium patients who viewed this system, we can concretely improve the quality of postoperative delirium video content and 3D immersive experiences.

3. Physiological data from clinical nurses involved in nursing care can be used to develop programs to prevent the onset of postoperative delirium. For example, by quantitatively evaluating the effect of prior physical condition on post-operative physical condition, we can increase the possibility of developing a program to prevent the onset of postoperative delirium.

Acknowledgements. We would like to thank Editage (www.editage.com) for English language editing.

References

1. Lipowski, Z.J.: Delirium. Acute Confusional States. Oxford University Press, New York, pp. 54–70 (1990)
2. American Psychiatric Association: Diagnostic and statistical manual of mental disorders DSM-5. 596 (2014)
3. Watanuki, S.: Algorithm development of assessment and care of postoperative delirium. As an example a typical surgery in the abdominal thoracic surgery. Nursing research **38**(7), 543–554 (2005)
4. Hasegawa, M.: Assessment structure of the nurses about the prediction of acute elderly patients of delirium occurs. Magazine of St. Luke's Nursing Society **10**(1), 1–10 (2006)
5. Hasegawa, M.: Current situation and problems of delirium care of femur fractures hospitalized patients in Kanagawa. Kanagawa University of Human Services Magazine **2**(1), 3–11 (2005)
6. Inouye, S.K.: Nurses' recognition of delirium and its symptoms comparison of nurse and researcher ratings. Arch. Intern. Med. **161**, 2467–2473 (2001)
7. Shimogawara, T.: Application of VR in nursing: fostering person-centered care through VR dementia experience. J. Japan. Soc. Nurs. Educ. **29**, 64 (2019)
8. Kameyama, K.: The meaning of simulated schizophrenia experiences for nursing students. using the Japanese version of virtual halucination. J. Japan. Soc. Nurs. **15**(2), 25–35 (2006)

Selection and Evaluation of Color/Depth Camera for Imaging Surgical Stoma

Michiru Mizoguchi[1]($\boxtimes$), Masatoshi Kayaki[2], Tomoki Yoshikawa[4], Miho Asano[3], Katsuhiko Onishi[4], and Hiroshi Noborio[4]

[1] Nara Gakuen University, Nakatomigaoka, Nara 631-8524, Japan
michiru-m@nara-su.ac.jp
[2] KAYAKI Studio, Nara-shi, Nara 631-8524, Japan
[3] Preemptive Medicine and Lifestyle-Related Disease Research Center, Kyoto University, Hospital, 54 Shogoinkawahara-cho, Sakyo-ku, Kyoto-shi, Kyoto 606-8507, Japan
[4] Department of Computer Science, Osaka Electro-Communication University, Kiyotaki 1130-70, Shijo-Nawate, Osaka 575-0063, Japan

Abstract. We aim to develop a system to evaluate pouch attachment to and removal from stoma (artificial anus). For preliminary evaluation, we devoted this study to verify if a color/depth camera can accurately capture the stoma shape. Specifically, a 3D scanner was used to take precise images of three stoma models made of human tissue-mimicking gel and with diameters of 3, 6, and 9 cm to obtain the corresponding point clouds. Then, three stoma models were imaged using a color/depth camera to obtain the point clouds. We used the "CloudCompare" software and its implementation of the iterative closest point algorithm to compare the point clouds. Furthermore, the point clouds in the 3D Euclidean space were represented in a polar coordinate system with origin at the center of gravity of the point cloud to obtain the corresponding histograms. Finally, each point cloud and histogram captured by depth camera and 3D scanner were compared. The evaluation results showed that a larger stoma model provides a smaller difference between the point clouds. Nevertheless, the histograms from the three models were similar. Therefore, histogram comparison may be effective for shape recognition of real stoma from point clouds toward the extraction of information for a system to guide pouch management.

Keywords: Stoma · Color/depth camera · 3D scanner · 3D point cloud matching · CloudCompare

1 Introduction

Cancer is the leading cause of death in Japan since 1981 [1], and the incidence of colorectal cancer is expected to increase. Surgical treatment often involves the construction of an artificial anus, also called stoma, in the abdomen to change the route of fecal evacuation depending on the damage site. Discharged feces are collected in a brace called pouch for daily use. Nevertheless, there are many problems related to stomas, with a major problem being the leakage of feces. Furthermore, the survival rate of stoma patients may decrease

© Springer Nature Switzerland AG 2021
M. Kurosu (Ed.): HCII 2021, LNCS 12763, pp. 601–614, 2021.
https://doi.org/10.1007/978-3-030-78465-2_43

during postoperative hospitalization following stoma construction [2], and some stoma patients are discharged without being informed about the basic stoma care due to short hospital stays. Moreover, patients who are not accustomed to the use of stomas may perform poor stoma management, which should be guided by trained medical staff [3].

To address the abovementioned problems, we aimed to produce a support system that allows stoma patients to appropriately attach and remove pouches. In this preliminary study, we acquired images of stoma models using a color/depth camera (RealSense D435 camera, Intel; Santa Clara, CA, USA) and a 3D scanner (Picza 3D scanner; Roland DGA, Irvine, CA, USA) and evaluated the imaging results. The stoma models were made of human tissue-mimicking gel.

In recent years, many compact and affordable color/depth cameras have been commercialized, such as Microsoft Kinect V2, Intel RealSense L515 LiDAR camera, Intel RealSense D415, D435, and D455 cameras, and OccipitalSCS (ARGO Co.). In addition, various types of 3D scanners are available for different purposes.

In this study, we compared the point clouds obtained from stoma models captured by a color/depth camera and a 3D scanner. For the comparison, we used a point cloud processing software that includes an implementation of the iterative closest point algorithm. In addition, the point clouds in the 3D Euclidean space were represented in polar coordinate systems to obtain their histograms to generate input data for a machine learning method to be implemented in future work.

In Sect. 2, we describe the 3D color/depth sensor and 3D scanner used in this study. In Sect. 3, we detail the evaluation of the point cloud shapes for three stoma models with diameters of 3, 6, and 9 cm. In Sect. 4, we report and analyze experimental results of the point cloud evaluation. Finally, we present the discussion, conclusions, and directions of future work in Sects. 5, 6, and 7, respectively.

2   3D Color/Depth Camera and 3D Scanner

2.1   Color/Depth Cameras

A color/depth camera can simultaneously capture consistent color and depth information. The Microsoft Kinect camera was released in November 2010 as a sensing system that captures color images along with pixel-by-pixel depth information. This camera uses active stereo and time-of-flight sensing to generate depth estimation with high pixel density [4, 5]. The Kinect camera can be used to capture human motion, identify faces, and recognize voices [6]. With the advent of Kinect, color/depth cameras have become lighter, more compact, and less expensive, enabling their widespread use in a variety of fields, from business, service problem solving, and entertainment to robotics, design, and technologies such as simultaneous self-positioning and environmental mapping [7, 8]. Moreover, approximately 77% of studies relying on data from color/depth cameras have mentioned the Kinect camera since 2011 [7].

2.2   3D Scanner

Since its introduction, 3D scanning has been a widely used method, despite of requiring contact with the target in its beginnings. Among its numerous applications, 3D scanning has been valuable for archaeologists and museum curators to restore, replicate, and enhance the preservation of valuable artifacts that have been recovered from excavations [9].

The Picza 3D scanner performs non-contact laser measurements through a laser beam directed to the target to be scanned. Thus, it allows to nondestructively acquire the target shape at high speed. In addition, it provides a software to combine two operation modes, planar and rotational scan, to improve the measurements from objects with complex shapes. Furthermore, it allows to extract data from characteristic points of the target [10].

3 Comparison of Sensing Accuracy

3.1 Stoma and Color/Depth Camera Selection

In this study, we assumed the target to be a stoma in the colon of a patient. Thus, the center of gravity is assumed to be slightly depressed and wrinkled. The stoma color looks red because it is filled with blood and moistened by mucus. In addition, the stoma becomes edematous after surgery by the disturbance of venous circulation in the intestine due to the surgical intervention. The size of the stoma decreases around 7 days after the surgery and usually settles to approximately 3 cm in diameter. The stoma also protrudes the colon into the abdomen and folds the inner colonic mucosa outward. A stoma pouch according to the final stoma size is then attached for evacuation. Therefore, the imaging target in this study resembles a real stoma with approximately 3 cm in diameter.

There are many compact and affordable color/depth cameras commercially available. Among them, we evaluated the Intel RealSense D415 camera (hereinafter referred to as D415 camera) and Intel RealSense D435 camera (hereinafter referred to as D435 camera). The main difference between these cameras is the depth field of view. The D415 camera has a narrower viewing angle due to its narrower focus, whereas the D435 camera has a wider field of view due to stereo cameras on its left and right sides, allowing to cover more area and reduce blind spots. Although the D435 camera has more than twice the depth noise in any given range, it can get closer to the target object with the same resolution and enables a shorter minimum shooting distance than the D415 camera. Therefore, we selected the D435 camera for imaging the stoma with 3 cm in diameter.

3.2 Comparison Between Color/Depth Camera Images and 3D Scans to Capture Stoma

The D435 camera is widely used in robotics, augmented reality, and virtual reality owing to its wide field of view and maximum depth distance of 10 m. However, for the comparative evaluation in this experiment, the target object was a stoma with a size of approximately 3 cm in diameter and 1.5–2 cm in height. In addition, we considered enlarged stomas of 6 and 9 cm in diameter as imaging targets. The surface of the stoma is slightly semicircular, and its periphery is in close contact with the abdomen. Therefore, to capture depth images of a real stoma, images from different viewing angles should be captured. In this study, the accuracy of the acquired images were evaluated separately for each size under the same imaging conditions.

We used the 3D scanner to capture the position of the laser beam as it hit the target surface by beam emission through a horizontal slit. The laser beam produces a point cloud consisting of tens or hundreds of thousands of points. This point cloud can be used to calculate the detailed distances to an object and obtain 3D coordinates. Furthermore, the Picza LPX-1200 3D scanner used in this study has a high resolution with a minimum scan pitch of 0.1 mm. We used the data acquired by the 3D scan as the ground truth for comparison and evaluation with the images from the stoma models of 3, 6, and 9 cm acquired by the D435 camera.

For the evaluation, we used "CloudCompare", a highly stable open-source software for point cloud meshing, manipulation, processing, and comparison [11]. "CloudCompare" can use the iterative closest point algorithm to align two point clouds (rigid body registration). Alignment is achieved by alternately finding the correspondence of the points belonging to the two point clouds and the parameters of the rotation matrix (R) and translation vector (t) and repeatedly minimizing the evaluation results. The basic concept is finding a candidate correspondence for each point in point cloud X with the closest point in point cloud Y. Next, the parameters of the rotation matrix (R) and translation vector (t) that transform point cloud X into point cloud Y are determined. Then, point cloud Y closest to each point of point cloud RX + t is then extracted, and the process is repeated until the distance between the corresponding point clouds is minimized. Positioning can only be performed if there is a shape match between the two point clouds of the target. Thus, a manual operation is required under discrepancies. When aligning multiple point clouds, the origin of the local coordinate system of the point cloud in the measurement frame is set as the origin of the global coordinate system, and the point cloud in the next measurement frame is aligned to it and integrated into the resulting point cloud. Finally, the point clouds obtained from the D435 camera and 3D scanner images are matched for the stoma models of 3, 6, and 9 cm in diameter, and the overlapping and point cloud distances can be evaluated.

4 Experimental Results of Imaging Accuracy

4.1 Experimental Setup

The experiment was conducted in a room resembling a hospital environment. According to the illuminance standard of the Japanese Industrial Standards, the illuminance of a hospital room should be 100–300 lx, and that of a treatment room should be 300–750 lx. In this experiment, the room was kept at a constant illuminance of 300 lx. The resolution of the depth map was set to 1280 × 720 pixels, and the D435 camera was fixed at approximately 40 cm from the target (Fig. 1(a)). A characteristic object is needed for positioning. As the stoma is almost spherical and cannot serve as reference, we fabricated a cubic (3 × 3 × 4 cm) reference. Then, the real stoma was placed on a base using the cubic reference as the characteristic object. (Fig. 1(b)). The D435 camera and real stoma were aligned with respect to the center of gravity of the stoma.

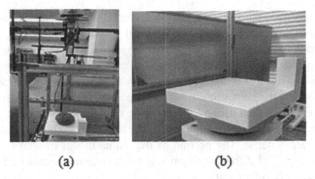

(a)   (b)

Fig. 1. Experimental setup. (a) Fixed D435 camera and (b) base with cubic reference for positioning

4.2 Coordinate Alignment Between Color/Depth Camera and 3D Scanner Point Clouds

The real stoma was placed at the center of gravity of the base (Fig. 2(a)). The stoma models with diameters of 3, 6, and 9 cm were rotated for imaging in angles of 0°, 90°, 180°, and 270° clockwise, and the base was tilted in angles of 0°, 20°, and 40° (Figs. 2(b), (c)). The images were taken after the stoma settled in a stable posture (Figs. 2(d), (e)).

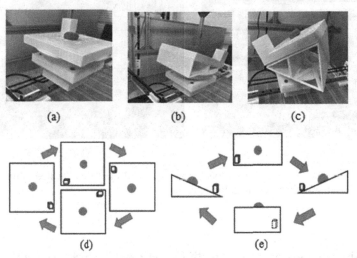

(a)   (b)   (c)

(d)   (e)

Fig. 2. Base tilted (a) 0°, (b) 20°, and (c) 40°. Clockwise rotations of 0°, 90°, 180°, and 270° (d) without tilting and (e) with tilting angle

Then, images taken with the rotated views of 0°, 90°, 180°, and 270° were converted into 3D point clouds. For each stoma view, the marked base where the real stoma was placed was retained, and the other points were excluded. We set "CloudCompare" to merge a pair of point clouds (Fig. 3(a)). We first merged the point clouds of the base and reference without the stoma for viewing angles of 0° and 90°, 180° and 270°. Then, two more point clouds were merged, one with the reference and stoma rotated 0° and 90°, and the other with the reference and stoma rotated 180° and 270°.

The merged point clouds were automatically aligned by the iterative closest point algorithm and manually aligned when the stoma model point clouds were inconsistent. An affine transformation was applied with respect to the cubic reference, and after merging and scaling, the point clouds were rotated and scaled (Fig. 3(d)). The merged base with reference was then removed to preserve only the stoma model.

Then, the 3D scanner was used to capture the real stoma. The point cloud captured by the 3D scanner is dense. The portion of the stoma model imaged using the D435 camera was set to 1/1000 of the imaging using the 3D scanner because the stoma model had approximately 40 to 50 point groups.

In "CloudCompare", the point clouds obtained from the D435 camera and 3D scanner images were compared with respect to the same coordinate system. The processed point cloud obtained from the D435 camera and the point cloud obtained from the 3D scanner were combined to determine the overlap and point cloud distance error. When imaging at base tilting angles of 20° and 40°, the real stoma moved to the lower side, which may reduce the imaging accuracy, but the iterative closest point algorithm allows overlapping in four directions. In addition, the position was fixed and constant for images acquired by the D435 camera, and the error remained in the distance range of the camera.

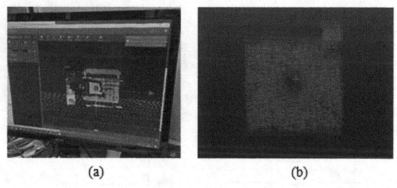

(a)   (b)

Fig. 3. (a) Point clouds merged in "CloudCompare". (b) Rotated and scaled point clods after merging and scaling with respect to cubic reference

4.3   Consistency Between Color/Depth Camera and 3D Scanner Point Clouds of Complete Stoma

We processed the images of the stoma model taken at clockwise rotations of 0°, 90°, 180°, and 270° and base tilting angles of 20° and 40°. First, the image of each rotation angle was viewed from the side, leaving the base with the reference where the real stoma was placed and removing the rest of the image. This was done for each rotation, and the images were converted into point clouds.

Again, we set "CloudCompare" to merge pairs of point clouds. We first merged the images containing the base with the cubic reference but without the real stoma for viewing angles of 0° and 90°, 180° and 270°. Then, another pair of point clouds was merged, one point cloud with the base with the reference and real stoma for viewing angles of 0° and 90°, and another one with the base with the reference and real stoma for viewing angles of 180° and 270°. Merging was performed manually by using the reference as marker, and the stoma model was removed from the merged base with the reference. All the processes for the stoma model at tilting angles of 20° and 40° were performed as for the tilting of 0°.

Each real stoma was imaged using the 3D scanner at tilting angles of 20° and 40°. The real stoma captured by the 3D scanner was converted from the STL format into a point cloud and combined with the stoma model captured by the D435 camera. These processes were performed as for the tilting of 0° (Fig. 4).

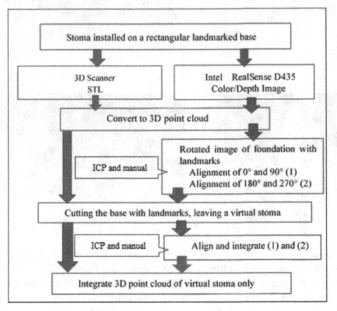

Fig. 4. Matching of point clouds obtained from color/depth camera and 3D scanner. (ICP, iterative closest point)

Each point cloud obtained from the D435 camera was processed in "CloudCompare". Then, we obtained the distance error between the two point clouds after matching, as shown in Figs. 5, 6 and 7. In the figures, the distance error is encoded in blue, green, yellow, and red from the smallest to the largest error. In the point cloud of the stoma model with 3 cm in diameter, the central excretory opening was indistinguishable (Fig. 5), whereas in that with 6 cm in diameter, the opening was only recognizable (Fig. 6), and in that with 9 cm in diameter, the opening was clearly distinguishable (Fig. 7).

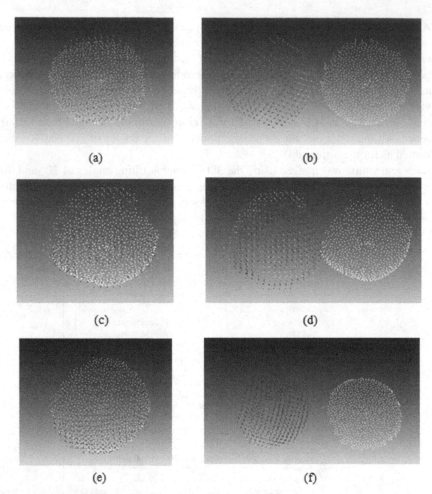

Fig. 5. Point cloud matching of stoma model with 3 cm in diameter. (a) Matched point clouds obtained from D435 camera at 0° tilting and 3D scanner. (b) Point cloud obtained from D435 camera at 0° tilting (left) and 3D scanner (right). (c) Matched point clouds obtained from D435 camera at 20° tilting and 3D scanner. (d) Point cloud obtained from D435 camera at 20° tilting (left) and 3D scanner (right). (e) Matched point clouds obtained from D435 camera at 40° tilting and 3D scanner. (f) Point cloud obtained from D435 camera at 40° tilting (left) and 3D scanner (right) (Color figure online)

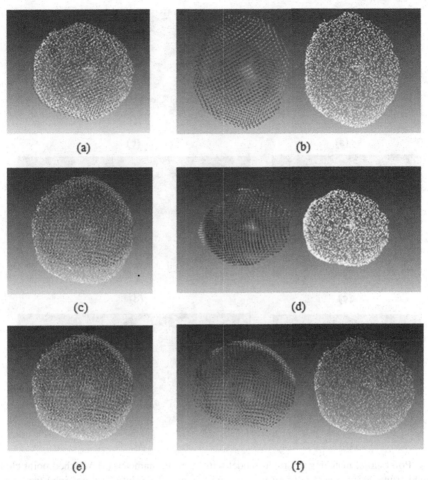

Fig. 6. Point cloud matching of stoma model with 6 cm in diameter. (a) Matched point clouds obtained from D435 camera at 0° tilting and 3D scanner. (b) Point cloud obtained from D435 camera at 0° tilting (left) and 3D scanner (right). (c) Matched point clouds obtained from D435 camera at 20° tilting and 3D scanner. (d) Point cloud obtained from D435 camera at 20° tilting (left) and 3D scanner (right). (e) Matched point clouds obtained from D435 camera at 40° tilting and 3D scanner. (f) Point cloud obtained from D435 camera at 40° tilting (left) and 3D scanner (right) (Color figure online)

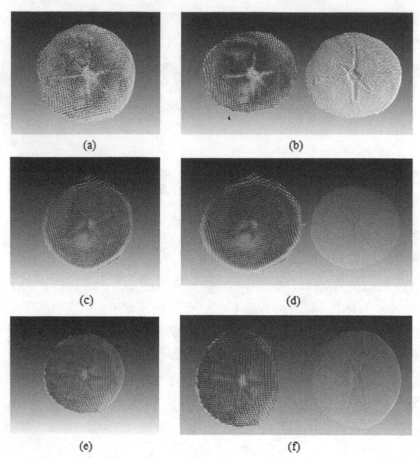

Fig. 7. Point cloud matching of stoma model with 9 cm in diameter. (a) Matched point clouds obtained from D435 camera at 0° tilting and 3D scanner. (b) Point cloud obtained from D435 camera at 0° tilting (left) and 3D scanner (right). (c) Matched point clouds obtained from D435 camera at 20° tilting and 3D scanner. (d) Point cloud obtained from D435 camera at 20° tilting (left) and 3D scanner (right). (e) Matched point clouds obtained from D435 camera at 40° tilting and 3D scanner. (f) Point cloud obtained from D435 camera at 40° tilting (left) and 3D scanner (right) (Color figure online)

We then compared the matching results between point clouds obtained from the D435 camera and 3D scanner according to size, as shown in Figs. 8(a)–(c), and tilting, as shown in Figs. 8(d)–(f). The figures show the point cloud consistency rate (in percentage) according to the distance error tolerance (in millimeters). By size, the point cloud of the 9 cm stoma model had a distance error of 3 mm and a consistency rate above 90%, even under tilting angles of 20° and 40°. On the other hand, the point cloud of the 3 cm stoma model had a high consistency rate under tilting of 0° and a rate of 80–90% for a distance error of 3 mm.

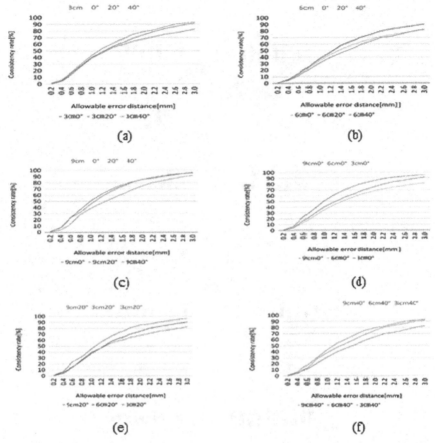

Fig. 8. Distance error tolerance and consistency of matched point clouds obtained from D435 camera and 3D scanner camera. Comparison by size for stoma models with diameter of (a) 3, (b) 6, and (c) 9 cm. Comparison by base tilting of (d) 0°, (e) 20°, and (f) 40°

The point clouds from the stoma model of 3 and 9 cm at tilting of 0° were further compared based on their consistency and distance errors. First, we obtained the center of gravity by averaging the X-, Y-, and Z-axis coordinates from the corresponding point clouds. Next, we calculated the difference between the coordinate points and the center of gravity and calculated the corresponding X-, Y-, and Z-axis vectors. Then, from the center of gravity, the vectors of points on the X, Y, and Z axes were decomposed into their respective components, and rotation angles θX, θY, and θZ around the X, Y, and Z axes were calculated using the arc tangent on the XY-, YZ-, and XZ-plane projections, respectively. The rotation angles between the vector and X, Y, and Z axes are shown as histograms in Fig. 9.

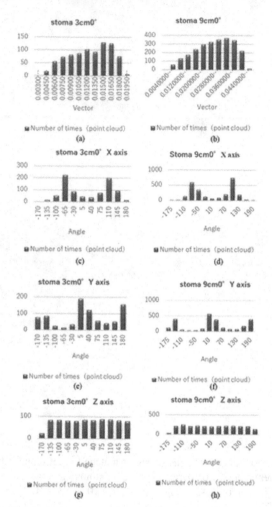

Fig. 9. Vectors and X-, Y-, and Z-axis angles of the point clouds from stoma models of 3 and 9 cm at base tilting of 0°. Vectors for point clouds of stoma models of (a) 3 and (b) 9 cm. X-axis angles for stoma models of (c) 3 and (d) 9 cm. Y-axis angles for stoma models of (e) 3 and (f) 9 cm. Z-axis angles for stoma models of (g) 3 and (h) 9 cm

5 Discussion

In this study, we selected the D435 camera as the sensor that best captures an actual stoma of approximately 3 cm diameter. To evaluate the imaging results in detail considering the small size of the stoma, we prepared models of 3, 6, and 9 cm and compared the corresponding point clouds considering those obtained from a 3D scanner as ground truth. From the evaluation results, the following findings were obtained.

1. Based on the point cloud matching of the stoma model, the smallest target (i.e., the real stoma of 3 cm) can be captured as an object by the D435 camera.

2. Considering the characteristics of the D435 camera, we acquired images from the stoma from various directions. By angle, the consistency rate of the stoma model point cloud of 9 cm was high in all cases. As expected, a larger stoma provided a smaller error and higher consistency rate.

3. The point clouds of the stoma models of 3 and 9 cm in the 3D Euclidean space were represented in polar coordinates. Then, histograms of angles θX, θY, and θZ were calculated. The point cloud distribution in the histogram is about three times larger in all cases for the stoma of 9 cm compared with that of 3 cm. Nevertheless, shape recognition of the stoma model of 3 cm, which is the same size as the actual stoma, can be done stably. In fact, the histograms for the point clouds of stomas of 3 and 9 cm were consistent. In future work, we will explore machine learning methods for nonlinear transformations.

6 Conclusion

No significant difference was observed in the distance error tolerance between the point clouds of the stoma models of 3 and 9 cm. Nevertheless, the point cloud had a higher consistency rate, and the stoma opening was clearly observed in the point cloud of the larger stoma model. Thus, the D435 camera provides the highest accuracy when capturing large stoma. However, various problems remain to be solved to capture an actual stoma.

1. When imaging an actual stoma, it would be difficult to use the setup implemented in this experiment because the D435 camera will have to be moved manually.

2. In this study, we used a cubic reference of $3 \times 3 \times 4$ cm because the circular stoma cannot be used as a reference. However, this reference will not be available when manually moving the D435 camera to acquire actual stoma images.

3. When imaging an actual stoma, conditions such as the light intensity should be carefully considered.

7 Future Work

In this study, we explored the possibility of using a commercially available color/depth camera for imaging stoma. Our goal is to develop a technique for proper and timely pouch removal by the patients through the evaluation of stoma color/depth images. In future work, we will address the following aspects:

1. In this study, we verified the possibility of measuring the actual shape of a stoma by linear expansion using a histogram of polar coordinates. In future work, we will use linear transformations such as affine transformations and nonlinear transformations possibly based on machine learning methods to stably recover the shape of the actual stoma even under poor imaging conditions.

2. In a patient, moisture from perspiration and excretion is absorbed, causing the skin protector to dissolve, decompose, or swell. These effects indicate that the skin protectant no longer works. In this case, captured images and machine learning or other

methods may be used to determine when to replace the pouch. The 3D shape evaluated in this study can be used as a learning input to determine failure of the skin protectant.

3. Once the 3D shape of the actual stoma is accurately obtained, a 3D printer can be used to create a female model of the stoma, and human skin gel can be poured into it to create a rheological stoma that reflects the softness of human tissues. Then, patient training on pouch wearing can be conducted. We are working to combine multiple Geomagic Touch devices [12] to freely manipulate 6-degree-of-freedom force/torque haptics. In addition, we will use the HTC Vive headset to guide procedures related to stoma management [13]. Then, we will create a system for training to properly attach the pouch to the stoma before discharge while the patient lies in bed.

References

1. Ministry of Health, Labor and Welfare, Basic plan for cancer control, https://www.mhlw.go.jp/stf/seisakunitsuite/bunya/0000183313.html. Accessed 28 Nov 2020
2. Takamizawa, E., et al.: A longitudinal study of changes in the subjective quality of life of patients after surgical construction of colostomy. J. Jpn. Soc. Cancer Nurs. **13**(1), 35–42 (1999)
3. Shigeno, T., et al.: Relationship of stoma self-care status with anxiety and QOL in ostomates. J. Jpn Soc. Stoma Continence Rehabil. **33**(3), 71–80 (2017)
4. Zhang, C., Huang, T., Zhao, Q.: A new model of RGB-D camera calibration based on 3D control field. Sensors **19**(23), 5082 (2019)
5. Henry, P., Krainin, M., Herbst, E., Ren, X., Fox, D.: RGB-D mapping: using Kinect-style depth cameras for dense 3D modeling of indoor environments. Int. J. Robot. Res. **31**(5), 647–663 (2012)
6. Han, J., Shao, L., Xu, D., Shotton, J.: Enhanced computer vision with microsoft Kinect sensor: a review. IEEE Trans. Cybern. **43**(5), 1318–1334 (2013)
7. Villena-Martínez, V., et al.: A quantitative comparison of calibration methods for RGB-D sensors using different technologies. Sensors **17**(2), 243 (2017)
8. Ataer-Cansizoglu, E., Taguchi, Y., Ramalingam, S., Garaas, T.: Tracking an RGB-D camera using points and planes, In: Proceedings of the IEEE International Conference on Computer Vision Workshops, pp. 51–58. IEEE (2014)
9. Intel RealSence Technology. https://www.intel.co.jp/content/www/jp/ja/architecture-and-technology/realsense-overview.html. Accessed 28 Nov 2020
10. Al-Baghdadi, M.A.S.: 3D printing and 3D scanning of our ancient history: preservation and protection of our cultural heritage and identity. Int. J. Energ. Environ. **8**(5), 441–456 (2017)
11. CloudCompare Homepage. https://www.danielgm.net/cc/. Accessed 26 Jan 2021
12. Phantom Omni – 6 DOF master device. https://delfthapticslab.nl/device/phantom-omni/. Accessed 26 Jan 2021
13. HTC Vive. https://en.wikipedia.org/wiki/HTC_Vive. Accessed 26 Jan 2021

Investigation of the Hashing Algorithm Extension of Depth Image Matching for Liver Surgery

Satoshi Numata[1]([✉]), Masanao Koeda[2], Katsuhiko Onishi[1], Kaoru Watanabe[1], and Hiroshi Noborio[1]

[1] Osaka Electro-Communication University, Shijonawate Osaka 5750063, Japan
numata@osakac.ac.jp
[2] Okayama Prefectural University, Soja Okayama 7191197, Japan

Abstract. We have developed some liver posture estimation methods for achieving a liver surgical navigation system that can support surgeons who needs to know very precise information about vessels in the liver. Those methods use 3D liver models scanned from patients and 2D images scanned by depth cameras for estimating the liver posture as accurately as possible. Since a new posture estimation method using simple and high-speed image hashing algorithm was developed last year, we are trying to improve the method in accuracy and applicability for the real-time liver posture tracking. In this paper, we examine how deep learning methods can be used for liver posture estimation and its tracking over the 2D images scanned from depth cameras. We study how can a multi-layer perceptron neural network learn and estimate the liver rotation expressed in quaternion form. The real-time surgical navigation system should be efficiently implemented by combining multiple estimation methods including the deep learning method.

Keywords: Liver surgery support · Navigation · Deep learning

1 Introduction

Livers contain several types of blood vessels that intricately interlace each other inside their soft organs. That makes liver surgery very difficult and requests surgeons scan livers in many ways such as X-ray imaging, computed tomography (CT) scanning, or magnetic resonance imaging (MRI) and so on, ahead of the operation. However, those images are usually displayed on a display in two-dimensional way, and exact correspondence between real vessels in the liver cannot be checked precisely. To improve that situation, we have proposed a liver surgical navigation system that helps surgeons to track the exact posture of a liver that is being scanned by a depth camera, by comparing it with a 3D liver model beforehand scanned from a patient body [1–4]. We have examined its performance from the aspect of the algorithm [5], from the aspect of the inter-process communication cost [6], and from the aspect of the shape characteristics of the liver [7]. We also proposed a new method using hashing algorithm that can simply identify the

© Springer Nature Switzerland AG 2021
M. Kurosu (Ed.): HCII 2021, LNCS 12763, pp. 615–624, 2021.
https://doi.org/10.1007/978-3-030-78465-2_44

liver rotation by calculating a hash value from the depth image and comparing the value with pre-calculated hashed values from 3D scanned liver model in high-speed [8].

In this paper, we examine a deep learning method for estimating liver rotation angles that can be used with the hashing algorithm. As we have clarified that the characteristic shape of the liver can help calculating identical values for different angles of liver rotations in the previous paper, the deep learning method can be supposed to be another way for estimating the angles of the rotation.

2 Liver Surgical Navigation System

2.1 System Overview

The liver surgical navigation system we have proposed uses two different types of cameras located above the liver. As Fig. 1 illustrates the system structure, a depth camera above the liver scans depth image of the liver, and another marker camera scans markers put on surgical knives. Those data sets are simultaneously sent and combined in a computer, and liver posture will be accurately tracked and vessels near the top of the knives are emphasized visually and audibly.

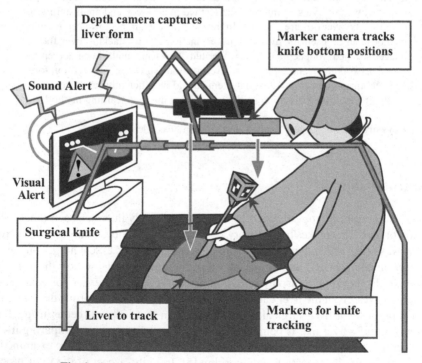

Fig. 1. System overview of our liver surgery navigation system

2.2 Liver Posture Estimation

Simultaneously as the depth camera scans the liver state, our system renders liver images using 3D liver data beforehand scanned from the patient. By comparing those images, the system estimates current posture of the liver. Figure 2 shows the data flow of the liver posture estimation system working with the depth camera and the OpenGL rendering system.

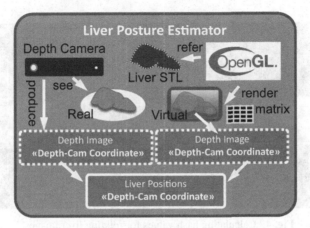

Fig. 2. Data flow of the liver posture estimator

We have clarified that the characteristics of the shape of the liver offers unimodality for estimating translations and rotations from two-dimensional images [6]. Figure 3 shows that the posture estimation process has a good convergence if it starts from any angles of rotations.

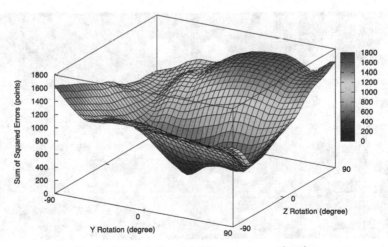

Fig. 3. Unimodality of the liver posture estimation

3   Hashing Algorithm for Posture Estimation

In our previous paper, we have proposed a hashing algorithm that hashes depth images horizontally and vertically and calculate the crossing points as that express the feature of the rotation angle [8]. Rotating a liver model from 0 to 360° stepping 10° on each X, Y, and Z axes, hashed values for all possible rotations can be calculated. Figure 4 shows how the hash table will be made by rotating the liver model.

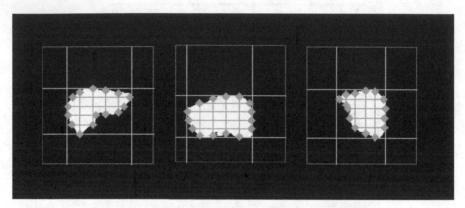

Fig. 4. Calculating hash values for rotating liver images

Similar angles can have the same hash value. In Fig. 5, the top center image shows the current state of the liver, and the hashed image is illustrated on its right side. Because of the unimodality of the liver shape, we can see that there is not any rotation candidate that is quite different from the true rotation.

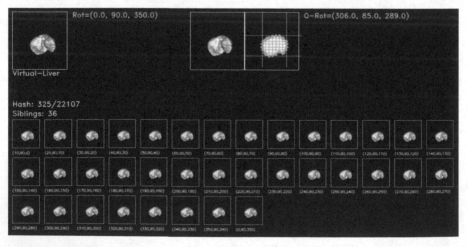

Fig. 5. A rotation can have some candidates for similar angles

By changing the hashing size, rotation estimation accuracy will be changed as well. Figure 6 shows how much the accuracy changes according to the hashing size. This indicates that this approach achieves close to 90% of the estimating accuracy.

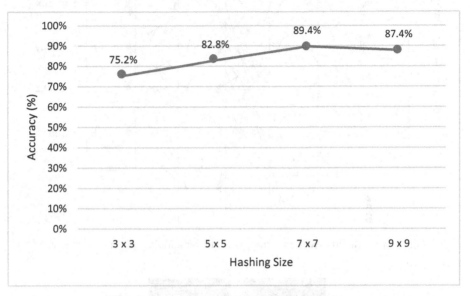

Fig. 6. Accuracy of posture estimation by hashing

4 Deep Learning for Posture Estimation

In this paper, we examine deep learning method for supporting the hashing algorithm explained in the previous chapter. Both the hashing algorithm and the deep learning method have constant amount of execution time; therefore, they could be combined to achieve more accurate estimation for real-time liver posture tracking.

We have adopted the simple layer structure that is usually referenced as MLP (multi-layer perceptron) structure for learning liver rotation angles. We assume that the rotation angles are expressed in quaternion as illustrated in Fig. 7. The pixel data of the depth image will be input to the learning network, and the four values of the quaternion that expresses the estimated rotation angle will be output from the network.

Two types of depth images are prepared as the input images as shown in Fig. 8. Both images have only black (0.0) or white (1.0) pixels, and the resolutions are different as the left one has 30×30 pixels and the right one has 60×60 pixels. Smaller size of images sometimes can help better learnings.

In this paper, we examine the influence of the image size and rotating angle resolution as explained later.

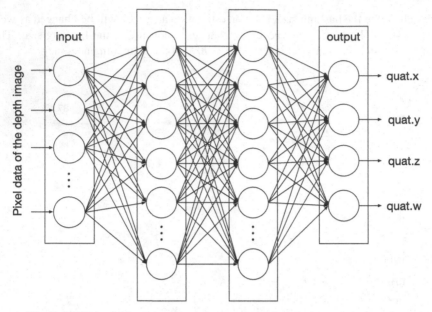

Fig. 7. MLP (multi-layer perceptron) structure for learning quaternion rotation

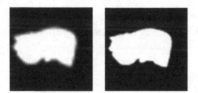

Fig. 8. Depth images with 30 × 30 pixels (left) and 60 × 60 pixels (right)

These images are made by rendering them in OpenGL as rotating the 3D liver model from 0 to 360° around X, Y, and Z axes.

Figures 9 and 10 show the learning histories using TensorFlow library with 70 epochs. As the MNIST example indicates high accuracy, two dense layers with 512 units are used in this paper. Figure 9 uses depth images with 30 × 30 pixels, and Fig. 10 uses depth images with 60 × 60 pixels. In both cases, the angle is rotated in 30°. Test data is prepared with randomly rotated angles in 1°.

There are 1728 images for training, and 10000 images for testing.

Blue circle points indicate accuracy improvements and blue dashed lines indicate the accuracy with test data. Orange triangles and dashed lines indicate learning losses.

Comparing these graphs, we can say that images with less size shows better accuracy.

In Fig. 9, test accuracy is 0.6063 and test loss is 0.0333. In Fig. 10, test accuracy is 0.5999 and test loss is 0.0338.

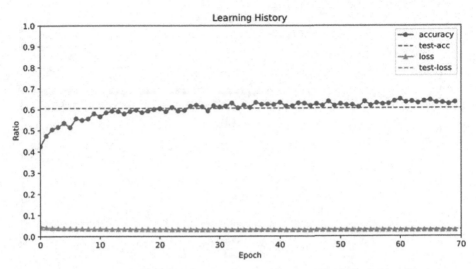

Fig. 9. Learning history for 30 × 30 images rotated in 30° (Color figure online)

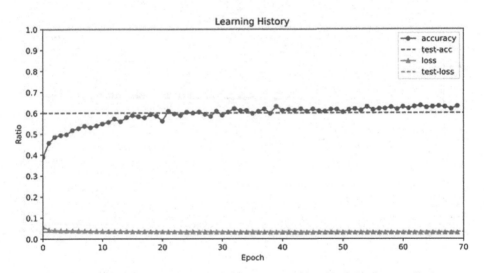

Fig. 10. Learning history for 60 × 60 images rotated in 30° (Color figure online)

Figure 11 and 12 show the learning histories with 70 epochs. Both use the same layer structure used for Fig. 9 and 10. Figure 11 uses depth images with 30 × 30 pixels, and Fig. 12 uses depth images with 60 × 60 pixels. In both cases, the angle is rotated in 10°. Both images show more converged status compared with Figs. 9 and 10. By increasing the resolution of rotation angles, convergence can be achieved.

In Fig. 11, test accuracy is 0.6952 and test loss is 0.0270. In Fig. 12, test accuracy is 0.6802, test loss is 0.0274.

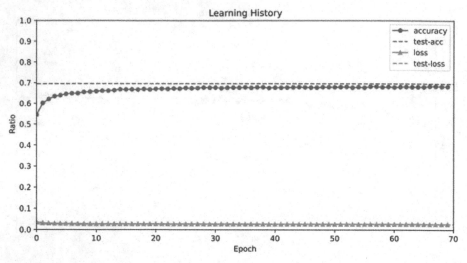

Fig. 11. Learning history with 30 × 30 image rotated in 10°

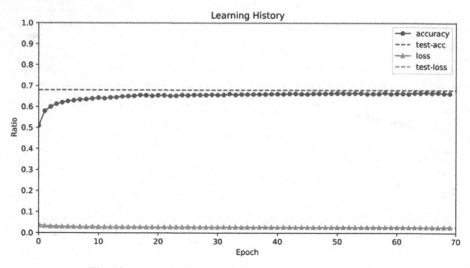

Fig. 12. Learning history with 60 × 60 images rotated in 10°

With figures above, we can conclude that less size images have possibility of better accuracy. We have tried images with 120 × 120 pixels as well, however, learning accuracy improvement was around 0.47, and test accuracy was 0.39. It can be supposed that larger size images can diverge learning curves with surplus pixels data.

5   Conclusion

We have shown the relationships between rotation angles and image sizes for the rotation angle estimation using deep learning method. It is clarified that larger size images can diverge learning curves and decrease the estimation accuracy, and less rotating angles can increase the estimation accuracy.

In this paper, we have adopted the simple MLP network structure. This is because that the MNIST (hand-written number image classification) examples prepared for TensorFlow library showed that the simple MLP network had advantages for the accuracy comparing to other complex structure such as convolutional networks; however, many types of layer structures should be examined for better accuracy in the future. The estimation accuracy of rotation angle was only around 60% to 70% in this paper, and that was less than the average accuracy of the hashing algorithm we have proposed previously. Therefore, we might conclude that the deep learning method with simple MLP network could not be directly combined with the hashing algorithm.

The number of learning epochs were 70 in all cases in this paper, but it is known that over hundreds or thousands of learning epochs can result in sudden improvement in the deep learning area. We might attempt to take such a large number of learning epochs in the future.

It is also important to notice that the quaternion is currently used for expressing and learning rotation angles. Using Euler angles could improve the estimation accuracy instead of quaternion, and that should be examined in the future.

For the future works, we would like to consider the complexity level of three-dimensional objects. From simple sphere or cube to the complex object like liver, the correlation between complexity level should give us a good insight about the rotation angle estimation.

Acknowledgement. This research was supported by Grants-in-Aid for Scientific Research (No. 26289069) from the Ministry of Education, Culture, Sports, Science and Technology (MEXT), Japan.

References

1. Koeda, M., et al.: Depth camera calibration and knife tip position estimation for liver surgery support system. In: Stephanidis, C. (ed.) HCI International 2015 - Posters' Extended Abstracts. CCIS, vol. 528, pp. 496–502. Springer, Cham (2015). https://doi.org/10.1007/978-3-319-21380-4_84
2. Doi, M., Koeda, M., Tsukushi, A., et al.: Kinfe tip position estimation for liver surgery support. In: Proceedings of the Robotics and Mechatronics Conference 2015 (ROBOMECH2015), 1A1-E01, (2015)
3. Doi, M., Yano, D., Koeda, M., et al.: Knife tip position estimation using multiple markers for liver surgery support. In: Proceedings of the 2015 JSME/RMD International Conference on Advanced Mechatronics (ICAM2015), 1A2–08, pp. 74–75 (2015)
4. Doi, M., Yano, D., Koeda, M., et al.: knife tip position estimation for liver surgery support system. In: Proceedings of Japanese Society for Medical Virtual Reality (JSMVR 2016), pp. 36–37 (2016)
5. Watanabe, K., Yoshida, S., Yano, D., Koeda, M., Noborio, H.: A new organ-following algorithm based on depth-depth matching and simulated annealing, and its experimental evaluation. In: Marcus, A., Wang, W. (eds.) Design, User Experience, and Usability: Designing Pleasurable Experiences. LNCS, vol. 10289, pp. 594–607. Springer, Cham (2017). https://doi.org/10.1007/978-3-319-58637-3_47

6. Numata, S., Yano, D., Koeda, M., et al.: A novel liver surgical navigation system using polyhedrons with STL-format. In: Proceedings of 20th International Conference on Human-Computer Interaction (HCII2018), pp. 53–63 (2018)
7. Numata, S., Koeda, M., Onishi, K., Watanabe, K., Noborio, H.: Performance and accuracy analysis of 3d model tracking for liver surgery. In: Kurosu, M. (ed.) Human-Computer Interaction. Recognition and Interaction Technologies. LNCS, vol. 11567, pp. 524–533. Springer, Cham (2019). https://doi.org/10.1007/978-3-030-22643-5_41
8. Numata, S., Koeda, M., Onishi, K., Watanabe, K., Noborio, H.: A hashing algorithm of depth image matching for liver surgery. In: Kurosu, M. (ed.) Human-Computer Interaction. Design and User Experience. LNCS, vol. 12181, pp. 625–634. Springer, Cham (2020). https://doi.org/10.1007/978-3-030-49059-1_46

Study on the Image Overlay Approach to AR Navigation System for Transsphenoidal Surgery

Katsuhiko Onishi[1]($\boxtimes$), Seiyu Fumiyama[1], Masahiro Nonaka[2], Masanao Koeda[3], and Hiroshi Noborio[1]

[1] Osaka Electro-Communication University, Osaka, Japan
onishi@oecu.jp
[2] Kansai Medical University, Osaka, Japan
[3] Okayama Prefectural University, Okayama, Japan

Abstract. In this study, we propose a system for assisting doctors with transsphenoidal surgery by understanding the positions of tumors during surgery. Transsphenoidal surgery requires examining endoscopic images to assess the situation depicted for surgery; determining the positions of tumors and organs is more difficult for transsphenoidal surgeries compared to other more general procedures. Under the proposed system, a three-dimensional (3D) model is created based on the patient's preoperative MRIs, and a superimposed image is displayed in real time. This system is expected to assist the surgeon in understanding the situation around the operating field.

Markers are used to obtain the data necessary to create an image overlay. The markers are affixed to an operating table and to the end of an endoscope. The patient's head is held in place during the intraoperative period. The positions of features within the patient's cranium relative to the operating table marker are obtained through a camera installed on the operating table. The positions of tumors and organs are then estimated from the data obtained and the data from the 3D model created from the patient's MRIs. The relative position from the marker at the end of the endoscope to the tip of the endoscope is obtained as well, allowing the position of the endoscope tip to be estimated even if the endoscope has been inserted into the body's interior during the intraoperative period; the tip cannot be seen from the exterior. The relative position of the endoscope tip and the patient's tumor is calculated, and a 3D model created from the MRI image combined with the current endoscopic image is displayed. The optimum number of simultaneous recognition markers for improving the accuracy of the measurements of the endoscope's position and orientation was verified, and results of a trial run of the image overlay system conducted using a simplified model were reported.

Keywords: Improving methods for estimating camera position and orientation · Marker-based augmented reality · Surgical support navigation system

1 Introduction

Transsphenoidal surgery is performed to remove tumors found in the "pituitary gland" (pituitary adenomas) of the brain. The pituitary gland is an organ related to hormone

© Springer Nature Switzerland AG 2021
M. Kurosu (Ed.): HCII 2021, LNCS 12763, pp. 625–643, 2021.
https://doi.org/10.1007/978-3-030-78465-2_45

production; it is attached to a slender stalk at the base of the brain core and can be as small as 1 cm. It sits within a cavity at the center of the brain (the sella turcica) and is positioned deep within the nasal cavity inside the nose. Generally, pituitary adenomas cause two major symptoms through hypertrophy: visual field defects and hormone secretion defects. In visual field defects, pressure on the optic chiasm causes bitemporal hemianopia, where the field of vision on the temporal side narrows and the field of vision decreases. Hormone secretion defects hold the potential for a variety of impacts on hormones, causing a variety of symptoms.

In transsphenoidal surgery, the physician approaches the brain through the nose to remove a tumor. Generally, an endoscope is inserted through the left nostril, and the resection tool is inserted through the right nostril. Bones in the nose are excised during the procedure, and a cavity called the "sphenoid sinus" is reached, from which the base of sella turcica, the bone in which the pituitary gland is cradled, can be visualized. When this bone is cut, a white membrane, the dura mater, is exposed; hence, the pituitary gland and the tumor are exposed. The incision of the intranasal mucous membrane and the excision of the tumor must be performed while viewing the endoscopic image. A hole directly in front of the tumor must be opened but maintained at an absolutely minimal size. The procedure therefore demands advanced knowledge and technical skill: the practitioner visually compares the endoscopic images with other images, such as the patient's MRIs to determine the incision site.

The current transsphenoidal surgical support systems comprise a simulation system for surgical training and a navigation system for grasping the environment surrounding the operating field for the procedure. For the simulation system, a variety of endoscopic surgery training systems using three-dimensional (3D) models that can provide an intuitive understanding of the position of the tumor in 3D have been proposed [1–4]. In contrast, for the navigation system, a system that displays the endoscope's two-dimensional image and, on a separate screen, the endoscope's current position, is generally adopted.

Therefore, to reduce the burden on the practitioner, we examined a navigation support system featuring a display of information regarding the area of the affected location superimposed on an image of the operating field [5, 6]. Using an image overlay to show a 3D model on the navigation system's endoscopic image supports the practitioner's understanding of the operating field environment. In particular, we considered a method for estimating the position and orientation of the endoscopic camera and developing a method that uses the measurement data to create a display that superimposes a 3D model on a selected position. In this paper, we report on the results of trial manufacture of an improved device using previously-examined content and a method of measuring the endoscopic camera's position and orientation, evaluating measurement accuracy, and creating an image overlay.

2 Proposed System

The proposed system combines with the intraoperative endoscopic camera image to create a real-time image overlay of the tumor [6]. This system is created from two algorithms. To obtain the information necessary to create the image overlay from the marker coordinates, two systems are required: a position and orientation estimation system that estimates the position of the tip of the endoscope, and an image overlay system that combines the positional relationships in the 3D model of the affected area in a virtual space with positions in the real-life affected area in actual space. A schematic of the proposed system is depicted in Fig. 1.

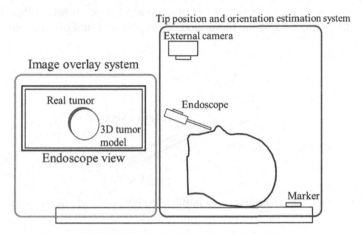

Fig. 1. Schematic of the proposed system.

The position and orientation estimation system estimates the position and orientation of the tip of the endoscope and the tumor and organs in the affected area. This method is based on it which is proposed in previous studies [7, 8]. Markers are affixed on the operating table and the endoscope, and a camera (external camera) is affixed on the operating table to recognize the markers. To estimate the position and orientation of the tip of the endoscope, the relative vector from the marker previously affixed on the endoscope (the end marker) to the marker affixed on the operating table (the tip marker) is obtained. It is possible to obtain the position and orientation of the tip of the endoscope from the end marker's position and orientation information, and the aforementioned relative vector.Next, the position and orientation of the tumor and organs are estimated. This estimation uses a 3D model created from previously-imaged patient MRIs. Vectors are obtained from the marker affixed to the operating table to features in the patient's cranium. The position and orientation of features in the cranium and the same features as projected in the MRI-derived 3D model are used to estimate the position and orientation of the tumor and organs. Because the endoscope is a rigid body, its relative positional relationship with the end marker remains unchanged. Moreover, as the head is fixed in place on the operating table, the positional relationship between the marker on the operating table and the tumor and organs in the cranium remains unchanged. Therefore, it is possible to estimate the position and orientation of the endoscope tip and the position of the tumor and organs within the cranium from the marker information.

Furthermore, regarding the image overlay system, it is necessary to combine a coordinate system in real space with a coordinate system in a virtual space to display a 3D model of the affected area. The tip of the endoscope is used as the point of reference for the virtual space coordinate system. The position and orientation of the tip of the endo-scope in the coordinate system recognized by the external camera (the camera coordinate system) and the values obtained regarding the position and orientation of the tumor and organs are converted into the virtual space coordinate system. Based on the converted data, an image overlay of the tumor and organs is created on the endoscopic image. An outline of the estimation of the endoscopic tip location is shown in Fig. 2, and an overview of the estimation of the tumor and organ positions and orientations is shown in Fig. 3.

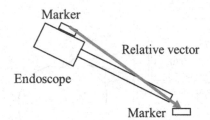

Fig. 2. Overview of estimation of position and orientation of endoscope tip.

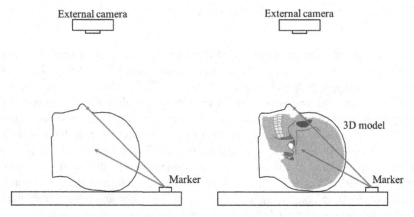

Fig. 3. Estimation of position and orientation of tumor and organs.

3 Implemented System

3.1 System Overview

An overview of the system created in this study is shown in Fig. 4. The external camera at the top reads the markers, for which ArUco markers are used (see Fig. 5) [9, 10]. ArUco markers can minimize the size of the markers to a minimum of 22 mm. Minimizing the size of the markers reduces the impact on the procedure. The relative vector from the marker affixed on the end of the endoscope to the tip is used to estimate the location of the tip. The relative vectors from the marker affixed to the operating table to the cranial features are used and combined with the features' locations in the patient's personal 3D model to estimate the positions and orientations of the tumor and organs. The estimated positional relationships are converted from the external camera coordinate system to the virtual space coordinate system and combined with the endoscopic images to display a 3D model. The performance of similar motions by positional relationships in real and virtual spaces make an image overlay possible. Here, training equipment modeling the head (see Fig. 6) and a simplified tumor model affixed to the equipment (see Fig. 7) are used to confirm the activity.

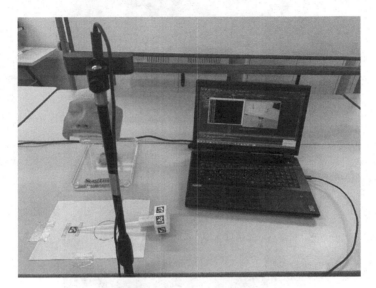

Fig. 4. System overview.

Fig. 5. Examples of ArUco marker.

3.2 Tip Position and Orientation Estimation System

The tip position and orientation estimation system estimates the position and orientation of the endoscope tip and of the cranial tumor and organs. The system uses a relative vector calculated via markers positioned on the points of interest. The relative vector is calculated from the marker affixed to the end of the endoscope preoperatively to the tip of the endoscope. The position of the end marker is represented as P_{mb}, the rotation matrix, as R_{mb}, and the reference marker, as P_{mt}. The orientation vector P_{relvec} from the end marker to the reference marker is represented via the following formula:

$$P_{relvec} = R_{mb} \times (P_{mt} - P_{mb})$$ (1)

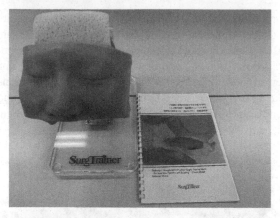

Fig. 6. Cranium training equipment.

Fig. 7. Simplified tumor model.

Calculating the relative vector makes it possible to estimate the position of the tip of the endoscope from the position and orientation of the end marker and the relative vector. The estimated position is calculated as follows:

$$P_t = P_{relvec} \times P_{mb} \tag{2}$$

The relative vector is shown in Fig. 8 and the estimation of the tip's position and orientation is shown in Fig. 9. Furthermore, when multiple end markers are recognized during relative vector calculation, an estimate of the tip's position from the average values for the relative vectors is calculated after the calculation of each individual relative vector. The position and orientation of the endoscope tip are estimated because the values are of great importance to the image overlay system. Using a coordinate system with the position of the endoscope tip as its origin, the positions and orientations displayed on the cranial 3D model are determined via the estimated tip position P_t.

In this study, we performed a stability comparison of a varying number of end markers in the 3D cranial model's image overlay. Six-sided, eight-sided, and 12-sided attachments

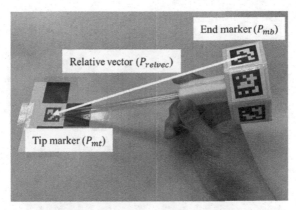

Fig. 8. Relative vector for the endoscope.

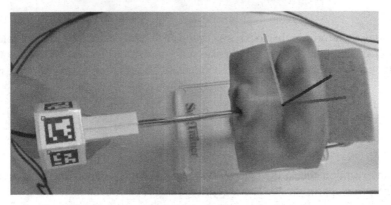

Fig. 9. Estimating the tip's position and orientation.

were affixed to the end of the endoscope, with six markers attached to each. Endoscopes with attachments other than the six-sided models are used because it is claimed that it is easier for the external cameras to recognize them. If the markers attached to the end are horizontal or exceed a certain angle to the camera, they become difficult to recognize, creating an issue. Because relative vectors for multiple items are estimated from average values, when the number of end markers drastically changes, it impacts the estimation of the tip position and orientation. Therefore, to decrease the frequency with which the issues with the external camera occur, eight-sided and 12-sided attachment models were added. Figure 10 shows each model of the endoscope.

In addition, regarding the orientation of the tip position P_t, an angularity correction for the endoscope attachment is applied to the affixed end markers, and the values are treated as the tip position orientation. Therefore, the rotation matrix is transformed into Euler angles. Euler angle transformations sometimes run the risk of triggering a gimbal lock issue: a problem where, when an object is repeatedly rotated using Euler angles, two of the axes end up overlapping, and the expressible angles of rotation decrease. However, this study uses only one rotation correction after the rotation matrix is transformed into

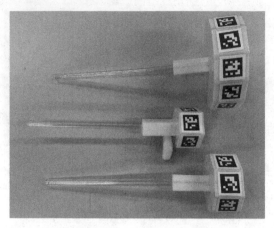

Fig. 10. Each model of endoscope.

Euler angles, therefore, gimbal locks are not considered to occur. There are multiple ways to express Euler angles, but this study uses a z-y-x rotation. To express z-y-x rotations uniquely, exception handling must be conducted. The rotation matrix is expressed as follows:

$$R_{mat} = \begin{pmatrix} m_1 & m_2 & m_3 \\ m_4 & m_5 & m_6 \\ m_7 & m_8 & m_9 \end{pmatrix} \tag{3}$$

As an exception check, the conversion formula changes depending on whether the value *exception* approaches 0. The *exception* value is calculated as follows:

$$\textbf{\textit{exception}} = \sqrt{(m_1 \times m_1) + (m_2 \times m_2)} \tag{4}$$

In the case where the Euler angle is expressed as $R_{euler}(x, y, z)$ and *exception* $\fallingdotseq 0$:

$$R_{euler}x = arctan\frac{m_8}{m_5} \tag{5}$$

$$R_{euler}y = arctan\frac{m_3}{\sqrt{(m_1 \times m_1) + (m_2 \times m_2)}} \tag{6}$$

$$R_{euler}z = 0 \tag{7}$$

In all other cases:

$$R_{euler}x = arctan\frac{m_6}{m_9} \tag{8}$$

$$R_{euler}y = arctan\frac{m_3}{\sqrt{(m_1 \times m_1) + (m_2 \times m_2)}} \tag{9}$$

$$R_{euler}z = arctan\frac{m_2}{m_1} \tag{10}$$

In this study, as the direction from the end of the endoscope to the tip is defined as the x axis and the markers are affixed, a correction is applied for the x value for each marker. For the Euler angle for each marker 1 through 6, R_{euler1} to R_{euler6}, the angularity correction is calculated as per the formulas below. Moreover, the values for the angle for each attachment are shown in Table 1.

$$R_{euler1}x = R_{euler1}x \tag{11}$$

$$R_{euler2}x = R_{euler2}x + \alpha_1 \tag{12}$$

$$R_{euler3}x = R_{euler3}x + \alpha_2 \tag{13}$$

$$R_{euler4}x = R_{euler4}x + \alpha_3 \tag{14}$$

$$R_{euler5}x = R_{euler5}x + \alpha_4 \tag{15}$$

$$R_{euler6}x = R_{euler6}x + \alpha_5 \tag{16}$$

Table 1. Table of corresponding angularity corrections.

	α_1	α_2	α_3	α_4	α_5
Six-sided attachment	$\frac{\pi}{3}$	$\frac{2\pi}{3}$	$-\pi$	$\frac{-2\pi}{3}$	$\frac{-\pi}{3}$
Eight-sided attachment	$\frac{\pi}{4}$	$\frac{\pi}{2}$	$\frac{3}{4}\pi$	$-\pi$	$\frac{-3}{4}\pi$
12-sided attachment	$\frac{\pi}{6}$	$\frac{\pi}{3}$	$\frac{\pi}{2}$	$\frac{2\pi}{3}$	$\frac{5\pi}{6}$

The estimated orientation of the tip as represented by these Euler angles is a mixture of positive and negative values. Therefore, the desired estimates cannot be calculated if the values are added and averaged unaltered. Therefore, the estimated orientations with the angularity corrections applied are reconverted to rotation matrices, then average values are calculated. The reconversion uses the following formulas:

$$R_{mat} = \begin{pmatrix} cos(R_{euler}z) & sin(R_{euler}y) & 0 \\ -sin(R_{euler}y) & cos(R_{euler}z) & 0 \\ 0 & 0 & 1 \end{pmatrix}$$

$$\times \begin{pmatrix} cos(R_{euler}y) & 0 & -sin(R_{euler}y) \\ 0 & 1 & 0 \\ sin(R_{euler}y) & 0 & cos(R_{euler}y) \end{pmatrix} \times \begin{pmatrix} 1 & 0 & 0 \\ 0 & cos(R_{euler}x) & sin(R_{euler}x) \\ 0 & -sin(R_{euler}x) & cos(R_{euler}x) \end{pmatrix} \tag{17}$$

The technique for estimating the position and orientation of the tumor and organs in the affected area also follows the formulas outlined in (1), and the relative vectors from the marker affixed to the operating table to the cranial features of interest are calculated. If the same features obtained from the MRI-derived 3D model of the patient's cranium can be identified within the patient's cranium, then it is considered possible for the position and orientation of the tumor and organs in the affected area to be estimated from the marker on the operating table.

3.3 Image Overlay System

For the image overlay system for the 3D model of the affected area, the values for the position and orientation of the endoscope tip estimated from the markers recognized by the external camera and for the position and orientation of the tumor and organs in the affected area are each converted from the camera coordinate system to the virtual space coordinate system and combined with the endoscopic images to create an image overlay of the 3D model. The position of the tip of the endoscope in the camera coordinate system is expressed as P_t^{camera}; the orientation of the tip as R_t^{camera}; the 3D model position as P_m^{camera}; the 3D model orientation as R_m^{camera}. Additionally, in the virtual space coordinate system, the 3D model position is expressed as $P_m^{virtual}$; the 3D model orientation as $R_m^{virtual}$. The conversion from the camera coordinate system to the virtual space coordinate system is conducted via the following formula:

$$P_m^{virtual} = R_t^{camera} \times \left(P_m^{camera} - P_t^{camera} \right) \tag{18}$$

$$R_m^{virtual} = R_t^{camera} \times R_m^{camera} \tag{19}$$

Using the position of the camera in the virtual space as the origin and the endoscopic image as the background, it is possible to create an image overlay using a 3D model by displaying the position $P_m^{virtual}$ in the 3D model and combining it with actual images. When using an image overlay of a 3D model, transmission processing is conducted. The 3D model used in this system is shown in Fig. 11. And the image overlay of the simplified model positioned in the training equipment is shown in Fig. 12.

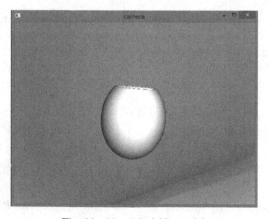

Fig. 11. Simplified 3D model.

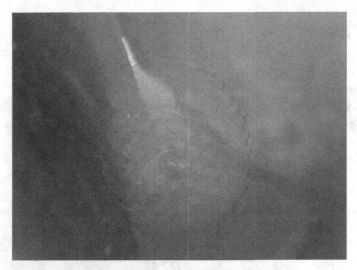

Fig. 12. Image overlay with simplified model

4   Basic Evaluation Experiment

4.1   Experiment Environment

In this study, we conducted a comparison using the 3D model images for each model in the image overlay system and a marker accuracy comparison for each model using a circle 7 cm in diameter. An USB camera (Logicool BRIO c1000e) was selected for the external camera used to recognize the markers. In the experiment, an accuracy comparison for a state of continuous motion was conducted by changing the number of end markers that could be reliably recognized. The experiment environment is shown in Fig. 13.

4.2   Evaluation Experiment

In this experiment, an accuracy comparison is performed by changing the number of markers during continuous motion. After calibration motions are performed for the estimation of the position and orientation of the endoscope tip, a perfect circlet, 7 cm in diameter, positioned on a desk is rotated one full turn for 10 s toward each endoscope model. A graph is created from the coordinate values obtained during the rotation, and the reference circle and the shape created by the measured values are compared. The external camera is positioned 500 mm from the desktop. In addition, calculations are performed under the assumption that a certain number of end markers is stably recognized by the external camera for each model. The number of markers stably recognized for each model is 2 for a six-sided attachment, 3 for an eight-sided attachment, and 4 for a twelve-sided attachment. Ten rounds of measurements were conducted for each model, and a graph was created from the results. An example of graphed results for each model on an x, y-coordinate system is shown in Fig. 14, 15, and 16. The results of translating these graphs to a z-coordinate system are shown in Fig. 17, 18, and 19. The average

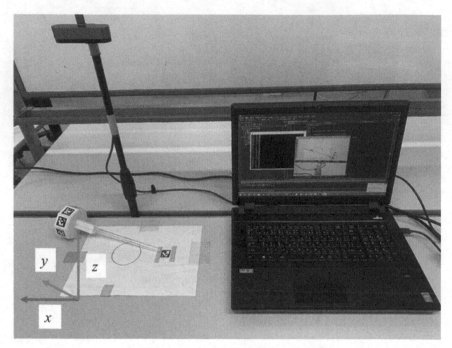

Fig. 13. Experiment environment.

values for the tip estimates obtained for each model are shown in Fig. 20, 21, and 22. Finally, examples of the graphs obtained for each model upon the generation of double circles from the obtained measurements are shown in Fig. 23, 24, and 25. Simultaneously, translated graphs for z-coordinates are shown in Fig. 26, 27, and 28.

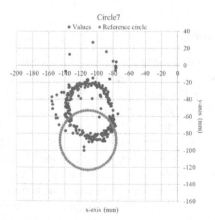

Fig. 14. Graph of measurements (x, y-coordinates, 2 markers, six-sided attachment).

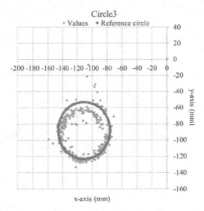

Fig. 15. Graph of measurements (x, y-coordinates, 3 markers, eight-sided attachment).

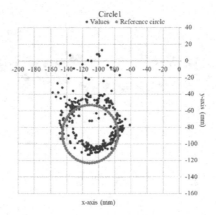

Fig. 16. Graph of measurements (x, y-coordinates, 4 markers, twelve-sided attachment).

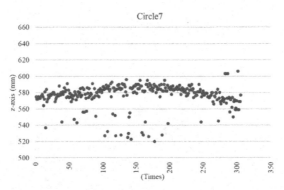

Fig. 17. Graph of measurements (z-coordinate, 2 markers, six-sided attachment).

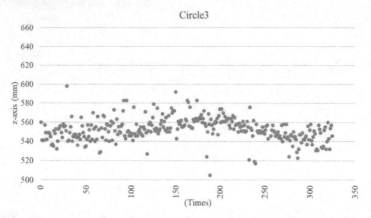

Fig. 18. Graph of measurements (z-coordinate, 3 markers, eight-sided attachment).

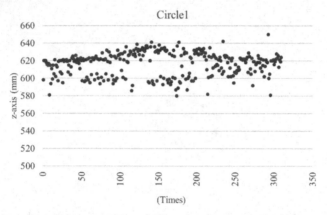

Fig. 19. Graph of measurements (z-coordinate, 4 markers, twelve-sided attachment).

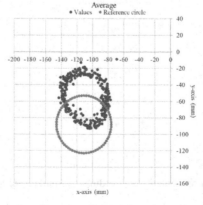

Fig. 20. Average values (x, y-coordinates, 2 markers, six-sided attachment).

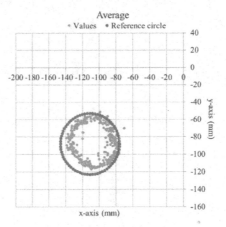

Fig. 21. Average values (x, y-coordinates, 3 markers, eight-sided attachment).

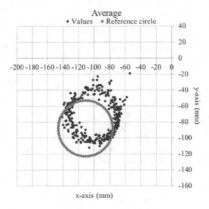

Fig. 22. Average values (x, y-coordinates, 4 markers, twelve-sided attachment).

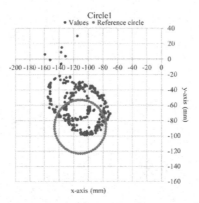

Fig. 23. Double-circle phenomenon (x, y-coordinates, 2 markers, six-sided attachment).

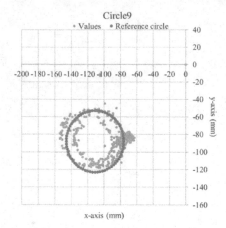

Fig. 24. Double-circle phenomenon (x, y-coordinates, 3 markers, eight-sided attachment).

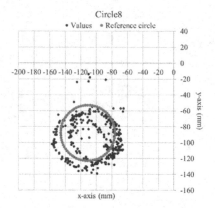

Fig. 25. Double-circle phenomenon (x, y-coordinates, 4 markers, twelve-sided attachment).

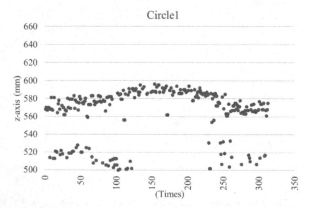

Fig. 26. Double-circle phenomenon (z-coordinate, 2 markers, six-sided attachment).

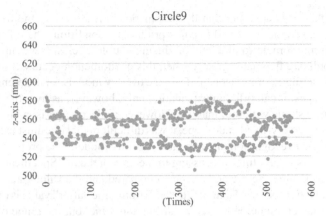

Fig. 27. Double-circle phenomenon (z-coordinate, 3 markers, eight-sided attachment).

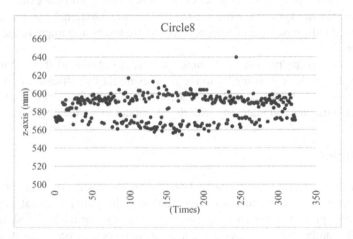

Fig. 28. Double-circle phenomenon (z-coordinate, 4 markers, twelve-sided attachment).

4.3 Discussion

When a decision was made to compare the accuracy for different numbers of markers, it was hypothesized that accuracy would improve when more end markers were added. However, after 10 sets of measurements for each model were performed, it became evident that the use of three markers tended to produce the formation closest to a true circle the most often. Moreover, in the experiment, measurements were taken at angles conforming to the boundaries outlined in Sect. 3, to avoid producing the phenomenon of the camera and markers being level with each other. However, the occurrence of a double-circle phenomenon produced from the measurements was confirmed in every model. After analyzing the results of 10 rounds of measurements with each model, it was determined that as the number of markers increased, the frequency with which this phenomenon occurred increased: six cases with two markers, seven cases with three markers, and nine cases with four markers. On screen, conditions are at first glance stable, but within, it is apparent that the end markers are reversing the front and back directions. As the frame rate is 30 fps, this produces a condition where front and back are reversed from moment to moment, producing double circles. It was also confirmed that the z-coordinate fluctuates greatly when this phenomenon occurs. As this study is limited to conducting a comparison of 3D image overlay models for different numbers of markers via images, it can offer an explanation only; however, as hypothesized, the 3D model is the most stable with four markers. However, as the comparison involved the use of an almost completely-fixed endoscope, it was difficult in that circumstance to produce the inverted marker recognition phenomenon with any model. One proposal for solving the phenomenon is to add filter processing to the obtained data. Specifically, under this processing, when values before and after are compared and the values are extremely far apart from each other (before: 50 mm; after: − 50 mm), the "after" value is excluded, and the measurements continue. However, regarding this function, the range of values that should be compared is unclear, therefore, further investigation is necessary. Apart from the addition of filter processing, it is believed that the use of multiple external cameras could confirm the markers. It is expected that the use of an external camera attached at an angle would reduce the rate of occurrence of future issues and improve the accuracy of the system.

However, given the problems encountered here, it is believed that accurate identification of the markers with regard to the features might be difficult. Therefore, it is believed necessary to propose a method for identifying cranial features without using the operating table marker and matching with the 3D model using the obtained algorithm.

5   Conclusion

To develop an augmented reality navigation system to provide support for the environment surrounding the practitioner's operating field in transsphenoidal surgery, this study created a prototype for an image overlay system using a simplified model and examined the number of simultaneous recognition markers necessary for estimating the position and orientation of the endoscope. For an evaluation experiment, a comparison was conducted for various numbers of markers in the 3D image overlay system depicting the position and orientation of the model of the affected area via imaging. Six-sided (2 markers), eight-sided (3 markers), and twelve-sided (4 markers) models were prepared; and an image overlay was created for each model of the simplified model positioned in the cranial training equipment. The results of the imaging comparison showed that the twelve-sided (4 markers) model produced the 3D model with the highest stability. The experimental comparison was conducted in an almost stationary environment. In addition, evaluating marker stability through comparison image overlay images only is considered difficult, and an experiment where the position and orientation of the endoscope were in continuous motion was conducted. Six-sided, eight-sided, and twelve-sided models for a circle 7 cm in diameter were prepared, and an accuracy comparison was conducted via the number of markers the external camera could recognize. Graphs were prepared of the estimated values, and it was determined that the eight-sided model was the most stable. The results of the two types of evaluation experiments are considered to indicate that the 3D model of the affected area was able to be created with a certain degree of stability. Future topics for research include improving the accuracy of the position and orientation estimation system verifying the accuracy of image overlay systems using simplified models.

References

1. Qian, K., Bai, J., Yang, X., Pan, J., Zhang, J.: Virtual reality based laparoscopic surgery simulation. In: Proceedings of the 21st ACM Symposium on Virtual Reality Software and Technology, pp. 69–78 (2015). https://doi.org/10.1145/2821592.2821599
2. Coles, T.R., Meglan, D., John, N.W.: The role of haptics in medical training simulators: a survey of the state of the art. IEEE Trans. Haptics 4(1), 51–66 (2011). https://doi.org/10.1109/TOH.2010.19
3. Shousen, W., Jun-Feng, L., Shang-Ming, Z., Jun-Jie, J., Liang, X.: A virtual reality model of the clivus and surgical simulation via transoral or transnasal route. Int. J. Clin. Exp. Med. 7, 3270–3279 (2014)
4. Li, L., et al.: A novel augmented reality navigation system for endoscopic sinus and skull base surgery: a feasibility study. PLoS ONE 11(1), e0146996 (2016). https://doi.org/10.1371/journal.pone.0146996
5. Onishi, K., Fumiyama, S., Miki, Y., Nonaka, M., Koeda, M., Noborio, H.: A study of camera tip position estimating methods in transnasal endoscopic surgery. In: Kurosu, M. (ed.) Human-Computer Interaction. Recognition and Interaction Technologies. LNCS, vol. 11567, pp. 534–543. Springer, Cham (2019). https://doi.org/10.1007/978-3-030-22643-5_42
6. Onishi, K., Fumiyama, S., Miki, Y., Nonaka, M., Koeda, M., Noborio, H.: Study on the development of augmented-reality navigation system for transsphenoidal surgery. In: Kurosu, M. (ed.) Human-Computer Interaction. Human Values and Quality of Life. LNCS, vol. 12183, pp. 623–638. Springer, Cham (2020). https://doi.org/10.1007/978-3-030-49065-2_43
7. Yano, D., et al.: Accuracy verification of knife tip positioning with position and orientation estimation of the actual liver for liver surgery support system. J. Bioinform. Neurosci. (JBINS) 3(3), 79–84 (2017)
8. Koeda, M., Yano, D., Doi, M., Onishi, K., Noborio, H.: Calibration of surgical knife-tip position with marker-based optical tracking camera and precise evaluation of its measurement accuracy. J. Bioinform. Neurosci. (JBINS) 4(1), 155–159 (2018)
9. Garrido-Jurado, S., Muñoz-Salinas, R., Madrid-Cuevas, F., Medina-Carnicer, R.: Generation of fiducial marker dictionaries using mixed integer linear programming. Pattern Recogn. 51, 481–491 (2015). https://doi.org/10.1016/j.patcog.2015.09.023
10. Romero Ramirez, F., Muñoz-Salinas, R., Medina-Carnicer, R.: Speeded up detection of squared fiducial markers. Image Vis. Comput. 76, 2016 (2018). https://doi.org/10.1016/j.imavis.2018.05.004

Evaluation of Depth-Depth-Matching Speed of Depth Image Generated from DICOM by GPGPU

Daiki Yano[1]([✉]), Masanao Koeda[2], Hiroshi Noborio[3], and Katsuhiko Onishi[3]

[1] denLabo LLC, Osaka-shi, Osaka 545-0011, Japan
d.yano+paper2021@denlabo.co.jp
[2] Okayama Prefectural University, Soja, Okayama 719-1197, Japan
[3] Osaka Electro-Communication University, Shijonawate, Osaka 575-0063, Japan

Abstract. We are developing a surgical support system to prevent surgical accidents in liver surgery. This system consists of three subsystems. First, The Liver Position and Posture Estimation System performs Depth-Depth-Matching of real depth image and virtual depth image to estimate the position and posture of the liver during surgery. The real depth image is the depth image of the real liver surface measured by the depth camera. The virtual depth image is the Z-buffer of the virtual liver generated from the DICOM captured preoperatively. Next, The Surgical Scalpel Tip Position Estimation System uses an optical 3D position tracker to measure the position of a grid pattern marker attached to the handle of the scalpel, and estimates the tip position by calculating the vector to the marker and the scalpel tip. And finally, The Liver Surgery Simulator receives the estimated position and posture of the liver and the position of the tip of the scalpel, and calculate the distance between the tip of the scalpel and the blood vessels. In this paper, we propose a high-speed Depth-Depth-Matching using GPGPU to estimate the liver position and posture using the real and virtual depth images. In the proposed method, a virtual depth image is generated from a 3D volume using GPGPU and Depth-Depth-Matching is continuously processed to speed up the position and posture estimation. We compared the performance of the proposed method with the conventional method, and confirmed the usefulness of the proposed method.

Keywords: Liver surgery support · Navigation · GPGPU

1 Introduction

Liver surgery is complicated because of the complexity of the blood vessels. The surgeon will refer to preoperative imaging using Computed Tomography (CT) and Magnetic Resonance Imaging (MRI) to understand the tumor and blood vessels' position. In preoperative imaging, Multi-Planer Reconstruction (MPR) can be used to observe the internal state of organs from multiple cross-sections, and volume rendering can be used to represent the interior of a 3D

© Springer Nature Switzerland AG 2021
M. Kurosu (Ed.): HCII 2021, LNCS 12763, pp. 644–655, 2021.
https://doi.org/10.1007/978-3-030-78465-2_46

image. However, it is not easy to grasp the organ's internal structure during surgery because the its position and posture are different from preoperative imaging.

There is a method of using a commercially available surgical system to grasp an organ's internal structure during surgery [1–4]. These systems can navigate the three-dimensional positioning of the tumor and surgical tools in real-time during surgery using the tomographic images captured preoperatively. The navigation system needs to fix landmark markers. Therefore, the use of Stereotactic surgery is appropriate and is used in orthopedic and neurosurgery. Soft and deformable organs cannot be used because landmarks cannot be attached to them.

Therefore, we are developing a surgical support system that targets the liver, which is difficult to attach landmarks to and deforms during surgery due to its softness.

2 Liver Surgical Support System

We are developing a surgical support system [8] for open liver surgery. The overall system diagram of the liver surgery support system we are developing is shown in Fig. 1.

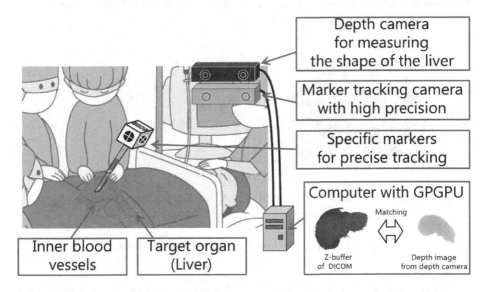

Fig. 1. System overview of our liver surgery support system.

Our liver surgery support system uses two cameras with different features to measure the liver and scalpel from the top of the operating table. The first is a depth camera (Kinect for Windows v2) to measure the shape of the liver surface in three dimensions. The second is an optical 3D position tracker (MicronTracker 3) to estimate the position of the tip of a surgical scalpel. The system calculates the distance from the tip of the scalpel to the blood vessels inside the liver by using the information from these cameras and the tomographic images taken before the surgery. If the tip of the scalpel comes close to a large blood vessel, a buzzer and light will alert the operator to prevent surgical accidents.

This system consists of three subsystems: The Liver Position and Posture Estimation System, The Surgical Scalpel Tip Position Estimation System, and The Liver Surgery Simulator.

2.1   The Liver Position and Posture Estimation System

The Liver Position and Posture Estimation System estimates the position and posture of the liver (actual liver) intraoperatively using two-dimensional Depth-Depth-Matching. Two-dimensional Depth-Depth-Matching requires two depth images.

One is a depth image of the actual liver surface shape measured with a depth camera (real depth image). A pseudo-liver made from an experimental ultra-soft modeling resin that mimics a real liver and an real depth image captured by a depth camera is shown in Fig. 2.

(a) Pseudo-liver made of ultra-soft modeling resin for experiments.

(b) Real depth image captured by a depth camera.

Fig. 2. Examples of resin liver and real depth images.

The other is a virtual liver Z-buffer (virtual depth image) generated from tomographic (DICOM) images of the liver taken by CT or MRI before surgery. The virtual depth image generated from the DICOM image slices and virtual liver is shown in Fig. 3.

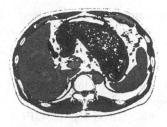

(a) DICOM slice section image.

(b) Virtual depth image generated by acquiring the Z-buffer from DI-COM.

Fig. 3. Examples of resin liver and real depth images.

To estimate the actual position and posture of the liver, automatic motion tracking with two-dimensional Depth-Depth-Matching is performed. The conceptual diagram of the matching algorithm [7] is shown in Fig. 4.

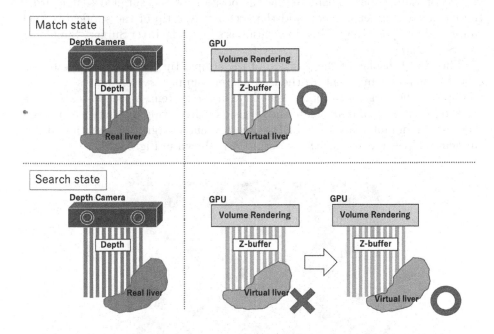

Fig. 4. Concept of two-dimensional Depth-Depth-Matching algorithm.

The search is performed by moving the virtual liver in parallel rotation in the virtual space and minimizing the score of the evaluation function using the annealing method. The score is calculated by summing the absolute value of the difference between each pixel in the virtual depth image and the real depth image.

Accelerating with GPGPU. For the high-speed calculation, virtual depth images are generated from the three-dimensional volume of the virtual liver using a general-purpose graphics processing unit (GPGPU). In GPGPU, the volume point cloud of the virtual liver is rotated and parallel translation, then perspective transformed, rendered and calculated in parallel to generate a virtual depth image (see Sect. 3.1). The estimated position and posture of the liver will be sent to the Liver Surgery Simulator (see Sect. 2.3).

2.2   The Surgical Scalpel Tip Position Estimation System

The Surgical Scalpel Tip Position Estimation System is a system that estimates the position of the surgical scalpel tip during surgery using an optical three-dimensional position tracker. Since the position of the scalpel tip could not be measured directly during surgery, a grid of markers was attached to the handle of the scalpel. Calculate the tip position of the surgical scalpel from the measured marker position and the vector to the tip of the surgical scalpel calibrated preoperatively. This tip position is sent to the Liver Surgery Simulator (see Sect. 2.3).

The visual display of the position of the scalpel tip and the distance to the object at hand is important for the liver surgery support system and is expected to improve the surgical support capability. In the system, a pseudo-scalpel was used to provide visual feedback to the surgeon by displaying the distance between objects at 1 mm intervals on an LED array. A pseudo-surgical scalpel (intelligent surgical scalpel) created for the experiment is shown in Fig. 5.

Fig. 5. Intelligent surgical scalpel [9].

2.3   The Liver Surgery Simulator

The Liver Surgery Simulator [6] receives the estimated position and posture of the liver and the position of the tip of the surgical knife, and incises and deforms a three-dimensional polygonal model of the liver according to the operation. The operation screen of the liver surgery simulator is shown in Fig. 6.

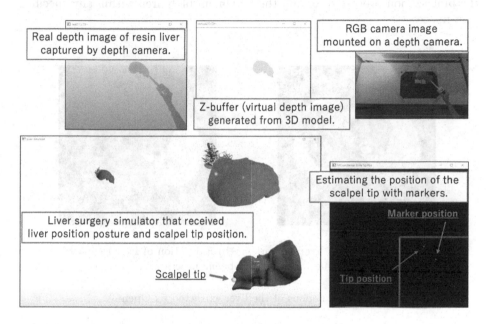

Fig. 6. Operation screen of the liver surgery simulator.

The three-dimensional models are represented in stereolithography (STL) format which is generated by segmenting DICOM preoperatively. The models consist of a liver STL, arterial group STL, venous group STL, and portal vein group STL. The simulator also can calculate the distance between the tip of the surgical scalpel and the blood vessels or tumor using the position and posture of the liver and the tip position. The calculated distance to vessels and tumors is sent to the intelligent surgical scalpel. The intelligent surgical scalpel has an LED level meter and visually indicates the distance to the tumor and vessels by illuminating LED.

3   Accelerating Position Posture Estimate with GPGPU

3.1   Depth Image Generation from DICOM

In the liver position and posture estimation system, the real depth image is compared with the virtual depth image using a matching algorithm. The virtual depth image is obtained by moving the DICOM captured preoperatively to an arbitrary positional posture using GPGPU calculations to obtain the Z-buffer.

As a preliminary step to acquire depth images directly from DICOM images [5], the liver region is binarized using OpenCV and extracted by labeling process. Figure 7(a) shows the result of the binarization process for each DICOM within the set gray values. Figure 7(b) shows the result of labeling the image after the binarization process to obtain the maximum blob area within any specified coordinates.

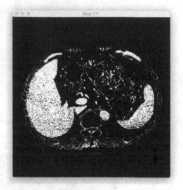 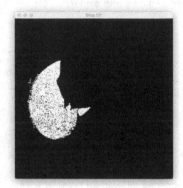

(a) Binarization of the liver region with a set threshold value.

(b) Extraction of liver region by labeling process.

Fig. 7. Blob regions of the liver extracted by OpenCV.

A set of blob regions (liver voxels) extracted by labeling is transferred to the GPU for rotation and translation, perspective projection transformation, and rendering.

The 3D coordinate of each liver voxel p_r after the rotation shift is

$$p_r = \mathbf{R}(p - p_g) + p_g \tag{1}$$

where $\mathbf{R}$ is the rotation matrix, p is the coordinate of each liver voxel, and p_g is the coordinate of the center of gravity of the voxel.

Coordinate p_p after perspective projection transformation is

$$p_p = \begin{pmatrix} f\dfrac{p_r^x}{p_r^z} \\ f\dfrac{p_r^y}{p_r^z} \\ p_r^z \end{pmatrix} \tag{2}$$

when f is the focal length of the depth camera.

The depth image is generated by rendering the liver volume. The rendering is done in such a way that the z coordinate takes the maximum value when p_p is at the window size.

3.2 2D Depth-Depth-Matching with GPGPU

In order to repeat 2D Depth-Depth-Matching continuously in real-time, the execution speed of the matching algorithm needs to be fast. In the matching algorithm, it is necessary to estimate the position and posture by comparing the real depth image with the virtual depth image for each frame of the depth camera.

Direct depth image generation from DICOM, which was computationally expensive and took a long time with CPU processing, was accelerated by parallel computing using GPGPU [5]. However, as shown in Fig. 8, the calculation of the score by the search algorithm is done by the CPU, and there was an issue with the real-time performance of the search algorithm. The reason for this is that the virtual depth image generated by the GPGPU is transferred to the CPU for each generated frame, and the score of the evaluation function is calculated by 2D Depth-Depth-Matching by the CPU. If the virtual depth image is transferred at each generation frame, there is a need for frequent data transfer between the CPU and GPU, which becomes a processing bottleneck.

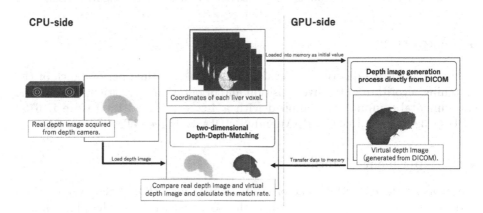

Fig. 8. The matching algorithm is being executed by CPU (real-time issues exist).

In order to speed up the execution speed of the matching algorithm and solve the issue of real-time performance, 2D Depth-Depth-Matching was performed with GPGPU as shown in Fig. 9. Using GPGPU, we generated virtual depth images from 3D volumes and continuously processed 2D Depth-Depth-Matching to speed up the position and orientation estimation. The processing is done continuously by GPGPU by synchronously executing two independent kernel functions of GPU.

CPU-side   **GPU-side**

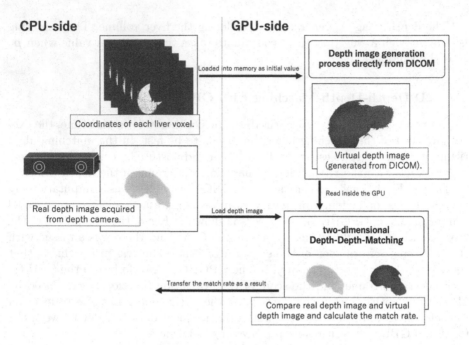

Fig. 9. The matching algorithm is being executed by GPGPU (solving real-time issue).

4   Experiment

In this chapter, we describe the evaluation of the real-time performance of the matching algorithm of the liver position and orientation estimation system. The experimental computer is equipped with a 4-core 8-thread Intel Core i7-6700 CPU (@3.40 GHz), 16.0 GB RAM and NVIDIA GeForce GTX TITAN Black.

4.1   Experimental Method

We measure the execution time of the matching algorithm of the liver position and posture estimation system when the score returned by the algorithm is sufficiently stable. The criterion for determining the stable state was that there was no change in the score for more than one minute.

The real depth image used for the evaluation was virtual depth image data rendered by OpenGL (evaluation depth image) in order to align the experimental conditions. The 3D model of OpenGL and the evaluation depth image are shown in Fig. 10. The virtual depth image was generated and used by using GPGPU with liver voxels extracted from DICOM (number of voxels: 2879092 points). The difference between the various methods is whether the Depth-Depth-Matching is performed on the CPU or the GPU.

In the experiment, the search cutoff time for the optimal value by the annealing method was set to 500 ms.

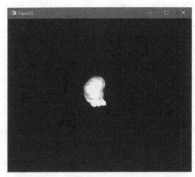

(a) STL model of a liver rendered in OpenGL.

(b) Depth image for evaluation, rendered in OpenGL.

Fig. 10. OpenGL 3D model and depth image prepared for evaluation.

4.2 Experimental Results

We measured the search time when the search algorithm was run on the CPU and when it was run on the GPU. Once the match rate was stable, we also measured the follow-up of the position and posture when the position of the 3D model liver in OpenGL, which was prepared for evaluation, was changed.

Figure 11 shows the change in execution time when the matching algorithm is executed and the matching rate is stable. The average values of the execution time when the match rate was stable are shown in Table 1.

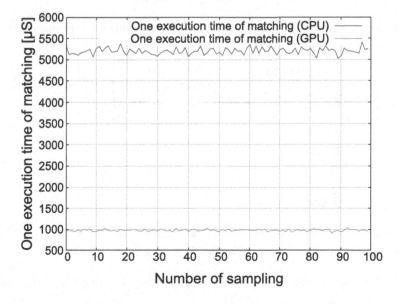

Fig. 11. Change in execution time when the match rate is stable.

Table 1. Average execution time when the match rate is stable.

Measurement conditions	Avg. [microsecond]
One execution time of matching (CPU)	5199.98
One execution time of matching (GPU)	978.42

After the matching algorithm is executed and the matching rate is stable, Fig. 12 and Fig. 13 show the follow-up of the position and orientation when the 3D model liver position of OpenGL prepared for evaluation is changed to the left by 100 mm.

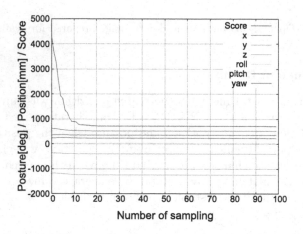

Fig. 12. Tracking of position and orientation when matching is performed by CPU.

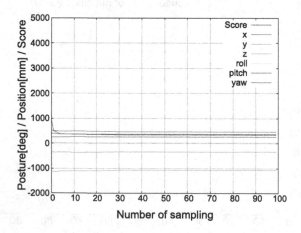

Fig. 13. Tracking of position and orientation when matching is performed by GPU.

5   Conclusion

In this paper, we proposed and implemented Depth-Depth-Matching using GPGPU and measured its processing speed. By using GPGPU to continuously perform Depth-Depth-Matching from depth image generation, we have achieved a speedup of about 5 times. In the future, we aim to take advantage of the real-time nature of the system to tune the search algorithm and improve the estimation accuracy.

References

1. Cranial Navigation - Brainlab. https://www.brainlab.com/ja/surgery-products/overview-neurosurgery-products/cranial-navigation/. Accessed 3 Feb 2021
2. Navix - ClaroNav. https://www.claronav.com/navix/. Accessed 3 Feb 2021
3. Surgical Navigation Systems - StealthStation — Medtronic. https://www.medtronic.com/us-en/healthcare-professionals/products/neurological/surgical-navigation-systems/stealthstation.html. Accessed 4 Feb 2021
4. Plan and Navigate - Surgical Theater. https://surgicaltheater.net/plan-navigate/. Accessed 3 Feb 2021
5. Koeda, M., Yano, D., Mori, T., Onishi, K., Noborio, H.: DICOM depth image generation using GPGPU for fast position and orientation estimation on liver surgery support system. In: TENCON 2019-2019 IEEE Region 10 Conference (TENCON), pp. 356–360 (2019). https://doi.org/10.1109/TENCON.2019.8929454
6. Numata, S., et al.: A novel liver surgical navigation system using polyhedrons with STL-format. In: Kurosu, M. (ed.) HCI 2018. LNCS, vol. 10902, pp. 53–63. Springer, Cham (2018). https://doi.org/10.1007/978-3-319-91244-8_5
7. Watanabe, K., Yoshida, S., Yano, D., Koeda, M., Noborio, H.: A new organ-following algorithm based on depth-depth matching and simulated annealing, and its experimental evaluation. In: Marcus, A., Wang, W. (eds.) Design, User Experience, and Usability: Designing Pleasurable Experiences, pp. 594–607. Springer, Cham (2017). https://doi.org/10.1007/978-3-319-58637-3_47
8. Yano, D., et al.: Accuracy verification of knife tip positioning with position and orientation estimation of the actual liver for liver surgery support system. J. Bioinform. Neurosci. (JBINS) 3(3), 79–84 (2017). e-ISSN: 2432–5422, p-ISSN: 2188–8116
9. Yano, D., Koeda, M., Onishi, K., Noborio, H.: Development of a surgical knife attachment with proximity indicators. In: Marcus, A., Wang, W. (eds.) Design, User Experience, and Usability: Designing Pleasurable Experiences, pp. 608–618. Springer, Cham (2017). https://doi.org/10.1007/978-3-319-58637-3_48

Author Index